SECOND EDITION

DOMINIC IGNATIUS EKANDEM

1917–1995

Prince-Cardinal
Nigerian Vanguard of Catholicism

PROMINENT
B O O K S
EDGE

5830 E 2nd St, Ste 7000 #9983
Casper, WY 82609
USA

Contents

CHAPTER ONE
IN MENTE DOMINI (IN THE LORD'S MIND)

CHAPTER TWO
POPULUM TUUM IN CHRISTO (YOUR PEOPLE IN CHRIST)

CHAPTER THREE
NATUS EST (HE IS BORN)

CHAPTER FOUR
IN FIERI (IN THE PROCESS OF…)

CHAPTER FIVE

GLORIA IN EXCELSIS DEO
(GLORY TO GOD IN THE HIGHEST)

CHAPTER SIX

PRIMUS ORDINARIUS PROPRIUS
(THE FIRST PROPER ORDINARY/BISHOP)

CHAPTER SEVEN

PATER FAMILIAS

(THE FATHER OF THE FAMILY/FAMILY HEAD)

CONGREGEMUR IN UNUM (GATHERED INTO ONE)

CHAPTER NINE
EGO SUM VIA, VERITAS ET VITA
(I AM THE WAY, THE TRUTH AND THE LIFE)

CHAPTER TEN

MISERICORDIAM DOMINI (THE MERCY OF THE LORD)

CHAPTER ELEVEN

MISSIO SUI JURIS (INDEPENDENT MISSION)

CHAPTER TWELVE

PRO CHRISTO LEGATIONE ERGO FUNGIMUR
(SO NOW WE ARE AMBASSADORS FOR CHRIST 2 COR. 5:22)

CHAPTER THIRTEEN

DEUS PROVIDEBIT (GOD WILL PROVIDE)

CHAPTER SIXTEEN

AD ASTRA PER ARDUA

(THROUGH DIFFICULTY TO THE STARS)

CHAPTER SEVENTEEN

VOX POPULI, VOX DEI (THE VOICE OF THE PEOPLE, THE VOICE OF GOD)

CHAPTER EIGHTEEN

IN VITAM AETERNAM (IN ETERNAL LIFE)

Books and Pamphlets by the Same Author

1. *CONFUSED VALUES IN NIGERIAN CONTEXT: RITUALS REVEAL MYTHOLOGY*, LAGOS, NIGERIA, JEROMELAIHO & ASSOCIATES, 1993.

    This book makes use of rituals and mythology as tools of interpretation of cultural, social, ecclesial and political situations and actions ina larger context and specifically in the context of Nigeria to portray the contradictory nature of what is said or done as opposed to what is professed. Rituals are to be simply understood throughout the text as actions and mythology or mythological as words conveying meanings and understanding. It calls for a reorientation of life and attitude. [*Out of print*]

2. *DECISION AND THE POWER OF GOD*, ILORIN, KWARA STATE, NIGERIA, DECENCY PRINTERS &S TATIONARY LTD, MARCH 1995

    This is a pamphlet that focuses on one's decision with regard to the power of God in nature, in his word and in his actions that is overwhelming and accomplishes what it sets out to accomplish. [*Out of print*]

3. *THE POWER TO DECIDE*, LAGOS, JEROMELAIHO & ASSOCIATES, LAGOS, NIGERIA, SEPTEMBER 1995

    The small decisions made each time and each day affect the larger or greater decisions that ultimately affect one's destiny or orientation in life. The minor decisions of life differ from the major decisions that have to be made or that have already been made. Discernment and revision of life or stocktaking play a vital role in making ultimate decisions of life.

4. *DRUG ABUSE AND DRUG PUSHING* IN *YOUTHS SOCIAL PROBLEMS: BY-PRODUCTS OF THE SOCIETY,* ILORIN, NIGERIA, DECENCY PRINTERS & STATIONARY LTD, KWARA STATE, 1999. [A CHAPTER IN A BOOK]

Drug abuse and drug pushing are social problems that can be induced by status symbol or relationships. The tendency can lead to self-destruction and ruining of one's future. The whole book highlights the problems that face the youth as a growing person. The youth should guard against peer pressure in this regard.

5. *CHRIST THE IDEAL OF CHRISTIAN SERVICE*, ABUJA, NIGERIA, *GAUDIUM ET SPES* PUBLICATION, 2005. [pamphlet]

Christ is the model of every form of service. He is the only one who offers a selfless, compassionate and loving service without counting the cost. This goes against all forms of selfishness and injustice. What is justifiable is serving as Christ served whether in the Church or in the society. No one should use office or religion as a cloak of deception. Service applies to both the ministerial priesthood or to the priesthood of the faithful.

6. *DECISION AND DESIRE: BLESSINGS AND CURSES*, UYO, AKWA IBOM STATE, NIGERIA, MACBENS, PRINTING PRESS, 2006. [pamphlet, out of print]

The decisions and desires of the individual contribute the blessings one receives or to the problems one encounters. Blessings demand obedience to the Lord whereas disobedience and stubbornness lead to the consequences of disobedience, the curses. Decisions and desires when properly combined bring blessings.

7. *DRUGS AND DEATH: DRUG TRAFFICKING, ECONOMIC, SOCIAL AND FAMILY IMPLICATIONS AND THE AGENCY'S RESPONSE*, LAGOS, SACRED HEART PRINTS, 2007, 2nd Edition 2013.

The book examines the term drug in specialised and general senses. Misuse of drugs that can easily be called drug abuse can lead to addiction and eventually to death if not properly handled. It looks at the percentage and the class of addicts and the range most prone to drug addiction. The factors encouraging drug trafficking and addiction, likewise various categories of alcohol addiction and those involved are examined. It aims at promoting a drug free society.

8. *THE USES AND ABUSES OF DRUGS* IN J. MADUEKE, J. EZEOKANA & B. OBIEFUNA, *EDS., CHURCH AND DEVELOPMENT,* NIMO, REX CHARLES & PATRICK'S LTD, 2008 [A CHAPTER IN A BOOK].

9. *CHRIST IN THE POOR,* UYO, AKWA IBOM STATE, NIGERIA, CLE PRINT VENTURES, 2010.

This book takes up the identification of Christ with the poor even in the most abandoned of the society. It calls for a deeper reflection of societal values.

10. *DECISION AND FULFILMENT OF GOD'S PROMISES,* PORT HARCOURT, RIVERS STATE, NIGERIA, MUSTARD SEED PUBLICATION, 2012.

This book examines the accomplishment of God's promises in the Old and New Testament and the decisions of individuals and groups and how that aided the fulfillment of the promises or its transfer to another person or to a future generation. One major question examined in the book is "Can God change his promises?"

Foreword

REV. FR. MICHAEL Edem, CM, tells the story of Dominic Cardinal Ekandem, a great missionary of the twentieth century in Nigeria, in Ikot Ekpene and in Abuja. Edem sets out to tell this story in a well-researched biography of the icon.

The biographer begins his story with the description of Cardinal Ekandem's times and age, his birthplace, and his contemporaries. Some people are born great; some people acquire greatness, while greatness is imposed on some people. To which category does young Tom belong in this biography? Read Michael Edem's story!

No man is an island. A child is born into a family, into a community and a village, into a country, into the world. The biography of Dominic Cardinal Ekandem begins in the Ibibio nation. The Ibibios of Akwa Ibom State, Nigeria, worshipped Abasi Ibom as a superior god in African Traditional Religion (ATR). Young Tom is of the royal pedigree of the Okuku Dynasty. Tom Ekandem was born on June 23, 1917, into Ibibio clan in the village of Obio Ibiono. His father was Chief Paul Ino Ekandem Ubo Etok, the Obong and chief priest of Obio Ibiono, and his mother was Nwa Ibong Umana Essien. He was born great into a royal family. From his boyhood days, Tom served at the sanctuary of the pagan religion assisting his father in the rituals performed to reconcile the deity of the land with the people and to settle disputes between families. As a believer of the

African Traditional Religion (ATR), he was allowed to carry the sacrificial victim (goat, chicken, and other items) to the altar of sacrifice.

The gift of faith, the conversion to Christianity, was a dramatic turn in the life of young Tom. He was baptized in 1925 with the name Dominic. In the third chapter of his book, the biographer has written in great details the parentage, birthplace, and religion. It was not easy to be the first convert from ATR to Catholic Christian in his town. The events of his juvenile life brought Dominic into close contact with the white man in school and church. He enrolled in a primary school to learn the white man's way of life contrary to the customs and traditions of his people. The Qua Iboe Mission Church, a missionary group of Christians, was Tom's first contact with the "white man's religion." He joined them but later converted to Catholicism. This was the beginning of great challenges in his life. Dominic was among the first converts in Obio Ibiono by the Shanahan missionaries of Southern Nigeria. Dominic met several obstacles in the practice of the Christian faith. He made serious attempt to change the traditional Ekpo society from a heinous cultist group to a cultural dance for entertainment. This met with great opposition.

To be a Christian in Ekandem's days was anathema. It was worse to contemplate the Catholic priesthood. The call of a young promising prince as a seminarian from the Okuku palace was regarded as an abomination that would call down the wrath of the gods on the Ibiono Ibom people. On the contrary, Dominic's priestly ordination was a momentous event, which set his tribesmen drunk with merriment. Reverend Father Dominic was ordained in 1947, the first priest of his tribe. Seven years later (1954), he was ordained the first auxiliary bishop in the Anglophone West Africa. The young auxiliary bishop was posted to Anua. In 1963, the new Diocese of Ikot Ekpene was created from Calabar, and Ekandem was installed as its first bishop. Pope Paul VI raised him to the status of Prince of the Church in 1976 to become the first Nigerian cardinal.

In spite of all, Dominic's life was full of trials, spiritual battles, and crosses in his personal religious life and that of the church. He drew strength from the cross of Jesus Christ, *In Cruce Salus*, "In the Cross is Salvation," which was Ekandem's motto in real life and commitment to service in the Lord's vineyard. At a certain stage of his life, he came face to face with the culture and traditions inimical to the Christian tenets. Ekpo masquerade was part of the menace. With God's grace arising from the strength of his episcopal motto, with his writings, Lenten pastorals, sermons, and speeches, he remained focused and committed to his people. He built schools for the normal and the physically challenged throughout the Diocese of Ikot Ekpene. Cardinal Ekandem's fatherly role comes out very strongly in chapters seven, eight, and nine connected with the Handmaids of the Holy Child Jesus (HHCJ) and the civil war. These chapters are *a must-read* in the book. The Nigerian Civil War (1966–1970) was a tragic period in the history of Nigeria. The cardinal had the care of the clergy and religious and, indeed, the faithful of Christ. It was a nightmare for the cardinal to guarantee the safety of the Handmaids of the Holy Child Jesus (HHCJ) in his war-torn diocese during the civil war. The Handmaids sought refuge in far away, relatively safe Lagos. The trials of the civil war brought tremendous difficulties to the HHCJ sisters. Being sisters from different ethnic groups in Nigeria increased the tension between them. Ekandem was caught in the midst of the trials and travails that would have led to a split in the HHCJ Congregation. With wisdom and experience in conflict resolution, Cardinal Ekandem solved the terrible war difficulties, revived unity among the sisters, calmed the storm, and healed the wounds inflicted by the war on the members of the congregation. The reconstruction of the war-torn country at the end of the war was a task that had to be done. Cardinal Ekandem helped to bring back the Generalate of the HHCJ to Ifuho and their Mother House to Calabar. The biographer has described in detail the events and effects of the civil war on Nigeria in general and on the church in Ikot Ekpene in particular.

At the end the civil war, the capital of Nigeria was relocated to Abuja. The church created Abuja territory *missio sui juris*. Without hesitation, Dominic Cardinal Ignatius Ekandem was appointed the first ecclesiastical superior to take charge of the Abuja Independent Mission. He was the pioneer, the leader, and the first to tread the new path to growth of the Catholic Church in the new capital of Abuja, Nigeria. His foresight and resourcefulness were brought to bear. This was another feather on his red hat and another "first." In 1992, Abuja was raised to the status of a diocese. Most Rev. John Onaiyekan, bishop of Ilorin, was transferred to Abuja as the coadjutor with the right of succession in 1990. At this point, Cardinal Ekandem's retirement was imminent. He retired in 1993.

Cardinal Ekandem initiated the idea of a missionary society of priests in Nigeria. The idea was accepted by the Catholic Bishops' Conference of Nigeria (CBCN), and Ekandem was in the forefront and played a leading role in the establishment and growth of the Society of the Missionaries of St. Paul, Gwagwalada. St. Paul's Missionary Seminary was opened in 1977 in Iperu Remo. The ordination of the first set of priests took place in 1986. Although there were several hurdles and teething problems associated with founding a pious association, Cardinal Ekandem nurtured the missionary society to great heights. The society having overcome all the obstacles held the first General Chapter in 1995.

Dominic Cardinal Ekandem remained an ideal servant of God, a renowned pastor, a meek and humble lamb like his Master Jesus, a victim of the difficulties of being the *first* in many situations in life, a light lit and put on a lamp stand to show the way, and a bridge builder among men. He spurred me to the priesthood being the first black Catholic priest that I saw in my life. He debunked the notion that the Catholic priesthood was the prerogative of the whites because all Catholic priests in the diocese were Irish. Today I am an archbishop. It is my privilege to write the preface to his biography. We pastors must remember that our lives are beacons of light and must be kept shining that all might see and give praise to God. The life of every priest should leave a legacy that is worth emulating; that says boldly of Cardinal Ekandem "imitate me for I am meek and humble of heart." It is a sermon on priestly vocation.

The cardinal's health deteriorated fast after his retirement in 1993. His light dimmed. Cardinal Ekandem passed away on November 24, 1995. May his soul rest in perfect peace. He was given a befitting funeral and buried in Our Lady Queen of Nigeria Pro-Cathedral, Abuja.

Fr. Michael Edem, CM has written and given us a vivid life history of a star of evangelization in Nigeria. Whoever reads this biography, and I encourage you to read it, will feel like a contemporary of Dominic Cardinal Ekandem.

+ Joseph E. Ukpo
Archbishop Emeritus of Calabar Metropolitan See Calabar
Cross River State, Nigeria

A Very African Cardinal (Foreword B)

I feel honored and privileged to be given the opportunity to write a foreword to the biography of Dominic Ignatius Ekandem, the prince who became a cardinal, the vanguard of Catholicism in Nigeria by Rev. Fr. M. Edem. Dominic Ekandem is a very African priest, bishop, and cardinal, a visionary who reversed the question "Can anything good come from Nazareth?" As a visionary and as an innovator and social pioneer, he showed that something good can come from Nazareth. This book is a labor of love. It was painstakingly researched and written. It's been a learning process for me too. Though a Catholic from birth, I plead ignorance to what is contained within this book before now. I knew nothing about His Eminence Dominic Cardinal Ekandem, the first Nigerian cardinal, to be appointed by the pope…That this man single-handedly initiated, planned, and carried out a large number of social and welfare programs in Nigeria, embracing all classes of people, including the disabled, is an eye-opener to me. It is something as a Nigerian I am hugely proud of and feel inspired by his actions. As a Nigerian, I feel that we owe him a debt of gratitude for what he accomplished for Nigeria/Africa in his lifetime through the Catholic Church. The role that the Irish missionaries and sisters played in establishing the Catholicism in Calabar Province is quite obvious.

The Catholic Church in Nigeria with the help of Cardinal Ekandem was at the forefront and instrumental in developing a lot of the welfare provisions in Nigeria in the areas of health, housing, schools, including disabled children, orphanages, and water, without which a lot of our people would not have made any progress or survived. Some people would not have received formal education of any type if not for the church. It can be argued that since the Catholic Church is no longer involved actively in the social/welfare programs or initiatives, there has been a lull in the development programs; and in fact, since the government took over a lot of these initiatives, there has been a decline in such provisions, and some have deteriorated. This is evidenced in the schools that have survived **without** adequate facilities for educational purposes. The book brings out an undeniable fact of the huge contributions of the cardinal with priests and sisters to nation building.

A fuller history of the role the churches/religious organizations have played in the development of Nigeria is yet to be documented. The pioneering spirit of these religious men and women has not yet been recognized. Are there any records of the sacrifices and the labors of love made by the cardinal and other priests/religious in the development of Nigeria apart from the scanty ones in biographical contexts? We are often told of what the government has done but not the clergy has. What became apparent especially in the section on the development of the FCT (Federal Capital Territory) Abuja is the cooperation of the cardinal as the superior of Abuja Independent Mission with a Muslim president (Shehu Shangri). They worked hand in hand to bring about the necessary change in the Federal Capital Territory in those early days. To think that in those days when they had so little, they were able to accomplish so much, armed with faith in God, they produced so much is a testament to their willingness to be used by God in shepherding the flock. Yet in these days and age with so much at our disposal, we find it very hard to do even the minimum with all Nigeria is blessed with.

What is stopping us? Is it that we have very little faith?

In many ways, the book seems like three books in one. The first is on the culture and tradition of the cardinal's background and the impact on his decision to become a priest, the second is on the activities of establishing numerous programs for the people, and finally, what he went through as a person, including his health problems, etc. One could almost lose sight of the focus of the book; however, the author has kept the various strands together to his credit. This leads me to the adage "to whom more is given, more is expected." Out of one man's sacrifice, many benefited, including the author.

The timing of publication of this book couldn't have been more apt, as it falls within the time when the new president of Nigeria has been elected on the platform of change, one hopes that the government will use this opportunity to reestablish links with the Catholic Church in particular and other religious organizations in general to work toward a unified program of national development for Nigeria and her people. The life of generosity, selfless sacrifice, and caring for the people of God both on the spiritual and social welfare level of Cardinal Ekandem is a great challenge to the Catholic Church and other denominations in Nigeria and, indeed, the whole world. Perhaps this is an opportunity for the Catholic Church and others to retrace their steps and go back to the original mandate of Christ who evangelized with power and authority and compassion and love instead of concentrating on themselves.

Juliana Ojinnaka-Osammor
Lecturer, The Sheffield College Sheffield, United Kingdom

Preface

I T IS JUST about twenty years since the death of our revered father, His Eminence Dominic Cardinal Ekandem. May his dear soul rest in perfect peace.

Already we have two full-length biographies in circulation by two of his spiritual sons, each with its own peculiar literary genre. The first to come out was by a priest of Uyo Diocese, Rev. Fr. Edidiong Ekefre. This publication was in the form of a classical "hagiography" aimed at projecting and highlighting the heroic life and virtues of a highly admired spiritual father. Almost simultaneously was the second book by Rev. Fr. Dr. Cosmas Nwosu, MSP, a professional historian and member of the Missionary Society of St. Paul, a society that prides itself to be spiritual sons of the cardinal. In this second publication, Father Nwosu attempted a first version of scientific biography of a great man of many parts. These two books somehow complement each other. But even put together, they have not said the last word on Dominic Cardinal Ekandem, the great pioneer indigenous missionary, pastor, patriot, and builder of church and nation.

It is therefore no surprise that another spiritual son has undertaken a new project of Cardinal Ekandem's biography. Nor will this be the last. We owe Fr. Michael Edem, CM a lot of gratitude for giving us another widely researched story of the life and times of this great "Prince, Primate and Patriarch of the Church." This work has covered some gaps in the previous works.

The long life and ministry of Cardinal Ekandem covered almost every aspect of the history of the well-acknowledged phenomenal development of the Catholic Church in Nigeria during much of the twentieth century. He had the burden of leadership thrust on him at all the crucial moments of this development before and after our political independence. His deep concern for the growth of the church shone through his entire active life, especially in his promotion of Christian life as a vocation—priestly, religious, missionary and lay.

His peaceful heart suffered through the horrors of the Nigeria/ Biafra Civil War. Like most Nigerians of his era, beyond the tragedy of an avoidable self-inflicted national calamity, he watched with recurrent disappointment as one hope after the other was dashed through greed and lack of concern for the common good. His dreams of a great Nigeria turned out to be a constantly receding mirage until his death, dreams that he had left with us to nurture into reality. When? Who knows?

Among the merits of this publication is the sustenance of those dreams and hopes of our pioneer Nigerian priest, bishop, and cardinal. His life is certainly the material of which saints are made, for the edification of the Church of God, to the glory of the Lord. He has run his own race. His reward is great in heaven.

+John Cardinal Onaiyekan
Archbishop of Abuja, **Nigeria**

Comments About the Book

Fr. Edem CM has offered all those who knew the Cardinal personally, those who heard of him, a vade mecum of sorts. He has served a dish that we must consume with relish. In this great work, he has patiently excavated and presented to us, a lot of background, some of it historical, some anthropological, theological, psychological and spiritual of the Ekandem persona.

This book is a great contribution to knowledge, but also to both the history of the Catholic Church and the history of the people, culture and environment that produced this great son of Africa who has really earned his place in the pantheon of the great. This book should find its place in the shelves of our public libraries in general and those of our religious institutions in particular. I highly recommend the book.

Most Rev. Matthew H. Kukah
Bishop of Sokoto, Nigeria

The world's upheavals in early 20th century affecting world politics, religion, etc. with a severe threat to human health and even to human existence which altogether culminated in the first World War, with the corresponding repercussions and ripples that did not totally die out before or during the second World War, cannot be completely written and contemplated upon without a key year of 1917 in the context of the apparition of the Blessed Virgin Mary at Fatima in the West, as well as serious matters such as the revolutions in Soviet Union in the East. All these put together and with a lot more cannot leave us in this part of the world and of Africa, Nigeria, ignorant of the impact of the birth of a boy: Dominic Ino Ekandem, in a remote and obscure village of Obio Ibiono in South Eastern Nigeria.

The boy in person unknown but, like little Jesus in Nazareth with a royal blood in his veins, will always remain for all of us in this part of the world, an icon, a luminary, a reference point in history, tradition, religion and culture to such an extent that the history of the said period can never be completely written without a mention of Dominic Ekandem even if such a writing is only an iceberg, a drop of water in the ocean or a mere mole of dust on the surface of a large office desk.

If the author of the Acts of the Apostles had to acknowledge that he had already written 'in his earlier works' all that Jesus said and did and that he had in that earlier work attempted to present a more orderly account of the life of the same Jesus since some others had already started compiling facts and data on Jesus, I must acknowledge that there are already works written on Dominic Cardinal Ekandem. Notably among them and more recently are books by Rev. Fr. Nwosu MSP and Rev. Fr. Ekefre. Now Rev. Fr. Michael Edem CM, aware that these works exist, presents to us yet another attempt but complementary to others, at an orderly account of the life of Dominic Ekandem. I am more certain that this will not be the last nail on the coffin because there are yet many aspects of the life of this God-chosen servant yet to be written. I cannot wait to read them even as I have read the two before and now this work. All and all, it will always remain an enriching experience to read the present work on Dominic Cardinal Ekandem: the first Catholic Deacon of our people; the first Catholic Priest of our land; the first indigenous Catholic Bishop of Nigeria and the first indigenous Cardinal of West Africa.

Most Rev. Joseph Ekuwem
Archbishop of Calabar, Cross River State, Nigeria

Lives of great people end with death like every other person but their greatness last longer in the stories people tell of them. The positive impact their lives and achievements had on people live on in memories and writings of those who cherish their greatness. Dominic Cardinal Ekandem had left behind his greatness on the tales and history of the Church in Nigeria, Africa and Uyo Diocese in particular. His stories can never be over flocked. Rev. Fr. Edem CM in his own perspective attempts in this book to tell the world more tales of the Life, achievements and holiness or spirituality of the late Cardinal. He had the singular privilege of being ordained by him and have had faceto-face encounter with the Cardinal while he was alive. This work is commendable in its originality and simplicity of accounts given. The life of a simple honest person is recounted from a humble beginning to how eventually he led many of the black race to the Catholic priesthood, episcopacy and college of Cardinals. The Cardinal was unique in many ways as the first and had been one who was in the conclave that elected the Great St. Pope John Paul II. His simplicity was outstanding, his spirituality astute, his holiness perceptive and his achievements outstanding. He gave Nigeria and the world, The Missionaries of Saint Paul to the greater glory of God. These are all embedded in this work for many to read, learn and emulate the great man of Africa and the Church.

Very Rev. Fr. Francis O. Essien
St. Joseph Major Seminary, Faculty of Philosophy/Theology, Ikot Ekpene, Akwa Ibom State, Nigeria

"It will be obvious to the reader that the author of this book has written about a subject very dear to his heart—he has chosen to write about one of the greatest men in the modern history of Nigeria, Cardinal Dominic Ekandem.

Father Michael Edem CM has spent an enormous amount of time and energy in compiling a tremendous amount of background information for use in this book, as well as fully researching the life and times of this amazing man of God and man of the people. This book details both the upbringing of Dominic Ekandem as well as his education and religious "career", together with the horrific catalogue of events that beset his country, and other countries in the vicinity.

A compelling read from beginning to end".

Michael I. Edem CM

Mr. Hugh Finnigan
Organist, St. Marie Cathedral, Sheffield, United Kingdom

This is a tremendous work. I cannot wait to read it.

Very Rev. Fr. James Shryane,
Holy Rood Catholic Church, Barnsley, South Yorkshire United Kingdom

An Updated Biography One of the identification marks of a great person is that after the person's death, many people spontaneously do certain things to immortalize his or her name. This new biography of His Eminence Dominic Cardinal Ekandem written by Rev. Fr. Michael Edem, CM, comes at an appropriate time to add to the growing biographies of our beloved late Prince, Primate and Patriarch. The work, which has the benefit of perusing previous biographies on the Ibibio born Catholic prelate would declare, like Luke the evangelist did upon writing another gospel of Jesus: "Inasmuch as many have undertaken to compile a narrative of the things which have been accomplished among us, just as they were delivered to us by those who from the beginning were eyewitnesses and ministers of the word, it seemed good to me also, having followed all things closely for some time past, to write an orderly account for you, most excellent Theophilus, that you may know the truth concerning the things of which you have been informed" (Luke 1:1-4). Fr. Edem's work, therefore, born out of a genuine desire to correctly immortalize the memory of Dominic Cardinal Ekandem, has brought new light to the life, words, actions and numerous achievements of this great son of Nigeria and Africa.

It is truly an updated biography of Dominic Cardinal Ekandem that is worth reading besides other biographies that one may already have read.

Anthony Iffen Umoren,
MSP Catholic Institute of West Africa Port Harcourt, Rivers State, Nigeria

"This book is a compelling narration of the context, life and enduring contribution of a great legend and true trailblazer. I recommend it to all who love the Roman Catholic Church and Africa and to those who seek inspiration to serve sacrificially. Many will be enriched by the largely unique historical records captured herein."

Professor Ifiok Otung
University of South Wales
United Kingdom

Preliminary Considerations/ Appreciations

Next year 2017, will marked the centenary of Cardinal Ekandem's birth. This book pre-empts that centenary celebration. This book marks the twentieth anniversary of the death of His Eminence Dominic Cardinal Ekandem (1917–1995). The first phase of his existence was during his life on earth. His death marks the beginning of the second phase of his life when he left for his Father's House during the Advent season of 1995. Happily, he had had enough time to prepare for the final lap of that journey. This book looks at both phases of his existence and what it entails.

This work on Dominic Ignatius Ekandem, the prince who became a cardinal and played an unforgettable role in the development of Catholicism in Nigeria, has taken almost two decades. It has eventually overcome many setbacks that hindered its publication before now. Such setbacks include the loss of original scripts, the search for the discarded scraps, and the emergence of other publications in the interim period. Meanwhile, other works have been published as this one was still in the process.

The pioneer work on the cardinal was that of Fr. Uduakobong Umoren published in 1976 shortly after his constitution into the consistory as a cardinal. Prof. Sylvanus I. Udoidem published his *Hospitality as Holiness: the Genius of Cardinal Ekandem, the Spirituality and Mission of Cardinal Ekandem*, which also touched the virtues and values of the cardinal almost a decade after his death in 2005. In 2013, Fr. Cosmas K. O. Nwosuh, MSP published the cardinal's biography from the point of view of evangelization as a pivotal instrument of the church's evangelization and expansion program, and in 2014, Fr. Edidiong Ekefre wrote on the cardinal from the perspective of his subtitle: *The Testament of Light.*

These works have contributed enormously to the understanding of the person and ministry of Cardinal Ekandem. This particular publication is not likely to be the last on him; more works might still follow. In Ikot Ekpene Diocese, *The Cardinal Ekandem's Lecture* has already been established, and about two or three have taken place in that series. These are likely to appear in printed form.

The title of prince came naturally to him from birth as a privileged son in the family of Okuku Ino Akpan Ekandem. When his father, Okuku Ekandem, was baptized, he bore the name Peter Akpan Ekandem. After baptism, he married in the Catholic Church, which involved a great personal sacrifice. This took place at the great cost of discipleship where his father had to do away with his very many wives so as to give Dominic the opportunity of being ordained. With the great sacrifice of the father sending the many wives back home to their villages, the ordination of Dominic went ahead.

Dominic abdicated his privilege of being an heir to the throne as a future Okuku. Yet a greater privilege was to come from God, for no one can outdo God in generosity. He became the prince-prelate of the church when he was consecrated bishop. This was a historic event that drew international attention since some of his co-consecrators came from other countries like Cameroon and Gabon to participate in that ceremony. Thus, he was prince by birth, prince-prelate by consecration as the first Anglophone West African bishop, and patriarch by elevation to the status of a cardinal in the Catholic Church, the first in Nigeria to have had that privilege. In this way, the prince became a cardinal. As a cardinal, he was regarded as the first citizen both within the church and in the society. It surely contributed to his being the vanguard of Catholicism, although he was not the first to become a Catholic in the country. His early firsts in many aspects gained him the unique position of being the vanguard of Catholicism.

The term "patriarch" is a very common one in the context of the Judeo-Christian religion like Abraham, Isaac, and Jacob. God decided to reveal himself to Moses as the God of their fathers—Abraham, Isaac, and Jacob—the patriarchs of Israel and, above all, as the "I AM" (Exod. 3:6; Matt. 22:32). Patriarch is a very common term in the Oriental churches but not so common in the Western Latin rite. In the Latin rite, this refers to heads of some autonomous churches consisting of several local churches. The title of personal archbishop granted to him by Rome would not have qualified him for this. It was his position as the very first West African English-speaking bishop and primacy of position as the oldest West African bishop that automatically conferred the title on him, coupled with the fact of being the groundbreaker of Abuja Metropolitan See. These circumstances combined to define him as a true patriarch. At one time, the title was even used for the pope as patriarch of the West, a title that is no longer in use in the Latin church for the pope.[1]

The title of patriarch does not demand much explanation in relation to the Catholic Church since by Divine Providence, he became the first Anglophone West African bishop, which gave him the privilege of being a patriarch of the whole country at a time when no other West African could be seen as a bishop. He was not the oldest among his contemporaries in St. Paul's Junior Seminary attached to Christ the King College, CKC Onitsha, but by God's providential plan, he was the first to be consecrated bishop.

He was not the first to be installed as a resident bishop. Bishop Anthony Gogo Nwedo, CSSp was the first Nigerian indigene to be installed as bishop of Umuahia. This does not deprive Bishop Ekandem of the eligibility to be a patriarch, especially with his conferment of the title of cardinal too as the first Nigerian cardinal. The aspects of prince, prelate, and patriarch fit in very well as he stood high among his equals. At his funeral, His Grace Abp. Albert Kanene Obiefuna publicly acknowledged that he was like a much beloved "headmaster"[2] of a school to very many over several years. He adopted a title rarely applied to clergy. All the same, he described him as such because of his influence and uniqueness when the ecclesiastical dignity in the hierarchical order was considered.

His eminence reinterpreted his name Ekandem by giving it a Christian significance. *Ekan-Ndem* originally means the mother goddess or mother of water goddess. With his reinterpretation, Eka, that is mother, and Ndem, the female water god or goddess, had been defeated or overcome. With this new understanding, Ekandem became the victor over the water gods and goddesses or even the gods or goddess on land.

This work encompasses matters beyond the physical life and works of the cardinal. It is more than a spiritual testament as such or a religious diary. The work covers his influence in civil society as well as in the church, his influence in the emerging Catholicism, his spiritual development, and his use of those gifts in various contexts. It recognizes the external and internal side of his life as a man who was very close to God, enjoyed extensively an infused knowledge like St. Thérèse of Lisieux, the Little Flower. He has something in common with the great mystics as God's gift. As part of his purification, he passed through several trials within and outside the diocese.

As for infused knowledge, that is incontestable. St. Paul speaking to the Colossians says, "That their hearts may be encouraged as they are knit together in love, to have all the riches of assured understanding and the knowledge of God's mystery, in Christ, in whom are hidden all the treasures of wisdom and knowledge" (Col. 2:2–3). The hidden wisdom of God (1 Cor. 2:7) can only be reached through contemplation. That was what led him into the depth of his knowledge and perception. Most Rev. Albert Kanene Obiefuna, the president of CBCN and archbishop of Onitsha Metropolitan See, publicly acknowledged this aspect of his life during the cardinal's funeral celebration on December 2, 1995, in Abuja, Nigeria.

His gentle disposition, circumspective, and prayerful attitude gained him the capacity to overcome the challenges of a crisis that nearly dragged his name to the mud. The same disposition and composure disposed his mentor Most Rev. James Moynagh, SPS, the first bishop of Calabar, to perceive a treasure in this African recommended for the office of auxiliary bishop. St. Teresa of Avila wrote: "All were pleased with me, for the Lord gave me the grace to be pleasing wherever I went and so I was much loved."[3] Like her, Cardinal Ekandem experienced many crosses, and he was greatly loved. As a trailblazer, he opened the door of hope to so many through establishment of many associations and societies for different categories of people.

His path of life brought many crosses. As he conceived the idea of the Cross of the Master, so did he live it out in his daily life to the extent that Abp. Brian D. Usanga, who preached at his funeral mass, said that "he lived in constant imitation of his Master Jesus Christ by obeying him and following his voice till his death.[4] He sought the Cross, he found the Cross and carried it throughout his entire life, during the Nigerian/Biafran Civil War through his care of the Handmaids of the Holy Child Jesus through false accusations, the internal crosses in his Diocese of Ikot Ekpene, as an Administrator of Port Harcourt Diocese including Abuja where he was a pioneer in very new circumstances; his sickness, his defence of the Church all brought with them elements of the Cross of his Savior and bore out the Gospel affirmation: "God makes light the burden we bear."[5]

His power to perceive a situation and translate it into action is what gave birth to Nka Adiaha Obong, the Catholic Women's Organization, the Teachers Guild, the Catholic Teachers' Association that provided the first Vono Beds to Afaha Obong Seminary, the MSPs, the Missionaries of St. Paul (MSP), and both seminary and society that have become phenomena of the twenty-first century. The perception and resilience of the prince-patriarch brought forth wonderful treasures from the depth from what appeared unlikely at first.

He was not the only one who perceived something. People also perceived the same things, but he pierced through to the depths with his infused knowledge that St. Thérèse of the Child Jesus calls an instruction by the "Doctor of doctors."[6] The divine instruction with his humility aided in discovering his exceptional gifts in many of the honors he received from society, from the church, and from further afield.

Cardinal Ekandem did not write much. What he wrote was incisive, penetrating, and full of wisdom but sometimes needing a commentary not unlike *The Flame of Love* by St. John of the Cross but always seeking to inspire and uplift. His thoughts were directed toward the upliftment of the people in all spheres of life.

What this work presents is only a tip of the iceberg. His true personality and worth will only be excavated slowly with time and with patience. The exit of this great man is like a big "iroko tree," giving way in a square where it used to provide shade for all that wished to take shelter under it. That exit was for the greater glory of God to establish the long-awaited union with the Father face to face (*panim el panim*) in God's House.

This work can be divided into three major segments: prewar that covers from the prologue to chapter six, incorporating the background, the seminary, the priesthood, the apostolate, the bishopric, and the first residential bishop of Ikot Ekpene; the second segment covers the war extending from chapters seven to nine, concentrating on the Handmaids of the Holy Child Jesus during the Nigerian/Biafran Civil War and the postwar, including the return of the handmaids and relocation of the Generalate to Ifuho in Ikot Ekpene; and the third section begins with the cardinalate in chapter ten till his death in chapter eighteen. This section looks at the cardinalate in chapter ten, Abuja Independent Mission in chapter eleven, the Missionaries of St. Paul incorporating chapters twelve to fourteen, while chapter fifteen looks at his episcopal motto: *In Cruce Salus*. Chapter sixteen looks at some of his pastoral letters and sermons, while chapter seventeen includes many tributes from people who knew him well together with some of his achievements. Chapter eighteen draws the curtain to his life on earth, looking at his last days, death, and burial followed by the Epilogue, Appendix, Bibliography, and Index.

This work owes a great deal to many contributors before its publication. The very first set of people who typed and copied the materials into a diskette were Anna and her cousin Viola together with Mrs. Francesco Giglioli, all of Vigna di Valle in Italy. That was the copy that never saw the light of day but got lost in transit. Our seminarians who have now become priests, namely, Frs. Augustine Abiagom, CM and Kevin Okonkwo, CM; Joseph Tumo Edem, my nephew; Rita L. Asuquo now married to Mr. Emmanuel Asuquo; the seminarians at Eternal Covenant Missionaries, Umuechem, Etche Local Government Area, Rivers State; Mr. Augustine Chidiebere Onuoha, ECM, Raymond, ECM, and Victor, ECM who helped tremendously in typing many of the materials for me; and Fr. Aloysius Udo, the second priest of Abuja, sometimes called *Filioque*, who provided some of the needed documents, they deserve special thanks. Fr. Emmanuel Bala deserves many thanks and appreciation for all his contributions for obtaining and making available the details of the funeral ceremonies. Especially indebted to are all those who granted interviews whether oral or written for their tremendous contributions. They are marvelous and exceptional.

The following deserve unalloyed appreciation for accepting to read, comment, criticize, and offer positive suggestions for the improvement of this work: Most Rev. Joseph Edra Ukpo, archbishop emeritus who agreed to write the preface of this work; His Eminence John Cardinal Olorunfemi Onaiyekan who accepted to write the foreword to this book; Abp. Joseph Effiong Ekuwem who took special interest in reading this work and making his comments and suggestions; and Mr. Hugh Finnegan who read and made corrections in this work. The same applies to Rev. Fr. Joseph Okeke from Orlu Diocese ministering at St. Marie Cathedral, Norfolk Road, Sheffield, England, and Rev. Fr. Dominic Udosen at the Spiritual Year Seminary at Obio Ibiono, Cardinal Ekandem's village, who helped in getting some of the documents needed and acted as the liaison officer to confirm certain required facts. Another group of people that need mention is as follows: Mrs. Juliana Ossamor who took pains to read, comment, and contribute even to the point of suggesting some useful materials for the work; her husband, Mr. Matthew Ogochukwu Ossamor, cannot be forgotten for synchronizing some of the fonts that did not tally for me; Mr. Terry Umoh and Mrs. Hanta Lessore who proofread the work and offered some suggestions; Msgr. Kenneth Enang who painstakingly read one of the chapters and made his contributions coupled with innumerable other contributions like granting interviews; and Rev. Fr. James Shryane for the insight he gave. The same applies to Rev. Fr. Terry Boyle who made a critique of the work and brought in very useful suggestions. Mr. Michael Galvin cannot be left out for his contribution in reproducing many of the old pictures used in this work; Sr. Regina Tombere, HHCJ for her contribution, Bishop Matthew Kukah granted a very incisive interview. He likewise commended this book to all and sundry. Special thanks go to Prof. Sylvanus I. Udoidem who granted permission for his review material to be used in the epilogue. He reviewed Fr. Edidiong Ekefre's book on Cardinal Ekandem during the launching of the book in Uyo, Akwa Ibom State. They all deserve special mention and appreciation. Special thanks go to Msgr. Joseph Ekarika for the materials supplied to me. The same applies to Sir Adam B. Nyong; Mrs. Veronica Okune and her son, Patrick Okune Ekpe; and Mr. Linus B. Edem. They aided the work immensely by their contribution. The associate professor, Rev. Fr. Donatus Udoette, and Rev. Fr. Donatus Ukpong, both of the University of Uyo, Akwa Ibom State, deserve a very sincere thanks for undertaking a specific task. Prof. Martial Jean Marie Staub of University of Sheffield needs special commendation and thanks for accepting to review this book.

Those who provided some materials for the work cannot be forgotten, for instance, Mother Mary Okpo, HHCJ, Mother Mary- Anne Iwoh, HHCJ, and Sr. Juliana Ekerete, HHCJ. All the Handmaid Convents that gave access to their community archives are greatly indebted to. Msgr. Godwin P. Akpan, the first rector and acting superior of the Missionaries of St. Paul Seminary, generously gave his archival materials that are profusely used in this book; his contribution was an indispensable one. Fr. Evaristus Igwe, CM, Fr. Cosmas Ukadike, and all the Vincentian seminarians in Abiakpo Ntak Inyang who made a concerted effort to find documents, scan, and make them available for this work all deserve special thanks too. Fr. Francis O. Essien, Fr. Imabasi Pius Okon, and Fr. Anthony Nyong deserve special mention for their immense contributions. Joseph T. Edem, my nephew, contributed by scanning many documents for use in this work. The same applies to Mr. Michael Nyong. They are greatly appreciated. Prof. Ifiok Otung of the University of South Wales is greatly remembered for his many contributions. Those who contributed to this work are so many that all cannot be mentioned by name, but they are specifically remembered and appreciated for their contributions that will remain evergreen as long as Dominic Cardinal Ekandem, the prince who became a cardinal, the vanguard of Catholicism in Nigeria, is read or spoken of. They cannot miss out in such infinite blessings. To all who contributed to this work, whether acknowledged or not, this simple refrain comes to you: many thanks, many thanks.

Prologue

IN PRINCIPIO
(IN THE BEGINNING)

Primate and Patriarch
In Principio, In the Beginning...Gen. 1:1

THE YEAR 1917 was the year of the birth of Dominic Ekandem with spectacular and eventful occurrences in many parts of the globe with various magnitudes. Some were with full blaze of publicity, others less so. The developments and events will unfold themselves in the pages below.

The First World War (WWI), which was in its third but penultimate year, was still raging with intense ferocity. But on April 6, of the year in question, the fortunes of the war changed in favor of the Allied forces. America that had remained neutral till date entered the war. Germany, which had reneged her pledge never again to attack neutral and passenger vessels, had provoked her. It will be recalled that Germany in 1915 had sunk a British passenger liner, the Lusitania. One hundred of the dead in the sunk ship had been Americans. At America's protest, Germany had reassured her and made the pledge only to breach it in this critical year. America, of course, responded by entering the war, as has been noted, on the side of the Allied forces, thus marking the beginning of the end of the First World War.

In this same year, the famous Balfour Declaration was issued. For nineteen centuries, the Jews had been dispersed throughout the world. It began in AD 70 when the Roman legions conquered and destroyed Jerusalem.[7] Of course, it had been foretold in the Holy Writ. Though in the Diaspora, that is, the Jewish dispersion throughout the world, the Jews never lost hope of Israel's ultimate reconstruction and their attachment to the land of Palestine, the city of Jerusalem, and their final return, which many of the prophets in the Sacred Writings prophesied and gave an unimaginable hope to the hopeless people that they would return and abide there forever. The First World War provided the right opportunity toward the realization of that prophecy and dream. It created an outlet for the pent-up aspirations of Jewish communities that was to have consequences that few could have foreseen in 1917.

A prominent Zionist writer,[8] Vladimir Jabotinsky,[9] urged the Jews to collaborate with the Allied forces for the liberation of Palestine occupied by Turkey, which fought on the side of the Central Forces. His proposal met with the approval of Great Britain, and the Jews contributed to the campaign of Gen. Edmund Allenby for the liberation of the Holy Land. The ground was thus prepared for when Britain would help to reciprocate in the realization of their agelong dream of a homeland. On the November 2, 1917, the Balfour Declaration was issued. It stated, "His Majesty's Government views with favour the establishment in Palestine of a national home for the Jewish people and will use her best endeavours to facilitate the achievement of this object." In time, this declaration formed a moral basis for the creation of the Jewish state on May 14, 1948, that was first recognized by Pres. Henry S. Truman of the United States of America after the proclamation of the declaration of the state of Israel by David Ben-Gurion, the head of the Jewish Agency.[10]

The Palestinians were not happy with the creation of the Jewish State ratified by the United Nations Commission adopted resolution that was also called Partition Resolution. The Arab states united together and threatened an all-out war in Palestine as soon as the United Nations passed the Partition Resolution. The whole land of Palestine boiled with an intensely heated and uncontrollable anger that portended conflict on an unimaginable scale.[11]

The Bolshevik Revolution[12] of Russia was another event of global significance in the same year led by Vladimir Ilyich Ulyanov, who, influenced by the works of Karl Marx and Friedrich Engels, became a revolutionary and put the theory of Communism into an organizational form. The Bolsheviks belonged to the Social Democratic Party of Russia that had a very large following. They eventually became the ruling party when Lenin succeeded with his revolution employing the slogan "All power to the Soviets." As the Bolsheviks (majority) revolted in March and October 1917, hell was let loose. They took over power in October of the same year. The czar (emperor) was first arrested and incarcerated then executed together with his entire family. The Bolsheviks only came to prominence after the provisional government called on them to come and render help to defeat the revolt of the pro-czarist army commander. The soldiers supported the proletariats (the commoners), and they became victorious when Lenin,[13] who was supported by Germany in whose country he was a refugee, offered the people "peace, bread and land"; and with the success in the uprising, Lenin insisted that the Soviets must rule. The catch-fire slogan with their popularity brought the Bolsheviks to power, and the aim of the revolution was achieved. The proletariats overthrew the bourgeoisie, the ruling class; took over power; and reaffirmed Communism and the Soviet Republic of Russia. They were to wield that power over an enormous area.

Subsequently, private properties and means of production and services were taken over by the state. Religion was banished or driven underground. Church buildings, including some of outstanding historic or architectural significance, were turned into warehouses, theaters, or civic assemblies. The religious communities,[14] especially the females, were driven away from their convents. Many communities of the nuns were lumped together with the intention of making them quarrel with one another and then cause an automatic disintegration owing to priorities and traditions, some being contemplatives and others being involved in active apostolic life with different types of apostolates together with their way of life. The secret aim of that project failed, for the sisters brought together developed a program that formed the basis of community life for them, including time for meals, recreation, prayer, and, of course, work that took a very great part of their daily program.

Their work, which took place twice a day, was excruciatingly difficult and demanding on them. They had to do everything manually from the clearing of the farmland, tilling, planting, up to the point of harvesting. There was nothing that was easy for them. Their existence together and success stunned the authorities as well as the spirit of acceptance. With their lives turned to that of beasts of burden, they could not but say "Welcome, Communism!" as a friend would welcome a friend. It was like making friends with the devil. They had no alternative than to embrace the forced labor. There were even stories of some being held for long periods in cold water in winter and subsequently dying of pneumonia. Communism spared no one, including the sisters.

After very many years of imprisonment and torture with the realization that they could not break the backbone of the sisters, they decided to select and send those who were teachers and nurses to accomplish a "useless task" as depicted in the film *Interrupted Lives*.[15] The useless task entailed teaching the little children regarded as "slow learners" in modern language, who might have been cruelly called "imbeciles" in the past where the sisters could not exert any influence. The same applied to the old who had become senile; yet the love and tenderness of the sisters who were so devotedly compassionate, kind, and loving had an impact that penetrated and affected deeply the lives of the patients and pupils.

At the same time, in another corner of the globe, the natural intensity and passionate inclination of one St. Maximilian Mary Kolbe, who was only a student at the time, was a very stubborn child. His stubbornness caused the parents to be very worried about him. He was pushed to cry and weep for the protection and passionate patronage of the Blessed Virgin Mary when his mother asked him a very challenging question: "What would become of you in the future?" He had a vision of white flowers and red roses given to him to choose, and he took both. That vision helped him to know that he would always be under the protection and guidance of the Mother of God.

As a student having the inspiration that he was to be a virgin that is chaste and pure as well as being a martyr, he started sharing some of his inner insights and inclinations with his friends by telling them that he had a great idea and that he wanted to consecrate his whole life to the Blessed Virgin Mary for the purpose of becoming a soldier of Mary, her intimate child, and to be able to live a holy life imitating her total surrender to God (Cf. Lk. 1:38). In 1917, the great idea took flesh in what he termed *Militia Immaculata*,[16] that is, the army/soldiers of Mary.

He started by embracing and enrolling six of his fellow seminarians so that he could accomplish the great idea of bringing the whole world to Christ through Mary, *ad Jesum per Mariam*, that is, to Jesus through Mary. His theology was theocentric but through Jesus under the directorship of Mary Immaculate as the army general fighting on the side of Christ. Total submission and dedication to the Immaculate Virgin Mary was the core of the entire salvific project. To fulfil this mission, total obedience to the will of God was paramount. To do this, a very pure intention was necessary in union with the Immaculate Virgin Mary.

Everything was to be accomplished with purity of intention giving glory to God. Maximilian Kolbe understood this divine project to be of utmost urgency to be brought to great success with great zeal and conviction. Realizing this, he sacrificed everything to make this great idea work. This momentous year saw the birth of *Militia Immaculata*, which was to expand with great intensity and rapidity that dumbfounded every person who later came across it. He went to Japan and built the same community and started producing the same magazine that rapidly spread and increased in demand. The grace of total dedication to God through the Blessed Virgin Mary with his expanded grace of charity was to lead him later to death cell at the concentration camp of Auschwitz where he was injected to die as a martyr.

However, perhaps the greatest event in this very unique year was the celestial visit in the remote town of Fatima in Portugal. In line with the dramatic events of global nature but very religious in nature was the apparition of "Our Lady Fatima in Portugal." It occurred on May 13, 1917. Three little shepherd children—Lucia Santos and Jacinta and Francisco Marto—witnessed the apparition of Our Lady of Fatima as they were in the fields taking care of their flock like the shepherds at the birth of Jesus Christ when the angels were singing in the high heavens and announcing the birth of Jesus Christ in Bethlehem (Cf. Lk. 2:13–17).

Eight days before the august heavenly visitor appeared to three little children, the reigning supreme pontiff, Pope Benedict XV, had directed the Catholic world to storm heaven in a fervent appeal to the Mother of God. That apparition called for conversion of heart, repentance, and turning back to Christ, the Lord. The recitation of the Holy Rosary was emphasized. As his continual appeal to the leaders of the warring parties to end the fratricidal carnage that was the First World War fell on deaf ears, his option was to turn to the Great Mother of Mercy, and it paid off! His stirring and impassioned pastoral letter addressed to the faithful of the universal church on May 5, 1917, and the eventful bombardment of heaven with prayers arguably resulted in the said celestial visit.

The Queen of Heaven visited the earth and made herself visible to three frightened shepherd children aged below ten. Our Lady chose these three simple and humble children to bring about the great message that will engulf the whole world in the flame of religious fervor and compunction of heart. She was to visit them regularly at the same spot—the Cova[17]—on the thirteenth day of the month for the next five months. On the last day of her terrestrial visit, seventy thousand people were reported to have gathered at the scene. Sign and wonders were witnessed. Those present witnessed that the sun zigzagged and rotated just above the head of the spectators, and petals fell from the sky. The heavenly visitor who had identified herself as the Lady of the Rosary to the children delivered a message and gave a promise. Her message was concerned with devotion to her Immaculate Heart for the conversion of souls. The triumph of her Immaculate Heart concluding with the conversion of Russia and peace was promised.

As hell was let loose in the bloody revolution in Russia, as the World War raged on decimating and vanquishing the world population in such a proportion that horrified the Holy Father in Rome, and as the visitor from heaven, the Blessed Virgin, revealed herself to the children in Fatima, Portugal, a child was born in an obscure, sleepy village, Obio Ibiono. Located in the then eastern region of Nigeria, it was to find itself later in the southeastern state and much later Cross River State before its present circumscription in Akwa Ibom State. The child's birth was significant in more ways than one not because he was born to a pagan, polygamous, and traditional ruler, Chief Ekandem Udo Etok and Madam Nwa Ibong Umana Essien, but because his father, occupying the throne as Okuku and wielding power and authority in and beyond Ibiono Clan, bought forth a bright, wise, and holy leader from the ancestral home of the Okukus, the prince by virtue of his birth, a primate by virtue of religion, and a nobleman by virtue of civil and public stance.

Perhaps, and just perhaps, it was because of the great and momentous events in the world in the year of his birth. But most assuredly, and decidedly too, because of the many great *firsts* of this child of a court sitting member. Take for example the following:

1. He was the first deacon of his tribe
2. He was to be the first indigenous Catholic priest of his then vicariate (later diocese) of Calabar
3. The first Catholic priest of his nation—Ibibio/Efik
4. The first African-born bishop in Anglophone West Africa
5. The first bishop of Ikot Ekpene Diocese
6. The first Nigerian and Anglophone West African to be elevated to the princely eminence of cardinalate; in other words, the first Nigerian cardinal
7. The first national president of the Christian Association of Nigeria (CAN)
8. The first president of the Association and Episcopal Conference of Anglophone West Africa
9. The first bishop to be the first superior of the first *missio sui juris* in Nigeria
10. The first bishop of Abuja Diocese, with a personal title of archbishop
11. The first Nigerian to moot,[18] articulate, and amplify the idea of a National Missionary Seminary
12. The dual founder of National Missionary Seminary of St. Paul, or, properly put, St. Paul Missionary Seminary, as well as the Missionary Society of St. Paul all located in Gwagwalada at the heart of the Federal Capital Territory, Nigeria

The child came to be called, known, and addressed as Dominic, a name he took at the reception of the sacrament of baptism eight years after his birth. His many firsts established him as prince and primate, and his unique position as a father in all ramifications made him unequivocally a patriarch. This was the Lord's doing, and it is marvelous to see.

Chapter One

IN MENTE DOMINI
(IN THE LORD'S MIND)

The Coming of the Maynooth Fathers, St. Patrick's Society, and the Erection of Calabar Prefecture

"**Y**AND DO NOT return without watering the earth, making it yield YES AS THE rain and the snow come down from the heavens and giving growth to provide seed for the sower and bread for eating, so the word that goes from my mouth does not return to me empty without carrying out my will and succeeding in what it was sent to do" (Is. 55:10–11).

Eternal plans are undecipherable by any human beings unless revealed at the proper time and place. That is why revelation in Christianity is paramount as the foundation stone of relationship and worship of God. His designs are inscrutable. St. Paul says, "How rich are the depths of God, how deep his wisdom and knowledge, and how impossible to penetrate his motives or understand his methods! Who could ever know the mind of the Lord? Who could ever be his counsellor? Who could ever give him anything or lend him anything. All that exists comes from him; all is by

1

him and for him. To him be glory forever! Amen" (Rm. 11:33–36; Cf. Is. 40:13; Job 41:3; 1 Cor. 8:6).

The vicariate of Southern Nigeria likewise the (circumscription) territory that was later termed Vicariate Apostolic of Calabar, which was to flower into a diocese, was already in God's mind, but no one knew until they came into being. That is why God's mind is inscrutable. It is all open to God while closed to human beings until he unveils what he has in mind for his creatures. God prepared the Blessed Virgin Mary ahead of the birth of Jesus Christ and kept her sinless so that she would be the worthy ark of the Lord. When God sent an angel to address Mary about the incarnation of Jesus, the Word that was to be made flesh in her, she was said to be "full of Grace" or "favored one" (Lk. 1:28) and blessed in a special way, his plans started unfolding. The angel continued, "The Lord is with you" (Lk. 1:28), thus indicating that God would never depart from her, and she would enjoy this privilege of being permanently in the presence of the Lord forever. This was in the pipeline, but everything unveiled itself when Mary accepted to be the Mother of God, Theotokos, by proclaiming her fiat that is her "yes." "Behold the handmaid of the Lord let it be done to me according to thy Word" (Lk. 1:38).

Little did the Maynooth Fathers know what was to unfold until they undertook to come for a temporary mission in Nigeria. Their acceptance fell into God's predetermined plan, which started shading light on what was totally sealed and inscrutable. Their "yes" resembled that of Mary, Mother of God, carried out in faith and total trust in God, and the inscrutable started becoming unveiled and comprehended although in a cloudy way.

The term "Maynooth Fathers" applies to the priests from St. Patrick's College, Maynooth, and the National Seminary of Ireland. In Nigeria, the Maynooth Fathers were "the ewe lamb of pleasure"[19] or to the pride and joy of Bishop Joseph Shanahan, CSSp[20]—that affable, personable, impressionable, and devout Father of all missionaries in Southeastern Nigeria and beyond. He physically brought them, the Maynooth Fathers, to Nigeria to his prefecture and later vicariate of Southern Nigeria. Aware and convinced that the Holy Ghost Congregation, to which he belonged, was not in a position to provide the priests badly needed in his prefecture, he set about to remedy the situation as soon as possible. The circumstance in which he was appointed was rather fortuitous. His celebrated one-thousand-mile trek to the Prefecture Apostolic of Adamawa then in Cameroon, and eventual hospitalization led to his historic mission.

Bishop Shanahan had been charged with the Prefecture of Adamawa in 1917 because of the First World War. That same year saw Lenin and the Bolsheviks solidifying the Soviet power in Russia. The British administration there had interned the German Holy Ghost missionaries who ministered in and staffed the area. The result of the action affected the church adversely, possibly commerce and finance too. The area was bereft of the spiritual support it enjoyed previously before the expulsion. The soul of that almost virgin and barren land, because **of** the expulsion of the missionaries, was left without a shepherd. This is in line with the Gospel saying of "being like sheep without a Shepherd" (Cf. Matt. 9:36–38). Some of the hostile chiefs and antagonistic townspeople had destroyed the buildings and most of what belonged to the church because of the absence of the missionaries as happened to Father Bubendorf when the chiefs in Cameroon gathered and sent him away to go home "to settle the palaver between the big chiefs in Germany and England,"[21] resulting in rejection and expulsion. The audaciousness of the chiefs emanated from the fact that all the missionaries were Germans who had been interned for nearly four years previously.[22] Seeing the opportunity provided by the war, they grasped it and expelled the missionaries without further ado.

The newly appointed administrator of the prefecture had no alternative than to begin a serious pastoral plan and spiritual revival of the souls there. In four months, he trekked a thousand miles visiting the abandoned missions beginning from Ossidinge in the Cameroons, administering the sacraments and encouraging the flock to persevere in the faith until the pope would send the missionaries to reside with them once again.

Thomas Higgins reported the following in his book *Maynooth Mission to Africa: the Story of St. Patrick's, Kiltegan*:

> In 1917 as a result of the First World War, Joseph Shanahan was given charge of the Prefecture Apostolic of Adamawa in Cameroon because the German Holy Ghost missionaries who staffed the Prefecture had been interned by the British administration there. In four months, he trekked a thou-

sand miles visiting the abandoned missions and afterwards he was so ill and exhausted that he had to go back to Ireland for a rest and for medical treatment.[23]

Monsignor Shanahan, as he was addressed then, trekked far and deep into the heartland of the prefecturate on account of an incident that was as bizarre as it was pathetic. Shanahan was at the verge of terminating his visit when these two men with complementary lists of sins met him on the way from a very distant place through the hills, and no white man could think of going there. However, now that they had met Shanahan, everything was fine since they wanted confession most. They could not be quietened or silenced in the midst of the people who were listening; they rather indicated that there was nothing strange since everyone knew about those sins. They rattled on quite unashamed. Monsignor Shanahan humorously remarked:

> They came out with such *hefty stuff*[24] that I began to get mystified and alarmed, especially as they both seemed to have the same list and were corroborating each other's story with vehement nods.

Shanahan walked away and told them that what they said was not true; they followed still, exuding "whoppers."

> "Father must listen," they said, "since we cannot go back without absolution!"[25]

Father Higgins described that humorous episode of Shanahan in a graphic manner indicating that these Cameroonians, who had been away from confessions for years because of lack of priests, had a "score" that was unduly high and included all sorts of "strokes."[26] The "score" and "strokes" are normally words used in the context of either tennis tournament or that of cricket. Higgins used them to underscore the seriousness of what went on.

When questioned, they said that they came on behalf of the whole village and would bring back absolution. When the visitor told them this was impossible, they replied, "God will understand and forgive without palaver. Therefore father would do the same."

The confession mentioned is paralleled to the Jewish high priest confessing the sins of the people on Yom Kippur, day of atonement, while placing his hands on the goat that would be driven to the desert by a specially designated person who would wash his clothes and take a bath before returning to the camp. Such confession was believed by the Jewish adherents to take away their sins while setting them free. Even though it appears that the Cameroonians might not have been aware of the procedure and existence of such a rite, it seems that is what they were repeating incognito in other words without realizing it until their confession forcefully impelled Monsignor Shanahan to embark on the extra two hundred miles trek into the hinterland of the Adamawa Prefecturate in the Cameroons.

Monsignor Shanahan, instead of giving absolution in absentia, as was demanded by the two villagers who dwelt on the mountains, promised to visit the mountain villages. He followed them as they requested even though he had come to the end of his strength with a growing abscess and internal pains. The journey was hazardous and exhausting, so full of hardships that he barely survived it. Upon reaching the waiting community, he collapsed. During the ensuing week, his faithful followers, through days and nights of torture, carried him. He broke down and collapsed as he reached the Cameroon port of Douala Hospital where he was strictly warned that he had to lie flat. Shanahan could not do that. He kicked himself up and jumped down, and the boil exploded after three days. He became relieved and traveled back to Nigeria through Calabar with a boat. He contemplated resignation, but his confreres or brothers vehemently told him that what was needed was to make him a bishop and not to resign. He went to Europe for treatment and rest by the close of the decade during the summer of 1919.[27]

A few months in hospital and a major operation restored his health. Then he remembered the nagging problem of the missionland priests to evangelize and minister to his flock. And he went to Maynooth, St. Patrick's College, Maynooth. It was a reputable National Seminary that produced "diocesan priests in hordes."[28]

The journey to Nigeria and eventually of St. Patrick's Missionaries began in 1920 after hospitalization and recuperation of Msgr. Joseph

Shanahan. The Kiltegans, as the St. Patrick's Missionary Society members recorded in their Diamond Jubilee (seventy-five years of missionary service) brochure, came to be called and known consequent to the generous and inspirational donation of a house by a Catholic businessman, Mr. John Hughes, at High Park Kiltegan, Co., Wicklow, Ireland, to Fr. Pat Whitney. The year 1927 was that eventful and groundbreaking year. Fr. Pat Whitney later consolidated the Kiltegan donation as a base for the proposed headquarters of the future missionary society. Kiltegan became synonymous with the group or individual member as a Kiltegan Father probably as those living in Kiltegan or those from Kiltegan as a place. This is akin to the identification of the Vincentian Fathers and brothers or the members of the Congregation of the Mission in France with St. Lazare who later were and are known in France and in many other places as Lazarists. From the point of view of nomenclature, the members of the society are called St. Patrick Fathers as a derivative of Fr. Patrick Whitney, the first volunteer; they are most widely known in Ireland as Kiltegans.[29]

Monsignor Shanahan cleared the ground to launch his passionate appeal in a manner that has never been done before in that seminary. The appeal was directed to the bishops of Ireland gathered in an assembly that later emerged as the Catholic Bishops' Conference of Ireland. Monsignor Shanahan sought for and was granted audience by those assembled Irish bishops. Leaning on the Irish hierarchy, he found a way to reach the hearts of the "would-be missionaries" before he actually met them.

In his words, "Here was my chance, and standing up, I faced all the Bishops of Ireland and spoke as never or since. When I finished they agreed to my proposal, and gave me permission to meet all the Maynooth students and seek volunteers among them."

A week later in February 1920, he addressed the students. Some of them expressed interest, among whom was one to be ordained in June of that year, Pat Whitney, whose diary was to relate thus: "Father Shanahan pleaded for Africa—Nigeria. He will give a temporary mission there to priests from Maynooth. There is immense work to be done and the pagans are asking for baptism. The appeal went to my heart. If I can, I will go— God direct me."[30] This is the type of passionate appeal that St. Francis Xavier made when he went to the University of Paris and appealed to the priests and students, telling them of the need for missionaries to go to

Japan and China whose citizens were hungering for baptism and desirous to know Our Father and Hail Mary, and there was no one to teach them. Priests were milling through the streets of Paris, while the people in mission lands were languishing in their ignorance. He shouted almost like Jonah in the streets of Nineveh for priests to respond to his passionate appeal. Some were touched to the heart, as it happened too in Ireland during the appeal of Monsignor Shanahan, but the response to the appeal of Shanahan was powerful, for it pierced through to the heart of his hearers.

There had been other appeals to the students shortly before Joseph Shanahan's. One was for China and the other for India. But Shanahan's appeal was more unique and offered an attraction. In its uniqueness was the extraordinary personality and aura exuded by the speaker, which impressed his listeners. The attraction was the *temporary nature of the mission*, which Shanahan offered. The volunteers would give a minimum of four years' service to the mission before returning to their home diocese. The other appeals had asked for a lifetime missionary service and did not accept volunteers on a temporary basis. The modus operandi necessitated the abundant influx of laborers to the harvest.

While still in Ireland organizing and praying for men and material for his beloved Prefecture of Adamawa, Msgr. Joseph Shanahan was elevated to the episcopacy.[31] The Prefecture of Southern Nigeria had been raised to a vicariate, and ipso facto, he, Joseph Shanahan, the prefect apostolic, became its first bishop. Technically, the prefecture could not be made a diocese since there was no Nigerian hierarchy.

The announcement was made on April 17, 1920. He elected to be consecrated in Maynooth partly because it would draw attention to his appeal missionaries, in sensitive and responsive quarters, and partly because it would cement the link between his vicariate and the Irish church. It worked, and the consecration took place on June 6.[32] He had come back to Ireland, a priest and a patient, for treatment and rest. He was going back a prelate and at peace with two Maynooth Fathers, Tom Ronayne and Pat Whitney, who were the first volunteers, and seven Holy Ghost missionaries, he had cause to be at peace. They set sail for Nigeria in November and came ashore at Calabar, part of Bishop Shanahan's vicariate, on December 15, 1920. Thus, the eventful missionary journeys of the Maynooth Fathers that would lead to the founding of the St. Patrick's

Society began. Meanwhile, Tom Ino Ekandem, who was to become His Eminence Dominic Cardinal Ekandem, was some three years old, a pagan and a prince by circumstances of his birth.

Fr. Pat Whitney was assigned to Emekuku, a rural station in the Igbo heartland opened in 1912. He was overwhelmed by the staggering number of people clamoring for baptism, some forty thousand catechumens[33] according to his own account. Adding the other baptized thousands needing pastoral care, he realized that the task of ministration was very daunting and intimidating for just two priests—himself and the parish priest under whom he worked. Father P. J., as he came to be fondly called, sensed a challenge—to win these importunate souls for Christ. But how can this come about without priests to work in the overripe vineyard? He remembered the many young men ordained in Maynooth, his alma mater, every year. He resolved to enlist them, "to launch a big offensive on Maynooth" as he wrote in his diary.[34] He wrote many letters to friends of Maynooth days and followed up with articles in the Holy Ghost magazines *The Missionary Annals*. Describing in great details the magnitude of work in the mission land, his one objective was to attract as many volunteers as possible. Then he authored a 128-page book, *An Irish Missionary in Central Africa*,35 giving even more a detailed account of opportunities for evangelization and the conditions in which the missionaries lived and worked. It was printed in 1923. By the end of this same year, Bishop Shanahan had a need to raise funds in Ireland for a congregation of sisters he was about to found—the Missionary Sisters of Our Lady of the Holy Rosary.[36]

Fr. Pat Whitney was made the fund-raiser, and so he returned to Ireland. While promoting the new venture in Ireland, the bishop commissioned him to appeal and recruit more volunteer priests. By the end of 1925, the strength of the volunteer Maynooth Fathers had reached eight. It was thanks to the great energy and efforts he put in the recruitment drive. His task of fund-raising over, Father P. J. returned to Nigeria in June 1926.

It will be recalled that in his first sojourn as volunteer missionary, before the fund-raising and recruitment commission in Ireland, Father P. J. had proposed to Bishop Shanahan some kind of independent status for the volunteer Maynooth Fathers.[37] The bishop, who was not averse to the proposal, had encouraged him to keep on writing. He was more preoccupied with his responsibility to evangelize his vast vicariate and did not seem to mind a separate diocese for Irish secular priests. Again, his congregation's inability to meet up with the priestly personnel needs of the ecclesiastical jurisdiction made it undesirable for him to hold on to it for them. Together with his fellow volunteer Maynooth priests, Father P. J., on his return, began to consider a separate society of priests. It would be set up like the Holy Rosary Sisters "for Africa but especially Southern Nigeria." It was very tough going founding the envisaged society.

Bishop Shanahan, who had at the beginning assented[38] and even consented to personally undertake the task of founding the society in time, backed out. Pressurized by his own congregation (that is, religious order) that opposed the founding of the new society, the bishop had little choice in the matter.

But Fr. Pat Whitney went ahead and was able to convince Rome through the help of Msgr. Arthur Hinsley who was raised to the cardinalate in 1937, the recently appointed apostolic visitor to British Africa. He left Nigeria in 1929 for Ireland and later in the year traveled to Rome for an interview with the prefect of *Propaganda Fide* in Rome, Cardinal van Rossum. In February 1930, the new St. Patrick's Missionary Society was announced by Cardinal van Rossum whom he had had conversation with a year earlier.

On St. Patrick's Day, March 17, 1932, the society was formerly established, and the first three members took the oath of membership at High Park, Kiltegan, before **the** bishop of the diocese, Bishop Matthew Cullen. Those who took the oath were Fr. Patrick J. Whitney, his cousin Fr. Francis Whitney, and an Irish priest who worked for some years in Melbourne Archdiocese in Australia, Fr. Francis Hickey.[39] The Spiritual Year program was opened that same year in September 1932. There were eleven candidates who began the program at High Park, Kiltegan, to the amazement and contentment of Fr. Pat Whitney and companions who saw this event as the handiwork of the Holy Spirit's procedural continuity in terms of the new Society of Missionaries in the church. Among the eleven seminarians, there were some who had already done part of their studies in other Irish seminaries. The establishment of the novitiate almost coincided with the preparation of Dominic Ekandem to take a major step the following year to begin his minor seminary training at Onitsha.

Propaganda gave approval for the society to be founded on February 6, 1930, with the name St. Patrick's Society for Foreign Missionary Priests.

But the issue of territory was yet to be settled. The volunteer missionaries had prepared the Igbo areas of what corresponded to the civil province of Owerri and Eke in Udi division. The assignment to Emekuku in the Igbo hinterland accounted for the tacit choice of Owerri and Eke in Udi division. Probably, they were aspiring to go to a known and familiar area rather than proceeding to a virtually virgin land they had no knowledge of. Yet they had to give up their preference to let providence carry out his work in a most effective manner.

The vicar apostolic would rather concede Calabar and Ogoja territories to them. In the resolution that was effected, Rome allowed Bishop Shanahan to divide his vicariate in the manner he saw fit. Thus, Calabar and Ogoja areas were assigned to the society, which came to be canonically founded on March 17, 1932.

Father P. J. was a man of vision, foresight with great resilience. He immediately knew that the survival and continuity of the work in Nigeria and other missions that will open up depended on the availability of personnel. To this effect, Fr. Patrick Whitney conceived the establishment of a seminary to attract vocations. The conception and establishment of a seminary did not deter him from making frantic appeals as ever to those who were willing to become volunteers by appealing in his alma mater Maynooth to join the missionary involvement of the nascent society in evangelizing the fertile territories of Nigeria ready for baptism and conversion to Christianity. Some of these volunteers came to staff the new seminary established at Kiltegan, and others went to work on the Nigerian mission.

The recruitment of volunteers has become a particular characteristic and a great approach of the Kiltegan Fathers missionary strategy. It is a type of aggiornamento, opening of the windows to let in fresh air as Pope John XXIII now canonized a saint used it. Aggiornamento, in its original context, means "bringing up to date or clarifying things so as to meet up with the present moment" for the purpose of survival, expansion, and existence. It began since that initial stage and has continued till today.

Some of the volunteers worked in Africa and Brazil.[40] In 2007, two Nigerian volunteers, Fr. Anthony Akpanessien and Fr. Paul Mendie, joined the myriads of volunteers throughout the world in evangelizing other people as the earlier ones did in coming to Nigeria. Father Anthony went to Tzaneen Diocese in South Africa likewise Father Paul. Both went to the same diocese. Fr. Anthony Akpanessien comes from Ikot Ekpene Diocese and undertook the volunteer missionary work during the time of Bishop Camillus Archibong Etokudo, and Fr. Paul Mendie from Uyo Diocese opted to join the volunteer missionaries during the time of Bishop Joseph Effiong Ekuwem. Since that time, Bishop Camillus had been transferred to Port Harcourt, while Bishop Joseph Ekuwem had become the archbishop of Calabar.

Two years later, Fr. Pat Whitney, who now has assumed the position of superior of the new society, saw the need to press for a separate ecclesiastical jurisdiction with its own prefect apostolic. Rome granted his request, and his inspired recommendation for Fr. James Moynagh as prefect was also accepted.

Father Moynagh was among the seven volunteers of 1930, among whom five were Maynooth Fathers ordained in June of that year, himself included. His first station was Ifuho where he was reputed to have introduced the first presidium of the Legion of Mary in the African continent with the help of a layman called Catechist Emmanuel Udom from Ikot Ifen in Afaha Obong in 1933. The year 1933 became a very significant number and date in Calabar Diocese because the private mail bag of St. Patrick's College, Ikot Ansa, Calabar, established in 1935 bore that number 1933, and the first vehicle, Mercedes-Benz, given to Dominic Ekandem as bishop bore that same number. The year 1933 was also the year that Dominic Ekandem began his junior seminary studies.

The following year, 1934, marked the establishment of the Prefecture of Calabar by *Propaganda Fide*, Rome, where Msgr. James Moynagh was appointed administrator of the prefecture. The prefecturate included the present Cross River State, Akwa Ibom State, Ebonyi, parts of Abia, and Rivers State. It was expansive, yet there were few priests who had to bear the heat of the day serving the people of God who were thirsting for the Word of God like the deer yearning for running stream (Cf. Ps. 42). Two years later, twenty seminarians began their theological studies at High Park, Kiltegan, in 1936. By 1937, the members of St. Patrick's Missionary Society, "Kiltegan trained priests," were ordained in March.[41] The joy would have been unimaginable. The God of providence had taken his course, started his work in a grandiose style, and had let his light shine for the good of the Gentiles in the foreign nations. They would have been seen as an answer of God to the prayers of those who took oath of membership and to the great contentment and further prayer of Mr. John Hughes and family. In a sense, it was the first fruits offered to God for a productive harvest and in line with the Jewish miniature creed in Deuteronomy 34 that the father of the family had to recite to the family members. God had visited his people and had opened the way for further fruitful harvests.

The four newly ordained St. Patrick's Missionary Society members were plunged into the already prepared fertile ground of Nigerian apostolate. They came in as replacements in the field of soccer with fresh energy, enthusiasm, vigor, and intent on winning numerous souls for Christ and accomplishing in practice what they had been dreaming of and contemplating deeply in their hearts as the fresh players go in with the intent of scoring goals and winning the trophy or getting the points. The arrival of these new men or the freshers automatically enlivened and granted succor to those who had been bearing the heat in the various fields and apostolates.

In 1938, the old provinces of Ogoja and Abakaliki were united to form a new and independent territory under Msgr. Patrick Whitney, the first superior general of the society, as prefect apostolic. Msgr. Pat Whitney's health deteriorated, and he had to return to Ireland in 1942. He was forty-eight years old at the time. To avoid a vacuum, Msgr. Thomas McGetterick succeeded him and kept the flag flying. Calabar became vicariate apostolic in 1947 and Msgr. James Moynagh became its first bishop. As Calabar became a vicariate, so did Dominic Ekandem become ordained a deacon and a Catholic priest that same year. It was another serious coincidence in the life of Dominic Ekandem. Calabar Vicariate Apostolic became a diocese in 1950 with Bishop James Moynagh as its first residential bishop. In 1955, Msgr. Thomas McGetterick became the first bishop of Ogoja Diocese[42] until Abakaliki was made an independent diocese in 1977 where Michael N. Okoro became the auxiliary bishop of Abakaliki. That same year, the St. Paul's National Missionary Seminary was established in November at Iperu Remo, Ogun State, on old Teachers' Training College site (TTC).

The mission of the St. Patrick's Missionary Society started expanding outside the circle of Nigeria to Kisumu in Kenya in 1952. The expansion program indicated the precedence of Nigerian mission over all others. The Kenyan mission matured to the level of a diocese in 1958 after growing from vicariate to prefecture of Eldoret in 1954 through a wonderful gesture of pastoral autonomy and expansion.

By 1962, Pope John XXIII appealed to the Irish bishops to send missionaries to South America. The response to that appeal witnessed the society sending a team of priests to São Paulo, Brazil, that same year.[43] The mustard seed taken from Ireland's mighty seminary, Maynooth, grew on the Irish soil with roots at the High Park, Kiltegan, developed its stem and branches when it was implanted on the Nigerian soil. The implantation like the branch from the root of Jesse (Is. 11:10) took root and extended to other parts of Africa and found its way providentially to other continents across the seas and oceans where the youngest branches were taken and planted there like the cypress of the prophecy of Ezekiel.

> [17] The word of the Lord came to me: [2] O mortal, propound a riddle, and speak an allegory to the house of Israel.
> [3] Say: Thus says the Lord God:
> A great eagle, with great wings and long pinions, rich in plumage of many colours, came to the Lebanon.
> He took the top of the cedar, [4] broke off its topmost shoot; he carried it to a land of trade, set it in a city of merchants.
> Then he took a seed from the land, placed it in fertile soil; a plant[a] by abundant waters, he set it like a willow twig.
> It sprouted and became a vine spreading out, but low; its branches turned toward him, its roots remained where it stood. So it became a vine; it brought forth branches, put forth foliage. (Ezk. 17:1–6)

Originally, this riddle was about the exiles from Israel in a foreign land, but it has now fitted in very well with the situation of the Kiltegans who spread very quickly because the ground was fertile and was well cared for. While the St. Patrick's Missionary Society was growing from strength to strength, the cultural, social, and anthropological background of Dominic I. Ekandem was developing and forming itself into a context that molded the illustrious son of Ibiono Ibom likewise the intricate polity or the life of

Obio Ibiono where Tom grew up. While the situation was ripe for evangelization, the cultural influence was equally waxing stronger. The missionaries had a great task before them.

Chapter Two

POPULUM TUUM IN CHRISTO (YOUR PEOPLE IN CHRIST)

The Origins

Every child that is born into the world is a mystery.
It comes with a mysterious entry that none can
decipher except at maturity and at exit.

—Wise Saying by an Unknown Author

A. The Ibibio People Vis-à-Vis Ibiono Ibom, Home of Dominic I. Ekandem

THE BIOGRAPHY OF Dominic Cardinal Ekandem will never be complete if it is not linked with the struggle to have a special vicariate called Southern Nigeria that came into existence on December 15, 1920. At the creation of the vicariate, Dominic was popularly known as Tom in his village, tribe, and clan. The young Tom was only three years old by then. As far as the faith was concerned, Tom was a neophyte. Hitherto,

Tom was a prince by birth but not a Christian by birth. Much water passed under the bridge before he became a Christian. All the same, he was one of the few from his clan and village privileged to share in that divine gift in those early days when many from his place were still deeply steeped in the African Traditional Religious (ATR) practices as well as the way of worshipping and living piloted by ATR.

Tom's princely status cannot be viewed aside from that of his clan, Ibiono Ibom in Ibibio land. It is only within this context that his life becomes properly situated and appreciated, thus opening it to many possibilities.

Ibiono Ibom is found in the southeastern part of Nigeria. The name South Eastern State was derived from this regional name that incorporated what is now Cross River and Akwa Ibom. That was the name before, during, and after the Nigerian/Biafran Civil War until the new division took place. The name South Eastern State was derived from the eastern region that metamorphosed into Cross River State and East Central State that embraced the whole Igboland and later gave birth to [metamorphosed into] Anambra and Imo State before a further splintering into Abia, Ebonyi, Imo, Enugu, and Anambra took place.

The southeastern region is now known and addressed as southsouth geopolitical zone. The denomination embraces many states like Cross River, Akwa Ibom, Bayelsa, and Rivers. The Ibibios are in the heart of the new nomenclature Akwa Ibom State. Ibibio land encompasses Ibiono clan in its entirety found in present Akwa Ibom State. The geopolitical coinage south-south is almost a recapitulation or recalling of what was known as COR State before the creation of the twelve states in 1967 in the country at the outbreak of the war. What was meant by COR State during the National Council of Nigeria and the Cameroons (NCNC) was Calabar, Ogoja, and Rivers, in other words, Port Harcourt. Calabar at the time incorporated what is now designated as Akwa Ibom State. The military head of state and commander in chief of the Nigerian Armed Forces, Gen. Ibrahim Badamasi Babangida, general commander of the federal republic of Nigeria (GCOFRN), created Akwa Ibom State on September 23, 1987.

The entity called (the Nigerian nation) Nigeria went through a process of sharing, which was termed the "Scramble for Africa" by the various European nations, whereby the western part of Africa was shared between Britain and France, while other parts experienced the powers of

Spain, Portugal, and Italy. What was termed Nigeria underwent a process of amalgamation that took place in 1914. The amalgamation process took place three years before Dominic Cardinal Ignatius Ekandem surfaced on earth as Tom. The amalgamation process brought about the combination of the northern, western, midwestern, and eastern regions. The four regions, which had their separate geographical, cultural, agricultural, religious, political, and governmental systems, were brought together under one name and nation—Nigeria. It formed the largest African nation and the most populated. Presently in 2015, it has an estimated population of one 178 million inhabitants, although during the time of Tom as a young person, the population was estimated to be less than 60 million, which was the figure of the 1963 demographical data. The population growth has almost tripled between 1963 data and the third millennium in 2013. The phenomenal population growth occurred within an interval of almost sixty years.

Tom, as he was known has progressed in God's vineyard, was from this great nation, Nigeria. His home was located in the eastern region at the hinterland of Ibibio tribe in the little village called Obio Ibiono. Obio Ibiono is the home of Ibiono clan and the home of the Okukus. Its location, notwithstanding the importance, forces one to ask, like the people of old, "Can anything good come out of Nazareth?" (Jn. 1:46) As it happened at Nazareth, so did it at Obio Ibiono!

The eastern region covered a widely and thickly populated area subdivided into east central and southeastern (parts) sections. It is the southeastern section distinct from the Efiks, Ogoja, and Port Harcourt zones that was and is called the Ibibio people. Ibibio covered five or six main divisions at the time—Abak, Eket, Itu, Ikot Ekpene, Opobo also called Igwenga or Egwenga, and Uyo divisions—Ikot Ekpene being the oldest of them all in Akwa Ibom State where other local governments are concerned. Across the water were those from Calabar, the Efiks. After the colonial era and the civil war that brought about the existence of Biafra as a separate nation and the civil war together with armed struggle between Nigeria and Biafra for three and a half years between June 1966 and January1970, that is, those that inhabited the eastern part of Nigeria under the name divisions became known and called (the) local government areas.

What was then known as Ibibio people incorporated Uruan, Ibibio, Eket, Annang, Ibeno, Oron, Okobo, and Opobo-Umani language groups.

Generally, all the groups of languages understood Efik and Ibibio. To understand Okobo and Oron likewise Eket and Ibeno that were closely related, one had to learn. The language that was in a class apart was that of Opobo Town that was commonly called Umani. This language group had boundary with another language group called Andoni now in Rivers State. In spite of the differences, they all understood and spoke Efik-Ibibio language.

A.   The Origin of the Ibibios

The origin of the Ibibios is uncertain. There are certain variations in the narrations and accounts given. One postulate[45] holds that the Ibibios are immigrants from the Southern and Central Africa, belonging to the Semi-Bantu group of languages that came to settle in the south-eastern part of Nigeria. Another is that they migrated from some part of the Cameroon called Usak-Edet or Afaha Creek or Edik Afaha, especially with regard to those from Uruan clan. It is also suggested that when these newcomers came to their present habitation, the original inhabitants of the land already existed there. Those who migrated from Edik Afaha traveled through the Afaha through the Atlantic Ocean to the Cross River and settled in "AkwaAkpa Uruan," their ancestral home. They dispersed from there into hinterland. Many left the ancestral home Akwa Akpa Uruan and settled in the waterine areas of Okobo, Oron, Eket and Ibeno, and Itu.

The place or spot of migration indicated as Afaha is very problematic. It has given rise to series of speculations and hypotheses. One of the propositions about Afaha is connected with "village names" in Ibibio land. The other aspect of Afaha when connected with the village names is one that claims that migration from Akwa Akpa Uruan and Afaha Atai in Ibesikpo clan as well as Afaha Etok as the progenitors of the Ibibios is just guesswork.

The second speaks of a part of the body "armpit"—Afaha as the origin of the word taken as "support" to account for the many Afaha that exist.[46] While many people attempted to trace the origin of the Ibibios to Edik Afaha in Cameroon, some traced the origin to Akwa Akpa Uruan, some to Igboland, and many other places to East and Central Africa.

Dr. Edet A. Udo following Prof. Joseph H. Greenberg locates the place of origin of the Ibibios at the Central Benue Valley.[47] The idea of the

Semi-Bantu group arises from the notion of having black curly hair, broad nose, and so on. Among all these opinions is the belief that the Ibibios originated from Israel! It is held that they are the lost tribe of Israel. The same applies to the Igbos. Their customs, especially the system of levirate marriage (Lev. 18:20),[48] are well explained in the book of Roland de Vaux called *Ancient Israel*.[49] Mourning the dead with regard to professional mourners (Cf. 2 Sam. 1:24; Ezk. 32:16; Lk. 8:52, 23:27–28),[50] special days of obligation (Cf. Deut. 5:12), sacred days and new moon (Is. 1:14; Nm. 10:10, 28:11–15; 1 Chron. 23:31; 2 Chron. 2:4, 8:13, 31:3; Ezra 3:5; Ezk. 46:13; Col. 2:4) that constituted a basis of some taboos[51] as shown by De Vaux,[52] the idea of having seven or eight days in a week, the fact of only one Supreme God (Deut. 5:6–9), Abasi Ibom, theocratic[53] system of government, the system of counting numbers, and use of theophoric[54] names[55] all point to the fact that they are part and parcel of the Jewish diaspora. Whether this opinion is tenable, it is one of those ones held by some as being more plausible. On the other hand, Ettang[56] says emphatically that the Ibibios migrated from Edik Afaha. There are some of the difficulties about the original spot of migration. Even though it is generally agreed that the Ibibios are of a Semi-Bantu group, it seems more plausible looking at the cultural manifestations that the Ibibios are part and parcel of the Jewish people. Probably, with further researches, explorations, and archaeological discoveries and excavations, the seeming mystery surrounding the actual place of migration and origin will be resolved. From the foregoing, it appears that some clans want to establish themselves as the proto-ancestor or the proto-home from which other clans in Ibibio originated. Whatever the case may be, Ibibio is the tribe from which Tom Ino Ekandem originated. The hidden tendency to portray Afaha clan as the place from which other clans emerged might just indicate a certain superiority complex.[57] Whether there is a tacit attempt to establish Afaha as the ancestral home of the Ibibios, it is generally accepted by those from Ibiono that Obio Ibiono is the ancestral home of all from Ibiono. Obio Ibiono, because of its position, has the right of coronation of the Okukus. Tacitly, nomination and coronation are the preserves of Obio Ibiono. Consequent to this, Obio Ibiono is regarded as the home of the Okukus. This understanding gives room for tracing the pedigree or genealogy of family tree of the Okukus to a common ancestor and founding father. This point will be developed later in this chapter. The mentality accounts for the intervillage wars in and around Ibiono clan as a form of opposition to this monopoly and tendency to lord it over others.

B.   The Worship of Abasi Ibom, the Supreme God

The Ibibios worship "Abasi Ibom" or "Akwa Abasi Ibom," that is, God Almighty as the only Supreme God, even though they may resort to a household, personal, or clan deity depending on the circumstances they find themselves. They are aware that the clan deity or personal deity is subordinate to the Supreme God—Abasi Ibom. Abasi Ibom literally means "the Almighty God, who lives for ever." The "Ibom" attached as a suffix to "Abasi" indicates supremacy or sovereignty or great magnitude, extraordinary, and wonderful in size. The religion is monotheistic by worshipping only one God, not polytheistic or pantheistic in the sense of worshipping many gods. They know that they worship and believe in one Supreme God—Abasi Ibom. This is he who lives forever (*Aba Ke Nsi-Nsi*). Put in the proper context, it is "the Almighty God who lives forever similar to the revelation of the Name of God to Moses in the desert: *I Am Who Am*" (Ex. 3:14). They are very religious people filled with the awesome goodness of Abasi Ibom. They are impelled to worship him whether in great or small things. The awareness of his presence arises from their experience during the various sojourns and settlements in various places, causing them to rely on their own God as the only source of existence, protection, and security. Since he is able to take care of them and can overcome all things, he is the Almighty God (*Abasi Ibom*). They know that all other gods are subject to him and can never be compared with Abasi Ibom or Akwa Abasi Ibom.

They are aware that they cannot begin anything without first consulting him and notifying him. This is expressed in the proverb *Etime ototot Abasi atuak Isong*. This is one of those ancient and ancestral proverbs that is common knowledge in Ibibio land. Literally, it means "the special peg or wood or instrument used in boring holes in the ground for building construction must first notify God before accomplishing the task." This is almost like the Augustinian manner of thinking and expressing things from the point of view of eternity or where everything points to eternity, *sub specie aeternitatis*. The acknowledgement of his supremacy, presence, and willingness to intervene and participate in their affairs makes it possible to invite him to share in their lives and projects at all times.

The family of Tom shared in this belief too likewise Tom himself who breathed this air of recognition and dependence on Abasi Ibom. They equally made and still make use of theophoric names as they live out their belief in the names given to their progenies. That is why most of the names are theophoric in nature, ending with either Lord or God as do those in Israel with either *el, iel,* or *ah iah,* indicating the beginning of the word *Elôhîm* or *Yahweh*. Names like Michael, Joel, Ezekiel, Daniel, Abijah, Elijah, etc., exemplify this in Hebrew. Examples of theophoric names in Ibibio have already been given in the footnote number 8 above.

C. Government

The Ibibios know they cannot rule without God. Although their system of government was not theocracy ab initio like that of the Jews in which their laws are held to be sacrosanct/sacred, the laws of God, that of the Ibibios, is a mixture of gerontocracy and democracy but with basic dependence on Abasi. In other words, the eldest are held to be honest wise men or women and the embodiment of the laws, customs, and traditions of the people ruling as heads of the family but always consulting other members of the ruling council before making important decisions. Consultation provides the common modus operandi in Ibibio and Obio Ibiono where Tom's, later Cardinal Ekandem, family originated. The mixture of gerontocracy and democracy was also exercised by Tom's father, Obong Ekandem, during his reign. The elders air their views, making their contributions, and come to a consensus or conclusion. No kindred or clan would be excluded so as not to give room to dissenters. The decisions arrived at are owned, considered theirs with the readiness to defend them while encouraging a patriotic spirit and willingness to participate and build up the family or village or clan or town or kingdom as the case may be. The ruler never presumed that he had all the answers even though the authority of his office invested power on him. He knew that he needed the help of others even though he embodied many things in the community. The office of Obong embodied wisdom, authority, power, justice, humility, and love. Others could help. Ekpo masquerade, a form of police force, was used in the past to maintain law and order, whereas in Uruan and Efik land, Ekpe, literally meaning "lion," was in vogue.

Generally, a certain patriarchal lineage called the ruling family held the mantle of leadership and passed it from generation to generation. That forms the basis of gerontocracy. Kingship rotated from one kindred to the other, especially in Ibiono Ibom in which Obio Ibiono remained a king-making community. In this type of system, monarchy will not have a chance at all. The ruler ruled with the welfare of his people in mind. They were always conscious of what they owed the people by being the leader, and they did all that was possible to bring it to bear. Inasmuch as there was autonomy in each segment of governance, there was always a very strong link with the center of power—the overall ruler. As such, the various categories of Obong go to demonstrate the strong link with the overall Obong with sovereignty. He is called Okuku in Obio Ibiono and in Ibiono Ibom.

D.   Obio Ibiono, the Home of the Okukus

It is from the background such as this that Ibiono Ibom and Obio Ibiono came. Tom was an Ibiono indigene. The belief of the people of Ibiono Ibom is that Obio Ibiono is the first ancestral home of all from Ibiono. It is held also that those who migrated from Cameroon departed from Edik Afaha, and Afaha plays a very important role in Ibiono Ibom as well as in Obio Ibiono as the kingly clan. The number of the villages in Afaha clan is sometimes estimated as ten or fourteen as the case may be. Afaha also has the primacy of position as the first son and the traditional head of all the clans. The overall ruler in Ibiono is called the Okuku. His palace is in Obio Ibiono. But there is an exception like the Okuku from Utit Obio who ruled from there when it was the turn of their own family to rule.[58] The title Okuku is equiparated or compared with the same title in Uruan called *Nsom Uruan*.

The full name of Obio Ibiono is Obio Ibono Ibom Akpan Ankine Akpan Obio Ukem. The full name of the village gives their ancestry up to the third or fourth preceding generations of the founding fathers. The name Akpan Ankine is sometimes rendered as "Akpan Ankit."[59] It appears the disparity arose from the oral transmission of the historical data from one generation to the other as was the case with many episodes in the Bible, for instance, the story of creation or the flood. The rendering is surely different in meaning. "Ankine" means "Have you wrapped it round me?" or "Have you bound it round me?" suggesting a belt, rope, or a loincloth around the waist. It may also mean "Have you put me round you or bound it round me?" in the sense of lifting the arms, looking upward while waiting for help, or speaking derogatorily or sarcastically in terms of having defeated or guarding or being in control of someone or putting the person as a loincloth or as a belt.

On the other hand, "Annkit" can mean "Have you seen me?" Supposing someone is throwing something or cutting with a knife, the passerby can say to the person throwing something or to the laborer "Ankit?" "Have you seen me? Be careful that you do not harm me." If someone is sweeping, such a statement is equally applicable. In whatever sense, there is an element of challenge indicating bravery and authority. In summary, Akpan Annkit or Akpan Ankine would have been a man of valor and authority.[60] The family members of Obong Ekandem always see themselves as descendants of the founding ancestors; hence, they trace their pedigree to Akpan Obio Ukem, the founding father who suggests autonomy, authority, and royalty. Tom Ekandem is from a royal stock, therefore a prince by virtue of his birth.

Akpan Obio Ukem is said to be the ancestor of Obio Ibiono according to the father of Tom. Akpan Obio Ukem, the hero who fought and defeated his enemies till he came to pitch his tent at Obio Ibiono. The account of victory and defeat reflects Abraham's pursuit of the raiders who carried as booty, slaves, and property; and when he came back and became aware of the situation, he pursued his enemies with haste, overtook them, fought and defeated them, and brought back all that belonged to him together with what the enemies had. On his way back, he met Melchizedek who was without predecessors and gave a tenth of his property as tithe to him (Gen. 14:18–24).

The boundary of Akpan Obio Ukem's domain was fortified by Utit Obio, which means boundary or the end of the village or habitation. At Utit Obio, Akpan Obio Ukem, the hero, good warrior, and founding father and a sagacious administrator, left some of his soldiers in order to ward off any intruding enemies who may attempt to infiltrate. He pitched another tent at Idoro, which is now a clan as a war camp, and did the same thing at Ikot Obio Ama, where he rested until he came to Obio Ibiono. He finally settled there because of the plain nature of the land without hills and mountains and devoid of much swamps. Akpan Obio Ukem, the patriarch, decided to use Afaha Idoro south, which has great warriors, as a fortress of Obio Ibiono where the scepter of kingship is preserved.[61] Tom, a patriarch, is a direct descendant of the founding patriarch.

The coronation ceremony of Okuku made use of many symbols.[62] It later included *edet ekpe* (leopard's teeth), symbol of power; *akangkang* (double-edged sword); *mmé* (bracelet); *ayang* (broom); *ofong ikpa* (white leather shirt indicating bravery); *nuk-enin* (tusk), symbolizing fame, wealth, prowess, and summoning people to respond to the king's (call) invitation; *sittim* (copper money or wealth to indicate how wealthy the person was); and *ntinya* (the special crown for "chiefs"), and the Okuku title can only be conferred at Obio Ibiono. Even if the incumbent ruler lives in another place, the coronation ceremony is destined to take place in Obio Ibiono at Enen Ibom Akpan Ankit Square that has now become the palace of the Okuku. The custom might remind us of the saying of Jesus: "No Prophet should die outside Jerusalem" (Lk. 13:33). Ekuriku, the scepter, which passes on from generation to generation, is handed over to the newly constituted Okuku in a colorful ceremony. Ekuriku is the mantle of authority that the Okuku uses in wielding his authority and power. It is also his insignia.

As the first residential place of the founding fathers and primacy of position among all others, Obio Ibiono had the inalienable right of exhibiting the face of a lion in the olden days when killed by brave warriors or hunters. It is the core village in the whole of Ibiono Ibom. It is the seat of the government. It may be one of the smallest villages with the population of about one thousand five hundred to two thousand inhabitants, but its importance cannot be denied. Obio Ibiono is one of the fourteen villages in Afaha clan. Their position is incomparable and a privileged one.

The four or five sons of the patriarchs constitute the royal families. The sons later begot families that developed into *ekpuk* (kindred). The kindreds have developed into royal families. Oral tradition once again leaves room for confusion. Some traditions speak of four sons forming four royal families, while some others hold on to five.

Another notable point is that who comes first among the sons is a big question. Among the group of four, the following are included:

Nung Akpan Obio Ukem Ibom Akpan Ankit or Akine
Nung Ekpo Mbiam Ibom Akpan Ankit or Akine
Nung Adia Mkpo Ibom Akpan Ankit or Ankine Nung
Okut Iko Ibom Akpan Ankit[63]

Among the group of five, the following are included:

Nung Adia Nkpo
Nung Akpabio
Nung Ekpong Ntak
Nung Ekpa
Nung Nkup[64]

Tom Ino Ekandem is from Nung Adia Nkpo, the "first" among others in Obio Ibiono. From all indications, Nung Akpabio is a shortened form of Nung Akpan Obio Ukem, while Ekpo Mbiam is the same as Ekpo Mbiam; Nung Okut seems to be the same with Nkup. The kindred that is left out is Nung Ekpong Ntak. Since oral tradition is the main source of information, the differences in the number of siblings are attributable to different priorities of those involved. The more detailed analysis of these differences is not within the competence of this work. It is hoped that later writings will deal with these. There is no dispute about Obio Ibiono as the center of coronation in Ibiono Ibom. Its significance is almost like that of Nazareth in the Promised Land; though small in size, it is very significant in what it symbolizes. Such was and is Obio Ibiono, the home of Tom. It is the first among equals. Their occupation is farming, fishing, tapping, and weaving.

E.   The System of Government in Obio Ibiono

Obio Ibiono's system of government is like that of Ibiono Ibom and that of Ibibio as a whole. Every village is a microcosm of the whole Ibibio land although autonomous in its own right. Their governmental system combines gerontocracy and democracy.

The kingship rotates from one family to the other among the kindreds' oldest members. The Obio Ibono is the *locus of coronation* in Ibiono Ibom. There are other grades of chiefs, Obong, that operate in conjunction with Okuku. They are Obong Obio or Idung, the chiefs who rule a particular village. In Obio Ibiono, the Okuku used to combine the two offices in the past—Obong Ekpuk, the chief who is in charge of kindred. The power of such chiefs depends on the number of kindreds. Obong Idiong is the overall soothsayer or adviser. The diviners are consulted when need arises. They like Obong Ekpo, who functions more in a traditionally cultic[65] context and security. They may or may not belong to the village council.

Obong Mkparawa, the youth leader, is the one who organizes the youth and whom they listen to. He is to help Obong Idung in organizing free and habitable village without troubles. They can discipline themselves and be authorized to discipline any person who goes out of order. He attends meetings of the village council, likewise consulting other youth leaders in other villages for the purpose of exchanging ideas.

Obong Ekpo is the chief of the masquerades who takes place during the season of Ekpo. Since it is part of the cultural heritage, he is generally consulted on issues pertaining to the commencement or closure of Ekpo season, its regulation when things go wrong, or the empowerment when something is to be enforced. The youth leader works hand in hand with Obong Ekpo for effectiveness.

Obong Mbre is the chief in charge of any form of organized recreation or entertainment or, simply put, the entertainment executive or recreational leader. He consults with Obong Obio and his advisers to see that things move on well and the people have beneficial and enjoyable days. Sometimes no specific person is appointed for the office. On the whole, the responsibility lies on Obong Mbre who acts as the liaison officer. These and others whose functions are vital are co-opted into the village council. A wise man, an orator, and a man of valor, preferably a warrior, one who can persuade in difficult situations people with a great wealth of experience and some skillful personalities, are also brought in for the smooth running of the event.[66]

Obong Obio and his council are the ones to see that peace is maintained in the village and law and order, protection of the people from neighboring attacks, sanitation properly taken care of, disputes settled, and necessary things done for the improvement of the community are carried out. Intervillage relationship is handled by the ruling council headed by Obong Obio. If Obong Obio is honest and just, his reign will be upheld and esteemed greatly; if not, it will be rejected as the kings of Israel before the Almighty God, the ultimate judge and ruler. The generation of funds will be greatly hampered, and the internal running of the village will not be smooth, and there will be a lot of resentment and anger. When Obong Obio acts in the capacity of a father, *pater familias*, the fatherly love will radiate, and the dwelling will be the abode of safety and refuge for all.

Obong Obio with his council are the ones to favor the establishment of new projects or to reject them. If they are foresighted, they will favor profitable projects or discard them if they do not see the need or sometimes if they will not favor the village. Sometimes in the past, good projects were rejected, owing to lack of knowledge. In places where land is greatly valued, profitable projects could be rejected in favor of land as it has happened in many villages. Those who see the need immediately rush to grab it. Land donated for the erection of churches is sanctioned by such a body as well as markets, parks, schools, hospitals, etc. Without their permission, even if a parcel of land is given, it cannot be used. With their approval, the use becomes automatic and free. They can agree to admit or to expel a religious body from the village as Okuku Ekandem did[67] depending on the performance of the religious body concerned.

In terms of security, they organized a "vigilante group" (*nka ukpeme*) to ward off "maggots" in the form of thieves or robbers who can possibly disturb the peace and security of the community. *Nka ukpeme* gives great support and collaborate the actions of the local law enforcement agency. The local law enforcement agency regulates the market days in times of conflict. They equally go on patrol when misunderstanding with other communities arises. The support of all the males in the community is generally needed to uphold the market days regulation. Obong Obio and council may use the veto power occasionally, but generally, the village deliberates on very important issues that affect the generality of the people.

Financially, they depend on their palm-produce sales or levies or taxation or loans in order to carry out the village or community projects. They can tap into the generosity of the citizens who want to demonstrate their patriotism and magnanimity.

When there is a need to open a new road or to expand the boundaries of the community or carry out general sanitation, communal labor is organized. The Obong usually handles such responsibilities and his council in conjunction with those designated for that particular purpose or the person in charge of labor or sanitation. They do not need to consult before making the decision. They need to inform others and disseminate information regarding the work to be accomplished and the date and the time through the village or town crier who goes around alerting the people of the forthcoming event. Sometimes a fine is attached to ensure a good turnout. The important market days are usually considered before fixing the communal labor to avoid clashing and unnecessary excuses. Once it is for the good of the community and the people are in the know, the work would be willingly accomplished.

This is where the moral authority of the ruler comes into effect. Important or foreign visitors to the place, who are likely to pass the night in the place, must pay a courtesy call to Obong Obio and his council for respect and security. In this way, the visitor would not be harassed by anyone but would be given a warm welcome.

This accounts for the visits of court clerks, district officers (DOs), and clergymen to Obong Ekandem, the Okuku of Obio Ibiono. The warm reception given to the visitors is an expression of love that will surely help the visitor to feel at home and dwell in the community tranquilly. On some occasions, depending on who visits the place, the Obong and his council may decide to confer a chieftaincy title on the person visiting as a sign of love, acceptance, and appreciation. It is never conferred on everyone.

The society is patrilineally organized. The patrilineal nature of the society also reflects that of the Israelites. The latter can be seen even in the account of the feeding of the five thousand (Matt. 14:13–21), where there was an addition "besides women and children" (Matt. 14:21). At that time in Ibibio land, women did not have much say. There was a presumption that the woman's place was in the kitchen. She was only to be seen and not heard. That picture has long changed in various Ibibio communities even though in various traditional institutions, women do not enjoy some privileges as men do, except in the ancient days in which a very old woman or the oldest woman in the village could join Ekpo group. That privilege indicated that she had passed the stage of being regarded as a female and was seen with the eyes of the elders of Ekpo as an elder only with regard to Ekpo. She was consulted and informed of what was going to take place in Ekpo group. It appears this was a way of minimizing the tension in Ekpo group. That exception later disappeared.

Michael I. Edem CM

UMIANA EKPO EKPO AFAI

AYARA EKPO

INYON EKPO

EKONG

ASIAN UBOIKPA

MBRE UBOIKPA

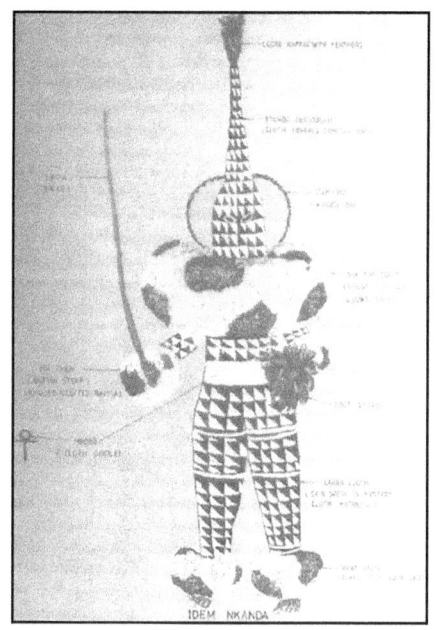

EKPE

INUEN EKPO/OBIOKPO

F.   Religion, Traditional Institutions, and Feasts

Like all the Ibibios, Obio Ibiono worships the Supreme God called Abasi Ibom. He is known to be all powerful, present, and all knowing, that is, omnipotent, omnipresent, and omniscient. There are no shrines or priests or priestesses dedicated to him. He is prayed to. His dwelling is not on earth. He is transcendent. He lives in the sky but hears those who call upon him. He is the Creator expressed in some contexts as Abasi Oboteyen. The God who creates or God the Creator of children. Literally, it means God makes or molds a child.

Before any prayer is offered, Abasi Ibom is invoked, even when libation[68] is to be poured. The typical traditional Ibibio prayer goes thus:

> Abasi Enyong, Abasi Isong, God of heaven and of earth
> Andinyie Odudu Nkan, The most powerful or omnipotent
> Andino Nkpo Inam, He who does things well or the capable doer Ema Ukot Fien Esin Ke Otu Nkpo, Nkpo Ofon Ama, When you are invited (into the group or to any event), all goes well. Immediately after the invocation of Abasi Ibom, the parents, if they are dead, together with the ancestors, would be invoked or invited.
> Ete Mmi, Eka Mmi Idi Idiwana, My father and my mother come and share (if they were dead)
> Mme Nti Ikan Iden Ye Iban Idi Do, Good men and women (ancestors) who departed come along
> Inno Ukpeme, Nsonidem, Uforo, Grant me protection, health, prosperity Mfoniso Ye Inyie, Good luck and wealth
> Eke Owo Obo Nkpo Amfon Mien, He who seeks my good Yak Nkpo Ofon Enye, Let something good happen to him Eke Obo Nkpo Andiok Mien, He who wishes me evil
> Yak Nkpo Odiok Enye, Let evil (something) come to him (This is almost like the psalm of curses against the enemy who seeks protection from God and destruc-

tion of the enemy.) Idiok Nkpo Aka Nsan, May evil stay afar off

Idiok Nkpo K'iso Ami Kedem, When evil is at the front, let me be behind. Abiba K'edem Ami K'iso, When it is behind, let me be in front. Ubok Ekpe Nnsana Nta Iwa, When my hands are clean, I am eating tapioca.

Ebi Mbat, Nkot Eyop, When my hands are dirty, I am chewing roasted palm fruit (because of rubbing away the ashes with the palms). This is also similar to prayer of confession of guilt and declaration of innocence in the traditional Jewish prayer context.

There are many other forms of prayers that express the people's belief and worldview. There are other deities who are given recognition or revered, and places of worship or where they could be sacrificed to are indicated as would be seen in subsequent pages. In Ibiono, the clan's major deity is Anantia Ibiono Ibom, but the shrine is located at Obio Ibiono. This is found in Akwa Obio Ibiono in the square where the Okukus' palace is located.[69] Frequently, Obong Ekandem, the father of the future cardinal, sacrificed to this deity whom Cardinal Ekandem later testified to when he said that they used to eat the yams and goats and cocks sacrificed to the deity.[70] Among the deities given recognition in Ibibio land are Abasi Obot Eyen and Abasi Obot Udia who may be called special attributes of Akwa Abasi Ibom instead of the nature gods who create children and make yams. Abasi Obot Eyen is generally sacrificed to in the special forest where a special pot is placed. Those who seek children go to the forest to drink from that pot as a sign of communion and subjection to the benevolence of the deity. The pot is only touched during the time of sacrifice. The sacrifice offered to Abasi Obot Udia takes place before the farming season. The clearing of the farmland to be cultivated usually precedes it. It occurs, preferably, at the boundary of the farmland concerned.

The sacrifice is offered to appease Obot and to secure good harvest. Obot is one of the theophoric names that is commonly used. Those who bear the name Obot are always linked with the God who creates or God the Creator of children, Abasi Obot Eyen, since no minor deity is associated with this function but the Creator (as such) per se. To bear the name

Obot is an indication of gratefulness to or gift from Obot. It could also be as a result of veneration or devotion to such deity. The name Obot became a common one with time. Later people began bearing such a name without being associated with Abasi Obot Eyen or sometimes from the family's genealogical tree or one bearing the name of the namesake; as a consequence, the name came to stay.

Another minor deity given recognition is Ndem, considered as spirit and associated with water. Ndem is a generic name for all the minor deities connected with water that may have small portions of the forest dedicated to them, especially near a common passage. There are many types of Ndem like Ekpenyong, Ekandem, and Afianwan, etc., in various places. Ekpenyong is a masculine form of Ndem, while Ekandem is the mother of Ndem, and Afianwan is a description of Ndem in a female context that is white Ndem or very fair and beautiful. They can have their dwellings on land, river, sea, or ocean or on a hill, a mountain, or a tree. They are offered sacrifices. When they are petitioned, they can become capricious in their reactions like invoking the spirit of the dead ones who were evil. If they do not respond positively to the pleas made, they are rejected; if what is petitioned is granted, they are given allegiance.

Ekpenyong is a common name in Ibibio as well as Ekandem or Ekanem, having an association with these deities or spirits. If a person dedicated to Ndem as a priest or priestess owns a child or somebody possessed by any such deity or spirit is termed *Awa Ndem*, likewise the person who sacrifices to Ndem and has an altar or shrine dedicated to Ndem. The child begotten during that period is named Ekandem or the anglicized form Ekanem. Okpono Ndem is the one who adores or worships Ndem, the great water spirit or deity. This applies to Ekandem or Ekanem. Ndem is construed to confer riches and wealth. This is why Cardinal Ekandem reinterpreted his surname, Ekandem, to mean Ekan Ndem, that is, Ndem has been defeated or overcome in the context of Christian Initiation-Baptism. He always saw himself as one who overpowers the minor deities with the help of God.

As can be seen from the foregoing, these minor deities have their temple or abode where they could be consulted or sacrificed to, but Abasi Ibom, the Great, Supreme, Almighty God, has no particular dwelling place or altar or place of sacrifice. He is everywhere. He owns the whole earth and the sky. If one were to dare to sacrifice to him, any place would be suitable since land as such is regarded as sacred and is an altar. These deities are only emissaries to Abasi Ibom. They can never be compared with Abasi Ibom who is in a class apart. He has no competitor (Cf. Deut. 5:6–9).

Apart from the minor deities, there is another class, the ancestors (*Mme Ikan* or *Mme Mbukpo, Mme Ekpo*), indicating the spirits of the ancestors—great grandparents, grandparents, or even fathers—that are long dead, especially those who led good lives (patriarchs) or the female (matriarchs). They are given reverence, and they can be sacrificed to and appeased or invoked for protection and care. They are regarded as part of the family setup. They are the living dead.

The loving and conscientious father, Okuku Ekandem, inducted the young Tom into these worships and sacrifices. The departed ones or the ancestors, both patriarchs and matriarchs, lived vicariously in their families and offsprings and successors. They cannot be ignored in any event, that is, within the traditional setting, libations are poured to invoke them, their intercession is sought, and their dwelling place after the physical world is secured in the form of a tombstone or a little building called *nwomo* to give them an abode in the spirit world. In other words, life after death is a continuation of the life on earth.

The Abode of the Dead, "Obio Ekpo." The conception of such a place is that of continuity with the current world of existence. That accounts for the burial of some slaves in the past with the casket of some important personalities as recounted in Bishop Shanahan's second burial[71] episode. [This is slightly different from the Hebrew conception of 'Sheol' which is a dark dwelling place of the dead.] The slaves were forced into the grave, probably four or six of them sitting on the floor of the grave stretching out their legs with fans in their right hands and the casket placed on their legs. This tradition of burying the living persons with the dead body of a king or chief or a special titled man is similar to the Egyptian burial custom of the pharaohs. The grave was then covered with sand, and the slaves died of suffocation or asphyxia. That is why the initiates carried out such a burial in the night only. Later, slain heads were used instead of burying human beings alive.

An initiate into *Ekong* society, that is, the group reserved for the warriors or those who slew the heads of slaves as in a war situation or cut the skull of a human being, symbolizing a real human being, is called *Ndi Nze* in Igboland. They had the privilege of being associated with nwomo together with the revered ancestors. Wealthy families constructed Nkuku or Iyoho, a gorgeously built pyramidal construction with variegated colored clothes of all kinds. Household items; war equipment; farming implements; heads of cows, goats, and chickens; shells of tortoise and snails; old pots; tripod stands no longer in use; plates; wooden spoons; machetes; spears; swords; and others would be left in that dwelling of the great personality concerned. Such ceremonies can be costly and can only be afforded by the very rich. Sumptuous feasting for the living and the dead takes place. The heads of the various animals, birds, and fish consumed during the ceremonies as well as the bottles of drinks, or *okoop*, the special calabash chords, used have to be deposited there. Nkuku is always constructed in the process of *Uwuongo-Owo*, the cutting of a physical relationship and giving a home to the deceased for the personality's use. Libation is very generously poured to the deceased for pacification and protection from harm.

Nwomo is small with a few mats and sticks in a form of hut. It is terribly low and close to the ground. Feathers of a cock offered are left behind, and the blood of the slaughtered cock is sprinkled there. The warriors have Abasi Ekong, the god of war. Nwomo is a little rectangular construction made of fresh raffia palm fronds, *eyei* or *ekpin*, beautifully woven with a particular design in a traditional manner with *itumo*, a type of tree that grows easily in the tropics. *Itumo* is a live tree easily propagated or grown and can survive for years. It is used as support together with dry bamboos and tie-tie, *Anyang*, in the construction of Abasi Ekong. Inside the Abasi Ekong house, a little clay pot (*usanidem*) with *okpoho* (copper), *ufon* (red chalk), and *nwewep* (a special leaf that is roundish in form construed to bring good luck and peace) are placed there. At the end of the construction, a small feasting is held. Obong Ekandem could not have been left out in such a situation since he was an initiate of Ekong.

Ekong is a traditional institution and carries along with it rights and privileges. One of the privileges enjoyed by the members was maintenance or sharing in the special portion of palm fruits called *Owok Ekong* reserved for initiates. Each member enjoyed that benefit rotationally. To have a share in Owok Ekong was a type of long-term investment to help defray the expenses incurred during the ceremonies. The initiates had the right to initiate all their male children.

To immortalize the fact of being a member of Ekong society, a son born at the time was automatically called Ekong or *Adiaha/Nwa Ekong* if a female. Similarly, any child born during the period of war was called or *Isua Ekong* or *Ufot/Ufot Ekong*, that is, the "Day of the war or the year of the war or *middle of the* war." The Ekong initiates had the regalia of a helmet, whether of iron or plastic or from special fiber; red long-sleeve shirt with pockets and the pocket covers on both sides, each pocket had a button attached; two crossbars of white and yellow clothes across the chest; an iron gong with sharp edges; a long sharp base that could be used in fighting or fixing the instrument into the ground with an open end for water, something to use in striking the gong; and a very mighty loincloth as well as shoes or boots.

When an initiate dies, fresh palm fronds would be beautifully woven and used for burial instead of a coffin. The origin of this appears to be emergency burial in time of war since it is presumed that the deceased was a warrior and died as a warrior. Since Obong Ekandem died as Obong Paul Ekandem, he could not be buried that way. Following the tradition, the deceased could be seated with all the regalia with a goat under his feet, one on the roof, and a cock attached to the right hand as well as a bell. Whenever the cock flapped its wings, the material, *Eto Ekere*, fixed to the right hand of the deceased, would strike the iron gong on the left. Both goats are strangled for the rituals, and the cock belongs to the initiates. An Ekong member's burial is always very late in the evening or in the night as at wartimes when a fallen warrior needed to be brought in the night for burial.

Sometimes instead of using the beautifully woven fresh palm fronds, *odong*, for burial, every thorny shrub or branch could be bound together and used to bury the person. Such burial indicates that the person died violently, suddenly, termed *Mkpai Afai*, without space to prepare a casket, and since burial must be carried out hurriedly, whatever is found is used for the burial. Since the person died violently, he/she must also be buried violently and hurriedly. The burial with thorns, called akpap, is also used for those who commit suicide to indicate that it is abominable.

Idiong is one of the traditional institutions found in Obio Ibiono. It simply means divination. The person who practices divination is termed *Abia Idiong* or *Abia Mfa*, while many of them are called *Mbia Idiong* or *Mbia Mfa*. They use an instrument called *ndomo* for divination. It is translated literally in the form of a question: "Should I measure or weigh?" It is the diviner's apparatus to ascertain the truth or falsity of the case. Idiong functions more in a controversial, uncertain situations and in determining the cause of a problem as well as determining the future possibility of a case.

Abia Idiong is one believed to be divinely inspired, a type of divine doctor who can ascertain or determine or unravel what is obscure. They play a very important role in a traditional society since they can foretell the future whether true or false and determine the cause of death or disease, which may lead to sacrifice in order to appease the situation or avert harm. Ndomo is similar to the Urim and Thumim of the Hebrew prophets of the Old Testament (Ex. 28:30). Idiong is for both males and females. They go through the process of entering Mbang Idiong, a type of enclosure/novitiate or separation in a little hut built and set apart for the person. It is a period of seclusion from the public. It could be compared to the desert experience or novitiate of St. Paul that he said he went to Arabia for three years (Gal. 1:17).

The person to be initiated stays in the seclusion for at least three to six months before emerging into the public after initiation. The person's body would be decorated with oil prepared from *Adan Umom*, a rhizome that when crushed and rubbed on the body gives a yellow or orange color, owing to its nature. Special food is prescribed by the ancient tradition as a constituent part of the initiation rite. The food has to be provided. The person in Mbang Idiong is never to be left alone in that seclusion. A little child has to be there with the person as in the case of Mbobo or Nkuho in the fattening room. For the person to go out and ease himself, he has to be preceded by the attendant who makes some noise to make sure no one is around and to ward off evil spirits. At the end of the seclusion, there is an initiation proper in which the person to be initiated lies down for some form of incantation and invocation of the various Idiong ancestors, during which the person undergoes what is called *Una Okpo Idiong*, lying like a corpse as part of the special ceremony.

It is a very perilous moment. One can easily pass away totally as popularly claimed that the person becomes unconscious by being struck down by the spirits of the ancient initiates till after that special ceremony comes to an end. The relations of the prospective initiate normally get worried until after the ceremony. When the person rises from the spot, it is a confirmation that the person has the divine mandate to arbitrate in the society in terms of judgment, dispute, and the like through divination. The lying down could be paralleled with *prostration* during the rite of ordination in the Catholic Church when the "Litany of the Saints" is sung.

There is always a great rejoicing when the initiate rises and did not die in the process. If death occurred in the process, it is always regarded as a bad omen that would usher in tremendous fear in the family and the entire (*milieu*) community. They would surely consult another diviner to tell them what they had to do next. The main instrument used is *ekput idiong*, a wooden instrument with openings at both ends and a portion for handling it with two pendulum sticks at both ends for swinging and producing sound. Other things associated with divination are *nkang* (charcoal) and *ndom* (white clay) chalk used to indicate favorable judgment. *Nsei* or *ufon*, somewhat reddish or yellowish-brown chalk, is used on the head of the person to indicate blessing and favors from the gods. The Idiong initiates have a special coronet called *okpono idiong* as an insignia.

Inam is another traditional institution in Ibibio land. Literally, Inam means "Must we do it?" or "Can we as a body do it?" or as a command addressed to the second-person plural, "You, do it." It is a priestly office, which demands great wealth in order to be initiated. Generally, those initiated are elderly people chosen by divine signs that have to be deciphered through divination as in the account of King Saul and the witch of Endor (Cf. 1 Sam. 28:7 ff). The Inam person must have been already initiated into Idiong. When series of misfortunes befall a person, the person goes to a diviner to find out what the situation is with the hope to avert it. He might learn in the process that he has to be initiated into Inam group. Only very few are in this group.

An Inam person is one who has been initiated into many institutions and societies of the lands and is living a good life both in secret and in public. He is without blemish in the eyes of the people that is why people go to him for prayer and for advice. He is a public figure and chief consultant in matters relating to moral life and good living. The office of Inam is regarded as a divine call through which the misfortune of a person can be turned into abundance. The prerequisite condition of election is moral rectitude or uprightness of the person. Inam forms the highest priestly office in Ibibio. Inam priests are revered and do not move from place to place. They are secluded, but they can be visited. They differ from *Omum Idiong* whose seclusion does not permit visits and is temporary. Since they do not move around or work, they can eventually become poor after having consumed most of their wealth in the process of initiation. Consequently, they can be dissatisfied, especially with their seclusion and penury. They do not own plots of palms like those in Ekong and Ekpe group.

The initiation process of Inam is very exacting and costly, especially as it lasts for several years. In some places, the duration is seven years, in others, forty-nine, that is, seven times seven like the Jewish Jubilee Year. After the period of seclusion, the outing ceremony, which entails going to the market, is part of what takes place. A sumptuous and an expensive celebration will take place. The person involved will go to one of their popular and greatly attended markets riding on a donkey or camel as the case may be. *Usanga ke enyong enang*, going on the back of the camel or donkey, is one of the major features of outing. If it can be afforded, it can be rented just for that occasion. Sometimes local Ibibio cows, *enang*, can be used. There will be twenty-one gun salute, that is, seven times three. The gun salute can be sounded even before leaving the compound, seven at the market to alert the people of his presence and seven at the house after coming back. Those who cannot afford the twenty-one can manage with seven only. Likewise, if a donkey or camel cannot be afforded or hired, strong and able young men could carry the person on the neck. The whole exercise has to be greatly publicized. Sometimes a cow will be slaughtered for entertainment as part of the ritual of initiation or, better still, seven cows. Abundance of everything will be experienced, for example, strong drinks, palm wine (*ukot*), goats, chickens, and yams. In short, everything has to be in multiples of seven commensurate to the number of years of initiation. Gifts are also given in return. Even his wives have to be up to seven. As part of the initiation rite, one of the wives has to be a woman with severe curvature[72] of the spine (Ekung) to indicate that he has married even the exceptional one. Oduk Inam is the only person who goes out of his way to marry the Ekung as part of the riches of Oduk Inam since the woman with severe curvature of the spine, Ekung, is believed to have mercury in the curvature. Whether that one gives birth or not, it does not matter. What matters is the marriage is part of the ritual. This gives rise to the saying "*Oduk Inam Odo Nkpo, Tutu Odo Ekung*," meaning "The Inam initiate marries to the extent that he marries an Ekung woman." Ekung is one of the most expensive wives to marry. They have to go in search for Ekung and negotiate her marriage wherever she can be found since they are rare. For Obong Inam to marry Ekung is a sign of wealth. In the process, a new house separate from the former one he was living will be built and *nwan ima*, the beloved wife, and the Ekung have to be the only ones to live in the new house with him. The building has to be within the same plot. The two women will be the ones to minister to him. The food is to be served by Ekung and water for his bath as well. In a way, Ekung is the one closest to him.

In a polygamous setting when there is Nwan Ima, there must be the opposite too, *nwan usua*, "the hated wife," especially the one who is jealous of nwan ima. The duo, nwan ima and nwan usua, constitutes a pair that is jealous of each other. The consequence of this is that the husband, *ebe*, can die of hunger because each of these would presume that the other would feed ebe as an Ogoja name *Anditung* indicates.

One day in a week is set aside for not going to the farm, *Usen Ubet Inwang*, a day that is a taboo to go to the farm on the market day called *Ata Etaha*. On that day, palm wine is not sold. It is shared freely by all the titled men and sometime by all men. The day is also called *Usen Ibet*, the day of prohibition that can be compared to Sabbath day's rest.[73] On this day, women are forbidden to drink ukot[74] (palm wine or pammy). The women can go to the stream but not to the farm. To reinforce the tradition, a story of how a woman went to the farm and saw a very mighty python symbolizing *Inwang* at the entrance and boundary of her farm scared a lot of women and made them stay away. A man can go to the farm with a boy and get vegetables and firewood but not to work. It is a day of rest. It was this idea of rest that caused Ata Etaha to be associated with Oku Inam as a day dedicated to Abasi Ibom.[75]

Every male and female, young and old, is entitled to this rest. Women used such a day for cleaning their houses and for beautifying their surrounding. Obong Ekandem and his family must have enjoyed this privilege. The day was originally dedicated to Abasi Inwang, the god of the farm. If Oku Inam is the highest priestly office as held, he could be associated with Abasi Ibom as his priest. On the other hand, if he were to be directly chosen as the priest of the Most High God, he could have been called Oku-Abasi Ibom, not Oku Inam. Only a process of *association* affiliates him. It appears this is more of a *projection*, that is, what the people claim it is than it actually is. Oku Inam is forbidden to eat new yams (*Obufa Udia*) until the ceremony of *Nsuk Udia* (taming the new yam), that is, making it harmless or controllable before he can consume it. Others can, but he cannot. There is no special symbol attached to the office or regalia. By virtue of his age, he dresses as elders do except Okpono Idiong like other Idiong initiates.

Ekpe[76] is a type of masquerade that uses a variegated type of raffia regalia for the costumes. Ekpe literally means "lion." It is among the powerful traditional institutions in the land. It is very prevalent in some areas but almost nonexistent in some others. There are many types of Ekpe, for example, *Obon, Mboko, Nyamkpe, Nkanda*, and *Nkpri-Ekpe*. Each of these has its distinctive style and manner of operation. Ekpe is more of a cult than just a society or an association even though it observes strict rule. Where it is frequently used, it involves sacrifices too.[77] Its membership is strictly controlled. One who is wealthy and trusted could be initiated into all the subgroups of Ekpe. It constitutes a type of traditional police force like Ekpo in order to maintain peace and order in the society as well as discipline.

An initiate has to spend a fortune to entertain all the existing members coupled with a standard fee, which has to be distributed equally. The initiate of Nkanda has to be decorated with white clay chalk, *ndom*, as well as *Ntang Nkanada*, the feather of a peacock to indicate its beauty, and the person has to beat a special drum dedicated for such occasions and for the use of the members. A fully initiated person is called *Oyoho Aban Ekpe*. At the time Tom and his brothers were initiated, it is not likely that they were mature enough to exercise their full rights. It is likely they were still minors.

One of the things peculiar to Ekpe as a cult during its initiation rite is *Udok Itiat Ekpe*. Literally, this means "climbing the stone of Ekpe." This rite gives the sense of satisfaction that an initiate has become a full member in Ekpe cult and has undergone full initiation rites. Beating the drum and decoration with Ntang Nkanda is a sign of full membership in the group, thus conferring special authority and title Oyoho Aban Ekpe (full initiate). As the name Ekpe implies, the members of the group can act like a lion or leopard taking animals away as compensation, especially when the owner of the animal is in debt. If somebody is to be ostracized, Ekpe, as an instrument, is used to confiscate the person's property, and that is called *Mbume Ekpe* (confiscation or forceful gathering or commandeering or struggling to get whatever is available). The initiated male children of a wealthy father will not suffer any embarrassments but will enjoy all the rights and privileges commensurate to their status. A minor will have to wait until maturity before assuming responsibility and undertaking the events of the cult and the climbing of Itiat Ekpe.[78]

In some places, Itiat Ekpe is not as big as the one shown in this diagram. It can also be conical with a flat base and black and smooth, generally located in *akai*, forest where the Itiat Ekpe is fixed to the soil. The particular spot where it is fixed is called *Akai Itiat Ekpe*, the forest where Ekpe Stone is located. In this conical form, Udok Itiat Ekpe, Climbing the stone of Ekpe or Ekpe Stone only entails stretching out one's leg and placing on it reverentially since Itiat Ekpe is regarded as something sacred by the initiates. No one is permitted to go to that vicinity unless an initiate. If one does, a very big fine that might render the culprit penniless can be pronounced. Of course, there are no pleas whatsoever once the fine has been imposed. One simply has to conform or face expulsion from the village and become a fugitive in a foreign land with no hope of return unlike the Jews who knew they would one day return to their homeland.

The initiates have enticements that are those things that attract them like plots of palm fruits (*Owok Ekpe*) owned and harvested in rotation among the members. The aim is to help defray the cost of expenses. There is a possibility that such plots were obtained through forceful usurpation of the plot and thereby creating an enforced ownership authority of the group. Another possibility is the allocation of the plot by the village to the group so as to enjoy the same privilege like that of *Owok Ekong*. Anywhere a fully initiated person goes and meets members of the fraternity as they sometimes know themselves, they regard themselves as brothers linked up through the initiation, provided the person passes the test of Nsibidi. Nsibidi will act as the secret signs used by those in AMORC or Ogboni or any other secret society to indicate their presence either through shaking of hands in the special way or through signs to gain entry to places forbidden to all others.

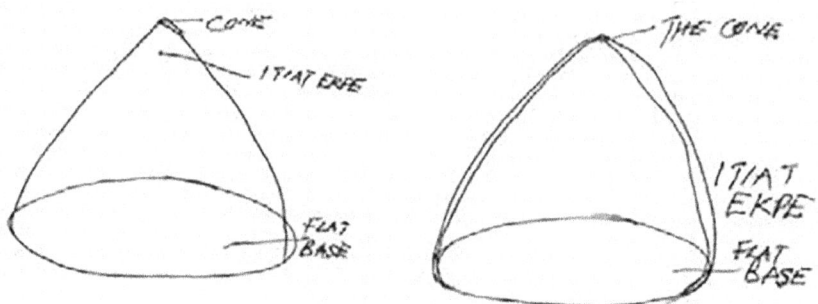

Figure 1 Itiat Ekpe with Flat Base

The figure below is the one found at Akpet in Calabar, Cross River State. Itiat Ekpe demonstrates its cultic displays and connection with occult symbols.

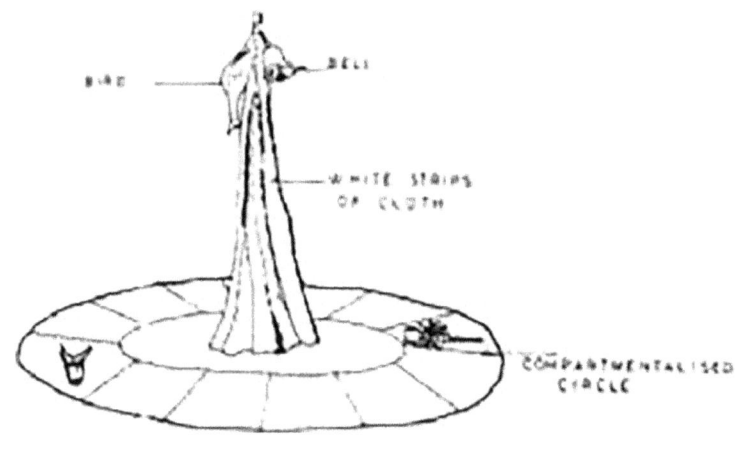

Figure 2

In the case of Ekpe cult, the *Nsibidi*, the secret sign, could be used to trap the uninitiated and maybe members who have been initiated but have not learned the secret signs very well. The process of initiating the secret or magical sign is called *Usin Nsibidi*, initiating a puzzle specifically belonging to the group goes with its collateral *Usiongo Nsibidi*, solving or unlocking the puzzle. Every fully initiated member must know how to "lock and unlock" the puzzle of Nsibidi. It can take the form of a sign or words. If Nsibidi sign is left near the door, especially in a bereavement setting, a noninitiate will not understand what is at stake. The person will match in only to tie oneself with the rope of the puzzle, thereby incurring a serious fine or punishment for his attempt. An initiate will immediately solve the puzzle and pass in without incurring any censure. Sometimes the solution to the puzzle may be just to give a signal with the hand or say something like *Tua Fi*, which is a verbal sign of spitting at Ekpe, thus reducing or neutralizing the power of Itumo, leaves signifying aggression and occult symbol when pointed at the person. Nsibidi has a type of entry and exit sign like stimulus and response or question-and-answer sequence. On the whole, Ekpe is used to force and enforce discipline where it is operative. When an initiate of Ekpe dies, various types of Ekpe society that he joined will be displayed. The same is applicable to Ekpo. The initiates will make their demand concerning entertainment. Since it is a type of force, destruction of property or catching of goats seen in the open places at the time also goes with it. If the specified things to be given to them are not correctly given, Ekpe will capture either goat or cock and go away. The animal or bird killed does not necessarily need to belong to the household of the deceased. Whoever owns the animal will later go to demand compensation from the family of the deceased. Once all the demands are satisfied, the sound of Ekpe will be heard if the initiate were to have been part of *Obon* group. Obon will then produce a sound that is heavy and frightening. Only the initiates will enter such a place. Swinging a piece of flat, thin, dry bamboo tied to a strong thread produces the sound. The swinging produces a horrifying sound like a lion. A bunch of leaves called *itumo* will be hung on the lintel of the house as an indication of the presence of Ekpe to ward off the noninitiates. Itumo leaves on the door are a common sign used for all the Ekpe initiates.

Ekoong is one of the traditional institutions that is almost on a par with Ekpe just discussed. It is a very dangerous and exclusive group that does not tolerate any infiltration. It is also one of the secret cults. It is similar to Ekpe. It has no secret signs like Ekpe, but it is much more dangerous than Ekpe. It could be compared to Freemasonry or any of the occult groups in Western society. Most of the things about Ekoong are carried out in the forest. The initiation rite as well as reception takes place in a special square in the village. On the day of the outing, no uninitiated or female is allowed to come out neither are they to pass through the square in which their gathering takes place. Any uninitiated who attempts getting out or even traveling that day will be seriously maltreated and later be killed by decapitation. A story was told of a major seminarian who landed at the square with his soutane and was instantly tortured and slaughtered. It is one of those unsubstantiated stories told to indicate the terror of the group and its dreaded nature of operation. They go on sailing like those in the Sea Dog's group. Sea Dog is one of those occult groups found in many places especially designed to attract the young. These Ekoong members can use axes, machetes, and bows and arrows to accomplish their torturing exploits while sailing. Nonmembers are not supposed to be seen; otherwise, they die.

It is believed that the person carrying or wearing the mask of Ekoong masquerade has to be through protected means and has to drink dry gin and other intoxicants heavily while on patrol so as not to fear any uninitiated who may come his way. It is strictly a male- dominated group. No woman of any age is ever admitted. Their attire is different from that of Ekpe and Ekpo. Ekpe and Ekpo make use of raffia although differently structured and decorated, but Ekoong makes use of dry banana or plantain leaves to indicate nearness to nature and hostility of spirit. Ekoong is almost like *Nkpoporo* practiced in Calabar area and as *Ayara* practiced in many other parts of Ibibio land.

When Ekoong is being displayed in the night, when most of their activities take place, no person is expected to open the door or window to peep at it. If one does and is noticed, that person automatically will be sentenced to torture and death. They are very strict. There are no half measures. They keep their membership secret. Only the initiates know themselves. They avoid open membership. Only those who have a natural inclination to such a group are the ones invited to join. The character of the person reveals their acceptability. No weak person can ever be admitted. Through their membership, they can advance their affair and try to implement publicly what they have agreed upon secretly. They can operate in a spirit of justice or simple revenge or extract what are seen as legitimate penalties. Ekoong operates freely in Ibiono. As part of the tradition, it is very likely that in the days of Okuku Ekandem, such things took place also.

Ekpo is included among the powerful institutions operative in the community. It is as dangerous as Ekoong and as Ekpe in its outlook, but Ekoong supersedes them all. Ekpo, as one of the means of maintaining law and order, was very strict in the precolonial days and after. Even though its cruelty is somehow subdued, it still has many dangerous practices that can wound, maim, or torture or beat a person or even shoot with arrow or cut with a machete or sometimes shoot with gun. The initiation into Ekpo group is extended to those who can keep secrets, and fathers can initiate all their male children. The young men qualified to dance are taught the special Ekpo dance according to the rhythm to jump and to demonstrate acrobatically to imitate the spirit world. They also learn during the process of initiation how to clad themselves in Ekpo attire.

Ekpo is mirrored on the spirit or spirits of a dead ancestor or ancestors. The word "Ekpo" means, very simply, "spirit" or the "ancestral spirit" that is not seen. When a suffix is attached, for example, Ekpo Mkpa, it means the spirit of the dead, in other words, ghosts. To call somebody Ekpo Mkpa means calling the person a ghost; in other words, the person is just nothing or that a ghost is better than the person or the person is acting or living like a ghost.

Ekpo, as a spirit of the dead, is supposed to come from the world beyond. It is otherworldly and not of this world through initiation in the real world. Consequent to such a conception, Ekpo masquerade is made to appear very frightful, terrifying, and dark or very beautifully dressed depending on the type of Ekpo displayed and the world outlook.

One of the original concepts of Ekpo was association with a dead brother or relation. If some food items missed in the house and could not be accounted for immediately, it meant that the Ekpo of the brother or relation had taken it to satisfy a need. It was simply called *Ekpo Eyin Eka*, the Ekpo or spirit of the brother. There was to be no quarrel about that since a hungry brother or relation had to be fed and catered for.

The system was devised to take care of the extended family system and neighbors to make sure they were not hungry. It was a form of social service toward the indigent. The aim was to avoid the poor starving to death.

With the conception that Ekpo is the spirit of the dead ancestor, it becomes evident that the orders of Ekpo had to be strictly observed. Using the authority of the dead ancestor's spirit, the idea of using Ekpo as a form of police ensued. Ekpo developed into the strictest police force one can ever think of without mercy or sympathy, without listening to pleas, and without any alternative other than what they have stipulated, which often is death by decapitation. With such a stringent penalty involving capital punishment, people feared to break the law. Even cases of husbands handing over their wives or fathers handing over their daughters to Ekpo for decapitation for infidelity's sake or for insubordination were reported in many circumstances in the past as some folklore songs indicate. It seems that as time went on, people started complaining about the operations of Ekpo, especially the killing aspect.

Where Ekpo was very tough, the rules and the implementation of the rulers were equally tough. Where the operation of Ekpo was not very effective, people felt a little bit of freedom. All the penalties incurred from wronging Ekpo were not of the same degree.

Some of the penalties of Ekpo entailed some fine. It appears the fine started coming in when the rules of Ekpo were somehow relaxed. Some people were fined seven goats, generally, the female goats, thirty- five yams, called *Iso Udia Itiaba*. The yams go in multiples of five into seven places, making up thirty-five yams. Everything demanded has to be in multiples of seven—seven pots of palm wine, jars of dry gin, even bunches of plantain, chickens, and some other items that were needed for the entertainment of the beneficiaries.

Depending on the gravity of the offense in some cases, only seven goats would be the fine. The reduction of the punishment gave birth to giving even a goat as fine. Failure to comply might incur the removal of doors of the person's house as the landlords do in some big cities when they want to forcefully eject tenants who owe rent for a long time. Apart from removal of doors, sometimes Ekpo defaulters experience the destruction of their roofs. In this way, the person is forcefully ejected out of the house. Sometimes the measure taken could be that of ostracization or banishment. The person can decide after being ejected out of the house to seek refuge in another place other than the village. This is similar to special villages mentioned in the book of Judges for those who committed an offense that necessitated death penalty, but as long as the person took refuge in the designated place called City of Refuge and remained there, the person's life was safe (Jg. 20:1 ff). If the defaulter wanted to escape death when capital punishment was in vogue within the Ekpo kingdom, one could decide to become a refugee by becoming an asylum seeker in a faraway place and never to return to the same village like the author of *Satanic Verses* and the Ayatollah Khomeini who passed death sentence on the Salman Rushdie in his absence.

It is believed that *Umiana Ekpo*, the blood masquerade, cannot be performed without shedding some blood either of a stranger or an uninitiated and getting the person's blood in a container. It is believed by the members that if no blood is poured, the person who put on the masquerade will die, or some misfortunes will come to them. In a way, it is a cult operated in fear. Small numbers join such a group. If no other person's blood is shed, the masquerade carrier must wound himself and shed some blood before putting off the mask. On *Ayara's* day, no person except the initiates is allowed to move out. A special concession is made for pupils and those in secondary school in some places, while nurses and other workers are exposed to serious dangers in some places. *Adiaha Adiana operates only in the night.* It operates very secretly and gently that one may not know it is operating. It can stand still near the entrance door in the night till someone opens the door, and it handles the person mercilessly. It does not kill. It tortures and flogs the person. After getting one person in the surrounding, it quickly changes its position and area of operation like the traffic police or road safety corps members.

Older children used to deceive and frighten the younger ones using Ekpo Ndem Isong. They use a heavy abandoned pestle to hit the ground and produce a heavy sound like that of the roller when a new road is being constructed. The hitting of the ground goes with a song that Ekpe Ndem Isong is coming. The masquerade covers itself with many rags and abandoned clothing to simulate a spirit coming out of the ground with great power and fright. The children become frightened out of their wits' end. The children lock themselves up in the house. In the process, spirit of the dead might go behind and consume the food of the younger ones in the name of Ekpo Ndem Isong and deprive them of their right. Deceit and cheating are part of the process. Children do not play that type of trick anymore.

Other forms of Ekpo may display and entertain by dancing. Among the groups that entertain is *Okpok Odoro Okon*, "the lizard that is on the roof"; after the display, a goat has to be slaughtered called *Ubio Ebot*. It is normally performed by a beautiful masquerade called *Ebe Uboikpa*, "the husbands of the damsels." The female gender called *Uboikpa Ekpo*, the "damsels of Ekpo," is among the entertaining group. Uboikpa Ekpo adopts the costume or regalia of the damsels with earrings, bangles, bracelets, the current style of shoes, and maybe dresses, but men perform all. It is carried out once in a leap year. *Inuen Ekpo* is Ekpo that is like a bird because of long legs and ability to jump. It precedes *Eka Ekpo*. Above all, there is Eka Ekpo, the mother of Ekpo, which appears only once in a leap year.

Before the season finally terminates, there have to be some sacrifices of goats and cocks to appease the gods and inform the ancestors and implore their intercession before terminating the celebration. Sacrifices are not as elaborate on the last day of the season as are offered at the beginning. That of the beginning asks for permission to be engaged in the play—life of the spirits. In every home, a special dish is prepared—*Usung Ikpong*, "the foo-foo prepared with cocoyam." Although cocoyam is regarded as women's crop, it is the one preferred on that day probably because of its smoothness or softness as foo-foo since much physical energy was not required for pounding it or since much physical work was not to be done that day. It is probable too because it digested faster than the yam or cassava foo-foo or because it was one of the commonest food items in the house or available nearby since it could be planted at any place and it flourished or because it underscored a sense of fertility since it was difficult to find cocoyam that was single without the shoots (*Nkok Ikpong*) attached or springing from the parent crop—Ikpong.

Usung Ikpong Nyongo Ekpo is the "cocoyam foofoo at the termination of Ekpo season." More precisely, they are cocoyam foo-foo balls since they were rolled for the intention of satisfying the consumer. Those who had good appetite could take up to two or three balls. Those with little appetite were satisfied with only one ball since the balls were made to be fairly big in sizes. Little children never managed to consume a whole ball. The children's balls were different from those of the adults. Usung Ikpong Nyongo Ekpo, the cocoyam foo-foo balls at the end of Ekpo's season, was never pounded in a mortar like yam or cassava foo-foo. It was always prepared from a type of tray, *Akwaa*, prepared specifically for that purpose. This type of Akwaa was made in the form of a small boat but not as deep and not as long. It had a special pestle called *Nyin Udung* with a very flat head, shorter than the normal pestle. It was after pounding it with *nyin udung* that **Okoop**, a type of calabash prepared with an open end from splitting the calabash chord for drinking palm wine that the rolls and balls of Usung Ikpong Nyongo Ekpo, was made from. It was a day of rest of its own right. This type of foo-foo normally goes with *Afia Efere* (white soup) prepared with special ingredients and enjoyed just for that day. The uninitiated and women could go out and watch Ekpo display that last day.

Mbre Ekpo, Mbre Afai (the Ekpo play, a violent play). Many who are inclined to Ekpo travel long distances to go and watch or participate in Ekpo society display, sometimes playing of sword to see the strongest whose sword would not fall from the participant's hand on being wounded. It is a crazy competition. Some can lose their hand for life in the process. It seems that the fun lies in the running, dancing, and watching the Ekpo and all that goes on during the festivity. Some of those who have established their abode overseas reserve some funds and their working holidays so that they could return home for this festivity and entertainment. In some sense, the whole display could be termed Ekpo carnival. *Ekang* and *Atat* are among the cultural organizations that operate in Obio Ibiono. Atat means wasp. It can sting as the name implies. As far as the traditional cults and societies are concerned, membership was seen as a sign of manliness, which is why the uninitiated were regarded as women even though some women are physically very strong. Obong Ekandem wanted all his male children as well as his entire family to be respected; hence, he initiated all of them, including Tom, the future cardinal into the group.

Among the feasts are *Usoro Nsuk Udia*, the feast of taming the new yam or simply the celebration of the new yam festival in which prayers, libations, and some small sacrifices were offered to Abasi Obot, the god who creates, and the *Ikan*, the ancestors, before the food was eaten.

The special computation of the yearly cycle situates *Usoro Obufa Udia* and Abasi Ekong, "god of war," during the period called Anyang, which occurs in the month of August. When it is said, "Anyang Odoro," that is, "the season for celebrating the feasts is ripe." It is a proclamation that comes up only once a year. This type of proclamation is similar to the promulgation of law after its publication. As a traditional ruler, Okuku Ekandem and his family shared in all these festivals also.

Usoro Ndok is the feast that comes up at the end of the year. It is the feast that marks the end of the old year and the announcement of the New Year. Sometimes fireworks prepared locally mark it. The arrow will be lit while shooting as it moves; it lights up its path and presents a very beautiful and fascinating scene. *Usoro Obufa Isua* is the one that celebrates the New Year with dances, songs, and music. Usoro Ndok goes along with Ekpo Ndok that comes up during the time of harvest. Its appearance is normally very brief. The moment the feast finishes, it terminates.

OBOIKPA EKPO

EKA EKPO

Usoro Obobom Akpan Anyoho is the initiating ceremonies of Ekpo season and the commencement of Ekpo display. These concluding ceremonies of Ekpo are the *Usoro Eka Ekpo*. It is during these concluding ceremonies that the various forms of Ekpo display and dance together, and the parade of various types of Ekpo takes place. The concluding part is entertaining, but the initial part coupled with the intervening season can be dangerous and bloody, especially when things are taken out of proportion. The concluding part provides occasion for recreation for those who want to be participants in the Ekpo masquerade carnival with its inherent danger even of paralysis.

G. Recreational Facilities

Obio Ibiono has many ways of recreating herself. One of the commonest ways is through storytelling (*nke*) even though it is fast disappearing from the village and family scenes. Some families where that still exists provide an opportunity to educate the children pass on the culture and moral principles to them at the same time. The stories could be done in the daytime or at nighttime. Storytelling as an exercise is most interesting during the moonlight night where children gather around the elders and listen to heroic stories, folk tales, and fables with all their moral implications. Storytelling period thus provides a moment for instructions through cultural folklores.

The popular place for common recreation is the village square—*Anwa Obio*. Anwa Obio is different from *Anwa Ekpo* where Ekpo masquerade display takes place. Anwa Ekpo or Ekpo Square is a hidden place in the forest so that the secrets of Ekpo discussed there are never overheard by non-members. Anwa Obio is a public square known by everyone and placed in a strategic position in the village. It is an open spot in the village where many displays take place. Wrestling (*mbok*) is part of that recreation. *Oyo* is a type of game played like badminton, but it is not returned to the opponent's court as is badminton. The opponent attempts to catch the bunch of this very soft and lovely grass called *nwa ebek ibong* bound together for that purpose and thrown to the contestant.

The contestant's aim is to catch the bunch being thrown with a type of reef knot drawing the rope to hold the bunch. It is a type of game that demands great dexterity and agility. A team of experts is normally chosen either from contending villages or from groups of families in the village if it is carried out on the village level only. Dances and songs with drums and clapping of hands according to the rhythm also take place. There are very many types of dances. The men have their specific ones likewise the females. If men participate in the women's own, it is to do the drumming for them, but in each case, the spectators will be there to encourage or congratulate those who do better and rejoice with them. Wrestling (*mbok*) is only for young men and boys, but *Mbre Uboikpa*[79] is only for young girls and ladies. *Ebre* is for the elderly women who join according to their categories. This is the background and worldview into which Tom was born. It was a calm and secure world that knew how to relax and how to work with its rules and regulations forming the backdrop. Ekpo and Ekoong contributed to the recreational life of the people, but since it was only once a year and because of their violent nature, they were not strictly considered in the same light.

Chapter two provides a good backdrop to the birth, growth, education, and Christianization of Tom as he became Dominic as the next chapter involves itself with these issues.

⁸⁰Chapter Three

NATUS EST (HE IS BORN)

Parentage, Birth, and Early Years

The journey of a thousand miles begins with a single step.

—Ancient Inspirational Wise Saying
by an Unknown Author

TOM INO EKANDEM was brought up in a very large and royal family of the Okukus. He was simply known as Tom. His grandfather, Okuku Ubo Etok Akpan, was the "paramount ruler" or supreme ruler of Ibiono Ibom. At that time, a paramount ruler combined the political, cultural, and legislative functions of governance and operated them with those in his council. As a paramount ruler, he had many other rulers under him who worked harmoniously with him to maintain peace and order in Ibiono Ibom.

The grandmother, Madam Nwa Idiong, on his paternal side had three daughters and one son, Ekandem. Ekandem was the father of Tom. The grandfather had many wives like his son, Ekandem. Obong or Chief Ekandem Ubo Etok was the Obong Obio, the village head, as well as the

Okuku of Ibiono clan like his father. He got married to the mother of the young Tom, Madam Nwa Ibong Umana Essien,[81] even though in the baptismal register, her name is indicated as Nwa Ebong. The family tree indicates royal descent likewise from the maternal side—Nwa Ibong signifying the second daughter born while the father was on the throne. In other words, Madam Nwa Ibong was a princess, while the father was a prince and later on became the Okuku of Ibiono Ibom.

Obong Ekandem, the father of Tom, was a court sitting member,[82] a chief of the village, and Okuku, the paramount (supreme) ruler. He had no formal education as such. His contact with the experienced ones enabled him to master the court decorum as well as the proceedings. This is an indication of the high level of intelligence of Obong Ekandem. He was a polygamist like his father. Okuku Ekandem married twenty- seven wives but not all at once even though some traditions mention thirty. From the narration of the cardinal himself, his father experienced this successive polygamy that left the number at twenty-seven.

The cardinal himself said, "I can remember the time he asked me to write down the number of his wives, it was something like twenty- seven but I grew up to see about fifteen in the compound. Some were sacked; other new ones were brought in." With such a big number of wives, there were bound to be many children, both male and female.

The father became converted in 1945, two years before the diaconate ordination of Dominic. Okuku Ekandem was baptized and wedded that same year. The mother of Tom, Madam Nwa Ibong, was second wife. That is why Tom had a dispensation before his priestly ordination. She gave birth to two sons and a girl. She had married before with a son, left the first husband, and married Obong Ekandem and gave birth to Tom and Rose. She was a trader and a farmer as well as being a dutiful housewife and a loving mother. She made use of the husband's palm fruits and trained her children with them. Madam Nwa Ibong Umana Essien died about 1927 at the time Tom was still very young. Tom said, "I was in elementary class two when my mother died." Tom was ten years old at the time. Many of the wives came to Okuku Ekandem after separation in the court. Being a court sitting member, he offered succor to them as a form of charity. As a traditional ruler and high priest in many respects, Obong Ekandem must have offered many sacrifices and libations to the gods of farming.

The father, Obong Ekandem Udo Etok, was a very religious man. He used to pray to the common deities and offer sacrifice for himself, his family, and the village. As young Dominic grew up, he participated in these sacrifices being initiated gradually into the services of the supernatural. Dominic recalled during the interview when he referred to the details in the seventieth birthday anniversary celebration: "I often shared the remains of the food of the gods with my other brothers and felt very hopeful of future good results." The details of this quotation are given under initiation into Ekong's traditional title.[83]

Obobom Ndem Ikot, Idio Udo Inwang, Udeekpe—the god of palm wine, Bacchus, the Roman god of wine; Anantia, the deity of Ibiono; and Abam, the god of government.[84] He was a titled man and an initiate into Ekong[85] group, Ekpo, and others. The initiation into groups entitled him to own palm fruit plots from which he and his wives and children benefitted immensely. The palm fruit plots were a source of income for the family. He had large farms and owned many animals and chickens. Obong Ekandem was a powerful, courageous chief and ruler at the same time, very influential.

Tom's family has the direct link with the founding ancestors (Ete Vitus Edet Ekandem, one of the brothers of Tom, is always very eager to recount their link with the founding ancestors.), thereby indicating direct descent from the patriarch and becoming a patriarch himself not only from the standpoint of the church but also from birth as a father who rules over his extended family. Obio Ibiono has four or five patrilineal groups, which are arranged according to the five sons of Akpan Obio Ukem Akpan Ankit.

> Nung Adia Nkpo—the first son of Akpan Obio Ukem[86]
> Nung Ekpong Ntak—the second son
> Nung Apabio—the third son
> Nung Ekpa Mbiam—the fourth son
> Nung Nkup—the fifth son

As discussed above, Nung Adia Nkpo is Tom's family, and it is the largest among the kindreds.

A. Birth and Family Setup

Tom was born in 1917. His birth was preceded by the First World War, abbreviated as WWI. The war commenced on July 28, 1914, after a combined force of Austria and Hungary allied with Germany invaded Serbia. Julian Gavagham says, Russia mobilised on behalf of its Balkan ally, which had offended Vienna after an ethnic Serb shot dead Archduke Franz Ferdinand in the Bosnian city of Sarajevo. Then Germany, which was allied with Austria- Hungary, invaded neutral Belgium on its way to France since it could expect the French to attack on behalf of Russia. The Germans, who had been spoiling for a war to increase their power amid growing imperial rivalry, hoped to defeat France quickly before Russia could gather troops from across its vast territory and attack her. Britain, which was allied with both France and Russia in its Triple Entente or Alliance and had been enraged by the "Rape of Belgium" that left 6,000 civilians dead and hundreds of villages razed, then declared war on Germany on August 4. A standing army of 733,000 men was called into action in August 1914, followed by a massive recruitment drive and later conscription.[87]

In 1914, when the First World War (WWI) began and was moving on like wildfire, Tom was still in the mind of God when it started. Tom was born three years later. The war brought an unprecedented destruction[88] of human lives and property likewise a retardation of human progress in history. The centenary of the WWI corresponds to 2014 that marks the Nigerian amalgamation period. The "Nigerian Amalgamation" celebrates a hundred years of that event. It also affirms the unity of Nigeria occasioned by that amalgamation. This is what Pres. Goodluck Ebele Jonathan focused on by designating a centenary village, a monument, and other significant items to mark the occasion a significant one.

The year 1917 witnessed the birth of Tom, the future Dominic Cardinal Ignatius Ekandem. His parents, brothers and sisters, and the whole village fondly called him Tom. Tom grew up in the family of this influential and powerful chief and Okuku. He enjoyed the adventurous atmosphere of the father's compound, the stirring tales of his father's heroism, and the influx of eminent visitors. Tom never loved cowardice. He preferred greatly esteemed courage. His father loved him very much and initiated him into societies.

The year of birth of Tom is given as 1917, but in the baptismal register still available at St. Joseph's Catholic Church, Anua, Uyo has his year of birth as 1918. An old missionary priest, Fr. James Kelleher, SPS, who was the parish priest of Anua at the time of the research, said, "When the year of birth is approximated it may be a year or two above or below or could even be far greater than that age." The missionaries had the tendency to simply look at the person and estimate or presume the age since the child or probably the relations could not give the exact date of birth since there were no written birth records at the time. Maybe that is why his year of birth appeared as 1918.

Apart from that, in Ibibio land as well as in Africa as a whole, the computation of the year of birth was according to the cycle of the farms cultivated rotationally. The farm rotation depended on whether it was according to a five-year cycle or seven-year cycle. If a child was born in a region that seven-year cycle was used, it would always be remembered that the child in question was born about that period. The computation of age is carried out according to that cycle. If a child is twenty-one years, it is often said that he has three farm cycles (*Isua Ikot Ita*). Sometimes the age estimation was linked with an event of great magnitude that occurred. Tom was born at a time in Obio Ibiono when recordkeeping was still oral, and the transmission of the information was through oral tradition.

Tom was not the first child of the mother since the mother had a child in an earlier marriage as will be seen later, but he was the first between his father and mother. Following the number of his wives that Obong Ekandem married, it is just obvious that Tom had many brothers and sisters who formed a very large family living a communal life. He has a senior brother Uko and Tom or Ndadda as fondly called by the dad. In other words, he was not the first son of his father. He was the second son who later occupied the position of the first son because of Uko's death. In Ibibio land, it is often said that when the first child dies, the second who is seen automatically becomes the first. The event goes to confirm an Ibibio proverb that the one who is visible and present (in an occasion of death) is the one named *Akpan* (first son).

B. The Family Communal Life

The family of Obong Ekandem was of no mean size. It was a very large one, yet all the wives and children were under the control of this courageous, influential, honest, strict, loving, caring, but mild father, husband, and ruler. He was able to balance strictness with gentleness. In this way, he knit the whole family together very closely.

The tradition in the family of Obong Ekandem was that when any of the wives finished cooking, she would bring the food to the husband's house where all the sons would gather together and eat. The girls normally ate with the mothers in the kitchen while helping to cook. Any other woman who finished her meal also brought it there. Following the number of wives, it means that many and varied dishes were expected, and, of course, that was a feast in itself. The children would eat and have more than enough. The sons who grew up married and had their own children were also fed from the general pot. Usually, there was a competition as to who would cook the best dishes among the wives or the daughters-in-law. That competition provided an opportunity for high quality and taste of the dishes presented.

The meals were brought in succession, and the feasting took place, especially in the evenings, when all the women would have returned from the day's farmwork or market. Food was never wasted owing to the number of children, but all had enough. As a chief priest, he had to offer sacrifices, and the victims of the offerings were consumed as communion sacrifice. This made the compound to be very busy. The young Tom recalls that there were always important visitors to the compound like the priests, the "DOs" (the district officers, the court clerks, and other chiefs from neighboring villages. Okuku Ekandem was a court sitting member. This accounts for the various visits from dignitaries of all kinds.

Each of the visits provided an occasion for feasting, and at the end of the visits, especially those of the DOs, the priests, and the court clerks always went back with a goat or sheep or ram and some yams apart from the ones that would be used to prepare a meal. The picture presented here is that of constant feasting in the family. No wonder Obong Ekandem decided to send his son Tom out of the family so that he could learn the art of formal education outside. "The family was totally non-Christian," Tom recalled. "I was completely born into a pagan family with all its sacrifices and feasts."[89] However, they were God-fearing in their environment.

C. Member of Qua Iboe Church

Okuku Ekandem was not simply contented with being a God- fearing person; he went a step further by becoming a Christian. He became a Christian by inviting the pastor of Qua Iboe Church, which is a denomination of its own right, to come and establish both church and school in the village. The pastor gladly responded, and Qua Iboe Church was founded in Obio Ibiono. The church survived for some time until the moment that Okuku Ekandem turned his back against the church and the pastor. Things had fallen apart. The details of this are found below under the section of initiating Tom and his brothers into Ekong group. At that point, the services of the pastor were no longer demanded. He was redundant and had to leave. Before the experience of separation, Okuku Ekandem and all his family formed a part of the church.

All the members of the family likewise the whole village shared in the Christian religion as obtained in the house of Cornelius in Acts of the Apostles chapter ten. Those who went to church had to be summoned every morning for prayer, not with an iron gong or by a town crier but through the system called *Umia Eto*—that is "beating the wood or stem" or in other words convoking/assembling the people as in the Hebrew sense of *qahal*. This means was used since there were no church bells at the time. In order to use the stem or wood for a signal as a bell, the construction had a foundation of smaller stems laid in a square form as a base. Two or three more of these squared foundation constructed in a descending order were laid before the main stem or wood that will produce the sound. Sometimes four forked strong sticks were used as support for the wood. In the morning, somebody in charge of sounding the alert would go and use another stick with a smooth handle to strike it, *Yom-Yom*, as many times as possible to produce the required sound. Since the sounding of the stem took place very early in the morning, about four o'clock, the sound was usually heard at long distances. The striking of the wood occurred that early to give chance to people to prepare and come in time for prayers at five o'clock. The sounding used to take place twice before the prayer began.

The church was built with mud, sticks, bamboos, and mat made from raffia palm leaves. It was this mud house with supporting pillars that was used as the church. It was oblong in nature with four doors, two at the front and two at the rear. People gathered and prayed. Qua Iboe was the main and only church in the village. The pastor was invited by Okuku Ekandem to come and live among the people. More of these details will be seen below during the initiation of Tom and his brothers into Ekong group. The pastor was a very good pastor.

The pastor was a very good one, but being so good and friendly did not prevent the rupture of relationship when he stepped on the toes of the Okuku in the process of initiating his children into the various traditional rites and titles he rightly merited. It was always a sign of prestige to initiate one's male children into these traditional rites as fringe benefits of being a full initiate. When the pastor boldly told Okuku that he could not be a "church goer" or a Christian and continue at the same time to initiate his children into the various traditional rites that they were incompatible, the Okuku became very angry.[90] He did not only cut of relationship with the pastor but also ordered him to move out of his village.

With this, Okuku Ekanem fell out with the pastor whom he perceived as trying to block his way and deprive his children of the fringe benefits of his position as a full Ekong member. He disassociated himself from the church that the pastor represented. Summarily, opposition to the pastor was opposition to the "white man's religion"[91] that sought to change the old ways and impose a foreign way of life on the people. That was the end of Qua Iboe Church for the family of Okuku Ekandem and the whole of Obio Ibiono till date. The influence of Okuku Ekandem among his people manifested itself powerfully here. It was a clash between the legitimate preservation of the authochthonous culture and traditional Christian values. This is what Bengu calls "opposition to the white man's religion."[92]

The rejection of the pastor and church is similar to what happened at Bodo in Ogoniland in Rivers State in terms of changing church. What occurred in Bodo was not as a result of clash of Christianity with African Traditional Religion even though that had its own toll in the late twentieth century. What sparked off the expulsion was education. For many decades, Anglican religion or what they sometimes term "Church of the Niger" had existed in Bodo for many years but did not establish any schools.

The church was built beside the river in the creek, which oil pollution has made impossible for fishermen to carry on their trade. The oil pollution is accompanied by terrible ecological hazards. Bodo used to send their children to the school in another village.

Many of them constantly failed Standard Six Examination or were driven away after completing Standard Five. Those driven away did not continue, except very few. They decided to do something.

They sent for the Catholic priest who was in Port Harcourt through contact established by one of their sons in Lagos. The young man saw the church and the schools established by the Catholic priests in Lagos, and one day he asked one of the priests if such a thing could not be done in their place. They promised to do something even though the distance was great. These were the Kiltegan Fathers. They decided to contact one of their men in Lagos who made special arrangement and was taken in a boat down there since there were no roads leading directly to Bodo. The easiest way was through the river. Upon arrival, the priest promised to build a school for them in the village and to establish a church. This is what they longed for. The chief of the village by the name Chief Berebon, whose only surviving last son, Chief Paul Berebon, still resides in the area, decided to convert to Catholicism, and thereby, together with all his cabinet and the entire village, turned away from Anglicanism to Catholicism and used the same church built for Anglican worship to commence Catholic worship.[93] Anglican church later regained entry into Bodo unlike Qua Iboe that never resurfaced at Obio Ibiono again.

Catholicism became the only and the official religion of Bodo until the crisis of 1988 opened the way for other denominations to spring up there. Such powers can usher in favors or disfavors depending on the way they are wielded. In the two circumstances, it opened the way of favor to one group and disfavor to another. God writes straight in a crooked line. Probably, if that uproar never occurred, Tom might not have become a Catholic, and the great prince, prelate, and patriarch would never have graced the face of Nigeria with his blessings or the Catholic Church. This is the work of the Lord; it is marvelous to see (Ps. 117–118).

D. Initiation into Ekong Traditional Title Taking

As a son of an Okuku who was fully initiated into many traditional societies and cults operative in the land, he sought for a way to get his son Tom and all the other male children initiated. The Protestant minister of Qua Iboe Denomination did not approve of that. Tom was not only a son but a prince too, following the various developments of events in the family and village.

The reaction of the minister infuriated the Okuku who immediately decided to stop going to church, stopped his wives and children, and asked the minister to leave the village immediately. It has to be recalled that at this time, Obong Ekandem was a traditional ruler to the core. Conflict of interests or rather the problem of choice of carrying the Cross and following the Lord or abandoning it is evident. This confirms the saying of the Lord Jesus Christ that a man cannot serve both God and wealth (Matt. 6:24; Lk. 16:13), for he will either uphold one or hold the other in contempt. His position as chief of the village as well as acting as the priest in his domain contributed greatly to this rejection and expulsion.

As the cardinal explained in the notes of the preparation for his seventieth birthday anniversary, it was out of ignorance that the father whom he qualified as a pagan acted. The father changed when he had the light of God's grace. The whole scene can be seen as a *felix culpa*, a happy fault, since out of that chaos, God prepared the ground and molded Dominic for a future cardinal, prince, and patriarch of his church. God writes straight on a crooked line.

After expelling the Qua Iboe minister who was invited to come and establish a school and a church, the Okuku proceeded to initiate his children into Ekong. As a fringe benefit to being a fully initiated member, he initiated his children as do members of Ekpe cult or secret societies or as seasoned Christian parents do to their children and wards so that the descendants can share in the rights and benefits of the parents. This is benevolent love.

As a result of the initiative of the father, Okuku Ekandem, young Tom became an Ekong member initiate together with some of his brothers. He simply said, "The event took place about 1921, I was not educated enough to remember the exact period and details."[94]

Consequent to the expulsion of the Qua Iboe minister, the Okuku went to Anua to negotiate with a priest to come and establish the Catholic Church in the town. The following excerpts are from the cardinal's personal notes, part of which he wanted to use for the Silver Jubilee Brochure and later excluded. He speaks strongly on "pagan virtues, sacrifice," polygamy, and food sacrificed to idols. The excerpts go thus:

> It is not always true to say that those who do not go to the Church do not practice virtues or are incapable of living virtuous lives. Many Africans are sometimes contemptuously referred to as pagans. Experience shows that certain African "pagans" are found to be the most god-fearing and honest-living men among us.

> My parents were pagans. I lost my mother when I was in Elementary Class 2 and my father played from that time on, the role of mother and father. He was a big "pagan"—big as regards the number of wives he had and the type of pagan sacrifices he offered and though he married many wives and performed many and frequent sacrifices to pagan gods, he appeared to be a naturally good man observing the laws as he knew them and was honest and devoted to his gods.

Pagans in African communities did not take on many wives merely for self-gratification. It was a sign of prosperity. They wanted children for defence in case of assaults during interfamily quarrels, village disputes or tribal wars. Each family aimed at self-sufficiency in as many ways as possible. In answering objections from Christians, the pagans of today maintain that they are at least honest by securing as many wives of their own as they want instead of interfering with young maidens or other peoples wives as the Christians do. In the light of the teaching of Christ and the gospels, those pagans have erred no doubt but their errors are not due to malice or down-right disobedience to the teaching of Christ and the Church. It is rather due to ignorance; hence as soon as they are sufficiently enlightened you see them courageously abandoning paganism for Christianity. They fear the gods and worship them and are always prepared to do what is right in the sight of their gods. They feel it is the duty to bring their children up under the protection of theses gods.

Early in my life, my father had associated me with pagan worship. I often carried the victims (fowls or goats, water or mashed yam) to be offered in sacrifice to the gods invoked to bless and protect us and help us to grow as virtuous children and useful citizens. I often shared the remains of the food of the gods with my other brothers and felt very hopeful of future good result. When my father sent us to school and we became introduced to the Christian religion, he encouraged us to embrace it viewing the Christian faith as a religion of the educated. He further encouraged us to observe the Christian rule of life, to refrain from what was forbidden, and he took pains to procure for us (the Church-goers) food and meat, as substitute for meat he had offered in sacrifice.

> Not long, the priest visitors to our Village became his friends, whom he often welcomed with presents (yams, fowls, goats, etc). This friendly relationship between my father (the Chief of the town) and the missionaries appeared to have prepared the way for my vocation.

E.   Early School Life and Catholicism

Obong Ekandem was a court sitting member as indicated in the opening page of this chapter. He was the chief of Obio Ibiono as well as the Okuku of Ibiono Ibom. He combined many roles in his person. Okuku Ekandem was very keen to have Tom and all his children educated in formal education. He was a very generous and welcoming man who kept his doors open for foreign as well as familiar visitors.

His contact with the court clerks, the interpreters, and the DOs (the district officers) or, simply put, his contacts with those who were formally educated inspired him to educate his children. The young Tom recalled, "My senior brother Uko was first sent to school but he did not do well. Then my father turned his attention to me and concentrated on me." Tom was neither the only one to go to school nor the first in the family but one of the three who were sent to school at Anua, after the school at Ikot Ada Idem. It is probable that he began his formal education in 1924. More will be said about this in chapter fourteen under the section "The Founder of the Missionaries of St. Paul."

The compound was always in festivity, receiving one guest or another. Following such a situation, the father decided to send him to go and live with people he perceived capable of helping Tom to be educated formally. The father noticed that since the compound was constantly busy, there would not be the required atmosphere for Tom to study. Tom did not perceive the father's gesture as punishment or cruelty or sign of hatred but as a means of enhancing his future. Although he stayed with other people later on in years, he first stayed with late Mr. Philip Inwang, an elderly schoolboy who was already in Standard Four at the time. He was the first master of the young Tom. Tom described him as "the dutiful, conscientious, zealous and very anxious to be educated young man."

The school was four miles away from Ikot Ada Idem. It was a government school. The school was moved to another place before the Catholics came and established another one. The dutiful young man used to rise at about 4:00 a.m. every day in order to arrive in time at the school after the four-mile trek. Since Tom was very young and small, he used to run after the tall, huge, dutiful young man and carry his books along while going to the school. At about 6:00 a.m., when the villagers would have arrived at the stream to draw water, Tom and his master, Philip, also arrived to have their bath before climbing the hill that led to the school. The daily journey through such roads when many others were in bed is indication that safety of movement and security were never doubted or even perceived to be a problem. They were taken for granted.

If these basics were lacking, Tom and his master could have been kidnapped or killed en route to the school. At the stream, Mr. Philip Inwang would help Tom to take his bath after bathing himself. Probably, the personal help rendered by Mr. Philip made Tom to remember him with great fondness and affection coupled with his capacity to bring up and teach the young Tom useful things about education. It is interesting to note that earlier rising of Father, Bishop, and Cardinal Ekandem at 4:00 a.m. daily had its origin from this early morning trek, which stamped him as an early riser and helped him to structure and regulate his life and horarium[95] daily.

The young man in question Mr. Philip Inwang was taking Tom to the school, and it can be presumed that it was the Catholic school that they attended since the government school had been transferred to another place. It is probable that Tom finished his preliminary studies at Ikot Ada Idem in 1927 and proceeded to Anua where he completed his primary education at St. Joseph in 1932. It is obvious that the school at Ikot Ada Idem was a feeder school to Anua. With the system of education at the time, he must have done initiating class ABC in 1924, elementary class one in 1925, and class two in 1926. This acted as the "transition" in nursery schools nowadays before beginning the "Standard" section that took six years and ending in Standard Six. From the saying of Dominic that his mother died when he was only in class two, the computation demonstrates that she died in 1926 during the period Dominic was undergoing the transition class.

Tom said, "I lost my mother when I was in elementary class two." It could be surmised that the incident took place in 1926 before he transferred to St. Joseph Primary School in Anua in 1928 and continued from then on.

The older schoolboy Philip was already a Catholic. There is no doubt too that he practiced his faith. Tom living with Philip as his master must have been influenced by the religious practices his master carried out just as he was influenced by the father's pagan practices. Since Philip taught young Tom many things about education, it is presumed that he must have taught him certain basic things too about Catholicism.

Before Tom came to live with Philip, he was already a Qua Iboe member before his dad severed the relationship as a result of the traditional title taking. To get into the life of this new worship, he had to be drilled gently and made to see the necessity of attending the Catholic Church.

St. Joseph Primary School in Anua where he transferred to school was a Catholic school. It was easier for him to learn some prayers before he began the proper catechumenate period, which lasted for about a year or two and later led to his reception of the sacraments. Even though his episcopal ordination Silver Jubilee Brochure bears 1925 as the year of his baptism likewise many other documents, his proper date and year of baptism indicated in the baptismal register still preserved in Anua Parish in Uyo directly bears the following details:

Number in baptismal register: 11750
Parents: Ekandem Udo Nwa Idiong and Mother Nwa Ebong

Name: Dominic Tom Ino
Year of birth: C1918
Place: Obio Ibiono
Date of baptism: June 23, 1926
Minister: James Hasson
Sponsor: Jacob Udofia

The baptismal register in which the details of the baptism are recorded has a thick, dark, solid cover bearing on the outside from 1927 onward, whereas in actual fact, he was baptized in 1926 as shown by the record and as can be verified by the photocopy of the page. What saves the situation is the number in the baptismal register; otherwise, it will be very difficult to find it.

Rev. Fr. Paul Biechy of Brazzaville took the initiative of sending Dominic to St. Joseph, Anua, to do his Standard Two there. In the same year, Bishop Joseph Shanahan, CSSp of Tipperary, Ireland, a renowned missionary, confirmed him and gave him the name of the Spanish founder of the Jesuits or Society of Jesus, Ignatius.96 Okuku Ekandem Udo Nwa Idiong was later baptized as Paul Ino Ekandem Ubo Etok.

The full name of the mother was Madam Nwa Ebong Umana Essien, although some render it as Nwa Ibong Umana Essien, exchanging the *E* with an *I*, thereby making it a different name. The mistake occurred in the baptismal register called *Liber Baptistorum*.

The problem with the year of birth has been taken care of already. His period of internship with Philip brought him to the great religion that opened great avenues to him. He was faithful in small things, and God placed him over many and important things later.

It is likely too that it was a year before his baptism that his mother died when he was in elementary class two.

Chapter Four

IN FIERI (IN THE PROCESS OF...)

Seminary Training, Priestly Ordination, and Early Days of Priesthood

It is the little moments that make life big/meaningful with
the possibility of blooming to maturity and fulfilment!

—Wise Saying by an Unknown Author

THE JOURNEY OF a thousand miles begins with a single step. An
Ibibio proverb says that "the first race is the master of all races."
Dominic was to take the very first step of a journey of a thousand miles
comparable to that of Monsignor Shanahan when he was made the prefect
apostolic of Adamawa. Such journeys are normally filled with eventualities,
uncertainties, joys, sorrows, humors, and sadness, but since there was an
aim, it had to be undertaken and continued till the desired location was
arrived at.

When Dominic started his apprenticeship with Mr. Philip Inwang,
he never knew that he would be journeying to the priesthood in a very

short while. As days went by, more things unfolded. The conversation of the Standard Three pupils had fired the heart of the young Dominic in such a way that it could be said with St. Padre Pio that his whole body was so hot with the fever of God that no human explanation was possible. The doctors who measured the temperature of Padre Pio simply concluded that no reasonable human being could survive with such a temperature. "The Young priest, Padre Pio, suffered severe bouts of extreme fevers which ran as high as 125 degrees Fahrenheit.

Documents and broken thermometers attest to that for which medical science can offer no explanation...I am aflame though with no fire."97 Sometime later, Padre Pio, while writing to his spiritual director, Father Benedetto, said,

> I feel myself burning all over, but there is no fire. I feel close to Jesus and bound to him by means of this Mother. But I don't even see the chains that hold me so tightly. A thousand flames consume me. I feel as if I am continually dying and yet I am still alive.[98]

The temperature of Dominic's life had been fired higher than normal and had risen so highly that the hand having been put into the plough could not look back (Cf. Lk. 9:62). He was ready to risk what was necessary in order to inform his father of what he was thinking of and inclined to. Like Jesus setting his face like flint going to the Cross resolutely (Cf. Is. 50:7), Dominic was ready to follow his Master, Jesus, not Philip, this time irrespective of what lay ahead. St. John of the Cross calls such a drive *The Living Flame of Love*,99 while from the point of view of St. Vincent De Paul, it is comparable to the *Flame of Charity* that stems from Christ and pushes Christians on the upward journey and relationship with others. It is love that conquers everything. With such a momentum, Dominic braced himself to make known his mind to his *Nna* as he usually addressed his father.

A.   Circumstances That Led to Priestly Inspiration

Dominic Tom Ino Ekandem started nursing the idea of becoming a priest in 1932 through the Standard Three pupils living in the same dormitory with him. He was in Standard Six himself. They were all "day boarders" who lived in the school from Monday to Friday and went home at weekends after classes on Fridays. The purpose of going home was to replenish the consumed food stuff during the week and to get what they would use until they went home again since they had to cook for themselves.

It was on one such trip that the Standard Three pupils discussed about becoming a priest that Dominic, as he was then called, overheard them. Dominic said, "It was in 1932 when I was in Standard Six that some pupils in Standard Three disturbed me with the idea of becoming a priest." The idea came from one of the teachers who went to TTC (Teachers' Training Course) at Onitsha. Three teachers went for that course as Dominic recalls. These were Mr. Bernard Mbaba and Andrew Utuk and one other teacher. They went for what is called the certificate course, which normally lasted for three months. There was no grading at the time. What was important was the certificate. Such teachers were called certificated teachers. It was one of these certificated teachers, Mr. Andrew Utuk, who encouraged the pupils to become priests. Mr. Utuk taught Standard Three at that time.

When the idea of "becoming a priest" was hovering in the air among the pupils and the teacher, Sr. Mary Charles Walker, who took over from the St. Joseph Sisters of Cluny in France that established the only girls' school in the vicariate, St. Joseph Girls' School Calabar, after their departure from Calabar, made plans to go to Onitsha to discuss educational issues with Bishop Shanahan.[100] She went in the company of her companions, the young aspirants, Lucy Williams and Kathleen Bassey, to discuss some important school matters with Bishop Shanahan at Onitsha. The other two, Agnes Ugoaru and Christiana Waturuocha, stayed back in the convent. The trip took place early in December 1930, a little before something very significant occurred on the Nigerian soil, the ordination of the first priest from Eastern Nigeria.

It was on December 8, 1930, when Rev. Fr. John Cross Anyogu was ordained priest by Bishop Shanahan of Southern Nigeria at the Holy Trinity Cathedral, Onitsha, now the Basilica of Holy Trinity, Onitsha. Pope Benedict XVI raised it to that status in 2007. Father Anyogu was the first and only Nigerian/African priest in the whole vicariate of Southern Nigeria.[101] The ordination of Fr. John Cross (who later became the first bishop of Enugu) took place four years before the departure of Sr. Mary

Charles Magdalene Walker, RSC, the foundress of the Congregation of the Handmaids of the Holy Child Jesus from Nigeria. Father Anyiogu went with Bishop Shanahan, CSSp to Anua for the investiture ceremony of the four pioneer members of the nascent Congregation of the Handmaids, which they called hooding of the first aspirants of the native sisterhood (More details of this are found in chapter six on the Handmaids of the Holy Child Jesus.). There at the little convent chapel in Anua, Fr. John Cross Anyogu performed the simple ceremony of blessing the hoods, while Bishop Joseph Shanahan, CSSp presided Mother Mary Amadeus, the superior general who came with her vicar general, Mother Mary Genevieve, SHCJ,[102] on a fact- finding mission to Nigeria after having decided to send missionaries to Calabar gave medals to girls[103] who now graduated from the first stage of aspirancy to that of postulancy.

In the midst of this euphoria of ordination of the first African priest, the certificated teachers arrived at Onitsha and imbibed the enthusiasm for native vocations from where it started—Onitsha. As good ambassadors, they did not keep the news for themselves but shared the idea with their pupils. The process of conscientization had begun with that sharing. No sooner had he shared the idea with the Standard Three pupils than they began ruminating in their minds what such a saying could mean. They pondered in their hearts like the Blessed Virgin Mary who kept all these things and pondered them in her heart (Cf. Lk. 2:51) what the saying could mean. The teacher shared, but the pupils expanded the information and embellished it. They were witnesses and messengers at the same time.

The reaction of Dominic was peculiar when he overheard the pupils' discussion. He questioned, "Obubit Owo ekeme ido Oku Abasi?" Simply translated as "Is it possible for an African to be a priest?" This is almost like asking in the Bible "Can anything good thing come out of Nazareth?" (Jn. 1:46) There was no African priest to be seen around at that time, and there was no news of any of them anywhere. It was a leap in the dark. The incident took place about 1929 when Dominic was about twelve years old. To hear such a thing was really a novelty. The incident of trying to know whether a black person could become a priest took place two years after Mr. John Hughes donated the High Park, Kiltegan, to Fr. Pat Whitney as a future place of the congregational headquarters in 1927.

Apart from that, it was evident that the young boys were not serious about their intention, and that was the reason why Dominic quizzed them whether it was possible for an African to become a priest. In addition, he encouraged the young boys in his usual humorous manner to go on and that he would support them as seminarians with seminary collection, which was already operative. This incident of the young boys returning to the dormitory prompted the young Dominic to nurse the idea of becoming a priest. The idea of becoming a priest started haunting him. On arrival on Sunday evening, Tom began to rehearse the question he was to put across to his English teacher, a volunteer priest, Reverend Father McDonald, who was also the manager of schools.

After the English lesson, Dominic approached the teacher, Father McDonald, and told him that some pupils were disturbing him in the dormitory about becoming a priest. He asked, "Is it possible for an African to become a priest as the Class Three pupils were saying?" Father McDonald did not respond to the question; he rather put a challenging question to Tom by asking, "Would you yourself like to become a priest?" At the spur of the moment, he responded simply, "I have never thought of that." It was a surprising question, and the priest immediately added, "Go and tell your father." The command opened the door and provided Dominic with an opportunity to become a trailblazer on the journey to the priesthood through the processes of his training.

a.   Disclosure of the Idea to His Father—the Okuku

For Dominic, communicating the idea to his father constituted a big obstacle. He did not know when and how to approach his father. He became greatly bothered, but he had to make the decision to disclose this unique and important idea to his father. That decision was to determine his future and go against his father's ambition for him as a court clerk or an interpreter that his father had been secretly nursing.

The young Tom was very circumspective and prudent. He did not approach the father the moment he went home at the weekend. He did not mention it on Saturday during the day until nighttime after having fed sumptuously and been taken to bed by the dad as the custom was.

When the paternal rite of putting the children to bed and bidding them good night had been completed and everyone had gone to bed, including the Okuku, whom they lovingly addressed Nna Nnyin or simply Nna,104 Dominic went very stealthily and with trepidation to the father's door. He tapped gently but firmly. Nna responded from inside where the door had been bolted, "Hm-hm, Anie?" "Yes, who is that?" Dominic responded, "Ami Tom ke odo." "It is I, Tom." Okuku, the father of Dominic, asked, "Nsido, Ukukaha ukuna tutu emi?" "What is it? Have you not yet gone to bed?" Dominic responded, "Iyoo, nkinaha dion!" "No, I'm not yet in bed!" The dad's question expressed some surprise because like every other child, Tom had been led to bed by the father and bidden good night. On hearing "not yet," the dad questioned what it was all about, and why he did not go to bed. Dominic simply answered him, indicating that he wanted to ask him a question. Dominic did not hesitate but spoke out boldly even though within him, he was afraid and uncertain of what was to come.

At this point, Dominic became very alert and happy that the door had been securely bolted. He was with the frame of mind that should the father wake, come out, and try to reach out to him, he would have found his way by running to safety. That is why he was happy that the door had been firmly bolted. Another advantage of disclosing the idea to him in the night was that it was dark, and the dad would not be able to pursue him. All his fears and calculations were dissipated when he heard the dad say "Go on." When he heard his father say "Go on," courageously, he said, "I would like to be a priest."

b. The Father's Reaction

The father paused for quite some time. The prolonged silence intimidated Dominic and caused him to be nervous again after the momentary self-confidence, especially when the dad retorted, "Nso Idiok Ekpo usin fien uto ekikere oro k'iwuot?" "What devil has put such ideas into your head?" Immediately, he added, "Obubit-Owo ekeme ido Oku Abasi?" "Can a black man (an African) be a priest?" The reaction and the question strongly portrayed that it was inconceivable and unheard of at the time for an African or black man to be a priest, especially since none had ever been seen. All the missionaries were Europeans. That is the background of the Okuku Ekandem's question and reaction. The manner in which the father addressed the question was almost a verbatim repetition of the question Dominic put to the Standard Three pupils who disturbed his conscience with such thoughts. The next question fired by the father, "Aya sidi ufok?" "Will you be coming home?" tacitly grants permission to go ahead with what Dominic was contemplating. The question once again calmed him down considerably, and Dominic responded by saying, "Ndiongoke!" "I don't know!" Dominic was very truthful to say he did not know. The Okuku was not satisfied with the "I do not know" response. Having given a tacit approval, he said, "Ka kedungo se," "Go and find out."

The Okuku mandated Dominic to go and find out from Father McDonald. The Okuku was used to being very generous to visiting priests. He gave chickens or goats or sheep and yams to visiting priests. He knew they did not marry and came from a different country and scarcely traveled home; being aware of this, he asked the son to find out. The mandate was a green light in the darkness.

Generally, the pupils were what was called day boarders. These were young people who stayed in the dormitory, cooked and ate their food, went to class, worked in the school, but when they dismissed from school, they went back to the dormitory to cook for themselves. They were obliged to go home every weekend after school on Friday. Of course, they had to trek whatever distance they had to cover or take a bicycle for those who were rich enough or capable of affording such luxury. Of course, there were none who could afford it. All of them trekked home together. On arrival at home, they had to go and harvest some cassava from the farm, come back, peel, crate, and tie it for the purpose of getting rid of the liquid in order to make it ready for frying on Sunday evening and turn it into *garri* while extracting starch from it for their khaki shorts and white shirts before going back to school either very early on Monday morning or more often on Sunday evening. As the beginning of the new week approached, Dominic went happily to inquire from Father McDonald when he returned to school on Sunday evening. It was really the next day being Monday that he approached the priest and asked if he would be going home should he become a priest. Father McDonald said he was not sure. The shuttling between the dad and the priest continued as long as clarifications were going on. On delivering the result of the inquiry to the dad the following weekend when he went home, the Okuku's reaction was more than expected. Even though Okuku put it sarcastically, the response was positive. The dad simply said, "Emekeme ika, sia adoho menyie uwak ndito," "You can go. After all, I have many children." With this utterance, Dominic was already sacrificed or, rather, he became a sacrificial lamb of the family, village, tribe, and country.

The perception of the life of the missionaries caused Okuku to point out the fact that he had many children (He won't miss him too much.). By that very fact of approving the idea of Dominic becoming a priest, Dominic had ipso facto assumed the role of a victim for sacrifice. It appears he was sold out or sent into perpetual exile or banished from the family fold or offered as a sacrificial lamb. With that response, Dominic was already set apart among all the children as the Israelite nation was set apart through God's covenanted relationship with Abraham that eventually engulfed the patriarchs and judges, prophets, and kings. Dominic was supremely happy with that response and deemed it a sign of total donation to the service of the Lord rather than rejection or being disowned.

The next contact with Father McDonald was a great and joyous one. The good news caused Father McDonald to go straight on to inform Father Ryan who was the superior of the mission while Father McDonald was the assistant. Hitherto, Bishop Heery, CSSp was the bishop of Onitsha. He was not yet made an archbishop. It was in 1950 that he became archbishop, barely three years after the sacerdotal[105] ordination of Dominic Ekandem as a Catholic priest and four years before Dominic was consecrated an auxiliary bishop of Calabar. Reverend Ryan, the superior of the mission, informed Bishop Heery of the intention of Dominic to become a priest. Bishop Heery CSSp started taking an interest in Dominic.

Toward the end of that year in 1932, Dominic was given the prospectus to enter the minor seminary. The process of inspiration that started as a rumor by the Standard Three pupils arose from the Standard Three teacher, Mr. Andrew Utuk. Mr. Utuk, who attended a certificated course in Onitsha, had discovered that an African could be a Catholic priest probably through his interaction with the priests there or through his fellow students. He did not delay to share the idea with his pupils on his return. Mr. Andrew Utuk was the one who started the succession of events that passed through various stages and began to solidify until it assumed a steady growth through listening; praying; fasting; obedience; suffering; patience; goodwill; good morals; reasonable intelligence; self-discipline; humility; an ingrained deep religious faith enlightened by hope, unctioned by charity, and propelled by dependence on God's providential care; docility to the Holy Spirit and the superiors coupled with openness to the same Holy Spirit, and eventualities coupled with series of vicissitudes.

God uses human instruments to accomplish his divine plan as exemplified by Moses, Abraham, Isaac, Jacob, and others. "When God makes his promises, he uses human beings, the apex of his creation as instruments for accomplishing them and this happens with their full cooperation and consent."106 The journey was long and arduous, yet the inner momentum inspired by the divine fire kept Dominic restless until what was an ember turned into a flame and what was glowing brightened up every place and retained a permanent brightness. It was a spark that was never extinguished. Inspiration is generally either God's action through human instrumentality or God's Word through human words. In the life of Dominic, we can see the increase of the divine spark before explosion into an uncontrollable divine flame.

B. Obong Ekandem's Predicament[107]

The commencement of the journey was difficult and tedious. Things were not very smooth. This could have constituted part of the reason for the choice of the motto: *In Cruce Salus*, "In the Cross is our Salvation." Dominic thought that with the reception of the prospectus, another problem was about to begin since the permission from the father to be a priest was "enough sacrifice." He was reluctant to show the prospectus to the father.

He wanted to spare his father, the Okuku, certain difficulties by not bothering him with the list of the items required; yet he needed the items in the prospectus in order to proceed. He somehow thought that if he approached his dad with the list, he might not be interested to purchase the required items. The Okuku as a court sitting member had been put in prison custody before the prospectus of the son came out. His incarceration experience accounts for the reluctance of Dominic to take the prospectus to the father together with the reasons he deduced. The Okuku was involved in a court case following the accusation of collecting bribes. The accusers were determined to see that the accused was imprisoned. The family members were equally determined to see that justice was done. The family said that they sold so many things in the compound to handle Okuku's case well by hiring a lawyer who never appeared even though he received the required fee. They also asked who knows if the lawyer had been bribed so that he would not show up, and the litigants could have their way as they eventually did. The Okuku was cleared of every charge except one that was reserved for the DO (district officer) to try at Itu. The family said that the accusers went as far as bribing the court clerk and the interpreter at Iyere in order to have the Okuku implicated and jailed. Still, the lawyer failed to appear in court. The Okuku was unjustly imprisoned for one year. Some years after they added, it was learned that the deceitful lawyer got drowned in the river at Akpabuyo after having escaped to Calabar like Judas Iscariot (Cf. Matt. 27:3–5). It is obvious that the tentacles of bribery and corruption had already infiltrated and permeated the Nigerian fabric before independence. Independence only liberated it and made it capable of reaching the age of maturity it has attained in the present age with its sanguine assassination, injustice, robbery, kidnapping, ritual assassination, and burying of human beings alive both in presumed sacred places for fruitfulness in the ministry and for quick money together with fraud.

Dominic, knowing the situation of things in the compound and knowing that the dad was sick in prison and had to be transferred to the general hospital at Ikot Ekpene for treatment, did not bother the Okuku. The situation of the family did not deter or dampen the enthusiasm of the young Dominic who was very eager and determined to go to the seminary. Fired on with a lovely and undaunted spirit, he asked one of his friends, a Standard Three pupil, to accompany him to Ikot Ekpene to meet his father, the Okuku, in prison. He had to trek from Ibiono to Ikot Ekpene since he had no money or any other means of transportation. The Okuku was imprisoned in 1932, and it was that year that Dominic was given admission into the minor seminary.

His sole aim of going to meet his father was to discuss his going to the seminary by breaking the good news of admission to him. He set out very early in order to arrive at Ikot Ekpene while the offices were still open. He had to cover a distance of about twenty-five kilometers to be there and the come back after the discussion. In other words, he had to cover sixty kilometers as a child the same day on foot to meet the father and discuss with him and then come back.

a.   The Meeting with the DO (the District Officer)

Dominic recalled with great humor his size at the time of trying to meet the DO at Ikot Ekpene. He said several times that he was very tiny at the time, and the court clerk was surprised that he wanted to meet the DO. Upon arrival at the district officer's office, the court clerk questioned him in English. "What do you want?" Dominic responded, "I want to see the DO." A further question followed. "For what purpose?" Again, Dominic retorted, "I want to see my father who is in prison." It seems this was an opportunity for Dominic to exhibit his mastery of English as a Standard Six pupil. He was very happy to have had that opportunity and to have used it well without any flaws or fear. Dominic and his friend were given a seat to wait, while the court clerk went in to inform the DO of Tom's intention and request.

The chronological calculation shows that the meeting took place in 1932 before Dominic began the journey to the minor seminary in 1933. It is to be recalled that Fr. James Moynagh and Utuk, a layman, established the first praesidium of the Legion of Mary on African soil at Ifuho that same year. That was the same place that the young Father Dominic was to carry out his apostolate as a newly ordained priest before his first transfer. It is equally sign of greater things to come despite the unfortunate circumstances in which his father found himself.

When the DO arrived, he questioned as the court clerk did before and gave a mandate that he should be conducted to the prison to see his father. Tom and his friend were escorted as well as directed to the prison. Upon arrival at the prison, it was discovered that the father was sick and was admitted in the general hospital at Ikot Ekpene. A warder was assigned to take Dominic and his friend there. The proper procedure was followed. This was what is often termed due process in many circumstances in today's Nigeria. Already there is a germ of nobility manifesting itself subtly in the life of the "small" Dominic as he described himself in the process of going to meet the DO.

b. Contact with His Father in Prison/Hospital Situation

The Okuku was lying in bed in the hospital when the young Dominic arrived. Dominic burst out laughing spontaneously seeing his father lying down in bed and cleaning the brass buttons of the warder's uniform. It could be his laughter arose from the fact that his father who was in control and was being served by others had now become controlled and was serving. They sat there quietly for quite some time after he greeted the father, until the friend urged him to say what he went for. It appears he was not in a great haste to deliver his message anymore. Perhaps he was circumspective waiting for the right moment to throw in what he went for. All the same, he mustered courage to inform the dad that he had good news for him. For Dominic, it was good news whether it was going to be so for his father. The father was excited and was anxious to know what was happening at home. Dominic said, "Concerning what I told you about my becoming a priest and going to the seminary, the time has come, and I have passed."

When Dominic said, "I have passed," he was referring to the Standard Six Examination, which twenty-eight candidates sat for, and only four were successful; and he was one of the four. It was really good news. From the look of things, there were no entrance examinations or formal interviews, except the informal ones carried out before the approval of Dominic for the minor seminary. Probably, the manifestation of the good intention and willingness sufficed having known Dominic in close quarters.

Having obtained a good result, his father would have insisted on the former career he wanted Dominic to undertake or even flare up with frustration as Dominic wanted to forsake and actually forsook the family that was very much in need of financial assistance at the time. Surprisingly, none of this took place. The dad's position was clear and simple: "You can see the place I am in. I hear that everything in the family, especially the palms that constituted the main source of income, had been sold to hire a lawyer who never appeared in court. There is nothing I can do. You may have to wait for a year till when I come out or look for someone who may like to help."[108]

The greatest relief was that the dad sanctioned his going to the seminary even though the possibility of financial support was very slim. The resoluteness of Okuku Ekandem is clear. It tallies with the Ignatian Principle of Spiritual Exercises that when in doubt or uncertain, decisions previously made should never be altered. Okuku Ekandem did not alter his former decision to see the son go into the seminary. That resoluteness would be manifested later when he would be required to do something very drastic concerning his marital situation before Dominic could proceed to the clerical stage of life.

c.   The Intervention of Father Ryan, the Father In Charge

The news of his father's approval of his going to the seminary was not kept secret. Father McDonald immediately shared it with parish priest, Reverend Father Ryan, who was always addressed as "the priest-in-charge" indicating the hierarchical nature of his position and responsibility. The priest-in-charge was the man responsible and answerable for the whole parish. All those working with him had to collaborate effectively and in a friendly manner to make things work out smoothly. The good news was shared with the father in charge. During the course of the conversation, he brought in the fact of his father being financially unable to take care of the financial burden at the time in question. The father in charge was very generous and gave him one pound sterling (£1) to purchase the items, which included underwear, white shirts, shorts and trousers, one white suit, towel, sandals, bedding, toiletries, plates, cutleries, as well as writing materials. The one pound (£1) covered everything together with a box in which all those things were stored.[109]

The reaction of the brothers when they heard that Dominic was leaving for the seminary was that of shock. They were shocked and inquired, "What is he going to the seminary for? Won't he marry?"[110] His brothers were mad with the idea contrary to the father's reaction who encouraged him to go on and to see if he could get help from anywhere. Perhaps the brothers were shocked and mad at the idea owing to the fact the whole affair was seen as unproductive in the economic sense since they knew there would be no salaries and no children since he was not going to marry and would not be able to support the family or contribute to the development of the family.

He got ready all the same in November and prepared to take off when the seminary was to open at Onitsha on January 15, 1933 (The year 1933 became very significant for Dominic from that time on.). The Mercedes car given to him during his episcopacy in Ikot Ekpene bore that special number, 1933, likewise the PMB of St. Patrick's College Ikot Ansa Calabar with which he was well associated at the pioneering stage.

i. The Seminary Situation

The seminary as understood by the Catholic Church is a training ground of candidates for the priesthood. In the early period of the church, the pastor or parish priest in the parish carried out the training. It was a type of apprenticeship whereby the candidate for the priesthood understudied the parish priest until the candidate could perform creditably well and was then said to be qualified and ready for ordination. There was no organized, coordinated, and systematic seminary formation program throughout the church before the sixteenth century.

The modern system of seminary formation[111] began with the emphasis of the Council of Trent[112] that took place between 1545 and 1563. It was one of the longest councils. The fathers of the council looked upon the establishment of seminaries as one of their major achievements. Before this time, seminary training employed the system of apprenticeship in parishes whereby the person who wanted to become priest understudied the priest in the parish until the person graduated and would be ordained priest sometimes after graduating in universities they proceeded to be ordained. To give them enough background formation and solid knowledge of what the church demanded, something had to be done. This is what led to the "retreats for (deacons) ordinands"[113] by St. Vincent De Paul in Amiens in Northern France. Every diocese was required to establish a seminary or join with others to establish one. The same requirement became paramount in the Nigerian church in the late eighties and early nineties after the international meeting of rectors and spiritual directors of major and minor seminaries of West and Central Africa at Yaoundé in Cameroon in 1988. The emphasis on spiritual year formation exploded and spread to the various diocese and archdioceses in the country. The Tridentine idea of establishment of seminaries embraced that of two seminaries, minor and major, in a large diocese. The provincial ones were to be taken care of by the ecclesiastical provinces, while the pontifical ones were to be taken care of by the Sacred Congregation for the Propagation of Faith (*Propaganda Fide*).

It was in an attempt to meet the demand of the council that St. Vincent De Paul, in line with others, organized a retreat for the deacons to be in France at Chateau Les Domes near Amiens Cathedral, which was regarded as the tallest cathedral in the world. The retreat lasted generally for a month. This was called retreat for the ordinands. At the initial stage, it was one week. Professors specialized in various fields were invited to come and drill the deacons before ordination at Chatillon Les Domes, later called Chatillon Les Challorans in Ain because of the river there. What happened in a small part of France later developed into a national and international phenomenon and finally evolved into what is now known as seminary.

In Nigeria, the first attempt to establish a minor seminary took place in 1909 at Iviani in Afemai in Delta State. Before the young Dominic was born and began his journey to the priesthood in 1933, others had already preceded him. The very first on this road in Nigeria was Fr. Paul Obodoechina Omecheta, born in 1888 and ordained in 1920 by Rt. Rev. Dr. Thomas Broderick, first vicar apostle of Western Nigeria. He made his first New Year's resolution on January 1, 1912, at the age of twenty-four. After six months, he renewed that resolution to become a priest and in 1913, which is thirty years before Dominic's project commenced. He was taken to England with his brother, Luke, at St. Mary's Junior Seminary Castle Head, Grange-over-Sands, Lancashire. There were priests ordained later in 1929—Reverend Fathers Joseph Onih, Kayode, and Adewuyi. Others had created the path of the priesthood that Dominic trod although not in the same setting.

ii.   The Journey to the Minor Seminary in Onitsha

His journey to Onitsha had to be via Aba since that was the only way he could get through to Onitsha. It is probable that his parish priest knew there would be other children going from there even though that information was not given until they arrived at the institution. He was instructed by his parish priest to get to Aba and find out where the Catholic mission was. After inquiring from some people, he was directed to the place. There, he met a catechist who went to inform the parish priest. The priest there instructed the catechist to take care of him till the following day. Another boy, one Moses Emerenini from Ubomiri near Owerri, had been offered admission to the same seminary where Dominic was heading. This gave the background to the long- standing friendship between the two later in life as Dominic recalled the situation during the interview when had been already a cardinal for many years.

Both of them left for Onitsha in the same lorry but did not know each other. They arrived Onitsha, and Emerenini took his box and began to move toward the bridge, and Dominic followed. It appeared Monsignor Emerenini arrived first in the seminary before Dominic, probably owing to the language advantage or familiarity with Onitsha. They arrived safely at St. Paul's Seminary, Onitsha, where Rev. Fr. Leo Brolly, CSSp, a Spiritan priest belonging to the Holy Ghost Congregation, was rector as well as the principal of Christ the King College, Onitsha. It was at Christ the King College, popularly known as CKC, that the students attended classes. Dominic fondly remembered the rector as a caring, loving, cheerful, disciplined priest whom he loved.[114] No wonder Fr. Leo Brolly, CSSp was present at the episcopal consecration of Dominic later on in years. The arrangement where the rector was also the principal also took place later at Holy Family College, Oku Abak, when it was established. The relationship gave rise to "seminary cottage." It was in this type of context that Dominic with his fellow classmates operated. Dominic recalled during the interview in 1995 with great delight that four of them arrived at the seminary on the appointed day to begin the journey to the priesthood. The four seminarians included the bishop emeritus of Owerri, Mark Unegbu; Monsignor Emerenini of Umuahia; Monsignor Meze of Enugu; and the cardinal himself. The group seems to have formed a little novitiate of its own because of the size and number.

Looking at the makeup of the group, Dominic Ekandem was the only Ibibio person who was a non-Igbo. He remembered those days and said, "I was the only person from my tribe. That was my fate. It was not easy." Maybe in private, the other three spoke Igbo but not when he was present.

English was compulsory in the seminary and hopefully during the official hours, but whenever they were dismissed from classes and were on their own, they did use their mother tongue for conversation. Dominic did not have that privilege since he was the only non-Igbo- speaking person there. This is likely to be the reason why Dominic said, "It was my fate." He had to try to learn a little of the language himself. Christ the King College (CKC), Onitsha, was opened on February 2, 1932. Before the official opening of CKC Onitsha, all the students who arrived before that time went to St. Charles College. The situation of the beginning of Queen of Apostles' Seminary, Afaha Obong, in Ikot Ekpene Diocese where the seminarians were quartered at Ediene Abak but held classes at Holy Family College, Oku Abak, until a permanent site was established. It was the same at CKC.

iii.   The Seminary Days

Dominic enjoyed his seminary days immensely and recalled quite a number of things that were not part of the program but had influence on him. Some of those things like training people in various fields other than education as such bore fruit in many organizations he later formed.

He enjoyed his studies very immensely as well as sports as he recalled his seminary days with gusto.115 He recalled first day of arrival at the seminary how a senior student took his box from him and helped him to make his bed. This is the type of joy and satisfaction that the psalmist witnessed in a joyously contented group of friends when he said, "Ecce Quam Bonum et Quam Jucundum habitare Fratres In Unum," "Behold, how good and pleasant it is for brothers to live in unity" (Ps. 133:1).116 What the psalmist extolled was perfectly realized in the experience of Dominic Ekandem as a day-old seminarian. That first impression was great and may have contributed to a large extent to his humble attitude despite the fact that he was a prince. This overflowed into many other things. Here are some excerpts from the cardinal's unpublished Silver Jubilee Memoir:

> As I was the only student from my tribe in the Junior Seminary at Onitsha when I started off, my career there would have been a sad and unsuccessful one, but fortunately I found myself among sincerely genuine friends and companions, devoted brothers, and deeply religious seminarians. The thought of giving up and running home quickly

deserted me. Nobody attempted to quarrel with me, I noticed no discrimination, small and young as I was, and nobody attempted to enslave or boss over me. In fact, to my embarrassment and confusion the very Senior Seminarians, like Monsignor Obelagu of Onitsha were serving me, making my bed, feeding me at table, washing and ironing my clothes and teaching me manners with all the tenderness of one's parents. It was my first experience of the old and senior serving the young and junior. The Seminary turned out to be such a happy home that I forgot all about my home in Ibibio Country. If all Seminaries in Nigeria today and the entire Priest trained therein continue to maintain such spirit and standard, then there would be no Church in any country of Africa, in fact, in the whole World that would be more fortunate than the Nigerian Church. It is such spirit of unity, genuine brotherhood, tolerance and service that does help many Seminarians to brave the hardships of seminary successfully to the day of ordination. It is that broadened outlook in life and religion, the anticipated, successful blending together of the excellent cultures of our many Nigerian tribes, that has inspired me to cry without ceasing for National Seminary where we could sink objectionable differences, developing affectionate respect for one another and together like brothers of the same parents work to consolidate and enlarge the magnificent edifice of the Catholic Church in our country.[117]

They attended classes at CKC and went back to the seminary for abode, meals, as well as spiritual exercises. One of the things he learned in the seminary and maintained to the end of his life was "meditation." In one occasion, he said, "How can a priest function well without meditation?" He did not claim it to be easy, but he did not throw it away because it was difficult. He saw it as a struggle and as a practice that needed seriously inculcated. It is more of an attitude formed after habitual repetition.

The long vacation period was very enjoyable. That gave him an opportunity to teach catechism to catechumens and learn a great deal from the priests who ministered tirelessly and went to the outstations with the zeal and love in spite of the difficulties to be found. Later, as a bishop, he adopted the same strategy while on pastoral visit to the parishes and stations.

The question "Will you be coming home?" raised by the father the night of declaration of his intention to become a priest was answered without any doubt by his coming home for holidays. Each of those periods provided him an opportunity to put into practice many good qualities he had acquired in the seminary like playing and reading. He also helped immensely in the sanitation and organization of the compound.

His recreation and games periods in the seminary were well enjoyed. He recalled those unique moments as being very delightful. According to him, he had nothing to regret about his seminary days or about his fellow students or the rector.

He simply said, "Those were glorious days and special moments."[118] From this statement, it could be said that he made the most use of the opportunities he had, leaving no stone unturned. Concerning the subjects studied, he said he could not remember, but he strove to learn them very carefully and conscientiously. He loved it. During one of the holidays when Dominic went home, he discovered that as a beloved son of the father, his father had for him decided to marry a woman and keep for him in line with African custom or with that of the Ibibios. He simply told the father that marriage was incompatible with priestly celibacy and that he could give her to any of his brothers, but for him, it was impossible to do so. The father was disappointed but gave up the idea afterward when he noticed that Dominic had started losing his gaiety and cheerfulness because of that attempt to get him a wife. When he realized it was the first test of his vow of celibacy to be made years to come, he became more resolute. He graduated from St. Paul's Seminary, Onitsha, in 1937.

iv. The Probation Period

His seminary days over and the examinations completed and the result of the London GCE out, he disposed himself for the task ahead. The determining factor for the success of the probational period was his docile disposition; otherwise, things would have been very difficult for him. The early period of priestly training in Nigeria was not easy at all. Things were difficult and delicate. For example, emphasis on family background to the priesthood, the example of the parents and family members, not going home easily on holidays, the simplicity of the candidate and genuine disposition that demanded total obedience, no particular friendship, the great periods of silence, no rejection of any food served, the capacity to adjust to situations and to live community life with others, the need to detach oneself from family and ties, living out of poverty, etc., were among some of the delicate or difficult things. There were many trials like that of Abraham or the people of God in the desert or even in the Promised Land. Anyone swimming in such a current had to be fully aware of the tide and discern whether to go against it or to float with it. Any little sign of insubordination or disobedience was considered a sign of lack of vocation. Parental problems were equally part and parcel of the entire system of training as will be seen in Okuku Ekandem's situation and decision.

In the midst of this crooked and rough and narrow road, which the Lord said leads to life, he was asked to go on probation to be one of the foundation members of staff for the newly established St. Patrick College, Calabar, quartered at Sacred Heart School beside the Sacred Heart Cathedral, Egerton Road, Calabar. The college operated there for some time before being transferred to the permanent site at Ikot Ansa, Calabar. The period of probation that is now called a pastoral year was meant to be a period of testing, deciphering, and sifting the genuine intentions from the false ones and to gain practical experience about the sacred priesthood.

Happily, he undertook the probation period, which at first lasted for one year when St. Patrick's College was still located at the same premise with Sacred Heart School, Calabar. Probably, he thought that after having completed the one-year probational period or two years, he would be asked to go on with his philosophical as well as his theological studies. Those expectations proved abortive and were premature. He was told to get on with the teaching job in the new college.[119] His special period in St. Patrick's College, Ikot Ansa, gave him a special connection with the college. He was a teacher in the college unlike His Grace Most Rev. Brain D. Usanga who did his higher school studies there while his secondary level of education took place at Holy Family, Oku Abak. Some even presumed that he was a fellow "old boy" of the college, whereas he was not. Things began to unfold gradually. He only became aware of the thorny road to the priesthood when he was told to repeat the probation already accomplished at the school. He then realized that it was not an easy road.

Having finished his minor seminary days in 1937, he did probation for two years, 1938 and 1939. If he had some misgivings, he did not express them, probably on the assumption that the bishop and all the expatriate priests were his superiors, and they had to show him what he was to do and teach him the way to the priesthood. The second year of the probation, still teaching at St. Patrick's College (termed "the university across the sea" by the old boys of the college), rolled to an end in 1939. Once again, he was poised to begin his studies in the major seminary with some indications from his superiors. Almost when everything was ready, the management discovered that there were not enough staff to handle the volume of work concerned; he was consequently enlisted as a teacher and member of staff for the third time after the training at Christ the King College attached to St. Charles College, Onitsha. The first bishop emeritus of Umuahia, Most Rev. Dr. Anthony N. Gogo Nwedo, CSSp had done his prefecting at CKC at the time the cardinal was a first-year student.

His period of probation was not as long as that of the Cardinal Dominic Ekandem. Bishop Nwedo, CSSp had started his studies at St. Charles and was a serious student at the time. He was senior to the cardinal in class and probably by age. Nwedo finished his probational period in two years and proceeded to the "senior house" as the major seminary was called at the time. Dominic, on his part, was requested to continue for one more year, increasing it to three years instead of two that his predecessor did. He embraced this third year of his probation with courage and equanimity. One of his students in St. Patrick's College, observing him and being aware of what befell him, said, "He remained calm but prayed all the more intently."[120] That was during the second phase of the probation that used up the whole of 1940. The probation period when combined with second phase covers three years from 1937 to 1940. He was also in charge of liturgical ceremonies in the institution.

It is possible he prostrated himself like Christ in the Garden of Gethsemane imploring God "if it is your will let this cup pass me by nevertheless not my will but yours be done" (Mt. 26:26–46). It was really an extreme test of probation. It was almost like loosening the gates and powers of hell against him. In the Lord's name, he overcame them (Cf. Ps.

118:13–14) and remained unperturbedly serene, setting his face like flint toward Jerusalem (Is. 50:7). Many a man or woman would have despaired in the face of such events or even given up. Many would have lost their vigor, slowed down their involvement in daily chores, avoided contact with the "supposed perpetrators of evil," prayed less and become despondent, and become detached but not in a positive sense but in a negative one; as far as Dominic was concerned, he was made of a sterner stuff he could not be subdued by such challenges. This special year of 1940 constituted the apex of the "three-year probational period." Hopefully, the decision of his father not to go back on his decision when he was in prison encouraged Dominic to go on irrespective of his father's situation at the time.

There is no doubt that the experience of the probation period partly informed his priestly motto, which read:

"A Priest "Alter Christus"—Be Thine the Master's Cross with love to bear so that in eternity endless with crown to wear."

The priestly motto was modified to suit the Episcopal one "*In cruce salus*"—in the cross is our salvation.

Most of his teachings had taken place during those three trying and arduous years. The undaunted spirit; the indefatigable character; the steadfast and enduring disposition; the unbroken personality; the hopeful vision; the overcoming outlook; the unstained demeanor and comportment; and a deeply spiritual, intellectual, moral, social, and pastoral man from the darkened nature of the unknown and became resplendent and sparkling like crystal. At the end of the dark tunnel, he emerged in the bright, warm sunlight and was greeted with the news that his probational period was over, and he could proceed to the major seminary. The news was received with joy, and his long-nursed desire was accomplished, and he proceeded enthusiastically to the senior house or major seminary.

v. Entry into Major Seminary

In 1924, the great missionary apostle and educator, Bishop Joseph Shanahan, (as the cardinal recalled in his sermon on the occasion of the Silver Jubilee of Bigard Memorial Seminary called St. Paul's Seminary at the time), started a senior seminary at Igbariam in a small village in Onitsha. The cardinal mentioned that Msgr. William Obelagu was one of the fruits of that venture. At the time Dominic went to the major seminary, it was no longer situated at Igbariam; it had moved to St. Paul's Major Seminary, Okpala. The Brochure of the Silver Jubilee of his episcopal ordination indicates that he did his philosophy course from 1941 to 1944 at St. Paul's Major Seminary, Enugu, and proceeded to complete his studies in the same seminary at Okpala-Owerrinta. If that were to have been the case, he would have studied philosophy for four years instead of three years and four years theology; the reverse would have been the case. He rather studied philosophy from 1941 to 1943 in Enugu. He started his theology in 1944 and studied till 1947 at St. Paul's Major Seminary, Okpala-Owerrinta. It was there he received his minor orders of tonsure, porter, exorcist, and lector as well as the major orders of acolyte, subdiaconate, diaconate, and finally, the priesthood.[121] The move to the major seminary was welcome news. There is no doubt that the relief and end of such a period of uncertainty were of great relief. The cardinal remembered very vividly the period of training in the seminary was appreciatively enjoyable. He remembered his contemporaries and the jokes and friendship they used to share.

Mother Mary Joseph Okpo, HHCJ, commenting on Dominic I. Ekandem as a seminarian said that when Dominic's sister Rose Ekandem whom she instinctively called Mmama introduced him to her at St. Theresa's Primary School, Edem Ekpat, in 1940, she did not understand what being a seminarian meant until Rose took time to explain it to her. She recalled, "Dominic Ekandem, the Seminarian, had three other Seminarians with him. They were Moses Efanga from Calabar, David from Idu Uruan and Gabriel Una from Afaha Oku, Uyo. Gabriel later died as a Seminarian while the other two discontinued and later got married."[122] It is difficult to say at what stage the seminarians left. All the same, it shows that Dominic was not the only student in the seminary at his time. If he went to the minor seminary from Ibibio section of the country, he might not necessarily have been the only senior seminarian or junior seminarian around. He must have been the most senior among them.

Dominic recalled that everything was studied officially in Latin. The subjects studied that he remembered included sacred scriptures, dogma, liturgy, moral theology, ascetical theology, canon law, and others that he could not recall. These subjects were studied in the then St. Paul's Seminary that commenced at Igbariam in Onitsha in 1924. The seminary later moved on to Ngor Okpala now in Owerri, Imo State, and eventually moved to its permanent site at Enugu, the present location in 1950. Dominic Ekandem started his studies in 1941 in the major seminary setting at Ngor Okpala and sailed on smoothly until an enormous decision was demanded of his father. That decision will be uncovered in a short while.

Dominic faced many grave difficulties on the road to the priesthood. His path was not easy and smooth. It was strewn with tones. The difficulties of the probation over one would have expected a problem- free journey to the end. It seems that the higher he went, the hotter it became, unlike climbing a mountain where the higher you go, the cooler it becomes. The earlier period of the seminary days witnessed many external problems both from his family as well as from his ecclesiastical family. No sooner had he approached ordinations had the deluge of difficulties surged again as if the basket had fallen, and all the content fell on the floor. Since he had already been through the crucible of suffering, he was not so much taken aback. He was undaunted by these happenings and difficulties. From his disposition and temperament, it could be said that he was prepared for it.

As already mentioned, Obong Ekandem's compound was often thronged with many visitors, some of them being the court clerks, the interpreters, and the Catholic clergymen to whom he was always generous with. It could be said that among the Catholic priests who visited was the parish priest who wanted the conversion of the Okuku. The zealous pastor did not relent his efforts in visiting. The cardinal stated in his memoir:

> Early in my life my father had associated me with pagan worship. I often carried the victims (fowl or goat, water and mashed yam) to be offered in sacrifice to the gods, invoked to bless and to protect us and help us grow as virtuous children and useful citizens. [123]

The involvement of the Okuku in traditional worship was one of the things challenged by the priests who visited him. Apart from the rejection of traditional worship, it was demanded by the parish priest that he should go to church. The Okuku did not reject such a novel idea but decided to send his whole family to Qua Iboe Church and join them later. He was still holding on to every other thing he was doing. The priest told him that going to Qua Iboe Church or even to the Presbyterian Church did not solve his problem. The Okuku thought that if he went to any of these churches and retained everything, surely, the demand of the parish priest would be satisfied. He was mistaken. Something more stringent than going to the church was to be required. For Okuku Ekandem, the demand was going to be horrendous. Such were the challenges that hovered over the Okuku.

Bishop James Moynagh SPS
1st Bishop of Calabar Diocese

C. The Obstacle and the Great Demand

Dominic had almost completed his studies for the priesthood in 1945 when his superiors told him that he had to return to his father since he could not be ordained in an environment such as the one his father was living in. Dominic, as an obedient seminarian, left the seminary. He had no choice. He had to return home. He left the seminary and went to his father's compound. The father had gone to court at the time Dominic arrived home. Dominic went to greet his father after his return from work. After all the day's feasting and sumptuous supper, the father demanded to know why he was at home and went on to inundate him with series of questions. He asked whether they were on break or not. What was happening in the seminary? What were the things demanded of him? Was Dominic looking for something? Dominic gave a negative answer to all the questions. He later told the dad in his usual humorous manner, "Endong Ubine fien ediyem utom oono," "I have been sent to you to find a job for me."

The dad exclaimed, "Job! What type of job? I married a wife for you, and you refused. What type of job do you want? Ayatime onyong seminary," "You have to get back to the seminary." Dominic went on. "It will not be possible as long as the conditions are not fulfilled." "What conditions?" At this Dominic had to restate all that was demanded of him before his ordination. The Okuku was very conscious of his becoming a Christian in the Catholic Church. Somehow he was aware of the need to wed with just one wife but not fully aware of the fact that he had to part with all his wives, except one with whom he would wed. At the third and last time, when Bishop James Moynagh, the ordinary of Calabar Diocese, came to him and mentioned something about getting rid of the wives, he humorously said, "Owo akpadia usung me ikemeke edidia edesi me iwuk abia ikoro?" "If one ate foo-foo, can the same person not eat rice or yam porridge or any other food too?" Obong Vitus E. Ekandem, one of the brothers of Dominic I. Ekandem, recollected. The reminiscence of Madam Rose corroborated what Vitus had said.

The difficulties on the way to the priesthood are unpredictable. They can be compared with the unpredictability of victory in the field of football until the final whistle is blown since anything can occur at any moment. This was the case with Sebastian Eyo when he was a seminarian. The predicament of Mr. Sebastian Eyo from Mbak Etoi was tumultuous and can never be said to have been a comedy as the case of Dominic Ekandem turned out to be but a tragedy from the human point of view owing to its end. The emerging problem of Sebastian became a total stumbling block for him to advance toward the priesthood.

What hindered him was not of the same magnitude as that of Dominic and his father Okuku Ekandem. Sebastian was almost at the point of completing his studies and getting ready for diaconate ordination. He could have been ordained the same year with Msgr. Silas T. Umoh who died in 2012 and buried the same day with Rev. Fr. Sylvestre Nkonduok who was ordained in 1978 with the present bishop of Port Harcourt Diocese, Most Rev. Camillus Archibong Etokudo. Sebastian faced a difficult situation not from his own point of view but because of the circumstances of his father. The standard was high, the demands were enormous, yet the faith was to be maintained in a pure state and had to be transmitted untarnished.

On the whole, Mr. Sebastian Eyo had no personal problems as such. The problem was his father's. His father, Mr. Eyo, had married in the church that automatically gave room for the young Sebastian to progress to the priesthood. Everyone knew and acknowledged that. They lived their lives as Catholics, and Sebastian progressed smoothly on the way to the priesthood until his father got himself involved in a serious problem that affected the son in the seminary. There was a widow whose husband died and was managing her life until Mr. Eyo, the father of Sebastian, had an extramarital relationship with her. She conceived and bore a son. The whole affair was reported to Bishop Moynagh, who said that the father of a priest-to-be should never have given such a scandal by living a loose life. Consequently, Sebastian was withdrawn from the major seminary/senior house out of no fault of his. He could not proceed with his training in the senior house even though he was almost ready for the diaconate ordination.

When Sebastian was withdrawn, he ceased to be a major seminarian; he went to teach at Holy Family College. There, he met a brilliant young man, Brian D. Usanga, who was a student there. Sebastian asked him to come and live with him. He did and was happy to stay with Sebastian and became very free with him to the point of going with Sebastian to his village, Mbak Etoi, to spend his holidays there. In other words, Usanga, who later became the second bishop of Calabar Diocese and eventually the first archbishop of Calabar, was a servant to Mr. Sebastian Eyo from Mbak Etoi, who was a tutor in Holy Family College, Oku Abak, that great, humble, and affable man who was very gracious in his general demeanor and very considerate in his relationships, while exercising his duty of justice and fair play was simply solid, courageous, and cheerful despite all odds. Brian Davies Usanga found a harbor or properly put a haven when he scarcely dreamed of it. Usanga was so fond of Mbak that he was admirably fond of the place and her people.

Probably because of his friendship with Sebastian and fondness about Mbak as a place, he decided to make Msgr. Emmanuel Umoetok his chancellor when Monsignor Umoetok finished his studies in Rome and worked for many years in Calabar Diocese. One good turn deserves another. This is almost like the friendship between David and Jonathan and how Jonathan, son of Saul, told David to "never cut off your faithful love from my house, even if the Lord were to cut off everyone of the enemies of David from the face of the earth" (1 Sam. 20:15). There was no covenant between Sebastian and Brian, but the bond of love was surely there.

Bishop Moynagh was firm with his demand that the Okuku Ekandem change his ways before the ordination of his son Dominic. Perhaps that was why Okuku did not react much when the young Dominic about the conditions informed him for his continuity since he was already aware of some of the demands before they entangled him (Cf. conditions for discipleship Matt 16:24–28, 8:16–22, 19:23–30). The ordination of his son depended on his positive response.

Another great demand made on Okuku was to stop sacrificing to the gods or deity he was affiliated to. He was to cease being a traditional worshipper. The Okuku was not to be a Christian and a traditional worshipper at the same time. He could not worship God and mammon (Matt. 6:24). No one can serve two masters at the same time. He was to be just a Christian and in the Catholic Church with one wedded wife without slipping back to the worship of the deities or returning to his former wives. After having considered all these things, he ordered the young Dominic informed him about the conditions for continuing his studies. Dominic went back as his father had instructed him and informed his ecclesiastical superiors that his father had agreed to carry out what was demanded of him.

Before Dominic left home, Okuku Ekandem questioned him in confidence to know whether he, Dominic, would be ordained a Catholic priest should he stop sacrificing to idols and send away his wives and wed in the Catholic Church with one. "Eya Udot Ubok mkpenam s'ebo?" "Would you be ordained if I carry out what I am asked to?" His father's answer was in the affirmative. "Sia adoho ekemek ido Oku Abasi, ka iso," "Since you had chosen to be a priest of God, go on." The deep and intimate discussion carried out between the father and the son created opportunity for credence and assurance. Dominic suggested to his father what he was to do. There were serious sacrifices on the part of the father and the son, yet they were bonded together by paternal/filial love. Since the father had declared that he had other children, and he was not going to lose Dominic if he became a priest, he stood on that ground without looking back.

Sometime after Dominic had gone back to seminary, Okuku Paul Ekandem asked one of his children to summon all his wives for him after supper. They all came. At this time, the wives were about eighteen in number. When they were all assembled, he told them that Dominic had almost completed his studies but was sent back because he could not be ordained while his family were living in the practice of paganism and polygamy.

He added that he wanted Dominic to be a priest, which he had chosen. He told them to find and discover where they were likely to go and settle permanently within the next two months. At that point, he told them that in two months' time, none of them would be staying in the same compound. He told them that they would all have to go back to their homes. The women roared, laughing boisterously as they left his presence. Each day he came back from work, he would remind them of the "D" day. The women started caricaturing the whole situation. Each time they went to the farm or to the market, they teased one another, saying that their time was limited and that their days were numbered. All was regarded as a joke. They did not believe it would happen. They took everything for granted until the big bang came. It could be, they were contemplating, that he would remove the pots, gather their property, and leave them outside as a sign that he did not need them again or that they were no longer his wives. What he did stunned them and went beyond all that.

D. The day the Sun Turned into Darkness

After having given allowance for more than three months, he came back one evening and announced to his wives that the next day would be the "day"; if there was anything they could do, let them do it. He said, "Tongo ke mkpong, owo mbufo ndomo kiet idikaha iso iba ke otung emi," "From tomorrow, none of you will be in the compound any longer."[124] At that, they burst out laughing again. Some questioned while chuckling, "Mme ebiwowot owo?" "Is he going to kill someone?"

No sooner had the day broken the following day than he began sharpening his machete. Any of the wives who saw him sharpening the knife wondered whether he was going to behead them for the sake of Dominic. The women were excited and alarmed about the ominous event that was due to overtake them. When he finished sharpening the knife, he went in to change and dress himself in labor clothes. He was soon ready for action with a long, strong ladder and his sharp machete. He did not have much difficulty in destroying the roofs since they werea ll thatched with mats, bamboos, tie-tie, piassava, and sticks.

The very first roof that he upturned was that of Mma Mary whom he later chose as his lawful wedded wife. Other roofs followed after—one after the other. It was a miserable sight. There were series of lamentations, and the wives who were caricaturing the situation before were then seen to be weeping helplessness. It was like "Rachael weeping for her children and refused to be consoled because they were no more" during the massacre of the infants during the Birth of Christ (Cf. Matt. 2:18). Many people came from the village to watch the great scene, the decision, and the drama of expulsion. The decision made by Okuku could only be called a serious cataclysm. It was no small decision. No man of weak character could make such a decision, neither could a person with a wavering mind or that of petty character. It was only a man of conviction, foresight with humble and moral courage, who could take such reactionary and revolutionary decision. No wonder the Cross played a very vital role in the entire life of Dominic.

The Okuku's decision could be likened to that of Abraham (Gen. 22) who was to sacrifice his only son. It was not only a great sacrifice but also a very great one indeed. In this case, the wives and children, in short, the whole family, were the cost of discipleship and service of God. This was a decision that, in the opinion of many, was unwise, futile, and too emotional. By making that decision, he had to abdicate his rights as a titled man and suffer rejection from many. Okuku Ekandem and his action became the talk of the day. He had made the great decision there was not going back. It was a moral courage of the first class. This was a decision of decisions. The crown to be gained was obtained at an incalculable price. No wonder the Cross meant so much for Dominic and was so dear to his heart.

E.   The Effects of the Decision

All the scattered women in the compound conglomerated with their children. Some went back to their families; others went to their relations. Generally, there was no one left in the compound. The various mothers were free to go to their farmlands owned before the dispersion and expulsion exercise to get whatever food materials they wanted. They could cultivate the plots and make use of the palm produce as well, but they were not having their abode in the compound anymore. Those whose male children had grown up quickly built huts for their mothers, but things were never the same anymore. The little children suffered. The Okuku had to play the role of father and mother. It was a great price that was paid for the first priest in Ibibio land to emerge. The following questions can be raised: Was this level of disruption given necessary since it was the son who was to be ordained and not the father? Is this similar to a situation where mothers were refused Holy Communion because their daughters were traditionally married and had not yet wedded in the Catholic Church? Could this have been averted in any way? Although the questions might be legitimate, they do not actually solve the problem since the main aim at the time was to lay a solid foundation built on Christ the rock. This is where African tradition conflicted very greatly with Christian tradition garbed in the European culture.[125] The conflict of culture always leads to suppression, assimilation, enculturation, or inculturation. In this case, it seems assimilation prevailed rather than the others.

The elderly sons helped in the chaotic situation until things improved. Rose Ekandem, Dominic's sister who was a nun at the time, left the convent and religious life to fill in the gap as a mother. This was the self-offering of Rose so that the brother could become a priest of God. That is martyrdom of charity like that of St. Maximilian Kolbe. The mothers took the very small children away. Their mothers who arranged a secret meeting place to serve food to their children surreptitiously supported the other ones. The unmarried daughters helped a great deal trying to keep the communal spirit going. The mothers who cooked for their children made sure that they did not enter the compound of Okuku Ekandem. They became afraid of him even though he never intended them any harm.

He realized the sufferings of the children and went out of his way to take care of them. He made sure he came back from work a little earlier than usual. It was the turning point of his life and that of the entire family. The consequences of that response, which he gave to "Tom" at night while in bed in 1932, were gaining momentum like flood and were determining so many things.

At the completion of the dispersion and expulsion exercise, he sent words to the parish priest and through the parish priest to the bishop that he was ready to see his son Tom ordained a priest. Presumably, the priest-in-charge had already learned of the cataclysm[126] in the kindred of Okuku Ekandem, but he did not act until he received official information sent by Okuku himself. The parish priest was delighted and sent an emissary to investigate. When the situation was confirmed, he went to find out which of the women he wanted to choose as his lawful wedded wife.

F.   The Choice

According to Chief Vitus Ekandem, who was the spokesman for the family of Okuku Paul Ino Ekandem Ubo Etok, his father, Paul, decided to choose Mma Mary as his lawful wedded wife in place of Mmatim, otherwise called Mmassah, who was the very first wife. Mma Mary Idung was from Ikot Ambon Ikono, not the one in Ibesikpo near Nung Udoe Ibesikpo but the one in Ikono. Okuku Ekandem chose Mma Mary first and foremost because she had lost all her male children[127] through death and was left with three daughters. He chose her realizing that if he drove her away, she would likely have to wander about since the female children could not take care of her. Apart from that, she was a good woman. In other words, it was out of consideration that he narrowed his choice to Mma Catherine. Mma Mary Idung, according to one of the nephews, Dr. Gabriel John Ekandem,[128] the son of the very first son before Dominic Ekandem, had three children: Ibanga, Afiong, and Atim. She became a wife after her menopause, so she could not give birth to any further children. Having only three surviving daughters caused Okuku to wed her to give her the protection and security, which she necessarily would have missed.

The idea of menopause seems to give room to some people to think that Mma Mary was barren. When the two accounts are carefully scrutinized, it can be confirmed that Mma Mary had children. In this context, the testimony of Obong Vitus Ekandem seems more plausible even though the names of the children could have included the ones named by Dr. Gabriel. At her death, the surviving members of the family buried Mma Mary Idung who became Mma Mary Ekandem. At that time, Martin Ekandem, who later died of diabetes in the United States of America and was brought back to be buried in Obio Ibiono, was part of the family that was seriously involved at the burial of Mma Mary.[129] It is to be noted that it was the roof of Mary's house that was first destroyed[130] and she being driven out. Providentially enough, she was the one chosen for that special role.

Mma Mary and Mmatim were the *Iban Ima* (the beloved wives) as distinct from the *Atai* (the first wife) with paramount position in the family. The first wife generally enjoys that position and privilege in a polygamous home. Since Dominic's mother was already dead, she could not have been the one even if she were to have been alive. But Mma Nwa Ebong, Dominic's mother, was the second wife; she could not enjoy that privilege. It had to be another of the mothers.

The two beloved wives[131] were directly in charge of the welfare of Okuku before the dispersion. That position made the two women a little closer to him than the others. Mmatim or Mmassah was a woman with a very strong will but very lovely and caring. She could mix with any group of persons at first sight. She was also very courageous and outspoken. She was fiery and tempestuous and could laugh at will or shout if she disagreed with a particular situation. She sometimes acted at the spur of the moment. She is the type that would be described in Myer-Briggs study of personality as the "gut person," but in actual fact, she was passionate. She was very lovely because of her charitable dispositions. Mma Mary, on the other hand, was very gentle, considerate, lovely, loving, and very thoughtful and was very much for others as well. Her charitable disposition like that of Mmatim was very clear. The two women, Mmatim and Mma Mary, formed what was called *Iban Ufip* (the jealous ones) or the wives who were jealous of each other and found fault with each other, quarreling and spying on each other while at the same time vying for a more intimate relationship with their husband than the other. Theirs was a healthy jealousy and competition between the two with regard to outdoing the other in acts of love toward the husband. This is a common thing in a polygamous setting.

Between the two, Mma Mary became the choice of the Okuku and eventually became the lawfully wedded wife after the catechumenate period and marriage preparation course. She was later christened Catherine Mary. In 1995, when the research began, she was the only surviving one among the wives of Okuku Ekandem. The Okuku himself became Okuku Paul

Ino Ekandem Ubo Etok after his baptism. He wedded the same year in 1945. It was a glorious moment achieved through sweat and sleepless nights decision. It was the decision that opened the way for the young Dominic to become Reverend Dominic at diaconate ordination in early 1947.

He completed his philosophical studies at St. Paul's Seminary Enugu in 1945 and began his theological studies at the same St. Paul's Seminary transferred to Ngor Okpala-Owerrinta.

G.   The Diaconate and Priestly Ordination

On December 8, 1930, Bishop Joseph Shanahan, CSSp ordained the young Rev. Fr. John Cross Anyiogu, a Catholic priest at the Holy Trinity Cathedral, Onitsha. After six years, Rev. Fr. Erameh Joseph Aigbodion was ordained in Asaba. He became "the second indigenous Catholic Priest in Nigeria, second to Rev. Fr. Emecheta from Illah town, Delta State."[132] Part of this information is not correct, especially the one indicating Emerah as the second priest in Nigeria. Emecheta, yes, but not Emerah. If Emerah becomes the second in Nigeria, what happens to Anyiogu who was ordained in 1930? If the presupposition is Delta, it is understandable, but if it is the whole nation, it is greatly mistaken. The year 1930 is a very important one since that was the same year that the volunteer priest, Rev. Fr. James Moynagh arrived in Nigeria with Bishop Shanahan, CSSp together with others who were to work in Calabar and its environs. It was two years before Dominic completed his Standard Six. That particular year, Dominic was in Standard Four at St. Joseph, Anua. Fr. John Cross preceded Fr. Dominic Ekandem in priestly ordination by seventeen years. Dominic was ordained a deacon by Abp. David Matthew, the apostolic delegate for East and West Africa early in 1947 at St. Anne's Church, Ifuho.

Later that year, on December 7, 1947, a day short of exact seventeen years of Fr. John Cross's Ordination, he was ordained a Catholic priest by Abp. C. Heery, CSSp of Onitsha as the ordaining prelate at St. Anne's Catholic Church, Ifuho, Ikot Ekpene, which was to become his episcopal see sixteen years after. All these took place under Calabar Diocese. St. Anne's Catholic Church was a parish church in Ikot Ekpene District by then.

The father's decision was the foundation on which all these other blessings of God were built. It is often said that grace builds on nature. In this case, the Okuku's disposition has made room for many things. Where grace abounds, thanksgiving increases as well.

After the great decision to send away his wives and choosing Mmatim to be the bride he was to wed, he had done with polygamy and committed himself to a monogamous life. Dominic made sure his father was baptized. Okuku Ekandem was christened Paul Ino Ekandem in 1945 at St. Joseph Catholic Church, Anua. The baptism occurred two years before Dominic's diaconate and priestly ordination in 1947. It was a great milestone in the family of the Okuku Ekandem.

H.   Dispensation Process

When Okuku Paul gave the green light for Dominic to be ordained in the church, his ecclesiastical superior decided to apply for dispensation because of the fact that he was the son of a second wife. Rome did not delay in granting the dispensation and opening the door of ordination to Dominic, thereby crowning the unique sacrifice of his father. His Holiness Pope Pius XI shortly before his deaconate ordination granted the dispensation.

It was on December 7, 1947, that His Grace Archbishop Heery, CSSp of Onitsha ordained Rev. Dominic Ekandem. So Tom became a priest at the age of thirty. He was the first native priest in the then Calabar Province. This was his greatest achievement. Throughout his stay in the seminary, he said, "I always prayed to become a Catholic priest." Addressing some Kiltegan priests, sometime in Holy Family College, Abak, Fr. Dominic Ekandem proudly said, "I am the first Nigerian priest among you…I am also the youngest.[133]

I.   The Benefactress

Bishop James Moynagh, taking a keen interest in the person of young Dominic, wanted him to progress without too much difficulty. He decided to get an Irish woman, Mrs. Annice Gordon, who was anxious to be involved in training priests in missionary countries, to help in the training of young Dominic for the priesthood. Mrs. Gordon married her cousin Mr. John P. (Jack) Gordon. Both had canonical permission from Rome to marry each other. The locals knew they had special dispensation. Both came from

Ballaghaderreen in County Roscommon in Ireland. They came from the Diocese of Achonry where the Annunciation and St. Nathy's Cathedral was located. Rev. Fr. James Shryane, a native of Ballaghaderreen who served at Holy Rood Catholic Church, Barnsley, England, for many years, remembered the visit of Bishop Dominic Ekandem to his town. Bishop Ekandem went to visit and to thank his benefactress, Mrs. Annice Gordon. Father Shryane recalled, "It was the talk of the Town."[134] Fr. James Shryane recollected that he was in the intermediate certificate class (three) in St. Nathy's College, Ballaghaderreen, at the time. He also vividly remembered that Bishop Dominic Ekandem gave a talk in his college even though he could not remember the details of the talk. He spoke with his contemporaries, Rev. Fr. Martin Jennings and Rev. Fr. John Doherty. It was Father Jennings who linked Father Shryane with Father John because of the position he held in the diocese and the records. Consequently, he could help with some information about the Bishop Ekandem's visit. Fathers John and Martin recalled that Bishop Ekandem addressed the students in the new oratory that was built in the college.

Figure 3 Mrs. Annice Gordon, the Benefactress of Dominic Cardinal Ekandem[135]

Father Shryane added that he could not remember what Bishop Ekandem said since it took place about sixty years ago. It was Father Martin who connected Father Shryane with Rev. Fr. John Doherty of Achonry

Diocese in Ireland. Father Martin and Father John recalled that Bishop Dominic Ekandem came to their diocese to see Mrs. Annice Gordon who paid for his entire seminary training. Fr. James Shryane noted that only God alone knows how many priests she trained for the African missions, particularly for Nigeria. She must have trained a number of them without mentioning it to people. Mrs. Gordon lived a very humble and virtuous life. She went daily to mass and received Holy Communion regularly. She was a very devout woman.

Bishop James Moynagh, the bishop of Calabar, was the link between Mrs. Gordon and Dominic Ekandem. The visit was very great and popular that the local newspaper called *Roscommon* carried the news. The visit took place about the time when the new college chapel was completed. Bishop Ekandem celebrated mass in the cathedral, and Rev. Fr. James Shryane was one of the children who served at that mass. Fr. James Shryane celebrated his Golden Jubilee anniversary of the priesthood in June 2015. All to the greater glory of God!

The Gordons did not have any surviving children. Each of the eight children born in that marriage died at infancy. The death of the last one, Denise Bride, broke her heart, for she had taken great care to provide a nurse for her. In spite of this, she still died at the age of nineteen in 1943, nine years after the death of the father.[136] Mr. Alex McDonnell, the cousin of Mr. John Gordon from the paternal line, corroborated the continuous death of the Gordons' children when he said, "Know that the Gordons did not have any children left as each died at infancy and as they were first cousins."[137] It is likely that they did not consider the constant death of their children as punishment from God. Otherwise, they would have experienced loss of faith instead of adopting spiritual children for the priesthood as they did.

They were a very wealthy family, having a very mighty store or what may be called supermarket today. In actual fact, these were departmental stores. Mrs. Annice Gordon became the chief executive officer (CEO) after the death of the husband. After many years, the grocery section and one other section were sold out. It was Mr. Teddy Gallaher who bought the grocery section. His son Michael Gallaher inherited the business. Even then, what was left was still very large. That shows the extent of the store. Mrs. Gordon owned very lovely Austin English- made car at the time when many could not afford a motorcycle. She was always neatly and smartly dressed. She decided to spend her wealth on training of Africans for the priesthood. The visit of Bishop Ekandem to her home in Ballaghaderreen was a confirmation of her good but silent work. Mrs. Annice Gordon, the benefactress, must have been very happy to see the fruit of her labor and to have a spiritual son becoming not only a priest but also a bishop. She must have had her own way of demonstrating that great joy.

"Mrs. Gordon never won any captain's prize on the golf links nor was she President of any organisation. She was a woman steeped in the spirit of prayer and in good deeds. She never sought any reward for her kindness, nor did she count the cost of anything she gave. She did it all for God."[138]

Dominic Ekandem paid a serious tribute to Mrs. Annice Gordon, his benefactress, when he said, "I remain ever grateful to her." He also said, "Bishop James Moynagh did this fantastic work without a word and I had no idea until after my ordination as a priest. He is a very kind and considerate person."[139] Dominic Ekandem revered Mrs. Annice Gordon and loved Ireland when he said, "The land that has done so much for me and for my country. I am deeply sensible of our indebtedness to the Irish people—our priceless Faith, our Christian education, culture, relief even from bodily infirmities."[140]

In imitation of his mentor, Father Dominic later found sponsors for many other seminarians when he became a bishop as chapter seventeen indicates.

There is an interesting parallel between the life of Cardinal Ekandem and that of Cardinal Bernadin Gantin (1922–1988) of Benin Republic. Benin Republic is a neighboring country having a boundary with Nigeria by the west. It is French speaking.

Cardinal Gantin was a contemporary of Cardinal Ekandem. Their paths must have crossed many times in the Vatican and in other places. Cardinal Gantin was five years younger than Cardinal Ekandem. Both had the same experience of sponsorship by a benefactor or benefactors. Cardinal Ekandem had a sole benefactress, but Cardinal Gantin had benefactors. He had two benefactors, one a priest, the other a woman. The sponsorship of Cardinal Gantin was when he went to Rome to study, whereas that of Cardinal Ekandem was when he went to study at Bigard Memorial Seminary, Enugu. Bishop Ekandem had the privilege of being introduced to his sponsor through his bishop, while Cardinal Gantin had the privilege of being introduced to his sponsors by some of his friends from France who came back to their parish priest and spoke of the brilliant young African seminarian who needed help. Father Aloyse became interested and decided to do something about it. Mlle Henriette Hoff decided to join the priest to sponsor Gantin. After his ordination, he equally visited Father Aloyse many times, and Father Aloyse had not only a great memory of him but also a great affection to the extent that he always kept the photograph of Cardinal Gantin on his table till the time of his death in 2007, a year before the death of Cardinal Bernadin Gantin in 2008.

Fr. Aloyse Seiler (1914–2007) was parish priest of the small village of Adelange in the region of Lorraine in France. The main city was Guessling-Hemering where the cathedral was. Father Aloyse was parish priest in St. Gangoulf from 1947 to his retirement in 1989. Toward the end of his ministry and, indeed, his life, Mlle Henriette Hoff (she is still alive but suffers from Alzheimer's disease) cared for him. They both supported Bernardin Gantin during his studies at Rome in the 1950s. Msgr.[141] Gantin visited them at least once, as far as Professor Martial recalls his conversation with them, and they both had a signed photograph of him in his cardinal cassock.[142] He later became the friend of the parish and visited once in a while. The last time he visited the parish was in 1999. He spent about a week with the family of Mr. and Mrs. Bernard Cuvillier in their home.[143] Cardinal Gantin was close to them.

His first posting saw him being sent as assistant priest to the same church he was ordained in, St. Anne's Church, Ifuho, where Fr. Joe Murray was father in charge. At the time of the Silver Jubilee in 1979, Father Murray was the vicar general of Eldoret Diocese in Kenya, one of the first places that the Kiltegan Fathers expanded to. Later, he worked with Fr. P. Laffey who took over from Father Murray when he was transferred.

J. Ordination and Early Years in the Priesthood

Dominic, after having been ordained, was very happy and enthusiastic as well as zealous. He lived and enjoyed a common life with Father Murray, SPS whom Dominic said taught him how to accept failure and not to be carried off by success.

Father Murray won more popularity through his actions. From Dominic's unpublished Silver Jubilee Memoir, the following is recorded:

> After spending a couple of months in Ifuho Mission, Rev. Father Murray, S.P.S. was appointed to go over to Afaha Obong and open a new parish, with me as his assistant. I was very fortunate to have Rev. Father Joe Murray, now a missionary in Kenya, as my Superior. "Having realized that I was by the grace of God a priest like himself, he overlooked all other differences between us and started to prepare for the task ahead. He ordered. I obeyed.[144] We agreed not to disagree, and this helped me very much not only during my years with him but in my relation with future Superiors and Subordinates. With him I had many pleasant surprises.

Though he was my Superior yet we lived like brothers. Though he was white and I am black yet there was no clash of colours. On the other hand there emerged a harmony comparable to that resulting from the combination of white and black on the keyboard of a harmonium-piano. With his pleasant and congenial disposition he taught me how to accept failure and not to be over-elated with success. As things were not laid down for us when we arrived in Afaha Obong, he lived in the mud house, ate our humble native food, slept in the open Church where neither a rest house nor a teacher's house was available, during our week-long trek or visit to Outstations. By so doing he became much more approachable, won the confidence of the people much more quickly than myself, and consequently became much more popular. In short he taught me how to be a missionary in my own country. So that the notion prevailing today among expatriate and some native priests, that native priests are much more acceptable to Nigerian Catholics than expatriate missionaries, is to me a false one. All Nigerian Catholics of goodwill, accept or reject a priest for what he is—a good priest, another Christ, or a bad priest, a false Christ, not because of colour, race or tribe which notion would destroy the Unity and the Universality of the Church. The goodwill I enjoyed from true Nigerian Catholics all over the country has made my years in the priesthood, very happy and really enjoyable despite the endless difficulties I encountered in the performance of the duties assigned to me. And indeed these difficulties, trials, disappointments and even big crosses are to be expected if we are honest with ourselves, for it was on the Cross that Christ redeemed the world. After twenty five years in the Lord's vineyard as a Bishop, the yoke appears so sweet and the burden so light that if it were God's will for me to continue, I will not mind beginning all over again and in any part of the world for that matter.[145]

In 1950, Father Ekandem was transferred to Afaha Obong Parish, Abak. Once again, he worked closely with Father Murray whom he spoke very reverently of and continued with his mentoring experience that was partially terminated at the transfer of the latter to St. John's Catholic Church, Abak. It was in this context that Msgr. Godwin Akpan, MSP, emeritus acting superior general residing at Iperu Remo, met him, had some interaction with, and made the following comments:

> My first close experience of the Cardinal started in 1944 on the Feast of St. Agnes, January 21st when I was admitted into Holy Family College, Oku Abak to study as a Seminarian in the newly opened Calabar Diocesan Seminary temporarily located in the compound of Ediene's Teachers' Training College, Abak. Reverend Father Dominic Ignatius Ekandem newly ordained in 1947 as the first Calabar Diocesan Priest who was appointed as the First Rector[146] of the Junior Seminary located in the compound of St. Mary's Teacher Training College, Abak.[147]

In 1952, Father Dominic was appointed rector of Queen of Apostles Seminary. Hitherto, the aspirants had moved to Ediene Abak, where the Teachers' Training College (TTC) was located. The seminary then moved from Ediene Abak, to Afaha Obong where Fr. Brendan Bolger was rector. When Father Bolger was transferred to Urua Inyang, Fr. Dominic Ekandem took over from him as the rector of the seminary at Afaha Obong. It is indisputable that Fr. Brendan Bolger was the first rector of Queen of Apostles Seminary, Afaha Obong, if Father Ekandem only took over from him after his transfer. Father Kiore was one of those who assisted him. Sylvanus Etok served as a senior seminarian auxiliary teacher of Latin and mathematics. The first set of students admitted into the seminary in Afaha Obong include Timothy Abraham Nwosu, Bartholomew Onu, Paulinus Jonah Essien, Bede Bernard, Clement Tinkang, and Nestor Nicholas. Others are Clement John and Thomas Sene Umanah.[148]

K. The Circumstances That Contributed to Father Ekandem Becoming Rector of the Minor Seminary, Afaha Obong

He was very interested in seeing young men opting for the priest-hood. He was not involved in seminary training, but he was very inter-ested in the seminarians themselves. Holy Family College was located at Oku Abak. The students who were interested in becoming priests lodged in the same compound but in a different section called seminary cottage. The priests living around the area used to go to the college to pick a sem-inarian to go and help them at masses in the stations. Father Hares was the principal of the college. One morning one priest asked Sylvanus Etok, who was aspiring to the priesthood, to come and help him at mass in Oku Abak. He went with the priest and was brought back afterward. As he alighted from the "big motorcycle" that priests used at the time, the principal came out of the office. By this time, the other priest had gone. The principal, Father Hares, asked Etok where he was coming from, and he said that father took him to Oku Abak to go and help in serving at mass there. The principal asked if he got any permission. Etok responded that he did not think it necessary. The principal said, "You did not think it nec-essary?" Etok responded, "No!" At that answer, Father Hares asked him to pack his things and leave the cottage. He pleaded and pleaded but to no avail. Sylvanus then went and packed his things and left quietly without informing the others and without alerting any person. He was afraid of causing the whole group becoming disturbed or walking away because of the unfair treatment. Leaving quietly in this manner, he acted the part of St. Joseph who obeyed the Lord quietly without any arguments and acted in faith.

When he left the college, he had no money to pay a cyclist. The cyclists used their bicycles as a means of transportation and charging money in the process to make a living out of it. Sylvanus had to trek. He had a quick breakfast that morning, so he was tired and decided to rest under a shade. As he sat there resting on this little hilly place, Father Ekandem passed with his motorcycle as he was heading on to Midim at an adjacent road to that of Abak. Sylvanus waved at him. He looked and turned back, and Sylvanus waved again. He came nearer and asked, "Who are you?" Fr. Dominic Ekandem then said, "I think I have seen you before." Sylvanus said yes, that he was from Holy Family College. At that point, Father Dominic recognized the uniform of college that Sylvanus Etok had on. Father Ekandem asked, "Why are you here?" Sylvanus narrated the story of his expulsion from the college because of going to serve at mass. Father Ekandem said, "How can somebody do such a thing? Tell me exactly what you did wrong." Etok repeated, "I did nothing wrong." With this answer, the priest asked, "What did you do right if you did not do anything wrong?" The whole story was narrated again by emphasizing that he followed the priest who asked him to come and assist at mass, and when he came back, he was asked to leave for not having obtained permission beforehand. The priest said, "Is that all?" The seeming exseminarian said yes. No person could have done such a thing. Father Ekandem asked if he had eaten. Etok said no even though he had a little breakfast. Etok was very hungry by now after the long trek. Father Dominic told him, "Do not go home yet. Go and wait for me in the mission." Father Ekandem had been sent to Abak at the time. When the priest came back, he took Sylvanus to the chapel where he said his midday prayer. He asked Sylvanus to stay and pray there. He did as he was told. Then Father Dominic came and asked him to tell him the truth of the matter, and the whole story was retold. He told him to go and eat and rest and that he would interview him again. In the evening, he went around the whole place with Sylvanus saying the Rosary as the priest's pious custom was. On finishing the Rosary, the priest took Etok to the chapel again and asked to tell him what he said at first. Sylvanus repeated the story over again. Father Dominic said after hearing the whole story again, "This is a serious case." Sylvanus stayed there until Father Ekandem went to Calabar through Oron to go and see Bishop Moynagh and tell him about the situation. Father Dominic came back the following day. Surprisingly, the bishop arrived the same day with his car, which was Mercedes-Benz. When Sylvanus saw the bishop, he said, "Oh, this is going to be a very serious case." He was surprised that Father Ekandem went that far.

Upon arrival, Bishop James Moynagh called and interviewed Sylvanus, and he repeated the same story afresh. The bishop asked Sylvanus to enter his car, which he drove himself. Etok took his place at the front seat and sat while the bishop drove. They arrived at the college, and the bishop drove to the front of the Father's House, while Sylvanus was sitting in the car. At that time, bishops were highly revered. Those without soutanes[149] normally rushed to put them on before going to stand around to greet the bishop. When they came out, they saw this little boy Sylvanus in the bishop's car at the front seat. They could not believe themselves even though they had heard that the bishop was on his way. Father Golgotha, who asked Etok to accompany him to mass later, mentioned the whole episode. He pleaded with the principal that he should not send Etok away. Father Hares had made his decision and was not ready to go back easily. When he came outside and saw Sylvanus in the bishop's car, he made signs to Sylvanus and said, "You went to Calabar and brought the bishop here?"

Father Dowling, who was a physics teacher, had also pleaded on behalf of Sylvanus Etok but to no avail. Father Dowling had later become the principal of Regina Coeli Secondary School when it was newly established. Fr. Michael Hares, the principal, was interviewed, and the bishop was seriously annoyed with him. The little Sylvanus was in the car listening to them. Bishop Moynagh, during the course of the conversation, said, "Look we were sent here to come and train those who will take over from us. We will not last here forever. We are to train them to take over from us." When the bishop finished speaking with the principal who was also in charge of the seminary cottage, he asked the young Sylvanus what was wrong about the place. Sylvanus did not hesitate to say that sometimes the aspirants were taken out of the class and sent to fetch water or to fetch firewood when others were studying or even sent to cut grass when others made noise in the class. According to Msgr. Sylvanus Etok, whenever Father Hares arrived when something went wrong, it was the aspirants from the seminary cottage who were deemed responsible; therefore, they had to suffer for it. The bishop, being aware of this situation report, was simply annoyed with Rev. Fr. Michael Hares, the principal. The thought of the indigenes taking over from the expatriate clergy was revolutionary. Fr. Emmanuel Uduakobong Chad Umoren called it program of indigenization.[150]

After their meeting, Fr. Dominic Ekandem was transferred from Afaha Obong to Abak to take care of the seminarians at the seminary cottage. That made Father Ekandem to speak of being the second priest to take care of the seminarians. This clears the mystery when the Cardinal Ekandem said, "I complained to the bishop about the situation that the young seminarians (or, properly put, aspirants to the priesthood) underwent," and the bishop said, "All right, you take over from Father Hares." Father Hares was still the principal, but he had no jurisdiction over the seminarians anymore since their spiritual welfare was strictly under Father Ekandem. Their duty was to attend classes and go back to the seminary cottage. His jurisdiction over the seminarians was only when they were at school but not when they were out. The decision did not bring a lasting solution since conflict soon arose between the principal and the rector or spiritual director. Sometimes Father Hares would order the seminarians out for labor, and Father Ekandem would ask the young seminarians to go back to the class. Fr. M. Hares had special jurisdiction, *potestas specificus*, over the seminarians, while Fr. D. Ekandem had ordinary jurisdiction, *potestas ordinarius*, over the same seminarians. They were torn in betwixt and between. It was an awkward situation, and something had to be done.

L.   The Necessity of Separating the Seminarians

That situation did not create an atmosphere conducive to a healthy coexistence for these growing saplings. The conflict situation created room for growth as it happened in Acts of the Apostles during the complaint about sharing of food where the Hellenists were neglected (Acts 6:1 ff) or like the persecution that provided opportunity for growth (Acts 8:1, 4 ff). The conflict necessitated a separation from bed and board and eventually from the same premises. Things worked themselves out naturally. Separation of jurisdiction in Holy Family College at Oku Abak did not end the interruption of their classes; hence, Father Ekandem had to devise a method of ending the vicious circle by seeking accommodation at Ediene Abak where the Teachers' Training College (TTC) was located. At Ediene, the seminarians occupied one dormitory all by themselves. The seminarians trekked to and fro daily for classes and carried out their spiritual exercises at Ediene Abak. The Vincentian seminarians living at Abiakpo

Ntak Inyang in Ikot Ekpene Diocese near St. Joseph Major Seminary do exactly what the young seminarians did in those days, except that they can talk while going or coming. The seminarians at Ediene did not have the same privilege.

The arrangement created another problem. First and foremost, seminarians were not to greet anyone in the morning while going from Ediene Abak to Oku Abak for studies. Seminarians generally have a standing rule that none of them is supposed to speak with any person until after Morning Prayer, meditation, sacrifice of the Holy Eucharist, and breakfast. For the seminarians, there was no great deal about it, but it constituted a very grave problem for the villagers they met on the way. The people began to look at the young seminarians in askance, cursing and saying at the same time, "What type of stupid and wicked children are you that you cannot greet people or respond to greetings? Are you dumb or evil in outlook and nature?" The people reacted this way because in African culture, the children are supposed to greet their parents and elders as the first thing in the morning. Unfortunately, the seminarians never had the occasion to explain to the villagers what their rule of life was. If they did, that would have exposed them to danger that could have caused "mass expulsion." To avoid that, they had to bear it in silence and carry the Cross in silence without any explanation.

What the seminarians did was to conform to the seminary rule of "the great silence," that is, *magnum silentium*, that was meant to be observed until after Morning Prayer, mass, and breakfast. None of the seminarians dared respond to all the insults. Their job was to continue on their journey and reach the school in time. The mission was so urgent that they did not need to speak with anyone (Cf. Mt. 10:1 ff). The command not to greet anyone or respond to the greeting of anyone is comparable to the order of Prophet Elisha to Gehazi, his servant, who sent him to the Shunammites's son who had died. He told him not to greet anyone on the road nor respond to the greeting of anyone but to go and stretch out his staff on the dead child even though the mother of the child refused to go with servant and waited until Elisha left with her (1 Kg. 4:29). Such disciplines had already existed before the church, in her wisdom, decided to devote special times of prayer and silence to God, although the circumstances were strange in this case since the seminarians were out of their habitat.

The second problem was the distance from the college to the dormitory/hostel that they lived in. All these had to be borne with equanimity and hopeful spirit. The seminarians were to meditate on their way to the college. That is why they did not greet anyone on the way even though none of the villagers was ever informed about it. The people who became annoyed with them did not realize this and were operating on a different wavelength. The move took place because of the love of Fr. Dominic Ekandem for those studying for the priesthood and his concern to defend the rights of the less privileged. That urge motivated him to go to see the bishop about the unjust governance and authority of the principal. Fr. Michael Hares, as a person, was a very good man and administrator. Perhaps he felt somehow threatened by the idea that the young Africans were coming up. He wanted to make things as difficult as possible for them, probably to see if they were genuine or determined to go on. The shifting of base from Oku Abak to Ediene Abak took place in 1952. At that time, Sylvanus was in his final year.

He and a host of others had to persevere despite the discouragement from other students who told them that the reason for their punishment was because they wanted to be priests and that if they changed their minds, they would not be punished. They would be treated respectfully as other students were. Sometimes when Father Hares went to the class and other students made noise, it was the seminarians who were to pay for that since the principal did not hesitate to take them out and flog them. The seminarians were given instruction by Father Ekandem—go to another class after one class, file back to Ediene, and do not delay there. It was a safeguard for the seminarians to act thus. Owing to the attitude of the principal, one Okokon Ekandem from Etinan, who was a Protestant, told the seminarians, "Why do you people not leave this idea of studying for the priesthood and be free since these people do not want you to become priests?" The seminarians persevered despite this negative exhortation and told the other students not to worry, for it was only a temporary situation. "Sic transitus gloria mundi," "The glory of the world is temporary." He was acting like Satan who wanted Christ to reject the way of the Cross (Cf. Matt. 4:1–11) or like Peter who told Jesus to forget about the Cross and death (Matt. 16:23).

Holy Family College fondly called by the students HOFACO[151] coexisted with the seminary cottage for about four years before the movement.

The constant movement took place till the final year when Fr. Dominic Ekandem, with the full knowledge and permission of the local ordinary, Bishop James Moynagh, started negotiating for a house and a land at Afaha Obong. The conflict of authority that arose concerning the abode of the seminarians was a *felix culpa* (a happy fault). The misunderstanding liberated the seminarians from their servitude and bondage. Even though they could not greet the people as they were moving along and feeling very uncomfortable and ashamed because of the awkward situation was a better option to lack of freedom, they would have had otherwise. The seminarians wished that Father Ekandem would become the principal of HOFACO, but he did. Eventually, it dawned on Father Ekandem that as long as the young seminarians continued going to Oku Abak, the problems would continue. He had to look for a lasting solution to the whole problem of conflict, which was very obvious to the students even though they did not point it out.

M. The New Dwelling Place at Afaha Obong, the Emergence and Autonomy of the Seminary

When Father Dominic got the permission to build a house for the seminarians at Afaha Obong, the three seminarians—Stanislaus Okoro, Silas Umoh, and Sylvanus Etok—meant for philosophical studies at Enugu for the major seminary formation did not move. They formed part of the first set of staff that taught in the new seminary. (Stanislaus Okoro later left the Catholic Church and joined a group that tried to model itself on the early Christians called in the local language *Ufok Abasi Uta Enang* [the Church that eats beef]). It was after the Nigerian/ Biafran Civil War that the situation was discovered. He went about begging since he had burned his certificates; consequently, he could not secure any job and could not get a reissue of it. He was married to Betta Okoro when he did not continue with the major seminary. Realizing that he could not gain any employment anywhere, Bishop Ekandem at the time offered him a teaching job in the minor seminary so that he could take care of himself and help his family. They were rather given a period of probation. They had to teach in the new seminary that was to begin at Afaha Obong in 1953. That could be said to be the official opening of the minor seminary at Afaha Obong. In actual fact, it had already existed at Oku Abak simultaneously with the HOFACO for four years before it emerged and become an autonomous institution. It existed as a city within a country in an embryonic form as a constituent part of that institution until the expulsion incident occurred. The expulsion only gave room to the seminary cottage to become like the Vatican City within the city of Rome, although Vatican is fully autonomous, whereas seminary cottage was still within the abode of HOFACO and subject to its rules and regulations. The official opening of Queen of the Apostles Seminary, Afaha Obong, came a year after the church's declaration of the dogma of the Immaculate Conception.

The new seminary was named after the Mother of the Lord and in connection with the disciples at the Upper Room and at Calvary. The nascent seminary was christened, Queen of Apostles Seminary, Afaha Obong, even though behind the scene, the seminarians normally couched it "University of Ikwek" because of the little section of Afaha Obong called Ikwek to boost their ego. It is probable that it became so named following the pioneer students of St. Patrick's College (SPC or SPACO), Ikot Ansa, Calabar in Cross River State established 1935. The pioneer students called their institution "university across the sea." Calabar had to be reached by boat or speedboat or ship or hovercraft or lighter or pontoon depending on the means available. The people reached Calabar by plying the thirteen nautical miles, which is fifteen statute miles of the Cross River to the other side. There was no alternative.

The name university across the sea was coined following the fact that one had to cross the Cross River from Oron on the mainland part of the state to get to Calabar. Even if one approached it from Ogoja side, a bridge had to be crossed. All the students from Enugu, Onitsha, Aba, Umuahia, Ikot Ekpene, Abak, Uyo, Eket, and even Oron itself had to cross the water before arriving at Calabar. That is how the name was derived. Gov. Jacob Udokaha Esuene, the first military governor of the state, commissioned the present road from Ikot Ekpene through Itu Bridge in 1977. The commissioning of the bridge was an epoch- making event that remains fresh in the minds of people. Lt. Col. U. J. Esuene was one of the best military governors, South Eastern State and later Cross River State, ever had if not the best governor. Before the completion of the bridge, every person going to Calabar had to cross the river by any of the available means.

When Sylvanus Etok finished his philosophical studies in 1955, the studies that lasted for two years and which utilized Latin as a medium of communication, he sustained an injury on the eye during soccer games in Enugu's major seminary. He could no longer continue with his studies. He was asked to go and teach once again at Afaha Obong Seminary. Father Kiore was the rector at the time. There, he taught mathematics and Latin from January 1956. Very Rev. Fr. Udom Ukpong was one of his students.

Ukpong recalled that he taught him Latin at Afaha Obong Minor Seminary. Sylvanus himself recollected Silas Bassey Edet as one of those he taught mathematics, a very intelligent student and mathematician now in United States of America. Silas is also teaching mathematics as a specialist in the field there. Sylvanus must have taught there for only one year since he had to leave his teaching apostolate in September of the same year when Bishop Moynagh came to the seminary and asked to see Sylvanus the same month. Generally, the school session ended that time in December, and the new academic year normally began in January. The arrival of Bishop Moynagh found Sylvanus teaching one of the subjects in the classroom. He beckoned on him to come out. Sylvanus had started using glasses, owing to his injury. He did not know how to maintain his glasses by keeping it clean. When the bishop realized that, he removed the glasses from him, took out his handkerchief, and wiped them clean and handed them back to Sylvanus who was very grateful but at the same time embarrassed and ashamed. The bishop told him, "You have to keep them clean." He was eager to know if he had become better or rather if his eye had improved. Sylvanus indicated that it was quite fine. The bishop said, "I am going to send you to Rome." Sylvanus said, "My Lord, I do not understand." The bishop started counting the words one by one. This was miraculous. "I am going to send you to Rome." He asked, "Do you understand now?" Sylvanus questioned, "Am I going alone, or is somebody going with me?" The bishop humorously said, "Are you not big enough to go to anywhere in the world by yourself?" He told him that Father Kiore would take him to Lagos to process his passport. Father Kiore was not very friendly like the very first principal of HOFACO whom the students and seminarians recall with great delight.

According to Monsignor Etok, the journey to Rome was not an easy one. It began with problems. On the appointed day, Father Kiore had prepared himself and called out Sylvanus from the classroom and asked him to enter the car so that he could take him to Lagos for the passport that the bishop spoke of. He asked if he could pick a few things from his room for the journey, and the priest said, "I have all the particulars. What do you want again?" Sylvanus said that he began the journey to Lagos unprepared. Being taken unawares, Sylvanus thought that they were likely to return that evening or the following day. The vow of obedience at the time was not dialogical or not being in the form of dialogue as it obtains today. Obedience to the authority was not questionable. It just had to be obeyed. Sylvanus said that he had no choice than to enter the car without any money in his pocket and without any spare cloth to change up with and no food with him. It was a true fulfillment of the Lord's instruction to his disciples not to take any haversack or spare tunic or spare tunic or sandals (Cf. Matt. 10:9–10).

They moved. At a certain stage during the journey, Father Kiore took out his flask and drank some tea and took some snacks already prepared and taken along with him at the commencement of the journey. They arrived at Onitsha, and the priest did not ask him whether he had eaten anything. Sylvanus stayed there in the car since he was not introduced to anybody. It was the driver who was very considerate and observant who asked him toward evening time whether Sylvanus was not going to eat; he said he responded with a question "Eat what?" The driver asked him, "Have you no money?" and he said that he had nothing with him. The question was repeated a second time, and he said exactly what he had said before. The driver said, "Do you know that this journey can take up to one week?" He added, "Do you know that you can die on the way?" According to Sylvanus, the driver said, "This man is terrible. How can he take somebody on such a journey without making adequate preparations?" The driver became angry and said, "I can leave this car here for him and go my way. Why should he treat a human being like this?" This is why some people question Christianity because of its ambassadors. Sylvanus said he was very hungry at this time and said that he did not know whether he would survive till the following day. The drivers knew themselves. He went and introduced him to the driver at Onitsha and told him, "I have a brother here, a very nice brother, my real brother."

When the driver came, Sylvanus recalled he told him everything that had happened. He went and prepared sandwich for him and gave him some *Krola* and *Tango* tablets to be diluted in water to produce soft drinks. The Krola and Tango tablets produced instant drinks once they were dissolved in water. Krola was like the present Coke drink, and Tango is like Fanta drink. They were the equivalents in those days. Sylvanus used these gifts and consumed them contentedly whenever he was very hungry and thirsty. The driver gave a warning that he should not allow the priest to see them. He thanked him in a very grateful manner and took the pack and hid it under the seat. He received that very happily and ate frugally and with gusto. Whenever the priest went out to eat, Sylvanus would take his pack, take a little of the sandwich and ate, and put it back. He said he made sure he wiped his mouth very well so as not to leave any trace for questioning. While going in the night, he always washed his shirt and wait for it to get dry for use the following day and sleep with his underwear. Sometimes he would wear his trouser while washing all the other items and drying them on top of the car till the following morning.

According to Sylvanus, the priest never once asked him whether he had eaten. That is how he managed till they got the passport and returned. Presumably, he thought that as long as he was with the driver, he would always be taken care of whenever the cook of the priest they lodged with fed the driver. On the day of departure for Rome, he almost did the same thing, but Sylvanus begged that he should be given one day to go and tell his parents. At this point, he became charitable and permitted Sylvanus to go and greet them before leaving for Rome. It simply shows that when God opens a door, none can close it, and when he closes, none can open it (Cf. Rev. 3:7 and 8). When Sylvanus left for studies in Rome in 1955, Fr. Dominic Ekandem had already been consecrated an auxiliary bishop of Calabar residing at Anua.

The young Father Dominic did not find it difficult to live community life. He found it rather easy because of his earliest experiences of communal life in a polygamous family life. That is why he is able to speak happily about his life with Rev. Fr. Joe Murray, his first parish priest in Afaha Obong. His missionary spirit was very much alive.

That is why he was able to say at his old age that if he had chance to go all over again, he would have no qualms about going to anywhere he would be sent. This is similar to what St. Vincent De Paul said to his confreres that he was willing to go on mission to Algeria when he was already seventy-five years old, at the time when many of his confreres were dying on the mission, and he was sending new missionaries. Some were questioning the rationale behind sending people when they were dying, and he, at that age, opted to go on mission himself; and he had to be restrained by his confreres. His opting to go on mission at that age motivated others who opted to go on the same mission. Great minds think alike. Maybe this missionary spirit rendered him available for the Ministry in Port Harcourt as an administrator immediately after the Nigerian Civil War and as the superior of the independent mission (*missio sui juris*) in Abuja that will be properly handled in chapter eleven, *missio sui juris*, the Abuja independent mission.

Chapter Five

GLORIA IN EXCELSIS DEO (GLORY TO GOD IN THE HIGHEST)

The Bishopric and the Episcopal Consecration

Ecce Episcopum Novum (Behold the New Bishop)

The Holy Spirit knows what a particular
age's most pressing need is far better than
men with their programmes.

—Han Urs von Balthasar

THE ROAD TO greatness is never an easy one. One has to overcome many a hurdle has to be overcome, many a mountain has to be crossed, before the goal is reached.

The path trodden by Dominic Ignatius Ekandem was never an easy one. It was always a very challenging one. Every stage of his life on the way to the priesthood was marked with thorns and difficulties that motivated his episcopal motto and coat of arms.[152] Chapter fifteen handles that aspect. Dominic could have breathed a sigh of relief when he was ordained a priest, but it appears that was not the case. Dominic could not and did not rest tranquilly on his laurels. He did not enjoy that desired rest. He was a man with a vision pulled by an invisible hand that he willingly cooperated with. That vision motivated him in everything he undertook.

Reverend Father Dominic was greatly surprised about the announcement of his episcopal nomination and eventual consecration. The nomination, which can be called announcement of the good news, automatically made him Msgr. Dominic Ignatius Ekandem. This is where the papal injunction *sub segreto pontificium* (under pontifical secret) applied very strictly. He did not consider himself worthy to be elevated to such an exalted and onerous office. That is why the news took him by surprise as a birth pang strikes a woman in labor. In actual fact, he was shocked. He said, "Who could have dreamt of the impossible in a situation in which I was the only African in the midst of so many expatriate priests who were senior in age, ordination and in experience. I was still expressing my thanks to God for the wonderful gift of the priesthood and there, in the context of enjoying God's favour, a surprise came out of the blues. An additional favour from God came. I had no alternative than to fall on my knees and surrender myself without reserve to God like the Blessed Virgin Mary while beseeching on him to accomplish his will in me, his unworthy priest." This is why priests in the past often signed *is* after their names, meaning *indignus sacerdote* (unworthy priest). This was to inculcate in the priest the idea of a free gift while exalting divine nature of the call and office. If any of them belonged to an order or to a congregation as the case may be, the initials of that order or congregation will also be appended after the *is*. There is no writing of Bishop Dominic in which he uses the *is*. His expression during that great event must surely have reflected itself in his heart but not in his writing.

A very interesting and fascinating episode took place long before the consecration of Reverend Father Dominic as an auxiliary bishop. His Proper Bishop, Most Rev. James Moynagh, SPS during one of the Bishops' Conferences, which was mostly of an expatriate-dominated hierarchy, threw a challenge to the bishops by asking why they did not look for auxiliary bishops for themselves. Spontaneously, a burst of laughter ensued.

One of the bishops retorted sarcastically that "if he had one, he would surely have made him a one." Bishop Moynagh took that up and said in the affirmative, "Surely I will make him one." Why did Bishop James Moynagh put this question to the episcopal conference at the time and on that very day? Was it a way of trying to sensitize the bishops to the great need of making the Gospel take root in the Nigerian soil by opting for promotion of the indigenes? Was it a way of manifesting his intention in a subtle way? Was it an open consultation like the Option A4 that Gen. Ibrahim Babangida, the military president and supreme commander in chief of the Nigerian Armed Forces, proposed as the best option for electing a candidate to any office in Nigeria? Was the Catholic Bishops' Conference of Nigeria not in favor of the proposal? They objected to it because of the inherent natural dangers of exposing the voter to various problems or, indeed, the candidate himself.

What was in Bishop Moynagh's mind as Bernard Lonergan in his book *Method in Theology* [153] pointed out that what is in the mind of the writer or preacher needs to be discovered and understood in order to get at the real message? What was in the mind of the bishop? Why did he sample the opinion of the other bishops before even making the proposal to send Dominic's name as the auxiliary bishop to Rome? Could it be that he was indirectly informing the other bishops that he was ready to be a trailblazer in consecrating an auxiliary in what was regarded and known at the time as the Black Africa? Could it be that the bishop was trying to consult without giving the air of consultation yet doing exactly that by throwing out the question? Was he attempting to consult as Pope John Paul II did when he was faced with a great difficulty he needed to resolve and make decisions before visiting South America, North America, Europe, Africa, Oceania, Eastern Europe, and Australia? He sent for the bishops of those continents, consulted and discussed with them,[154] and came to conclusions about many issues before visiting. The process of such interaction took the forms of *ad limina apostolorum* (to the threshold of the Apostles) visit. Generally, this is called *ad limina* visit. It provides firsthand information to the supreme pontiff before going to any country. It gives him knowledge of what to emphasize during his visit.[155] Conscientization is the best word to describe what Bishop Moynagh was involved in and what he was aiming at.

He conscientized his brothers in the episcopacy while carefully and secretly revealing, his intention.

A. Indigenization Process

The process of indigenization is the process of making things to take the form of the indigene concerned; increasing local participation/ ownership by involving the culture, the beliefs, and the values of the local community; and making the Gospel take flesh in the culture of the people as St. Paul did in Athens (Acts 17:16–34). This process that was carried out by Bishop James Moynagh began when he boldly told Father Hares that their main duty was to get those who would succeed them. That statement colored everything he did and made real all his undertakings. His love of the seminarians did not create room for mediocrity but endeared them to him as a father. He was not only interested in promoting vocations to the priesthood but equally encouraged females to embrace the religious life also. He knew that the native sisterhood was an indispensable tool of evangelization and indigenization. It was this urge to promote the native sisterhood and process of evangelization that prompted him to obtain the decretum for the recognition of the Congregation of the Handmaids of the Holy Child Jesus and its erection in 1937. Chapters seven and eight devote great attention to this issue. When the congregation became autonomous in 1957, Bishop Moynagh presided over the first General Chapter of the Congregation in which one of the four original members was elected as the first superior general on December 28, 1957. The sister who became the superior general was Mother Gertrude Waturuocha, HHCJ.

Fr. Uduakobong Umoren commenting about Bishop Moynagh's role in the indigenization process noted that "long before Africanisation became an ecclesial household word, this man of foresight, this prophet who is able to see the needs of the hour for a better future undertook a programme of indigenisation."[156] Bishop Moynagh was not only a man of foresightedness and missionary vision but also a man of extraordinary courage. He broke the status quo of expatriate dominance through his missionary zeal and foresightedness by making the only African priest in his diocese an auxiliary bishop.

In this respect, he emerged as a charismatic figure in the Dark Africa, making light to shine where there was none. The people who dwelt in darkness have seen a great light (Is. 9:2; Matt. 14:6). He pursued his charismatic inspiration vigorously to the end, lighting a flame that would not be extinguished.

When the Holy Spirit teaches and reveals things, he does in a very simple and plain manner. He causes what is hidden to be known or become common knowledge. In his presence, everything is known. It will no longer be like seeing things as in a mirror but face to face (Cf. 1 Cor. 13:12; 1 Jn. 3:2, 3).

It did not take too long after that disturbing question before Bishop Moynagh started revealing what was hidden in his mind. He proposed and recommended Father Ekandem to the pope through the Roman Curia for the service in the church as an auxiliary bishop in Calabar Diocese. Calabar Diocese later became a metropolitan see as an ecclesiastical province on March 26, 1994. The proposal was a welcome one, and the candidate proposed was accepted and approved after due ecclesiastical investigation and examination of the proposal by competent ecclesiastical authorities. It can be construed that Bishop Moynagh was a great missionary with optimism and readiness to go ahead with what he perceived to be good for many and for their spiritual transformation so as to be constantly on the Mountain of the Lord.

B.   Parable or Joke of Bishop Moynagh?

Many of the bishops were surprised to witness what they regarded as a joke that eventually came true. Recommending the only African priest in his presbyterium was an act of bravery that conveyed an unhindered yet enlightened force of will. The conviction of Bishop Moynagh who asked for an auxiliary bishop had an audacity that sprang from the Gospel values of Matthew 28:19 and Mark 16:15: "Go out to the whole world and proclaim the Good News, baptising them in the name of the Father and of the Son and of the Holy Spirit." This mandate, together with the ingrained attitude of knowing and believing that the indigenous clergy were the ones to succeed the expatriates, impelled Bishop Moynagh to begin laying a foundation for the future. The foundation was laid for effective evangelization. To achieve this, an indigenous clergy was necessary. The indigenous clergy versed in the language and culture of the people would form a good basis for evangelization.

This is inculturation in practice. He took this step not only to foster evangelization of the people but also to give the desired education that the Efik/Ibibio people craved for. What this means in practice is making the Gospel to take flesh in the culture of the people in order to enhance the evangelization and education of the people in the proper context. It corresponds to what Pope Paul VI said in his encyclical titled *Evangelii Nuntiandi*[157] *on announcing the good news to the people of today that people teach more by action than by words. Teaching by action becomes more imperative and effective than by mere words. Bishop James Moynagh, SPS constantly insisted on this in every aspect of formation and evangelization. He saw it as an effective tool of evangelization. By insisting on indigenization, he did not intend to make the candidates for the priesthood sacred cows. Despite the fact that he was desirous to see the indigenous clergy grow, he never compromised the quality of the candidates and what the priesthood signified.*

Rev. Fr. Dominic Ignatius Ekandem served as a priest for seven years before Bishop Moynagh proposed him to be elevated to the level of an auxiliary bishop of Calabar. The bishop did not make the proposal single-handedly. He consulted his priests as few as they were at the time. They were mostly expatriate missionaries. It was not very easy, and Father Dominic was quite unaware since everything was carried out under strict pontifical secret. The consultation took place under very strict confidence and pontifical secrecy (sub segreto pontificium) under pontifical secret. The proposal was made to Pope Pius XII who wrote the encyclical letter, "Munificentissimus Deus," in 1950, defining the dogma of Assumption and Immaculate Conception of the Blessed Virgin Mary.

In 1947, Msgr. James Moynagh, SPS was named the vicar apostolic of Calabar. He was consecrated bishop thereafter. Incidentally, that was the same year, 1947, Dominic I. Ekandem was ordained a deacon and a priest. It took place three years before the declaration and promulgation of the dogma. The year of the declaration of the dogma of Immaculate Conception, 1950, was the same year that Calabar became a diocese. Fr. Dominic Ekandem's episcopal consecration took place four years after the definition of the dogma of Assumption of our Blessed Mother, the Virgin

Mary. No wonder Bishop Dominic was so devoted to the Blessed Virgin Mary, especially in his recitation of the Holy Rosary that he carried out in a devout manner throughout his entire life. He can conveniently be described as a Marian bishop[158] since he was consecrated within the Marian period of the declaration and definition of the dogma. With the definition of the Marian dogma, many parish churches and station churches with the various titles of Mary sprang up. At that time, in Calabar Diocese, Ndon Ebom Parish, now in Uyo Diocese, started in 1950 and was named Parish of Assumption. The same applied to Ukana Iba in 1955 and Ikpe Annang in 1957. Naming these parishes after Our Lady assumed into heaven soon after the definition and declaration of the dogma demonstrates how seriously the whole church considered the dogma. It shows that Bishop Ekandem was a direct beneficiary of the dogma since his consecration fell within the first four years after the definition. Msgr. Sylvanus Etok rightly pointed out that "He would have been one of the pioneer Bishops to explain the Dogma and to live it out."

Figure 4 St. Anne's Cathedral, Ifuho, Ikot Ekpene

C. The Consecration of Dominic Has a Solid Link with the Mother Diocese of Calabar

The consecration of Fr. Dominic Ekandem was fixed for February 7, 1954. The year 1954 also marked the milestone or rather the bridge linking Calabar Diocese, the Mother Diocese, with Ogoja, which became a diocese in 1955. Historically, Msgr. Dominic I. Ekandem's consecration as the auxiliary bishop of Calabar made him a year older than Ogoja diocese. With the nature of things in those days, phoning was very limited, transportation was very difficult, flights were rare, and cars were not very many as it is now. Only few people in a particular place owned cars as in the story of Mrs. Annice Gordon who owned a car in Roscommon County in Ireland mentioned in chapter four. There were no traffic "holdups" or "heavy traffic," or as it is normally expressed in Nigeria, "traffic jam" was not there. The roads were narrow. At that time, driving was at the left-hand side of the road. Distance was measured in miles, and volumes were calculated in gallons and pints. Things were really different. The main means of communication were bicycle and canoe or by trekking or walking. Car or lorry or ship or horse or chariot was luxury, and only the rich could use it. Moreover, movement was limited because of the tedious nature of things. The arrangement took some time before the information reached the bishops in other countries who had to attend the consecration.

The appointed day of consecration was a joyous one. It combined the earthly joy with the heavenly one. The venue interestingly enough was the cathedral at Calabar, the seat of the diocese; but Anua, where the Medical Missionaries foundress,[159] Mary Martin, first established an infirmary, became his residential home. The little village of Anua as insignificant as Bethlehem became as important as Bethlehem. It was at Anua that the Medical Missionaries of Mary established an infirmary that later graduated to a clinic and eventually to a hospital, St. Luke's. Calabar was the chosen venue and the point of intersection for the nation Nigeria, for Africa, and for the whole world since it was an epoch-making event.

The atmosphere was charged. It was similar to what E. N. Amaku described in his "Efik Reader": "*Otop Ntuen Isimke Isong*," "If an alligator pepper (seed) is thrown up, it will not reach the ground." The little village of Anua, which was as insignificant as Bethlehem, became as important as Bethlehem itself. It is normally said in the history of the old Roman Empire that "all roads lead to Rome." In this case, all roads led to Anua. The village was so peopled that movement became difficult, but the event had to take place. Everyone was excited. The air of expectation was decisive yet thin. Many pertinent questions were raised.

Before the day of consecration, the old question "Can an African become a priest?" was being asked: "Can an African become a bishop?" In other words, can anything good come out of this Dark Continent and pagan country? Is it not the reserve of the expatriates? That is why Prophet Isaiah says that "God's ways are not our ways" (Is. 55:11). Why was he chosen? Who will attend the consecration? The answer to the question "Can an African become a bishop?" is redundant since it has answered itself through the instrumentality and foresight of Bishop Moynagh, SPS. He deemed it fit to have an African as his auxiliary for the purpose of handing on the baton and for effective evangelization. The next question "Who will attend the consecration ceremony?" equally answered itself as the people from the various walks of life from far and wide attended it.

Rev. Fr. Dominic Ekandem remained faithful to his priestly duties for seven years. At the age of thirty-seven, His Bishop James Moynagh, SPS proposed Dominic for bishopric as his auxiliary. Rome generously acquiesced to that and granted his request. On February 7, 1954, at Sacred Heart Cathedral, Calabar, Bishop Moynagh, the principal consecrator; Co-Consecrator Bishop Peter Rogan, MHF of Buea, British Cameroons; and Bishop P. Biechy of Brazzaville, French Equatorial Guinea, Africa officiated at the consecration of Dominic Ekandem as the auxiliary bishop of Calabar.

With a very slight difference, the consecration of Bishop Dominic Ekandem fell short of "caesaropapism"[160] since there was a joint effort between the government and the church to celebrate the event. Chief Beka A. T. (Akpan Thomas) proudly recalled that "The consecration of Bishop Ekandem was not just the Church's affair but a national affair since even the Governor of Nigeria at the time, C. J. Mayne was there in person." He continued, "The DO, that is the District Officer commanding Uyo, Oron, Eket, Opobo was also there."[161] Since it was the first of its kind in West Africa, many people came from various parts of Africa and Nigeria in particular to witness the event.

D. The Nigerian Independence Celebration

In 1958, as Sir A. T. Beka returned from studies in England, he was with many Africans who boarded the same ship. There were some from

Ghana, Sierra Leone, Senegal, Nigeria, and many other countries. He met one Englishman who was traveling in the ship also. The Englishman asked those from Nigeria whether they were from the Northern or Eastern or Western Nigeria. They responded according to their various regional locations. He went on to tell young Beka that he heard Nigeria would be having independence in 1960. He said Nigeria would face three major problems, namely, lack of love for the country, lack of love of one another, and the problem of time and punctuality. Beka asked how he came to these conclusions, and why he was so interested in Nigeria. The man said that he was returning from holidays and that he was a teacher in Uyo TTC or Teachers' Training College. The Englishman responded by saying that at the TTC, there was a way that the whistle would blow; it would be for teachers only, another way would be for students only. Finally, there was a way it would sound, and the attention of the whole college would be needed. One day the whistle for all was blown, and all assembled.

Mr. F. Hales, who was the principal by then, introduced the purpose of the assembly. He pointed out the men, the chiefs from Abak, who would need to go back with some people to help them carry out elections. The chiefs objected immediately by noting that they would not like any African to be involved in the procedure so as not to play some games. The method was to point out the name of the persons, and the voter would use a pen and mark x. The chiefs went with the foreigners only. On the ground of not loving the country, the man said that once someone is from Uyo, he is only concerned about Uyo. The same applies to Ikot Ekpene, etc., that the one who comes from another place is left outside the circle of decision-making. Concerning time and punctuality, the man said that if things were scheduled for three o'clock, the person would come at four o'clock, while others would be very circumspect. Probably, the man was right in his analysis or maybe not. It appears some of his observations were right, especially concerning African time, which is something ridiculous.

Six years after the consecration of Bishop Dominic, the independence of Nigeria came in 1960. A meeting was held in Abak with four stall wards, including Eyo and Akpabio; Nyoyoko; Beka, the youngest person among them; and one European forming a committee preparing for the celebration of independence. After the discussion on the entertainment in terms of the displays, food, drinks, and speeches, the only European among them, who presumably was the DO, said before the dismissal that on that day if anyone touches the British flag, the Union Jack indicating their presence and rulership by bringing it down, he will shoot that person to death. Everyone kept silent, and they finished and took up their bags and were ready to move when Beka, like the young Daniel in the Story of Susanna in the book of Daniel chapter thirteen, said, "How can you leave the meeting place without finding out why the DO said he will kill the person himself?" They all dropped their handbags, sat, and inquired what he meant and why he said he himself will shoot the person bringing the Union Jack down while hoisting the Nigerian flag of green white green. The man explained that it will be an insult to Britain if the flag is just brought down without any ceremonies. The ceremonial aspect of it would entail singing the British national anthem, saluting the flag, bringing it down ceremonially, and then the Nigerian flag will be hoisted and the Nigerian National Anthem sung before hoisting the flag. In this way, there will not be any trouble. After the explanation, they all dispersed, and everything went as was scheduled on the day of independence. It was the preparation for the same independence that gained Bishop Ekandem the recognition by the British Empire's honor of OBE (Order of the British Empire). The conferment of the honor arose from organizing the women to make a match pass that deeply impressed the British on the Independence Day. His initiative and ingenuity greatly manifest themselves in the areas of pastoral involvement and civic responsibility. These were blended to foster women's emancipation. It occurred at a time when women's place was seen in the context of domestic work only. The women's matching was only a prelude to greater things to come. That singleness of purpose and vision led to the formation of the Adiaha Obong Society, which has now become a national as well as an international association as far as the African continent is concerned.

The year was 1954. The event was the consecration of young Rev. Father Ekandem as the first West African Bishop. In this picture the young Bishop now Cardinal posed with his father chief Ekandem.

Figure 5

E.   The Consecration and First Posting as Auxiliary Bishop

Rev. Fr. Dominic Ekandem was consecrated a bishop in 1954 after his priestly ordination in 1947. His consecration as a bishop took place two years after the St. Patrick Fathers expanded their missionary territory to Kenya while still laboring in Nigeria. They deemed it fit to launch out to East Africa from the shores of West Africa. The first place he was posted to as an auxiliary bishop was Anua Parish. It is interesting to see the difference between what was upheld that time and what exists today. He became parish priest of Anua as an auxiliary bishop. He was not posted to a place where he was able to reside and help in the administration of the diocese as such but was made a parish priest. There, he took care of the flock and sought after the lost flock and immersed himself in the care of souls. He put in his best in the apostolate.

Some may ask, "Why was he posted there as parish priest after having been consecrated an auxiliary bishop? Why did the bishop not keep Bishop Ekandem with him at Calabar?" To be noted is that Bishop Ekandem was not sent there by his mentor for punishment nor was his posting a form of victimization. He was rather sent there because it was the Mother Parish of all the parishes in what was called the mainland, incorporating Ikot Ekpene and Uyo Districts, which incorporated the following major areas: Eket, Ikot Abasi, Abak, Ukanafun, Uyo, Oron, and Opobo. Anua was and is a stone's throw from Uyo, which was a divisional headquarters and now a state capital. What was just one parish has given birth to two independent dioceses, namely, Ikot Ekpene and Uyo Dioceses. His work was enormous. As an auxiliary bishop, he had the priests working in these areas as his co-collaborators as enunciated by the decree on the bishops in the Second Vatican Council document, *Christus Dominus*.

F.   Auxiliary Bishop Ekandem Ordained the First Priest

Being an auxiliary did not deprive him of his rights as a bishop. Of course, his involvement in ordaining a priest for the first time in his life was because of the openness of the substantive Bishop Moynagh who was always ready to be a trailblazer in the pastoral field. His episcopal duties with great pastoral responsibilities were properly and diligently exercised. He was mandated by his Ordinary Bishop James Moynagh to carry out all his pastoral concerns. He could ordain and was capable of ordaining a priest as he did when he ordained Rev. Silas Titus Umoh who became a priest in 1961 at St. Anne's Catholic Church, Ifuho. Fr. S. T. Umoh later became Monsignor Umoh, and for many years, he was the rector of Bigard Memorial Seminary. It was during his tenure as the rector at the Faculty of Philosophy, Ikot Ekpene, that the seminary became autonomous and bore the name St. Joseph Major Seminary, Ikot Ekpene. Young Silas was born on October 1, 1933, the year that Bishop Ekandem started his minor seminary training. Silas was born into the family of Titus and Emilia Umoh of Ikpe Ikot Ekpe in Ikpe Annang clan now in Essien Udim Local Government Area. Silas lost his mother at the age of two and his father when he was five.

He was cared for and brought up by his uncle Gregory Umoh. His parents, being ardent Catholic members, decided to send their child to a Catholic institution for his primary education that took place from 1940 to 1945 at St. Thomas Catholic School, Ikpe Annang. He finished the elementary aspects of his education there and proceeded to St. Anne's Primary

School, Ifuho. He completed his Standard Six Examination in 1947. His secondary education took place at Holy Family College (HOFACO), Oku Abak, from 1948 to 1952.

It is to be noted that by the time Silas finished his primary education, Dominic Ekandem had been ordained a Catholic priest. Silas's inspiration to the Catholic priesthood did not come from HOFACO but from a blind teacher and catechist, Emmanuel, as he was popularly called, from Ikot Ufen, Afaha Obong. Silas used to tell people the story of his vocation emanating from Catechist Emmanuel as the man who used to teach them about the priesthood.[162] Although there was this strong desire to become a Catholic priest, he was not so free because of his uncle who was an ardent Methodist member, and he planned to make him continue in the Methodist Church's tradition. Bishop James Moynagh recommended that he should go to Enugu for senior or major seminary. Major seminary was also called senior house for the priesthood at that time. It was called senior house because they wanted to distinguish it from the junior seminary.

This took place between1953 and 1959. At Anua, Bishop Dominic Ekandem was the priest-in-charge. At the completion of his major seminary training, Silas was sent on probation for two years from 1959 to 1961 to St. Mark's Catholic Church. There, he ministered till his sacerdotal ordination that took place on July 30, 1961, at St. Anne's Catholic Church by the auxiliary bishop of Calabar Diocese, Bishop Dominic Ekandem. St. Anne's was still a parish church by then. It was a momentous day and a groundbreaking event as he became the fourth indigenous priest from what became Ikot Ekpene Diocese later.

This was the first priest he ordained as a bishop after his consecration. He had rights to confirm and carry out other pastoral duties as a bishop. Rev. Fr. Silvanus Etok was ordained in 1959 in Rome, while Fr. Silas T. Umoh came next in 1961, two years after. His ordination was an epoch-making event since this constitutes the first ordination ever carried out by Bishop Dominic, two years before he became the local ordinary of Ikot Ekpene Diocese and seven years after his consecration as a bishop. Father Silas was first posted to St. Marks's Parish, Oron. Bishop Ekandem was still under Calabar Diocese as the vicar general and as priest-in-charge of Anua Parish. He saw his apostolate as service. That accounts for his disposition to be the vicar general and priest-in-charge of Anua Parish. He perceived the episcopal office as that of serving the people with greater diligence, pastoral charity/care, and attention to the flock of God. Bishop Ekandem recalled that this was an unmerited favor granted to him by God. He said, "I ever remain grateful to him." As a very humble person who was always ready to learn, submit, and listen to his seniors as he had been doing in his father's house before he went to the seminary, he acted as the scribe who bought out of his house, both the old and the new, and harnessed them for the promotion of the kingdom of God on earth. "Therefore, every Scribe who has been trained for the kingdom of heaven is like the master of a household who brings out of his treasure what is new and what is old" (Mt. 13:52). It seems that after Bishop James Moynagh had observed Bishop Ekandem for six years and put him through strict scrutiny, he was authorized on the seventh year to ordain Fr. Silas T. Umoh. Among the pioneer missionary priests fondly remembered by the people at the time of ordination include Fathers Kraft, Biechy, Stiegler, and J. L. Hanson. It was Father Hanson who baptized Dominic Ekandem. He was the one who signed the baptismal register. These were Holy Ghost Fathers who functioned at the pre-diocesan creation era. Msgr. Silas T. Umoh died in February 2013 with a few months to complete exactly the age of eighty. May he rest in perfect peace. Amen! He was buried the same day with Fr. Christopher C. Nkonduok who died at almost the age of sixty-three. May his soul rest in peace.

Figure 6 The first four seminarians from Ikot Ekpene Diocese who became the first four priests and Brian D. Usanga who became the second bishop of Calabar.

At the time that Bishop Dominic I. Ekandem became the ordinary of Ikot Ekpene Diocese, there were only ten parishes in existence.

There were four Nigerian priests, Fr. Isidore P. Umanah of Blessed Memory, the first priest of Annang land to be ordained; Fr. Emmanuel Afangideh; Fr. Sylvanus Etok; and Fr. Silas T. Umoh. If there were ten parishes, it means that the St. Patrick's Missionaries manned six of them. The parishes that were in existence at the creation of the ecclesiastical jurisdiction of Ikot Ekpene Diocese were the following:

- St. Anne's Parish, Ifuho, established as a parish in 1918 but with a resident parish priest in 1920. It became the mother of all the parishes in Ikot Ekpene Diocese. The establishment of Ifuho as a parish came a year after the birth of Tom Ino Ekandem who was to be baptized seven years afterward though not at Ifuho but in Anua, where Ifuho sprang from as an outstation until it was made a parish.
- St. Patrick's Parish, Urua Inyang, 1939, which is nineteen years after the creation of Ifuho Parish
- St. Theresa's Parish, Nko, 1947, corresponding to the year of the bishop's consecration
- St. Brigid's Parish, Urua Akpan, 1950, falling within the Marian year before the dogma of Immaculate Conception
- Parish of Immaculate Conception, Afaha Obong, 1947. This was the same year that Rev. Dominic Ignatius Ekandem was ordained a Catholic priest.
- Assumption Parish, Ukana Iba, 1955, having the same birthday celebration with Ogoja Diocese
- St. Andrew's Parish, Nto Edino, 1956
- Assumption Parish, Ikpe Annang, 1957, came three years after his consecration
- St. John's Pro Cathedral, Abak, 1958, came four years after consecration
- St. Vincent de Paul's Parish, Ikot Obong Edong, Ikot Ekpene, 1960. This was the last of the parishes established before the erection of the new diocese dated March 1, 1963, and given in Rome and mandated by the Bull[163] of His Holiness, Pope John XXIII.

Chapter Six

PRIMUS ORDINARIUS PROPRIUS (THE FIRST PROPER ORDINARY/BISHOP)

First Residential Bishop

Gaudium Magnum Anuntio Vobis
("I bring to you news of great joy,"

—Lk. 2:10)

A.   Introduction

THE SAYING THAT the journey of a thousand kilometers begins with a single step holds very true of the *ecclesiastical circumscription*[164] *named Ikot Ekpene Diocese. The creation of a new diocese always goes with lots of anxieties, surprises, and expectations. The creation of Ikot Ekpene Diocese was not an exception. Many things can take place during those early days.*

In 1963, Bishop Dominic I. Ekandem was appointed the first residential bishop of Ikot Ekpene Diocese after having served for seven years as a priest in various capacities and nine years as an auxiliary bishop as priest- in-charge at Anua. Before he became the first residential bishop of Ikot Ekpene, the bishop of Umuahia, Most Rev. Anthony Gogo Nwedo, CSSp[165] had already been consecrated and installed the first residential bishop of Umuahia Diocese in July 1959. Umuahia Diocese came out of Owerri Diocese where Bishop Joseph Brendan Whelan, CSSp was the first ordinary of the diocese. Most Rev. Mark Unegbu, the first Nigerian bishop of Owerri, took over from Bishop Whelan, CSSp as the second bishop of Owerri after the Nigerian/Biafran Civil War. The war took place between July 6, 1967 and January 15, 1970. Gen. Yakubu Gowon headed the Nigerian side, while Col. Odumegwu Ojukwu headed the Biafran side.

The two bishops were ordained after Bishop Dominic Ekandem. Bishop Unegbu was his classmate at Christ the King College, Onitsha, while Bishop Nwedo was his senior. Considering Bishop Dominic's manner of approach to and doing things, he did not bother whether he was made a residential bishop. His concern centered on God's favor as minister in his church as an auxiliary bishop. He was occupied with the idea of serving God as a bishop and how to lead forward, the newly carved-out ecclesiastical territory under his care as chief shepherd of souls.

a.   Bishop's Residence at the Creation of the Diocese

Naturally, at that time where everything was modestly carried out and in a low key, there was no bishop's house. Bishop Dominic had to live with the other priests at the present parish house where the cathedral administrator is living in Ifuho outside Ikot Ekpene town. The very first parish house, which was smaller, was pulled down at the creation of the diocese in 1963. Priests like Frs. Biechy, Plunkett, and some others lived there before the construction of the new parish house, which is the present one,[166] and the very one that Bishop Dominic Ekandem lived in when the diocese was "carved out" of Calabar.

Fr. John McGuiness was the priest-in-charge of the Ifuho Parish before it became St. Anne's Cathedral, and he became the cathedral administrator at the time. Bishop Ekandem lived with him, and when Sylvanus Etok came back from studies in 1964, he equally lived there with the bishop. At the time that the bishop began piloting the affairs of the newly created diocese, there were very few Nigerian priests.[167] All the others were expatriate priests from Ireland belonging to the Kiltegans or St. Patrick Fathers.

It was only years later that Bishop Ekandem built the bishop's house located along Cardinal Ekandem's avenue, now used by Msgr. Cosmas Udomah as St. Dominic's Chaplaincy. This is to maintain the memory and presence of the cardinal. When bishop's house was renovated in 1984, he moved into St. Vincent Catholic Church as his temporary residence and the diocesan administrative headquarters until after the reconstruction. There, he lived with Very Rev. Fr. Xavier P. Ekutt who had taken over from the Vincentian Fathers. Very Rev. Fr. Paul Roche, CM was the parish priest of St. Vincent Catholic Church, Ikot Obong Edong, Ikot Ekpene, at the time of taking over. Fr. Xavier Ekutt was ordained the same year with Fr. Joseph Uko in 1981. He worked with Very Rev. Fr. Roche, CM for a while before being mandated to take over when the Vincentian Fathers left the parish. Fr. Ekutt became the first Nigerian priest to work there as a parish priest.

b. Means of Communication and Transportation

At the creation of the diocese, everything was simple; there were no sophisticated devices or technologies. Means of communication were very simple but rare. Most of the communications had to be done in person by traveling down to the place or by sending a messenger or posting a letter that took ages before arrival. In some occasions, the event passed before the mails arrived. Such was the situation with communication. Telephones were uncommon, if there were any. Telegraph and telephones were carried out in the post office, except where a diocesan headquarters was capable of installing one. They had to wire the message through a cable made of copper wires. Wherever the pole fell down, there was an interruption in the line of communication. Generally, the post office was the central place for such system of communication. There were some telephones but in very strategic places. Ifuho Parish had one since it was equally the bishop's residence. What operated mostly was the telegraph message, which was not very effective either. Sometimes there were many disappointments. Means of transportation were difficult. Bishop Ekandem had a little lovely radio that he carried along with him wherever he went. He took time to listen to news for the purpose of being current and sharing news of the worldwide affairs with the flock.

Few people were able to afford motorcycles, which took the form of the mighty motorcycles still found in some quarters like the military and the police force even though it is a common phenomenon in Europe and in some other places. Bishop Ekandem had a motorcycle that he used in touring the whole mainland section of the diocese. The first time he went to Okon on pastoral visit, he went with that motorcycle and stayed in the oldest school block almost opposite the present parish church. Even bicycles were of great pride for those who were able to afford them. The roads were not very wonderful. There were series of struggles at every inch so as to manage and survive.

Writing was done mostly manually. Those who could afford them used manual typewriters. That is why handwriting as a subject counted very greatly in schools. People developed wonderful or beautiful handwritings. The style of writing of Bishop Ekandem was cursive. His had the uniqueness that characterizes Bishop Dominic. Many of those speeches and homilies and many of his sermons are extinct except the presidential addresses as Catholic Bishops' Conference (CBCN) chairman of Nigeria. The addresses have been published as *Shepherd among Shepherds*. Msgr. Sylvanus Iniobong Udoidem carefully looked at the publication containing those speeches in the paper he presented on the cardinal's anniversary in Ikot Ekpene Diocese.[168] He prepared his homilies and talks and rendered them ad libitum, that is, "at will." When there was need, he wrote most of his speeches and homilies by hand and typed some of them. In such circumstances, he wrote down the key points in the form of a sketch and delivered them spontaneously. He read out his homilies and sermons only in very rare occasions.

c. Funding

He had very little funds at his disposal. That was part of the very strict adherence to poverty following the injunctions of the Lord (Cf. Matt. 10:1 ff) in sending out the twelve. However, what he had was sufficient to manage the diocese and his clergy. He lived a life of poverty and an austere one for that matter. It was the characteristic of the period and of the good shepherd (Cf. Jn. 10:11–18). This trained him to live frugally. He desired that his fellow workers lived that way also following the example of the Master. Since the priests were not very many, whatever fund he had for the maintenance of the bishop's court was used for the few priests and the laity. This was supplemented by whatever trickled in from the diocese to serve the people of God and to promote evangelization and the spread of the Gospel in order to fulfill the injunction of the founder, Christ the Lord (Cf. Matt. 28:16–19).

Msgr. Kenneth Enang, who was at the center of the diocesan finance and finance committee, said, "The Diocese survived from the contribution of the Cooperation Mission Fund (CMF). This took the form of Mission Appeal. The expatriate priests, mostly from Ireland working in Nigeria and in Ikot Ekpene Diocese in particular helped a great deal in raising funds. They sent forms to Bishop Dominic to sign and return same to them. With the returned forms, the Missionaries and their collaborators carried out serious campaign that raised some funds from their home countries for the development of the Diocese."[169] Owing to the aid provided from such campaigns, some projects or even the maintenance of the priests and members of the church were carried out. The faithful were not financially burdened.

In those days, people saw the church as the great provider, where one received rather than giving. It had its positive as well as negative impacts. The situation changed when many of the expatriate priests left. The indigenes had to provide everything for the maintenance of their priests. The unfelt burden became an obvious one.

d. The Indigenous Priests at the Inception of the Diocese

Bishop Ekandem started the diocese with four Nigerian priests, namely, Rev. Fr. Isidore Umanah, who was the first in dignity as far as Ikot Ekpene was and is concerned; Reverend Father Afangideh, the uncle of Rev. Fr. Thomas Ebong, the present dean of communications in Ikot Osurua Polytechnic, Akwa Ibom State; and Rev. Fr. Sylvanus Etok and Rev. Fr. Silas T. Umoh were the first four indigenous priests who formed part of the initial takeoff crew. These were the four indigenous priests with a handful of St. Patrick's Missionaries who collaborated with Bishop Ekandem to launch the diocese into deep waters. The troubled waters were tough. As the saying goes: "When the going is tough only the tough get going." This is a common proverbial saying that has come down to us through the ages.

The dependence on foreign subsidy as it still happens in many parts of Africa was prevalent. Since the bishop did not have many choices, he relied much on the few he had in terms of personnel. For instance, Fr. John McGuiness, SPS was the vicar general, bursar, finance administrator, education officer, teacher, and many other appointments he had to be saddled with. His hands were overfull, yet he was able to fulfill all of them diligently and efficiently. How he did it marveled many. He loved the bishop, and the bishop trusted Very Rev. Fr. John McGuiness. Since he handled very many posts, it appears that such a position was an enviable one. Sometimes his position made it difficult for some to get directly to the bishop. Any person who wanted to see the bishop had to see Fr. John McGuiness first. He also acted as the secretary. The difficulty of not reaching the bishop directly and immediately without having to pass through an intermediary angered some people and created an atmosphere of animosity or even jealousy whether imaginary or real.

e.   Pastoral Vision

i.   Development of Pastoral Strategies

Realizing the number of priests in the diocese, the bishop had to work hard to develop a solidly sustained *pastoral strategy*.[170] He knew the importance of catechists and made use of them in establishing new stations and in sustaining the faith of the people by conducting Sunday services for them, teaching catechism, and sustaining the tempo of the catechism by incorporating volunteers to help in teaching it. These are the things that should have been carried out by a resident parish priest but because of scarcity of priests at the time, the catechists had to play a very central role in the process of evangelization. It was generally called CCD, the Catholic Christian Doctrine.

Fr. Edward McNamara, a legionary priest and professor of liturgy in Regina Apostolorum University, Rome, answering some questions on the lay participation in the liturgy where there is scarcity of clerics, highlights the importance of the lay faithful in carrying out many of the duties that are supposed to be done by the clerics while at the same time indicating something about their dressing, which is not supposed to be like that of the clerics.[171] He gives a lengthy résumé of what the instructions of *Redemptionis Sacramentum* and *General Instruction to the Roman Missal* say. It was after the explanation that he addressed the question of abuse of vesting as an extraordinary minister of the sacraments vesting as an ordinary minister of the sacraments. This type of abuse did not arise in Ikot Ekpene Diocese since the catechists knew their boundaries. They were instructed on mode of dressing and decorum.

They were very conscientious and eager to evangelize the people according to the mind of Christ and of the church. This is why they were trusted servants. With this, it was possible to learn the faith of the church, know it, and practice it. In the bid to convert the people from paganism to faith, the teaching had to be consistent. Part of their duty was to conduct morning prayers at the stations and exhort the people on the right manner of worshipping God. Since many of the people they taught were not lettered, the manner of teaching catechism was by rote. They repeated it over and over until they were able to remember and recite on their own. They were strict not to promote anyone who was not qualified to receive any of the sacraments since they knew that the parish priest could decide to interrogate the candidates himself before conferring any of the sacraments. They knew they were agents who needed to do everything with fidelity and trust.

ii. Establishment of Marriage Centers in Parishes

Before the implementation of Rites of Christian Initiation of Adults (RCIA), involving the long period of training of adults in preparation for the sacrament of initiation of adults, emerged in the seventies from East Africa, Bishop Ekandem had ingeniously developed a pastoral plan reflecting such strategy. He built marriage centers in parishes where the wives went in for training for about six months in preparation for wedding. The training included the church's teachings, relationship with the husband and others, spiritual life, developing marriage spirituality, hygiene, home management, and bringing up of children. They were taught many prayers and how to lead the Rosary while committing many Psalms to memory. It was an intensive period. Apart from cleanliness, an essential element, punctuality was one of the things greatly emphasized. The education of the women strongly entailed the education of the entire family. That is why women are very important and play unmitigated roles in the family. Married women are the heart of the family, while the men are the heads.

It was a very good choice to train the women while the husbands took care of the home and had to provide for the children. The men went to visit the wives at the marriage camp and provide for her upkeep from time to time. They attended the sessions scheduled for men. Their training did not last as long as that of the women. The women were more eager to learn and to get wedded and were more disposed positively to making a good home. Each of them knew that the marriage was indissoluble and was for life. That is why they prayed earnestly to God to sustain their homes and marriage. The idea of divorce was something that was unheard of in the context of such marriages.

That is why it took such a long time. The men learned to take care of the home in the absence of the wives just as they took up the daily chores in the home when the wives gave birth. The men had intensive training during the day and went back home, while the women stayed most of the time at the center. They were not supposed to have any marital relations within that period until after their wedding. The rule of no extra marital relationship was greatly enforced and adhered to by both parties. They were aware that they were taking a divine step and act they were engaging in. At the center, married women who had good marriage homes were part of the team of trainers. The marriage center or camp in Ikot Ekpene Diocese was at Nko. Going there was a type of retreat. It was period of establishing the foundation of proper and long-lasing marriage based on the principles of God.

B. Priestly Decorum

Bishop Dominic was very anxious to see his priests dress well and appear neat in public places, comport themselves well, speak well, and live well, controlling themselves not to let bouts of anger mar the work of God; to be very prayerful, pastorally zealous in carrying out the apostolate, love the flock, listen to them, and visit them in times of need, he did not find it funny or take it lightly when things went the contrary. It is the duty of every priest to be neat and polished to avoid being a distraction to any person.

One of the middle-aged priests of Ikot Ekpene Diocese described the late cardinal as a mature, solid, and pastor par excellence. Bishop Dominic Ekandem had the tact of governance and diplomacy coupled with integrity in his person. He governed his priests as well as his flock with love, compassion, and understanding. He was careful to spice his governance with firmness despite the fact of love and concern. He never presumed any person but treated each distinctly and as person. As a father, he covered all under the mantle of his paternal care as Jesus did. One of priests recalled him as a "good shepherd who never left his flock untended."

He respected the people. He loved them, the little no less than the great. It has to be noted that his position was unique because of his age and years in priesthood. From the point of view of African culture, he already had the preeminence of position that was incontestable. He provided the father figure for all, both in the government and in the church. He had the capacity to call any of his priests and scold him seriously for any wrongdoing or for anything he perceived as unbecoming of a priest. He still did that up to the point of his death in 1995. As a benign father, he had his own ways of carrying it out. He never allowed a situation of conflict to make him to adopt a vindictive approach. He had an open heart full of love for his own as a good shepherd imitating the Lord Jesus Christ. He always spoke in private at such times to the ones concerned. He did this type of correction in a place called Efe. Efe was his former garage that was later covered with blinds to guarantee some security and protection while using the place. The place was originally open and exposed to danger like reptiles. It had to be restructured for the new purpose it was intended.

Some blocks were erected and the heavy curtain furnished to make it appear a little habitable. Any person invited to Efe would generally begin to question oneself and examine the conscience to see what he did that did not go well with the ethics of the priesthood or the priestly decorum. It took the form of a headmaster summoning his people to his office for official interrogation. The invitation to Efe always had that undertone.[172] Sometimes the good news to be delivered could demand being summoned to Efe. At Efe, he could talk in very strong terms to the priest while they were by themselves. He did not fail to point out the weaknesses and faults of the person. All this was done with the aim of correcting and hope of a better life and apostolate. The same man, who was very stringent with his coworker previously if what the priest did demanded commendation, can easily turn round and be supportive of the same coworker publicly. He treated every priest respectfully but did not hesitate to point out the faults of the person if there was need.

C. The Capacity to Affirm, Correct, and Identify

During one of the presbyteral meetings, there was a proposal to use the national uniform as the diocesan one. The priests spoke for and against. One of the priests argued strongly on the irrelevance of a national uniform becoming a diocesan uniform. He argued that the purpose of its distinctiveness would be defeated since it is already used nationally. Even if the same material were to be used with the name of the diocese on it, it would still not make any difference. In that case, it would be identified with the nation and not with the diocese. Furthermore, it would be better to go for something totally new and different. One senior and revered priest in the presbyterium supported the idea of abandoning the entire idea. The whole presbyterium supported it, and the idea was laid to rest. The argument was powerful enough to conclude all the discussions on the matter.

After the meeting, the priest who moved the motion was summoned to Efe in the evening. On his arrival, he was ushered in to the house. He was conducted to the presence of his bishop at Efe where his Ordinary Bishop Dominic Ekandem sat waiting for him. The priest's attention was drawn to what happened during the presbyteral meeting. After the preamble, the bishop said to him, "You used your intellectual power to destroy all the arguments in favour of the National uniform being used for the diocesan uniform, even the revered priest Father X supported you. Why did you not use your intellectual power to support the argument? If you had done that, the idea of the National uniform for the diocesan one would have scaled through. Always aim at building instead of destroying."[173]

The priest went back to his parish and continued in his mission without being carried away by the situation. A few days later, an official visit to the parish called pastoral visit took place. It was the official opening and inauguration of the parish at Iwukem. The bishop arrived and was cordially received. During the homily, he spoke about the priest he reprimanded some days earlier in glowing terms. He told the people:

> I sent this priest to your Parish because I know him. He is a solid, intelligent, pastorally minded and zealous. I knew he will be able to take care of the Parish before I sent him. Whatever he tells you, I am the one telling you just as the Lord Jesus said that whoever hears you hears me and whoever listens to you listens to me and what I say to you is given to me by My Father (Jn. 12:49; 14:20; 16:23). When you see him, you see me. He is my eye and my mouth. Your kindness to him are only showered upon me. So treat him as you would treat me. Love him as you would love me. He is my able representative.

The priest in question was Very Rev. Fr. Emmanuel Udonwankwo from Abiakpo Ntak Inyang where the Vincentian Fathers and brothers or the Congregation of the Mission have a House of Formation. Father Emmanuel finished his term in that parish without any problems because of the tone set by the chief shepherd with whom he collaborated for carrying out his pastoral ministry. Bishop Dominic Ekandem was able to combine the tact of a father—disciplinarian, love, and concern—in that very act. Father Emmanuel was not happy with what he experienced at the Efe. He never noticed the niceties expressed by this man who was as simple as dove but wise as a serpent (Matt. 10:16, Douay-Rheims version). He spoke to the priest within closed doors as a hard man and disciplinarian. He interacted with him as a father and mentor in the field of apostolate. The bishop went as far as identifying with the parish priest by saying, "Whatever he tells you, comes from me." He showed his trust of the priest by his words. He did not victimize him or throw away the baby with the bathwater. He respected the dignity of the priest as a person and upheld that dignity at the same time. That is the characteristic of a true shepherd and father who beats the child with a cane while, at the other hand, draws the same child close to himself. He disciplines and shows love at the same time.[174]

In another context, he called another priest of his to Efe. He lamented as a father would when his child is not doing well. To correct this particular priest who was not comporting himself well regarding priestly discipline and cleanliness, he told him, "You are a male pig. Is that what you were ordained for? Will you comport yourself and face what you promised or face the music?"[175] The priest left his presence crushed. The prelate did not relent his effort in monitoring how he was getting on to make sure there was an improvement. He called the attention of any of the priests and pointed out what he became aware of and looked at it with his priest to aim more at a life of holiness, reformation, and integrity rather than allowing oneself to degenerate and lose fervor and the tasty nature of being salt of the earth and light of the world.

He loved and cherished his priests while not only pointing out their weaknesses and sins but also indicating ways of remedying the situation. He employed the tact of challenging the priest, bringing his weakness and sins to the fore and providing alternative manner of living that adopted personal discipline and serious life of prayer. He never kept quiet and allowed the situation to drift on. He did not believe in transferring priests in order to avoid scandal, but he made the one concerned to see the futility of his actions and the need for renewal and growth. It was the one priesthood of Christ, the good shepherd he felt called to propagate and extol and share with the others. Heaven was the goal for all Christians, and every clergy had to work toward that. No one is exempt he used to say.

D. During Annual Priests' Retreat

The prince-prelate always attended the diocesan priests' retreat organized yearly. During those retreats, sometimes some of the priests who had not met for a very long time used the period to converse and plan their programs together and resolve pastoral issues during those periods. The likelihood of having some undesired distraction was there. If a priest caused the distraction of others during the input/ conference/ talk or at any other time, he would surely take note of it and act accordingly. The moment the prelate noticed some people discussing during the retreat, he would slip a little note into the hand of the priest or priests concerned to come and see him after the talk. This did not make him to be distracted or preoccupied with the disturbances; he was rather fully in control of the whole situation so as to maintain peace and order and help all to participate effectively in the spiritual exercise retreat. Sometimes this made him unpopular, but he was concerned for the general good instead of tolerating distraction.

This type of invitation did not take place at Efe but in his room during the retreat. Once any person realized that a note had been given to one or two people, the rest will be very careful lest they received the summons to go to his room. In this way, the retreat period would be very quiet, and those who really want to devote themselves to the prayerful atmosphere and profit from it would surely do so. The spiritual exercise for spiritual renewal authentically accomplished its effect in this way. That was the effect of early intervention. It may not have solved the problem totally, but at least it went along way to minimize it and keep it in check.

E.   Encounter in a Marriage Context

One young priest had just taken over a parish vacated by expatriate priests who ran since its inception. He did not work there for long when he experienced a very serious opposition by an intended bridegroom because the priest told him that it was not right for him to marry a young girl who could have been his child. The intended bridegroom threatened and vowed to destroy this priest who at the same time stood his ground by telling the man who incidentally was a judge that what he was intending to do concerning the supposed bride was incorrect. This resembles the situation of John the Baptist and King Herod (Cf. Matt. 14:1–12; Mk. 6:14–29; Lk 9:7–9). The quarrel escalated, and each decided to have recourse to the paterfamilias, the ordinary of the diocese. The bishop told the judge, who is to be known as Judge UN in this context, that the priest was right in his demands and questionings about the location of wedding for validity and licity. He also had to undergo the marriage instructions.

Judge UN was confused, but having heard from the chief shepherd, he had to undergo the normal training facilitated by the catechist. He had to complete the course within the normal duration. The young priest had told the judge that it was not proper for him to go and marry a little girl who could have been his daughter or granddaughter. If he insisted and went on, he would likely see himself being abandoned by this very young person. The response was "It is none of your business. All that you need to do is to facilitate my marriage with whom my heart delights." The priest said, "No, that will only make you to enslave this girl who will not be able to stand up to you or argue when there is contention." In these days, that can be construed as pedophilia.

The man was bent on marrying the same girl. The priest gave him an alternative of going to wed at any other parish of his choice. He continued with his threat and said he was going to show the priest who he was if the priest did not do what he demanded of him. The priest decided to go and consult with his ordinary who told him that he should not worry that the man would eventually come to him. It happened as the prince-prelate had predicted. Judge UN discussed lengthily with the prelate. Judge UN was told that for pastoral reason, he should refrain from adopting his former approach so as not to bring scandal to others. He was asked whether he wanted to cause scandal to the old and the young in the parish. It was that aspect of becoming a stumbling block that caused Judge UN to relent. It shows that even though he was angry with the priest, he was still deeply religious. He was asked to go and reconcile with the priest whose name he had started defaming.

He was equally asked to apologize to the priest and make amends because the priest he was dealing with represented Christ the teacher. He was reminded that even though the priest was young, he was his spiritual father in faith. The approach of Jesus in terms of treating those who came to him was applied here, especially in the context of asking Judge UN if he wanted to scandalize people in the parish and be a stumbling block to the others. The nondirective approach brought the man to a sense of recollection and self-awareness.

Judge UN left a little more consoled than he would have originally been if he only ended up with the young priest. Judge UN finally married the young girl after fulfilling the conditions he was subjected to and went to another parish for the wedding. He reconciled with the young priest and even made the young priest his confidant to the extent that he helped forestall the penetration of Islam into Ikaland, in an interior part of the diocese, which the bishop subtly eroded by organizing Catholic pilgrimages to Marian Shrine established in that area for the purpose of making Catholicism to become a prominent religion there. Bishop Ekandem established a secondary school for females in the area. That was part of the strategy to spread Catholicism while presenting seemingly harmless celebration in the area.

The bishop's astuteness manifested itself here too. He used one stone to kill two birds, stop the spread of Islam in the area, and consolidated Catholicism at the same time. Having fulfilled the requirements, he went on to marry the girl. When he grew older, feeble and sick, the girl abandoned him as the priest had predicted. He died in isolation and agony.

F.   Resolution of Conflict of Authority

In a certain parish where one of the priests was newly posted, things were not very smooth. The members of the Parish Pastoral Council (PPC) were not ready to work with the new priest. They always had a meeting before the PPC meeting. Their secret agenda was always there as Plan A, while the agreement to execute anything with the new priest was regarded as Plan B. The secret tussle of power continued, and the priest in question was becoming disillusioned. He tried many strategies, but none worked. He continued strategizing and failed repeatedly. They came up with a very fantastic plan to try and fence the parish since every place was open, and many people were encroaching into the church's land. At last, he felt happy that he was beginning to make an impact and to experience some inroad into the administration of the parish. No sooner had they arrived at this point of seeming congruity than the secret agenda started manifesting itself again. When he asked for an explanation, there was no response. It was similar to the situation in which Jesus was telling the disciples that the son of man was to suffer many things in the hands of chief priests, the elders, and the scribes and the pharisees (Cf. Matt. 16:21). The disciples were busy thinking of who among them was to be the greatest (Cf. Matt. 20:20–28). They were more wrapped with the material pursuit than understanding Jesus.

At this point, he asked the vice chairman of the parish if he knew why the difference and the coldness of feet arose, and he said nothing tangible. The only sensible thing he said was that higher authorities had decided that fencing should stop, and the clinic project should continue. The priest flared up and nearly wept at the same time, but he held his peace. He contemplated changing the executive members of the pastoral council to aid things function better. When the old members became aware of his intention, they resisted all the more and threatened any person who would cooperate with the priest in terms of becoming a member of the parish council. There was tension in the parish. This time, the tension extended to the parishioners. It was not only restricted to the parish priest and the PPC. The old members of the PPC reported to their mentor who told them that they should not worry, that nothing would destabilize them. With that assurance and self-confidence, they went back and tried to tie the loose ends of the knots and make sure that the parish continued in that quasi-peaceful situation. Such intervention constituted a bold affront. That was the last straw that broke the camel's back.

All the while, the parish priest dared not approach the bishop. He thought that approaching him would be a disturbance. Consequently, he decided to stay clear of the bishop's residence. When things turned sour, he could no longer bear it. He went to book an appointment with his ordinary, but to his apparent surprise, he heard the invitation from the bishop himself: "Come right in." There he sat and began to discuss what he went for. He did not have to repeat the journey before meeting the bishop. He started by saying, "My Lord, Bishop, I will like you to remove me from this parish and make an assistant wherever you wish, for I cannot work there because of the higher authorities who are undermining my efforts to progress. There is nothing that I try that works. I am frustrated to the last point. Just let me leave the place so that I can begin life afresh."

By the mere mentioning of the word "higher authorities," the bishop interrupted, "Who is the authority, or who are the authorities? There is no higher authority in this diocese other than me except God." The priest responded by giving him the name of the priest behind the disobedience of the parishioners. The cardinal then retorted, "I am the bishop. There is no other bishop in this diocese. I am the ordinary of this diocese. Since you speak of changing the executive, go ahead and do it as soon as possible. As to the case of the authority, I will handle it myself." He then decided to change most of the PPC members and retain only one or two who showed some sign of sympathy. He made out the list and carried out the reshuffle-ment of the council.

The next time they had a meeting, he walked in confidently, being armed with the authority of the ordinary. He made his pronouncement with audacity. He dismissed the group. He told them that the change took effect from the last time they had a meeting. He told the old members who were not retained to leave. They were told that the new members would function till the proper elections were carried out. The old members wondered what gave him the effrontery to act in such a manner. He did not consult them except that he sought the opinion of those to be appointed members. They could not imagine the change and authoritative manner of acting. Yet they suspected that something serious must have taken place. This is the priest who was so mild and gentle, pleading with them to do something, to cooperate, and asking their opinion at every stage, and was now acting with impunity and without any reference. It appears that is what happens when people are kind. They think the person is a fool and may walk all over them. Nevertheless, that should never derail one from being kind.

They said, "He must have had authority from somewhere," like the apostles who became bold after the resurrection of Christ (Cf. Acts 2:1–11). These were the very people who locked themselves up and stayed in closed doors. They were the ones who opened all the doors and windows after the descent of the Holy Spirit. They were said to have been filled with new wine. The parish priest in this case was surely filled with new wine, and that is what empowerment does. This was the situation. The cooperation with his priests gave that implicit trust and paternal love that formed the foundation of their relationship and existence. When the priest who undermined the peaceful coexistence of the parish heard of the changes, he asked, "Father, so you changed everything about the PPC (Parish Pastoral Council) without even a word or reference to us?"[176] The parish priest simply said that it was necessary for efficiency and effectiveness in order to avoid conflict.

Concerning the case of the priest who was regarded as the higher authority by his fellow parishioners, the bishop did not lose time at intervening. He did not send for the priest nor did he discuss it with him since he knew that the head of the snake had been cut. He was expecting to hear the supposed higher authority react but did not find any reaction. Since then, things continued smoothly. He was conscious of the fact that the progress of the diocese was marred by constituting himself an obstacle to the progress of the parish; as such, he acted when it was due without trying to please anyone to the detriment of the parish or the diocese. The priest regretted his supposedly good and patriotic action and refrained from such interferences in the future. He knew his boundaries from then on.

The parish moved on unencumbered under the new parish priest. People started noticing progress in the parish. Members of the PPC worked with and trusted him. The ordinary did not dance to the tune of any person or interest group or groups as Herod did to the tune of Herodias and the daughter (Cf. Matt. 14:6 ff). He allowed no one to dictate to him what needed to be done in the diocese even though he consulted widely and listened attentively before carrying out any important actions. He knew when to step in and when to say "no" in order to arrest a situation of an impending chaos. He moved with the spirit of the times. He did not just act to frustrate any person but acted in the interest of the diocese. Fortunately, the priests working under him perceived some of that. Calling their attention about a particular thing was frequent and was for their own good and that of the entire diocese. The modus vivendi (mode of living) had to interact and mix up completely with the modus operandi (style of operation).

G. Disagreement of Parishioners with a Priest

Whenever a report was brought against any priest, the chief shepherd in the diocese listened with rapt attention. Often, such complaints like not being present in the parish or shouting at people or at the top of his voice or not being gentle with people had a hidden agenda of removing or changing the priest. He usually defended his priest while the report was going on. Generally, Bishop Ekandem would say, "I have no priest to give you. If you have any yourselves, you can go ahead with him. Once I withdraw him, I will not have any other one to send to you."

As soon as the representatives of the parish leave, he would send for the priest concerned. Often, he sent his secretary to bring the priest. Depending on the gravity of the report, the priest would be brought down without delay. The secretary always waited until the priest returned from wherever he went. He never went back without the priest in question. No matter how serious the situation was, he always treated the person with diligence and in a dignified manner. He always introduced the conversation with a question of how things were in the parish. At the end of the preliminaries, the prelate would introduce the reason for inviting the priest. He never rushed into any condemnation. He equally listens to the priest with serious attention while taking note of the points brought against him by the body of parishioners. After listening to him, if he was wrong, the bishop would speak in very strong terms to the priest and ask him to go and retrace his steps. If the priest made divisive statements or injurious points that hindered the growth of the people or their faith, he would look at the situation with him and guide him on how he would put it across to the people. If it needed apology, he would ask him to render it to the parishioners by himself and withdraw the statements made earlier. It was the priest's responsibility to correct the wrong impression created in the parish. It was not the bishop's duty. This was a personal pastoral approach he used in administering difficult situations in parishes.

H.   Practice at Liturgical Functions and Correction

Before any celebration, the cardinal always had practice with the people involved. Even if he was sick himself, he would always avail of the opportunity offered and be present punctually for the practice. After the practice, if the master of ceremonies indicating the places for the prayers makes mistakes, he would overlook the mistake and get on till after the celebration before making a jest of the person involved. Sometimes, when the master of ceremonies (MC) opened the wrong place for prayer, he would delay before **he** proceed to pray and adjust the prayer. It is incredible that he would not react to such a situation.

The man could not easily be moved by little changes. He remained steadfast and immersed in the celebration without flinching in any way. Once he was asked, "Why do you do this when you know there was a mistake?" He responded by saying that it was to avoid distracting the people. "If I begin fumbling over the pages, I will distract myself, and the faithful would be distracted. They will lose their concentration." He added, "I do not want to be the cause of any person's downfall. I prefer to bear the burden alone than to smear it on others and cause them to throw away the grace of active participation."[177] This is a great sense of *sensus fidelium* (the faith of the faithful) and *ecclesia supplet* (the church supplies).

I. His Trust of Functionaries

He had a great capacity to trust and establish confidence in the person he worked with. This was based on the knowledge that the master of ceremonies or the MC was supposed to have studied or known the text of the ceremonies in such a way as to master it properly. Familiarity with the text was considered a foregone conclusion.

Freedom of operation without goading the MC along or attaching strings to the duty entrusted to him shone out very brightly in his life. If any person was given the function of the MC in the diocese, he would not hesitate to do what the MC indicated to be carried out. If he realized that there was a serious mistake, he will read the one shown him then will open to the right one and continue normally. He was always conscious of *sensus fidelium* (the faith of the faithful).

Once there was an ordination to the priesthood, and he was not well. He asked the Late Abp. Brian Davies Usanga to carry out the ordination. Rev. Fr. Inyangetor, now Msgr. Peter Inyangetor, was the master of ceremonies. They started smoothly until the time for the ordination rite. Bishop Ekandem was present at the altar. When the MC took the *Roman Pontifical* to Bishop Usanga to indicate to him what he was to do, he said, "You can keep the book. I have carried out many ordinations before." Bishop Ekandem sat at the other side and said, "My Lord, do whatever the MC tells you. That is how we do it here." The MC had to take the rites to him once again. This is similar to the scene of the wedding feast at Cana in Galilee where the Blessed Virgin Mary told the attendants, "Do whatever he tells you" (Jn. 2:5–7). Bishop Usanga had to adhere to everything the MC showed him from then on. Once he entrusted something to any person, he always supported the person, especially when what was done was in order.

J. His Faith and Devotion to the Blessed Virgin Mary and Prayer Life

Dominic Cardinal Ekandem had a simple and realistic faith. His prayer was based on that simplicity of little children's trust. This is the type of trust he experienced from his father who trusted and loved him. Likewise, he trusted and supported those he assigned to carry out certain functions or duties. Fr. Patrick X. Ekutt recalls that Bishop Dominic Ekandem packed down to the Presbytery of St. Vincent Catholic Church, Ikot Obong Edong, Ikot Ekpene, in 1986 following the renovation of the bishop's house by Very Rev. Fr. Innocent Umoesinwang who was the bishop's secretary by then. The renovation entailed reroofing the house too. Relocation was imperative pending completion.

Hitherto, the prelate moved to St. Vincent as his temporary abode. Many things had to be hurriedly done to make the place conducive till the completion of his house. A chapel had to be improvised. The long hall that forms part of the house had to be partitioned to create a chapel out of it. It was there that the statue of the Blessed Virgin Mary was kept. Every evening, the prince-prelate used to go there with Father Ekutt to recite the Rosary in Latin. Having cultivated the habit of praying the Rosary in Latin since minor seminary days at Christ the King, Onitsha, he continued with that habit even after his episcopal consecration and cardinalate. Fr. Patrick Ekutt, who was younger, would usually kneel, while the chief shepherd would sit facing the statue of the Blessed Virgin Mary. They meditated deeply while praying the Rosary. It usually took time to complete the decades since they spent time reflecting on the various mysteries. It was not a prayer said by "rot" as one expatriate priest once said. It combined meditation and contemplation, thus making it alive and involving. That is why Father Ekutt said, "We prayed it according to the Cardinal's Method of Prayer."[178]

a.   The Spiritual Life of the Prince-Prelate

The courageously firm prince-prelate was naturally bold. Such combination of quality is rare, yet he possessed them. Those who knew him saw him as a man of rare qualities. His conversion and insertion into Christianity made his hidden qualities to emerge. Rome was not built in a day. His spiritual life and virtues grew gradually but steadily since growth in the spiritual life is never conclusive.

Even though Bishop Ekandem did not like to talk about his spiritual life, everything was evident in his daily life and comportment. He never wanted anything good to be attributed to him. He wanted everything to be attributed to God, the source of all good things.

The ordinary did not like to delay actions, but at the same time, he did not like to rush things. He preferred giving chance to things to unfold themselves while allowing the imprint of providence to be manifest itself. He prayed always for the enlightenment of the Holy Spirit in everything so as to be taught and illumined in his actions and words. Following and doing the will of God in everything was his delight and quest. Sometimes he was criticized as being slow while in the process of discerning God's will.

In one occasion, he said, "Who told you that I have something special about prayer. I have difficulties in prayer like others. I only carry out meditation as I was taught in the Seminary. Sometimes God decides to look on me with his countenance of illumination. It is none of my doing. I only remain grateful to him. Do not let anybody put it into your mind that I have special methods of prayer I have none. I have God and that is my all."[179]

Despite the fact that he was unwilling to speak about his prayer life, many people testified on how transfixed and resplendent his face became whenever he prayed starting from the time he was a seminarian. Mr. Sebastian O. Eyo, one of his former students during the probation period, writes:

> I was a student of Mr. Ekandem for two years (1939–1940). During this period, he had duties as an Auxiliary and over us young Seminarians. These apart, he had many other duties to perform both in the college and outside but he always squeezed time to pray three timesa day with the Seminarians despite his day-to-day crowded programmes. His prayer life was not done with performance within the stipulation. He was often seena t prayer privately in his room. Watching him at prayer one would wonder whether he ever had any distractions. Tranquil and angelic he did his best through advice and example to transform our disposition. Erring students were always called into private audience and advised on how to compose oneself for effective prayer. While he was personally charming in his prayer life he did his best to inculcate into us good prayer habits.[180]

It is obvious that in spite of his objections, Bishop Ekandem could not hide God's transforming power.

In the same vein, Mr. Paul E. B. Inyang, a student of his at the same time with Mr. S. O. Eyo, recapitulated:

> I studied under young Ekandem in the then Sacred Heart College (which was later called St. Patrick's College and transferred to Ikot Ansa-Calabar) in the present premises of Sacred Heart Cathedral Calabar from 1939—to the end of 1940. He was an Auxiliary over young Seminarians. Apart from his teaching assignments, which he performed with additional devotion, he had other duties within and outside the College. The wonder of it is that he had so many duties to perform but he performed all of them with perfection and promptitude. Some of us always wondered at his ability to keep time so effectively; yet he never missed nor came late for prayers. (Ekandem was just himself at prayer there was no hypocrisy about it). Whenever he was at prayer we realised that every part of him was praying. No amount of noise and movements could distract him. He was a powerful man at prayer. We all wanted to be like him. Everyone tried not to be late for meals in order not to miss the prayer before meals. If anyone did he had to pray first before sitting down to eat for Ekandem would not tolerate such.[181]

At the time of "visit to the Blessed Sacrament," he was almost always the first to be there. His relationship was always to transform rather than find faults with us.[182] The Bishop Ekandem, by being reluctant to speak about his prayer, did not intend to hide his gifts; he rather wanted those talents to speak for themselves as Jesus wanted his works to testify on his behalf.

In another context, Pa Lawrence Ogbuah, a contemporary of the Bishop Dominic Ekandem at CKC Onitsha, although a junior student to Dominic from Enugu at the time, described the young Dominic as "the smiling morn."[183] He was always happy, smiling, fast, and punchy. It could be seen that he was internally free. He was known and loved by both students and staff. Pa Lawrence recalled an episode that took place in 1965. At that time, Dominic was already the ordinary of Ikot Ekpene Diocese. This elderly statesman shared this wonderful memories of the cardinal in 1997 with the author when in the company of Sr. Immaculata Offiong, HHCJ coming back from Eruku in Kwara State where she finished a workshop on Enneagram with the students of seminary of St. Peter the Apostle called in to meet Pa Lawrence for some information. During the conversation, recognizing that his mentor and revered father in faith Cardinal Ekandem was the topic of discussion, he shared his intimate experience of faith and prayer mingled together.[184] Lawrence was on his way to the hospital for operation and met Bishop Ekandem who was a great friend. Lawrence was the provincial secretary in Uyo division. He was afraid of going in for the operation. When he met Bishop Ekandem, he expressed his fears. The bishop spoke a little with him and told him to go on to St. Luke's Hospital, Anua, that he would meet him there and that he would celebrate the Holy Mass for his intention while the operation would be going on. Lawrence proceeded, and bishop Ekandem went to the hospital authorities and asked the medical team to wait for him to dress up for the celebration. The concession was granted. When he finished vesting and arranging everything, he sent words to the authorities that he was ready. The operation began simultaneously with the celebration of the Holy Eucharist. When Lawrence heard that the bishop was outside the theater celebrating for the success of the operation, Lawrence was rid of his fears, and the operation ended successfully.[185]

Lawrence considered him as a man who placed the highest premium on spiritual things. His sensitivity toward Lawrence was a great demonstration of caring for the body and soul—the physical and spiritual affairs. He treated Lawrence likewise any other person as a brother. His comportment stemmed from his recognition of sharing the fatherhood discovered at the foot of the Cross. His prayer life opened many avenues for him.

In 1970, at the end of the Nigerian/Biafran Civil War, there was an American called Bob Coop, a Catholic Relief Service (CRS) worker who lived near the prelate. At the time he functioned in Nigeria, rendering his services in Ikot Ekene, he used to speak admiringly of the bishop as an eyewitness to his prayer life and consistency and regularity of purpose. He often expressed his high regard for Bishop Dominic Ekandem as a man of prayer and regularity. Bob Coop went on to say, "Bishop Ekandem, that man, he prays so much."[186] Being asked how he came to that conclusion, he said that whenever he passed the bishop's house, he used to see lights on in his chapel. The occurrence was frequent and regular too. Most Rev. Ephraim S. Obot gave the testimony of Bob Coop about Bishop Ekandem in Idah in 1996.

His Excellency Jerome Pvigione is the Pope's Personal Representative in Nigeria and Ghana. During his visit to Ikot Ekpene Diocese in 1974 the Annang people at their Colourful Ceremony conferred the Chieftaincy title on him. Here he is flanked by his Hosts during that visit : Cardinal Ekandem (right)

Image below idah in 1996

Bishop Camillus A. Etokudo took over as the ordinary and successor of Cardinal Ekandem at Ikot Ekpene in 1989 even though he was ordained an auxiliary bishop since 1988. He later became the substantive bishop of Port Harcourt Diocese on May 4, 2009. He succeeded Bishop Alexius Makozi who translated from Lokoja Diocese to Port Harcourt. It was at the same place that Bishop Ekandem was an administrator immediately after the Nigerian/Biafran Civil War. Bishop Etokudo simply said, "The Cardinal was my father. I knew him to be a great man of prayer."[187] Bishop Joseph E. Ekuwem, the ordinary and first bishop of Uyo Diocese, said that "what sustained the Cardinal and kept him alert was his ingrained deep spiritual life."[188] In the same vein, Bishop Ephraim S. Obot said that the prayer life of the cardinal arose from his perception of Christ's suffering, death, and resurrection. In other words, the humanity as well as the divinity of Christ's life were succinctly linked during his moments of prayer and in life. He said, "The Cardinal was a seasoned man of prayer. He knew how to combine self discipline in prayer and in real life."[189]

His Grace Brain D. Usanga, the first metropolitan archbishop of Calabar, said, "The Cardinal's deep prayer life was revered in his daily life since prayer life and actual life cannot be separated."[190] Msgr. Gregory Akpan said that for anyone to pass the night at the cardinal's house, he had to be ready for early rising and for early mass since the cardinal would rise at 4:00 a.m. for office and lauds then meditation before the celebration of the Eucharist. Msgr. Kenneth Enang said that "he was able to carry his crosses with the power of his prayer since he suffered greatly in his life."[191] Fr. John Oscar Uko, one of his former secretaries, said in passing, "Whenever the Cardinal entered the Chapel with any problem or difficult thing to handle or project to be accomplished, he would always come out with a wonderful solution. When he is there, he would be charged, the ideas would seem to come from the four corners of the earth to fill his mind and he will come out very relaxed, composed and ready to move ahead. He could not have been more favoured."[192]

It is obvious that there was a trusting, loving surrender to God together with total self-giving during his moments of prayer while facing difficulties. He took his insoluble problems to God while waiting in utter expectation and trust on the Lord. As a contemplative in action, he admitted that some of the problems were beyond him. At the same time, he was always hopeful that God would grant him an inspiration and creative solution to handle the situation.[193] He did not go into contemplation because of the magnitude of the difficulties challenging his ministry but because it was his way of life, and he trusted in him who was capable of everything. This contemplative characteristic accounts for Father Uko's conception of "being charged" whenever he went into the chapel.

Prayer had become his second nature. It was his "attitude," so to speak. His contemplative attitude was meant to "see God," which is the fulfillment of the beatitude. "Blessed are the pure in heart, for they shall see God" (Matt. 5:8). Contemplation in his life was to lead him to see God in every situation and in all things so as to be able to fulfill God's will. He simply had a heart full of God and full of faith. That accounts for his achievement of magnificent things in very simple ways colored by the influence of the Cross as a starting point of all asceticism.

Mother Mary John Okpo, HHCJ, the first Handmaid Sister to obtain a doctorate degree, said that "he combined his ascetic life with his deep prayer life that won him success in every situation and above all the admiration of his admirers and his enemies as well."[194] He baffled his contemporaries in so many ways and in many things. Some used to wonder where he got all the wisdom. It was from no other source than from the fountain of wisdom who gives generously to those who ask him. His life was subject to the movement of the Spirit. He became a new creation (Cf. 2 Cor. 5:17) by that very means. In this way, he was disposed to bearing witness even in the smallest events of life.

The various testimonies about his prayer life are only a tip of the iceberg. The gift of discernment is another very important feature in his life linked very strongly with his prayer life. Properly put, it is the offshoot of his prayer life. The gift manifested itself in his personal experience as the bishop of Ikot Ekpene Diocese. It was one of the things that reinforced his ascetical life as regards siesta in the afternoon.

b.   Ascetical Disposition

The relationship that Bishop Ekandem had with Bishop Geoffrey May Paul Okoye, CSSp as a classmate went so deep that they shared intimately and joked about many things. It was in one such moments of deep sharing that Bishop Okoye told Bishop Ekandem of a man who was on his way to committing suicide when he had gone in for siesta. He had heard the comment of the suicidal candidate who said, "I think he was ordained to go and sleep. Let him sleep on and neglect his duty as a pastor of souls." Bishop Okoye could not contain himself he had to send out the gateman to go and look for the man until he found him. One day he had just finished his officework for the morning session likewise his meal and went in to rest before the afternoon session. No sooner had he gone to bed than he heard the ringing of the doorbell. The bell was rung vigorously and repetitively that no one in the house could resist its insistent noise.

The man who rang the bell insisted on seeing the bishop when a member of the household attended to him. The attendant told the visitor that the bishop was resting. The visitor frustratingly and angrily retorted, "Let him sleep on, but he will never see my face again."

Since the man spoke in a very powerful voice, the bishop heard the man very clearly. He was so moved that he wanted to go down immediately but for the fact that he had already unvested. He hurriedly dressed up and went down. The man had left. He went to the road to see if he could find the man but did not see any person immediately on the street. He asked his helpers to go and look for the man while he waited impatiently. It appears what pushed him to take that quick decision was his care of the flock. The man was found and brought back.

The conversation that ensued frightened him out of his wits. The man started the conversation by saying, "Tell that priest that I came to inform him that I am on my way to commit suicide. My aim of coming was to bid him farewell."[195] The bishop looked at the note the man left before going away and discovered it was written in a very scratchy and unreadable handwriting that revealed the psychological imbalance, a sign of serious pathological situation. The battle between the two took place for a very long time. Every other person who wanted to see him had to wait or leave until the battle came to an end after three hours. When the man changed his mind at the end, he asked for the bishop's blessing and departed.

The episode became a landmark in the life of the prelate and patriarch and changed his programs and entire pattern of life. From then on, he ceased to observe his siesta. He broke down every form of protocol. The only rule that was left was "first come, first served." There is time for everything. Even when he was out of his environment, he found it difficult to rest in the afternoon. He had to occupy himself with either reading or writing. His concern for the flock was so great that he prayed daily for increase in vocation that God may send holy and conscientious priests among his flock so that the flock would be guided according to the direction of the Holy Spirit on the way to life. His use of scriptures was like that of the Fathers of the church for exhorting, teaching, correcting, and encouraging the flock.

Daily scriptural reading furnished him with materials for his homilies, sermons, talks, likewise for his fruitful meditation and an insertion into the life of Christ. He continued with what he learned in the seminary. The spiritual reading was also given its proper place. With such dispositions, he was able to counsel people pastorally and direct them spiritually.

Despite his deep comprehension and insertion into the mysteries of God, his enlightenment notwithstanding, he always said that he found meditation difficult in the seminary and still found it difficult. He said that he always made use of whatever was useful in the prayer life of the expatriates who taught him. While talking in one occasion, he recalled that his manner of handling difficulties at prayer and in life generally was simply to take it to God. He is all wisdom and all seeing, all loving. Nothing is impossible with him.[196]

As a perfectionist, he never left any stone untouched. He always wanted the best out of every situation. With the simplicity of the saints, he stressed the fact of his being ordinary and not extraordinary. But it is a well-known fact that the most ordinary things are the ones that become very extraordinary. He never wanted anyone to perceive him as being extraordinary since such a perception would not reveal his true self. He was strict with himself even in the area of eating and drinking while at the same time liberal with people. Maybe his sickness was part of his dietary strictness. He offered himself totally to God and pleaded that he might be accepted together with his sufferings as an "acceptable sacrifice pleasing to the Lord" (Rom. 12:1 ff). His trust in providence acted as a strong support for him during his whole period of trial as a diabetic patient. When he spoke of the burden that was sweet and light, he had at the back of his mind "come to me all who labour and are heavy laden and I will give you rest. Take my yoke and learn from me for I am gentle and lowly in heart and you will find rest for your souls" (Matt.11:28–30).

There is no real prayer in which nothing happens or is done. Active prayer is the whole person made alive in God and converted to God. It seems he was greatly tied to this saying of St. Paul that for those who loved God, everything works together on to good (Rom. 8:26). He was always optimistic that God would come to his help no matter the situation. His filial trust formed the basic foundation of his actions. His degree of perception of the necessity of unity in the Nigerian Episcopal Body, among the clergy and the laity and the whole nation at large, formed his incisive, penetrating patriarchal disposition. Here, the saying of Paul is fulfilled: "If God be for us who can be against us for he did not spare his own but gave him up for the benefit of us all" (Rom. 8:35–37). His greatest difficulty was to do away with his prayer and live a prayerless life. He was aware that his prayer was an orientation of his whole being—body, soul, heart, mind, spirit, and imagination—on conversation with God.

Such a relationship, whether inadvertently or advertently, expressed itself in humility that was one of the fundamental characteristics of Bishop Dominic Ignatius Ekandem. His humble attitude made him to be attracted to all and sundry. Those who came close to him experienced not only his humility but also his warmth of love. Such a love was both affective and effective. At the same time, it was personal and concerned about the well-being of the whole person. That love was effectively constant. His love was affective in the sense of here and now and effective in the sense of necessity to be met. It was a practical love.

A certain anecdote is predicated of the prince-prelate when he was on holidays at home as a cleric (hopefully he was tonsured[197] at the time). A man who wanted to show his magnanimity went and organized some women in one station to bring water to Reverend Ekandem and informed him of the date beforehand. When the deed was done, the man went around, announcing to others what he had done for Reverend Ekandem. When Ekandem became aware of what the man was doing, he sent for the man and paid him the equivalent of his service, and no one succeeded to plead to the contrary.[198] It is very probable that he was moved by the biblical injunction that your left hand must not know what your right hand is doing (Matt. 6:3). With that, he stopped the man from unnecessary popularity he wanted to gain while portraying the cleric as one who could not take care of his basic needs without depending on others.

K. The Diocesan Gathering of Nka AdiahaO bong and the Birth of Utom Abasi

Nka Adiaha Obong is a diocesan organization envisioned to be an "umbrella for all" women. It is also called CWO (Catholic Women's Organization). It has a special greeting with the following slogans: *Iban Idey?* response, *Idey*; *Iban Igood*, response, *Igood*; *Iban Ifine*, response, *Ifine*; *Iban Iget Complain?* response, no complain. The questions and answers are normally in pidgin English. Once this special greeting is used, the place becomes heated up like boiling oil in a drum because the women's enthusiasm has been ignited. The women come from various parishes, quasi-parishes, and autonomous communities. At one such gathering at Ifuho during their annual Mother's Day program and "get- together" that generally begins on Thursday evening[199] with registration and lasting till Sunday afternoon after the Eucharistic celebration, lots of activities usually take place.

On that Thursday evening, the women normally recite the Rosary while going on candle procession. The full Rosary of twenty decades is often recited interspaced with hymns and chants as well as intercessory prayers following the intentions presented. The Rosary procession with lighted candles sometimes takes a long time and may end late before the women retire. The influx of women has the potentiality of overstretching the seams of the accommodation provision. Consequently, improvisation can arise, leading to restlessness and noisemaking. Some of the women do go with their cooking utensils, especially at the time each person was to cater for herself. That process changed with time, having realized the cumbersome nature of the whole operation coupled with the tendency and actual causing of lateness to the various programs. The easiest way to curb the problem of cooking and excessive noise was to make sure that every person who registered for the program bought food cooked centrally and ate. Lateness and noisemaking were stemmed to a very great extent.

The next day's program, which was Friday morning, began with fasting and prayer, ending about midday with Eucharistic celebration. Again, the recitation of the Rosary in the evening after biblical quiz competition, dancing competition, and drama and singing competition took place. The following day being Saturday, the mothers went on match past, launching, and many other events. The afternoon and evening periods witnessed the diocesan meeting in which the executives play a very important role in galvanizing and directing the proceedings of the meeting until it terminates very late in the night.

It was in such an occasion that *Utom Abasi* (the "work of God" or, simply put, "God's work") was born at Ifuho. The women were so excited and extraordinarily happy that they decided to send representatives to go and inform their chief shepherd of the birth of the child. When they arrived at the gate, the gateman would not let them in. Some of the women had taken the initiative of going to inform the cardinal of this eventful occurrence. When the gateman refused them entry by announcing that the bishop had gone to bed and should not be disturbed, the prelate heard the commotion and sent for the gateman who reported what had just taken place. He told the bishop that the Adiaha Obong women came to report to him that a new child was born during their annual mother's meeting and gettogether. He inquired from the gateman where the women were; the gateman or the night guard responded that they had gone back to the camp at Holy Child Girls Secondary School, Ifuho, where they stayed. The bishop simply told the night guard to go and call them. The man hesitated knowing that it was dark and late. He later mustered courage and went in search of them. He arrived and started asking for the women who came to look for the bishop while identifying himself as the bishop's night guard. He told them that he had a message for them from the bishop. The women emerged. They were informed to return immediately to the bishop's house and that he was waiting for them.

Upon their arrival, the prelate was the one who opened the gate for them. He took them in as late as it was almost like the guard in the prison who took Paul to his house, bandaged his wounds, and gave them what to eat, and he and his entire household were converted and baptized (Cf. Acts 16:25–34). Bishop Ekandem gave them seats and proceeded to go and look for the key for the store where he gathered blanket, powder, soap, towel, crème, wrapper, whatever little clothing he could find for the baby, and whatever he laid hands on for the mother of the baby. He brought those things and gave them to the women emissaries who took them with great joy, singing and dancing while returning to their abode. Before the departure of the women, the chief shepherd told the women that he would visit the child and the mother and the other women the following day. On arrival at daybreak, with the spree of joy and gladness, the mother and child were brought to the accompaniment of dancing throng to the bishop who prayed for the mother and the child and named the child Utom Abasi[200] because it was in the course of God's work she came into the world. The bishop did not mind his rest being disturbed in order to take care of his flock in a very humble yet joyous way that exuded deep paternal love manifesting in germ the God-fearing spirit and shepherd who never leaves his flock untended (Cf. Jn. 10:11–18).

L. His Sense of Humor

Cardinal Ekandem had a natural sense of humor garnished with witty sayings although in a very simple manner. In all his writings, it is noticeable that he was always very simple like his Master, the Christ in speech and actions. Sir Adam Bassey Nyong, KSJI recounts how he taunted him when he was to go for the election of Pope John Paul I, and what would happen should he be elected pope as he went into the conclave. He spontaneously retorted, "Ado afo usudoho? Nkana nkama etok adaiosis emi mma afo edibo ke nkpodo Pope, Ka keben do!" "And you yourself, can't you be one? I have not even finished shepherding this small diocese, and you say I should go and be pope. Go on and be one yourself." Both of them laughed boisterously and left the matter there.

In another occasion, the same Adam said to him, "Your Eminence, why did you go for a double operation of your eye instead of one at a time? Supposing you become blind, what will happen to the great work you are carrying out?" He looked at him and smiled. Then he affirmingly said with humor and faith, "I will not become blind. Is it not his work I am doing?" In actual fact, he did not become blind, but as time went on, his eyes became far better, and he was able to read toward the end of his life without glasses. This recalls the joke of a Vincentian priest from Ireland, Father John, who died at the age of 101. When he was asked why he was not using lenses anymore when he was above ninety years, he said humorously, "When you are before eighty, you need glasses, but when you go beyond that age, you do not need glasses anymore since the body would have corrected its defects." These great men have great wits.

M. Humble Service

When he was at Sacred Heart College before it moved to Ikot Ansa and assumed the name St. Patrick's College, he used to go as an auxiliary to dig the trenches and foundation with his students. He taught by action. His action was enough to stimulate the young students to see him as a proper human being and as a role model. His humility made him to be submissive to whoever was put in charge of him, whether young or old.

About 1957, Ntisong Vincent and his wife, Mrs. Rosemary Uwemedimo, who was always proud to acclaim herself thus "Ami ndi nwan Ibibio," "I am an Ibibio woman" (even though she was English to the core when she married the young Nigerian lawyer), together with some Irish priests went to visit the young Bishop Dominic at Anua. Bishop Dominic was a family friend of Ntisong Vincent. There were no Nigerian priests in the area by then as the family recalled. Upon arrival, Bishop Ekandem, barely three years a bishop, went around and shook hands very warmly with them and asked each person, "What would you like to drink?" When he had ascertained the response from each person, he proceeded to serve him or her despite the fact that he had servants in the house who could have done that job. He did not call them. One Irish priest protested, "My Lord, you should sit down, and we should be serving you."[201] The bishop answered, "No, that's all right. Thank you." Here, he demonstrated the quality of Christ who said in Mark's Gospel 10:45 that he came not to be served but to serve and to give his life as a ransom for many. Bishop Ekandem exemplified in his life what Jesus teaches as a pattern of life and as one who washed the feet of the disciples (Jn. 13:1–17). He continued to serve until he finished serving all. That was in pre-Vatican days when bishops were very few and were really grand, yet the family recalled there was no air of importance about him even though he was the first anglophone bishop in modern times. The combination of service and humility embraced themselves in this great man. Matthew reports thus:

> But Jesus called them to him and said, "You know that the rulers of the Gentiles lord it over them. It shall not be so among you; but whoever would be great among you; must be your servant, and whoever would be first among you must be your slave; even as the Son of Man came not to be served but to serve, and to give his life as a ransom for many" (Mt. 20:25–28).[202]

N. Combination of Simplicity and Humaneness

Bishop Ekandem is a man who lived his life realistically and not theoretically. He tried to make the Gospel injunction his life principle. He strongly believed that what is preached is what is to be lived. This is in consonance to the instruction given to any candidate for ordination to the sacred priesthood. "Meditate on the law of God, believe what you read, teach what you believe and put into practice what you teach."[203]

One day one Irish, Rev. Fr. James Sharkey, popularly tagged Jim Sharkey, was traveling to Aba from Ibiono. On his way, he called in to greet the bishop at Ifuho in Ikot Ekpene. He was courteously received by one of the helpers in the bishop's house who told him that the bishop was not available. With this, Reverend Sharkey, SPS left and continued his journey. Shortly after that, the young man went to inform the bishop of the visit of the priest. The response of the bishop was "Why did you not call or inform me about it?" The young man said, "I thought you were resting or doing some work. Consequently, I did not want to disturb you." The Bishop was not happy. Responding to this, he said, "Even if I were to be working or sleeping, should I not be called? Am I having a nursing baby at hand?" He gave that humorous reply and took off in search of Reverend Father Sharkey. He went straight to Sharkey's parish and found him absent. He inquired when the Reverend Father Sharkey would be back and left for Ifuho.

At about 8:00 p.m., he went again to meet Reverend Father Sharkey. Upon arrival, Bishop Ekandem apologized to Father Sharkey that he was around, except that he was not informed when he came. Sharkey was surprised and started apologizing for causing him inconveniences, making him to come twice to the parish. Soon after the exchange, he left and went back to Ifuho where the episcopal see was.[204] The bishop demonstrated that he was a servant of Christ and of his people.

Figure 7 Cardinal's Interaction with His Flock at Jude and Catherine Ekpo's House

O. Dedication to Pastoral Care

Sr. Regina Tombere, HHCJ, a member of the Handmaids of the Holy Child Congregation, recounts very vividly her encounters and experiences with Bishop Ekandem thus:

It was in Abuja that I learnt the name of my eldest Maternal Aunt, when the Cardinal asked me of her and how she was doing and sent me to give his apologies to her for the difficulties she was experiencing in her marriage. Prior to that incident I never even knew that he had any acquaintance with her! I was amazed. The story of what followed after I reached home and delivered the message is long. That incident showed me that the Cardinal was "a down to earth pastor," able to establish a deep personal rapport with his flock. My aunt knew him as her pastor, a child in Afaha Esang station, when he was the pastor in Afaha Obong Parish.

Throughout my days as a teenager schooling in Goretti Girls Secondary School, I used to visit the Cardinal regularly. Two occasions come to mind. One was to do "Legion Work." The other was on outing day. My family was not located in Ikot Ekpene at the time so on some outing days I would go with my friend, Rita Inyang to visit her family. At other times I would go to visit the Cardinal, at that time, the Bishop of Ikot Ekpene. On such visits he would spoil me with memorable paternal affections that would encourage me to go there often. On one of such visits he gave me his personal passport photograph with the instruction that I should put it in my prayer book and leave it there as a reminder to me to be praying for him. It was a picture of him as a much younger person, maybe even as a Seminarian. I treasured that photograph as a relic and kept it with me all my life, preserving it religiously in my "Divine Office." One day in 1990, Sister Mary Liguori Okure set her eyes on it by chance in the chapel and took it away. That was the last I saw the photograph, to date. Despite all my repeated requests for that photograph Sr. M. Liguori, HHCJ has refused to return it to me. All my attempts to get her to give it to me have proved abortive. I am still grieving the loss of that photograph.[205]

> That gesture from the Cardinal as my Bishop shows me what a humble man he was. His unassuming humility was also displayed to me when he told me he would like the Jehovah's Witness members to come and preach to him. He did not perceive himself as being too high to be beyond the preaching or prayers of the little ones.

> Two weeks to the death of the Cardinal here in Abuja I was at home with my mother. She told me of a dream she had. A very big tree fell down by the station Church in her village, Afaha Esang. I interpreted it for her that I view it to mean that the Cardinal will soon die. That was how rooted the Cardinal was in the hearts and minds of the people he was their shepherd in his very first station as a priest till his death.[206]

The chief shepherd left an indelible mark on the sheep he pastured since his early days as a priest. They followed him around in their minds and continued to hear his voice long after he had left them. Christ had said that the sheep that belonged to him listened to his voice. He knows them, and they know him (Jn. 10:27). He led his flock with genuine love that produced abundant fruits.

Chapter Seven

PATER FAMILIAS (THE FATHER OF THE FAMILY/FAMILY HEAD)

His Fatherly Role and the Handmaids of the Holy Child Jesus Congregation

Not to oppose error is to approve it; and not to defend
truth is to suppress it, and, indeed, to neglect to confound
evil men—when we can do it—is no less a sin than to
encourage them.

—Pope Felix III

FIRSTLY, ONE MAY rightly ask why the origin of the Handmaids of the Holy Child Jesus Congregation appears prominently in a book about Cardinal Ekandem when he was only a seminarian at the time of its foundation. Secondly, why bring in the handmaids and the civil war situation when his life as prince, prelate, and patriarch is the central point? Thirdly, why bring in the handmaids' return [**check**] to Ikot Ekpene after the secession into the picture? The first reason, the second reason, and the third reason is Ifuho. Ifuho forms the connecting rod to all three circumstances since it was the locus, place from where the handmaids began the serious spiritual journey called novitiate. Their novitiate shared the same building with the Medical Missionaries of Mary.

It was also at Ifuho that Rev. Fr. Dominic Ekandem started his first pastoral duty before being posted to other places and then to Anua. It was to Ifuho that he returned after being appointed the bishop of Ikot Ekpene. He left Ifuho during the war and returned there after the war. There, he received the handmaids back after the war and period of separation. They established their Generalate there. Ifuho is an ancient and a historical place linked to ecclesiastical matters. That is why the life of Bishop Ekandem together with that of the handmaids can be seen in three compartments of the same prism of before, during, and after the war. It forms a trio that reinforces the connectivity between the ensuing situations and contexts as events unfold themselves.

The Latin term "paterfamilias" literally means *the father of the family/ family head*, but for proper understanding, *the head of the family* is better. Paterfamilias is a term that encompasses many things in this writing. It is adopted to embrace chapters seven, eight, and nine. These three chapters form a continuum and enjoy a common link. They have an internal connection that binds them together. These three different chapters are made so for the purpose of convenience. The division occurs to avoid monotonous reading of a very lengthy chapter.

Paterfamilias is an umbrella term uniting the three chapters that are coordinated but totally distinct in content. Some of the chapters are heavy, owing to the materials and discussions, controversies, and correspondences associated with them. Reading chapter seven on the origin of the Handmaids of the Holy Child Jesus without proceeding to the two subsequent chapters will make the work disjointed. Proper comprehension and appreciation of the link demands a patient and unrelented reading.

The role of paterfamilias and the Handmaids of the Holy Child Jesus is crucial to the understanding of the handmaids in Southern Nigeria and their development. The history of development of the Congregation of the

Handmaids of the Holy Child Jesus and the corresponding growth can be found in many of the archival documents and books of the congregation. The same applies to other publications by members of the congregation or even from extra handmaids' sources that give allusions and writings by nonmembers. The activities of the prelate in conjunction with Bishop Brian D. Usanga, the auxiliary bishop of Calabar, together with those of the handmaids assume a common relationship as well as a discordant one in the arena of apostolic and paternal zeal. Such happenings promoted incomprehension and wrong interpretation that did not close all the doors. It had an opening toward what was to endure. The relationship embraced a reconciliation and acceptance on the paternal and filial sides. The popular saying of "back to land" crowned the journey home with a golden crown instead of with thorns as Jesus was in Pilate's court (Matt. 27:27–31; Mk. 15:16–20; Lk. 23:11; Jn. 19:2–3). The handmaids are not an island. They can only be understood in their proper context.

A.   Origin of the Handmaids and Growth: The Prewar Situation

The Congregation of the Handmaids of the Holy Child Jesus would never have seen the light of day but for the *providential plan of God* that brought Sr. Mary Magdalene Charles Walker. Her heart was pierced by the passionate appeal of Bishop Shanahan. She did everything possible to respond to that call. She volunteered to come and run a school at Calabar where vacancy was created as a result of the departure of the *Cluny sisters* of French origin. The Cluny sisters were properly called Congregation of St. Joseph of Cluny in France. Blessed Anne Marie Javouhey founded the congregation in 1807. The members of this congregation distinguished themselves in missionary commitment and establishment of indigenous African clergy. The Cluny sisters arrived the prefecture of Southern Nigeria in 1889 and settled at Onitsha, working in the colonial hospitals and teaching in schools. They arrived four years after the arrival of Fr. Le Jeune, Bubendorf and others of the Holy Ghost Congregation from France. The Congregation of the Holy Spirit, CSSp were the ones who evangelized that part of Nigeria called East of the Niger. The Cluny sisters established a girls' school in Onitsha from the beginning and founded a similar school in Calabar in 1905, six years after their arrival in Nigeria. Two of the sisters worked in the European hospital for some time and withdrew, owing to relationship with the administration of the hospital.

The convent in Onitsha was closed in 1908, three years before extending to Calabar, while the community at Calabar continued at St. oseph's School till March 1920 when the only English speaker among them became sick, and they were withdrawn back to France.

The school was left without any steersman as such.[207] It took almost a year and some months before another person to continue the apostolate came in the persons of a young nurse, Marie Martin, and Agnes Ryan. Agnes was older in age. Both arrived in Calabar in June 1921. These two young women came to hold brief for the religious sisters that were to come later. They were lay volunteers, so to speak, for Marie Martin was a nurse on training when she arrived in Calabar. She became the foundress of the Medical Missionaries of Mary many years later, having experienced the necessity of a congregation to take care of the situation of the women in the area. To avoid "confusion," the two women had to adopt the title "sister,"[208] although they might not have conceived the idea of becoming religious at the time. The adopted title eventually became the proper one as years passed by. At the same time, Marie Martin became a foundress to a new congregation.

While Marie Martin was working on the habit of her new congregation soon after its establishment, Sr. Mary Charles Walker featured in the scene. Her congregation had already declined from undertaking the apostolate at the prefecture of Southern Nigeria in Calabar. In her eagerness to go on mission to Africa, she volunteered without delay. To the greatest surprise and chagrin of the congregation, Mary Charles Walker volunteered and even appealed to Rome[209] to grant her the privilege of coming to Nigeria, having been encouraged by Msgr. Joseph Shanahan to appeal to the pope. The rescript (special written permission) was granted by Pope Pius XI on May 23, 1923, two years after the arrival of Marie Martin and Agnes Ryan. Sr. Mary Charles Walker arrived in Calabar on October 2, 1923 through M.V. Akabo that was bound for Calabar from England.[210] Her arrival gave hope to the young women who had been left like sheep without a shepherd and like a ship without a steersman. Now the steerswoman had come to rescue the floating ship so that it could be captained through competence. God writes straight on a crooked line. The providence of God always takes care of everything. When one road closes, another opens that none is able to close (Cf. Rev. 3:7). That is the mystery of the evolution of the many religious communities, and the handmaids were not an exception.

On her arrival, Sr. Mary Charles Walker engaged herself in the educational sector and medical, pastoral, and catechetical apostolates. Her missionary courage and immersion into the various activities endeared and enticed the young pupils who studied in the school. The girls keenly observed her. The only practical evidence of their observation was the emergence of the postulancy that was to flourish into a congregation.

a.   Circumstances Surrounding the Emergence of the Postulants

The true origin of the Handmaids of the Holy Child Jesus can properly be said to have taken place in the context of Eucharistic adoration. Mother Mary Charles Magdalene Walker as she came to be called and known used to encourage the young women who attended her school to write letters to Jesus present in the Most Holy Sacrament. This initiative reveals the special love of Jesus present in the Most Holy Eucharist that Mother Mary Charles Walker left as a legacy for the future congregation she was to form. Among the pupils who wrote to Jesus, those who expressed their wish to serve as religious sisters, were explicitly noted.

The letters to Jesus in the *Sanctissimum* or Most Holy Eucharist revealed the intention of the young women who secretly nursed the longing to be like Mother Mary Charles Walker of the Religious Sisters of Charity (RSC).[211] Their intentions were revealed separately, but all geared toward becoming religious and consecrating themselves totally to the Lord by becoming religious. As Mother Mary Charles Walker revealed to Gertrude Waturuocha about 1929, there were others who had the same desire. It appears she was waiting for Gertrude to express it to constitute the fourth member of the group before thinking of laying a foundation.[212]

b.   The First Postulants

Gertrude did not know that the bigger and older girls like Kathleen Bassey, Lucy Williams, Agnes Ugoaru, Maria Anyiogu, and Clara Oranu used to go to Sr. Mary Walker for special prayers as aspirants. These big-ger girls were "pupil teachers," and some of them even taught Gertrude Waturuocha who was far younger in age and in class. The "four to make the foundation stone" were Kathleen Bassey, Lucy Williams, Agnes Ugoaru, and Gertrude Waturuocha.[213] These four, when Sr. Mary Charles Walker left after the arrival of the Sisters of the Holy Child Jesus, formed the foundation members or the corner stone on which the edifice of the Congregation of the Handmaids of the Holy Child Jesus rested.

It was that same year, 1929, when Sr. Mary C. Walker, RSC dis-cussed the need to lay the foundation stone that she wrote to Mother Mary Amadeus, the superior general of the Sisters of the Holy Child Jesus, inform-ing her of the progress of the work and her failing health while appealing for assistance because of her age and health.[214] Mother Amadeus was Sr. Mary Charles Walker's classmate. She used that privilege to contact her. The General Chapter of the Sisters of the Holy Child Jesus in June 1930 gave a positive and unanimous response to the appeal of the Nigerian mission. After three months, Mother Amadeus and her vicar, Mother Mary Genevieve, made a maiden and "fact- finding" visit to Calabar and were immediately followed by the three pioneer sisters of the Holy Child Jesus: Mothers Mary Edith Rudwick, Mary Lawrencia Dalton, and Mary Vianney Raftery. Bishop Shanahan, who accompanied them while on voyage with twelve Kiltegan Fathers, among whom was Rev. Fr. James Moynagh, SPS, who later became the bishop of Calabar,[215] led the group to the shores of Calabar.

After some discussion with Bishop Joseph Shanahan on school mat-ters in Onitsha, Mother Mary Charles Walker used the opportunity to speak about the nascent religious group in December 1930. By this time, the little group had already existed for about a year.

She intensified her training and formation of the young aspirants, preparing them for hooding as postulants in 1931 after four days' retreat. January 15, 1931, Bishop Shanahan came in the company of Fr. John Anyiogu to carry out that simple ceremony. Fr. John Cross blessed the hoods of the postulants, while Bishop Shanahan presided at the liturgical celebration of that day in the little convent chapel of the sisters in Anua.

There was a division of labor. It was Mother Amadeus who gave the medals to the postulants. This constituted the epoch-making event of Bishop Shanahan before he left Nigeria for Nairobi, Kenya, in 1932, while

Mother Mary Charles Magdalene Walker left in 1933. The Holy Child Sisters took over the formation of the young women and did everything to see them progress and imbibe at the same time the principles and life of the religious in spirit and in truth. The postulants automatically assumed the name sister. The four were now addressed as Sr. Kathleen Bassey, Sr. Lucy Williams, Sr. Agnes Ugoaru, and Sr. Gertrude Waturuocha.[216] In an epoch that the modus operandi favored adoption of a new name in the religious life to indicate the new life and status of the person as obtained in the case of Simon to Peter during his confession of Jesus as the Son of God (Cf. Matt. 16:18) and Saul to Paul during his conversion (Acts 9:1 ff), change of name in the religious life at the time conveyed with it the unique sense of breaking with the past with a corresponding initiation into a new sphere of life. It entailed a new family, namely, the religious community, one belonged to. Adoption of a new name can reflect the tonsure of the candidate on the way to the priesthood where the candidate's portion became the Lord's before the advent of the *Motu Proprio: Ministeria Quaedam* of Pope Paul VI. It was this document that changed the vision of priestly processes.

c.   Laying of the Foundation of the Congregation of the Handmaids of the Holy Child Jesus

The foundation mentioned here is not referring to blocks and mortar but the four young women who had been clothed as postulants. They were the ones who advanced to the next stage to begin their canonical novitiate program. Their spiritual journey began from the convent school at Calabar under the tutelage of Mother Mary Charles Walker to the new novitiate complex in Ifuho.

With the four postulants, the foundation of the Congregation of the Handmaids of the Holy Child Jesus was laid on January 15, 1931, and progressed because it was laid on solid rock. On April 24, 1937, the postulants moved from Calabar after their investiture to Ifuho where the novitiate was built. On April 25, 1937, the first Holy Mass was celebrated in the novitiate chapel. The handmaids novitiate commenced on that day before the decree establishing the handmaids novitiate arrived in June 1937. From the outlook of things, it means that the postulants operated for six years before they officially began the novitiate.

The Holy Child Sisters who took over from Mother Charles Walker did not leave any stones untouched in making sure that the newly hooded young women properly imbibed and followed the religious traditions so as to lay a good and solid foundation for those who would come after them. The handmaids' novices took new names. Lucy Williams became Sr. Mary St. John, Kathleen Bassey became Sr. Mary Ignatia, Agnes Ugoaru became Sr. Mary Aloysia, and Christiana Waturuocha became Sr. Mary Gertrude. From that time, the congregation grew, and many members joined them probably through the concerted effort of the four frontliners.

When Marie Martin finished the canonical procedure, likewise the habit of the Medical Missionaries of Mary in Dublin, the novices, namely, Sr. Joseph Moynagh, Sr. Mary Magdalene O'Rourke, and Sr. Mary Patrick Leyden, were formed in the same building with the handmaids' novices at Ifuho.[217] Both novitiates began in April 1937.

d.   Internationality of the Handmaids at its Foundation

From the very beginning, the Congregation of the Handmaids of the Holy Child Jesus was international in nature, owing to the composition of the very first sisters who joined. Sr. Mary St. John was from Cameroon. Her presence reinforced the internationality of the congregation coupled with the expansion program within the country covered by chapters six to ten of the memoirs of Mother Gertrude Waturuocha, HHCJ. The expansion reached Ghana.[218] The first General Chapter took place in 1959.[219] It brought Sr. Mary Gertrude Waturuocha, HHCJ to the helms of affairs as the first mother and superior general of the Congregation of the Handmaids of the Holy Child Jesus. It was an occasion that made the congregation enjoy her full autonomy for the first time.

B.   The Great Transition

The first General Chapter brought with it an avalanche or occurrence of great magnitude. The autonomy of the handmaids entailed enormous responsibilities that were totally unforeseen. The forebears of the Handmaids of the Holy Child Jesus learned to depend on God's providence from the very first moment of their autonomy. It is obvious that doing of God's will or dependence on his providence is never easy, except when the individual's will corresponds to God's will can peace of mind ensue; otherwise, there will be serious unresolved conflicts between one's will and God's. Willing what God wills is what gives the transforming power that leads to sanctity since willing what is contrary to God's will leads one away from God and ends up in sin.[220] In the sisters' case, abandonment to God's providence is what gave a solid foundation to the future of that nascent community with untold prospects and promises of future growth and development.

The Sisters of the Holy Child Jesus did not want to bog them with their system of government but left everything open for the young sisters who groped along being led by the light of faith only. The handmaids, learning through daily experiences, led to the art of dependence on God and to work out everything with great patience and trust that God will surely show the way. With the already expanded program in view, they had to begin training their members to fill the gaps and do away with the inadequacies that normally go with inexperience and lack of professional training in the proper field of work.

There is no doubt that Mother Mary Charles Walker confided in and discussed the initial conception and formation of the religious for the southeastern section of the country in Calabar with Bishop Shanahan who resided at Onitsha. The initial contact did not eliminate Msgr. James Moynagh from the context at all. There is no gainsaying that when James Moynagh took over the administration of the vicariate's section as envisioned by the superior general of the Kiltegans who requested Rome to entrust it to James Moynagh as the prefect apostolic of the new prefecturate carved out of the vicariate of Southern Nigeria, Bishop Shanahan happily conceded it since he was anxious to evangelize. The concession eventually became a diocese. The process did not cause James Moynagh to remain at the periphery. No, he was very much involved in major decisions and events of the new congregation. The congregation's development, existence, and growth flourished in his presence, direction, and guidance. All leaned heavily on him.

That atmosphere witnessed the advancement from the state of being a pious association to the attainment of the diocesan status and eventually the international status of having approval from Rome where the

Handmaids Congregation enjoyed a pontifical status. This is what Rev. Fr. Cosmas K. O. Nwosuh, MSP calls *blessing from life in exile.*[221] It is common knowledge that the prominent role of Bishop Moynagh did not extend to the moment of witnessing a pontifical status since it occurred during the heat of the Nigerian/Biafran Civil War. Nevertheless, his contributions as a father and mentor can never be underestimated. It was Bishop Ekandem who weathered the storm and witnessed that great event. Moreover, Bishop Moynagh's role and influence still held sway during the early days of the war, as he was the ecclesiastical superior when Mother Gertrude consulted him about the situation of the sisters who were scattered around many places in Calabar and Ikot Ekpene Dioceses at the early stages of the war. It was he, Bishop James Moynagh, SPS, who suggested that when the students and pupils were sent home if the war persisted, the sisters should all gather in one convent should the sisters be frightened in any way.[222] They needed to have waited till the war subsided, and they were to stay together and be close to one another.

The same fatherly role continued with Bishop Ekandem who was a more senior prelate than Bishop Usanga who took over from Bishop Moynagh during the war, contrary to the presentation of Nwosuh[223] that Bishop Usanga was always "boisterous, colourful, loquacious and had a charming wit and a sarcastic sense of humour. He never failed to grab the limelight whenever the opportunity presented itself. He never shied away from acting or presenting himself as an intellectual."[224] Even though he was cute and witty in his observations and comments, he was naturally an intellectually enlightened. There was no duplicity in him that the idea of acting or presentation of self implies. Bishop Usanga would shout out if he disapproved of a situation or something. He did not pretend or act as if there was nothing wrong. He reacted to situations, but it was not out of pomposity with underlying domineering pride but with the intent of rectification and streamlining. He sought the best in each situation and with the aim of uplifting or protecting the persons concerned. He made use of the situations and, while working, persons to reach God and not to terminate at the persons and things. Things were given their proper places. In other words, he had a great sense of humor and the capacity to see through things[225] in their proper perspective.

He was simply intelligent, and that is why some Protestants in Cross River State at the time were always planning a strategy against Bishop Usanga. Once in 1971, while traveling from Calabar to Oron in the ferry from Elder Dempster Wharf in Calabar through MV Eket, two prominent Protestant leaders from different churches were strategizing how to overcome and overpower Bishop Usanga when one of them said, "For example, we need to get someone who is bold and intelligent to withstand Bishop Usanga who always overpowered us. We need somebody to stand up to him."[226] If his intelligence were to be a "seeming" or "acted" or "presented" or "presumed" one only, such a plot would not have taken place.

Bishop Usanga knew how to be tough and also how to be simple. When he disapproved of a situation, he did it vehemently, and then when he approved of it, no one was in doubt. He loved and respected people, but he never tolerated any person who wittingly or unwittingly disrespected or tried to him. He always corrected the anomaly there and then. His self-confidence enhanced his output and interpersonal relationship. He had a strong personality quite capable of leading naturally and when used in the context of service became very protective to the weak, the lame, the blind, the orphans, the widows, the strangers, the sick, and all classes of the vulnerable. He was a father with many capacities. His sense of justice and peace inspired by the teachings of the Second Vatican Council had a serious impact on his episcopal motto: *Servire in Justitia et Pax*, "Serving in Justice and Peace," or as he translated it into Efik: *Ndinam Utom K'Unen Ye K'Emem*. His episcopal motto formed the bedrock of his pastoral vision. His sense of justice extended to that of protection and security also. His idea of protection and security tallied with the necessity of Bishop Ekandem who became greatly troubled about the security and the protection of the sisters. Bishop Usanga was that pastor or the chief shepherd whom God gave to the people of Calabar Diocese as an auxiliary bishop at the exit of the lovely Bishop Moynagh who equally had a strong and protective personality.

Bishop Usanga had a very good relationship with Bishop Ekandem irrespective of the differences in age and ordination. He was very close to Bishop Ekandem. They supported each other in diverse ways while remaining independent and autonomous. If Bishop Ekandem listened to the advice of Bishop Usanga, it was out of respect and recognition of human dignity and not out of the timidity of not being educated and "respect for the highly educated." Divine knowledge is greater than the acquired one. Bishop Ekandem was imbued with divine wisdom, and that is what is termed *infused knowledge*. That is the reason he spoke with authority to any group without fear or favor. He received his knowledge from the fount of knowledge. That type of knowledge is pure and untarnished, full of surprises yet very simple, and straight to the point. Such knowledge or wisdom or words cannot be contradicted (Lk. 21:15).

The fatherly role of Bishop Ekandem was exercised with the agapeic love of a prelate, prince and patriarch, mentor, and confidant. This understanding formed the backdrop of the drama that developed as the war progressed with series of upheavals that almost became cataclysmic both for the nation and for the citizens of various categories.

Bishop Ekandem had been constantly passing from one battle or trial to another. Here is another with its peculiarity during the Nigerian/ Biafran civil crisis in the country. The Congregation of the Handmaids did not exist for a very long time when the events of war and scattering of the sisters sprouted like a mushroom.

Chapter Eight

CONGREGEMUR IN UNUM (GATHERED INTO ONE)

The Sprouting Events and Coming Together of the Sisters

> Let us not waste time reflecting so much upon our
> troubles, either past or present. We must think about
> them as little as possible, for they have less power
> to harm us when we disregard and ignore them.
>
> —St. Margaret Mary Alacoque

I T IS NECESSARY to view the various events that sprouted in line with earlier occurrences. The handmaids existed just about a decade or so before the frightening event of secession and the scattering of the sisters occurred. For a very young congregation trying to stabilize, it was devastating, but the God of providence was guiding them. Psalm 23 can easily be applied here. "Even though, I should walk in the Valley of Darkness, No evil will I fear, for you are there" (v.4). The trials came not only for the handmaids and the Chief Shepherd, Bishop Ekandem but also for the entire nation.

It was on January 15, 1966, when a group of young Nigerian soldiers who abhorred the corruption, nepotism, bribery, and vandalization of the nation's resources staged a coup d'état, intending to rid the nation of these anomalies. They intended to wipe out the rulers—the president, the prime minister, and the premiers and governors—of the three regions—northern, western, and eastern. Maj. Chukwuma Nzeogwu led the partially successful and partially failed military coup. It later degenerated into the Nigerian/Biafran Civil War after a counter coup that bred pogrom upon pogrom. The effected coup failed to achieve its aim of riding the country of those designated as the perpetrators of the bribery and corruption and nepotism. That sparked off great anger that escalated to the point of bringing about a counter coup that killed Maj. Gen. Agwuiyi Ironsi who became the first head of state and military ruler. Having got rid of him, a systematic slaughtering of military officers from the east and the civilians in thousands upon thousands ensued. This was called pogrom. The dissatisfaction of the northern officers who plotted a counter coup probably stemmed from the need to retaliate and curb the supposed Igbo expansion and domination in the army and many other areas. The federal government paid a deaf ear and held a blind eye to the atrocities. This infuriated the easterners who felt very insecure in any other places except in the east. The result of the resentment was the mass exodus of easterners from the north to the east. The returnees were concerned about their safety. They arrived empty-handed, fleeing the massacre only with their lives. Such situation created an untold poverty even the actual war situation ensued.

These were people who had established themselves wherever they found themselves. Many of the Igbos and some other easterners were murdered mercilessly. The leaders in the east sought a peaceful solution and failed after the Aburi-Ghana peace accord. The aim was to restore peace and order, compensation, and reintegration and foster the unity of the country. The failure of the various international and national attempts at reconciliation and resolution of the problems led to Ahiara Declaration on May 27, 1967. That declaration opened the way to the declaration of Independence of Biafra on May 30, 1967. The Independence Declaration worsened the situation as Yakubu Gowon leading Nigeria at the time construed independence declaration as secession. He reacted to it by aiming at crushing what he saw as rebellion. At this point, the ground was fertilized for outright war of reunification and the struggle for Biafra's autonomy. Biafra launched the civil war with little or no ammunitions, while Nigeria had the superiority of sophisticated weapons and international allies at her disposal. The atmosphere was oblique. This is reflected in Chinua Achebe's *There Was a Country* under the section on "The Military," pointing out Frederick Forsyth's BBC documentary *Biafra: Fighting a War Without Guns*."[227] The war developments mounted pressure on all and endangered the lives of the citizens in the eastern region, sparing neither the religious in the convents nor others in the society. This background led to the trials of the handmaids and the chief shepherd of the flock, Bishop Ekandem.

A.   His Trials during the Civil War

It is an old adage that says that adversity brings out either the best or the worst in a person. For Bishop Ekandem, the civil strife or crisis brought out the best in him. His activities, speeches, and entire behavior underscored his pastoral stance as the chief shepherd and father his flock in an unmitigated fashion. As a father, he did not want to align with any of the sides but chose to remain neutral. At the same time, he tried to intervene to avoid disastrous consequences by making a very bold but unsuccessful attempt to meet Maj. Gen. Odumegwu Ojukwu, the secessionist leader and military head of state and commander of the Biafran nation for a peaceful resolution. Biafra, as a nation, still exists in some old maps.

He was committed to justice and peace spurred on by his Christian outlook of charity and patriotic outlook. The civil war began on May 27, 1967, with the declaration of Biafra as a nation after all attempts at peaceful resolution failed. The determinant was the Aburi Declaration.[228] The consensus of the special Advisory Committee of Chiefs and Elders saw secession as the only viable path[229] when consulted by Ojukwu. The war lasted for thirty months and finally ended in January 1970. In the interim, many atrocious and horrendous things took place. Many people were executed (*en mass*) and buried in common shallow graves as part of the atrocities of war. Some were buried alive in wells, others were maimed, property including vehicles confiscated, while human beings were captured or conscripted into the army. Churches were vandalized. The soldiers used some of the church's documents in some places as firewood. Many lives were lost. Fear and terror reigned, while Bishop Ekandem was praying for peace and making series of efforts to foster reconciliation and termination of the arms conflict and destruction of lives and property. He was greatly worried seeing that his flock was at risk of starvation and death apart from dying as a result of the war or even stray bullets that killed many or being caught in between the conflict as the war advanced.

Among those kidnapped were Rev. Fr. Isidore P. Umanah (RIP), the first indigenous priest of Ikot Ekpene and the first from Ikot Ekpene Diocese to teach in Bigard Memorial Seminary, Enugu, and Rev. Fr. Sylvanus Etok, the then Rector of Queen of Apostles Seminary, Afaha Obong, Aba.[230] Many people were either abducted or captured and sent to Umuahia, Owerri, Ututu in Umuahia and many other places. The two priests were taken to some villages in Ngwa[231] land with the intention of killing them purportedly because of siding with the Nigerian forces, which they had no contact with. In a word, they were considered saboteurs because that was what merited instant death and execution without any appeal. They escaped death by whiskers and by the grace of God. Their Ordinary Bishop Ekandem was very worried as a human being and prayed even more insistently for their safety as Jesus did in the Garden of Gethsemane as he pleaded with his Father with great self-abandonment to his will to let the cup pass him by (Matt. 26:36–46). While there, they took care of the orphans in the place until after the war as the persecution in the early church led to expansive primary evangelization in Samaria (Acts 8:4–40). Only Monsignor Etok was left in the place of kidnapping and temporary domicile. The place could have properly been called the land of death since that was the original intention until God changed the mind of the kidnappers when the Nigerian soldiers captured the place.

Fr. Isidore Umanah was sent to Ututu (which formed part of Calabar Diocese and later back to Umuahia) after the war in 1970, ministering to the people of God there in misery, while some captured ones returned after the liberation of the mainland part of the then South Eastern State of Nigeria, now called Akwa Ibom State or Akawa Abasi Ibom State as distinct from Cross River, a sister state. The old Cross River gave birth to Akwa Ibom State and after that reached menopause and stopped bringing to birth. The idea of kidnapping reveals the situation in life, operative during war period or conflict, but the one in the present-day Nigeria is used as a substitute for robbery by extorting a very high sum from the victim or from the victim's relations with the threat of *Boko Haram* bombing at the corner.

As these two priests and others ministered in what might be called mission land away from one's home (*missio ad extra*), the Chief Shepherd, Bishop Ekandem ministered with the other priests at home front (*missio ad intra*) under great difficulties. That was one of those situations he danced at the foot of the Cross with the wounded crying, the bleeding, the suffering dejected and rejected Christ as well as the Crucified Christ.[232] The Cross of Christ intimately enshrined in Bishop Ekandem's episcopal motto or coat of arms, *In Cruce Salus*, "In the Cross is Salvation," became very resplendent and meaningful even as it unfolded itself in reality. He could not be neutral to the Cross since no one can be neutral to it. Jesus had once told Sr. Maria Faustina, "I suffer even greater pain than that which you see."[233]

The suffering of his members made him to become more worried and restless than ever before as long as the conflict lasted. He was like Jesus who told Saul on his way to Damascus that Saul was persecuting him (Acts 9:4 ff). One must either be on the Cross or be under the Cross. One is on the Cross suffering with Christ or under the Cross suffering with other human beings and sharing in the redemptive action of Christ, the head of the body, the church. For the sake of his flock, he had the privilege of dual sharing; "being on," that is, being crucified with the Lord and "standing under the Cross"[234] so as to be a full participant in the suffering and pain of the flock while reaping the fruit of the suffering redeemer. He did not only share in the sufferings of others in Christ's name but also identified with the Crucified Lord as he went through his daily passion with the Lord. That was his lot as the chief shepherd of the flock.

B.   Responsibility for the Handmaids of the Holy Child Jesus

Things were not easy for anybody. The chief shepherd found it equally difficult as all did. The clergy and the religious were no exceptions nor were the laity. They all swam in the same bitter, toxically infested water of war and suffering. The chief shepherd swam along with the Sisters of the Handmaids of the Holy Child Jesus, the first indigenous congregation in Nigeria and in West Africa founded on April 15, 1931, even though Mother Mary Joseph Okpo, HHCJ indicates 1937.[235] Bishop Ekandem was greatly affiliated to the congregation even as an auxiliary bishop of Calabar before he assumed full responsibility during the war as the bishop of Ikot Ekpene after Bishop James Moynagh, SPS, the first bishop of Calabar, was driven out of Nigeria and not allowed to return. Bishop James Moynagh was blacklisted like many other expatriate priests and brothers who assisted the afflicted populace during the civil war.

Many of the "blacklisted" expatriate priests were incarcerated before expulsion. Bishop Moynagh did not suffer such fate. He was barred from returning to Nigeria together with Bishop Godffrey M. P. Okoye, CSSp after the trip to see the Holy Father, the pope, for the purpose of reconciliation and peace resolution of the conflict, which General Gowon[236] construed the Catholic Church to be fueling the problem in Nigeria. Bishop Moynagh incurred the wrath of the Nigerian government because of that peace mission perceived as a declaration for Biafran Independence. That singular action unleashed the wrath and hatred toward the Catholic Church as a great supporter of Biafra. With the barring of Bishop James Moynagh, SPS from re- entering Nigeria, Bishop Usanga, who was the auxiliary bishop of Calabar, assumed responsibility for the handmaids but much more so with Bishop Dominic Ekandem. This happened because the sisters were taking refuge in Ikot Ekpene Diocese during the war as discussed below under "The Shift to Eriam/Urua Inyang."

Before the repatriation and final expulsion, the expatriate priests were incarcerated. While in prison at Ikot Ekpene, Rev. Fr. Roderic Michael Vincent Crowley, CM (a member of the Congregation of the Mission or the Vincentian Fathers and brothers), generally called Father Rod, used to take food to the expatriate priests imprisoned in Port Harcourt. He had a special "military pass" with him whenever he went there. With the "military pass," he was able to go from Uyo to Port Harcourt where the first superior of the missions, namely, Very Rev. Fr. Frank Mullan, CM, was detained by the military in the process of imprisonment and repatriation. In the detention camp, a soldier guarded him[237] as Paul was in his own, rented lodging in Rome (Acts 28:30).

During the discussion with Father Mullan, he noticed somebody in the room and that was the guard who ordered him to leave immediately, and Father Rod obeyed. Other expatriate priests were later charged to court. Their charge was "illegal entry into Biafra." They were given varying terms of imprisonment before Fr. Frank Mullan, with three Holy Rosary Sisters, came up for hearing. The last group was given bail, but they had no money to pay. Father Rod had to go around the Europeans to beg for money to bail them but to no avail. He was lucky to meet a Lebanese who told him to go to his drawer in the Cedar Palace Hotel to get the money there. Fortunately, it was enough, and the four were bailed within minutes of the expiration of the one-hour grace period. The Catholic secretariat eventually paid that sum.[238]

Others including Bishop Whelan of Owerri Diocese and many more were sentenced at subsequent periods and deported back to their countries. While in detention, Father Rod with some Daughters of Charity of St. Vincent De Paul, Sr. Louis Steen, DC with another Daughter of Charity, and many others organized feeding for the missionary prisoners.[239] Meanwhile, Bishop Ekandem was still moving from one place of the settlement of the Handmaid sisters and the various refugee camps to visit his flock and give them words of consolation to the detriment of his life.

Father Rod was temporarily detained in the company of Fr. Denis Corkery, CM and Fr. Eamon Raftery, CM, two Vincentians who suffered the same fate with others. Father Eamon later became the provincial director of the Daughters of Charity in the Nigerian province. He was only there to help them. He was not part of the group. That excuse was not cogent enough to grant him freedom. They detained him the whole night long till morning period. Father Rod extricated himself by telling them that he had to celebrate mass for the Gov. Dieter Spiff that morning before he was released but with an injunction that he had to leave everything behind.[240] All these took place from January 1970 soon after the war till sometime in December of that year.

The crime of these priests and sisters was serving their flock and risking their lives for their spiritual benefits and physical survival with the aid of Caritas International and other agencies that opted to help instead of abandoning them to die of starvation as the Nigerian Federal Army staged a siege of circumventing the territories, blocking roads and airstrips that could have conveyed food to those victims of war. The federal army contrived the gesture of the various organizations to supply food as a prolongation of the war; hence, the tactic of starvation, as a military strategy, was adopted so as to bring the war to an immediate end. Maj. Gen. Alexander A. Madiebo has a lot to say on this.[241] At such a point, it was the spirit of survival more than nutrition that sustained the rebel soldiers and civilians.

With the exit of Bishop Moynagh, the ordinary of Calabar Diocese, a vacuum was created. The auxiliary bishop of Calabar, Bishop Usanga, operated at Calabar, while Bishop Dominic Ekandem took full responsibility of the sisters' situation, especially when the shift was made at Ikot Ekpene. Some of the sisters think that the Congregation of the Handmaids of the Holy Child Jesus, which was diocesan and international at its origin, had four members[242] and had Rt. Rev. James Moynagh, the bishop of Calabar, as its founder, while others hold that it was Sr. Mary Charles Walker, an English voluntary missionary of the Religious Sisters of Charity (RSC) who came out to Nigeria, was the canonical founder. The handmaids have all come to an agreement that Mother Mary Magdalene Charles Walker is the canonical founder of their congregation, while Bishop Moynagh was the ecclesiastical superior. That is why the members are promoting the cause of her canonization. During the civil war, Bishop Dominic Ekandem was greatly responsible for the safety of the sisters in Ikot Ekpene Diocese with the auxiliary bishop of Calabar, Bishop Brian D. Usanga, in Calabar. Bishop Ekandem took special interest in the Igbo sisters whose lives were in danger because of the atrocious acts of the yet pestering Biafran soldiers who infuriated the innocent nonIgbo civilians and provoked them to hate many of the Igbos and want to eliminate them. In the face of such great peril, he stepped in as a benevolent and concerned father by bringing them nearer to himself at Eriam in Ikot Ekpene Diocese, visiting, encouraging, and celebrating, the Eucharist for them where the sisters had gathered by the hand of "providence." He exhorted them to rely on God who was capable of protecting them and to whom nothing will be impossible (Lk. 1:37).

C. War Turmoil and Scattering of the Flock

Every cause has an effect. Sometimes the effect can be very tremendous, sometimes light in magnitude. The effect of the scattering of the handmaids was seismic in nature that brought about many consequences.

At the time the Nigerian soldiers dropped the first bomb at TTC (Teachers' Training College) Ifuho,[243] the sisters were still living in their different communities. The TTC later turned to Holy Child College, Ifuho, Ikot Ekpene. The bomb dropped between the school and the sisters' chapel and destroyed the arts room and library.[244] The expected fright became a reality, and the counsel of Bishop J. Moynagh came into force. Bishop Ekandem instinctively came around to quieten their fright and encourage them. He was like the stone of Gibraltar to them while demonstrating his paternal care and love. This is the type of love that God told the people of Israel that even if a mother forgets the baby at her breast, he would never forget them (Is. 49:15).

The scattering was precipitated by the closure of schools in South Eastern State. This was preceded by the regional closure sparked off by the bombing spree in Owerri before it tapered down to South Eastern State. Mother Mary Joseph Okpo says, "The first shocking experience was the closure of all the schools in the Eastern Region of Nigeria in September 1967. Eastern Region, apart from the Western and Northern Regions constituted what was proclaimed Biafra as a nation. The sudden announcement by the Eastern Government was due to the dropping of the first bombing attack at Owerri Girl's Secondary School a day before the school re-opened. This was supposed to be a temporary measure but a prelude to unprotected catastrophe."[245]

When the bomb was dropped at Holy Child Teachers' Training College, Ifuho, Ikot Ekpene, in 1967, it was dangerous to continue residing at the convent there. Safety in that environment could not be secured. The sisters panicked. They had already been instructed by Bishop Moynagh to "evacuate and gather in one Convent to provide support and encouragement to each other after the closure of the schools and the children sent away should the Sisters become greatly frightened.[246] It became imperative for "the Novice Mistress, Sisters [sic] Mary Genevieve Cudjoe, the Novices and all the Sisters then resident in Ifuho to move out to Eriam."[247]

a.   The Reaction of the Sisters During the War Situation

The Nigerian/Biafran War was a great disaster from the social, educational, financial, economic, human health, and, in fact, existential point of view. It affected the society as well as the church. There was no peace and no serenity but agitation and anxiety, misery, poverty, restlessness, and insecurity. The more this went on, the more frequent Bishop Ekandem visited the sisters at Eriam to confirm them in faith and hope.

The sisters followed strictly the instruction of Bishop Moynagh, SPS before he and Bishop Godfrey Mary Paul Okoye, CSSp,[248] the bishop of Enugu, departed for Rome to plead with the pope to intervene in the catastrophic war situation that had already taken the lives very many coupled with hunger and disease. The two bishops went as envoys of Maj. Gen. Odumegwu Ojukwu, the secessionist military leader of the Republic of Biafra, the country that the "diplomatic plot" of superpowers never allowed to see the light as Emefiena Ezeani portrays in *In Biafra, Africa Died*.[249]

When Bishop James Moynagh, SPS could not return to Biafra/Nigeria, the Auxiliary Bishop Brian Davies Usanga took over in the interim until he was officially appointed bishop of Calabar and installed in 1970 after the war. Bishop Usanga later became the first archbishop of Calabar before his successor, Abp. Joseph Ukpo, who previously was the bishop of Ogoja. Archbishop Ukpo retired in 2013, and Bishop Joseph Effiong Ekuwem, who was the first bishop of the Catholic Diocese of Uyo for twenty-three years, took over as the third archbishop of Calabar Metropolitan See. When Bishop Usanga took over, he automatically became the ecclesiastical superior of the Handmaids of the Holy Child Jesus. The central seat of government was at the original site at Calabar. The Dioceses of Ikot Ekpene and Uyo sprang from the Mother Diocese of Calabar.

The presence of Bishop Moynagh, an expatriate and a European, gave credence to the Peace Corps team. They went as emissaries to Rome to plead with the pope to aid in stopping the massacre of the innocent people through indiscriminate bombings and shellings that affected markets as at Nkwogwu, Mbaise, in East Central State, what is now Imo State; hospitals as in Ituk Mbang, Uyo, in South Eastern State at the time and now in Uruan Local Government Area, Akwa Ibom State; and churches as in Uli in Orlu Diocese, still in East Central State, now in Imo State, so that peace could return, and the people could live normally. The effects of the war had no exception, including the religious and the clergy, as indicated in the imprisonment scene and repatriation. Bishop Ekandem was almost at the center of events when the war reached the mainland.

Hitherto, the sisters took the advice of Bishop Moynagh and made preparations to move to a somewhat more secure place. At that time, Mother Gertrude Waturuocha, HHCJ was on official visitation to Itak Convent and Immaculate Conception Girls Secondary School where the convent was located. She completed the visit having come from Calabar for that purpose and was on her way to the convent at Oron[250] when she was reminded of the good counsel of Bishop Moynagh and the necessity of being together in one community.

b.   The Shift to Eriam/Urua Inyang

The sisters evacuated the school and convent and moved to Eriam, which is still in Ikot Ekpene Diocese. The rest of the Handmaids of the Holy Child Jesus from Edem Ekpat, Oron, Anua, Ekpene Ukim, and Ndon Ebom, with the superior general, Mother Mary Gertrude Waturuocha, and her council went to stay at Loretto Girls Grammar School, Eriam, Afaha Obong, where Sr. Mary Elizabeth Umoh, a member of the general council, was the principal. The contingent from the various houses arrived at Eriam the same day the students were sent home after being addressed by Mother Elizabeth Umoh, the principal. With the convergence of the handmaids at Eriam, the onus of protection on the part of Bishop Ekandem became more pronounced, the inquietude of the surrounding became more apparent, and the possibility of eruption of some vicissitude became more ominous. The whole atmosphere was being in the "lion's mouth" as the Italians often say, *in bocca al lupo*, whenever one was to go in for examinations. This is their own way of wishing the person good luck. In other words, the person should not fear but should go in boldly and accomplish what is at hand.

With increase of tension and uncertainty, many of the sisters made their way to Loretto Girls Juniorate, Eriam, Afaha Obong, on the way to Abak from Ikot Ekpene. The sisters, aspirants, postulants, novices, and professed sisters converged at Eriam. Some of the sisters in Ogoja and Abakaliki were cut off. No one could communicate with them because of the war that was raging at Ikot Okpra.[251] The sisters made very quick decisions by shifting their base from Ifuho that had wittingly or unwittingly become a war front as a result of the bombing. With the shift, Bishop Ekandem had no alternative than to be fully in charge of the sisters and to take responsibility for them from the diocesan point of view, knowing how important the spiritual life of the sisters was to him.

Upon arrival at Eriam after a short while, the sisters thought that the best and safest place to send the novices and postulants to would be in Urua Inyang, which was relatively calm. When it was reckoned that Eriam was no longer convenient for the formation of the novices who deserved a quieter and a more serene environment for their training in pursuance of their novitiate program, they shifted their base to Urua Inyang, especially as Eriam is close to Abak town. It was no longer very safe either. The only safe haven for the mistress and the novices was Urua Inyang, which is far from Abak and from Eriam but close to Azumini on the way to Aba through the interior roads via Iwukem. The formation section moved to Urua Inyang where another TTC was located on instruction.

The result of this departure was splitting the sisters instead of living together. Those from Edem Ekpat had gone over to Urua Inyang since there was ample space there. The other sisters with the general councillors stayed at Eriam.

c.   Eriam as the Temporary Generalate of the Handmaids

The Generalate moved temporarily to Eriam since the general councillors and the Mother General were there. The novitiate together with the novice mistress had moved too. Eriam became a microcosm of the entire congregation. In the wake of all the events, Bishop Dominic Ekandem was open to the sisters' coming and welcomed them heartily to his diocese, although no particular place in the wartorn areas was free. The day that the aforementioned group arrived at Loretto was the very day the students were to evacuate and return to their homes until the situation improved. The author recalled that the headmaster of their school had alerted them of the necessity of closing the school till further notice. The government's request must have affected all the primary and secondary schools in the eastern region. This should have been after the failure to uphold the Aburi Accord that is well documented by Chinua Achebe in his last publication *There Was a Country*.[252] The announcement came at the time their school was preparing for final examination. That was meant to be the last essay type of examination before the multiple choice questions of examinations took over. That should have been the same time that Mother Elizabeth received the message and shared the same information with her students before they dispersed to their different homes. As the sisters moved from their former communities to a temporary one, so did Bishop Ekandem move from Ifuho to Abak where he established his temporary residence at Ediene Abak. He administered the diocese from there.

As Mother Elizabeth Umoh, who was the principal of the Juniorate as well as the secretary of the general council, was at the verge of finishing her address to the students who were about to leave, the sisters started arriving. The sisters at Edem Ekpat Secondary School near Etinan had gone to Urua Inyang for safety. Consequently, some of the sisters were at Eriam, while others were at Urua Inyang. The division caused them anxiety over the safety of one another. Realizing the worries of the sisters in the two places, Bishop Ekandem gave instruction that all the sisters needed to be at the same place, namely, at Eriam. The process of bringing back the sisters began. Those from Edem Ekpat had taken all their necessary belongings, including some trunk boxes, while evacuating. The journey was cumbersome but safe. The prayer life of every Christian, including that of the bishop, intensified, owing to uncertainties that surrounded every person. Bishop Ekandem in whose territory the sisters were residing became responsible for the sisters even though their Generalate was located at Calabar Road, Calabar.

They were all united in faith though not physically. Every war goes along with its atrocities, and the Nigerian/Biafran Civil War was no exception. As the Biafran soldiers suffered more and more casualties and defeat from the Nigerian troop, they became very hostile to those who crossed their path. They suffered defeat mostly from lack of arms and sabotage. Their partners often, because of fear, dumped the ordered ammunitions in the high seas. They were afraid of being bombed at the airstrip while landing at night.

d.   Preparation to Bring Back the Sisters from Urua Inyang

Two drivers with two vehicles had the onus of bringing back the sisters from Urua Inyang to Eriam so that all could stay together. The roads were dangerous with Biafran soldiers in every nook and corner. Who would make the journey to Urua Inyang? Sr. Mary Anne Iwoh, HHCJ, though with fear, volunteered to undertake it. The first part of the journey was to go to Abak town and buy petrol. There were corpses on the roadsides to the town that was almost totally deserted.

Sr. Mary Anne Iwoh, HHCJ was mandated to go and bring back the sisters from Urua Inyang after volunteering to do so. She was traumatized after having seen what was at the roadsides. Sr. Mary Anne rushed in to inform Bishop Ekandem of her experience. She met the bishop at Midim in Abak. The bishop probably went to visit the parish quietly and see things for himself. At that time, Bishop Ekandem had changed base from Ifuho to Ediene Abak where the TTC was located. The TTC later became school of arts and science, Ediene Abak. On calling in to see the bishop, Sister Mary Anne was hoping that the prelate would tell her "Eyen mi fiak edem, kuka do koro usung ifonke," in other words, "My daughter, do not go there. Turn back because the road is not safe." Instead of confirming her reluctance and telling her not to go, he rather encouraged her to go. He said to her. "Sia Edohode fi aka, ka yak Obong Abasi ekpeme fi," in other words, "Since you have been asked to go, proceed, and may Almighty God protect you." He then imparted his paternal blessings. She mustered courage and left while continuing on the journey.

Fortunately, the tanks of the two vehicles were filled with fuel. At the same time, the fear and feeling of insecurity was increased, especially as vehicles could not easily be seen on the road. Coming back from fueling the vehicles, they met a group of Biafran soldiers holding their hand grenades, suspecting an attack from the Nigerian soldiers at Abak- Afaha Obong junction. Sister Mary Anne was eager to help, but she could not imagine herself being swamped by the soldiers. She invented something that appeared plausible in order to set herself free from their insistent and persistent request. When she appealed to Rome like Paul before King Agrippa and Festus in Acts of the Apostles, Paul was told to Caesar (Rome) "you must go" (Acts 25:11–12). In Sr. Mary Anne's case, Rome became an exit route for her. She told the soldiers that Rome had not given her permission to carry soldiers in the car; if they wanted, they could be at any part of the car but not inside with her. The soldiers succumbed. As long as they moved away from the scene, they did not care about convenience, provided they went to safety. She helped all the same but not according to soldiers' terms of reference.

e.   The Return Journey from Urua Inyang and the Hazards

There were two vehicles arranged to go on the rescue mission. The driver of the sisters drove one of the cars. Sister Mary Anne herself drove the other. Upon arriving at Etim Ekpo junction, Sister Mary Anne met this group of retreating soldiers who were anxious to flee the environment at all cost. Some of them boarded the first vehicle driven by the driver. When they came to the one driven by Sister Anne, she told them that she was not given permission to drive men how much more soldiers. How would she be able to drive them if she had not yet obtained permission from the pope in Rome? If they wanted to travel with her, they could be at any part of the car but not inside. They agreed to jump on the bonnet of the car. She drove along until she came to the diversion from the major road. They got down and thanked her and went on their way. That shows the soldiers were desperate to escape by any means. They were happy to flee from the hostile natives as well as from the advancing Nigerian troops. The natives became hostile, so owing to the atrocities of the Biafran soldiers toward their people who were friendly to them at the beginning. Many of the people in the surroundings were killed with impunity, and some were thrown alive into wells. Others were piled on them until they died a slow and painful death through suffocation as it occurred at Ndukpoise, Ibesikpo, in Uyo District at the time.

The two vehicles traveling to Urua Inyang where a transitory convent had emerged arrived safely. The sisters were taking refuge there, and assuming the condition of refugees like Jesus Christ on his way to Egypt with Mary and Joseph now realized, they had to pack immediately and move. At the time, means of communication was difficult. The sisters had no clue that they had to move until the arrival of their sisters. After arranging and packing the few items they had, they started the journey to Eriam. Meanwhile, the bishop was going about his pastoral duties but discretely to avoid handing himself over to the soldiers who were looking out for any suspicious movements that could arouse their interest.

f.   Contact with the Retreating Biafran Soldiers

During the war period, it was very dangerous to travel. Those who could avoid it traveled very little or not at all. The best means of transportation at the time was trekking since one could easily take refuge in a building or in a nearby bush to allow any oncoming vehicle to pass without spotting the person. This was a precautionary measure. As a necessity where one had no alternative and had to travel by car, the person was necessarily disposed to meet with various types of difficulties on the way. This is what faced the sisters while on their return journey from Urua Inyang.

The first vehicle leading the way conveyed the items used by Mother Mary Joseph Okpo, HHCJ who was the principal of Girls Secondary School, Edem Ekpat in Etinan before the scattering of the flock. The retreating soldiers heading to Aba met the first vehicle driven by the sisters' driver. The soldiers presumed that Mother Joseph was intending to return to Etinan from where the soldiers were fleeing. They noticed the trunk box of Mother Okpo bearing "St. Theresa's, Edem Ekpat"; hence, they asked for the owner and started using abusively humiliating words with lots of molestations. A great pandemonium ensued. They did not believe what Mother Okpo was saying that she and the others in the car were heading on to Eriam, which was a stone's throw from that place. The national army had laid siege on Etinan; the only way out was to flee from there. That is what the Biafran soldiers did. It was in the process of retreating from Etinan when the soldiers met the returning sisters/refugees with their luggage.

Mother Joseph was on her knees, begging the soldiers and weeping at the same time. War crime could range fleeing from one place to another and embracing anything at all that the soldiers were not pleased with and could cause instant death. Mother Joseph knew that her life was in serious danger, and she could be killed at any time. She was trembling with fright when the vehicle of Sister Mary Anne arrived. She jumped out of the car and went straight to the soldiers and reaffirmed what Mother Mary Joseph Okpo had told them that they were coming from Urua Inyang to Eriam where their convent was located. At that intervention by a neutral person and group of sisters, Mother Okpo was set free, and the convoy proceeded and reached Eriam.[253]

When another proposal to go and get the remaining sisters was made, Sr. Mary Anne Iwoh, who later became the Mother General of the Congregation of the Handmaids of the Holy Child Jesus in the 1980s, declined going a second time having seen what she and the others passed through before arriving at Eriam. It was Sr. Mary Agnes Bassey, HHCJ who was one of the councillors, who went and brought back the sisters to Eriam, and the whole group stayed together. Here is the personal write-up of Sister Mary Anne about the trip:

g. The Return Journey from Urua Inyang and Efforts to Rescue the Sisters in 1967[254]

Here I narrate my Experiences

From here my trepidation increased. This was the road I was to take to bring the Sisters from Urua Inyang and these "Biafran" Soldiers were going the same way to escape to Aba. When I had passed this group of soldiers at the junction, I was puzzled what to do should I meet more of them on the way, as I was aware of the fact that the retreating "Biafran" soldiers would likely take the same route to Aba. With my Rosary in hand and faith in God's protection, I continued the journey. Since I knew Bishop Dominic I. Ekandem, the Bishop of Ikot Ekpene Diocese was "taking cover" in St. Michael's Catholic Mission, Midim, I called to see him and tell him of my mission. I had hoped that he would discourage me from making the risky journey to Urua Inyang. On the contrary he said: *Eyen mi sia edohode fi aka, sanga ye Obong. [My child since you have been mandated to go, go with the Lord [May the Lord go with you].* I knelt down and he blessed me. With that I set out when I met another group of soldiers trekking to Aba. They stopped the cars and wanted lifts. God gave me the courage to argue face to face with them that Reverend Sister does not travel with soldiers in the same car and if they insisted, they would have to wait for me to go to Rome and get clearance from the Holy Father. After much pleading and to save time, I permitted them the use of the empty vehicle and the rest did not mind sitting on the bonnet of the car in which I drove. I did not let them sit in the car with me. And so we continued till we reached Urua Inyang junction where I parted company with the soldiers who were grateful and continued their onward journey to Aba.

I branched off to St. Augustine where the Sisters were and they hurriedly packed their luggage brought with them from Ifuho. The two cars were filled with as many Sisters as could fit in and there were still some Sisters who had to wait for the second trips [sic]. The first car started the homeward journey. The second car in which I was followed some thirty minutes later. Some distance before the Etim Ekpo bridge, the Sisters who had left Urua Inyang earlier were stopped by a group of retreating "Biafran" Soldiers from Etinan, who I was told, wanted to see their luggage and saw among others, a suit case addressed to Sr. Mary Joseph Okpo, St. Theresa's Secondary School Edem Ekpat, "ETINAN. Furious at the name ETINAN from where they were retreating, they would have rough-handled the Sister but for God's protection. When I arrived at the spot, Sr. Mary Joseph was already on her knees begging the armed retreating "Biafran" Soldiers. I joined to plead that we were not going to ETINAN but to Eriam to meet our other Sisters. It was a tough and frightening experience to have this encounter with irate soldiers. By God's help, they let us pass but we were all quaking with fear and in the midst of it all, I forgot to call and report our return journey to Bishop Ekandem.

> Right, glad I was and with thanks to God I arrived at Eriam with the first badge of Sisters from Urua Inyang. Unfortunately, there were still some Sisters to be brought down too. From the nasty experience I had had that day, I was so scared to repeat the journey. Sister Mary Agnes Bassey HHCJ was requested to undertake the mission of rescuing the remaining Sisters in Urua Inyang, which she did. To the glory of God, she successfully brought the Sisters safely to Eriam before the Etim Ekpo Bridge was blown up by retreating Biafran Soldiers.

Dominic Ignatius Ekandem

Sr. Mary Anne Iwoh HHCJ

As the last batch of sisters moved along, they met the retreating Biafran soldiers who were not ready to listen to any pleas as a result of their frustration and defect at the war front. The sisters were held at the checkpoint for a very long time. They miraculously escaped being killed and crossed the bridge to the other side just before the Biafran soldiers blew up the bridge on March 31, 1968. The link was destroyed. Crossing had to be done by canoe. The sisters went down to Eriam and continued to remain in prayer while the war raged on.

Eriam once again housed all the sisters in the mainland as Uyo, Ikot Ekpene, Abak, Etinan, Oron, Okobo, Eket, and Ikot Abasi were termed at the time. Bishop Ekandem visited the sisters regularly. He used to go through the bush path from Ediene Abak to Eriam to see the sisters, celebrate the Most Holy Eucharist for them, and encourage them or rather put new hearts into them.

Bishop Ekandem saw his sufferings in the light of eternity as St. Pio of Pietrelcina often said that one should prefer to get his reward not here on earth but in heaven, and if one were to be asked whether the reward should be given here and now, the person should say, "No, I want it in heaven."[255] The underlying reason is the transitory nature of earthly reward. His hunger for compassionate love, justice, and collaboration and the need to relieve others' sufferings was unimaginable.

In a situation in which the regulation of two weeks before burial was fixed, he, in conjunction with the presbyteral council, preferred to lay down principles that would help the church to look critically, morally, and justly at the situation by establishing that, first and foremost, immediately death occurred, the members of the family had the moral right to inform the church president in the village or the catechist who will go with two other members to examine the situation and proceed to inform the priest who will then fix the burial date and that nothing was to be changed in the house. If the person was not properly taken care of while alive, there was no need of building a new building apart from the thatch house the person was accustomed to and providing a wonderful bed when the person was sleeping on mud bed or broken bamboo bed. He emphasized that it was not the ostentatious burial that would lead the person to heaven but the way the person lived. It was not an imposition. It was rather the paternal concern that in many circumstances where poor families are concerned, the worry of burying a beloved one generally caused the living to impoverish themselves in order to impress others and boast like them that they gave a befitting burial to their loved ones. Humility was to be experienced in all circumstances whether in life or in death.

Nothing was expected to change in the room or the house. Everything was to be left intact. Part of it was to avoid excessive expenditure that generally impoverished the mourners after the burial and not to incur serious debts or begin to sell things to take care of the bills. They were to remain simple. His sense of justice did not permit him to leave his flock unattended but to go the extra mile to take care of them. This is where the proclamation of Christ, "You are the salt of the earth and the light of the world" (Matt. 5:13–16), really found a place in his life. He first lived the beatitudes out in his life while allowing the proclamation of the salt and light to naturally take their place and flow in his life with a blending that synchronized everything without much ado. It was the same love of the flock that was extended to these religious sisters. He could not leave his lock untended. That had to be done with the simplicity of the dove and with the wisdom of the serpent. His fatherly role was better experienced than spoken of.

D. The Entry of the Nigerian Soldiers intoL oretto Girls' Juniorate, Eriam

Since Bishop Ekandem was not resident at Eriam, he was not there when the Nigerian soldiers came to Eriam. The day the Nigerian troop reached Eriam, it was like a miracle. There were no shootings at all. Some officers who entered the Loretto Girls' Juniorate compound found the sisters praying in the Queen of Peace Chapel. Mother Elizabeth Umoh, together with the chief of Eriam who was always present and visited the sisters often to make sure that nothing happened to them, met the soldiers. "Captain Moses, a Catholic as he introduced himself,"[256] even asked the sisters to pray for them as well. There are many accounts of the sisters on this issue. The account of Mother Mary Joseph Okpo highlights the bravery of the sisters, namely, Sr. Elizabeth Umoh, Sr. Agnes Bassey, and Sr. Immaculata

Offiong, the Efik-speaking sisters, together with Chief Alphonsus Akpan Udo, the only man present in the compound when the soldiers entered Eriam. Chief Alphonsus prostrated as the soldiers approached.[257]

According to Mother Okpo, the soldiers had raised their guns as they approached but lowered them and greeted the sisters when they noticed the gesture of the sisters and the chief. It seems Alphonsus is the same one described by Sr. Elizabeth Umoh in her memo as Tom Udo Udo. The soldiers later left without troubling any of the sisters. They walked around the compound and asked a few questions and left. All the shootings, bombings, canons, and mortars that were used in Ikot Ekpene never had occasions in Eriam. It was a "Passover." It took place suddenly and ended suddenly. The area was "liberated."[258] The people accompanied the soldiers with singing, dancing, drumming, and conveying their things along the road. It was jubilation galore.

E.   The Blunder of Love and Concern During the War

Motivated by his ardently paternal love, he went extra mile to see that the sisters had some sense of security during that period of war. He wanted to be able to say with Christ, "I have lost none that you have given to me" (Jn. 17:12). St. Peter exhorting the people of God said, "Tend the flock of God that is your charge, not by constraint but willingly; not for shameful gain but eagerly; not as domineering over those in your charge but being examples to the flock. And when the chief Shepherd is manifested you will obtain the unfading crown of glory" (1 Pt. 5:2–4). Since this was part of the manifestation of the symbolism of the episcopal ring of being wedded to the Body of Christ, the church, he willingly did it without minding whether he was going to lose his life. He had put his hand into the plough he could not look back and still be fit for the kingdom.

When Bishop Usanga and Bishop Ekandem realized that there were lots of commotions, killings, and molestations, the duo decided to offer to the sisters what they considered a way out of the problematic situation of war, hatred, and retaliation. They proposed to the sisters the choice of going back to their places of origin until the war came to an end. They did this out of paternal love and concern with full knowledge that if any problems arose in the area where the sisters took refuge, even though consecrated, they were might not be spared. Frightful as the prognostication was with its ominously pregnant situation, they paternally suggested that the sisters left Eriam that ostensibly assumed a "comfort zone" posture to where they would be more secured, and their lives would be spared despite the fact that the soldiers had passed over Eriam, and the chief was very close to the sisters. What was needed to see through the whole situation was not just a brutal courage of the soldiers but also a moral courage that goes with circumspection and fortitude as a gift of the Holy Spirit.

The piece of advice given concerned mainly the Igbo-speaking sisters. Other nationalities like the Togolese, the Ghanaians, and the Cameroonians were not affected. The Igbo sisters were asked to leave. What complicated the situation was the demand that on leaving, the Mother General, Mother Mary Gertrude Waturuocha, should resign her office till after the war while giving chance to one of the indigenous sisters from southeast to take over and rule till the end of the war. The sisters were very astute when they demanded from Bishop Ekandem to write what he had said verbally. He consented to do that on behalf of Bishop Usanga as well. Mother Gertrude has this short but powerful letter in her memoir: The letter does not indicate any date or address, it is plane, simple and straight to the point. The letter reads:

> Dear Mother Mary Gertrude, for your safety and that of the other beloved Ibo Sisters, we think you should resign from your office as the Superior General, for the present, since you have to go with other Ibo Sisters to Lagos. Meanwhile, one of your Sisters of South Eastern State Origin will take your place and govern the Congregation as the Superior General till the end of the crisis.[259]

This simple unalloyed letter penned at the insistence of the sisters, especially Mother Marie-Thérèse Adude Akwe, HHCJ,[260] the vicar general[261] of the Congregation of the Handmaids of the Holy Child Jesus at that time, highlights the simplicity of the dove embedded in the prelate according to the demands of the Founder of Christianity and Savior whom Bishop Ekandem lovingly followed. It is very probable that there would not have been too much difficulty if the bishops had excluded the terms "resign" and "indigene." That was the point of their crucifixion and demand of an indigene from the state to govern until after the war. The sisters were right to have revolted because of suing such a terminology after a lawful election carried out licitly and validly. Probably, this was utilized for want of a better word. It was Dag Hammarskjold who said, "Never for the sake of peace and quiet deny your experience or convictions." In another context, he said, "To have humility is to experience reality, not in relation to ourselves, but in its sacred independence. It is to see, judge, and act from the point of rest in ourselves. Then how much disappears, and all that remains falls into place."[262] The prelates did not want to be silent in the face of impending disaster for their flock. They had to see, judge, and act before it became too late. This was to forestall solvable problems.

The appendix indicates that Bishop Ekandem who wrote that letter, extemporaneously borrowing a paper from the sisters to do that at the spur of the moment, never intended to debase, deform, eliminate the legitimate authority, or destabilize the congregation that he joined to work so hard for its growth and existence. This was caused by the burning desire to see his children freed as Moses did not mind the obstacles when he consistently went to pharaoh's court to intercede for the Hebrews. It was at a time like that he vowed to see his children safe and decided even to die instead of seeing any harm come to the flock entrusted to him.[263]

Chief Justice Aniagolu, during the toast he made to the cardinal in 1979 during the Silver Jubilee Celebration of his episcopal ordination, said, "Perhaps the best practical demonstration of the firm character of which Cardinal Ekandem is made is found in his conduct during the Nigerian Civil War. In order to protect all the Religious, Priests and all the people of God under his care during that period, Cardinal Ekandem, the Bishop of Ikot Ekpene, suffered innumerable privations, both physical and mental, and at one time offered to lay down his life rather than suffer any harm to come to any of them, no matter from what ethnic group he or she had come."[264]

The appendix clearly indicates that the sisters who knew the modus operandi should adopt that for proper and smooth operation of events. That indication exposes the wisdom of the ancients in a nutshell. He did not claim to be omniscient but submitted humbly by pleading with the sisters to use the best means possible. It is even to his credit and that of the sisters that he added the appendix. It is also for posterity to excavate the treasure hidden in that heart, the seat of wisdom, or the inner mind, *lebab* as the Hebrews termed it. This is where the fatherly blunder of love features inexorably and for the main purpose of saving life so as not to answer for negligence before the Lord of Host.

That is why God looks at the heart and not the countenance. It is the motive in this case that matters more than what was perceived, contrived, or interpreted. It is a glaring fact that as far as Bishop Ekandem was concerned, there was no duplicity in him because of his simplicity of saying the truth the way he saw it and always not for the purpose of destroying a person because of truth but to let Christ reign. Maybe they wanted to front an indigene in case of any attacks. What they perceived as obvious danger was still far-fetched as far as others were concerned.

Their visionary horizon differed; thus, bitterness and misunderstandings arose. Since they did not state that as an intention, it was difficult to fathom the entire context. There were series of transactions, communications, goings, and comings before the fluid situation of departure coalesced into a practical movement that took the sisters to safety that the prelates intended although with gross misunderstanding and interpretation. Presumably, the letter recorded by Fr. Cosmas Nwosuh dated April 8 preceded that of Mother M. Gertrude. The letter below is the one written extemporaneously by Bishop Ekandem who came as an emissary on behalf of Bishop Usanga. It reads:

> *Bishop's House*
> *Ikot Ekpene 8*[th]
> *April 1968*

> *The General Council,*
> *Handmaids of the Holy Child Jesus, Novitiate House, Ikot Ekpene, Mother House, Calabar.*

> *Dear Sisters,*

> *Having discussed the present situation with His Lordship Bishop Usanga of Calabar, we have come to the conclusion in*

the interest of and general welfare of the Congregation, a substi-
tute should be made for Mother Gertrude who will serve as the
Superior General until things return to normal.

There can be no doubt that Rev. Mother Gertrude has
been so far the best Superior that the Congregation has got
and in suggesting this change for the meantime, I am sure you
do understand.

Dear daughter in Xt I am
+Dominic Ekandem,
-Bsp of Ikot Ekpene. [265]

The appendage to the letter insists that the sisters employ any valid method they are acquainted with to accomplish the request. The appendix reads:

Ps266

Please in doing this make use of any method you know to
be valid according to your rule. D. E. [267]

The adjustment of the prelate indicates that he was not dogmatically dogmatic; he was open to Father to change to something better for the good of the sisters, the congregation, and the entire church. Nwosuh enumerates the various people who were present when Mother Gertrude called the councillors together and gave the information from Bishop Ekandem. Sr. Mary Immaculata Offiong is one of those mentioned in his book as being present for the briefing on the message of Bishop Ekandem as a member of the General Council. [268] Alas! When contacted in person, Sister Immaculata emphatically said, "I was not there; neither did I know what transpired since I was only taking refuge there." It is not only that "she was not there" but that she was not a member of the General Council when Bishop Ekandem gave the information. There seems to be a mix-up of facts. The interaction was between the bishop and the superior general and council members present at the time. Sr. Mary Anne Iwoh, who later became the superior general of the congregation, said that she had just come back from the University of Ibadan because of the civil war situation.

Even though she had reacted when a new superior general was proposed to be elected, she was not a member of the general council by then. She only reacted as a concerned member of the congregation.

Sr. Mary Immaculata Offiong later became a member of the interim government, and since their constitution did not permit any sister at the time who was not legitimately elected into the council to be given the title of "Mother" even though she became the acting secretary general, she never signed Mother, except "Sr. Immaculata," as numerous mails of the congregation at the time testify in the various houses and in the congregational archive. For instance, the circular letter of June 25, 1969, announcing Juniorate entrance examination and the necessity of the superiors of various houses to alert the parish priests about the entrance examination and giving it wide publicity together with other matters pertaining to the congregational internal organization, is signed as Sr. Immaculata Offiong (Ag. Secretary General).[269]

It is either that Father Nwosuh got the wrong information or presumed that was the correct situation or that the contrivance was to build up to the crescendo not of "anti-Semitism" but of "anti-Igbo" and the awkwardness of segregation. Probably, this was a subtle way of assassination without any guns or knives or bombs. Ostensibly, this bomb or, rather, letter bomb was more insidious than the Hiroshima bomb blast. The misrepresentation conglomerates everything to adduce the conclusion of "anti-Igbo," and this is the same person to whom the sisters returned at the end of the war and finally shifted their headquarters to the original place of foundation. Mother Elizabeth Umoh was not voted for as opined by Father Nwosuh. She was reluctant[270] to accept office even when others urged her to do so because she felt that Mother Akwe was the rightful person to do. Mother Akwe was sick and was to go to Ireland for treatment. That is why Mother Umoh wrote her resignation letter when she came back well and better. That was the *Meraviglia Dei* (the great work of God) who writes straight on a crooked line. It was not possible for the sisters who reacted most against the proposed idea of an interim indigenous Mother General from the state were those from South Eastern State as his book indicates. After Mother Gertrude intimated the council members of what was brewing, they took a decision to get the sisters to Ifuho for the exercise of choice.

F.   The Preeminence of Choosing to Stay or to Leave and the Intervention of the Ordinary of Ikot Ekpene in the Face of the Impending Troubles

When the situation became very intense, Bishop Ekandem called the sisters together and addressed them, giving options for them to stay or to go back to Igboland for the sake of security and safety. He went straight to the point and made the sisters to see the need of taking such decisions. He advised all the Igbo sisters to return to the convents in Igboland.

If any of them was afraid she would be killed, let her make haste and depart. She can return to the sisters of the Handmaids of the Holy Child Jesus after the war. Some of the aspirants, postulants, and novices took his advice and returned home.[271] There were eleven sisters who decided to remain. Among those who remained were three finally professed sisters, two on temporary vows or those who made the first vows, three novices, and three postulants. One of the finally professed was the first superior general while the other was the assistant superior general. The third finally professed was Sr. Margaret Mary Opara, popularly called Sister Nwanem. She later died at the age of eighty-one while living at Abak Hospital Community House of the Handmaids. Among the postulants who remained, one of them became the vicar general in the early nineties. Having made the decision to stay, Bishop Ekandem, however, decided to address all of them in Queen of Peace Chapel in Eriam where all the sisters were quartered.

The bishop requested that they should put their resolutions into writing before Jesus Christ present in the Blessed Sacrament. Putting their decision in to writing simply portended the necessity of individual responsibility and avowal before God. This was to be carried out voluntarily without consulting any other person. Each of the sisters had to write a letter to Gen. Yakubu Gowon (1967–1975). Gowon was the first military head of state and commander of the Nigerian Armed Forces. Each of them was to attach an endorsed passportsized photograph. Whatever they wrote was known personally by the head of state and by the individual sisters. However, it seems that they did indicate that they were consecrated to God's service in the Congregation of the Handmaids of the Holy Child Jesus and that they were Igbos working in the warring part of the country—South Eastern

State of Nigeria. The sisters believed that Bishop Ekandem must have taken those letters personally to Gen. Yakubu Gowon.

With the saying of Paul that the love of Christ has brought us together and has made us out of many one (Col. 2:2), Christ has broken the wall that separated us, and there is no more Jew or Gentile or Greek or Scythian (Col. 3:11; Cf. Gal. 3:27–29). Bishop Ekandem went beyond the confines of the war period to extending charity and concern to both civilians and soldiers no matter what part of Nigeria they came from. This is a personal testimony of Mother Okpo, HHCJ who saw Bishop Ekandem as was then known as a hero and a living martyr.

Figure 8 Bishop Ekandem with Mother Gertrude Waturuocha and the HHCJ Sisters, some SHCJ, MMM, and IHM Sisters

G. The Solidarity of the Sisters, Some Voices, and Plotting of the Path

It is a well-known fact in law that "exception disproves the rule," whereas in logic, "exception proves the rule." If the prelates, Bishops Ekandem and Usanga, asked the superior general to resign in the interim and imminence of terrible disaster so as to save life, which even in moral philosophy and moral theology when it concerns life, an operation can be carried out, that could destroy an essential part of the person's body or even womb or baby. The main aim was not to destroy the organs or the baby but to preserve the life of the mother or the person, but where the main aim is to destroy the life of the unborn child or the organ of the body, it is morally wrong. This is called the principle of double effect. It can properly apply in this context since the demand was only for the interim period. It was not meant to be forever.

The nota bene or "note well" added to the letter "Please do it according to your rules" has a great deal to do with the blunder of love and the idea of convoking a chapter in order to elect a new Mother General. The reason for this additional statement shows that there was no intention of destabilizing the congregation. It might have come as an afterthought. Even then, it was to make sure that things went well and according to their rules. The addition took place before handing over the letter to the sisters. The reaction was an aftereffect. It was after the letter was shown to the sisters that many of them started writing in no uncertain terms to express their disapproval of the very idea proposed. Father Cosmas documented the various sisters who wrote disassociating themselves from such request.[272] This shows very clearly their disavowal of the entire situation. They expressed their bitterness that turned out to be an unveiling of their solidarity. It equally plotted the way forward. The sisters were unanimous on their stand. They carried out the exercise independently of one another, but their goal was the same. Their reaction was genuine and purposeful because they knew their rules and constitutions more than the two bishops did. If the sisters did not react, it would have meant that they did not love their congregation nor did they understand what they stood for.

The sensitivity of the prelate is very glaring in this matter and exonerates him of the high-handedness and overstepping of power[273] that the Republicans accused Pres. Barack Obama of America. The accusation of overstepping his power made them to plan to sue him to court. Bishop Ekandem could have been accused of high-handedness at the time he asked them to embark on the new chapter, which many of the sisters reasoned was inappropriate. Also, the duration of the Mother General in office had not yet expired. These situations provided cogent reasons for the bishop to be sensitive to the points raised, retrace his steps, and let things move on. All was for the sake of love, concern, and safety. The love and concern override everything and put him into danger.

The crisis revealed the solidarity of the sisters, their commitment to their community life, and a reaffirmation of the solid foundation and the guidance of the Holy Spirit their community was built on. In the light of the Holy Spirit, the prelate stood solidly behind them as *Pastor Bone* or "a good shepherd." That accounts for his interest after the war to take the initiative of summoning the Mother General back in order to continue the mandate she received from her sisters when they voted her as their superior general.

Chapter Nine

EGO SUM VIA, VERITAS ET VITA (I AM THE WAY, THE TRUTH AND THE LIFE)

The Journey to Lagos and All It Entailed

*He who would climb to a lofty height must go
by steps, not leaps.*—Pope Gregory the Great
in a Letter to St. Augustine of Canterbury

A. The Accusation and the Journey of the Sisters to Lagos

BISHOP EKANDEM WAS accused of harboring Biafrans; hence, he was called a saboteur. The penalty of those termed "sabo" or "rebel" during the war was death sentence by firing squad, and in some circumstances, the culprit or the "sabo" had to dig his own grave. He was forced to go there and be shot while his body fell into the grave without giving trouble to anyone to bury the remains. This might remind us of Jesus being forced to carry the Cross on which he was going to be crucified (Jn.

19:17). If the "sabos" were many, one of them would be asked to cover the grave of the already executed "sabos." The last surviving person might be asked to cover the penultimate victim before he was shot or released to carry the message home. Such was the perilous situation of the saboteurs or the presumed saboteurs during the war. His detractors labeled him "sabo." They actually handed him over and denounced him as Judas handed over Jesus to the Jews. He was sentenced to be brought before the firing squad for execution.[274] However, he was miraculously spared execution at the last moment.

The life of Bishop Ekandem was greatly and constantly in danger, yet he never abandoned the sisters neither did he stop being charitable and fatherly to all. Every bishop is given a ring to indicate that he is married or espoused to the church as Christ is the Spouse of his Bride, the church (Cf. Eph. 5:23–27; Col. 1:18). The bishop has the duty of defending the church till death. That is why many of them were martyred or exiled from their dioceses. That is why Bishop Ekandem never gave up even when his life was in danger even after having been released like Tobit (Tob. 1:16 ff). He was determined and courageous like the martyrs of old who became so infatuated with Christ's love to the extent that they were ready to die, and they did die for the sake of Christ. In a very real sense, the Pauline statement of "caritas Christi urget nos, the love of Christ pushes us on" (2 Cor. 5:14) applied to him and exemplified itself when it came to the ultimate test. He was ready to pass to the great beyond when he went to the place of execution even though he reluctantly allowed his secretary to accompany him. He did not mind being executed, provided that his flock survived. The secretary turned out to be the voice that shouted, "This man is innocent!" and he escaped death miraculously. "A good shepherd lays down his life for his sheep" (Jn. 10:11 ff.). A hireling runs away as soon as the lion approaches. The sheep do not belong to him, he cannot die for his flock, but a true shepherd like Bishop Ekandem was not ready to abandon his flock. He was ready to defend them; to protect, feed, and water them; and to bandage the wounded or even carry the ailing on his neck like Christ the Good Shepherd.

He knew the sisters personally and called them by their names. The sheep do not know the hireling, they run away from him, and he does not know them personally and by name as does the good shepherd. Since he is a good shepherd, his flock will also be good because they feed from the bounty of the shepherd who opens the gate of the sheepfold for them to go out for pasture and watering and walks before them. The sheep follow him because they are familiar with him and know his voice. The shepherd takes pains to examine each while calling them out by name, scrutinizing each in case any had been wounded, so that he can give special care and attention (Cf. Jn. 10:1–10).

Psalm 23 comes to play forcefully in this context as the psalmist renders this psalm of confidence and trust:

> The Lord is my shepherd, I shall not want. Fresh and green are the pastures where he gives me repose. Near restful waters, he leads me to revive my drooping spirit, he guides me along the right path, he is true to his name. Even though, I should walk in the valley of darkness, no evil will I fear, for you are there with your crook and staff, with these you give me comfort; my head you have anointed with oil, my cup is overflowing, surely goodness and kindness shall follow me all the days of my, in the Lord's own house shall I dwell for ever and ever. (Ps. 23)

Bishop Ekandem, DI, as people sometimes abbreviated his name or sometimes just speak about DI, put in everything at his "wit's end" to protect and save the life of his flock and show the way in the midst of darkness. His life was in constant peril until he succeeded in sending the sisters safely to Lagos through Calabar Airport. He did not mind what people were saying or doing. He had fixed his eyes on Christ and on the Cross. He was not ready to look back.

Unfortunately, the sisters compelled to travel in a military aircraft that had no seats except one, which was given to their sick sister. The sick sister was Sr. Margaret Mary Opara, HHCJ (Sister Nwanem).[275] All the others sat on the floor of the plane without seat belt or anything to hold them when the plane either jerked or passed through a bumpy sky or turbulent weather or while taking off or landing. They managed it that way until they got to Lagos. It was an uncomfortable journey, for the plane in question was meant to convey ammunitions and not travelers; hence, it was a "seatless plane." The circumstance in which they found themselves and in the face of an alternative of life or death, they took that risk.

All those who lived during the war period, especially the civilians, underwent daily vicissitudes; such that made it very difficult to know whether one would survive till the following day. Because of being marked as a "rebel" against Nigeria and a "pro-Biafran" by his detractors, everything about Bishop Dominic must have been "circumscribed" in the area he lived in and operated. Consequently, he went with the force and power of a non-partisan to sternly warn all those involved in violence never to use his name again to gain popularity for themselves or try to cause him any unmerited harm through labeling. Hitherto, the federal troop as the Nigerian soldiers were called advanced rapidly from Uyo heading for Ikot Ekpene.

Bishop Ekandem was advised by his well-wishers to leave his abode in Ikot Ekpene to a more secure place. It was that advice that took him to Ediene Abak where he took refuge until the end of the war. He went to Ediene Abak where the Teachers' Training College was located in Abak Local Government Area. This was the first place that the minor seminarians who evacuated the seminary cottage at Oku Abak stayed temporarily till Afaha Obong Seminary was established. Bishop Ekandem decided to go and pitch his tent there. The ad hoc dwelling was not too far from Abak or from Loretto in Eriam where the sisters converged. The sisters had a temporary Generalate in Eriam, and Bishop Ekandem had a temporary secretariat and bishop's house at Ediene Abak. The ordinary of Ikot Ekpene who had shifted his residence to Teachers' Training College (TTC) Ediene Abak, where the present bishop of Ikot Ekpene, Most Rev. Camillus Raymond Umoh, who was an altar boy, stayed with him at the time. Meanwhile, DI was still carrying out his pastoral duty despite all the instability. Moreover, he went to Midim Parish to see how things were getting on there and to confirm the parish priest, Rev. Fr. Harris, SPS, and parishioners and strengthen them to keep faith in God while praying earnestly for peace to return. The sisters were overjoyed to see him on April 1, 1968, after many miles trekking. Theirs was a mixed joy. They soon recovered themselves and spontaneously sang together the hymn to the Blessed Virgin Mary, "The Magnificat" (My soul glorifies the Lord).[276] Shortly afterward, Bishop Ekandem celebrated the Holy Eucharist with and for them. Even in the midst of sadness, accusation, misunderstanding, and frustration, there could be some joy. Since the area was under Biafra but was peaceful again, the people could move around, but that did not affect the Igbo sisters. They moved around in Loretto compound but not in the village. They were under a semi-house arrest until word came from Gen. Yakubu Gowon that the sisters should be flown to Lagos. The preparations began promptly, but things were not as smooth as were previously envisaged.

B. The Ordeal of Evacuation

Bishop Ekandem made no delays. He moved with the speed of lighting to secure the "passes" and "military permission" for the sisters and himself to aid in the evacuation process. The process was discouraging and protracted. Mother Gertrude was not the only person to make the journey.[277] Others were involved. The journey to Lagos began by going to Oron to board a ferry to Calabar. At Oron, they met a very unfriendly soldier who refused them free passage even after having been shown the "passes," permission and authority from the general officer in charge, Adekunle Fajuyi. He was the man in charge of the amphibious brigade that took Calabar, Oron, and its environs. The soldier at the wharf refused them embarkation of the ferry. They had no alternative than to pass the night at Oron, owing to the danger of having to travel back to Eriam late that day. Meanwhile, the bishop exhorted the sisters to entrust everything to God. He remained calm himself throughout the whole journey and prayed more intensely than before. The following day, they left for Eriam.

They traveled back to Eriam in the same bus with others from the same South Eastern State. Their courage increased with imminent danger. After a week of renegotiation, the journey to Oron began again. Probably, a message had come from Adekunle to the officers at Oron. They were allowed to board the ferry to Calabar. The Igbo sisters were not to speak at all through the entire journey so as not to betray themselves and attract unnecessary embarrassment. Those who spoke Efik or Ibibio or Annang fluently without accents betraying them conversed freely with others. One thing that was not to be taken away from any of them was laughter. They could laugh but were not to talk.

The time the sisters crossed to Calabar was the period the Nigerian troops were planning an assault on Port Harcourt. The ammunitions were conveyed through Oron via Opobo. It was a moment that could not easily be forgotten. Upon arrival at Calabar, they had to report to the military headquarters before the sisters went to their convents in Calabar Road. They had a wonderful and fraternal welcome from their sisters who were separated from them for about seven months.

Mother Ignatia Bassey and Mary St. John Williams, two of the foundation members, did everything possible to help the sisters relax. Bishop Ekandem, after having made sure that the sisters were safe, went to the bishop's house to pass the night and to greet his brother, Bishop Brian D. Usanga. He spent the night in the Bishop Usanga's company.

C. The Final Lap

The following day, they went to the airport in Bishop Dominic's car driven by the bishop himself. On April 27, 1968, upon arrival at the airport, Captain Dickson refused them embarkation on the ground that the Igbos were not only rebels but also spies. After a prolonged plea, which met with refusal coupled with anxiety, tension, exhaustion, and restlessness, one of the sisters, Mary Mercy Opara, in her seventies, collapsed. It was a very trying moment. There was no medical help. Bishop Ekandem had to embark on a powerful, deeply rooted heaven-storming prayer that lasted for about thirty minutes. At the end, the sister was revived and taken back to the convent. None of the altercation seemed to touch the soldier concerned.

Following the Lord's teaching that whoever puts his hand into the plough and looks back is not fit for the kingdom of God, the bishop wasted no time going back to negotiate again. On April 29, all the sisters boarded the ammunition plane and left for Lagos. The bishop went back to Ikot Ekpene to continue his care of the flock, while the sisters had an occasion of breathing an air of freedom at Lagos. His trials during the civil war did not diminish his zeal for the flock nor reduce his determination, neither did it extinguish his spiritual fire. They were rather enriched and enlightened.

Mother General of the Handmaids during the war,
Mother Gertude Waturuocha HHCJ

D. An Avalanche of Correspondence

The mails exchanged at the time were many both within and from without. Many wrote to Mother Gertrude, who was governing from a distance but with a substitute or a delegate *en lieu de Superiore Generale*. Some of the writings will feature in subsequent pages below as the discussion continues. Some of the documents are apologetic in nature. All the same, the "work of God does itself" as St. Vincent De Paul said while addressing his confreres, "If the works he has done are works of God, as they seem to be, God must have given him His Spirit to do them. And consequently, they should be seen as God's will and accepted like manna from heaven."[278]

a. The Rectification and Withdrawal Letter of Mother Gertrude

In this letter, Mother Gertrude revisits the whole situation in the context of the war, not *itinerarium mente in Deum* but *mente in bellum*, pointing out the extraordinary circumstances that rendered everyone incapable of knowing exactly what the appropriate response was in the given circumstance. Concerning the bishop's intervention, she says that it was love for the church, the congregation, and the sisters that persuaded the bishops to act thus all for the good of the flock because they did not want any harm to come to any of the sisters. The action of the bishops made the sisters go back on their constitutions even though they knew exactly what to do, but because of *blind obedience*, they had to agree to the bishops' position.

When the bishops realized through the enlightenment of the Holy Spirit that they were intervening in the life of the sisters, they paved the way for rectification of the mistake made. Because of blind obedience, things assumed their proper order after many upheavals. The bishops were aware of what GK or Gilbert Keith Chesterton pointed out in his book, *A Short History of England*, in chapter 10: "To have a right to do a thing is not at all the same as to be right in doing it." They wanted things to work out well for all concerned.

The solidarity of the sisters manifested itself likewise their faith. The disposition of the sisters strengthened Mother Gertrude. The union of the sisters gave her the impetus to act and speak with one voice despite the troubles. The crisis situation revealed the oneness of the sisters and their love for the congregation. Their closeness to one another manifested how close God and the Providential Hand of God over them had been all these years. Mother Gertrude wrote as one enlightened by the Holy Spirit despite the seeming darkness. Here is her letter in full:

C/O Holy Child College, P.O. Box 510.
Lagos, Nigeria.
16th July 1968. J. M. J.

My dearest Sisters,

The content of the attached document were very much feared by all of us from the beginning, and all along the extraordinary happenings in our Congregation since the month of April.

We know the right course of action to take, but we had to obey! However, we must be thankful to God that the Bishops got the light to see, and the inspiration to detect and take steps to stop the great danger of arrangements contrary to our Constitutions. I think that the light and the inspiration had been given to the Bishops because of our *blind obedience* all along and in all the issues.

There could be no greater sign of God's real love and wish for our Congregation to stand and to remain what it has been from its first foundation-International, than this timely realisation by their Lordships, of the impending doom of our Beloved Congregation, a Congregation founded and supported by many unknown heroic sacrifices of our beloved Sister.

However, we do not and should never blame our always well meaning Bishops. They felt the Church, the Congregation and the personal safety of all of us were very much at stake, and as loving shepherds of these God's precious properties they acted. We all know how dear the Congregation is to their hearts, and how anxious they are to see it grow and flourish spiritually and temporally. The circumstances were too extraordinary for anybody to know the correct thing to do in a short time.

I fully realise the embarrassment which the going back to Constitutional arrangements could mean to those of us who were directly affected, but thanks be to God, these have always, been very liberal besides, have we not had enough evidence and experience to realise that THIS is our TIME,[279] planned from all eternity by our divine Lord and the Master to test our faith and love—our loyalty to the Church and the Congregation? He knows the weight and measure of the Cross He sends to each one of us, and each of us has in her own way had her measure of this Special Cross sent and meant by our Lord, for the making of each one of us and the Congregation what He would wish.

Let us continue to meet God's challenge with cheerfulness, let us refuse him nothing for it is in giving that we receive, and in obeying that we reign in and with him. The Congregation was founded in suffering obedience and excruciating detachment by our valiant Sister, so like mother must be the children.[280]

He had allowed what had happened for the purification and fertilisation of our Congregation for richer harvest of grace and virtues, like the Harmattan Wind, which sweeps through thick forests and bushes and blows away all the undesirables and purifies the land for a rich harvest. A greater future lies before our Congregation; this fact should render our crosses supportable.

I am most grateful for your letters; they have been a source of great consolation and encouragement to me. Your demonstration of love and loyalty to the Congregation must have pleased our Lord and filled our Sister with pride.

I am happy, genuinely happy, not because I am far away from you, but because God wills me to be where I am. Many of you so beautifully put in your letters bits, which have been most uplifting. Yes the will of God has no "why" especially for us who have by our religious Vow of Obedience made *total* surrender of our will to God. From all eternity He knew that the present Cross would come our way. The prayer one of you made and sent to me not long before I left Eriam, has been my constant watchword: "My God within me, let me see in all events Thy Will for me." So you see I owe you the extraordinary grace of the perfect peace which I enjoy in the midst of thorns.

Keep well and happy always. I refer you to my last Easter letter; little did I realise what was coming when I wrote that letter, but God who inspired it saw the need.

I need not tell you that my heart is with you, and how I look forward each morning to our meeting at the Table.

Keep ever close to him and see His Will in all events, big or small. Let fraternal love continue to guide us!

> With all my love and prayer.
> I remain, my dearest Sisters,
> Yours Very devotedly in J. C.
> *Mother Mary Gertrude, H.H.C.J.*
> (Superior General) A. M. D. G.

Withdrawal of Formal written Resignation from the office of the Superior General of the Congregation of the Handmaids of the Holy Child Jesus

*   *   *

At the request of His Lordship Rt. Rev. Brian D. Usanga, AG. Bishop of Calabar, and His Lordship Rt. Rev. Dominic I. Ekandem, Bishop of Ikot Ekpene, on the 8th day of July, in the year nineteen hundred sixty-eight:

I hereby withdraw my formal written Resignation from the Office of the Superior General of the above mentioned Congregation, which I tendered to the above mentioned Bishops, on the 23rd day of the month of April, in the year nineteen hundred and sixty-eight, at their formal written request.

On the 16th day on the month of July, in the year nineteen hundred and sixty-eight, the same Bishops further requested that we go back and deal with the situation in accordance with the Constitutions of our Congregation. To use their own words: "As the prevailing conditions which necessitated the action have been considerably modified, *you* have to *appoint* a *delegate*, either the Vicar General or any member of the General Council, who will be given unlimited authority to deal with all the affairs of the Congregation, in *Calabar* and *Ikot Ekpene* Dioceses, during the emergency separation of the Superior General from the Mother House; follow your Constitutions."

By the "'ACTION" is meant the Bishops' Formal written request to the Superior General to resign her Office, and their formal written request to all the Professed members of the Congregation in Calabar and Ikot Ekpene Dioceses, to elect a new Superior General or a Substitute, according to our Constitutions.

Now to deal with the situation in accordance with the Constitutions of our Congregation:

1.   The Official election by votes of a delegate for the Superior General in her absence is not in keeping with the Constitutions of our Congregation.

2. It is not in keeping with the Constitutions of our Congregation to address the delegate as "Mother General" anywhere.

3. In the absence of the Superior General from the Mother House, the Vicar General normally acts in her place, but in rare cases and for ill health, the second in office falls in.

4. So in this case Mother Mary Elizabeth Umoh, who is second in office of the Assistants General, is appointed to act for the Superior General in her absence from the Mother House, as the Vicar General, Mother Marie Therese Adude Akwanson, cannot do so owing to ill health.

5. Mother Elizabeth Umoh has authority to deal with all the affairs of the Congregation, with the General Council, in Calabar and Ikot Ekpene Dioceses.

6. In accordance with our Constitutions, substitutes for absent Assistants General are not given the title "Mother."

Copy to: Mother Mary Gertrude Waturuocha
(Superior General, H.H.C.J.)

1. His Lordship

Rt. Rev. B. D. Usanga, AG. Bishop of Calabar C/O Holy Child College, P.O. Box 510, Lagos, Nigeria. 16th July 1968.

2. His Lordship

Rt. Rev. D. I. Ekandem,
Bishop of Ikot Ekpene
Each House of the Congregation
(Calabar and Ikot Ekpene Dioceses)

The letter of Mother Gertrude exonerates the two bishops on the ground of blind obedience and their well-meaning intention. They acted in good faith irrespective of the methodology. Bad faith cannot be imputed inasmuch as good faith predominates, remembering the fact that God looks at the heart and not at the countenance or outward appearance (1 Sam. 16:7).

b.   The Accusation and Reaction of Mother Mary Elizabeth Umoh

The upheaval that arose as a result of the war situation created tensions and suspicion everywhere. Even though the external cohesion was still very strong, the internal cohesion had started giving way to misunderstandings and interpretations. To dispel them, Mother Mary Elizabeth Umoh had to write and clarify her position and put the records straight. This letter below is clarificatory and came eight days after Mother Gertrude's letter:

Convent H.H.C.J.
Eriam—Afaha Obong,
P.O. Box 24 Abak.24 July 1969.

Ikoyi.
P.O. Box 510, Lagos.

Dearest Rev. Mother,

I meant to write this letter much earlier but all the -same I hope you will accept it in good faith.

In April 1968, due to the unforeseen and rather unfortunate circumstances brought about by the current crises, I was officially asked, for the interest of the Congregation and of the basis, to hold your office in South Eastern State on temporary basis, until situations improved. Your letter of authority and confirmation and authority refers.

Since then, circumstances have changed, thanks be to God, and I am happy it was possible for you to assume your former position in the entire Congregation. This being the case, I wish to inform you that I have decided to discontinue holding the office of Acting Superior General in the South Eastern State as it no longer serves *any practical* purpose.

I shall still serve our dear Congregation as before in my first and present office of Assistant General, and as an interested member of this family of God.

Thanking you for your kindness and begging your prayers and blessing.

I remain,

Your Loving and grateful child in J.C.

———————————————

Mother Mary Elizabeth Umoh H.H.C.J.

Copies to:

1.   The Houses H.H.C.J. S.E.S.

2.   His Lordship Most Rev. Bishop B. D. Usanga, Acting Bishop of Calabar.

3.   His Lordship, Most Rev. Bishop D. I. Ekandem, Bishop of Ikot Ekpene.

For your information please.

———————————————

Mother Mary Elizabeth Umoh H.H.C.J.

This letter predates her analysis of the prewar, war, and post-war situations. It explains her becoming the acting superior general. It could be conjectured that she refused to take up the post not because she would have been incapable of carrying out the task the role demanded but because she did not want anyone to see it as usurping the position a more qualified person. Mother Marie Therese Akwe, the vicar general, would have occupied or incur accusation of ethnicism, which was in the air during the intervention of the bishops. It is likely that no one explained immediately why Mother M. Therese refused to assume the responsibility that she was constitutionally eligible to hold but because of ill health and the need to travel to Ireland for treatment; she declined the post. Even though what Mother Elizabeth Umoh was afraid of in the congregation later smoldered as rumor that was destructive both to the congregation and to Bishop Ekandem still moved on in good faith. The write-up of Mother Elizabeth Umoh cleared the gloomy atmosphere likewise the unsavory odor that pervaded the congregation and the entire environment and persons living around. The situation became clearer in the letter of Mother Mary Gertrude that served a dual purpose of elucidating the truth and eliminating falsehood.

E. Various Interpretations of the Situation Akin to a Character Assassination

St. Paul's writing to the Philippians from Rome said that some preached Christ from envy and rivalry, out of partisanship, so as to cause more troubles for him while others preached out of genuine love and from good will, that his joy was that Christ was preached all the same whether in pretense or in truth (Phil. 1:15–19). The role of Bishop Ekandem and, subsequently, Bishop Usanga in relation to the sisters and the entire congregation has evoked very many contradictory reactions coupled with deliberate and malicious misrepresentations and interpretations intended to damage the reputation of the bishop.

The excuse was the supposed principle of *qui tacit consentire* (silence means consent). Such a position is unacceptable because it fails to distinguish a deliberate and culpable silence from a wise decision to withhold comments when a decision is uncertain.

Nwosuh churns out myriads of questions in an attempt to posit the problem of ethnicity and tribalism as the basic backdrop of the letter of Bishop Ekandem and Bishop Usanga that called for the resignation of the legitimately elected superior general.[281] The imposition of tribalism and ethnicity coupled with the proposal to convoke a General Chapter when it was not due and in the midst of the war period that led to the disagreement of the sisters and backpedaling of Bishop Ekandem[282] does not only insinuate but also presumes a premeditated situation that tantamount to uprooting exercise while maintaining the appearance of continuity. Bishop Ekandem would never have "backtracked" if he was as full of himself as the writer claims. It is the man with genuine simplicity and humble spirit that acknowledges his mistakes and retraces his steps. He never claimed to be perfect since God only is perfect (Cf. Matt. 5:48).

The man full of himself can never do that because of pomposity and the attempt to cover his tracks or blur the situation. When Bishop Ekandem became aware that the time of General Chapter was not the right time when the sisters reacted, he withdrew from that position and added as a postscript, which the sisters should do it in the best way possible and according to their own rules. There was no imposition of any kind. That is the man of substance. The worst thing in life is to make mistake and not realize that it is a mistake and die with it, that is stupidity, but the man who knows that he knows not is a wise man, for it is in dying that one rises to life.

Those who claim that Bishop Ekandem was tribalistic in his approach are the very ones who are tribalistic but transfer that accusation on that great man even though he did more than he spoke or said. There was no need of forcing defects on this soft-spoken, compassionate, and humble man who was ready to serve yet ready to challenge and correct injustice or work against it for the sake of the poor or relieve the people living in poverty with the sole aim of uplifting them. He was like a lamb led to the slaughterhouse that opened not his lips, and in his humiliation, justice was denied him (Cf. Is. 53:7). His motto, *In Cruce Salus*, molded and remolded him like the potter that Prophet Jeremiah was ordered to go to in Jeremiah 18:1 ff in such a manner that followed in the footsteps of Christ hung upon the Cross yet alive to give life to the world.

Bishop Ekandem always arbitrated in conflict situations and made himself available to both young and old. He never sought for a crossless religion[283]; otherwise, he would never have adopted *In Cruce Salus* as his episcopal motto that portrays him both as a priest and as a victim like

Christ himself. The Cross implied for him the Crucifix, which reminds the world of eternal love that is so extravagant as to shed his blood for the forgiveness of sins of the whole world. In this light, conversion is ever necessary for renewal.

As a bridge mender, he never withdrew any day from his children. Owing to the fact that he embodied the beatitudes in his life, "Blessed are the poor in spirit for theirs is the kingdom of heaven," he never allowed poverty or riches to divert his attention from the right path. He was indifferent to poverty while choosing to be poor in a situation he could have been rich. The same spirit of indifference to poverty or riches characterized his auxiliary, Most Rev. Silas Obot, the bishop of Idah who at death was discovered to have only seventeen thousand Naira (N 17,000) in his account (equivalent to one hundred Euros only). This is something totally incredible to modern readers in the age of materialism and secularism. Bishop Ekanem preferred poverty to riches like his Master Jesus Christ. "Blessed are the meek for they shall inherit the earth" (Matt. 5:4). His meekness, simplicity, and humility were bound together to generate a down-to-earth person who looked for the good and convenience of the other more than he sought it for himself. "Blessed are the peacemakers for they shall be called children of God" (Matt. 5:9). He always sought for peace and promoted it with all his heart, with all his being, and with all his strength. This is what the traditional rulers perceived and conferred on him the title of chief or king of peace, *Obong Emem.*

He left no stone unturned; in other words, he did whatever was within his power to be done when it came to seeking for peace and in resolving conflicts. He was never afraid of conflict, but he never preferred conflict to peace. "Blessed are the merciful for they shall obtain mercy" (Matt. 5:7). He felt very uncomfortable in the face of suffering of others while he did not regard his own suffering as anything important. He was not a stoic but simply preferred the greatest good to the greatest number of people or as St. Paul says, "Always consider the other person as being better than yourself, so that nobody thinks of his own interests first but everybody thinks of others interests instead" (Phil. 2:3–4).[284] In other words, always consider others first before considering yourself. This breeds altruism instead of egotism.

F. Refusal to Compromise with Conscience

Bishop Ekandem was adamant when it came to truth, the teachings of the church and the pope, justice, and right of the poor. He was so obedient and docile to the church; her leader, the pope; and the sacrament par excellence—the Most Holy Eucharist that nothing could separate him from the love of God (Rom. 8:35 ff). As a human being, he had his fears, but he never permitted such human fears to jeopardize his relationship with his God. When the criticisms bombarded him, that could have been the time to give up, but he didn't because he knew that history would blame him all the more as Eleazar said in the face of pretense (2 Macc. 6:1 ff) if he did not safeguard the lives of the sisters from Igboland by giving them the opportunity of going to safety. He was not intending to become a shadow of the unfulfilled dreams of the people but remained himself. In other words, he was authentic so as to become a revelation of the real selves of those who were seeking his conformity to their expectations and behavior. Many a man or woman sells his or her conscience to conform to the expectations and opinions of others instead of clinging on to the truth he or she is conscientiously convinced of and conforming to the will of God that liberates and gives authenticity. Truth, authenticity, and conviction give way to love of God and neighbor.

> Others have no right to demand that I be anything else than what I ought to be in the sight of God. No greater thing could possibly be asked of a man than this! This one just expectation, which I am bound to fulfil, is precisely the one they usually do not expect me to fulfil. They want me to be what I am in their sight: that is, an extension of themselves. They do not realise that if I am fully myself, my life will become the completion and the fulfilment of their own, but that if I merely live as their shadow, I will serve only to remind them of their own unfulfilment.[285]

The capacity to withstand pressure in times of great difficulty is the courage of faith exhibited by ardent followers of God. This can only be learned at the foot of the Cross. Bishop Ekandem would have failed very woefully if he did not save the lives of the sisters. After all, when Moses led the people of Israel out of Egypt, was it not in the midst of difficulties, traumatic experiences, and sufferings, yet all these took place so that they could inherit the Promised Land, which had to be won through warfare? Victory is always achieved with a great price. No Cross, No Crown.

G. Mother Elizabeth Umoh's Document and Defense Entitled "The HHCJ Before, During and After the Nigeria/Biafra Civil War"

Congregation of the Handmaids of the Holy Child Jesus Before, During and After the Nigeria/Biafra Civil War 10th July–15th January 1970

Written by Mary Elizabeth Umoh, HHCJ, Delegated to Act for Mother Mary Gertrude, HHCJ

The Congregation of the Holy Child Jesus is the first Indigenous Congregation in Nigeria. One of her outstanding characteristics is **Unity in Diversity**. Her Foundress was Mother Mary Charles Magdalene Walker of happy memory: English by birth and religious of Irish Sisters of Charity. She started the Congregation of the HHCJ with four foundation members of different countries, tribes[286] and background. They were:

1. Mother Mary St. John William of the Republic of Cameroon
2. Mother Ignatia Bassey of Calabar-Nigeria
3. Mother Mary Aloysius Uguaru of Umuahia in Abia State, Nigeria
4. Mother Mary Gertrude Watuouacha [sic] of Nguru in Imo State-Nigeria

As religious, they served God in peace and in unity. On 28th December 1959, the Congregation hitherto, under the Sisters of the Holy Child Jesus SHCJ held her first General Chapter to elect her Superior General. Mother Mary Gertrude Waturuocha, the fourth of the Foundation

Members was elected the first Superior General. Thus the Congregation gained independence.

With God's grace and trust in Divine Providence, Mother Mary Gertrude and her Council aimed at keeping the Congregation one in spite of initial hardships experienced by the first members. While the Foundress, Mother Mary Charles Magdalene Walker lived in Calabar, the Mother House since 1923; she opened Convent HHCJ in Anua on 9th July 1929. Other houses were opened at Edem Ekpat, Ifuho, Asong, Ndon Ebom where Foundation Members worked. After the Congregation's independence in 1959, other houses were opened in different parts of Nigeria and (in) other African Countries; such (houses) are: Cameroon, Ghana, Togoland, Sierra Leone giving the Congregation *Before the actual war started* (an international character). Rumours mounted all over the country. Sisters (SHCJ) from foreign countries left Ifuho, later on Nigeria. There was unrest in Institutions like University of Ibadan. At a stage all HHCJ were asked to make up their mind individually either to stay on the Convent or be released to go home and come back after the war if they so wished. I know of only one Handmaid who left. After the war! saw her in a habit of another Congregation: I heard[287].

Parents were worried about their children in school. Tension mounted higher following the decision of the national leaders, "On Oburi [sic] we stand" with the first drop of bump [sic] in Gakem in Ogoja, Government gave orders to close schools in South Eastern State on 10th July, 1967.

On that very day 10th July 1967, many of our students in Loretto Girls Grammar School (now Loretto Girls Juniorate) Made their First Holy Communion, some of them were in their white dress and veil taking photograph when the message came. Thus the school closed abruptly on 10th July 1967.

During the War

When "Biafran" Soldiers began to retreat from Oron/ Uyo area to Aba area, Ifuho Convent was closed down. The Holy Child Sisters had already left to their own countries. The Novice Mistress decided to carry the Novices to Urua Inyang Catholic Mission with almost all the movable property in Ifuho Novitiate. A poor cripple Mma Theresa Essien also went with them. Unfortunately going to Urua Inyang so far away across a river, seemed more dangerous than staying near Ifuho.

The Superior General Mother Mary Gertrude Waturuocha and her Council came to stay at Loretto Girls Grammar School Eriam Afaha Obong, with Sr. Mary Elizabeth Umoh, a Councillor too. Ifuho and Ikot Ekpene became dangerous zones, because of air raids and shootings.

The General Council decided that our drivers should go to Urua Inyang and bring to Eriam the Novice Mistress and all the Novices with her. Thanks to God, all of them and the Sisters who went to Urua Inyang with via Okon were brought to Eriam through Etim Ekpo. As soon as they crossed Etim Ekpo River, retreating Biafran Soldiers blew down the bridge.

Sisters-Refugees in Loretto Eriam

Eriam Convent was by now cut off from Ikot Ekpene town, Uyo, Oron Calabar, Etinan. Civil War is such a terrible thing cutting off brother from brother as such, we were separated physically from other Sisters in the country. Later on, Calabar, Etinan, Oron areas were liberated[288] using (the) war expression; Abak was our only safe town.

Sister Mary Elizabeth Umoh, the Principal of Loretto Girls Grammar School, a member of the General Council and Local Superior, together with her young companion hosted the Superior General and the Council and all the Sisters refugees. There were altogether thirty-three (33) Sisters. Since there have been good relationship between the Sisters and the Village, the head of the village made a promise that he and Eriam Villagers will protect all the Sisters from danger as far as they were concerned. They kept this promise to the letter.

By this time Uyo area, Oron, Calabar were quite safe. Eriam was very much threatened by air raids that used to bomb part of Ikot Ekpene and Central Annang. Military planes used to reverse in Eriam compound shelling and shooting increased as soldiers moved into Central Annang. As situations grew worse in the villages around, people who were nearer to the war front began to move in groups. Nigerians as a whole (those in the "liberated" areas) became more conscious of the Sisters who came (from) non-Efik Speaking areas. The Civil War did not affect the Congregational unity of the Handmaids of the Holy Child Jesus. Instead love and concern increased. The Novice Mistress and all the Novices went to our Convent in Ghana to continue their formation.

Since the war affected our Ibo [sic] and Efik Speaking Sisters geographically, at this time when the war front was very near to Eriam, steps were taken to protect the Sisters more. The two Bishops: Bishop Dominic Ekandem (later on Dominic Cardinal Ekandem) of Ikot Ekpene Diocese and Bishop Brian David Usanga of Calabar Province decided, as Mother Mary Gertrude Waturuocha, the Superior General told us, to move our Ibo [sic] Sisters away from South Eastern State to Holy Child Convent, Obalende, Lagos.

Acting Superior General

One day in 1968, Mother Mary Gertrude Waturuocha-Superior General, and Mother Marie-Theresa [sic] AkweVicar General were in the enclosure of the veranda of the first building in Eriam Loretto House discussing matters. Present with them were: Sister Mary Joseph Okpo-Principal of St. Theresa's Secondary (School), Edem Ekpat and Superior of Edem Ekpat Convent and Sister Esther Ogugo, who was a student in the University of Cork, Ireland. She had visited Edem Ekpat and accompanied Sr. Mary Joseph to Eriam. Mother Mary Gertrude called me—Sr. Mary Elizabeth Umoh in. After sitting down, she told me that they had something serious to discuss with me. She then told me that the two Bishops: Bishop Dominic Ekandem of Ikot Ekpene Diocese and Bishop Brian Usanga of Calabar Diocese had discussed with her about the safety of our Ibo Sisters in Eriam. It would seem certain people had disclosed that the Principal of Loretto was hiding Sisters in the Convent. The Bishops thought it safer to transfer the Superior General and other Ibo Sisters at Eriam to Holy Child's Convent, Obalende, Lagos. Sr. Mary Elizabeth already a member of the Council, to act for Superior General, during the period she would be in Lagos.

Re: Action

Sr. Mary Elizabeth Umoh [sic] was so shocked to hear of such a situation and rejected the idea immediately, she told Mother Mary Gertrude that in her absence, the Vicar General, Mother Marie-Theresa Akwe should act according to our Constitutions, better still, a non- Nigerian. Many Sisters agreed that she should act, Mother Marie-Theresa bluntly refused to act, in spite of pleading, she refused to act.

Mother Mary Gertrude, Mother Marie Theresa, Sr. Mary Joseph Okpo and Sisters [sic] Esther, jointly begged Sister Elizabeth to act as she had held out in the past when Mother was very sick and her vicar was away in Ireland. When Mother Gertrude wanted to kneel down, Sister Mary Elizabeth stopped her and told her that if it was the only thing that would save our Sisters, she should think about it. Meanwhile word had reached Mother St. John who was at Calabar that Sister Elizabeth Umoh had refused to act for the Superior General. Mother St. John wrote to Sister Mary Elizabeth through Agnes Afangide (Miriam). She encouraged Sister Elizabeth to accept the situation as a sacrifice. Sister Mary Elizabeth thought that Mother Mary Gertrude would take her to the two Bishops but she did not. Neither Bishop Ekandem nor Bishop Usanga ever said anything to Sister Mary Elizabeth about the Situation and the idea of Acting Superior General for Mother Mary Gertrude.

Assembly of Sisters at Convent H.H.C.J. Itak

Mother Mary Gertrude, the Superior General, and Council invited the Sisters to Itak for a special meeting. All the Sisters were informed of Acting for the Superior General. There again the Vicar General refused to Act. At this point Sister Mary Elizabeth was *forced*[289] *to act for Mother Mary (Gertrude)*.

Military Entry Into Eriam Convent[290]

Whenever the soldiers entered a town or village the inhabitants were said to be "liberated". Some youths would help the soldiers to carry bags or follow in procession as if for a village play, such was the picture of a procession that was passing to Afaha Obong junction from Eriam. The Sisters including Mother Gertrude, the Superior General were praying in the Chapel before the Blessed Sacrament. The Chief of the Village came in and addressed all the Sisters with words of con-

solation. Shortly after this heavily-armed soldiers slipped from a long procession form [sic] by (the) villagers. They cut through the school playing field towards the building where the Sisters were praying. Sr. Elizabeth Umoh and the Village Head Tom Udo Udo, went out to meet them, the leader drew near and when he was told that Reverend Sisters were praying he became calm and assured the Sisters of safety, he begged for their prayers.

Transfer of Sisters to Lagos

Bishop Ekandem and Bishop Usanga made transport arrangement for the transfer of our Ibo Sisters to Lagos. Mother Mary Gertrude Waturuocha wrote a letters [sic] of Authority to act for her to Sr. Mary Elizabeth Umoh and addressed the same to all the Communities in South Eastern State.

On the day of departure, Bishop Ekandem, Sr. Mary Elizabeth Umoh in company with other Sisters, escorted the Superior General—Mother Mary Gertrude to Oron *enroute* Calabar—Lagos. It was a sad separation; the consolation was that it was only for a while.

Communication with the Superior General

Even though Mother Mary Gertrude the Superior General had left for Lagos, Communication in writing still continued. Examples of such letters to her are those of 5th June 1969 and 24th July 1969, from her we got those of 23rd[291] November 1969 and of January 10th 1970. Since, (Sr.) Mary Elizabeth Umoh made a special journey with war plane carrying wounded soldiers to Lagos to visit the Superior General and Sisters. They had settled down and seemed happier and more comfortable than those in the "War front". Members of the Council and others wrote letters and were anxious about the Sisters in Lagos. Solidarity was still very strong. As war progressed towards Ukana, Ekpenyong Attai [sic], and Central Annang, refugees increased in our compound. The Minor Seminary at Afaha Obong was closed, and the Seminarians were asked to come to Loretto because the soldiers had occupied their school compound. The Seminarians after overcoming their initial feelings of strangeness gradually fitted in with the girls.[292]

School as Refugees

As more refugees raised [sic] from Eriam school Compound, it became unsafe to keep the students. Bishop Ekandem advised that we moved to St. Mary's T. T. C. Compound, Ediene Abak. Mr. Ayakem, the Principal, kindly admitted us, so that the Bishop, Rev. Fr. Patrick Essien with him, the Sisters and the Students were all Refugees. There were twenty five (25) boys with us. We organised ourselves in such a way that our stay at Ediene became joyful, we formed a beautiful choir which sang during our daily morning mass. The Sisters managed and controlled both the girls' and boys' quarters. It was a testing opportunity for those who aspired to become either priests or religious. The Students behaved very well, where we were assured of safety in Eriam, we went back to School after four months. Refugees went back as their areas were liberated.

The Seminary Re-opened and the boys went back to their Compound.

General Effects of the War

Besides loss of innocent lives, the Civil War brought great disaster to many in the Country especially in the areas that actually faced the gun, many parents[293] were forced to abandon some of their children as they ran away for safety, and families were forced to separate. Some husbands were forced to abandon their wives to armed soldiers. Mass destruction occurred and we owe gratitude to the Church and charitable Organizations such as Caritas, Red Cross Society, religious Organizations and other helpers, some soldiers were very kind and generous to the poor civilians. Mother Mary Vianney of the Society of the Holy Child Jesus came out alone to Nigerian [sic] from America with the Red Cross Society. In the Congregation of the Handmaids of the Holy Child Jesus, we cannot forget the wonderful care given to refugees and orphans in Anua by Sr. Mary Veronica Enang. Soldiers brought abandoned Children in the bush and other places to Anua Convent. Sister Mary Veronica and other Sisters took care of them. In general the War period gave us, extra-ordinary opportunity for human-itarian acts.

End of War

The Civil War ended on 15th January 1970. It ended abruptly so that while the signal for end of war was given, some soldiers were still fighting until messages we [sic] sent. Orphans in Anua were taken to Ifuho Convent, Sr. Lucy Ekwere looked after them. Cardinal Ekandem built an Orphanage for the children. Late Sr. Mary Stephen Inyang, and Sr. Mary Gabriel Akpan looked after them. Sr. Mary Rosario Umoh continued this good work. All the orphans have settled down in life—some are graduates. Besides work among orphans, some Sisters went to Ihiala to collect refugees from South Eastern State. They distributed bread as they went along the roads in Ibo lands. We visited families of our Sisters in Ututu.

War Blessings and Manifestation to the Congregation of the Handmaids of the Holy Child Jesus[294]

Those who have strong faith have seen the many good things God has manifested to the Congregation during and after the Civil War.

1. Throughout the war period no Handmaid was killed or died in the enter[295] [sic] Congregation.
2. Love and unity grew stronger
3. War ended on 15th January 1970 and after some period, the Superior General-Mother Mary Gertrude came back to the Generalate at Ifuho to continue her work.

At this point I like to clarify a few areas for the sake of those who had misconceptions about acting for the Superior General during the war and her absence from the Generalate.

1. The Civil War was between Nigeria and a section of the Country called "Biafra" but not in the Congregation of the Handmaids of the Holy Child Jesus where love, peace and unity reigned.
2. Bishop Dominic Ekandem and Bishop Brian David Usanga moved us 160 Sisters to Lagos in good faith for the Sisters' own safety.
3. That none of the two Bishops ever consulted Sr. Mary Elizabeth Umoh or make known to her the matter of acting for the Superior General.

4. She heard of it for the first time when Mother Mary Gertrude called her as said above. The "acting" Superior General had absolutely nothing to do with usurpation of one's office. See Mother's Letter of 16th July 1968 to Communities. As we continue to count our war Blessings we remember that we owe our **Pontifical Status** of the Congregation granted by Pope Paul VI in 1971 to the Unity in Diversity, which existed in the Congregation.[296]

To the two Bishops, Dominic Cardinal Ekandem of Ikot Ekpene Diocese, Bishop Brian David Usanga—Bishop of Calabar and to the Sisters who were ready to stick out their necks for the safety of their Superior General and other Sisters should need for the supreme service arise (we are grateful to Divine Providence).

The Congregation has grown in strength and numbers, to reach Provincialisation[297]. We have every reason to thank God for increase of vocation after the war. Among the girls who were with us as refugees in Eriam, seven became Sisters including 2 refugees. Among the 25 boys, 12 became Priest [sic] one of whom is a Bishop. Many Missions have been established such as in England, Germany, Kenya, U. S. A., Italy, and Canada. Sisters are mixed and sent out to many parts of Nigeria paid [sic] foreign countries. Unity in Diversity Continues and is stronger after the War and Provincialisation. We owe our survival to Divine Providence and our generous sisters.

May God be praised now and forever more.

Why Did Vicar General Not Take Over in the Absence of the Superior General?

The Vicar General Marie Theresa Akwe who should have acted on behalf of the Superior General and in accordance with the Constitutions of the Handmaids of the holy Child Jesus could not carry out that mandate of delegation for **health reasons** as hinted in the letter of the Mother Gertrude Waturuocha, the Superior General. Sr. Elizabeth Umoh who was one of the Assistants General was delegated in the letter of 16th July 1968 to act on behalf of the Superior General, Mother Mary Gertrude Waturuocha. This letter was sent to all the Local Communities in South Eastern State.

That question answers itself and extricates both Bishop Dominic Ekandem and Bishop Brian David Usanga likewise Sr. Elizabeth Umoh who was purported to have ganged up (had been in collusion) with Efik Speaking Sisters and usurped the powers of the Mother General at the insinuation, imposition and insistence of the two late Bishops.

Mother Mary Elizabeth Umoh HHCJ,
Delegated to Act for the Superior General in S.E.S.

The foregoing portrays Mother Mary Elizabeth Umoh as a solid, undaunted Handmaid of the Holy Child Jesus Congregation whose horizon was never woolly nor blurred concerning the goal of her congregation or the country and beyond where clash of interest was at stake. She stood her ground when she was under pressure to deviate from what she stood for. The following is recorded in her funeral brochure:

> In 1956, she was given the Eastern Nigeria Scholarship to study more on education in St. Mary's Teacher Training College, Fenham, Newcastle Upon Tyne 4, England. As part of her study, she visited schools in North of England, Sunderland where she experienced the Montessori Method. The Ministry of Education London sent her a letter of appointment to remain and teach but she declined the offer. In her own words: *"I told them that I was on Nigerian Scholarship and that I owed the government of Nigeria service and that my superior needed me back."*[298]

She was straightforward in her dealing with the congregation and the hierarchy of the church, her Superior; the nation; and the international community. Even though she was a simple handmaid, she was a groomed handmaid of the Lord who held on to her fiat as Mary, her model, did. She decided to leave behind this monumental document that contradicted the supposed poisonous atmosphere that prevailed.

She penned a few facts in a simple way. Her intention was not "apologetics" as such but a clarification of facts that could have been forgotten. The clarification exonerated both Bishop Ekandem of Ikot Ekpene

Diocese, South Eastern State, during the Nigerian/Biafran Civil War, and the auxiliary bishop, Brian David Usanga, of Calabar Diocese, South Eastern State. She has succeeded in eliminating two birds with one stone. Her desire to straighten facts and put things in the proper light tallies with Bishop Dominic's total and open embrace of all.

The bishop recalled his fondness of his schoolmates. He remembered his contemporaries and the jokes and friendship they used to share. All his friends at the time were the Igbo brothers since there was no other person from his Ibibio tribe or region.[299] The comment about his contemporaries, jokes, and friendship is a happy prognostication of his social relationship with all and sundry as he grew from strength to strength and from one stage of life and apostolate in the hierarchy of the church to the other. He could not have been so friendly to his Igbo friends and turned round to hate the sisters at the same time. He used to go and spend his holidays with his friend Monsignor Meze. This was one of those friends whose company he particularly enjoyed.

Fr. Cosmas Nwosuh, MSP testifies to this when he states:

> Bishop Ekandem, in contrast was an introvert and reticent. He was regal and grave. In speech he was highly taciturn, simple and unpretentious lacking the bombastic and flowery style of his younger confrere. Bishop Ekandem valued and greatly respected the educated…, Ekandem was both expansive and inclusive. He cultivated a reputation for himself as one who built bridges across ethnic, racial, and creedal [sic] divides. He championed unifying causes and projects.[300]

It is difficult to be a bridge mender and builder and, at the same time, work against a particular ethnic group, the Igbos. It is precisely because of this sterling quality that Rome appointed him to be the very first administrator and bishop of Abuja as an independent mission and later as a diocese and archdiocese.

Bishop Godfrey Mary Paul Okoye, CSSp, who later became the founder of the Daughters of Divine Love Congregation, was a very close friend of his. He was one of the first bishops who received him very warmly in Enugu after the consistory that designated Bishop Dominic Ekandem as Dominic Cardinal Ekandem. It is presumed that the author did not intend any misrepresentation but could have been a serious mistake or an oversight. He used to go and spend time with Monsignor Meze of Enugu. The pair got on very well and enjoyed the company of each other.

Fr. Cosmas Nwosuh, MSP, a great historian, has done a wonderful exposé of the life and works and involvement of the cardinal from the point of view of evangelization of the nation to the growth of the Catholic Church, the various institutions, and religious developments in general. He views everything through the prism of the cardinal as the number one Christian in Nigeria. It is a work that he has put in a great deal. He has traveled far and wide, consulted many people, visited many an archive, and perused innumerable libraries both public and private to obtain the pieces of information he pieced together to produce this monumental work on Cardinal Ekandem, the founder of the Missionaries of St. Paul, which Fr. Cosmas K. O. Nwosuh, MSP is a member.

Time and talent have been immensely put into this work. It is all to the glory of God and a worthy congratulations to Father Cosmas. His chapter on the cardinal and the Handmaids of the Holy Child Jesus has made series of revelations, but there are certain facts that demand a careful examination as well as interrogation of some of those facts and assumptions presented. The sarcastic manner of presenting the cardinal smeared dirt not only on the cardinal as such but also on him as a beneficiary of the fruits of the cardinal's achievements likewise his entire congregation. Objectivity is important, but prudence, which is a concomitant of wisdom, is much more desirable and upheld. Prudence and wisdom cannot reign without examining the facts properly in their contexts so as not to give a one-sided view of a situation.

H.   Memories of Bishop/Cardinal Ekandem by some Who Knew Him

Some religious have decided to share their memories of the person of Cardinal Ekandem with those who will read this work. The depth of encouragement, paternal love, compassion, nonexclusivity, outreach, spirituality, collaboration, and use of very apt images abound. Some of the memories that portray the person of the bishop of Ikot Ekpene Diocese and later as an administrator of Port Harcourt and eventually as the pioneer superior and bishop of Abuja feature in this section. This subsection presents some voices that reflect the person of Dominic Cardinal Ekandem as an open person ready to welcome others in the spirit of the early church. What all who knew him record about the ordinary of Ikot Ekpene is his closeness to the religious, his personal view of them, and the depth of love toward them, respect of their sanctity and dedication coupled with his prayer life. He never viewed the religious except in the light of the religious par excellence, the Blessed Virgin Mary.

There are many who have wonderful memories of Bishop/Cardinal Ekandem. One of them is Mother Mary Joseph Okpo, HHCJ who highlighted the care and love he showed to the sisters during the war and the risks he took to visit them and the joy experienced by the sisters after the entry of the Nigerian soldiers into Eriam Community. The sisters spontaneously sang "The Magnificat" in praise of God for his wonders. Her personal note about Bishop Ekandem bears witness to the bishop's closeness to the sisters and his paternal love. A lot is noted above about her perception of Bishop Ekandem, her admiration of him as a seasoned prelate and selfless servant of God. There is no need to repeat such points here. They have been elaborated above. He personally cared for his priests and the family of his priests as a lone male voice, Very Rev. Fr. Paul Roche, CM, remembers him at prayer beside a dying very close fellow worker.

The various voices of the sisters testifying to this go a long way to attest to his unbounded love despite one pastoral blunder that expressed love more than hatred. The voices speak for themselves.

Sr. Theresa Nwanruo, the very first female religious to work in Abuja Independent Mission shares her memory[301] of Bishop/ Cardinal Ekandem's perception in terms of his deep love, hospitality, appreciation of the religious and close collaboration with them.

Sr. Regina Essiet portrays the cardinal as seeing the female religious as a treasure and as those who need to be constantly happy. In this little memorial, the amiable capacity of the cardinal is very clear toward all the religious and not just to the handmaids alone. Sr. Mary Tuku exemplifies him as getting to the depth of religious perception of linking the religious with the Blessed Virgin Mary and her capacity to recall what the cardinal said to her and others when they were to begin their mission in the independent mission. She underscored the seriousness with which the cardinal presented the Abuja mission that necessitated the planting of the seed of faith. Here, his faith perception is brought to bear. Sr. Lucy Afangide brings out his vision, generosity, and closeness to the sisters in general. Sr. Regina Tombere recollects the impression that the cardinal made on his parishioners during his first year of apostolate—his capacity to call each sister by name. Sr. Mary Anne exhumed from the archive his perception and appreciation of the religious from his interaction with the sisters during the publication of the book on the foundress and during the golden anniversary. Sr. Juliana Ekerete portrays him as a man of rare qualities. Also leaning on Justice Aniagolu brought out the sacrificial life of the cardinal as a good shepherd willing to lay down his life for his flock:

a.   Our dear Cardinal

Our Father in Faith was a gracious man, lived graciously and died same.

The gracious man used such words to address religious such that those who were not happy were encouraged to live up to it; "my dear daughter, what can I do to make you happy, just tell me; are you hungry? Who caused you pain? You are my treasure, my precious one if I can have more of your type, I will be a happy man. Mbokpo mi! I missed you so much, never stay so long without my seeing you. You are my future hope and that of the Church. Keep together, love one another and pray always for me". I put you in the chalice at every Mass. My comfort, my princess, I love you and God and Edisana Eka (The Holy Mother) love you too. God bless you my dear child. May his gracious soul rest in peace.

Sr. Regina Ebukidiok Essiet, HHCJ Generalate of the Handmaids of Holy Child Jesus, Ifuho, Ikot Ekpene, Akwa Ibom State, Nigeria.

b.   One Memory of Late Dominic Cardinal Ekandem

My first encounter with Dominic Cardinal Ekandem was as a very young girl in 1967. I was just contemplating being a religious Sister after my Secondary School Education. He was the first Bishop I ever came close to. Earlier, I saw Bishop James Moynagh, SPS, who resided in Calabar but came to my parish—St. Paul's at Ututu, Arochukwu LGA, Abia State, from time to time to confer the Sacrament of Confirmation on deserving candidates. I was one of the lucky ones.

Precisely in January 1967, I went to Ikot—Ekpene, the Headquarters of the Handmaids of the Holy Child Jesus (HHCJ) and then met Bishop Dominic Ekandem the then Bishop of Ikot—Ekpene Diocese as a Postulant.

Bishop Dominic Ekandem had a special paternal love for all of us desiring to be Rev. Sisters at our tender age. He had endearing names for us such as "Mbopo" especially if you were robust like some of us. Mbopo in Efik means a well fattened lady prepared for marriage.

I had great respect for Bishop Ekandem. All the Sisters found him very approachable. Bishop Ekandem even as a Cardinal would never let any Sister go away without having the opportunity of seeing him, even if it was siesta time. He would send message to the Sister to wait for him and when he met with her, he would treat her as a queen, giving her the warm feeling that she is the only person he had to see that day. If you made a move to go, he would say "wait". Without seeking the assistance of his servant, he would take you to the dining table, bring out some drinks, biscuits, etc, by himself and would sit down with you to entertain you, and unless he was informed that another visitor was around to see him, he would wait until the Sister was ready to go.[302]

Humility

I admired His Eminence for his great humility. Once when he was named the Archbishop of Abuja Mission, he gave me a ride from Ikot—Ekpene to Abuja. Around Lokoja, he said, "My dear, let's stop and see what my cook packed in the food flask. I hope it will be good enough for you. You deserve something very nice as my Mbopo" I blushed, I thought it was a flattery. But when we stopped, he insisted I be served first and added much more for me.

On a personal note I saw Cardinal Ekandem as a man of God, who placed high premium on virtuous life. He was always concerned about me maintaining a high standard of virtue in my religious life and never to allow anything to interfere with my Vows. I am sure he was concerned about other religious women too, because when I lived close to his house at Ikot—Ekpene, Sisters would often visit him for counselling and sometimes

Michael I. Edem CM

he would tell me "Mbopo, Sister so or so will be coming to visit. Take good care of her. I won't be back from my trip by then." Such visitor would stay in our Convent for a while before leaving. He was very concerned about Sisters who encountered problems in their vocation and paid special attention to those who left the religious Life. He would counsel and help settle them by getting them some jobs or even be involved in teaching.

He was very interested in our spiritual growth. As pioneer Sisters in Abuja, even though we were only two then, Sr. Mary Tuku and I, he appointed late Fr. John McGuiness to be our Confessor and Spiritual Director.

Generosity

Dominic Cardinal Ekandem (then Bishop) was also quite supportive. I remember when he visited us at FCDA, Federal Capital Development Authority, Life Camp where we started life in Abuja. He gave us forty naira which was good money in the 1980's. He never came to Abuja without giving us some gifts in cash or kind, albeit small, but we appreciated it because his Diocese was a rural one and not very prosperous.

Collaborative Ministry[303]

Dominic Cardinal Ekandem had a high sense of appreciation for collaborative ministry. He appreciatedt he work of Sisters especially the pioneering Sisters because Abuja was not an easy place to be in those days. He encouraged us in our different apostolates and wasf ull of praises for whatever we did well.

In a personal note, he had great respect for me and this was reciprocal. He always saw me as a great woman while I saw nothing great that I had done. He wrote to me quite often and encouraged me in my religious life. I so appreciate those letters that I still have a number of them. His letters always made me feel good, appreciated and encouraged to work harder in God's vineyard.

HIS DEMISE

When I heard that Dominic Cardinal Ekandem had died in 1995, I felt very bad but somehow relieved because when I last saw him in his residence at Area 2, Garki, I shed tears, Diabetes had taken a toll of his toes, he had sores which I knew were causing him serious pains seeing the way he came down the staircase to meet me in his parlour. In spite of his pain, he cracked jokes with me and called me endearing names as is his usual style was whenever we met. "Adamma", "Mbopo", "My spiritual Mother." "I am happy you are here at last".

It is my hope and prayer that one day, not too far from now, this great man will be declared a Saint of the Catholic Church.

May God rest his soul in perfect peace.

Sr. Theresa Nwanruo, HHCJ
(His Spiritual Daughter) Handmaids Convent, Abuja.

Sr. Lucy Afangide brings out the special love, the vision and the humor he exhibited toward the religious. The fascinating part of it was the spiritual dimension, which he saw as a paradigm of growth and fervent spirit in the field of apostolate. Cardinal Ekandem's benevolent disposition extended to all and sundry; he was not sectionalistic, nepotistic nor discriminatory; he was open to all-men, women, youth and children, male, female, strangers and acquaintances. Sr. Lucy became more aware of these qualities when especially she worked closely under his supervision in the Abuja Independent Mission.

c. A Brief Account on late Dominic Cardinal Ekandem—Archbishop of Abuja

Cardinal Ekandem was a good Shepherd that loved, cared, showed concern and compassion to his flock. He was a man of great faith and disciple.

I happened to come close to him when I was assigned to work in Abuja Independent Mission on the 3rd of May 1983.

He was fatherly to the religious women, always encouraging us and giving hope and support.

He was a man of great *vision* and would be showing the religious the right way towards the Apostolate of women, and children, widows and the poor.

He was so special to the religious in his humorous manner of interacting with us. Making us laugh and joyfully carried out our duties.

He was concerned about the state of being and spiritual progress of the religious. He was generous and kind to the religious and always firm in his good decisions.

In the early days of Abuja Independent Mission, he would sometimes give the religious lift from Abuja to Ikot Ekpene and back.

He was generous with his time, resources and knowledge.

In his generosity, he allotted a piece of land in St. Mary's Parish Karu Abuja to Handmaids Sisters to build their convent and that was accomplished through the help of Foreign Agency who sent money for the building of the Convent in 1996.

The memory of late Dominic Cardinal Ekandem cannot be forgotten.

He was a great spiritual father who worked tirelessly for God and the faithful people of God.

He led the religious by his exemplary life and virtues. He was the father of the orphans, the poor and widows. He was instrumental to leading and inspirational to all the Women in Nigeria. The Rich and the Poor benefited from his ministry.

I believe our great father is rejoicing in Heaven with the Angel and the Saints.

SR. Lucy K. Afangideh HHCJ
Handmaids Convent, Garki, Abuja.

In her own capacity as one who knew the Bishop Ekandem as a very young person, as an aspirant, postulant and as a Sister that worked side by side with him in the Abuja Independent Mission, Sr. Mary Tuku gives not just the sayings of Bishop and Cardinal Ekandem but his depth, love, compassion and kindness. His thoughts of the religious and views remain indelible in her mind coupled with dedication to duty like the

Blessed Virgin Mary. His capacity to encourage and help the Sisters to overcome their difficulties and focus on the actual things they need to do is equally prominent.

d.   My Daddy Dominic Cardinal Ekandem 1966–1995

I came to know His Eminence Dominic Cardinal Ekandem as an aspirant in 1966 when I accompanied Sr. Dominic Catherine Archibong to Ikot Ekpene from St. Theresa's Secondary School Edem Ekpat.

It was a meeting whose memory has remained green in my mind until date. "Eyen" he called me, "have you chosen to be a Sister?" Strive to be a good one. Simple, loving, dedicated and ever cheerful, that's what our Mother Mary expects from you. Strive always to be like her. Ever obedient, ever ready to help and anticipate the needs of others as she does, She did that when she went to visit St. Elizabeth and also as she did for the married couple at the wedding feast at Cana. These words helped to shape my spiritual journey to the "religious Life".

I came to know him more during the war, when on the 21st Nov. 1967, the feast of the Presentation of Our Lady in the Temple, he asked Rev. Fr. Patrick Essien of happy memory to perform the Rite of Hooding. So it was that at 6.00 pm at Ifuho Chapel, Sr. Agatha Mozie and myself were hooded. Throughout the war period he was up and doing, over-seeing the Diocese and making sure that the Priests, religious and children especially were well taken care of. This is what gave birth to Children's Home in Ikot Ekpene Diocese during the war. Children were abandoned on the roadside or in the bush, and the Sisters would go round picking and bringing them to Children's Home for care. I also remembered vividly when the soldiers entered Eriam to capture us, to our greatest surprise; there he was with the Chief that morning to protect us. Surely he must have trekked on foot from Ibiono to Eriam and arrived just before the soldiers entered the compound.

We the Sisters had all assembled in the Chapel struggling to sing and pray. He was there as a good shepherd who tended and cared for his flock. I often marvel at his simplicity. Someone could easily be swayed by his tender loving care which he strove to show to everybody. You felt loved and important, as he would often say those sweet words Eka (Mother) or "Eyen" (child) (you are my all and all) as the case may be. Be that sweet smelling scented Rose in the Lord's garden, so bloom where you are planted and let those who see you experience the lord and Our Lady in your way of living, be a mother or sister to everyone. Charm them with your self- dedication and commitment to your apostolate.

In 1981, while I was in Benin in the School of Nursing, I dreamed we were on Corpus Christi procession, His Eminence Cardinal Dominic Ekandem was carrying the Monstrance, he felt very tired and could not walk further, so he knelt down and beckoned for help. I quickly ran up to him and he handed it over to me. I then carried it to the end and after the procession he blessed me, smiled and walked away. However, I could not interpret what it meant. (It took about one year to become aware of the possible meaning of the dream that of coming to the aid of the Cardinal).

ABUJA MISSION

A year later at the completion of my training I was posted to Abuja where he had passionately pleaded with the Congregation to send Sisters to work in Abuja as Nurses and Teachers. On the 27th August, 1982 he commissioned and sent us forth as the first Missionaries to Abuja with the team leader Monsignor Dominic Inyang, Sr. Theresa Nwanruo and myself, his words were, am sending you out to that virgin land to plant the seed of Christianity. Plant this with your life and your great dedication to your apostolate. Remain the model you have been, good, loving spouse of Christ. Once more, bloom now more than ever in all aspect of your life let them see in you that great love and service which is your motto. Live your lives as true daughters of our Mother Mary. God favoured her and you too are specially chosen and favoured. Live in peace with one another and radiate that loving smile everywhere.

While in Abuja, we strive to keep the flag flying, in each of his visits, he always gave that fatherly advice. He will also say don't be ever discouraged with the difficulties you may encounter. The road is rough I know, but take up the challenge, the Lord will always bandage your wounds, go to him in the Blessed Sacrament daily, be a woman of prayer and like the mother of Jesus whose name you bear, remain at the foot of the Cross carrying him and all will be well again.

Until his death in 1995, I remained close to him as I carry out my nursing activities and apostolate in Abuja.

Daddy rest in Peace.

Rev. Sr. Mary Tuku HHCJ
Handmaids Convent, Idah, Kogi State, Nigeria

e.   On Cardinal Ekandem

It was in Abuja, that I learned the name of my eldest maternal aunt, when he asked me of her and how she was doing and sent me to give her his apologies for the difficulties she was experiencing in her marriage. Prior to that incident I never even knew that he had any acquaintance with her! I was amazed. The story of what followed after I reached home and delivered the message is long. That incident showed me the Cardinal was a down to earth pastor, able to establish a deep personal connection with his flock. He knew my aunt as her pastor, a child in Afaha Esang station, where he was the pastor at Afaha Obong Parish.

Throughout my days as a teenager schooling in Goretti Girls Secondary School, I used to visit the Cardinal regularly. I remember doing that on two occasions. The first was to do Legion Work. The other was on an Outing Day. My family was not located in Ikot Ekpene at the time so on some Outing Days I would go with my friend, Rita Inyang to visit with her family; but at other times I would go to visit the Cardinal, then the Bishop of Ikot Ekpene. On such visits he would spoil me with memorable paternal affections that would cause me to want to keep going there often. On one of such visits he gave me his personal passport photograph with the instruction that I should put it in my prayer book and leave it there as a reminder to be praying for him always. It was his picture as a much younger person, maybe even as a seminarian. I treasured that photograph as a relic and kept it with me all my life, preserving it religiously in my divine office even though I later missed it.

That gesture from the Cardinal as my Bishop, shows me what a humble man he was. His unassuming humility was also displayed to me when he told me he would like the Jehovah's Witness members to come and preach to him. He did not perceive himself as too high to be beyond the preaching or prayers of the little ones.

Two weeks to the death of the Cardinal here in Abuja I was at home with my mother. She told me of a dream she had. A very big tree fell down by the station church in her village, Afaha Esang. I interpreted it for her that I view it to mean that the Cardinal will soon die. That was how rooted the Cardinal was in the hearts and minds of the people he was their Shepherd to in his very first station as a priest till his death.

May he rest in peace!

Handmaids of the Holy Child Jesus Convent, Garki.
Abuja (Catholic Secretariat of Nigeria, Abuja)
Sr. Regina Tombere HHCJ

f. Bishop Dominic I. Ekandem's Relationship with the Handmaids of the Holy Child Jesus

Dominic Cardinal Ekandem as the first Bishop of Ikot Ekpene Diocese was a great supporter of the work started by Sister Mary Charles Magdalen Walker, Foundress of the Congregation of the Handmaids of the Holy Child Jesus. He was eager to assist the Handmaids develop spiritually and materially to meet the standard expected of a religious congregation and in line with foundation laid by their Foundress.

Hence it was that at the first General Chapter of the Handmaids in 1959, Bishop Dominic Ekandem, the Auxiliary Bishop of Calabar Diocese, visited the Capitulars of the Chapter in Ifuho, who were in adoration of the Blessed Sacrament before the election of their Superior General. The main purpose of this visit was to give the Sisters enlightenment on the gravity of the step the Handmaids of the Holy Child Jesus were going to take. He gave them promise of prayers and wished them every success in the choice of their first Superior General. Sister Mary Gertrude Waturuocha, HHCJ was elected the first Superior General.

It was his desire that this first indigenous Congregation in West Africa, the Handmaids of the Holy Child Jesus, will do well in every aspect of religious living, in good understanding of the implications and commitment of the religious Life. By the grace and plan of God, the Congregation was granted in February 1971, the "*Decretum Laudes*" by the most Holy Father, Pope Paul VI, to the glory of God.

Archives: Generalate HHCJ, Ifuho

It was a great joy to His Lordship, Bishop Dominic I. Ekandem, when in his paternalism, friendship and generosity; he expressed his appreciation to the Congregation HHCJ who in their thoughtfulness had published in 1973 the book titled, "A Tribute to a Valiant Missionary," on the life and work of Sister Mary Charles Walker, the Foundress of their Congregation. This he saw as a treasure which could have been kept in the safe of the Congregation but by which publication, "Opportunity is given to all who are seriously engaged in the work of the Church in Nigeria to learn her ways and profit by her success."

Other paternal sentiments and exhortations by Bishop Dominic I. Ekandem, Bishop of Ikot Ekpene Diocese regarding the successful religious Missionary of the HHCJ as a result of the deep foundation laid by their Foundress and transmitted through the four foundation members of the Congregation, can be gathered from the "Preface" written by his Lordship, Bishop Dominic I. Ekandem on "The Tribute to a Valiant Pioneer Missionary" at the celebration of the Golden Jubilee of the arrival in Calabar of Sister Mary Charles Walker, 1923–1973.

Mother Mary Anne Iwoh HHCJ,
Former Mother General of the Handmaids of
the Holy Child Jesus, Ifuho, Ikot Ekpene,
Akwa Ibom State, Nigeria.

g.   Dominic Cardinal Ekandem, A Man of Rare Qualities

When Rev. Father Michael I. Edem C. M. asked me to write something about His Eminence Dominic Cardinal Ekandem, I rejected because it was difficult to write about such an eminent person, not knowing the aspect to write.

Afterwards, I reluctantly accepted to write because of Father Michael's incessant request, I continued asking myself for a long time what kind of a person Dominic Cardinal Ekandem was.

The answer came when I read the First Letter of St. Paul to Timothy Chapter 3:1–7 about LEADERS IN THE CHURCH:

> "…A Church Leader deserves excellent work, he must be above reproach, be sober, self-controlled and orderly, he must welcome strangers and must be able to teach, he must not be a drunkard or a violent man, but gentle and peaceful, mature in faith so that he must not swell up with pride, he must not love money…He must be a man who is respected by people outside the Church…"[304]

Yes, this is the man, Dominic Cardinal Ekandem, whose character and life style fits into this category of Pastors. He was a fervent missionary, a model Prelate and a dignified gentleman.

According to Late Bishop James Moynagh in his reflections when the Cardinal celebrated his Anniversary of Episcopal ordination on 10th February, 1979, wrote "the Cardinal was a pastoral Priest, the man of prayer, the humble man filled with love for his people, the man who as Priest and Bishop and Cardinal was always willing to spend himself for Christ's flock."[305]

I came in contact with Cardinal because I was fortunate to be present at his priestly ordination at Ifuho, as a child in the primary School. Again I was privileged to witness his Episcopal ordination at Calabar as a representative of my school in 1954. None of these events really meant much to me at the time.

Another event that brought me closer to the Cardinal was that he officiated at my Hooding at the Prince of Peace Chapel, Ifuho, on 6th January, 1956. My impression of him that day was that he was a very kind man, humble and simple because of the way he spoke to me. He was softspoken, sympathetic and approachable. Even though these events somehow exposed me, I was always shy to get close to him. Moreover in those days there was not the type of collaboration between the people and the hierarchy as there is now. However, being a religious Sister I often came in contact with him whenever possible.

After the Cardinal's Episcopal ordination he was posted to St. Joseph's Parish, Anua as the Auxiliary Bishop of Calabar. There he exercised his pastoral ministry until in May 1963, when he became the first Bishop of Ikot Ekpene Diocese.

At Anua one of the most significant events he performed was the erection of the statute of Our Lady of the Immaculate Conception at the entrance of St. Joseph's Parish to replace the so called "Deity" of the area named "Ukana Offot". Originally, there was a small forest and stream at the entrance of the Church believed to have harboured this "deity".

Since the Church was established, I presume little or nothing was done to destroy or remove the deity from that environment, otherwise it would not have continued to exist there until the fifties. So the Cardinal being a strong prayerful man negotiated with the Chiefs and convinced them to remove the deity to any environment of their choice. This was done after which the statute of our lady was mounted at the spot.[306] This is a true fact that many people do not know.

I am narrating this because I was an eyewitness. My little village, Ikot Ekpenyong in Ibiono, was then an out station in Anua Parish and people used to trek from there to Anua, the Central Mission. On two occasions when I was in Primary School I went to Anua, saw the forest and stream, stepped into it and scooped the water. Looking back to this event, I have great respect and reverence for the Cardinal because it takes the courage of a strong, spiritual person to perform such an act. Again it shows the extent he was respected and honored by the people to whom he had endeared himself.

The Cardinal also brought a significant development to the Diocese by founding the Catholic women's Organization (CWO), which eventually spread to other parts of Nigeria and beyond. This organization in no little way accelerated the emancipation of the women and they can never, never forget their beloved Cardinal Ekandem.

Alongside this development, his zeal and passion for the development of the youth was very strong. So he embarked on an all-round education for them. When he declared at the re-union of the Holy family College, Abak, Old Boy's Association that: "our educational system must reflect our pre-occupation with making man grow as a person."[307]

To fulfill his ambition he embarked on building up such schools as Kizito Comprehensive School, Adiasim, Goretti Girls' Secondary School of Domestic Science and Commerce, Ikot Ekpene, Loreto Girls' Grammar School, Eriam. He also set out to maintain such schools as Holy Family College, Abak, St. Mary's T. T. C, Ediene Abak, Holy Child T. T. C. Ifuho and others.[308]

Another aspect that the Cardinal exhibited a great zeal and enthusiasm was the promotion of vocations to the Priesthood and religious Life. He left no stone unturned to pursue this course. Seminaries and Juniorates were encouraged to be established and he supported the building of Loreto Girls' Juniorate at Eriam and gave scholarships to girls who opted for the religious life, though some of them discontinued.

He encouraged different Congregations to work in Ikot Ekpene Diocese, as a result, diversified apostolates were carried out in the Diocese. In general there was mutual understanding and collaboration between each Congregation and the Diocese.

Here, the Congregation of the Handmaids of the Holy Child Jesus, whose Generalate and Novitiate are in the Diocese, where he became the first Bishop, needs special mention. It is very interesting and inspiring to learn what the Cardinal wrote about the beginning of the Congregation. He wrote in his Congratulatory Message to the Handmaids during their Anniversary Celebration thus:

> "Looking back at my last year of primary school education in St. Joseph's School Anua, 1932, one of the most inspiring spectacles that left a lasting impression on me was that of the Aspirants or Postulants of the Handmaids (foundation members) dressed in white with white veils. I had never seen any black Sister before, nor even a Seminarian, not to talk of an African Priest so for me they looked like angels, and really they were angelic in their movement and behaviour.

"...We cannot but admire in the first place, those four African young ladies, who, born and bred in paganism, not only embraced the Catholic Faith and the Catholic Way of life but went further to aspire to the religious Life consisting of the three Evangelical Counsels (virtues) of Chastity, Poverty and Obedience.

"They gave Nigerian Church a vigorous brilliant start, while serving as an example and an inspiration to the men of my tribe who were not as quick as themselves to perceive the beauty of the life of complete dedication to God's service..." He continued, "The beginning of the Congregation of the Handmaids of the Holy Child Jesus came upon us as a miracle and nothing was responsible for such a miracle except the missionary spirit of the Church". He then praised—"Sr. Mary Charles Walker, who, with a true Missionary Spirit braved every obstacle and opposition to answer Bishop Shanahan's invitation to come to the Mission Station of Calabar where she successfully sowed the seeds of the first Nigerian, indigenous female religious vocation, the Handmaids of the Holy Child Jesus."[309]

He concluded that "The Congregation of the Handmaids of the Holy Child Jesus has been abundantly blessed, and has served as a torch to the various religious female Congregations springing up all over the country now, and sending missionaries to other parts of Africa and beyond".

This indeed is the fulfilment of the prophecy of Bishop Shanahan in his letter to Sr. Mary Charles Walker 12th October, 1929:

"...My hope has always been to have many convents of the Native Sisterhood scattered throughout the Country..."[310]

Through God's Providence the Congregation had attained her autonomy before the Cardinal was made a Bishop. It was therefore possible for the Congregation to benefit from his good administration. The Cardinal was fatherly, very understanding and benevolent towards the Congregation. His support spiritually and materially, encouragement and above all his life style enabled us to achieve a lot.

One of such outstanding examples was the Mission at Abuja Federal Capital when he invited the Congregation there to start our apostolate which eventually has developed to be what it is today.

On behalf of the Congregation. I want to use this medium to hail and express our very sincere appreciation to the Cardinal for his love, support, prayers, encouragement and for all he did for the Congregation. I earnestly thank him for what he did for us and our people, especially during the

Nigerian Civil War. This contribution would be incomplete if this aspect was left out, even though many misconstrued his activities then.

I would better express this in the words of his friend and classmate, Hon, Chief Judge of Anambra State, Mr. Justice A.N. Aniagolu OFR KSS, which he declared when he proposed the toast of His Eminence, Dominic Cardinal Ekandem at the luncheon of the Feast of Christ the King on 21st November 1979 at Onitsha.

"If ever there was a pleasant assignment I was called upon to exercise, it is this of His Eminence Dominic Cardinal Ekandem D.D., O.B.E., CON, Prince of the Church and faithful servant of Christ. It is to me a pleasant assignment because I am talking of a man whom I fervently believe in, not from a standpoint of mundane sentimentality but as an ideal priest, a man who crystallizes in his personality the true tenets, and symbolizes the very epitome of practical Christianity...[311] The Chief Judge further said: "Perhaps the best practical demonstration of the firm character of which Cardinal Ekandem is made is found in his conduct during the Nigerian Civil War. In order to protect all the religious, Priests and all the people of God under his care during that period, Cardinal Ekandem, the Bishop of Ikot Ekpene, suffered innumerable privations, both physical and mental, and at one time offered to lay down his life rather than suffer any harm to come to any of them, no matter from what ethnic group he or she had come."[312]

CONCLUSION

My writing has presented only a snap-shot of our illustrious son and prelate and I thank Rev. Father Michael I. Edem CM for giving me the opportunity to write about my experience of Cardinal Dominic Ekandem.

I am thankful to the Almighty God for choosing Dominic Cardinal Ekandem to be His Chief shepherd and endowing him with all the blessings and graces for his Ministry.

I salute and hail the Cardinal himself for being a suitable recipient of these honors and making the best use of them.

I register my sincere appreciation to his family and all and sundry who have contributed in any way to the fulfilment of his priestly vocation. Lastly I pray that the good seed that he had planted will continue to bear abundant good fruits till the end of time. Amen! **Sr. Juliana Ekerete H.H.C.J**

Immaculate Conception Secondary School, Itak/Handmaids of the Holy Child Jesus Convent Anua, Akwa Ibom State, Nigeria.

h.   Distant Memories of Dominic Cardinal Ekandem

During nearly twenty years as a missionary priest in Nigeria I had of course heard a great deal about Nigeria's first cardinal, and had met him in passing at various functions, but it was only during my three years (1977–'80) as parish priest in Ikot Ekpene that I came to know the cardinal directly and personally.

He had been made cardinal in 1976, and lived not far from St. Anne's cathedral in Ifuho; after all he was Bishop of Ikot Ekpene. Down the road I was Parish Priest of Ikot Ekpene. The Vincentians had begun the Parish of St. Vincent de Paul, when they first arrived in 1960. A fine church was built, and a large community house. It was not a parish house, but one that was to be a base for several priests who would be engaged in giving retreats and parish missions far and wide, but with Ikot Ekpene as their home base. However the Cardinal found it strange that priests of the Diocese ran the parish of Ikot Ekpene—at the heart of the Diocese of Ikot Ekpene—by a Missionary Congregation rather than directly. My predecessor Fr. Harry Smyth CM had been told that the Cardinal wished the Vincentians to vacate St. Vincent's in favour of the Diocese. So on arriving I realised my basic task, apart from running the parish, was to prepare the handover of the parish to the Diocese. This of course was to color many of my meetings with the Cardinal.

Regular meetings.

Someone who knew the Cardinal well told me that if during a meeting, the Cardinal began to tap his feet, I should know he was unhappy with how things were going. This did in fact occur from time to time, but overall our meetings were courteous and became more and more relaxed and friendly. I can recall one occasion when the Cardinal—realising I came to Ikot Ekpene from Benue State in Central Nigeria—told me the following story. From 1970—'73 as Bishop he was serving as Apostolic Administrator in Port Harcourt. On one occasion he went to the senior military officer to complain about the conduct of the troops who were still occupying Port Harcourt since the end of the Civil War. The Officer was from Benue State. The Bishop complained to him that instead of defending the people and keeping peace, many soldiers were looting and stealing, and a favourite target seemed to be the Catholic Church with the Churches and Schools offering good pickings. The Colonel expressed his outrage at the very idea, and made a firm promise to stamp out such behaviour—with immediate effect. Bishop Ekandem was too polite, or maybe so diplomatic, that he did not point out to the officer that the table at which they sat as they drank cups of tea had once been in the Bishop's front room! He roared with laughter at this and it seemed to relax our subsequent meetings.

Handover of St. Vincent's parish.

Little by little the plans were made for the handover. The Vincentians were to be given a piece of land in Abiakpo Ntak Inyang, about 2 miles to the west of the town. It was offered because it was just walking distance from where the philosophy Faculty of the Bigard Memorial Seminary had newly been built. This was to be the place where the Vincentians would send their seminarians for their philosophical studies, but we wished them to live in community and simply to attend the Seminary for their studies. From that point of view the place was ideal. There was a Church there, St. Joseph's, and the Vincentians were told they could care for it, rather than the priests from the Cathedral Parish. However the road in was scarcely motorable. There was no good supply of water and no electricity. What there was however, was lots of palm trees. But these were important to the people from the village who used them either to produce palm-wine or palm-oil. Compensation would be demanded if we began to clear the place to build. In addition of course, no funds were made available from the Diocese to begin the building.

In St. Vincent's parish, a diocesan priest Fr. Patrick Ekutt was appointed as assistant priest and he moved into the house, early in December 1981. It was becoming clearer to the parishioners that soon the Vincentians would be leaving. The Cardinal was hurrying along things, as the expected visit of Pope John Paul II to Nigeria, was hopefully to include a visit to Ikot Ekpene. The cardinal of course wishing to welcome him without the confusion of a Missionary Congregation in the town parish. In the event the Pope did not come to Ikot Ekpene, but our move out gained momentum none the less.

In February of that year I became ill with what was thought to be a tropical abscess of the liver. When a bit better I was sent home for medical attention (missing the Papal visit) and did not return till almost the end of March. On return I suggested to the Cardinal that Fr. Ekutt be appointed Parish Priest of St. Vincent's and I would remain on as assistant. This is what happened, the Cardinal readily agreed. We worked together and the Easter celebration was especially memorable. By October I was able to leave Sr. Vincent's and move into the new house "Blessed Ghebre Michael's"— our student house now under the protection of our Ethiopian Vincentian Martyr. The house was blessed in November 1982. Lots of problems followed of course as we were settling into a not completed building with 15 seminarians, but Thank God we were blessed, the community settled, the village people welcomed us and the handover was complete.

Diocesan Retreat.

In July the Cardinal asked me to preach the annual retreat to the priests of the Diocese. A big undertaking, as I had only given a couple of priests retreats before. The Cardinal himself made the retreat along with the priests. He gave a couple of talks during the retreat, and it is from this that I especially remember his great concern to foster a missionary spirit among the Nigerian priests. He was very much responsible for initiating the Missionary Society of St. Paul, begun in 1976, the year he was made a Cardinal, and based in the new Federal capital, Abuja. A visit of Pope Paul VI to East Africa and his call there for African Missionaries was also part of his inspiration. The new movement was to gradually take shape with lots of assistance from the member of St. Patrick's Missionary Society. I recall that during the retreat the Cardinal spoke about the spirit of the missionary which free him or her from home and family and gives them fully to a new people and new place. He spoke of a meeting he had with the mother of a St. Patrick's Missionary from my home town, who had died at a young age. He related how the mother apologised to the Cardinal that she had no other son to give him to replace the one who died. He held this up to his priests as a heroic example of the missionary spirit. It is good to realise that now all these years alter the members of St. Paul's Missionary Society are doing marvellous work in many countries far from home, and not least in the Diocese of Southwark, London.

Night of vigil and prayer.

One day, while I was still alone in St. Vincent's and was having my lunch, a caller came to the door. He was a messenger sent by the Cardinal. He gave me an invitation, sent to all priests, summoning us to an emergency meeting the following afternoon. Phones were not working, and so any gathering that had not been pre-planned had to be announced by sending out messengers to all would be participants. No hint was given as to what the emergency might be, the Cardinal crafty enough to realise that this absence of information would ensure a full turn out. So it turned out. Mud splattered cars arrived from all over the Diocese.

The emergency was about a Fr. Emmanuel, a diocesan priest who was seriously ill in the hospital at Urua Akpan, a Missionary Hospital run by the Medical Missionaries of Mary. Fr. Emmanuel was an only child. His parents were not baptised Christians, and never really understood the life of a Catholic Priest, and the apparent abandonment of family which it seemed to entail. He had a lonely life and had little support from family and relatives. Now in hospital he had no one to really care for him. It was for family members to provide food to their sick relatives in the hospital and look after all their needs. Fr. Emmanuel lacked such care. The Cardinal said that starting from that evening he wanted priests, two at a time, day and night, to be with Fr. Emmanuel.

In the event it turned out that the Cardinal and myself were to start that evening and remain till replaced next day by two more priests. It was a very memorable experience for me. We arrived at the hospital before sunset, and found Fr. Emmanuel who was lying on a bed in a corridor, and more or less unconscious. As night came and the place became quiet the Cardinal asked to prepare for Mass. I got a bed table and put it over the foot of the bed. On the table I set up the altar from the Mass box we had brought. Then to my surprise the Cardinal told me to vest and offer Mass, and he would serve me. Some hours later about midnight, he said Mass and I served him. The whole night as passed in prayer, in times of silence, and in conversation.[313] Fr. Emmanuel died in March 1981, but that night has remained with me ever since. I felt my faith was straightened, and we each found our basic vocation—not that of Cardinal or priest—but as disciples of the Savior who came to give life to the world.

Paul Roche CM.
Provincial Director of the Daughters of Charity,
England and Ireland Palace Court, London, England.
February 2015

I.   The return to Ifuho and the Relocation of the Generalate

When the end of the civil war was announced and proclaimed in the media, Mother Mary Gertrude was still in Lagos. Things started settling down; still, she did not return. Bishop Ekandem was worried. He was obliged to invite her to come back. The invitation to come back reveals the open-mindedness of the prince-prelate. It took a while before she returned.

When she came back, she did not go down to Calabar where the seat of the government was since its foundation. It is akin to what is found in the Sacred Writ about Jesus and Herod where Joseph and Mary were asked to rise and go back to Israel, for those who wanted to kill the child were dead, but realizing that Archelaus was reigning there, they decided to settle at Nazareth (Cf. Matt. 2:19–23). She decided otherwise, to settle at Eriam, the place of temporary refuge where the sisters were quartered during the heat of the war.

As a human being, she was afraid and did not yet take neither Bishop Brian David Usanga nor Bishop D. I. Ekandem into confidence. She was simply watching to see which way the pendulum swung to as she waited at Eriam. By then, the military governor of South Eastern State, Col. Jacob Udokaha Esuene, was ruling at Calabar, the state capital. She took her time together with the general council before she made her decision to go down to Ifuho, the place where the first novitiate of the Congregation of the Handmaids was situated.

Ifuho had great prominence like Calabar, which was the cradle of the congregation as seen in chapter seven about the origin of the handmaids where the remains of Mother Mary Charles Walker was exhumed from England and brought to rest even though they are still contemplating bringing her body to Ifuho where the Generalate is at present. While Calabar enjoyed the privilege of harboring the Mother General and many of the council members, Ifuho had the primacy of position as the place where many offices of the congregation were located. In terms of property and antiquity, Ifuho ranks next to Calabar since it witnessed the first novitiate house of the congregation. After due consultation with the general councillors, the Mother General, Mother Gertrude Waturuocha, HHCJ, and the members of the general council decided to move to Ifuho and occupy the place as their new Generalate. The novitiate was then moved back to Ifuho as it was before the war. All these took place in 1971 after the war.

The movement took place to reciprocate the kind gesture of Bishop Ekandem. It brought the principle of *Kentronics*[314] to bear. In other words, not kicking against the goad as Jesus told Saul/Paul on the way to Damascus while going to persecute, arrest, and imprison the "Followers of the Way." Kentronics is used by Fulton Sheen to mean struggling against pain and so causing oneself even more pain like an ox kicking against its shackles or goad. According to him, the word derives from Greek *Kentra*, meaning goad, and applied in the context of kicking against the goad, that is, kicking against God, which was impossible. God pitied Paul who was ruining himself in the process because of his resistance, while Bishop Ekandem pitied the sisters not returning because of their fear.

Rethinking the situation made Mother Mary Gertrude and councillors not to want to kick against a genuine love and compassion demonstrated by the paterfamilias who, inviting her back, did not have any hidden agenda of animosity toward her as an Igbo sister but regarded the Mother General and her council together with all the sisters as his beloved children that he considered part of his flock. No matter the historical innuendos, the chief shepherd, Bishop Dominic Ekandem, did not intend to stifle the convictions of conscience.[315] He wanted the sisters to act with utmost freedom, but as a father, he had to draw his children back to himself after the scattering during the fog and darkness of the night.

The Generalate left Calabar the foundational place to Ifuho just as the provincialate of the Daughters of Charity of St. Vincent De Paul moved from the original place at Eniong Offot near Anua to Nchia- Eleme in Rivers State because of constant molestation and more than one experience of being burgled. At that point, Ifuho enjoyed dual privileges of being the cathedral see of the diocese and the center where the Generalate of the Handmaids of the Holy Child Jesus is located.

Probably, the Mother General did not want to return to Calabar because of her going to Lagos consequent to the "forced resignation" construed to have originated from Usanga who used Bishop Ekandem as a supporter to accomplish his plans. That misunderstanding gave rise to the expression of Father Cosmas in his book on Cardinal Ekandem, *Friends and Fellow Countrymen*.[316] That was a wrong understanding. Bishop Usanga was still well disposed to the sisters and desirous as Bishop Ekandem was since the main point of contention was the safety of the sisters, but human nature played its part. While Calabar lost, Ikot Ekpene gained. Finding a more benign reception, she wholeheartedly returned with Bishop Ekandem to foster the growth of the congregation as well as the bond of love among the sisters proudly demonstrated during the war.

The riddle of Samson, son of Manoah, from the tribe of Dan, clearly plays out itself here. "Out of the eater came what is eaten and out of the strong came what is sweet" (Jg. 14:14). One maybe wondering what the riddle means in the context of the whole episode of war situation, parting and returning, cutting off and reattaching, disconnecting and reconnecting. The story of Samson tearing a young lion that was roaring and coming toward him to devour him while on his way to Timnah creates the link. Samson tore it with his bare hands without any weapons when the Spirit of the Lord came upon him, and eventually, the carcass of the young lion produced honey when bees came and inhabited it. Samson, on passing through the same road another time, went out of his way to look for the carcass of the young lion.

On finding it, he realized the bees in the hive. When he put his hand, he got some honeycomb; he took some, ate it, and gave some to his father who ate it without knowing where and how it came about. At the marriage feast that lasted for seven days, he then bought out the riddle and told the kinsmen of his wife to solve it. He told them that if they gave the answer, he would give them thirty pieces of fine linen and thirty festal robes; if not, they would give the same to him. They struggled for three days and could not get the answer. They went to the wife, Delilah, to cajole or coax Samson and get the answer from the husband for why should he come to rob them because they responded to their invitation. The wife got the answer in her own way and told those invited. They gave the solution to the riddle to Samson who went down to Ashkelon, killed thirty men, and took their robes and gave the festal robes to those who answered the riddle of what is eaten coming from the eater and what is sweet coming from the strong (Jg. 14:1–20). The same statement can be applied to Saul who became Paul who was breathing threats everywhere; but when he became converted, he was the one who was experiencing persecution from many fronts, including stoning, even though he did not die, flogging, being surrounded in peril of his life. He was a chosen instrument of God, for he was meant to suffer many things on behalf of the Lord Jesus (Acts 9:10–19; 14:19–20). He who was a persecutor had now become the persecuted and vulnerable. Roles had changed.

What was considered a threatening, unfriendly, and unbearable environment had become the cherished place of resort. It is like the stone rejected by the builders that has become the cornerstone; it is marvelous to see. It is the work of the Lord, a marvel in our eyes (Acts 4:11; Matt. 21:42; Ps. 118:22). God has his ways of doing wonderful things in a simple way. That is part of the wonder of the ways of God. When forgiveness is given with a sincere heart and received with open mind, it breeds peace and reconciliation. Dag Hammarskjold said, "Forgiveness breaks the chain of causality because he who 'forgives' you-out of love-takes upon himself the consequences of what you have done. Forgiveness, therefore, always entails a sacrifice…The price you must pay for your own liberation through another's sacrifice is that you in turn must be willing to liberate in the same way, irrespective of the consequences to yourself."[317] Forgiveness was given, and forgiveness was received. It is the wonderful exchange that breaks the chain of reprisals leading to freedom for both parties.

The gentle, unassuming, humble, and fatherly role of Bishop Dominic Ignatius Ekandem was not just observed within the confines of his ecclesiastical jurisdiction but extended beyond his diocese; his country, Nigeria; West Africa as the region; and Africa, the continent, and reached the Vatican that recognized his qualities and appointed him as the first Nigerian cardinal underscoring his position as prince and patriarch of the church.

Chapter Ten

MISERICORDIAM DOMINI (THE MERCY OF THE LORD)

The Cardinalate

Non Nobis Domine Non Nobis Sed Nomini
Tuo Da Gloriam (Not to us Lord, not to
us but to your name give the glory).

—Ps. 114/115:1

Ability may take you to the top, but
only character keeps you there!

—Wise Saying from an
Unknown Author,
July 2014 Calendar,
Marietta Georgia, U.S.A.

THE ANNOUNCEMENT OF Bishop Ekandem as the first Nigerian cardinal was surprising but at the same time very gratifying. Nigerians had been hearing of cardinals from other countries but never had one of theirs. They prayed very earnestly for God to grant them one. The news of getting a cardinal accounts for the national joy that ran like wildfire across the country. It went beyond creed and religion or even the past three regional structure of Nigeria of north, east, and west. Rome takes many things into consideration while nominating people for various positions and honors in the church. Bishop Ekandem was not an exception.

He was the first from Ibibio to be ordained a priest; the first Nigerian priest to be consecrated bishop; the first Anglophone West African bishop; the first president of AECAWA (Episcopal Conferences of Anglophone West Africa); the first president of the Episcopal Conference of Nigeria; the first Nigerian bishop to be an administrator of Port Harcourt Diocese immediately after the civil war; the first young bishop to have muted the idea of a national seminary in 1956, nine years as priest and two years as a Bishop; the first national president of Christian Association of Nigeria (CAN); the first Nigerian prelate to be assigned the task of pioneering the Abuja Independent Mission; the founder of the Missionaries of St. Paul Society/Seminary and approved by the Episcopal Conference of Nigeria; and a very astute and courageous administrator with seasoned capacity to penetrate the core of the matter in a twinkling of an eye. In a word, Cardinal Ekandem was a man of great integrity and sound judgment of situations, favored with mystical and endowed with infused knowledge.

A.   Announcement and Recognition as the First Nigerian Cardinal

The Vatican City released the good news on April 27, 1976, at noon as the custom is of all announcements of elevation or appointments. He was not aware of the announcement. He was attending a meeting of the Bishops' Conference as he was the current president and was deeply involved in that meeting when there was an interruption or what may be called a breach of protocol. In today's language, it is called *breaking news*. This came with the congratulatory message of Monsignor D. Causero, chargé d'affaires of the apostolic nunciature in Nigeria, deputizing for His Excellency Most Rev. Girolamo Prigione who was the pro-nuncio at the time. It was a solemn but joyous moment where the atmosphere was charged with great excitement and surprise at the breaking of the news.

The chargé's letter reproduced by Uduakobong Umoren[318] on the day the good news was announced goes thus:

Cardinal Ekandem after investiture ceremony

Message of Congratulations to His Eminence, Most Revd. Dominic I. Ekandem By Msgr. D. Causero, *Chargé D'Affairs,* The Apostolic Pronunciature

The Holy Father has appointed His Excellency Most Reverend Dominic I. Ekandem, a Cardinal of the Holy Roman Church. On account of a series of delays (both of delivery of diplomatic bag and in the delivery of calls[319]) I was not in a position of breaking the good news to His Eminence and to you in due time, that is, yesterday at twelve noon when it was officially announced in Rome.

Anyway, I wish to be present here today to share in the joy of the newly elected and also in that of the whole Church of Nigeria gathered and represented here by all its Pastors.

I congratulate you your Eminence, on your promotion to the rank of Cardinal. It is a high and, deserved recognition to your tactful judgment. A canon of the code of Canon Law reads: "The Cardinals must be priests of understanding, learning, piety, judgment and ability". And we love to say it, that the Holy Father did not depart from the rule.

Many will certainly refer to your election, Your Eminence, as an historical event in the life of the Church in Nigeria and rightly so.

You are the first Nigerian Cardinal and I feel deeply moved and, no doubt, all Bishops and the faithful of this country are proud that one of the Bishops of Nigeria has entered the Senate of the Roman Pontiff and is expected to assist him as one of his chief counsellors and helpers in governing the Universal Church.

On behalf of His Excellency the apostolic pro-nuncio, and the new Secretary, Rev. Fr. Lozano, I renew to you, Your Eminence and the whole Church of Nigeria represented here by its Archbishops and Bishops, my congratulations—cordial, sincere and joyful, 28th April, 1976.

The response of the newly proclaimed cardinal came later but full of originality[320] and simplicity based greatly on faith vision, pragmatic, and selfless yet profound in nature and in context. The response of the new cardinal underlines the mercy or goodness of God through the church as the basis of his elevation. It went thus:

For me this is a moment made possible only by Almighty God, our Heavenly Father through our Holy Father Pope Paul (VI).[321] I give thanks to God for the great honour bestowed on my country.

For myself, I can only repeat that I am a Catholic Priest. This is what is really important. Whatever honour may be attached to that priesthood in my humble person, I accept it on the solemn understanding that I was ordained a priest of God to minister to the people and if necessary to die for the people. This serious and holy commitment which we priests make publicly every Holy Thursday, I share with priests everywhere.

Prayerfully, I would borrow the beautiful and prophetic words of the Virgin Mary: "Because He that is mighty has done great things to me." Prayerfully, I borrow from the recent call of the Holy Father and I am emboldened to say that this is a time for strong prayer. This is a time for storming heaven with our prayer. It is the strong who shall inherit the Kingdom of God. I plead with all men of good will that we at this time give ourselves up to and make **strong** to Almighty God.

I ask for the prayers of all. I ask for prayers for my brother Bishops and myself that we may rightly lead the Church in this great country at this critical time of our history. May God bless us all.

28th April 1976.

A lot can be discovered from this speech of the cardinal. "The greatest good for the greatest number of people" is one of the philosophical backdrops of the message. It has the Pauline theological insight in the letter to the Philippians: "Always putting others first and regarding them to be better" (Phil. 2:3–3) as a catalyst. It is very obvious in this address that he sees God as the author of all good things. He called for prayer. The episcopal conference was to be the first beneficiary. This became clear when he said "brother Bishops." He requested prayers for himself and for the entire nation. That is why God predominates and forms the undertone linking every move and vision. It is a theocentric address offered by a humble man in a spontaneous manner.

B.   The Reception at Port Harcourt International Airport

The reception at Enugu came after that of the International Airport in Port Harcourt. This came after the reception of the Cardinal's Hat in Rome. There were many prelates and clergy of other ranks who graced the occasion. Those who went to receive him at the airport were from Ikot Ekpene, Calabar, Ogoja, Uyo, and Port Harcourt Dioceses. The named places are under Calabar Metropolitan See now. There were at least three prelates, Bishops Ukpo, Fitzgibbon, and Silas Obot, his auxiliary at the time before being translated to Idah Diocese in 1978. It was in December 1977 that Pope Paul VI raised the prefecture to a diocese. Most Rev. Ephraim Silas Obot became the first bishop of Idah in Kogi State.

It was a glorious day. There were many monsignors, priests, and religious men and women; the knights and their ladies not to talk of lay eminent Nigerian citizens who joined the group. As usual, Cardinal Ekandem was very modest in everything. He was calm. He did not throw away his humility nor did he forget to use the occasion to exhort the people of God who came to welcome him. He thanked them for their kindness and appreciated the sacrifices made to come from all the places mentioned to receive him. From there, the convoy wound its way down to Ikot Ekpene, "the Raffia City" or the little Bethlehem of Nigeria. Some prayers of thanksgiving for what God had achieved in his life together with the safe journey were offered. They had refreshment before parting to their different places.

C. Reception at Enugu

After that joyous celebration at Port Harcourt Airport and at St. Anne's Cathedral, Ikot Ekpene, many dioceses invited the new cardinal for reception. One of the very first ones was Enugu Diocese under the Ordinary Most Rev. Geoffrey Mary Paul Okoye, CSSp. The reception, which was a diocesan affair, was a grandiose one at Holy Ghost Cathedral, Ogui Road, Enugu. The ceremony was a colorful one at the "Coal City" and former capital of Eastern Nigeria. Bishop Okoye, who left Port Harcourt Diocese during the civil war, became the second bishop of Enugu after Bishop John Cross Anyiogu, the first bishop of Enugu. As the first Nigerian citizen by virtue of his elevation, Ikot Ekpene could not monopolize him or claim him for itself anymore. From the beginning, he had been a man for all. The elevation aided its comprehension. It placed him in the limelight. The *Daily Star Newspaper* covered the event at Enugu:

> RECEPTION OF DOMINIC CARDINAL EKANDEM, THE FIRST NIGERIAN CARDINAL IN ENUGU AT THE INVITATION OF BISHOP GODFREY MARY PAUL OKOYE CSSp, THE CATHOLIC BISHOP OF ENUGU DIOCESE.
>
> At the reception accorded the first Nigerian Cardinal, His Eminence Dominic Cardinal Ekandem at Holy Ghost Cathedral, Enugu, East Central State on Tuesday, 30th November 1976, a Pontifical Eucharistic Celebration preceded every other event. The joy of Bishop Okoye CSSp., GREAT FRIEND AND COMPANION of the Cardinal was immense since he saw the occasion of the visit and reception as a special blessing from the Lord and a great

union of the Church that lived out unity in diversity. It is obvious that the positive response of Cardinal Ekandem to his invitation to visit the Diocese and to come for reception must have bonded their old time friendship more forcefully and gave room for a more prolonged, supportive, positively fraternal and amicable coexistence. He and the Diocese gave a very warm and powerful reception to the Cardinal. Enugu marked herself as the very first place aside of the Catholic Bishops' Conference of Nigeria and his home Diocese that received and congratulated the Cardinal after the Consistory Declaration of Pope Paul VI and Investiture.[322]

No wonder His Excellency, Most Reverend G. M. P. Okoye CSSp. preached powerfully and convincingly and eloquently[323] on that day putting new hearts into the people and encouraging them to live a new life. In his sermon, he "charged all the Christians to be practical, live lives worthy of emulation and give to charity, receive more in return." At the same time, he lamented over the "multiple sins in the world today and called on all Christians to give (up) their lives to God and prepare for the Second Coming of the Lord who would come to execute judgement." He went further to say: "If you have given to corruption, oppression, cheating, bribery, robbery and all that is evil, give it up, amend your ways and be prayerful."[324]

Bishop Geoffrey Okoye, CSSp was one of those very powerful preachers who touched the hearts of his hearers with his homilies and sermons. In this little extract, he focused on newness of life demanded by the season of Advent that emphasized the Second Coming of the Lord. He did not limit his homily to the good people of Enugu Diocese but extended it to all. He used the pulpit as a platform to give the message of salvation to everyone.

At the civic reception that took place immediately after the Eucharistic celebration, responding to all that was said and given to him, Dominic Cardinal Ekandem inserted his cardinalate into the Body of Christ, the church, and tailored it to the local church in Nigeria. He went on to say, "Further more, as the Vatican is a world recognized State, my appointment as a Cardinal puts Nigeria into the Executive Board of the World's most influential state in the Diplomatic World."[325] He implored all Christians to thank God for the honor conferred on the nation by his election while begging God to continue to endow the nation with countless blessings and peace.

Turning to Enugu as a place of his studies as a seminarian, he told the people to continue to fertilize the land with good works and generosity so that grace might abound all the more. On the same vein, he implored all Christians to exercise charity, thoughtfulness, and maturity in facing Church problems[326] so as to bring about meaningful growth.

The genuine spirit of interchange of ideas and pleasantries is indicative of the fraternal and loving coexistence without any manipulations or deception. The sharing was genuine, deep, and all embracing. Freedom of speech as well as openness of heart toward the people and one another in the episcopate were obvious. Such an attitude could not have been possible except in an atmosphere of mutual understanding and trust.

This goes to buttress the fact that the long existent friendship in the episcopacy went beyond tribe, ethnic, and language barrier. That is why the friendship was deep and lasting. Love and unity expressed themselves in the "guard of honor" mounted by the Knights of St. John International that the cardinal proposed that serious consideration be given to its existence. It was the powerful support of Bishop Okoye, CSSp and Bishop Mark Unegbu, the bishop of Owerri, which caused that group of knights to exist in Nigeria. They saw the need. They moved for it and opened infinite doors of blessings for the interested Christians in Nigeria. These three were the link between the hierarchy and the new order of Knights of St. John International. The dream of the new set of knights was realized through their foresight. A person like Bishop Okoye or Bishop Mark Unegbu would not have gone out of his way to associate with the cardinal if they considered or held him to be anti-Igbo either during the prewar, the war period, or the postwar time. They discovered none and held on to none but moved ahead to foster their unity and single vision for the good of the flock and growth of the kingdom of God.

As the chargé d'affaires indicated in his congratulatory message, that the honor was done to the nation, the conferral of that honor became a national celebration. Many people who did not know the cardinal in person were eager to meet or see him. Such was the situation when His Grace, the archbishop of Onitsha (one of the most populated Catholic areas in the country), Most Rev. Francis Arinze, who later became the second Nigerian cardinal, invited him for a reception in the archdiocese. One of the Knights of St. John International after the visit of Cardinal Ekandem to Onitsha boasted that he shook hands with the newly appointed cardinal and even took a photograph with him. Another who had known the cardinal for a long time stunned the rest when he said that he had eaten with him in his house. On hearing this, others who wanted to meet the cardinal face to face asked if an appointment could be booked for them to go and visit him. Such was the air of the celebration. This could be likened to the beatification of Blessed Cyprian Michael Iwene Tansi whose joy of beatification swept through the whole nation as the first "beatified brother." It was a great encouragement to all and sundry. Even the non-Catholics rejoiced that, at last, Catholicism had gained root in Nigeria through the recognition of one of her members.

D.   The Seminarians' Congratulatory Message

Here is the brief congratulatory message that Cosmas Udoma, the primus of Ikot Ekpene Diocese, sent to the newly constituted cardinal in consistory on behalf of the seminarians. He reminded the cardinal of the need to pursue the idea of the national seminary and bring it to completion:

IKOT EKPENE

28th April 1976

Dear Lordship,

We congratulate you on your recent elevation to the status of a Cardinal by His Holiness Pope Paul VI in Rome. We are especially grateful to God for conferring this office and honour on you and we wish you long life and God's blessings in the ministry.

We hope that your new appointment will give you the opportunity to propose and effect the establishment of a National Seminary where many Nigerians from different tribes and languages will study for the priesthood in our country.

May God bless your appointment and ministry. Amen.

Yours respectfully
Cosmas M. I. Udoma
(For and on behalf of Ikot Ekpene Seminarians)[327]

E.   Some Outstanding Events

As a humble and principled man, Cardinal Ekandem was always open to the various events that took place. He never died with the situation. Like the Lord Jesus Christ in his Paschal Mystery who knew the way out of the tomb, he always emerged in light after darkness. He was a great listener. From his listening, he learned from others and tapped from their resources and wealth of experiences. He never regarded himself as having it all. Whenever the good of the people and or the principles of God established by divine law or ecclesiastical jurisdiction, the magisterium, he was always there to defend, correct, teach, and inspire people toward what was best and desirable without seeking his own good. That is what his selfless services gained for him. Sometimes that disposition brought him great troubles, but he was always at peace. He knew how to adjust and how to be firm at the same time.

a.   Diplomatic Speech at the Governor's Visit to the Rehabilitation Center, Ukana Iba

The year was 1985, twelve years after the establishment of St. Joseph Rehabilitation Center, Ukana Iba, Ikot Ekpene Local Government Area now in Essien Udim Local Government Area of Akwa Ibom State. It was in that year that the executive governor of Cross River State, Brig. Gen. Dan Archibong, decided to visit the center and to see the children being trained in carpentry, welding, sewing, shoemaking, typing, and literacy studies in order to provide a foundation for their future and authentic living. The institution focused on the physically impaired.

Before the arrival of His Excellency, the military governor, the security officers came early to the scene to check everything, examining the seats, tables, and whatever was there. After their thorough examination and scrutiny, they rearranged the items and sat. Some of them were standing, while a few of them were patrolling until the arrival of the governor. He arrived the premises with fanfare and blaring of siren. Before his arrival, Cardinal Ekandem, who was always punctual at every event, was sited waiting for him as the chief host.

As part of the protocol after the arrival of the governor, the cardinal was requested to say the opening prayer, which he happily did. He begged God to assist in the whole celebration and visit and to bless the governor and his entourage, the state, the children and staff of St. Joseph Rehabilitation Center, and all their benefactors and benefactresses. He also asked for God's special grace and guidance in all things, especially in the process of doing his will, promoting the welfare of the poor ones of the society, and raising deep consideration and concern for the poor in all generations so that his name may ever be glorified. At the end, he submitted all to God the Father through Jesus Christ his Son and Lord who lives and reigns forever and ever.

After the prayer, the introduction of the various dignitaries; the welcome speech by Sr. Xavier Daily, DC now Sr. Alice Daily, DC, the coordinator of the center who outlined the work of the institution; how it was funded by Misereor,[328] the CBM (Christoffel Blindenmission) in Germany with two members of staff sent by them as specialists to train others in skill acquisition and rehabilitation; together with some voluntary workers in the place, the number of students, and so on took place. She showed the institution's deep appreciation for the visit of the governor and pleaded that it be made regularly since the children and the institution were very pleased to receive him.

Then came the moment for the governor to make his speech. Governor Archibong made a powerful and impressive speech. As part of his contribution to the work and solidarity, in order to demonstrate the good will of the government, he gave automatic government employment to a staff who was also physically impaired but worked in the place. The applause was thunderous, and the whole arena was lit with joy, and all wished that the governor visited frequently to improve things for these physically impaired members of the society so as to show them a greater sense of belonging and love.

When Cardinal Ekandem was given the opportunity to speak, he stood as his custom normally was. He thanked God the giver of life who sustains everything in being even in moments of difficulties. He provides for his children at all times whether they are helped or not. He foresees that they are alive whether taken care of or whether remembered. Before God, the physically impaired or physically challenged are the same before him. Even though the diocese may not have much, she tries to provide from her meager resources, trusting the benefactors and benefactresses who are moved to support these lovely children of God who have a bright future as long as they struggle through the huddles of life and their inhibitions. They remain cheerful and grateful to God despite their situation. They become a source of inspiration and joy to those who come in contact with them.

The missionaries like the Daughters of Charity who recognize the worth of these children do not hesitate to help the children in every way possible. They become the mothers and fathers in the absence of their biological parents. Since many of these children do not have their parents, the sisters occupy that role and do not only fill the gap but lead them to God as well. Whether their institution is recognized by the government and whether the other institutions are returned to the proprietors, supported or not, the children do acknowledge that they are recognized by God and are equally cherished by him. The children develop a sense of pride and love that they consciously or unconsciously transmit having learned it in the atmosphere of love. The government has done well to remember them today. It is a great gesture of solidarity with the children and with the church; we are grateful. The children are Nigerians like every other child. They deserve just and equitable treatment as others.[329]

His words were weighty and well chosen. The speech produced the desired effect. The governor's visit paved way for many things that took place later. Hitherto, the battle to return or retain schools and hospitals taken over by the government after the Nigerian Civil War created a battleground and caused the proprietors to fight for their rights. Although the Anglicans and some others who established schools and hospitals did not bother very much about the return of those institutions, the Catholic Church was vehement on getting back her institutions. The government, on the other hand, held tenaciously on to them and would not release or hand them over. Mr. Ukpabi Asika, the only civilian (governor) administrator of East Central State, made the first move to take over schools and hospitals in East Central State. He succeeded in claiming what was not proper to the government. The gesture of depriving the proprietors of their institutions was later extended to many places in the country when he became minister of education. That was properly Mr. Asika's contribution to his state and nation.

Educational policy incorporated the takeover of schools into its system, and it became a national policy by confiscating them. Even in that awkward situation, some states did not adopt the system. The former Benue Plateau State that incorporated Benue State, Kogi State, and Plateau State did not adopt it. Some teachers in private schools were still paid by the government as it used to happen during the prewar period. The same applied to Kogi State that was cut off from Benue. The Catholic institutions were still receiving the subvention, and some of the Catholic teachers in those schools were still being seconded to the institutions concerned. Like mother, like daughter.

In the east, that is, east central, and the southeast, what is now eastern zone, and the south-south zone, received the greatest dose of the educational policy and takeover. Abp. Anthony Olubunmi Okogie of Lagos Archdiocese, who is now Anthony Cardinal Okogie, went to the court several times against the government, fighting for the return of Catholic schools and hospitals, all to no avail. The people presumed that the problem was partly fueled by the Anglicans who spearheaded the takeover and resisted the return of the institutions together with some Catholic teachers who felt that the private schools had too much authority over the teachers and limited their freedom.

It is probable that some of these factors lay behind government retention of schools and the refusal to hand them back to the proprietors. It is a battle fought tenaciously by Dominic Cardinal Ekandem even though he did not see its outcome. He abided by the injunction that the missionaries can open new schools, but the others would not be returned. Fortunately, the second civilian governor, Chief Godswill Akpabio, has authorized and handed over the institutions to the proprietors who were willing to receive them back despite the deplorable situations. He went as far as giving a huge amount to each of the schools as takeoff grant to help in rehabilitation and restructuring. However, after some time, some people went backward and engineered him to take back some of the institutions like the Mercy Hospital, which he promised to take proper care of and pay the staff in time. Of course, that did not happen.

The church still retained that hospital since it was already handed over. During the days of Cardinal Ekandem, the only green light was in the area of hospitals although that did not materialize except in the appointment of key personnel in the area of management and governance in the hospital setting. That is what led to the appointment of Mrs. Elizabeth Ekong as commissioner for health during the military regime of Gov. Eben Ibim Princewill, the military governor of Cross River State. Mrs. Ekong was loyal to the church and loyal to the government. It took her a great deal of energy to maintain that balance properly because of her deep Catholic faith and recourse to the cardinal as her spiritual father in important decisions. Fortunately or unfortunately, she was the only female commissioner among all others in that regime.

The diplomatic speech delivered by the cardinal opened the way for dialogue that normalized the relationship between the church and the state. It was during the time of Brig. Dan Archibong that the seed of negotiation was sown. The governor visited St. Joseph's Rehabilitation Center where the prince-prelate was there. He received the governor and spoke in his normal gentle and uncoarsed voice, making his points one after the other. The prelate's speech opened a door of dialogue that became fruitful later on.

During that particular visit, the aides of the governor who came to arrange everything and see that all was well wanted the seat of the prelate to be kept together with that of the governor. The secretary of the prelate knowing the situation on the ground refused to put the two seats together and immediately rushed to the cardinal who said, "No, the seats should be separated. If they are kept together, I will not sit there. They have to be separated." The disagreement was about handing over of schools and hospitals. This underlined the diplomatic speech that yielded the desired effect at the end. The prelate did not want to exchange the right of the poor children of God for his own glory. He stood his ground but for the sake of the children of God.

This calls to mind his questioning of the land officer in charge of land distribution in the Ministry of Lands and Survey in Ikot Ekpene Local Government Area who boasted that a particular priest could have been beaten because of his refusal to surrender the land bought by His Eminence Cardinal Ekandem himself to some villagers. It could be the land officer wanted to manipulate things in conjunction with the villagers. The cardinal asked the land officer, "So you would have stood there watching the villagers lay violent hands on the Priest of God because he was fighting for land for his father or members of his family or for himself, was it not for the Church of God? All right, go ahead and let them beat him. What will you gain from that? As long as there is no justice, there will be no peace. Do the just thing, you will have peace likewise every other person."[330] This took place in 1984. In this case, he could easily have said with the psalmist: "Non-nobis Domine non-nobis sed nomini tuo da gloriam," "Not to us Lord not to us but to your name give the glory" (Ps. 115:1). The priest involved sang with the Israelites the psalm of victory in recognition of God's benevolence and salvation: "In exitu Israel d'Aegypto, domus Iacob de populo babaro," "When Israel came out of Egypt, the house of Jacob from people of strange language..." (Ps. 114:1).

The desire of Cardinal Ekandem was not only to work with diocesan priests alone but also made great efforts to accommodate those in congregations like the Vincentians that his predecessor invited to the Diocese of Calabar. The negotiation started in 1959 and materialized in October 1960 and their arrival in early November 1960. It was part of the foresight of his predecessor, Most Rev. James Moynagh, and the incumbent in the person of Cardinal Ekandem.

b.   The Ordination of the Vincentians and an Abuja Priest

The Ordination of the Vincentians by Cardinal Ekandem and blessing of the Cardinal by Fr. EDEM CM, one of the newly ordained priests.

The Diaconate Ordination of Rev. Michael Edem CM The year 1983 was a momentous and an epoch-making year for the Vincentian Fathers and brothers in Nigeria. That year formed a bridge and laid a subsequent cornerstone for the growth of the Vincentians in Nigeria. In 1960, His Excellency Most Rev. James Moynagh, SPS invited the Vincentian Fathers to Nigeria. The negotiations started in 1959, passing through Vatican City, coming back to Dublin, and connecting Calabar where Bishop Moynagh lived. The missionaries arrived Nigeria at the end of October 1960. Since that time, there were no priestly ordinations till 1973 when Cardinal Ekandem as the ordinary of Ikot Ekpene Diocese ordained the first Vincentian priest, Very Rev. Fr. Timothy Njoku, CM at St. Vincent De Paul Catholic Church, Ikot Obong Edong, Ikot Ekpene, South Eastern State, the place that the Vincentians first settled and built up.

A big gap existed between that first ordination and the second one of Very Rev. Fr. Anthony Njoku who was ordained at St. Paul's Catholic Church Owerri in December 1975 by Bishop Mark Unegbu. Father Anthony later went back to his diocese in Owerri. After these, two ordinations came, the set in 1983 ordained by His Eminence Dominic Cardinal Ekandem, ten years after the ordination of the first Nigerian Vincentian. The 1983 ordination took place at the Cathedral Church of St. Anne, Ifuho, Ikot Ekpene. Fathers Richard Ikechukwu Diala, CM and Michael Imediedu Edem, CM, ordained in July on the feast of Our Lady of Mount Carmel, formed the second set of Vincentians in Nigeria. The two Vincentians were ordained with Rev. Fr. Wilfred Ojukwu, the first priest of Abuja Archdiocese, originally from Nnewi in Anambra State, Nigeria.

In his reflection, the cardinal was very grateful to the missionaries in general and particularly grateful to the Vincentians whose sons were ordained to work in the Nigerian church. Fr. Richard Diala, CM from Oguama- Ihenworie Ikpa in Owerri Diocese, now Archdiocese of Owerri, and Fr. Michael Edem, CM from Ibiaku Obio Ndobo, Uyo, ordained under Calabar Diocese now in Uyo Diocese, formed the second set. Father Edem, CM is the very first Vincentian priest from Ibibio/ Efik/Annang language group. He is the very first from what is now Calabar Ecclesiastical Province. It was an epoch-making event that drew the Vincentians and the Daughters of Charity of St. Vincent De Paul from all parts of the country and beyond. Father O'Hergaty, CM came from Ireland representing the visitor or provincial superior of the Congregation of the Mission in Ireland at that ceremony. The link had to be made since the missionaries came from Ireland to evangelize the eastern part of Nigeria, especially Owerri area, and southeastern part of Nigeria in Calabar Diocese. The base from where they functioned was at Abiakpo Ikot Essien in Ikot Ekpene. Since the cardinal ordained the first Vincentian priest by virtue of the Vincentians presence in the diocese likewise the second set, he can easily be called the father of the Vincentians in Nigeria.

c. Cardinal Ekandem and the Coming of the Knights of St. John International

One may be wondering why the origin of the Knights of St. John International in Nigeria should feature in the biography of Dominic Cardinal Ekandem and not the Papal Knights of St. Gregory or St. Sylvester that started with six people, and only one of them, Sir A. T. Beka, is the only surviving original member. The simple answer is because of his specific involvement in its establishment in Nigeria even though he also established that of Saints Gregory and Sylvester.

In 1976, there was a move to establish the Knights of St. John International in Nigeria. It was that same year that Bigard Memorial Seminary, faculty of philosophy, Ikot Ekpene, was to commence at Ikot Ekpene. Students and staff, both the academic and nonacademic staff, including the domestic staff, were transferred from Uwani-Enugu to Ikot Osurua/Abiakpo Ntak Inyang site in Ikot Ekpene Local Government Area. Its beginning prepared a seminal ground of molding the future autonomous major seminary called St. Joseph Major Seminary. God blessed Nigeria that same year by granting the first Nigerian cardinal in the person of Dominic Cardinal Ekandem by Pope Paul VI, now St. Pope Paul VI. It took happened during the consistory of 1976. It was a year of great favor from God for Nigeria and for the Catholic Church. The National Missionary Seminary/ Society witnessed the approval of the National Episcopal Conference of Nigeria during the Kaduna meeting. It was also the year that preceded the foundation and establishment of the Missionaries of St. Paul in Nigeria in 1977.

The blessing showered on the Catholic Church was not limited to the official inauguration of the major seminary in Ikot Ekpene; it also extended to the establishment of the Knights of St. John International in the country. During the annual CBCN (Catholic Bishops' Conference of Nigeria) of 1976, one of the major discussions about the implantation of the ancient and noble order of the Knights of St. John International featured prominently embracing various degrees of divergent motions. The nascent group in Akwa Ibom State noted in their souvenir program of events that "in spite of early teething problems, it has grown from strength to strength…"[331] The discussions about the establishment of the new order seemed to be moving forward and backward. The Knights of St. Mulumba had been established in the country for almost twenty- three years. It tried to effectively stop the various prominent Nigerian laity from joining secret cults that counteracted their faith and caused it to become a counterfeit one. Great tribute is to be paid to them.

When the proposition to establish the Knights of St. John International came on the agenda, it aroused a very strong and open discussion. The opposition by some bishops backed by the officers of Knights of St. Mulumba together with other eminent members of the already existent order was fierce. One of the main objections was that the order of Knights of the St. John International was a foreign one and should not be allowed to come and mingle with the one founded in Nigeria since 1953. The main aim of the opposition was to make sure that the incoming order of Knights of St. John International never took off since the old wine is better. Could it be that selfishness played a role? Convincing arguments were proffered embracing the pros and the cons. The arguments had almost tilted toward the annihilation of that seminal idea when Cardinal Ekandem stood to speak. This is what made Col. A. E. N. Izuwah, the vice president of the Owerri Grand Commandery, during the installation of new aspirants to describe the establishment of the order as taking place "under intense pressure and criticism."[332]

It was in this atmosphere that Cardinal Ekandem proposed that each bishop should make it optional and voluntary for those who want to join the new order of Knights. Since the Knights of St. John International belonged to the Catholic Church, and the whole church is universal, there is nothing foreign about the Knights of St. John coming to Nigeria since

Nigeria is part of the universal church. The whole church is one. The Knights in Nigeria are part of the knights in Europe or in America or in any other part of the world. They are one. He also added that if there were any candidates who were interested in the new order and lived in a different diocese and felt like going to join the order existing in another diocese, they should be free to do so. The proper bishop should not hinder such persons but should facilitate and aid such desire to come true. If they were pleased to join the already existent one of St. Mulumba, there should be no hindrance whatsoever.

The first thing to be noticed is the persuasive power of the cardinal. His ability to simplify complex problems and proffer very simple and solutions stands out.

Secondly, the freedom of the individual was underscored. This is similar to the approach of Bishop Shanahan when he visited Maynooth proposing a short-term period of missionary work that fascinated the students and gave them opportunity to respond positively. The ordinary or the candidate should not be under any compulsion to act. There should be no coercion by anyone as long as the person freely chooses to opt for Knights of St. John or St. Mulumba. The ordinary needs an open heart to accommodate those who choose to take the optional exit instead of the conventionally recognized one.

Thirdly, the intrinsic link between the knights and the universal church should never be overemphasized or neglected. The necessary emphasis should be made. His great sense of logic and the principle of unity in diversity expressed themselves clearly. As long as the church is universal and Knights of St. John International are part of the church in her universality, they are not restricted to any particular tribe, nation, or region. Such characteristic defies unnecessary circumscription and circumspection.

The proposal met the support of Bishop Godffrey Mary Paul Okoye, CSSp of Enugu and Bishop Mark Unegbu of Owerri. At this point, the matter was laid to rest, and freedom was given to the members to go ahead. The man who came up with the idea of the knighthood of St. John was Sir Kevin Ejiogu. He witnessed the operation of the Knights of St. John when he was in Togo, and coming back to Nigeria, he wanted to experience what happened over there. Consequently, he started making enquiries, and eventually his bishop brought it to the Catholic Bishops' Conference for discussion.

d.   Its Establishment at Enugu, Owerri, and Ikot Ekpene

Since the two bishops who supported Cardinal Ekandem on the necessity of establishing the new order, Bishop Okoye of Enugu, who already had the personnel that was capable of piloting the affairs of the newly found order, gathered the people concerned and formed the seminal group there, giving room to the first establishment of Knights of St. John International at Enugu, which eventually became the national headquarters having its *temple* there. Owerri became the second place of establishment at the invitation of Bishop Unegbu. The main person who made the proposal and sought for its establishment on the Nigerian soil, Cardinal Ekandem formed a small group that began the Knights of St. John in Ikot Ekpene Diocese later. Ikot Ekpene became the third place to have the Knights of St. John.

The cardinal called Mr. Cletus A. O. Etim, the general secretary of Ikot Ekpene Diocesan Council; Chief A. T. Beka, the president at the time; Mr. Sylvestre Esu; Mr. Adam Bassey Nyong; and Mr. Fidelis Akpan to join and start the new order in the diocese. The cardinal had problem of establishing the Knights of St. John in the Diocese of Ikot Ekpene because most of those who wanted to be involved in the foundational group were mostly teachers. That is why he did not opt to establish it first at Ikot Ekpene. He gave room to the two bishops, Okoye and Unegbu, who had the personnel to start the commandery in their diocese. The formation of Knights of St. John International in each diocese is called commandery, paralleled with the group of St. Vincent De Paul Society in a parish that is called conference; and the one in the diocese is called the council, while archdiocesan one is called the metropolitan council. Each group has its nomenclature and modus operandi.

It is to be noted that the one man who moved the motion for acceptance and establishment of the Knights of St. John, that is, His Eminence Dominic Cardinal Ekandem, now became the third in order of establishment. That is why Christ the Lord said that the greatest must be the servant (Matt. 23:11–12). It is clearly manifested here. Ikot Ekpene Commandery has #423 as the present code, Commandery #423, Ikot Ekpene.[333] It took four years from the date of the discussion to the time of establishing the commandery in Ikot Ekpene.

The procedure of admitting members into the Knights of St. Mulumba was "by invitation" of certain elderly persons into the group, especially after having looked at the person's practice of faith, social life, and general comportment, including financial stability. The financial aspect comes in because of contributions and dues together with charitable works that the group may decide to embark on. It is not meant to show affluence or to show who is rich or financially buoyant. It aims at the humanitarian and promotional goal focused on evangelization. The members carried out the invitation and sought recommendation from the parish priest and, eventually, a confirmation of the bishop. From the information about the beginnings of Knights of St. John International, the bishops invited the people they deemed fit to form the nucleus of the new knighthood and groomed them to what the church wanted. A slight difference but very important.

e.   A Brief History of the Coming of the Knights of St. John into Nigeria

The ancient and noble order of the Knights of St. John was established by the early crusaders of Amalfi in the Kingdom of Naples in 1048 to provide a haven for and to defend the sick and weary pilgrims to and from the Holy Land. Naples became a very important port and point of intersection for the pilgrims of the time because of sea voyage. This order of Knights then progressed from just providing succor to the pilgrims and defending them to the spiritual level where the order became dedicated to the services of the Mother Church to create and foster true fraternal relationship among its members while practicing faith, hope, and charity as the cardinal principles of the order. The order is semi military in nature with military rankings; for example: officer cadet, second lieutenant, lieutenant, captain, major, lieutenant colonel, colonel, brigadier, and the various groups of generals that are applicable.

The group established in Naples soon disappeared and was revived in the United States of America in the last quarter of the nineteenth century, precisely in Dayton, Ohio, in 1870. As a result of voyage, immigration, seeking for greener pastures, Christian religious revival, visits, interaction, and discussion motivated the reconstitution of the group. The reawakening aimed at inculcating Christian principles; encouraging practice of virtues; respecting the clergy; protecting ladies; assisting widows and orphans; developing better conceptions of public duty; infusing the society with the concept of loftier morality; fighting against advancing bulwark of social disorder; inspiring love for the country and its constitutions; and imitating of the virtues of the medieval knights whose good sense of honor and love for the truth, piety, courage, respect for women, boundless Christian charity, that is, Christian charity toward all irrespective of creed, color, sex, race, language, or religion.

In the United States of America, owing to their determination to support the constitutions of the country and a host of other ideals, it was recognized and incorporated by the senate on May 6, 1886, as "Knights of St. John, the Roman Catholic Union of Knights a 'body politic and corporate, with perpetual succession.'"[334] St. John the Baptist became the patron of the order, a patron of the most chivalric order, the Knights of St. John Hospitallers later known as Knights of St. John of Jerusalem, Rhodes, and Malta. The order spread to many places and was later introduced into West Africa at Saltpond in Gold Coast in 1937.[335] Cape Coast is now known as Ghana.

The first port of call after Ghana was Liberia before spreading to Togo. It was at Togo that the first worthy president, Sir Kevin N. O. Ejiogu, from Nigeria came in contact with the group. He expressed interest in having the order in his country, Nigeria. The interest was examined, weighed, discussed, and given approval by the West African Grand Commandery based in Ghana under the leadership of Brig. Gen. Sam Aggrey, KSJ, grand president, West Africa Grand Commandery Knights of St. John.[336]

After the expiration of Sir Kevin N. O. Ejiogu, KSJ's term as the first president of the order of Knights of St. John International and founder of the Holy Spirit Commandery #414, Enugu,[337] Sir Robert E. Odinkemelu, KSJ became the second worthy president of the Holy Ghost Commandery #414, Enugu, and Grand Deputy Organizer for Nigeria—Ladies Auxiliary-Knights of St. John.[338] Mr. Odinkemelu was generally known and addressed by fellow members of the order as Bob, being an abbreviation of his first name. He was very popular among them.

Cardinal Ekandem was aware of the misunderstanding that ensued during the Nigerian/Biafran Civil War. He knew that many Igbos, because of lack of understanding the proper situation, misunderstood him. The misunderstanding found itself into the book of Father Cosmas on the cardinal. He portrayed the cardinal as being tribalistic and anti-Igbos. Asking the Igbo sisters to return home until after the civil war and appoint an Efik-speaking person in the interim as superior general, as discussed in chapters eight and nine, inflamed that misunderstanding. Some could have lynched him if they had the opportunity. Fortunately, it never occurred. One of those who had misconstrued the situation was Chief R. Odinkemelu. He was prominently placed before the ensuing conflict in the country. He was still influential during the civil war. With his bias about the cardinal carried over from the war propaganda and lack of correct facts, he continued in that spirit until he became the commander in charge of the Knights of St. John in Nigeria.

On the day of his visit to the cardinal after his election, he went to consult with the cardinal. The cardinal was surprised to learn that he was coming to visit him. He was conscious of the fact that Odinkemelu had some reservations about him. As a shepherd and father, he was disposed toward his son's visit while being circumspective at the same time. When Odinkemelu came in, Cardinal Ekandem had resigned himself to whatever fate had in store for him at that moment.

Could it be that Odinkemelu had come to molest him or what? He resigned and sat there. Surprisingly enough, the visit of Sir Robert Odinkemelu had a different aim. It was a mission connected with Knights of St. John International.

His approach was totally different. What ensued during his visit to the cardinal was that of filial relationship nourished by genuine love that arose from the newly gained understanding or conversion when he discovered the truth. The truth came from the two bishops, Okoye and Unegbu, who regarded the cardinal as their brother bishop. Instead of hating or nursing hatred as he probably did in the past, things rather worked out differently. It could be surmised that Bishop Okoye, who was a very close friend of the cardinal, advised him to approach the cardinal and present himself as an officer of the order so as to help resolve some issues in the process of establishment. Necessity drew him closer to the cardinal who was ready to receive him.

Since after that visit, he never withdrew the demonstrated filial love. He showed genuine and real love till death.

If this influential man who did not have the proper disposition at the initial stage eventually changed his mind when he discovered the truth, does this entail ethnicism and hatred of the Igbos? Surely, it cannot be! If Bishop Unegbu, who was his contemporary in the minor seminary, did not get on so well with him, he might not have supported the cardinal's idea of establishing the new order of Knights of St. John. He could have abstained from supporting the cardinal's proposal, and the order could have died a natural death. Perhaps there would never have been the ancient Order of St. John International in Nigeria, but it came to stay. A misconception should never be considered as truth.

Mr. Emmanuel Eleanya, KSM, a senior and respected knight of St. Mulumba, is an enthusiast and great lover of Cardinal Ekandem. He opted to write this biography himself. He made the proposal to the cardinal about writing this biography before the present author joined him to start the research. He was the man who made most of the outline and questionnaires used in the various interviews. The prologue and the Maynooth Fathers or the Kiltegan Fathers bear his imprint with some moderations as found in the present form. He is a typical Owerri indigene, an Igbo man of the first order, who never experienced the supposed hatred of the cardinal but the loving tenderness of the prelate. Mr. Eleanya worked very closely with Cardinal Ekandem in Abuja till the time of his death. This goes to demonstrate his openness toward all. Is that not the reason why Rome chose him to be the first administrator and bishop of Abuja, making him head high in the midst of his brothers? The paternal and fraternal love between the cardinal and Sir E. Eleanya, KSM made him to start this biography. The whole venture is a living testimony of its own.

The very first priest he met at St. Mary's Parish, Zuba, as part of Minna Diocese at the time was an Igbo. He stayed with him and conversed and interacted and dined with him. The priest in question simply remarked the simplicity and affability of the cardinal. They lived as friends and as equals. The cardinal stayed there most of the time until buildings were erected at Gwagwalada and much more later in Garki in the Federal Capital Territory.

f.   Concerning the Catholicity of the Church

The thoughts of Cardinal Ekandem about the universal church gives an insight into what he had in mind about the church and the members of the church founded by Christ himself. He says:

> Those who have chosen to be Catholics want nothing but Catholicism in its entirety. We Nigerians do not like adulteration, whether of food or drinks hence the sincere Catholics do not want and do not need a watered-down Catholicism either by ignoring of healthy principles or in the name of adaptation. Nigeria needs faith, the whole faith and nothing but the faith. Only faith in its entirety will be meaningful and good enough for Nigerians, nothing mutilated, nothing disfigured, nothing derogatory. Here I like to borrow an expression I read once from Dr. Nnamdi Azikiwe's writing when in his rendering of verse 4 of chapter one of the Old Testament Canticle of Solomon, he said, "I am African, I am black but beautiful".[339]
>
> The perception of the Catholic Church and its Catholicism embraces what is authentic, what is universal, what is amiable, what is united, what is pure, and what is noble. Linking up philosophers and theologians with the formation of the future clergy, he likens it to the British Commonwealth, which the Catholic Church is to borrow from. Only what is good or positive in the commonwealth is to be borrowed but not the limitations of the organization. Even though she "belongs to all the Nations of the world and is destined to serve all, hence in the theological language of the Church she is described as Catholic or Universal. But in so far as she belongs to every Nation equally, it is a National Church and so for us the Catholic Church is our National Church and we are determined to keep her so, but without national vices or limitations."[340]

With the strong sense of Catholicism opening up to its universality and unity in diversity, he undertook the task laid on him by the supreme pontiff, Pope John Paul II, of piloting the affairs of the nonexistent mission but which was to commence in earnest and reach the point of fruition. That is the Abuja Independent Mission.

Chapter Eleven

MISSIO SUI JURIS (INDEPENDENT MISSION)

The Abuja Independent Mission[341]

*The best perfection is to do ordinary things in
a perfect manner. Constant fidelity in little
things is a great and heroic virtue.*

—*St. Bonaventure*

THE IBIBIOS SAY, "Yam can only be planted where a suitable support is found so that it can conveniently climb." Cardinal Ekandem was such a tree with a such a plant with such a support. The pope as head of all the congregations operating in the Roman Curia and through the *Propaganda Fide* did not hesitate to appoint Dominic Cardinal Ignatius Ekandem as the first ecclesiastical superior of Abuja Independent Mission. The necessary qualities and attributes required were exemplified in the cardinal. The task to be accomplished was a very difficult one.

Knowing the material from which Cardinal Ekandem was constituted, the following distinguished him: his experience as the first bishop of Anglophone West Africa; his being the first bishop of Ikot Ekpene Diocese from its inception to its flowering; his experience as the first president of the Catholic Bishops' Conference of Nigeria (CBCN), the first Nigerian cardinal; his obedience to the church, to his superiors: the pope and the Roman Curia; his docility[342] of heart, mind and spirit; his love of the church; his readiness to learn and to sacrifice; his acceptability by Catholics and non-Catholics alike including the government; his foresight; his admiration by young and old; his exemplary life, friendliness, firmness, paternal love; and his principles of standing up courageously with passion for the truth and the ability to pursue it vigorously to the end marked him out as the candidate who could weather the storm as he effectively collaborated with the St. Patrick Fathers.

This type of trust and confidence had already been exercised by the pope in the Vatican through *Propaganda Fide*, Congregation for the Propagation of the Faith for the Evangelization of Peoples, in the sixties when he was given the mandate to be the administrator of the Port Harcourt Diocese when the late Bishop Godfrey Mary Paul Okoye, CSSp was asked to leave Port Harcourt at the end of the Nigerian- Biafran Civil War. He was the substantive bishop or the ordinary of Ikot Ekpene Diocese when he became the administrator of Port Harcourt. He was far younger when he took charge of the Port Harcourt Diocese together with his proper diocese of Ikot Ekpene. The charge to be the administrator of the Abuja Independent Mission was in line with what he had done earlier. In Port Harcourt, there were a substantial number of priests but in Abuja, he started administering the vast territory with only three priests. This was almost like one diocese in Liberia immediately after the civil war manned by only the bishop and his vicar general. The vicar general, normally termed VG, was the only surviving missionary priest operating in the entire diocese. Each of them had to celebrate four masses between Saturday evening and Sunday evening to try and touch at least some section of the diocese. It was like coming back to the crossroad to check where one started as Jeremiah 6:16 has it. This time he was far older and more advanced in age coupled with the diabetic condition of his health that nearly prevented his presence at the Second Vatican Council.

A.   Emergence of Federal Capital Territory

The idea of the Abuja Capital Territory was the brainchild of the head of state and commander in chief of the Nigerian Armed Forces, Maj. Gen. Murtala Mohamed who was assassinated by the coup d'état of Dimka in order to topple the government. The conception of this idea took place in 1976 before his assassination. Mobolaji Ajose-Adeogun was the first minister of the Federal Capital Territory (FCT). He administered the FCT for three years from 1976–1979. At this stage of the creation of Abuja Federal Capital Territory, everything was still in a fluid stage even though the idea of the FCT had come to stay owing to the territorial boundary that was already created and the extent it covered. The work of the minister at the time was to actualize the dream of the FCT. John Jatau Kadiya, 1979–1982, who immediately succeeded him and went on for the following three-year term before shorter periods of administration took place. The idea of an independent mission became stronger and started taking shape during the administration of J. J. Kadiya.

Murtala Mohamed wanted a place where everyone would feel the sense of belonging as a citizen and one that would be central to the whole nation. The decree that promulgated the movement and the transfer of all the federal ministries from Lagos to Abuja came afterward. After this first phase of the construction of skeletal structures, many of them of temporary nature, the move to relocate to Abuja began. The relocation period can be called Phase Two of Abuja where John Jatau Kadiya took over as Minister of FCT. Many ministries moved to the Federal Capital Territory.

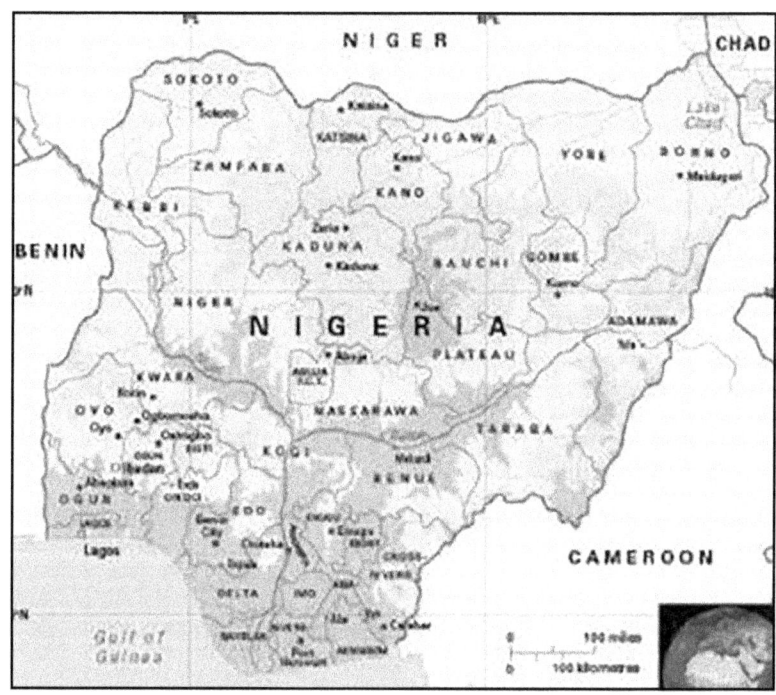

Figure 9 Map of Nigeria indicating Abuja FCT, Niger in the North, Atlantic Ocean in the South, Cameroon in the East, and Benin Republic in the West

Figure 10 Map of Nigeria Showing Various States and Boundaries
When this idea started materializing, the Catholic Church did not
hesitate or delay to move with the *signs of the times* as recommended
by *Gaudium et Spes*, a document of the Second Vatican Council held
between 1962–1965. The Catholic Bishops of Nigeria did not want
the flock going to the Federal Capital Territory to roam about there
like sheep without a shepherd. The Catholic hierarchy recognized
the need to tend, follow, and feed the flock as Jesus asked Peter to
let him feed, tend, and feed his flock. The Catholic Bishops sought
the approval of the Sacred Congregation for the Evangelization of
Peoples, *Propaganda Fide*, to have an Ecclesiastical Mission Territory
incorporating the Abuja Federal Capital Territory. *Propaganda Fide*
did not delay to grant that request made for the interest of the people
of God for the growth of the church in Nigeria.

The reign of Mobolaji Ajose-Adeogun as minister of the FCT was the constructive stage and the attempt to move from Lagos to Abuja. The construction began at Gwagwalada, and certain offices and establishments were located at Suleja in Niger State that was already operative until the changeover. That is why one of the prisons belonging to the FCT is still located in Suleja.

The Abuja Independent Mission took off when the various ministries started moving, everything centered at Gwagwalada and Suleja. Even though Suleja belonged to Niger State and still belongs to Niger State as such, it became the cradle of the FCT because of proximity. It was one of the first places people found accommodation when they arrived at the Federal Capital Territory. Gwagwalada played a prominent role since it was the first place that most of the things commenced from. That is why offices like the immigration still has its headquarters in Gwagwalada, although it has recently been shifted to Kuje near the airport. The Government Day Secondary School (GSS), the Federal Road Safety Commission (FRSC), Federal Radio Corporation of Nigeria (FRCN), and the University of Abuja are all located in Gwagwalada. The specialist hospital, the high court of appeal, the main post office, while the first prison, even though it later acquired the name of Medium Security Prison has lost its first position. Krikri Prison is now called the Maximum Security Prison. The international airport named after Dr. Nnamdi Azikiwe is located near Kuje. These are some indications of what Gwagwalada was meant to be—namely, the hub of the entire Federal Capital Territory. The excessive heat rising from the low altitude and gradient of the place gave it a characteristic valley temperature and cost it its primacy of position as the first among equals. Gwagwalada was meant to be like Ikeja of Lagos.

B. The Arrival of the Catholic Church in the Federal Capital Territory

Generally, the arrival of the Catholic Church in Federal Capital Territory, or what is known as Abuja, was slow. The steps to begin the missionary work there were fast. When Abuja started evolving at the initial stage, it started to demonstrate features of a city. The Catholic Church did not delay in appointing Cardinal Ekandem to administer this extraordinary mission. November 6, 1981, witnessed "the official erection of Abuja as an independent mission" by the Vatican and simultaneously appointed Dominic Cardinal Ignatius Ekandem as the first person to man it as the first ecclesiastical superior of that mission with full rights and benefits with the authority to perform all necessary acts in conformity with the rule of the mission and in accordance with the Code of Canon Law. Any ecclesiastical jurisdiction is erected by the Vatican and not by the episcopal conference of the country in question. That is why the Catholic Episcopal Conference of Nigeria could not establish that independent mission. They had no *potestas ordinarius*, ordinary power and authority to do that. It was welcome news when the Vatican made that pronouncement.

The formalization and approval of Abuja Independent Mission emerged during the second year of John Jatau Kadiya as the minister of the FCT. The independent mission was to embrace the whole area called Abuja Federal Capital Territory bordering the Kaduna Diocese in Kaduna State in the north, Minna Diocese in Niger State in the west, Lokoja Diocese in Kogi State in the south, and Keffi in Laffia Diocese in Nasarawa State in the east, respectively. The cardinal was appointed the ecclesiastical superior of the new jurisdiction.

Originally, Rome wanted the mission to develop into a sovereign archdiocese with no suffragans depending on it or the archdiocese itself depending on others but was meant to be autonomous like the archdiocese of Washington or the one in Brazil. It was supposed to have a very unique position, equal to none in the country. That would not have cut Abuja Independent Mission away from active participation in the CBCN affairs except that as an independent see, it needed a special relationship with the pope and the Roman Curia. That did not happen and had to be developed in line with other dioceses.

C. The Temporary Status of Abuja Independent Mission

The cardinal would have had an opportunity to be attending the meetings of the Catholic Bishops' Conference of Nigeria (CBCN) while reporting directly to the Vatican, but the Nigerian Bishops' Conference was not comfortable with that situation and objected to it that the cardinal would become too powerful especially during the appointment of a successor. There was no ulterior motive to the proposal or a subversive one. There was no question of colonial mentality involved. It was the nature of the place as a *missio sui juris,* an independent mission that necessitated that. To counter that objection, Dominic Cardinal Ekandem suggested that "to appoint a successor, names could be submitted by each of the three former Ecclesiastical Provinces of Lagos, Onitsha and Kaduna and forwarded to Rome for eventual action and appointment of a successor. In this way, the unfounded fear generated can be resolved and dismissed."

The CBCN did not give its blessing to that suggestion. The cardinal being a docile and an obedient son of the church did not count anything as a loss but considered it as the voice of the church, which he obeyed. Noticing that there were serious objections, he laid the matter to rest. The idea of an autonomous archdiocese disappeared as quietly as it came. He did not manipulate things or mobilize some people to work on his behalf for the achievement of that goal. He realized the necessity of unity and solidarity that he fought for many years. He wanted that to grow and symbolize the independent mission.

After having put things in their proper context, he immediately embarked on planning the evangelization of the independent mission without delay. The first thing he did was to search for priests who could minister in the mission territory. Being aware that the place was dominated by indigenes who were supposed to speak Hausa, he sought for those versed in the language to begin the ministry of evangelization there. This was to forestall the people of God suffering for lack of knowledge of God and living as sheep without a shepherd.

He never allowed his apostolate as the ordinary of Ikot Ekpene to becloud his work as the administrator of Abuja Independent Mission. His first move was to approach the Most Reverend Peter Yariyok Jatau, the archbishop of Kaduna Ecclesiastical Province since Abuja was ipso facto under his jurisdiction. Abp. Peter Yariyok Jatau was very disposed to help his senior brother in the episcopacy. He was obliged to go with Cardinal Ekandem to St. Mary's Parish Suleja so as to introduce him to the area called Abuja. It was necessary to do that since the Most Reverend Peter Jatau was familiar with the terrain. Both arrived at St. Mary's Suleja and spent the night there.

D. Request for Priests from CBCN, Catholic Bishops' Conference of Nigeria, and the Arrival of Msgr. Dominic Inyang

In the summary of the presidential address of Archbishop Okogie during the meeting of the CBCN, he noted as one of his major points, "Abuja needs our joint support to ensure its material and spiritual development." Responding to the address, Archbishop Obiefuna thanked Archbishop Okogie who later became Cardinal Okogie for the points raised while observing that the points were already in the Agenda.[343] To demonstrate the importance of what Archbishop Obiefuna commented on, the second session, which began at 4:30 p.m. on Tuesday, March 6, 1990, resumed the discussion in the previous meeting treated as No. 4.4. It went thus: "A Hausa-speaking priest to be posted to Abuja." In response, Kaduna Province said, "Father Kukah had been earmarked for this position."[344] With that affirmation, the discussion on the necessity of posting a Hausa-speaking priest to Abuja was closed.

The cardinal had written to the CBCN requesting the various bishops to give him priests from their various dioceses to help in beginning the new mission. That appeal letter did not produce the desired response. The letter of appeal tendered to the bishops dismissed the tacit accusation that Cardinal Ekandem filled the mission territory with priests from his ethnic group. Fortunately, his appeal met with Archbishop Jatau's favor. That is how Rev. Fr. Matthew Hassan Kukah of the Kaduna Archdiocese (at the time Kaduna embraced the present three Ecclesiastical Provinces of Kaduna, Jos, and Abuja). The Kaduna Archdiocese itself incorporated: Kaduna, Jos, Ilorin, Makurdi, Minna, Lokoja, and Sokoto. Fr. Matthew Hassan Kukah was nominated with the approval of his ordinary, the Most Reverend Peter Yariyok Jatau. Father Matthew's name was forwarded to Rome. Rev. Matthew H. Kukah, who later became the second bishop of Sokoto was known and recognized by Rome, at least theoretically as the official person to begin the missionary activity in the newly erected jurisdiction. The recognition took place shortly after the erection of the Abuja Independent Mission. Abuja is estimated at eight hundred thousand square kilometers with an estimated population of over one million and Catholics being over ninety thousand.

Meanwhile, Cardinal Ekandem was still fully responsible for Ikot Ekpene Diocese as the local ordinary. This seems to go with the popular *parlance* that as far as the church is concerned, if the person is good and is trusted, greater and greater responsibilities are entrusted to the person. "For to him who has will more be given, and he will have abundance, but from him who has not, even what he has will be taken away" (Matt. 13:12). Such a practice accounts for overburdening of some persons in the church to the discontentment of many who can develop a serious spirit of jealousy that they forgot the tasks assigned to them.

E. The Zeal to Begin the Work of Evangelization in the Territory and the Process of Appointing Fr. Matthew Hassan Kukah

As soon as the discussions about Abuja Independent Mission came to an end, Cardinal Ekandem was very eager to begin the work of evangelization in the mission territory. The moment he finished discussing with the Most Reverend Peter Yariyok Jatau and learned that he was willing to release Father Kukah for the mission, Cardinal Ekandem became more eager to meet Father Matthew. His ordinary, Archbishop Jatau, had arranged with the cardinal when he and Father Kukah would meet.

After the information that he, Cardinal Ekandem, was traveling to Rome the following day, he did not tarry or hesitate to dispatch a letter to Fr. Matthew Kukah the following day, requesting him to report at Abuja to begin work since he had graciously accepted to come as a pioneer priest there. Archbishop Jatau had not even discussed this with Fr. Mathew Kukah when the cardinal dispatched the letter. That enthusiastic approach actually slowed down the process it was intended to speed up. Father Matthew could not move as quickly as the cardinal had envisaged. A vacuum was created. Fr. Kukah conjectures that the cardinal must have written the letter soon after their discussion and posted it that same day.

Even though the Vatican had approved everything about Abuja, beginning the project was very problematic. The Jews, when they came from the land of Egypt, were like nomads roaming the whole desert region until they crossed the Jordan and entered into the Promised Land. Their situation was unstable. Nothing was certain except the promises of God, God himself, and his constant protection. Their dwelling places were makeshift ones. They dwelt in tents, which also housed the Ark of God. Their destination was certain, and they knew that their leader, Moses, and his mouthpiece Aaron, his brother, were in control of affairs even though the people revolted against them.

The instability of the Jewish situation in the desert is parallel to the experiences of the first beginnings of the Abuja Independent Mission. Rome appointed Cardinal Ekandem to take charge of this new territory over and above his normal duty of being the chief shepherd of Ikot Ekpene Diocese. Rome knew him as the man on the spot. Cardinal Ekandem had the duty of seeing that the virgin mission territory that appeared as an outstation developed to a station church and from station church to parish church and finally to the status of diocese with the capacity of becoming an archdiocese, as it did at a later date.

The cardinal was a man of foresight who "worked more with his heart than with sentiment" as Rev. Fr. Matthew Kukah remarked, did not leave any stone unturned in the evangelization of the independent mission. He used all his many abilities to see that things worked out well.

Rev. Fr. Matthew Kukah, a priest of the Kaduna Ecclesiastical Province had heard of Dominic Cardinal Ekandem but had never seen or met him. He knew that Nigeria had a cardinal. The fact of not knowing or meeting the cardinal before made things more complicated for Father Kukah, who, when his ordinary, Archbishop Jatau, told him on the preceding day that they would travel the following day to Abuja to meet Cardinal Ekandem, exclaimed unconsciously, "I hope there is no trouble." Such an exclamation was indicative of his great surprise at what was happening. On the morning of the following day, Archbishop Jatau and Father Kukah left for Abuja and met with the cardinal at St. Theresa's Catholic Church, Suleja, a parish in Minna Diocese while belonging politically to Niger State. Father Kukah recalled that the cardinal was a very gracious, gentle, and humble person. These virtues galvanized their meeting and rendered their discussion so cordial that although they met for the first time, it seemed as if they had been friends for ages. However, the friendly and cordial meeting did not eliminate the shock he was experiencing.

The moment he gave his consent, Cardinal Ekandem became very joyful and thanked him very sincerely for having accepted to work in Abuja Mission. There and then, he told Father Matthew that he would be traveling to Rome the following day. Although they had spent quite some time discussing, it seemed to pass quickly; such was the cordial atmosphere that prevailed.

The shock became greater when Cardinal Ekandem told him during the discussion that he wanted him, Fr. Matthew Kukah, to help him look after the new Abuja Independent Mission. Father Matthew's spontaneous reaction was like that of Jeremiah who told God (Jer. 1:6) that he was too young and did not know how to speak. Father Matthew did not declare his incapacity to speak but did mention the impediment of being too young and inexperienced to accomplish such a task. From the look of things after having raised what he considered a legitimate objection, he immediately suggested that he would gladly work with him if he appointed a more experienced person, or rather, a more senior person, who would carry such important responsibility. Cardinal Ekandem quickly retorted by telling Fr. Matthew Kukah that he could only appoint somebody after discussion with the person. He immediately added that Father Matthew was his first choice. There was a mutual agreement between the two of them that they would both think about it.

Then he informed Father Matthew that he was on his way to Rome to see and inform the Holy Father, Pope John Paul II, that he had found a companion who would work with him in the mission. It was a big shock to Father Matthew when the disclosure was made. It is very likely that his bishop already held a previous discussion with the cardinal on the matter before intimating Father Kukah of the need to go and see Cardinal Ekandem. This accounts for the positive response of the Archdiocese of Kaduna during the CBCN meeting that Fr. Matthew Kukah had been "earmarked" for the Abuja Independent Mission.[345]

The shock continued, however. Cardinal Ekandem had dropped the message that he would soon be on his way to Rome, but before his departure, he wrote a five-page letter, which Father Matthew was unfortunately unable to find when he returned from studies in Rome. The boxes he left behind at Holy Rosary Catholic Church Wuse, Abuja before going for studies had been misplaced and could no longer be found. The letter was in one of those boxes. In the said letter, Cardinal Ekandem congratulated Fr. Matthew Hassan Kukah for accepting to work in the Abuja Capital

Territory. The letter further stressed that his name would be given to the Holy Father in Rome as his closest fellow worker and collaborator. The letter arrived two or three days after the meeting at Suleja. Meanwhile, the cardinal was already in Rome. This corroborated the point that Father Matthew's name would be given to the Holy Father.

Father Kukah conjectures that the cardinal must have written the letter immediately after their meeting and probably posted same before departing soon afterward to Rome. At that time, Father Matthew had been appointed by the Catholic Bishops' Conference of Nigeria to start the Justice, Peace, and Development Department Commission in Lagos, and here was another burden put on him coupled with the fact that he was given a special assignment by his ordinary to reorganize the various departments in the chancery/archdiocesan secretariat. That being the case, Father Matthew had developed a triangular type of life between Kaduna, Lagos, and Abuja. He had to shuttle between Lagos, Kaduna, and Abuja frequently. He stayed some days in Lagos, go to Kaduna to put in some days, and shuttle to Abuja to try and do the same until he was able to finally move to Abuja.

F. The Transition Period

The protocol was completed but the movement failed in its promptness. The progress was inescapably delayed. The logistics of sudden transfer and the failure to set things in their proper places and making the necessary handing over increased the delay. Things had to be tidied up. In the process, the faithful were lamenting about lack of ministers and their hunger for spiritual food. Some of the people went to St. Mary's Catholic Church Suleja, which was an outstation of St. Kizito's Parish that was later called St. Theresa's Catholic Church Bwari, while those who had no means became stranded, and they cried out all the more intensively like the deer pining for running streams (Cf. Psalm 42:1). The frantic effort to have a resident Catholic priest among them stimulated the faithful to write a letter to Bishop Abbah of Minna Diocese. He did not delay to forward the letter to the cardinal since he knew that the Federal Capital Territory was under his care and competence.

a.   The Arrival of Msgr. Dominic Inyang in Abuja

Cardinal Ekandem, being a man of action who liked striking the iron while still hot, made a very quick decision to ask Msgr. Dominic Ekeng Inyang of Calabar Diocese, who had just retired from the Catholic Secretariat of Nigeria in Lagos as the secretary general, to come over quickly to help out in the Abuja Independent Mission. The cardinal cleared with his proper bishop, the Most Reverend Brian Davies Usanga who later became the first archbishop of the Metropolitan See of Calabar. He requested that Monsignor Dominic should be released for the new mission. The bishop of Calabar gave his blessing and consented in "faith and with good conscience" (1Tim. 1:19) by releasing Monsignor Inyang who was asked to move as soon as possible to the mission territory. He had no alternative but to obey. St. Paul says, "Keep on working with fear and trembling, to complete your salvation, for God is always at work in you to make you willing and able to obey his own purpose. Do everything without complaining or arguing that you may be innocent and pure, as God's perfect children" (Phil. 2:12–15). The words fit very much to the emergency situation that Msgr. Dominic Ekeng Inyang found himself in.

The situation is somehow enigmatic. Natural curiosity can easily cause someone to ask for the reason why the cardinal went to Msgr. Dominic E. Inyang to come to his rescue in the difficult situation in which he found himself. Whatever caused the cardinal to approach Monsignor Inyang to come to the rescue mission is not easy to understand. Was the choice dependent on the presupposition that his bishop, Brian D. Usanga, would willingly release him as part of the response to the cardinal's appeal for priests? Could it be that he went to somebody that bore the same name with him, believing that he would be able to endure and persevere with a resilient spirit like himself? Was it because of proximity? Was it because of the needed Hausa language in the place? Was it because of previous contact and relationship? All the other questions might easily be dismissed with a simple answer of no, while the last one seems more probable than all the others.

The first meeting of the two Dominics took place in 1950. Dominic Inyang was living with his senior brother who handled the mantle of authority as the father of the family since the death of their father. Dominic and his sister were very young at the time. They grew up to see their senior brother playing the role of the father of the family, *pater familias*, as Joachim Jeremias calls the head of the family in the Passover context in his book *The Eucharistic Words of Jesus*.

Dominic ran away from the clerk quarters in Ikot Ekpene. He took a lorry to Aba where the next-in- command lived after a serious quarrel with his brother's wife at Ikot Ekpene. After the terrible quarrel, he told his sister in-law that since she had made him insult his senior brother by insulting her, he could no longer live in that house because he would not be able to look at the face of his brother he had insulted through her. Immediately, he left for Aba.

The whole family was Protestant. They belonged to the Methodist Church. Before leaving Ikot Ekpene, the sister had met a friend of hers who was a Catholic and decided to become a Catholic with the help of the friend. She was living in Aba with the brother whom Dominic went to meet. It was the sister that lived with the brother in Aba who became inclined to the Catholic religion. She was at Holy Child Convent School Ifuho. There she met her friend that wanted to wed. She was a Catholic. The lady lived almost opposite the school. The sister helped Dominic become interested in Catholicism. Dominic met Father Mahoney who became very eager to help Dominic become a Catholic. While living in Aba, Reverend Father Mahoney was greatly endeared to him. Father Mahoney was the parish priest of CKC, Christ the King Church Aba. He used to take Dominic to the places and to outstations and centers he had to celebrate the Eucharist. It was in one of those occasions that Father Mahoney told Dominic that there was a Nigerian Catholic priest from his own area called Dominic working in Abak.

Since Dominic E. Inyang was brought up in a Protestant context in the Methodist Church, his senior brother did not want him to leave the Methodist Church. Dominic continued living with his brother while waiting for an opportune moment to depart on reaching a mature age and choose his religion. The opportunity arose because of the dispute. When he met the sister at Aba, he quickly realized that without delay. At this time, Ekeng was not very much grounded in Catholicism, yet he set out to meet Father Ekandem. The search and the finding seem to point to the action of Jesus toward the disciples of John the Baptist who asked him, "Master, where do you live?" and Jesus said, "Come and see" (Jn. 1:39). "Going to see" took longer than just seeing and leaving. The disciples of John became the disciples of Jesus. Ekeng having found Father Dominic decided to move on from there.

It appears that Ekeng took the name Dominic for his baptism because of the influence of Rev. Fr. Dominic Ignatius Ekandem whom he met for the first time. The year 1950 became the date Dominic fixed for his exodus from the brother's house after a former failed attempt so that he could go and practice a religion of his own choice.

b. The First Meeting of the Two Dominics

When Dominic found him, he told him that he wanted to become a priest. Fr. Dominic Ekandem, who worked in the minor seminary in Afaha Obong, Abak, in the then Eastern Nigeria, asked him why he wanted to become a priest. Dominic Inyang told him that "priests live a simple life, or rather that priesthood is a simple life." Father Dominic never asked him any further questions or queried any further. He gave him the benefit of the doubt. Maybe Father Ekandem did not want to discourage him that is why he sent him to Ifuho. Dominic Inyang, being armed with a letter to the famous Marian priest set out to meet the parish priest of Ifuho. He did not go back to Aba after getting a letter. He went to Ifuho and delivered the letter to the priest who was popularly known as Fr. Una Eka, that is, the priest without a mother or motherless priest since the Blessed Virgin Mary was his mother. Fr. Una Eka's real name was Fr. Patrick Keeflehan. Dominic Inyang lived with Father Patrick for some time before his journey to the priesthood began through the junior seminary.

The relationship still continued and became greatly cemented when Msgr. Dominic Ekeng Inyang became the secretary general of the Catholic Secretariat of Nigeria. The longstanding relationship with his recently completed assignment at the Catholic Secretariat of Nigeria increased the link, fortified the affiliation, and gave the needed disposition of moving like a soldier without delay. No sooner had his bishop, the Most Reverend B. D. Usanga, given him the permission than he moved to the designated territory.

G. St. Mary's Catholic Church Suleja, the Touchstone of Abuja Independent Mission

St. Theresa's Catholic Church as a parish had many outstations. One of them was St. Mary's Catholic Church, which was in Suleja along the road to Kaduna from Abuja. Cardinal Ekandem led Monsignor Inyang to St. Mary's as Monsignor Inyang recalled. Monsignor Inyang arrived at Suleja on Easter Wednesday of 1982 with Dominic Cardinal Ekandem indicating that, like the apostles of old, he had to operate with the authority of the one who sent him. This is the day that the Abuja Independent Mission commenced outside its proper territory though Monsignor Dominic finally reached his destination a few days later.

H. Mr. Ansa's House, the First Residence of Priests in the Federal Capital Territory

Instinctively, Msgr. Dominic E. Inyang was curious to know where Abuja was and insisted on going to know the place. His instinct of curiosity drove him to his final destination. Somebody took him to Gwagwalada, and immediately, word went round that their long- expected priest had arrived. The instantaneous meeting was one of the most thrilling episodes of the mission of the famished people of God. Before the monsignor knew it, the faithful had met together trying to locate where he was going to stay in order to begin the mission so long expected. They came up with questions and choices for the monsignor to answer and decide upon. Before they put the question to the monsignor, one of the faithful had already volunteered to lodge Monsignor Inyang in his house, a three-bedroom apartment.

The volunteer was Mr. Ansa whose son, Mr. Emmanuel Ansa, later went to the major seminary for some time before discontinuing. Emmanuel became a teacher and taught at Saints Simon and Jude Seminary in Kuje after some years. He married Jacinta, a nurse that worked in the seminary. Mr. Emmanuel Ansa enjoyed the presence of Monsignor Inyang, who was accommodated by his father for many years in their home. That relationship caused Msgr. Inyang to be present at the wedding of Mr. Emmanuel Ansa and stayed to the end of all the celebration and reception before going back to Garki where he ministered as the vicar general of the Diocese of Abuja when things stabilized.

At that initial stage, the Catholic faithful asked Monsignor, "Which one would you prefer, to live with a family or to live in a separate apartment or to stay in a school?" Monsignor Dominic did not hesitate to say, "With a Family."[346] That answer brought great jubilation, and the people applauded heartily. They showed how happy they were by allowing the man who volunteered to accommodate him to show himself. At that point, Mr. Ansa revealed himself as the man that would be willing to accommodate him. From the jubilation of the people of God, it is obvious that the decision had already been accomplished before testing Monsignor Dominic to see the choice he would make. It is obvious that the faithful were already stimulated to maintain a high level of zeal for evangelization not only of themselves or the Federal capital Territory only but also of the world so that with teaching and preaching with religious instruction, Christ would be properly proclaimed to the world.[347] Their cooperation was simply marvelous.

Mr. Ansa told Monsignor Dominic to give him a few days to organize things in the house. Mr. Ansa saw this not only as a religious responsibility but also as a moral obligation to accommodate his priest. He traveled the following day to Uyo in Akwa Ibom State and told the wife to come and evacuate the master's bedroom since they had a higher master, Monsignor, who was to live with them. He also told her to pack her things and come down to Gwagwalada as soon as possible. The whole arrangement was completed in about three days. Msgr. Dominic Inyang packed into Gwagwalada about Friday or Saturday of the Easter week and celebrated the first Eucharist at Government Day Secondary School in Gwagwalada. There the mission in the Abuja Independent Mission took off. When the cardinal learned that Msgr. Dominic Ekeng Inyang had moved to Gwagwalada and taken residence there, he went to St. Mary's Catholic Church at Suleja, which he was accustomed to do. In the evening, he went to Mr. Ansa's house where Monsignor Dominic lodged to meet and address the people. He had a Breviary in his hand and had no other item with him. After addressing the people, he wanted to see where Monsignor Dominic stayed and was taken to the room. He never left that night but spent the night there with Monsignor Inyang in the same room. They had only one bed, and they shared it. This shows the missionary spirit of the cardinal and his simplicity. What he noticed in the life of his parish priest at Afaha Obong, he put it into practice in Gwagwalada after many years had elapsed. He revealed his true missionary character even at old age. The following day, he left and went back to Suleja and later left for Ikot Ekpene.

I. The Arrival of Fr. Matthew Kukah in Abuja

Dominic Inyang labored indefatigably for three months before the arrival of Fr. Matthew Kukah. It could be Father Matthew decided to hurry up since he learned that there was a priest from the East already working in Abuja, or perhaps he had rounded up things in his diocese of origin and in Lagos before moving to the independent mission. The arrival of Rev. Fr. Matthew Kukah ushered in a great joy just as it did when Monsignor Inyang arrived at Gwagwalada. The people were delighted. Cardinal Ekandem told Rev. Fr. Matthew Hassan Kukah and Msgr. Dominic Ekeng Inyang to go and inform Pres. Shehu Shagari that he had been posted to Abuja and that he needed a house. Although the two were told to accomplish the task, it was Fr. Matthew Kukah who eventually went to the Federal Capital Development Authority (FCDA) and informed them of the cardinal's message. They were ordered to go and look around and choose a house. They chose one in an area called the Accelerated Center. That is the present building where the education office for Abuja Archdiocese and the *Good Shepherd Newspaper* are located.

J. The First Offertory Collection, First Bazaar in the Federal Capital Territory and the Disobedience of Monsignor Inyang

The first offertory collection on Sunday amounted to twenty-five Naira nil Kobo (N 25). This was for food and for fueling of Monsignor Dominic's car. Life went on normally until the time they organized the first harvest and bazaar sales. Out of excitement, Monsignor Inyang decided to use the proceeds of the harvest, which came up to one thousand five hundred Naira (N 1,500) to travel to Rome and look for some money. When the cardinal heard that such an amount had been realized, he told

Monsignor Dominic to use that money judiciously since that was going to be his only income for the next year. At the same time, the cardinal told him if you travel with it, you must get three people to stand surety for you and guarantee you when you travel. Monsignor Dominic risked traveling with the money.

On his arrival at Lagos, he met Rev. Fr. John Burke, who became the bishop of Warri, later archbishop of Benin and an administrator of Warri Diocese. Father Burke told Monsignor Dominic that he was going to guarantee him and can even stand for him in place of the three people the cardinal spoke of. He added that he should not take the normal flight. He would see if he could find a tourist flight for him, which would make it far cheaper. Monsignor Inyang eventually traveled at the cost of five hundred Naira return ticket and saved one thousand Naira (N 1,000). He did not spend so much since his transportation in Rome was assured. Before his departure from Lagos, Father Burke spoke with his confreres in Rome and explained the situation to them. The St. Patrick Fathers offered to pick Monsignor Dominic from the airport and lodge him in their house. Unfortunately, that was the day that Francis Cardinal Arinze from Nigeria who was working at the Vatican at the time, wanted to travel home and had asked the same house to convey him to the airport.

The house responded that they were waiting for a very important visitor, and they would not be able because of the availability of the car. When Msgr. Dominic Inyang met him at the airport, he went and greeted him warmly and later learned of the travel arrangements. He was sorry about it, but the Abuja Mission was beginning to go places. The following day, he was taken to the *Propaganda Fide* where he had to apply and fill out some forms and go back waiting expectantly. Sometime after his return, as he was working, he received from the post a slim envelope bearing his name. He opened it and discovered that the content was a check for fifty thousand Deutsche Mark (DM 50,000) addressed to him. He went to the post office and changed the money. It came to eighty-five thousand Naira (N 85,000). He used that to buy cement and commence the nursery/primary school in Gwagwalada. From all indications, the school was built before the church. That was the first phase of Abuja Independent Mission.

K.   The Arrival of the First Female and Male Religious

Msgr. Dominic Inyang had earlier worked with Sr. Theresa Nwanruo, HHCJ in Lagos at the Catholic Secretariat of Nigeria. It was easier to co-opt her into the Independent Mission in the Federal Capital Territory. He spoke with her and invited her to come and see the place just as Jesus told the disciples of John the Baptist who followed him from a distance, and Jesus turned around and asked, "What do you want?" and they retorted, "Where do you live?" Jesus gave an invitation "Come and see" (Jn. 1:39). The "come and see" in the context of the religious life is normally associated with Aspirancy Phase. It could be said that Sister Theresa, at this point, was aspiring to go to the Abuja Independent Mission when she paid a visit. She cannot recollect whether she spent the night at St. Mary's Catholic Church or not, but she certainly recalls that when she eventually came with Sr. Mary Tuku, HHCJ, they spent the night at Life Camp in the house of Mr. Okpanachi whose junior sister was a novice under Sister Theresa when she was the novice directress. Sister Dorathy became the provincial superior later in her life. Mr. Okpanachi was in charge of lands in the Federal Capital Territory at the time.

It is probable that Sr. Dorathy Okpanachi, HHCJ must have informed Sisters Theresa and Mary of the presence of her brother at Life Camp as a possible place of refuge before things settled. Sister Theresa was the very first female religious to feature in Abuja Independent Mission before she came to work with Sr. Mary Tuku after the cardinal had officially asked from their Mother General for permission for them to come and assist in the virgin mission. The two sisters are members of the Handmaids of the Holy Child Jesus congregation. With their presence, they did what the priest could not accomplish—for example, starting the first school and clinic as they did, and they made sure those establishments were functioning. Sisters Theresa and Mary arrived at the mission territory on August 18, 1982, although Sister Theresa was already there on a visit before coming to settle. Iro Abubakar Dan Musa was the minister of the FCT during this period. He administered from 1982–1983.

The next one to arrive at Abuja for the special mission was also a Handmaid of the Holy Child sister. Sr. Lucy Afangide, HHCJ was the third female religious to arrive in Abuja. She arrived in the company of a major seminarian, Aloysius A. I. Udo from Ibiono Ibom in Akwa Ibom State. Mr. Joseph Akpan, the cardinal's driver in the company of the cardinal's cook, Mr. Peter U. Essien, were part of the contingent. They arrived on May 2 and 3, 1983. Sister Lucy was taken to their community where Sisters Theresa and Mary lived. Aloysius, Joseph, and Peter proceeded to a guest house, Area 1, Section 2 in Garki where they passed the night.[348] The arrival of this group witnessed the toil of Msgr. Dominic Inyang and that of Rev. Fr. Matthew Kukah that was beginning to bear fruit. Father Matthew was already there for about a year before the arrival of this new group in the Federal Capital Territory since he himself arrived Abuja in May 1982. He had St. Mary's Catholic Church as his first port of call like Msgr. Dominic Inyang and like the cardinal himself before making alternative arrangement.

Following the request of the ecclesiastical superior of the *missio sui juris,* (the independent mission) to the Nigerian hierarchy for priests in the territory because of the acute shortage of priests, Rev. Fr. Richard Devine, SMA (Society of African Missionaries) was seconded from Ekiti Diocese where he had served for twenty-one years before proceeding to the independent mission. His arrival made him the very first male religious in Abuja. Fr. Richard enjoyed the company of his parishioners who fondly abbreviated his name as Richi, Ricky, or simply as "Mighty Fellow" because of his girth and energy.[349] Father Richard arrived three days before Sister Lucy and Aloysius. It shows that the month of May 1983 was the beginning of a bumper harvest for the mission territory and for the Catholic faithful. The seed had started spreading and covering the ground. Many spiritual plants were sprouting and enjoying new growth. The insistent prayers of the faithful and their thirst were gradually being assuaged. The second male religious to arrive was Rev. Fr. Casmir Ezeh, CSSp, a Spiritan. On his arrival, he started working with Rev. Fr. Wilfred Ojukwu, who was ordained in 1983 as the first Abuja priest.

L. Constant Shuttling between Ikot Ekpene and the Federal Capital Territory

The cardinal had become accustomed to shuttling between Ikot Ekpene Diocese and Abuja Independent Mission. The shuttling consumed a lot of his energy in an attempt to fulfil his pastoral ministry. Sometimes, he spent up to one month or two months in each place or two weeks in each of the places but making sure no part was deprived in any way of his presence and paternal guidance of teaching, of correction, and of instruction (2 Tm. 2:25). He tried to become all things to all in order to win some at all cost (1 Cor. 9:22). St. Paul says, "All Scripture is inspired by God and profitable for teaching, for reproof, for correction and for training in righteousness" (2 Tm. 3:16). The Vatican Council II strongly exhorts the bishops to "be especially concerned about catechetical instruction. Its function is to develop in men a living faith enlightened by doctrine. It should be very carefully imparted, not only to children and adolescents but also to young people and even to adults."[350]

Such consistency in instructing the people of God is to lead to better understanding, a deeper faith, and nearness to the shepherd.

The nearness to the flock avoids the type of heresy called Gallicanism, whereby the bishop lives very far away from the flock and had little or no contact with the flock placed under his care. This led to so many problems in the church for want of leadership, teaching, and correction. That accounts for the constant shuttling between the two posts. To carry out the journey between Gwagwalada and Ikot Ekpene every now and then, covering a distance of about 640 kilometers each time by car, he needed lots of God's graces and protection. He also needed to be resilient to accomplish that on the terrible Nigerian roads. The interesting thing is that he always left Ikot Ekpene the same day and arrived at Abuja the same day. Sometimes, he even began his pastoral duties without any delay. Indeed, it was a divine intervention. The next morning, he began his normal activities and reception of both priests, the religious, and the laity without any exception and without booking.

All this was done when he was already advanced in age. He was equally suffering from diabetes, which he had grown up with for many years and which was to bring his life to an end some years later. That was part of his cross. On some occasions, he was asked by some of the priests and the laity why he did not fly some part of the journey to ease part of his problems, he used to say, "What would the Lord Jesus Christ have done if he were to be here? Would he have flown or would he have used the ordinary means like every other person? What of all the others that travel to the Capital

Territory, do they fly? They are just human beings like I. I am not doing anything extraordinary by driving." He loved to identify with the common people and the poor as Christ did. For him following the footsteps of Christ was not distinct from carrying out what he was ordered to accomplish in the church. As he was happy to follow the poor, simple, and suffering Christ, so was he happy to follow him in carrying out his mandate of bringing people to Christ. Since he was not different from those he served, it was very easy for people to approach him with freedom and cordiality.

One of the things often remarked by friends and foes about the cardinal was his impeccable obedience to the church. He often said, "Who am I to disobey the Holy Father when he demands of me to do something? Who can resist his voice and still remain part of the communion of the church? To resist the Holy Father is to resist God. I cannot put myself into such a situation. That would be declaring war on God and on the church. Will I still be a son of the church in fact and in truth?" The respect he had for his biological father and the respect he exercised toward him was transferred to the church and her leaders without question. The reverence he had for his father as the okuku of the clan coupled with the honor given to his father by others and the respect and obedience the father commanded gave him that air of royalty and obedience mingled[351] with love that became devotion. Only the royalty know the respect and honor to accord the royalty in a given context. Others can learn, but it will not flow naturally as it would have flown with a member of the royalty who had experienced such life.

A person of lesser rank would not have been able to accomplish that. The royal blood supported by authority is manifest in the unique outpouring of love for the Holy Father, the pope, and the church. In the context in which the Prince-Prelate functioned, the church's fathers exhort bishops: "They should be especially solicitous of those parts of the world in which the word of God has not yet been proclaimed or in which, on account of the scarcity of priests, the faithful are in danger of falling away from the obligations of the Christian life or even of losing the faith itself. Bishops should, do their utmost to ensure that the activities of evangelization and the apostolate are zealously supported and promoted by the faithful."[352]

The Abuja Mission was a very peculiar one. In many circumstances in Nigeria, dioceses are created where local government headquarters already exist, or where a town is operating, or where a great historical or heroic site is. This applies to all other countries. Abuja was an exception. It was like creating a diocese in the ocean or in the desert. Abuja as an independent mission acquired its name from the intention of the Holy Father, Pope John Paul II, who wanted it independent and autonomous but complete in itself. The Federal Capital Territory was a vast land that the federal government was trying to develop out of nothing. The occupants of the little hamlets that existed there were pushed further afield. The massive landmass around the center of the nation was designed to suit a plan that was to be developed later. It was in this barren terrain that the archdiocese, which eventually emerged, was to be implanted with less than the number of the apostles that Christ used to preach the Gospel. The mission was that of a mustard seed, but it had to be in the form of a mustard seed to fall into the category of the Lord's description of the kingdom.

His impeccable obedience had to be put into practice as he exercised it when he was to begin philosophy during his probational period. At that time, he was given three years' probation that differed from the normal two years. It appears since he came from a background that is unique, peculiar, and extraordinary, extraordinary demands came to him as well. To he whom much is given, much is expected. He had received so much even from his background of a complex polygamous family. It was this same family that experienced expulsion of all the women. Only one of the women who were left with female children became the wedded wife so that Dominic could be ordained a Catholic priest.

The peculiarity of his position singled him out from the beginning. He took up the task with an undaunted spirit. He waded into an unknown land with the strength of the martyrs and with the courage of a lion. His targets were the souls of men, women, and children that arrived in the Federal Capital Territory with the intention of beginning life in the place. His search was not for himself but for the Lord and the salvation of souls.

He can be called, in truth, the Pioneer Pastor of Abuja Independent Mission. He was a pioneer in every sense of it. He did not mind where he stayed. The inconveniences were many, yet he made his bedroom to be both office and bedroom. Cardinal Ekandem had a big bed. Part of it was his bed while the other side held the files he needed to work with. He operated this way without grumbling, knowing that accommodation was very difficult. Pres. Shehu Shagari who appointed him a member of the National Ethical Commission gave the building he operated from to him. The cardinal used this. He was driven by the zeal of a *Pastor Bonus,* Good Shepherd.

M. Pastoral Strategy Adopted by Dominic Cardinal Ekandem

Dominic Cardinal Ekandem utilized the same strategy he adopted when he became the pioneer bishop of Ikot Ekpene Diocese in the then eastern region to evangelize the Abuja Independent Mission. His method of evangelization was through *schools and hospitals and Catechists.*

To effect this, he sent Msgr. Kenneth Enang who helped him seriously at Ikot Ekpene to bring medical personnel and an educationalist from there to Abuja to help in deciding where the various places, hospitals, and schools were to be located. Monsignor Enang was brought to Abuja at the request of the Vatican. The cardinal did not single-handedly bring him there. Rome asked the cardinal if he is the person that had been doing all the submissions to Rome or if it was some other person that used to help him. When Cardinal Ekandem said that it was Msgr. Kenneth Enang who used to help him, they asked if he could bring him to Abuja to help in this new mission. Cardinal Ekandem did not have any difficulty in inviting Monsignor Enang to Abuja. From then on, he started helping in whatever way the cardinal wanted him to. Msgr. Kenneth Enang was the rector of the minor seminary, Queen of Apostles Seminary, Afaha Obong, Abak Local Government Area in Akwa Ibom State and project coordinator in the diocese of Ikot Ekpene before being asked to report in Abuja. Very Rev. Fr. John McGuiness, SPS who was the vicar general in Ikot Ekpene Diocese came to Abuja about this time too to give a helping hand in the all-embracing mission. He was the one that the cardinal asked to be the confessor of the religious that had arrived in the mission territory.

At that initial stage following the evangelization strategy of the cardinal, he had to think of siting hospitals at strategic points after looking at the map of the Federal Capital Territory. Four hospitals were to be built in the territory. One was to be located at Bwari; one at Gwagwalada; one at Garki, the center; and the other at Kuje. Misereor gave the money for feasibility study, and when that was completed, religious congregations were asked to apply to come and run it. Bwari Hospital witnessed the

Immaculate Heart Sisters applying and working there, while Gwagwalada witnessed the entry of the Handmaids of the Holy Child Jesus congregation applying and running it. The clinic at Garki came much later. It is run by a group of catholic women organization (CWO) with two religious women as part of the hospital management board. The three others had taken off, but the land acquired for that purpose in Kuje could still be utilized for some other purpose unless the planning is still on. Rome was not built in a day.

The hospital project or clinic at Garki had not taken off during his days but eventually did during the days of his able successor, the Most Reverend John O. Onaiyekan, now His Eminence John Cardinal Onaiyekan. He led the place step by step to the green pastures by acquiring land and establishing a secondary school, Regina Pacis for girls in Garki, CKC, Christ the King Secondary School for boys in Gwagwalada. He thought of education as an essential tool for development. Church and state in Nigeria are still using education for development in many parts of the country. It is still a key element.

His experience in the created diocese of Ikot Ekpene inspired him to turn the red sand of the Federal Capital Territory into lovely buildings relying on foreign aid and internal contributions. He set forth to acquire parcels of land as he saw his predecessor, Bishop James Moynagh of Calabar, do, and as he did at Ikot Ekpene. He acquired the unallocated lands in the strategic areas from the minister of the Federal Capital Territory, Mmaman Vasta, and started his networking of institutions that served the entire territory when many people started pouring into Abuja. He did not do all alone. He employed the assistance of his priests and members of the church to accomplish this.

Before he vacated the see of Abuja as cardinal archbishop of Abuja, a title given *ad personam*, in other words, given to him in a personal capacity for who he was. He showed his unsullied and unalloyed obedience to the church by signing whatever papers the pro-nuncio, Abp. Paul Tabet, concerning his succession to the See of Abuja, prepared. As a matter of principle, the successor was to be versed in Hausa, Igbo, and Yoruba, the three major Nigerian languages. He submitted the documents at the nunciature and returned home. His ingrained devotion and obedience to the church and the church's authority caused him to experience some misunderstanding with some of those from his homeland concerning the nomination of a successor. He had no regrets about his decision even when those who questioned the proceedings of succession after the announcement sowed the seed of confusion in his mind.

The only thing he said was that the church is one; and whoever serves, provided the name of Christ is extolled, is doing the will of Christ. An Ibibio proverb says that "whatever is palatable in the mouth of a sick person is what the person eats until death." The aspect of untarnished obedience as far as the cardinal was concerned was none negotiable, *Roma locuta causa finita*, Rome has spoken, there is no appeal (the cause is finished). A man's or a woman's greatest strength is sometimes his/her greatest weakness. This is very much ad rem as far as Dominic Cardinal Ekandem is concerned. With his unquestioning obedience, he could not expect anything less from his priests and laity.

What he lived is what he expected others to live and share since everyone shared in the same divine life of Christ—the head of his body, the church—and shared in the same redemptive power and gift.

N. The Ordination of the First and Second Priest for Abuja Independent Mission

Since Cardinal Ekandem was still operating from Ikot Ekpene and sharing the same length of time between Ikot Ekpene and Abuja till he retired from Ikot Ekpene Diocese and took up residence in Abuja and was installed later in 1990, he could not ordain the first Abuja priest in Abuja itself. Rev. Fr. Wilfred Ifedili Ojukwu, or fondly called Fr. Willy Ojukwu, is originally from Agulu in Anambra State. He was the very first priest Cardinal Ekandem ordained for Abuja Independent Mission. His ordination took place at St. Anne's Cathedral, Ifuho, in Ikot Ekpene Diocese during the third set of the Congregation of the Missions (Vincentian) ordinations where Rev. Fr. Richard Ikechukwu Diala, CM and Rev. Fr. Michael Imediedu Edem, CM were ordained priests for that congregation.

Cardinal Ekandem ordained these three priests that same day. Among the three, Reverend Father Ojukwu was older since he had already been a reverend brother with the Marist Brothers of the schools for a long time before opting to become a priest. His situation can be likened to that of Rev. Fr. Donatus Ezike who was originally a businessman from Orlu Diocese who later became a reverend brother through his contact with Bishop Godfrey Mary Paul Okoye, CSSp in Port Harcourt. Bishop Okoye later introduced him to Archbishop Arinze, the second Nigerian cardinal that helped Donatus join the brothers of St. Stephen. As a brother, he expressed a desire to become a priest. He was equally assisted by the same archbishop after a long period to start preparing for the priesthood by studying subjects that would lead him to a major seminary. He even had to start studying Latin in All Hallows Seminary Onitsha. He started the major seminary training as a late vocation and became a priest. Fr. Donatus Ezike was ordained that same year of 1983 for Onitsha Archdiocese.

Fr. Wilfred Ojukwu was ordained with the two Vincentian priests on the feast of Our Lady of Mount Carmel on July 16, 1983. He was the person designated to give the "vote of thanks" to the diocese of Ikot Ekpene for organizing the ordination and for the gifts in kind and cash donated to the newly ordained coupled with the congratulatory speech, which was read and signed by Sir A. T. Beka, the chairman of the planning committee and diocesan president at the time. They congratulated the three new priests and rejoiced with them. They stressed the need to uphold the teachings of the church, obedience, and holiness of life. Father Ojukwu responding to the message, thanked the people of God on behalf of the three, and expressed appreciation for their magnanimity and sacrifices. He begged God to bless them for their kindness toward those ordained in the name of the Lord and pledged on behalf of the newly ordained that they will put into practice what they preached. The jubilation was so great that immediately after that, traditional displays took place all around the cathedral compound before people began to disperse.

From the point of view of the administration of the Federal Capital Territory, a very transitory method of operation ensued owing to the duration of term of office. At the time of Father Ojukwu's ordination, Haliru Dantoro (1983–1984) was the minister of FCT. It seems he interacted more with Mamman Jiva Vatsa (1984 to December 1985) later in connection with land acquisition indicating that all hands were on deck to make sure that things moved smoothly.

Rev. Fr. Wilfred Ojukwu arrived at Abuja on September 15, 1983, after his two months holiday. On September 18, 1983, he was appointed the assistant parish priest of Our Lady Queen of Nigeria Pro-Cathedral, Garki under Father Kukah, now the bishop of Sokoto. Both Father Kukah and Father Ojukwu were using Dumes Canteen in Area 1, Garki, Abuja as their place of worship. The use of the canteen as a place of worship gives a clear idea of the origins of Our Lady Queen of Nigeria Pro-Cathedral Parish in Garki. It is certainly the second oldest parish in the Federal Capital Territory with St. Paul's Parish Gwagwalada with primacy of position. This was an innovation. Father Wilfred was the first rector of Saints Simon and Jude Seminary Kuje. As one of the pioneers, before he went for studies, he collaborated in establishing many stations that became parishes later. In 1991, after intense pastoral engagement in the independent mission, he was granted permission by his ordinary, Cardinal Ekandem, to go and study in America where he obtained a master's degree in education and another in pastoral counseling, and doctoral degree in moral and pastoral counseling from the Catholic University of America (CUA) in Washington DC. When he went out, he was to engage himself in fund-raising for the independent mission also. It appears that was not successful at all, and the appeal yielded nothing since robbers robbed Father Wilfred of the proceeds. He was left alive to tell the story. Father Ojukwu even lectured in the same university before retuning in 1995.

Reverend Father Wilfred was not the only one ordained specifically for Abuja Independent Mission. The next in rank who was the second priest to be ordained for the independent mission was Rev. Fr. Aloysius Atkinson Idiwot Ikpong, UDO originally from Calabar Diocese. His Lordship Brian Davies Usanga loved sending his seminarians to many seminaries. One of the Seminaries he patronized was St. Augustine's Major Seminary, Jos; apart from Saints Peter and Paul Major Seminary, Ibadan; and Bigard Memorial Seminary Enugu. At the time, St. Joseph Major Seminary, Ikot Ekpene and Seat of Wisdom, Owerri came up, he equally sent his seminarians there. He loved variety, or rather unity in diversity for the enrichment of the presbyterium. Aloysius Udo was one of those sent to Jos.

He was there till his fifth year in St. Augustine's Seminary before he applied to the Society of Jesus, better known as the Jesuits. Aloysius greatly admired the members of the congregation before his application to become a member. They simply advised him to go back to his diocese of origin. It so coincided that at the time he contemplated joining the Society of Jesus, he met Cardinal Ekandem and discussed the possibility of joining the Abuja Independent Mission. At the point of acceptance, Cardinal Ekandem took over the center stage and became the one who approached Bishop Usanga, the ordinary of Aloysius, for permission for Aloysius to become a candidate for the independent mission.

When Bishop Usanga granted the permission, Aloysius had no difficulty in switching over to the Abuja Independent Mission with Cardinal Ekandem as the ecclesiastical superior. He arrived at Abuja on May 2, 1983.That was almost one and a half months before the first priest, Fr. Wilfred Ojukwu, was ordained. Aloysius was sent to Our Lady Queen of Nigeria Parish, Garki with Fr. Matthew Hassan as the priest-in-charge. He also worked in Karmo and Nyanya, being outstations of Garki at the time. Apart from working in these places, his other duty was cooking whether he knew how to cook well or not.

He just had to learn and to make ends meet. Aloysius worked for four months in the independent mission before he went back to Jos to complete his theological studies.

His deaconate ordination took place at Queen of Apostles Seminary, Afaha Obong, Akwa Ibom State on Easter Tuesday within the Octave of Easter, 1984. His priestly ordination occurred on July 7, 1984, at St. Anne's Cathedral, Ifuho, Ikot Ekpene by Dominic Cardinal Ekandem. Rev. Fr. Aloysius Idiwot Ikpong, UDO is *the second priest* ordained for Abuja Independent Mission. His ordination at Ikot Ekpene together with that of Ojukwu shows the close tie between Ikot Ekpene Diocese and Abuja Independent Mission/Archdiocese.

At this point, many other priests and religious started trickling into the mission territory, reinforcing the handful of priests and religious already laboring in the intense heat in that arena. Their arrival was a welcome news of joy that reinforced and relieved the earlier comers. The mental fatigue that their arrival took away was greater than the physical relief since they had to select the most pressing need before engaging in it. Prioritization of needs always took precedence over all others in the midst of scarcity and emergency. They were concerned only with the essentials and what was absolutely necessary.

O.   The Necessity of Land Acquisition

The arrival of Rev. Fr. Matthew Hassan Kukah prompted an emergency meeting being held at St. Mary's Catholic Church, Suleja in Minna Diocese where Abp. Peter Yariyok Jatau of Kaduna Metropolitan See and Bishop Christopher Abbah of Minna Diocese with Fr. Matthew Kukah were in attendance. At that meeting, the prelates and the priest saw the necessity of embarking on land acquisition for the good of the church and for future projects. It was resolved that Father Kukah's immediate assignment was to liaise with the federal government to procure land and register the presence of the Catholic Church in Abuja.[353]

This group paid a courtesy call to Mr. John Jatau Kadiya, the FCT minister, and Rev. Fr. Matthew Kukah was formally introduced to him together with his land officers. That opened the way for further contacts and encounters. The introduction to Pres. Shehu Shagari was not difficult because the moment Fr. Matthew Kukah's name was mentioned, he gave him total support, confessing that he, the president, had been reading the write-ups of Fr. Matthew with interest in the *Guardian-Nigerian* newspaper. That familiarity made things easier. He then gave a general invitation to come to him anytime he wanted and let him know anytime a difficulty arose. Pres. Shehu Shagari was very friendly and supportive even though he was a Muslim. It was with the same disposition that President Shagari received Pope John Paul II when the pope visited Nigeria for the first time in 1982. That disposition caused the Italians in Rome to recall the reign of President Shagari with great appreciation as the one who received the pope into Nigeria.

Father Kukah, being a very close fellow worker of the cardinal, must have learned a great deal by reading his thoughts coupled with the day-to-day exchange of ideas they often had in terms of the areas that needed development and the siting of some basic amenities for the people of God. The tête-à-tête discussion prompted the International Conference on Development. Rev. Msgr. B. A. Okodua, national director of the Pontifical Missionary Aids Society (PMAS) later changed to Pontifical Missionary Society (PMS) delivered a paper on the subject. The conference was held from April 27 to 30, 1992,[354] almost sixteen years after commencing the independent mission. Father Matthew says, "In one of those occasions,

I used the privilege given to me by the president, Alhaji Shehu Usman Shagari, when I went to look for a house for the cardinal. After having located a smaller building, I told them that I had spoken with the president, and he had given me authority to go round and pick any house of choice, and that if anyone disturbed me, I should report back to him." With that statement, he was given the right to pick any house of his choice.

Fr. Matthew Kukah added significantly, "In actual fact, I had not spoken to him the day before. It was his general statement that 'if I were ever in trouble or needed anything I should always get back to him' that empowered me." With what the president said, Father Matthew worked on the assumption that if permission was needed (*epikeia*), he would surely have granted it without delay. With that, he was allowed to go scouting for the building of choice. The building he chose was the one Cardinal Ekandem lived in till his last moment on earth before going to the house of his Father. One of the people Fr. Hassan Kukah mentioned very frequently was Mr. Uganden of the Lands and Survey. He was very helpful concerning land acquisition for the church in the mission territory.

P.   Erection of Abuja Diocese and Transfer from Ikot Ekpene

Dominic Cardinal Ekandem, full of pastoral charity in all ramifications, could not rest on his laurels as long as the mandate to be the superior of the Independent Mission of Abuja was concerned. He had to work till the last moment he was relieved officially of that duty (*servitum*), as pastor of souls in the territory. He was anxious to satisfy the needs of the people in Ikot Ekpene as well as those of Abuja. Even the distance, the bad roads, his health, and many other inconveniences did not hinder him from carrying out his duty. His constancy was like that of the saints, while his courage was like that of the martyrs who never cared about their suffering and impending death so long as they were drawn by the love of the crucified Christ. He was simply consistent. If he told those in Ikot Ekpene that he would be there in two weeks' time, he surely would be there unless admitted in the hospital or was out of the country or was responding to the supreme pontiff's call. His words were as certain as the morning sun in West Africa. During the time of the erection of the new Abuja Diocese, Hamza Abdullahi was the FCT minister. His tenure began in 1986 and extended to 1989, the very "Year of the Erection." Gado Nasko began from there onward as the new minister (1989 to 1993). It shows that there was some type of systematization of the duration of the ministers, probably with a guiding principle instead of the one-year term that featured prominently in the past—for example, Haliru Dantoro, 1983–1984, and Mamman Jiva Vatsa, 1984 to December 1985.

What aided him most was the presence of his coadjutor,[355] the Most Reverend Camillus Archibong Etokudo. The Most Reverend C. Etokudo succeeded Cardinal Ekandem as the second bishop of Ikot Ekpene. He later became the ordinary of Port Harcourt Diocese and served as the fifth bishop, taking over from the Most Reverend Alexius Makozi, who was formerly the ordinary of Lokoja Diocese before he became the fourth bishop of Port Harcourt. Bishop Etokudo's presence and his experiences as a papal diplomat in various parts of the world, with so many languages and cultures he encountered, gave him an advantage in dealing with many pastoral issues that surfaced, coupled with his listening ear and the capacity to combine academic life with pastoral charity. Like Moses and the seventy elders in the desert, he handled all cases within his authority and reserved a few for the cardinal's handling. He had a wonderful respect for Cardinal Ekandem whom he fondly referred to as "my father." This was to indicate the dignity, reverence, and filial relationship that existed among the two of them.

When Dominic Cardinal Ekandem received the Apostolic Bull of Erection of June 19, 1989, from His Holiness Pope John Paul II appointing him the ordinary of Abuja Diocese as suffragan of Kaduna Ecclesiastical Province, Cardinal Ekandem knew that the time had come for him to leave Ikot Ekpene and its administration and governance for Abuja, and settle down there for more intensive work. With the new bishop at his side, he was ready to sing the Nunc Dimittis like Simeon in the Bible after seeing the baby Jesus in the Temple. Cardinal Ekandem left after having served Ikot Ekpene Diocese for twenty-six years as a bishop. That was a very considerable commitment.

Shortly after receiving the bull that authorized him to be installed as the first bishop of Abuja Diocese, another Apostolic Letter came. The interval was about a month and eight days when that Apostolic Letter signed by the prefect of the Congregation for the Propagation of the Faith and by the cardinal concerned with the public affairs of the church, the *missio sui juris,* the Independent Mission of Abuja shaded off that notion of mission territory, and it became a brand new diocese. The Apostolic Letter of erection of the diocese of Abuja was issued on July 19, 1989.

Bishop Camillus Etokudo was ordained a bishop in 1988 but was installed in 1990, on February 3. The installation of Bishop Camillus Archibong Etokudo from Okon Parish in Ikot Ekpene Diocese came after a period when the See was vacant owing to the transfer of His Eminence Card. Ignatius Ekandem to Abuja. His Lordship Most Rev. Camillus Etokudo waited for Cardinal Ekandem to be installed as the bishop of Abuja on December 16, 1989, after almost six months' interval of issuing the bull and about five months after the Apostolic Letter erecting the diocese of Abuja. The filial and paternal relationship can be seen even in this situation. With these procedures in place, Cardinal Ekandem left Ikot Ekpene Diocese in 1989 and officially went on transfer to Abuja as a diocese, no longer as a mission territory. The earlier and pioneer missionaries used to call such establishments bush churches. By this time, Abuja was developing into a city, not even a town but a planned city. The eight long years of shuttling were over. Anytime he went to Akwa Ibom State, he went for a different purpose, not because of pastoral needs. Cardinal Ekandem remained at Abuja till his installation. He left Ikot Ekpene Diocese finally after the reception of the Papal Bull appointing him the first ordinary of Abuja Diocese to go and prepare for the erection of the new diocese. At the erection of the diocese of Abuja, the name of *Propaganda Fide*, Congregation for the Propagation of the Faith had been changed to Congregation for the Evangelization of Peoples, *Congregatio pro Gentium Evangelizatione.* The change took place in 1967. The cardinal prefect by then was Jozef Tomko who was appointed April 24, 1985, till April 9, 2001. He was the prefect of the congregation for sixteen years. Cardinal Tomko was the prefect that signed the Apostolic Letter of erection of the new diocese of Abuja. The secretary of the congregation at the time was Jose Tomas Sanchez who functioned from 1985 to 1991. Cardinal Ekandem was made archbishop *ad personam* on his own merit long before the diocese of Abuja matured to be named a metropolitan See. The conferment of the special title "archbishop" added to the number of recognitions that he enjoyed from civil and religious authorities of many nations and peoples.

Q. Congratulatory Message

The Catholic Bishops' Conference of Nigeria (CBCN) under item 2.5, as part of the new agenda, created a space for congratulatory messages after goodwill messages to the pope, the president of Nigeria and the military governor of Oyo State since the second plenary meeting of that year took place at the Pastoral Institute, Ibadan on October 16 to 19, 1990. Cardinal Ekandem, Bishop Usuh, and Bishop Etokudo were congratulated for their official installation and Bishop Ekuwem for his episcopal ordination and installation. It was also disclosed that Bishop Patrick Kelly, SMA, former bishop of Benin City, was to celebrate his fiftieth year as a bishop on June 2, 1990. The president congratulated him through his successor, Bishop Ekpu.[356] On page 3 topmost before the opening address, the following is recorded: "His Eminence Cardinal Ekandem was installed Archbishop of the Diocese of Abuja, and was honored with an Honorary Doctorate degree at the Loyola University, Chicago."[357]

The phenomenal growth of the new diocese caused the Mission Territory established in 1981 to be erected as a diocese in about eight years. This is a marvelous work of God coupled with the unrelenting zeal of Cardinal Ekandem; Msgr. Dominic Inyang; Rev. Fr. Matthew Kukah; the three pioneer sisters of the Handmaids of the Holy Child Jesus: Theresa Nwanruo, HHCJ, Mary Tuku, HHCJ, and Lucy Afangide, HHCJ; together with Reverend Father Ojukwu and the seminarian Aloysius Udo as the pioneer missionaries in the territory before others came to lighten the load and make things easier for the people of God.

The phenomenal growth did not slow down for many schools of various categories, nursery, primary, and secondary sprang up. Parishes developed from very insignificant posts to become mighty stations and evolve into many big parishes, hospitals, clinics and a minor seminary including Gaudium et Spes Institute where many seminars and workshops take place regularly. The structure of Gaudium et Spes Institute was meant to be the retirement home of Cardinal Ekandem, but since he preferred to continue living in Area 2, the house selected at the initial stage, that retirement home became the site for the institute. It became very appropriate for that because of its surroundings and location. What was meant to house the cardinal and give a little comfort till death became a new center of giving life while projecting his vision and ideals into the future.

All these facilities were established so as to balance the intellectual with the physical as well as the spiritual developments of the members of the church to generate a holistic approach to effective evangelization. The foundation for a solid diocese with all the necessary structures had been put in place for continued growth. The church, the individuals, and the government were all involved in housing to take care of the influx of people into the territory.

R. The Succession Plan

By the time Cardinal Ekandem retired as the ordinary of Abuja on June 23, 1992, at the age of seventy-five, things were already put in place for the speedy progress and growth of the diocese. The population of Catholics had arisen to 22 percent of the 423,000 inhabitants of FCT. The Catholics numbered 9,390. There were 10 parishes by 1990, 14 diocesan priests, 93 male religious, and 16 female religious, 10 religious priests.[358] By the time Cardinal Ekandem retired, he made sure that a coadjutor was appointed. The appointment of the coadjutor, the Most Reverend John Olorunfemi Onaiyekan, took place on July 7, 1990. His episcopal motto is Fiat Voluntas Tua, Thy Will Be Done. His Holiness Pope John Paul II, who later was canonized as St. Pope John Paul II on April 27, 2014, carefully carried out the appointment of the coadjutor. It was the same pope who gave the pallium to His Grace Most Rev. John O. Onaiyekan after the elevation of the diocese of Abuja to a metropolitan See with the suffragan bishops in Lokoja, Makurdi, Idah, Lafia, and Otukpo, later with the creation of new dioceses out of Makurdi, Gboko, and Katsina-Ala were added. Abuja Archdiocese then became one of the biggest archdioceses in the country with the greatest number of suffragan bishops. The elevation of Abuja to a metropolitan See took place before the final lap of the earthly journey of Cardinal Ekandem. At the elevation of the diocese to an arch-diocese, Bishop John Onaiyekan was made an archbishop by His Holiness John Paul II on March 26, 1994, and was installed the same day as His Grace Most Rev. John Olorunfemi Onaiyekan.

Archbishop John Onaiyekan, who was later created in consistory as a cardinal on November 24, 2012, by His Holiness Pope Benedict XVI, is originally from Kabba, the place that the local people like to describe as "the center of the universe from where God created the world" is under Lokoja Diocese, one of the suffragan bishops of the Abuja Metropolitan See. He was born on January 29, 1944, to the family of Bartholomew and Joanna Onaiyekan. He started his primary education at the age of five at St. Mary's Catholic School, Kabba from 1949 to 1956. In 1957, he began his secondary education at Mount St. Michael's Aliade, Benue State, and completed it in 1962 with a grade one certificate.

The Muslim leaders called the emirs in the northern part of Nigeria went around searching for him to go and take an engineering course or medicine in Ahmadu Bello University, Zaria on a federal scholarship, but he turned it down and proceeded to the major seminary of Saints Peter and Paul, Bodija, Ibadan in 1963. The emirs were greatly disappointed, but they could do nothing. He was sent to Rome to complete his philosophical and theological studies between 1965 and 1969. His ordination to the sacred priesthood took place on August 3, 1969. He taught at St. Kizito's College, Isanlu, and in 1971, he was appointed the rector of the minor seminary in Lokoja. September of 1971 witnessed his going back to Rome for a specialized study in biblical studies. In February of 1973, he completed his licentiate in sacred scriptures (LLS) and obtained a doctorate degree in biblical studies in January 1976. He came back to Nigeria afterward.

On his return, he was posted to his alma mater, Saints Peter and Paul Seminary, Bodija, Ibadan. By September of 1977, he became the vice rector of the seminary. In 1980, he was appointed by Pope John Paul II to the pontifical International Theological Commission, a body of thirty theologians from the entire world for a period of five years—that is, from 1980 to 1985. By November 1981, he was appointed once again by Pope John Paul II as one of the seven Catholics on the International Methodist-Catholic Dialogue Commission. In July 1982, he was made the cathedral administrator of Immaculate Conception Cathedral, Lokoja Diocese. In November of the same year, he was named the auxiliary bishop of Ilorin Diocese to succeed Bishop Mahoney who was retiring. Bishop Onaiyekan was made the titular bishop of Tunusuda. On the feast of the Epiphany, January 6, 1983, Pope John Paul II ordained him as an auxiliary bishop of Ilorin at St. Peter's Basilica, Rome. He became the second residential bishop of Ilorin on October 20, 1984. When he was named the coadjutor of Abuja on July 7, 1990, he was asked by the Holy Father, Pope John Paul II, to be the administrator of Ilorin Diocese that had now become vacant until a successor in the person of His Lordship Most Rev. Ayo Maria Atoyebi, OP was appointed.

He became the archbishop with the elevation of the diocese of Abuja to an archdiocese on March 26, 1994, whereas the appointment took place in 1993. To crown it all, he was named the third Nigerian cardinal on April 26, 2012, where he participated in the consistory that elected Pope Francis in 2013. At the time His Grace Most Rev. J. O. Onaiyekan became a cardinal, the population had risen over a million Catholics. It was during the administration of Bala Abdukadir Mohammed who became minister of the FCT from 2010 that His Grace Most Rev. John Onaiyekan became His Eminence John Cardinal Olorunfemi Onaiyekan. This confirms what St. Vincent de Paul said that the work of God does itself. That terse and insightful saying can be seen fulfilled in reality in the development of Abuja and in its existence. The CBCN did not make any mistakes when they perceived the need for that mission territory. God equally guided Pope John Paul II, who gave the approval together with the Sacred Congregation for the Evangelization of Peoples that approved its establishment.

S.   **Special Invitation Given to the Daughters of Charity of St. Vincent de Paul**

Having realized the type of apostolate and the charism of the Daughters of Charity and their ability to work with people who are poor and having personally witnessed it in St. Joseph Rehabilitation Center, Ukana Iba in Ikot Ekpene Diocese, likewise at St. Louise's Special School for the Physically Impaired, also in Port Harcourt Diocese when he was the administrator, he wasted no time in issuing a very special and urgent invitation to the daughters to come and begin the apostolate for the physically impaired. A special school for the physically impaired, which was inaccurately called in the past the deaf and dumb, "was to be established without delays." A plot of land together with some funds for the construction was provided for this purpose. The daughters needed only to go and develop the land and get in the children to the school. The cardinal was spurred by the benefits of the school he personally witnessed. When he saw the physically impaired children who were educated become happy, communicating by using sign language, who could have been languishing at home, he wasted no time in inviting the sisters to come and establish a similar institution together with a clinic in the mission territory. Unfortunately, the Daughters of Charity could not respond positively to the invitation at the time because of a lack of personnel. Archbishop Onaiyekan issued a new invitation letter in 1995 after the cardinal's retirement. The work was undertaken the following year.

This is part of the letter of invitation that the archbishop of Abuja, now John Cardinal Onaiyekan, wrote: "You are invited to commence [an] apostolate for the poor and disabled in the Archdiocese of Abuja I am requesting that you take immediate steps to implement the project of special Education for the disadvantaged children and particularly for the deaf children."[359] Since the sisters could not respond immediately, they lost the opportunity of being one of the earliest groups of consecrated women to be involved in the pioneering work of Abuja Mission. They equally lost the land and the money reserved for them. The land that was meant for the school was originally at Wuse. Since they delayed in arriving at Abuja, the government took it back and converted it to a recreational facility in Wuse. The land was close to the pastoral center in Wuse. The benefit of having immediate cash that was attached to the invitation was also lost.

When the Daughters arrived in 1996, they took up residence in a rented building near St. Paul's Catholic Church, Kubwa. On May 28, 1996, Sister Francesca, EDET DC and Sister Theresa, MADU DC were sent to take up the apostolate of special education and the clinic. They began in a rented building provided by Christoffel Blindenmission (CBM) through Mr. Paul Caswell until the sisters bought their own land and built their own house at Kubwa. The two sisters worked with CBM. The special apostolate of Sister Francesca was working in the community-based outreach program for children with disabilities, while Sister Theresa began an outreach primary health-care program.[360] The two sisters sent were qualified in education and in health. They formed a pair to begin the foundation of a new community of Daughters of Charity to express their special charism of serving Christ in the poor.

The sisters are located at Biazhin Road in Kubwa in their house called St. Vincent's Community Kubwa, Abuja, with a clinic or St. Vincent's Hospital, Kubwa and a short distance from there, the School for the Slow Learners, St. Vincent's Special School is found within a walking distance. In this way, the mind of the cardinal was carried out. The Daughters of Charity arrived in Abuja after the final exit of Cardinal Ekandem.

## T.	Memo on the Necessity of Active Involvement in Abuja Apostolate by the Missionaries of St. Paul

The Independent Mission of Abuja started because of the direct wish of the Catholic hierarchy of Nigeria. It began with full approval from Sacred Congregation for the Evangelization of Peoples. The independent mission covers 8,000 square kilometers or 3,090 square miles of the Federal Capital Territory. The population of the country was estimated at the time as having 50 percent Muslims, 40 percent Christians, and 10 percent of traditional religionists. These figures were greatly disputed. In January 2015, Christians were estimated at 50.5 percent, Muslims were estimated at 43.5 percent, while those that practiced Traditional African Religion were estimated at 6 percent.[361] In the whole nation, 8.2 percent are Catholics; the percentage is very small. Protestants are 19.9 percent, Churches of Christ are 12.3 percent, and Anglicans are 10.1 percent.[362]

By 2012, the estimation of Catholics in Abuja was 542,105. It formed only 17.5 percent of the total population of 3,096,000. The population of Catholics in Abuja is relatively small compared to the total population; as in the nation, so is it in Abuja. The number will surely be greater than what has been estimated because of population growth, which was estimated at 177,155,754 in 2014 instead of 168.8 million in 2012.[363]

The projected population of the territory when fully developed is put at 3 million. The total population of Abuja by 2015 has come to 3,324,000, far greater than the projected population. It is likely it will still grow bigger than what it is at the moment. It means that the percentage of each of the groups has also increased considerably.

The fact that the Independent Mission of Abuja was established by decree from Rome on November 6, 1981, after which followed the official movement of the Missionary Seminary/Society of St. Paul to Gwagwalada,

Abuja on October 13, 1984, was more than a mere coincidence. Series of questions and suggestions arise concerning the involvement of the Missionaries of St. Paul in the missionary life of the independent mission. As far as bringing the good news of salvation to the indigenes of Abuja is concerned, Abuja is, par excellence, a missionary territory. If the first indigenous missionary institute has, providentially, its home in a missionary territory, what justification has this missionary institute for not being actively involved in the apostolate of its home based territory, which is obviously missionary?

Besides, whatever the rhetoric, Islam is the real threat to Christianity in this country (even though Pres. Shehu Shagari gave the Catholics a free hand to access houses and land). Who could be more qualified to counteract this threat than the personnel needed for this type of apostolate?

Two possibilities were open to the Missionary Institute of St. Paul by which active involvement in the Apostolate of Abuja can be effected:

1. An Initial Response

    The society has been formally invited to take up the pastoral care of Yaba in the Abaji Local Government Area (of the cardinal's letter dated April 14, 1989), entering into negotiation with the cardinal as to where one could make a start and on what terms Yaba would be administered.

2. On a Long-Term Basis

    In keeping with our constitutions (chapter 1, No. 3) by which members of the Missionary Society of St. Paul are committed "to the apostolate of the printed word," a lot could be done by MSPs by making the presence of the church in a territory that will be the center of ideas that is bound to have an impact in the religious sociopolitical life of Nigerians. The effective use of the news media to evangelize can form a part of the program.

The Missionary Society of St. Paul will be contributing in no small way to the future of the church in Nigeria by being actively involved *now* in a planned evangelization for the New Capital Territory, Abuja.

Rev. Msgr. Godwin P. Akpan
Ag Superior
21. 6. 89.

Bearing in mind the need of the Missionaries of St. Paul in Abuja, the background of the seminary likewise that of the Missionaries of St. Paul will go a long way to brighten the prospects for evangelization in the missionary territory. The Missionaries of St. Paul cannot but be seriously involved in the apostolate of the media and the pastoral life of the mission.

Chapter Twelve

PRO CHRISTO LEGATIONE ERGO FUNGIMUR (SO NOW WE ARE AMBASSADORS FOR CHRIST 2 Cor. 5:22)

The Development of the National Missionary Seminary/ Society of St. Paul

It is very hard to convince those whose lives are dominated by feeling that faith has nothing whatever to do with emotion. Nor does it have anything to do with "feeling good," because very often faith recommends something that is very difficult, such as taking up a cross.

—Venerable Archbishop Fulton Sheen

EVERYONE IS AWARE that all gigantic projects that ever existed began in a very humble manner or at least conceived initially in a very humble way, or in a well-laid-out fashion. Sometimes the inspiration of such conceptions or projects comes in a flash, disappears, and resurfaces after some time. At other times, the inspiration stems from what is perceived, thought of, and developed in a gradual or systematic manner. At other times, the inspiration imposes itself with such intensity that one becomes restless until every detail is perceived. Here is what Robin S. Sharma says as he quotes an Indian philosopher, Pantanjali.

> When you are inspired by some great purpose, some extraordinary projects, all your thoughts break their bonds: your mind transcends limitations, that your consciousness expands in every direction and you find yourself in a new, great and wonderful world. Dormant forces, faculties and talents become alive and you discover yourself to be a greater person than you ever dreamed yourself to be.[364]

A. The Origin and Inspiration of the Idea of a National Seminary

His very first visit to Ireland in 1950 and the second one after his episcopal consecration in 1956 generated lots of reactions in his mind that kept him pondering over them like the Blessed Virgin Mary (Cf. Lk. 2:19). What he saw and experienced in Dublin and in many other parts of Ireland inspired and kept him reflecting on the next course of action. The processes of implementation began but slowly. That year of great inspirations could be likened to *plate tectonics,*[365] *which is "the movement of the crust that builds mountains and opens ocean basins," changing the physical features of the surface of the earth. Plate tectonics can be very rapid in manifestations, but the inspirations that Bishop Ekandem had during his visit did not occur with such rapidity.*

Cardinal Ekandem showing plans of the
missionary seminary to Pope John Paul II

Some of the implementations experienced delayed reactions, while others took off speedily, especially the organization of the women that developed into Catholic Women's Organization originally called Nka Adiaha Obong that built a school for girls with the aim of helping them compete favorably in the society. The next one was the St. Joseph Catholic League that gave many scholarships to indigent students, the Catholic Teachers' Association that started with the provision of the first Vono beds to the Queen of Apostles Seminary, Afaha Obong coupled with many other occurrences and developments. These form part of the whole picture. Among all these, the inspiration to have a National Missionary Seminary ranked topmost. It became a dream like the popular saying of Martin Luther King Jr., "I have a dream," that was unfolding but waiting for the proper moment of fulfillment while experiencing difficulties and transformations.

B. Conception, Prospects, Failures and Obstacles

The conception began with his visit to Ireland. The idea of the National Missionary Seminary was a burning issue that could not be implemented immediately. The initial proposition after the conceived idea took place when Cardinal Ekandem was the only African bishop in 1956 during a meeting of bishops held in Kaduna.[366] He was the only non-European bishop. In other words, he was the only African or Nigerian bishop among the ecclesiastical hierarchy of Nigeria. His proposal was shelved. He persevered just as Gen. Muhammadu Buhari, who failed the Nigerian presidential elections thrice, did until he won it at the third attempt on March 31, 2015.[367] The failure of Abraham Lincoln on the road to the presidency took place two times, once as a member of the Whig Party and another as as opponent of Sen. Stephen A. Douglas in the Republican Party. These failures did not deter him from restrategizing, but he redoubled his efforts until his popularity led him to the presidency in which he had a victorious outcome.

Ten years passed. Cardinal Ekandem was still nursing the idea. In 1966, after a provisional approval and the idea was about to mature, the Civil War broke out. Things became chaotic, and the idea went into a cooler for the second time. The dream he had of a National Seminary did not die off with time like the Rebellion of Theudas (Acts 5: 17–40, especially 34–37) that disappeared with his execution. The followers of Judas the Galilean disbanded after being killed. The case of Jesus Christ superseded both space and time. Gamaliel warned the Sanhedrin to be careful that if the undertaking was of human origin, it would surely fail on its own accord, but if not, they would be found fighting against God (Acts 5:33–39).

During his visit to Ireland, Dominic noticed that the whole nation came together to form a society of priests known as the St. Patrick Fathers or the Kiltegan Fathers.[368] That seminary was to cater for missions within and outside the country. From that moment, he started wondering whether the same could not occur in his country. Commenting on what he witnessed in Dublin, he said, "It became greatly inspired."[369] The inspiration took place during his second visit in 1956 as an auxiliary bishop. He proposed what he had in mind that same year when he came back, but the seed fell on rocky and thorny soil. The second attempt as a residential bishop of Ikot Ekpene occurred ten years later.

All the proposals took place in Kaduna. He probably did not wait for an opportune moment. It could be his desire to witness the implementation of the inspiration motivated him to push ahead without considering all the logistics. Probably, passing the first proposal through the right channel by following due process made him presume success. It suffered prematurely. There are many who observe without following up on their observation and translating it to reality. There are others who observe and follow up systematically until they reach a practical step of invention. It may take long, but such fire never dies out till it sees the light of day. Fortunately, Cardinal Ekandem lived to witness his dream realized despite great delays. It tallies with an Efik proverb that says Usen mkpa ofon akan usen emana, The day of death is more glorious than the birthday.

The first proposal he made to the Bishops' Conference of Nigeria was about the Unity of Formation Program, knowledge of one another, the country, and the liturgy.[370] There were three main seminaries at that time—namely, Bigard Memorial Seminary Enugu in the east, Saints Peter and Paul Seminary Bodija-Ibadan in the west, and St. Augustine's Mayor Seminary, Jos in the north. Philosophy was to begin at Ibadan, theology in Enugu, and Postgraduate faculty in Jos.[371]

What he proposed to the Bishops' Conference was to have some years of studies done in one seminary, a certain number of years in another, and the remaining years in the last seminary. That proposition would then incorporate the unity of formation and knowledge of one another, the country, and liturgy. The fire of one nation in unity and the one Catholic Church was burning powerfully in him. The proposal did not meet any approval owing to various difficulties—namely, the problem of numbers and the seminaries were run by various religious congregations. The Holy Ghost Fathers (CSSp) ran Bigard Memorial Seminary, Enugu situated in the eastern part of the country. The Society of Missionaries for Africa (SMA) ran Saints Peter and Paul, Ibadan, representing the western part of Nigeria, and the Augustinians (OSA) ran St. Augustine's Seminary, Jos founded for the north. Such factors militated against the implementation of the proposal. The shelved idea did not imply a pronouncement of a final death sentence.[372]

When he noticed that the idea did not scale through, he made another proposal. The second time, he proposed the National Missionary Seminary. It gained support. He was seconded by Bishop E. Fitzgibbon who was the administrator of Port Harcourt Diocese at the time and later became the bishop of Warri and retired from there. The proposal gained the support of many bishops with the hope of sending out missionaries later. It could be Bishop Fitzgibbon seconded the motion to demonstrate sign of solidarity as the one who succeeded the cardinal in Port Harcourt or because he saw the necessity of the missionary seminary as he belonged to the St. Patrick Society, an offshoot of Maynooth College that is the emblem for the whole of Ireland that served nationally and internationally. Whatever was the motive, he had perceived the need to pursue such a course with all vigor.

Having succeeded with the Catholic Bishops' Conference of Nigeria—the proposition moved up to its apex. In 1976, during his reception after being created in consistory as a cardinal, he made the same proposal to Pope Paul VI. The response of the pope was in the form of a question. "What is the opinion of the Nigerian Bishops?" He mentioned that, in principle, it was discussed, but not much was done about it. It was then necessary to go and finally consult them on the matter.

At the conference in Kaduna, the cardinal recalled the proposal was brought again to the bishops for ratification. "There were twentyseven Nigerian bishops present at the conference," he said. "Twentytwo of them voted in favor, three voted against and two abstained. The result was sent to Rome." The pope responded by saying, "By all means, go ahead." The Bishops' Conference started putting things in place. Since the seminary was meant to assimilate the whole nation for the purpose of missionary action in the country and outside, it could also have been called Emancipation Seminary. The bishops did not think Emancipation Seminary has a ring to it. They rejected it. The Bishops' Conference eventually accepted the name *National Missionary Seminary*. In a way, he saw his dream of unity being implemented bit by bit in the Missionary Seminary. Here is the memo he submitted for that purpose.

C.   Approval and Permission

Introduction

The Missionary Society of St. Paul signals unity in the Nigerian church, as its members face the challenges of living out this unity in a community setting regardless of their diverse ethnic origins. The dream of having a Missionary Seminary for the nation was re-enkindled by the call of Pope Paul VI in Kampala, Uganda, when he stressed the need of Africans becoming missionaries to themselves. When Bishop Ekandem came back to Nigeria, he began to reoil his ammunitions and set them ready for eventualities. He leaned very heavily on the saying of the vicar of Christ on earth while mustering courage to re-present his proposal to the Bishops' Conference. This third time, he did not want to fail. He did his background work by presenting the idea to the pope who told him that he needed the approval of the episcopal conference for such an idea to sail through. He was now empowered by the highest authority to strike while the iron was hot. He waited for the right moment, which took place at Kaduna once again. Then Bishop Dominic submitted the memo on the subject during the 1976 meeting at Kaduna when he was the president of the Catholic Bishops' Conference of Nigeria.

It is very likely that life must have become very satisfying for Bishop Ekandem seeing that his dream was gradually becoming a reality. What was only an ideal slowly took flesh in a concrete manner, and what seemed impossible became realized. It is under this type of situation that Bishop Ekandem tendered his memo, which was partly historical and partly an appeal with the conviction that something very great was taking place within the global history. He did this without looking back.

a.   The Inspirational Memo of Cardinal Ekandem

CATHOLIC DIOCESE OF IKOT EKPENE

Phone 21

Bishop's House
Library Avenue,
P.O. Box 70,
Ikot Ekpene Nigeria.

A NEW IDEAL OF AN OLD IDEAL AN IDEAL NEVER ATTAINED

The idea for a National Seminary for Nigeria remains an ideal imprisoned by the emergence of three major seminaries, roughly serving three metropolitan areas. The three major seminaries at Jos, Ibadan and Enugu bear testimony both to the growth of the church in Nigeria and to the differences in the church.

At a conference in Kaduna back in 1956, the idea of a National Seminary was first mooted by me in a letter to the Nigerian Bishops through the then Apostolic Delegate, Archbishop O. Knox.

The events of the first half of 1966 served to promote an enthusiasm for, and an acceptance of, one major seminary that would achieve a pooling of personnel, resources and materials.

A decision was taken in Ibadan by the committee set up to examine the proposal; a start was made in the fall of that year. Philosophy would be housed in Ibadan, Theology in Enugu, and a post- graduate faculty was projected for Jos. The civil war intervened and the plan was achieved. When the bishops met in conference after the war, the idea of a National Seminary engendered a heated debate, making the idea an emotive and divisive issue.

The fifth year theology is a palliative that appears to be unworkable. A federal Advisory Commission on seminaries met once, only to discover that the idea of National Seminary was unacceptable to the majority. The matter was then referred back to the National Episcopal Conference.

But the matter must not rest there! The Church in Africa and in Nigeria remains haunted by the clarion call of the Holy Father in Kampala, 1970—the Church in Africa must, in its turn, become a missionary church.

Inspired by this prophetic challenge, demanding a worthy and necessary response to the Holy Father's call, this new idea of an old ideal is born. What is now proposed is a National Missionary Seminary, training candidates and priests for evangelization, not only in those parts of Nigeria where vocations are not plentiful, and indigenous priests are few in number, but in all of Africa. And those of the African continent will not limit its horizons; they will extend to those of the universal church. There are compelling and attractive arguments in support of the idea. Firstly, it is namely: the church in Nigeria, by reason of her bright future in vocations, has a responsibility towards the whole of Africa. At the present moment, while secularist trends do not dictate events, is surely the opportune time for the church to live up to her divine calling- to bring the Good News to all places in the continent, and even further afield.

In terms of vocations, calling upon the pioneering generosity of the young, there is every reason to expect a ready answer at the national level. The home churches can only benefit from such a new impulse, a new missionary movement that makes the local church look beyond its own boundaries and send its emissaries beyond its own boundaries with the Gospel of Jesus Christ.

There would be in existence a new national seminary, national in the best and challenging sense of calling upon the church in Nigeria to supply personnel, candidate for the priesthood, for a venture that would, without doubt, bring in its wake immeasurable spiritual benefits, not only for the local Nigerian churches, but for the church in Africa and beyond its shores.

To realise the ideal demands immediate action and speedy realization. The new Nigerian Federal Capital in Abuja suggests the location of the proposed National Seminary.

The young National Organization of the Propaganda of the Faith would gain an immense impetus from the presence of a federal missionary seminary. There is no doubt that the laity would be ready and willing to support such a truly great project.

The training of the seminarians would take cognizance of the African situation, where the religious content of the Muslims and the Animists would be studied, and Ecumenism in Africa would be treated in depth. The major achievements of Vatican Council II, will, not alone encourage and inspire, but will see their full implementation, in the seminary envisaged.

The important Secretariats and Commissions in Rome would act as catalyst for such a National Missionary Seminary which, in its turn, would be extremely useful source for dialogue with, and feedback to, them.

There is little danger of an emotive and divisive debate occurring and threatening the realisation of the ideal of the National Missionary Seminary here proposed, and, with the numerous vocations, especially in the south of the country, the church in Nigeria need not suffer from a lack of vocations.

Friday, May 15, 1976.

His Lordship, Bishop D. I. Ekandem.

Appendix

At this initial stage of the proposal for a National Missionary Seminary a number of questions arise, e.g., what place does the Holy Ghost Congregation, already sending priests to Sierra Leone, have in the planned National Missionary Seminary?

Again, a National Missionary Seminary would need a sustaining organization or society to prosecute a missionary programme. What form would this take?

1. The Holy Ghost Congregation is, so far, unable to be truly national. Igboland remains the catchment area of vocations. There is little hope of this situation changing to any great extent for some time to come. Consequently, the Holy Ghost Congregation might benefit greatly and significantly by being called upon to broaden their horizons by relating to a National Seminary. At present, the Holy Ghost Congregation is tied very much to those Dioceses with Igbo Bishops.

2. A National Seminary needs a supporting National Agency or Organisation. In itself, this would constitute a new challenge and a most rewarding departure. The Church in Nigeria would be expected to forge an instrument of unified action that operated over and above local, diocesan and regional interests, operating even beyond the boundaries of Nigeria itself. Such an operation would improve its own disciples and make for an instrument of unity, which might well succeed, where other efforts have failed.

3. The implementation of this proposal, which should not be delayed due to the urgent need of an African Missionary Apostolate, must not await the setting up of the new Nigerian Federal Capital at Abuja. A temporary institute should be set up in the meantime, while awaiting the transfer to Abuja.

4. In the event of this proposal meeting with the approval of the Sacred Congregation for the Evangelization of Peoples, I would appeal to the Sacred Congregation to take the necessary financial initiative. Otherwise, the poverty of the Nigerian.

5. Church, which has in no way been alleviated by the much publicised oil revenues, may be the death-knell of the idea, as there is no possibility that we can initiate the project, if left to our own meagre financial resources.

Friday, May 15, 1976.

His Lordship, Bishop D. I Ekandem
President-Episcopal Conference, Nigeria

The appendix precisely expressed the major points and mode of operation, the approaches coupled with the fact the Holy Ghost Fathers were unable to be truly national in character owing to their insertion in the eastern part of the country, hence the necessity of opting for another group that would handle the project in the desired manner. He spoke boldly but at the same time sympathetically while touching the hearts of his brothers—the bishops. The Appendix pointed out the way to be followed. It later became a document to be referred about the development of the National Seminary and the Missionary Institute.

b. Historical Background[373]

The initiative of a Missionary Institute with the sole need "to fulfill missionary apostolate in and outside the country" generated a very enthusiastic discussion at the 1976 Kaduna Catholic Bishops' Conference.[374] With the weight of argument on the part of those who say that such a missionary institute would go a long way to "foster national unity and solidarity," it was evident that the overwhelming opinion was in favor of the proposal.[375] The crucial decision of the Conference for a Missionary Institute was sealed off by voting which "out of the 27 members present, 22 voted YES, 3 voted NO, and 2 abstentions."[376] This historic event was on September 15, 1976, at about 11:20 a.m. with the acceptance of the project, a committee of three bishops (Usanga, Ganaka and Adelakun) with the right to co- opt any member into it and a mandate to consider the matter in all its ramifications was formed.

The work of the initial committee yielded fruit such that the National Missionary Institute of St. Paul was opened at Iperu Remo in Ogun State and the first students admitted on Mission Sunday, October 23, 1977. In October 1978 the Congregation for the Evangelization of Missionary Priests was formed. The society has the constitutions and organization of similar missionary societies in the church throughout the world.

The Society's Coat of Arms

The coat of arms of the society—Pro Christo Legatione Ergo Fungimur, So We Are Ambassadors for Christ—summarizes the apostolate of the society as the symbolism depicts.

MSP LOGO

- The world map within the circle represents the field of evangelization;
- At the north of the circle, the Cross symbolizes salvation;
- Below the Cross, the dove symbolizes the spirit of Christ renewing the face of the earth;

- The open Bible at the center of the map, with a stole on the right-hand page, signifies the mission to preach and sanctify;
- The pen on the left-hand page indicates the various contributions of the written word to the apostolate.

Membership

Membership of the new society is open to priests already ordained, and to students of the National Missionary Seminary at a certain stage in their course. Msgr. Godwin P. Akpan, formally a priest of Calabar Diocese, became the first member of the society in January 1984.

Students of the National Missionary Seminary of St. Paul are admitted to temporary membership two years after admission to the seminary. They take the permanent oath of membership immediately before they are ordained deacons. Priest wishing to become members of the society are admitted as temporary members for three years before taking the permanent oath of membership.

The Promotion Program

Over the years the society has boldly embarked on a promotion program both among the Catholic faithful in Nigeria itself and overseas. To the extent that its limited resources allowed, it has also sent some of its priests for training with a view to joining the seminary staff and filling other society posts.

Figure 12 The Logo of the MSPs

The Ambassador Publications

A very significant part of the society's promotion effort has gone into that area of communications. The society's publishing arm, Ambassador Publications, now brings out a quarterly missionary magazine titled *The Catholic Ambassador* (*ISSN 1115-8832*), a calendar with scripture and vocation guide, and a liturgical desk diary containing a directory of the Catholic Church in Nigeria. It also does reprints of religious books by agreement with authors and publishers concerned. The director of communications has responsibility for all this.

The Missions

The Missionaries of St. Paul are given a specific missionary formation and training. Under God, this enabled a missionary charism to emerge in the members so that their training and charism may bear fruit. The main question is: Will the forthcoming assembly be plenipotentiary? Will it be able to make full and binding decisions for the society? The commitment of SPS is to the transformation of the Missionary Society of St. Paul into a full-fledged society of apostolic life.

D. Appointment of Acting Rector

The consensus reached by the bishops to embark on the initiative of a National Missionary Seminary motivated them to appoint an acting rector that was to oversee the initial takeoff. That entailed a powerful disposition on the part of the bishops to release one of their priests for the post and arduous task. After some consultation, Bishop Usanga opted to release one of his senior priests, Msgr. Godwin P. Akpan who was at the time serving as the cathedral administrator at Christ the King Catholic Church, Barracks Road, Uyo to take up the post. Monsignor Akpan received the letter of appointment submitting himself to the powerful and providential care of God with equanimity and obedience to his bishop and the Catholic Bishops' Conference of Nigeria with great disposition and trust. The mission was eventful in nature, but he trusted fully in the God who always cares and took the Israelites to the Promised Land with powerful and outstretched arms.

The letter sent by the Catholic Bishops' Conference was written and signed by his proper bishop, His Excellency, the Most Reverend Bishop Brian D. Usanga of Calabar Diocese who was the chairman of the seminary commission at the time. Bishop Usanga was equally appointed chairman of the National Seminary Committee Episcopal Conference of Nigeria. The letter had a dual authority, that of his bishop and that of the Catholic Bishops' Conference of Nigeria.

a. Letter of Appointment

DIOCESE OF CALABAR

Bishop's House
P.M.B. 1044
Calabar,
C.R. State Ndinam
Nigeria.

Motto: To serve in Charity and Justice
Servire in Caritate et Justitia
utom (Abasi) ke ima ye edinen ido
21ˢᵗ August, 1977
Your Ref....................
Our Ref....................

Rt. Rev. Monsignor G. P Akpan, V.G,
Christ the King Church
Uyo

Dear Rev. Monsignor Akpan,

APPOINTMENT AS ACTING DIRECTOR NIGERIAN NATIONAL
SEMINARY

You are hereby appointed Acting Director of the Nigerian National
Seminary temporarily cited at Iperu-Ijebu Ode Diocese effective September
1, 1977.

You are to meet His Lordship, Dr. Anthony Sanusi, Bishop of Ijebu
Ode before September 1, and Rev. Monsignor Alphonsus Obine, Secretary
General Catholic Secretariat, Lagos for accommodation funds, transport,
etc., in connection with your work.

On behalf of the National Episcopal Conference of Nigeria, I wish
to congratulate you on this very important Apostolic assignment for the
Church in Nigeria, in Africa and the universal church.

Sincerely Yours in Jesus Christ
+ Most Rev. Dr. Brian D. Usanga Bishop of Calabar

CHAIRMAN   NATIONAL   SEMINARY   COMMITTEE
EPISCOPAL CONFERENCE OF NIGERIA.

cc   His Eminence Dominic Cardinal Ekandem
+   Most Rev. Dr. A. Sanusi, Bishop of Ijebu Ode Rev. Monsignor
     Alphonsus Obine—Secretary General.

**b.   The Initial Protocols and Necessity of Securing a Site for
     Commencement**

With the approval of the idea of a National Missionary Seminary
and appointment of the acting rector, the need for getting a site to start

this big project became a teething problem for the bishops. They were not particularly concerned about the geographical location although it was part of their consideration. They just wanted a place with some buildings to commence and implement the idea of a National Missionary Seminary.

Bishop Anthony Saliu Sanusi of Ijebu Ode, bishop emeritus who was succeeded by Bishop Albert Fasina, generously opted to give the old Teachers' Training College (TTC) at Iperu Remo, Ogun State that was not immediately in use for its implementation. It was the same Bishop Sanusi who preferred to stay in the old Bishop's House after his retirement instead of transferring to a new Bishop's House. He did not want to overburden the diocese.

Msgr. Godwin Akpan, having been appointed acting rector of the New National Missionary Seminary, had to relinquish his post as the Pro-Cathedral administrator. He was ordered to make contact with the host bishop, the Most Reverend Sanusi, to see the place and see what needed to be done so as to put things in place to prepare for the inauguration ceremony. It is obvious that the bishops were on fire about inaugurating the seminary having put the various structures in place. They did not want any hindrances toward the desired goal. That is the reason for the cooperation of the stakeholders involved. The initial finances were to be met by the Catholic Secretariat of Nigeria. Monsignor Obine, the secretary general was instructed to meet the needs of the newly appointed acting rector in terms of accommodation and transport.

i.   Early Involvement[377]

Monsignor Akpan got officially involved on August 16, 1977, in the unfolding process of the Missionary Institute of St. Paul. The Bishops Committee for the National Missionary Institute of St. Paul invited him to that Committee Meeting in Port Harcourt. His Eminence, Dominic Cardinal Ekandem, who was the Chairman of the Committee and current President of the Catholic Bishops' Conference of Nigeria (CBCN) took the decision and invited him to their committee meeting. At the meeting, Cardinal Ekandem expressed the wishes of the Bishops inviting him to accept the directorship of the proposed National Missionary Institute of St. Paul. Monsignor Akpan had already expressed a willingness to accept the appointment while promising to do his best. He also asked for cooperation and prayers. At the Bishops' Conference held in Benin from September 13 to 17, 1977, the conference confirmed the committee's report, thereby giving full support to Monsignor Akpan to take charge of the National Missionary Institute of St. Paul's project starting at the temporary site at Iperu Remo.

The main concern at the time was to rehabilitate the old St. Mark's Teachers' Training College compound in Iperu for the formal inauguration of the Missionary Institute with the nine pioneer students on Mission Sunday, October 23, 1977. It was a significant event heralded in with an open-air concelebrated mass attended by representatives from the dioceses in the country to mark the formal inauguration of the Missionary Institute of St. Paul.

ii.   Preparation to Visit Iperu Remo

25th August,
Rt. Rev. Msgr. A. Obine
Secretary General Catholic Secretariat Lagos.

Dear Rev. Msgr. Obine,

I shall be visiting Iperu on the 31st, of this month. If all goes well, hopefully I shall be in Lagos on the 1st, of September 1977. Otherwise, it will be possible to come to you on the 2nd of September.
While asking for your prayers.

Sincerely Yours Rev. Msgr. G.P. Akpan,

c.   Meeting with the Bishop of Ijebu Ode, Most Rev. Dr. Anthony Sanusi

In the late seventies, things happened in quick succession. On August 11, 1977, Msgr. Godwin Akpan was invited the Bishops Committee Meeting. Having completed the initial protocols of acceptance, receiving a letter confirming the appointment, he proceeded to inform the church council at Uyo of the new assignment on August 27, 1977, where he was the father-in-charge. The reactions of the council were mixed, but he had to leave because of the urgency.

On August 31, 1977, the maiden visit to Ijebu-Ode with respect to the project was undertaken from the cardinal's residence in Ikot Ekpene, arriving at St. Sebastian's Cathedral in Ijebu-Ode at 3:30 p.m. from there, he was escorted to the Bishop's House. There he met Bishop Sanusi who received him and his driver, Gregory Asuquo Pius Udo, very warmly. He and the Bishop went at 4:30 p.m. to see the expected compound at Iperu Remo. They met in the parish house of an Irish SMA priest, Rev. Patrick Barry. From there they went to the site, which was in the same compound except that the site had been abandoned over the years. The rehabilitation work had to start right in earnest with the active cooperation of the parish priest Rev. Patrick Barry.

When on July 20, 1977, it was first mentioned that he would be directly involved in the proposed seminary, the National Missionary Seminary of St. Paul, a chain of events was gradually unfolding. It sounded revolutionary to talk of a fourth major seminary in Nigeria when the three existing ones were serving the then priestly training needs of the church in Nigeria well.[378]

The 25.5-acre compound once used as St. Mark's Training College looked more like a deserted village than a site[379] to be rehabilitated so as to be ready for nine pioneer students and two member staff on the fourteenth of October of that year in preparing for the official opening of the new Missionary Seminary on Mission Sunday, October 23, 1977. The amount of work in the compound was alarming. The time within which the work was to be completed in order to meet the immediate objective (opening on Mission Sunday 1977) was desperately short.

With the unqualified cooperation of Bishop Anthony Saliu Sanusi and of Rev. P. Barry, not only was the essential part of the work completed on schedule but it was also possible to get NEPA to install light a few days prior to the date.

The opening date, October 23, 1977, started with an open- air con-celebrated mass. Under the brightly shining tropical sun, many bishops and a host of priests concelebrated together with lay representatives of the then twenty-eight dioceses in the country at the time attended. The event of the day heralded the birth of the first Missionary Seminary in Africa. To mark the formal opening of the Missionary Seminary, the then president of the Bishops' Conference of Nigeria, Dominic Cardinal Ekandem, in a simple but significant ceremony, solemnly declared, "With profound gratitude to the Almighty God, it is my privilege to declare the National Missionary Seminary of St. Paul open for the greater glory of God and for the salvation of souls." Thus, the National Missionary Seminary of St. Paul started and grew in the temporary site in Iperu till it moved to its permanent location in the new federal capital territory, Abuja, on October 13, 1984.

d.   The Choice of St. Patrick's or Kiltegan Fathers

The prince who became a cardinal, conceived intuitively that the Holy Ghost Fathers in Igboland were operating within a certain geographical location and circumscription, the same applied to the Missionaries of Africa in the west and the Augustinians in the north, he decided to opt for something specifically unique to the Nigerian situation, the National Seminary. That was not to be compromised at all. He envisioned a neutral group that will be able to take care of the situation and the new group. His mind-set moved to the Kiltegans owing to their background and experience in the field of evangelization and proximity of spirit and value.

Concerning the choice of the Kiltegan Missionaries, Archbishop Joseph Edra Ukpo, the emeritus archbishop of Calabar Metropolitan See says, "As a man of perception, the cardinal moved to ask the Kiltegans, St. Patrick Fathers to see to the running of the Missionary Seminary of St. Paul since they have a similar charism with that of the Missionaries of St. Paul."[380] This is the foundation behind the statement of "the Holy Ghost Congregation being attached to the dioceses in Igboland and to the bishops in Igboland."[381] For that reason, they were not disposed to carry out or implement the idea of a Missionary Seminary that had no boundaries within the country nor restricted to a particular locality or region but such that would embrace the entire nation.

i.   Funding of the Repairs

This is what Monsignor Akpan called Partners in Progress.[382] Before the 1976 Kaduna decision of the Catholic Bishops of Nigeria to establish the National Missionary Seminary/Society of St. Paul, the initiator of the project, Cardinal Ekandem, had done the spadework. In the early seventies, in his contact with the superior general of the St. Patrick Fathers who was the superior of SPS at the time with no written agreement, he was able to get the St. Patrick Fathers to agree to assist in the training and spiritual formation of the young members of the society to be, from then on, the involvement of the Kiltegan fathers in the life of the young society was very crucial. In a way, in terms of the initial development of the National Missionary Seminary/Society of St. Paul, the Missionary of St. Patrick's was a gift to the society. The St. Patrick Fathers, who generously served in various midwifery capacities, were so many extensions of that gift to which we remain eternally grateful. The first in the scene in practical terms was Rev. Thomas Greenan, SPS who assisted especially in respect of submitting the estimate for the rehabilitation of the existing buildings in the 25.5acre land of St. Mark's, as it was now undergoing a radical change to becoming the first home for past, present, and future Missionaries of St. Paul. Admittedly, progress was being made in making the National Missionary Seminary/Society a reality.

ii.   The Formation of the Various Boards and Committees

To effectively establish the seminary and society, many boards and committees and subcommittees with the capacity to co-opt others into them sprang up. The very first board to be formed for the smooth beginning of the seminary and the Missionary Institute of St. Paul was the ad hoc committee that met in Port Harcourt comprising Cardinal Ekandem, chairman and president of the Catholic Bishops' Conference of Nigeria, and the CBCN committee on the new institute. There were mainly three different types of boards or councils until both came of age. These were: the internal governing council, the governors board or governing council, and the Catholic Bishops' Conference of Nigeria (CBCN), the general umbrella that foresaw and supervised everything. It was the ultimate port of call since all the reports had to go back to them for implementation, for guidance or scrutiny as they deemed it fit. The conference gave freedom to the various councils' operation to operate in its name, *in nomine suo.* For practical purposes, the ordinary of the locus of the seminary automatically became the ordinary of the seminary and society as indicated in the letters of the Most Reverend Anthony Sanusi, the Bishop of Ijebu Ode.

e. Formation of the Bishops' Committee on the Seminary after Approval at Kaduna

After the approval of the idea of the National Missionary Seminary/ Society by the Catholic Bishops' Conference, there was a strong need to put some structures of operation in place. One of such structures included the nomination of some bishops to the National Missionary Seminary Committee. The following were appointed:

Bishop Brian David Usanga—Chairman,
Bishop Gabriel Gonsum Ganaka—member,
and Bishop Julius Babatunde Adelakun—member.

Since the country had three major regional divisions at the time and three ecclesiastical provinces of east, north, and west were appointed. The three were to coordinate things and report them to the plenary session of the Catholic Bishops' Conference of Nigeria.

The Bishops' Committee that interviewed and sought the opinion of Msgr. Godwin Akpan about the directorship of the National Missionary Seminary included Cardinal Ekandem as chairman together with the three members of the bishops' committee. It appears Cardinal Ekandem featured as chairman because of his unique position as the one who made the proposal to establish the National Missionary Seminary and as the president of the Bishops' Conference. The letter written to Msgr. Godwin Akpan after accepting to be the rector of the National Missionary Seminary bore the name of Bishop Usanga as the chairman. This is in conformity to page 5 of the minutes of the Bishops' Conference that sat at Kaduna during that historic commencement of the National Missionary Seminary. Since the seminary was national, it had to reflect that national character too.

f.   The Governing Council

This council took care of the overall planning, financing, and execution of the institution's project. They acted as the overseer over the actions and decisions of the internal governing council while collaborating effectively with it. They had to give a report to the Catholic Bishops' Conference about their undertakings and progress. Bishop Anthony S. Sanusi, the first bishop of Ijebu-Ode was the first chairman of the governing board. In as much as the seminary, the novitiate, philosophy, and theology training remained in Iperu Remo, Bishop Sanusi remained the chairman of the governing board. In terms of the membership and vows of Monsignor Akpan, he was the man on the spot. He was the ordinary of Iperu Remo, likewise the ordinary of the society until the institute moved to Abuja. In the chain of production and execution, Bishop Sanusi was the person to report things to. It was his responsibility to take care of the necessities concerning the growth of the nascent body in the Nigerian Church. The governing council chairman only changed with the leadership in the place that the seminary was located.

Cardinal Ekandem with Fr. P. O'Reilly, Superior of the St. Patrick Fathers

Figure 13 Bishop Ekandem and the Superior General of the SPS

g. The Internal Governing Council

The CBCN set up the internal governing council for the smooth running of the society and the seminary. It had the following *Terms of Reference*:

- Getting the Missionary Society on its feet
- Laying the Foundation of the Society
- Organizing the Formation of the Students
- Doing Research on the Future of the Missions.

With the specification of the terms of reference, the job of the council was somehow simplified, but they still had a lot on their plates to chew. The internal governing council had the responsibility of accounting to the Bishops' Conference. The president of the internal governing council had to attend the meetings of the bishops regularly especially when a report was to be given about the seminary and the society. The number of personnel involved was small and concise. It was a form of think tank to engineer the evolution of the society and seminary.

The following members constituted the internal governing council:

- Msgr. Godwin P. Akpan, MSP—President
- Rev. Fr. James Sheerin, SPS—Secretary
- Very Rev. Gabriel K. Yankoya—Member
- Rev. Fr. Leonard Kasanda Lumbulu, CICM—Member

It is interesting to note the constitutive mélange. Two members of the staff of the seminary, Monsignor Akpan and Fr. James Sheerin were involved. There were two outsiders who looked at things with external binoculars utilizing their experiences and expertise. The outsiders were: Very Rev. Gabriel Yankoya and Fr. Leonard Kasanda Lumbulu, CICM. Father Leonard was generally known as Fr. Leonard Kasanda or simply as Father Kasanda.

The council had the duty of taking care of planning the day- today running of the seminary and its growth. This accounts for the important decisions arrived at and executed by the council. The secretary of the council, Fr. James Sheerin, normally signed mails before delivery, affecting

Monsignor Akpan as the president. The members of St. Patrick Society formed part of the seminary. The regional superior Very Rev. Fr. Dermot Connolly, SPS who lived at Ebute Meta at the time sent them.

The internal governing council did not operate alone. It functioned in conjunction with the *first three Kiltegans/St. Patrick Fathers* namely:

- Rev. Fr. John Lawlor, SPS
- Rev. Fr. James Sheerin, SPS
- and Rev. Fr. Hugo McBride, SPS.

Among these three, the very first to arrive was Fr. John Lawlor followed by the other two. Monsignor Akpan and Father Lawlor received the first set of students together with Fathers James Sheerin and Hugo McBride who arrived on October 14, 1977.[383] It is not surprising why Fr. John Lawlor, SPS became the first vice rector of the seminary, owing to uniqueness of position and early arrival. Monsignor Akpan and Father Lawlor started swimming together in the rough waters of pioneering the establishment of the society and seminary. The advisory council was one of the boards formed to help in the smooth running of events especially at the appointment of Msgr. Godwin P. Akpan as the acting superior general.

i. The First Set of Students at Gwagwalada Seminary

The first set of students[384] were nine in number. They are the nine pioneer MSP seminarians that joined the major seminary, Missionary Seminary of St. Paul at Gwagwalada that started at Iperu Remo, Ogun State, Nigeria. These are their names:

- Philip Dung,
- Dominic Ekandem,
- Sylvestre Ibuot Ete,
- Nicholas Ibuot,
- John Jiges,
- Lawrence Nwafor,
- Anthony Ojakaminor, Andrew Toyinbo, John Osom.

The nine candidates that graduated from Iperu with Msgr. Godwin Akpan proceeded to Gwagwalada. They constituted the foundation members of the National Missionary Seminary, Gwagwalada. Among the nine that started philosophical courses, five became priests: Jiges, Dung, Osom, Ibuot, and Toyinbo. The five that became priests excelled in various contexts and some in their "Diocese of Origin" like Fr. Nicholas Kokoette Ibuot. He was ordained for Calabar Diocese before it gave birth to Uyo Diocese. Father Nicholas died as a priest of Uyo Diocese at the age of fifty-one.

Since students were being sought urgently, the necessary places to turn to were the seminaries. Many of the first batches of students came from Calabar and Ikot Ekpene Dioceses (Nicholas, Dominic, Sylvestre, and John). Rev. Fr. John Osom, MSP emerged as the first fruit of that venture. The National Missionary Seminary has since grown to a very large extent having missionaries in almost all the dioceses in Nigeria, Gambia, Cameroon, Sierra Leone, South Africa, Botswana, America, Britain, and Ireland, etc. They are still exploring the possibility of going further afield.

The mustard seed that started in part with St. Patrick Fathers, the Kiltegan Fathers as the Initial Formation Team in Iperu Remo, Ogun State, has since evolved and extended to Gwagwalada where Philosophy and Theology are studied. Monsignor Godwin Akpan was the first rector. Since he joined the society as a foundation member, he was appointed the first acting superior general till the first chapter and general elections took place in September 1995 where Very Rev. Fr. Felix Elosi, MSP was chosen and elected as the very first elected superior general of the Missionary Society of St. Paul (MSP). Since the base is Gwagwalada in Abuja, it is proper that John Cardinal Olorunfemi Onaiyekan, the metropolitan archbishop of Abuja, should be their ordinary. By virtue of that position, he automatically became the chairman of the governing council.

At Kuje in Abuja, Cardinal Ekandem established the minor seminary—Saints Simon and Jude Seminary Kuje, Abuja—to foster vocations in the diocese. He equally established hospitals in Gwagwalada, Bwari, and Garki to take care of the health of the people of God, likewise nursery primary in Garki, Gwagwalada, and Nyanya with secondary schools in Gwagwalada for boys and in Garki for girls—namely, Christ the King for boys and Regina Pacis for girls. He was always concerned with the holistic development of his flock that is why the idea of National Seminary beyond frontiers became uppermost in his mind long before he was charged with the onus of beginning the Abuja Independent Mission. The Catholic Church is to be credited for establishing many of the welfare services taking care of various people in the country. That is a positive contribution. The seminarians functioned in Iperu for over a year before the grand opening finally occurred.

The governing council meeting of July 21, 1993, held at the Eucharistic Heart of Jesus Convent (EHJ) had four archbishops although two were not present, five bishops, two were absent, two monsignors, and four priests. The constitution of the priests was very important since one represented the Missionaries of St. Paul, Fr. Otoide; the other represented the St. Patrick Fathers in Nigeria since he was the superior, Very Rev. Fr. Dermot Connolly; Fr. Etafo, a Canonist, was the technical person there; while Fr. John Joyce represented the internal governing council and staff. Other details can be seen at the footnote together with those absent.[385]

The chairman went on to say that the Missionary Society of St. Paul wanted to become a society of apostolic life. Church norms demanded that this be effected under the authority of a diocesan bishop; there was no provision in law for an episcopal conference to play such a role. The Abuja Diocese had been requested to take on this responsibility and he, as archbishop of Abuja, had accepted that responsibility. The Catholic Bishops' Conference of Nigeria would therefore need to transfer authority to the ordinary of Abuja, who would then take the necessary steps toward a canonical erection of the society. It presupposed a consultation with the Holy See and the obtaining of a nihil obstat from the same Holy See.[386] These steps were taken to effect good foundation for proper establishment of the society and its growth.

Chapter Thirteen

DEUS PROVIDEBIT (GOD WILL PROVIDE)

Implantation and Growth of the Society

Unless the Lord builds the house, in vain
do its builders labour (Ps.127:1)

THE IMPLANTATION[387] OF the Missionary Society of St. Paul and the National Missionary Seminary of St. Paul both owe their origin to God's grace. The action of God is very obvious even in the turn out at the opening ceremony shortly after approval and planning. St. Vincent de Paul was right when he said that "God's work does itself."[388]

A lot transpired during the official opening of the National Missionary Seminary, Iperu. The seminarians and the priests present captured the situation vividly by giving a captivating description and information about the events. The reports and activities speak for themselves.

A. The Grand/Official Opening[389]

Over two thousand representatives of Nigeria's twenty-nine dioceses at the time, including distinguished visitors from overseas, gathered at Iperu from May 26 to 27 for the formal opening of the National Missionary Seminary of St. Paul by the Catholic bishops of Nigeria. Bishop O'Meara, the national director for the Propagation of Faith in the United States of America, delivered one of the speeches at the grand opening ceremonies. He stressed the need to live a life of union among the Missionaries of St. Paul and with others, since missionaries are always linked with others, holding on to faith and persevering on their commitment. If they do this, they will surely be a very happy group joining other happy population of missionaries in the church.

> Life, and so they must learn how to stay alive and survive spiritually. They must learn how to pray so that they will never lose the vision that brought them here…the vision of sharing the riches of Christ Jesus with others who do not, as yet, possess that grace and offering loving service in his holy name. They will have to remember also that they are part of a community because missionaries never go it alone. They are sent by the church of Nigeria, and they are sent to the church in the place to which they go, and beyond that they, themselves, among themselves, must have a sense of community which will enable them to bear each other up through temptation, through discouragement, the human weaknesses that are the common lot of all human beings who walk this planet.
>
> I make them a promise that if they persevere in this beautiful vision, that if they keep alive their faith, and work hard to overcome its obstacles, they will always be happy people. For the past twenty-three years, my priesthood has been devoted entirely to dealing with missionary personnel, and I want to tell all of you and the laity here present that I know of no happier group of men and women than that group we call our missionaries. They have given everything

away and the Lord rewarded that with an abundant measure
of his peace, of his joy and his fulfilment.[390]

—Bishop Edward T. O'Meara
National Director of the Propagation of Faith, USA

a. Missionary Dimension

His Grace Most Reverend Francis Arinze, archbishop of Onitsha
and chairman of the Episcopal Conference of Nigeria, who later became
Cardinal Arinze, emphasized the missionary dimension of the new institute. He pointed out the role played by Nigerian priests and sisters as vanguards in the missionary field before the Missionaries of St. Paul came
into being. The group of Nigerian missionaries included the diocesans
as well as the religious who went to countries like Sierra Leone, Ghana,
Liberia, Gambia, Congo, and Kenya. He noted that the establishment of
the Missionaries of St. Paul was a great milestone that would release mobile
forces in the army of Christ the King.

b. Local versus Universal Church

The emphasis of Most Reverend Anthony Saliu Sanusi, the bishop of
Ijebu Ode, noted that the dioceses were having a single vision of evangelization previously, and at the time of establishment of the Missionaries of
St. Paul, they were beginning to look at things globally distinct from the
former ways of concentrating on the various dioceses. He went on to say
that there was no contradiction in the development. The needs of the local
church should never be permitted to jeopardize the needs of the universal
church since the service of the entire church will bring abundant fruits to
the local church in Nigeria. In this manner, the local church in Nigeria will
be contributing to the life of the universal church.

c. Poised for the Future

The newly appointed rector of the seminary looked with optimism
and enthusiasm at the future and the effective participation of the Nigerian

church at the world's evangelization by sending out missionaries and observed that Nigerian church was poised for action.

> I look on the national missionary seminary of St. Paul as a sign, a healthy sign, that the Church in Nigeria is poised to enter effectively the new missionary era to which Vatican II invites the young churches of the world to take part in the universal mission of the church as soon as possible, by sending missionaries to other countries even though they themselves are short of clergy.[391]

> —Msgr. Godwin P. Akpan, Rector

B. Extracts from Ambassador Magazine on the Grand Opening

The contribution of His Eminence Dominic Cardinal Ekandem touched on a number of issues that gave direction to the Missionary Society of St. Paul a cognate existence of the missionaries. The spirit of St. Paul and the necessity of the National Missionary Seminary were seriously underscored. With this, he gave a guideline that was to influence the development and implantation of the missionary wing and the society. It was a perceived vision at a distance and yet close but closer than Balaam's perceived Star of David.

> I shall see him, but not now: I shall behold him, but not nigh: there shall come a Star out of Jacob, and a Sceptre shall rise out of Israel, and shall smite the corners of Moab, and destroy all the children of Shethites (Numbers 24:17).

It was Saint Thomas Aquinas that said that for a believer, he does not need any proofs; but for an unbeliever, even the proofs are not necessary. In the same vein, Prophet Habakkuk says,

> Then the Lord answered me and said: Write the vision; make it plain on tablets, so that a runner may read it. There is still a vision for the appointed time; it speaks of the end

and does not lie. If it seems to tarry, wait for it; it will surely come, it will not delay (Habakkuk 2:3).

Cardinal Ekandem beheld what others were trying to grapple with. Intuitively and perceptively, he beheld what was quite afar, and what was quite afar became closely beheld and cherished.

The *Spirit of St. Paul* was the speech delivered by Cardinal Ekandem during that inaugural celebration of the grand opening of the Missionary Society of St. Paul and the National Missionary Seminary at Iperu—Remo, Ogun State. The attendance in the celebration was over two thousand people, including the prelates, namely the cardinals, archbishops, bishops, priests, religious, and the laity, as well as foreign participants. Many of the speeches given above are by Bishop O'Meara, the American director of the Propagation of Faith. In his address, Cardinal Ekandem mentioned the initial financial contributors to the project and expressed deep gratitude to them all.

Under the spirit of St. Paul, the cardinal gave a brief historical survey of the development of the seminary. He demonstrated how three popes were involved at the various stages and each performing a definite task in the process of expansion and development of the twin project, the society and the seminary in the light of Pauline missionary inspiration.

a.   Spirit of Saint Paul

It was another Paul who continued where St. Paul left off. It was Paul VI who traveled to Kampala of the Ugandans and charged the African bishops: "As missionaries to yourselves, you Africans must now continue, upon this continent, the building up of the Church." It was Paul VI who bequeathed to us the most historic and precious treasure of missionary endeavour in our time, "Evangelii Nuntiandi," which distilled for us, for all time, the 1974 Synod on evangelization in the world today.

It was Pope Paul VI of blessed memory who gave the official blessing to, and permission for this, our National Missionary Seminary venture. It was Pope John Paul I who received from my hands, at the first opportunity I had with him, a report on our infant Missionary Seminary. And now it is the vigorous and dynamic Pope John Paul II who is the present guide and protector of our Seminary of St. Paul. I am not surprised to find that the spirit of Paul is strikingly evidenced by the enthusiasm and practical involvement of the people of God in Nigeria. How encouraged we have been to witness how the National Laity Council is making inspired and generous provision in setting up a five million Naira Trust [fund] to finance this seminary! Our prayer now is that their efforts may be a success. I cannot forget my debt of gratitude for the equally inspired encouragement given by the CKC old boys association in Onitsha, who, on hearing the proposal of the National Missionary Seminary, raised on the spot over seven thousand naira with a promise of doing more. The Knights of St. Mulumba and imbibing too the spirit of Paul already come out to help with sponsorships.

Thus, with the initial efforts of all the Nigerian bishops, coupled with donations from overseas benefactors, represented here today by the American director of the Propagation of the Faith, His Excellency Most Reverend Bishop O'Meara, the subsidy from the Sacred Congregation for the Evangelization of Peoples and, of course, from the Holy Father himself. It has been possible to make this splendid and most encouraging beginning.

Dominic Cardinal Ekandem

It is interesting to note the two road maps of the society and of the National Missionary Seminary mapped out by Cardinal Ekandem in this speech. His input is and was of vital importance as the trailblazer of the entire project and visionary. All he needed to do was to unfold what was embedded in his mind so that others could share in it. In his speech, he pointed out the road to be followed, indicating what he perceived that was to take place and emphasizing the vocational outlook and orientation of a missionary in the context where mostly a diocesan spirit had dominated. This calls for proper understanding and reinterpretation.

b.   The Necessity of a National Seminary in Nigeria

By Cardinal Dominic Ekandem

The National Missionary Seminary of St. Paul has now completed its fourth year with forty students in philosophy and the spiritual year and with bright prospects for a good representative intake in the next academic year. Over the past two years, the seminary has been made known by parishes and schools in twenty-nine dioceses in Nigeria and had received generous response from bishops, priests, religious, and people of these dioceses. The seminary magazine, *The Ambassador*, is gradually making way as a link between the parishes and the seminary, establishing that partnership of interest, prayer, vocation, and support so necessary for growth of a missionary institute.

i. Something New

When the bishops of Nigeria embarked on this project, we knew we were establishing something new in the Nigerian church: a seminary that was national and essentially missionary. If it were a question of something equivalent to any of our existing seminaries, we would not have started it at all. We were already well served by three major seminaries for the training and formation of diocesan priests: Ibadan, Enugu/Ikot Ekpene, and Jos. There was no need for another seminary unless we had a special objective. It was this missionary objective that won the great enthusiasm of the late Pope Paul VI and brought the encouragement, support, and backing of the Congregation for the Evangelization of Peoples.

ii. Specifically Missionary

We wanted a seminary to give a specifically missionary training and a special staff to inculcate the missionary ideals, which mold the missionary vocation, the "vocation for life" which Pope Paul VI asked the bishops of the world to keep continually before the people (*Ecclesiae Sanctae* III, August 6, 1966, No. 6). Unfortunately, in the country, at the moment, we seem to have just one idea of the priesthood: to become diocesan priests. The missionary vocation is not yet planted. Anyone who offers himself for missionary work goes and gets out.[392] This should not be the case. The missionary vocation is a seed to be sown and a plant to be nurtured, and we felt the establishment of a Missionary Seminary would prove effective in promoting and establishing the missionary vocation in the Nigerian church.[393]

iii.   Missions Outside Nigeria

If we had missionary priests at St. Paul's today, we would decide on what mission area to send them. When we have missionaries, we will decide where they should go. We have many invitations from South Africa and other parts of the continent, from North and South America. There is no need to decide to which territory we are going until we are ready to go. The seminarians can be assured we have their missions in mind. What is important for them is that they will be well trained in the spirit and mold of missionaries.

If it is possible, because experience is a great teacher, we would want to work abroad first with other missionaries. This is the way it has always been. St. Patrick Missionaries, for example, began with the Holy Ghost Fathers. Something similar could happen with the Missionaries of St. Paul even though circumstances have changed considerably in fifty years.

iv.   The Parish Clergy

The parish clergy here, as elsewhere, has a very significant role in the development of the missionary seminary, a role they are already generously playing in many places. Through them, the people will know that to share is to expand, that we are all in the service of the universal church, that missionaries are messengers sent out by the Christian community with all her love, sacrifice, and support. In the beginning, St. Paul was resented for going to the Gentiles. In time, there will be a great bond between the priests and people of Nigeria and the Nigerian missionaries going out. Already, Nigerian diocesan priests are working in African countries, such as Liberia and Sierra Leone and in Grenada, West Indies. Others will follow them. They will be joined by and they will join the Missionaries of St. Paul.[394]

The seminarians recalled the grand opening and the historical events of their foundation as they knew it in a graphic manner.

C.   Our Story

In September 1976, the Catholic bishops of Nigeria, meeting in Kaduna, decided to establish a National Missionary Seminary and a

Missionary Society. Cardinal Dominic Ekandem was then president of the bishops' conference. Earlier in Rome, he had mentioned to Pope Paul VI the idea of establishing a Nigerian Missionary Seminary to be placed under the patronage of St. Paul. The pope immediately recalled his encouragement to the Africans to accomplish and gave his blessing to the proposal.

The bishops' decision in Kaduna to establish a national missionary seminary was in line with the pope's intention and the intrinsic nature of the church as missionary. The new seminary and society would be a microcosm of the nation, establishing the bond a cohesive force among the people of Nigeria. The society and seminary were to follow in the footsteps of the forebears by bringing the good news to foreign nations It was decided that the headquarters of the society should be at Abuja, the new federal capital.

Providentially, the Rt. Rev. Dr. Anthony S. Sanusi, the bishop of Ijebu Ode, Ogun State had offered the former St. Mark's College, at Iperu Remo, the probability of beginning the new seminary became more obvious. The first set of students arrived at Iperu on Mission Sunday, October 23, 1977.

In October 1978, the Congregation for the Evangelization of Peoples approved the Nigerian bishops' decision to establish the Missionary Society and Seminary of St. Paul, likewise the appointment of the bishop of Ijebu-Ode as the ordinary of the society and seminary. In May 1979, the National Missionary Seminary of St. Paul was formally opened by the Bishops' Conference of Nigeria at Iperu at a two-day event that brought together over two thousand worshippers, including the clergy, the religious, and the laity from all the dioceses, together with visitors from outside the country.

On Mission Sunday 1979, three students in their third year in the seminary at Iperu made their mission promise to Bishop Sanusi during a concelebrated mass.

Rev. Msgr. Godwin P. Akpan from Calabar diocese was accepted into the Society of St. Paul. The seminary has admitted the third set of spiritual year students.

a.   Iperu-Remo as the Home of the Missionaries of St. Paul

John Jiges, one of the very first seminarians to be admitted and who witnessed the grand Opening, narrated his experiences. He looked at modules of operation and structural infrastructure before the opening. The old students joined the staff to welcome the new arrivals. All joined to prepare for the official opening. They had something exciting to look up to at that initial stage. It was a good beginning.

b. Our Present Home

We arrived at Iperu-Remo on October 15, 1977, the first set of students for the Missionary Seminary. The place was completely unknown to us, and when we found the compound, it was like a forest with buildings in the middle of it and bush paths leading to them. There was no electricity or water, and the place seemed infested with ants and mosquitoes. The mission house stood alone near the main road, which Fr. Barry, the parish priest, shared with the two members of the staff who had been preparing for our arrival.

We were accommodated in one of the main buildings. There was a small chapel ready and a class hall, where the writing on the blackboard showed that this was once a center for training catechists. Workers were busy repairing, reconstructing, and painting. Shortly after our arrival, we were connected to NEPA (National Electric Power Authority). Mission Sunday of October 23 brought hundreds of visitors to the compound for a concelebrated mass that Cardinal Ekandem was the principal celebrant. It was the official beginning of the seminary, a day we will always remember. We will remember too our first threeday retreat given by Bishop Job of Ibadan. In different ways, we came to realize the great interest that the bishops had in the new seminary and in us. Gradually, we got a clearer understanding of our own training, especially during the thirty days retreat given by Father Dolan.

Since then, there has been progress on all sides. We have been connected to Iperu Town Water Supply. A generator has been installed to help NEPA, National Electric Power Authority. The chapel has been extended to accommodate about sixty persons. Adequate quarters for the spiritual year have been provided. A new dormitory has been built. The library is growing. We now have a resident staff of five and three visiting teachers. Each week we see improvements in class halls, recreation rooms, and games facilities. We know all this has been made possible by generous benefactors in Nigeria and in many parts of the world. We hope our prayers and our lives will show them gratitude.

The missionary seminary is at Iperu because Bishop Sanusi, who has been our father in so many ways, gave the buildings of the former St. Mark's Teachers' College for this purpose. Saint Mark's was built in the 1950s under the direction of Father Daily SMA. For twelve years, teachers were trained here. We would all like to know more of its student teachers during those years. We know of one of its very distinguished visitors in 1962: Cardinal Montini, later Pope Paul VI. After being closed as a teachers' college, it was an interdiocesan training center for catechists and later still an agricultural center under the Catholic mission. Then it was vacant for a few years until we came in October 1977.[395]

—John G. Jiges

The following is the papal blessing given at that occasion:

POPE JOHN PAUL II'S BLESSING OF THE SEMINARIANS

Father,

In your plan for our salvation, you provide shepherds for your people. Bring to fulfilment the good work you have begun in these young men. Raise them up as worthy ministers for your altar and gentle servants of your gospel.

D. Historical Background of the National Missionary Society of St. Paul

"Go, therefore, make disciples of all nations" (Matt. 28:19). In obedience to this mandate of Christ, the local church in Nigeria, through the Episcopal

Conference of Nigeria, is seeking a major but decisive step in a planned evangelization on a national level and beyond. The National Missionary Seminary of St. Paul was opened at its temporary site at Iperu Remo in Ijebu-Ode diocese of Ogun State on Mission, Sunday, October 23, 1979.[396]

In 1956, His Lordship, Rt. Rev. Dr. Dominic Ekandem, who later became His Eminence, Dominic Cardinal Ekandem, made the first proposal about a National Missionary Seminary in the Kaduna meeting of the bishops. It took another twenty years before the bishops' conference took a final decision in 1976, after the aborted one taken in 1966 before the Civil War. Msgr. Godwin Pius Akpan of the Diocese of Calabar was appointed acting rector of the seminary by the National Episcopal Conference of Nigeria during the meeting in Benin on September 13, 1977. To assist the acting rector was Rev. Fr. John Lawlor of St. Patrick's Missionary Society.

1. Objective: Missionary orientation is the strong emphasis for missions and evangelization within and outside Nigeria.
2. Qualification for entry: For academic qualification, a candidate is expected to possess the West African Examination School Certificate or its equivalent and has to be of sound health, proven character, and with average intelligence.
3. Method of Application: All applications must pass through the bishop of the candidate seeking admission. The bishop, in turn, will comment in writing on such applications.
4. Basic Requirement for Entry:

• Candidates will be expected to acquire the spirit of prayer, self-denial, and obedience by a willingness to take part in the spiritual exercises of the seminary and by keeping the rules.
• Every candidate will begin the seminary with an intense one year spiritual formation in the spirit of the great missionary of St. Paul.
• During the first year, each student will study the constitution closely with a view to abiding by that.

Course of Studies: After the spiritual year, the normal seminary course in philosophy and theology will be systematically passed.

Sponsorship: It costs a minimum of N500 per annum (in 1979) to maintain a seminarian in Iperu.[397] With the often devalued situation of the Nigerian currency, a lot more will be needed, probably ten times that amount.

Maintenance: While in the seminary, the maintenance of the candidates will be borne by the seminary.

Ownership of the place: This will be treated in detail later on in the work. The National Missionary Seminary/Society of St. Paul belongs to the Episcopal Conference of Nigeria and can be reached through

The Acting Rector

National Missionary Seminary of St Paul
PO Box 11
Iperu-Remo
Ogun State
Nigeria

E.   A Special Appeal for Support of the National Missionary Seminary of St. Paul, Iperu-Remo, Ogun State.

To support the seminary appeal for aid to support the Seminary by the laity and various associations had to be established. This was approved by the Episcopal Conference of Nigeria, and the appeal was open to as many as possible and extended to willing clergy and even donors outside Nigeria. It was expansive, yet it was very necessary. That foresight eventually gave birth to the Associates of St. Paul Missionaries, probably tapping from the experience of Bishop Shanahan and that of the founder of St. Patrick Fathers, Very Reverend Father Pat Whitney, SPS.

The benefactors and benefactresses have to address their donations to the rector. The distribution of the envelopes for the appeal in aid began on November 20, 1977.

The day witnessed the "cablegram of His Holiness, Pope Paul VI," part of which reads

Holy Father sends paternal greetings for inauguration of National Missionary Seminary of St. Paul. He praises the generous missionary spirit that finds expression in this initiative of the beloved church in Nigeria; to share the light and joy of Christ's message with so many other sons and daughters of the continent. His Holiness is particularly pleased that the ceremony will take place on Mission Sunday during the week commemorating the tenth anniversary of his own historic achievement of love and solicitude for all peoples of Africa. Praying that this institution will be a Center of Eucharistic piety where men will deepen their faith and charity in prayerful study of God's word and be strengthened to communicate the life-giving and uplifting Gospel to their brethren. The Holy Father cordially imparts a special apostolic blessing invoking grace and peace upon all assembled.

His Eminence Dominic Cardinal Ekandem, in his inauguration address, while praising the great sacrifice on the part of the expatriate missionaries, noted,

It is gratifying that as expatriate missionaries entered Nigeria towards the end of the last century, we are beginning our preparation, and that on a national scale of sending Nigerian missionaries out to join the main stream of Catholic missionaries, flowing into Africa and beyond. It seems then that the opening of the National Missionary Seminary of St. Paul, heralds the dawn of a "new missionary era" at least in Africa, with all the attendant commitment of every son of Africa who should be legitimately proud, nay, regard it a rare privilege in his life-time to be called upon to champion a cause which has not only an international but an eternal bearing on an emergency operation.

The speech portended a happy prognostication uplifting the spirit and inciting zeal to be part of the whole missionary trend evangelizing the entire world. Msgr. Godwin Akpan then shared his experience while traveling to Texas to see the parish that the missionaries were to minister in.

On his arrival, he met the Josephites who decided to send him to a parish. After spending two more days in the state of Mississippi, he arrived in the vacant parish of Breaux Bridge toward the border with Texas, which was his last station. While there, he contacted Fr. Peter Hogan who visited Nigeria the year before.

Concerning the Josephite Fathers, Monsignor Akpan has this to say:

> I knew almost nothing about them. That point did not form a part of any objective for visiting the United States at this time. Consequently, I did not ask any question into the foundation of the society. But as I watched them from day to day it became increasingly necessary to learn something about them. I had asked them too many questions already. Lest my visit should look like a sub-panel of an inquisition I decided to fill up the gap with reading from the expanding library that I found in every mission house. It was an authentic observation that the library in each mission house is growing faster than the growth of any seminary library in this country. That was a personal lesson to me as an individual. The above in the main, are areas that call for immediate action. The spectrum of needs is such that every Nigerian Catholic should deem it an honour to take the pride of place among the pioneer donors in aid of the first National Missionary Seminary."[398]

Formation of Associate Missionaries of St. Paul Monsignor Godwin remarked,

> So it is encouraging that you the laity, are here this morning, and that you have taken upon yourselves the burden of being the support of this Missionary Institute of bringing to it the alms of the whole Nigerian church, the love, the prayer the understanding, the sacrifices and the financial donations that will make this thing work, because the Rector, the staff and the students cannot do this by themselves. What they are doing is part of your Church…[399]

The appeal was reinforced by Bishop Edward O'Meara at Iperu on May 27, 1979.

Become an associate missionary of St. Paul by:

1.   Reading a small portion of the New Testament each day.
2.   Praying daily for the missionary work of the church.
3.   Participating in the liturgy of the Eucharist as often as possible.
4.   Becoming a subscriber to *The Ambassador*
5.   As a sacrifice in gratitude for your own faith, making an annual contribution to the training and support of St. Paul's missionaries.

All communications were to be directed to

THE RECTOR
NATIONAL MISSIONARY SEMINARY OF ST. PAUL
P.O. BOX 11, IPERU-REMO, OGUN STATE

Membership and donations were to be acknowledged in Seminary Magazine, *The Ambassador.* The bishops' contribution was acknowledged first and foremost for authorizing collection in all the parishes in the country to aid the seminary to grow and what individual bishops contributed. It was a moment of great solidarity and touching those who were sensitive enough to the plights of those who were to begin life on the rough terrain with the future known only to God. This is where serious faith was needed. Their optimism propelled them until they overcame all the major difficulties.[400]

F.   **The First Rector's Processes of Excardination/Incardination, Incorporation, Temporary and Perpetual Vows/Membership.**

To consolidate what has been begun, due process had to be followed for authenticity and legality so that Monsignor Akpan can function as an insider and as a proper member instead of functioning as a hired servant or as an extern.

Having been charged with the great duty of piloting the affairs of the newly constituted National Seminary, Monsignor Akpan thought it wise to be a part of the newly born Missionary Society of St. Paul. First and foremost, he asked his ordinary, Bishop Usanga, to grant him the permission to join the society as a pioneer member. Later, he wrote asking for permission to be excardinated from Calabar Diocese so as to freely join the Missionary Society by being incardinated there without hindrances. The next major step he took was to write a letter to the chairman of the governing board, requesting to be admitted as a temporary member of the society and later to be admitted into temporary vows and eventually to final or perpetual vows that will confer full rights and privileges on him as a full member.

On the same day, August 8, 1977, he wrote to his bishop, Most Reverend Brian D. Usanga, the bishop of Calabar from Christ the King Pro-Cathedral, Uyo, where he was the administrator, asking to be given leave to become a member of the National Missionary Society of St. Paul. The letter was copied to His Eminence Dominic Cardinal Ekandem. It clearly demonstrates his eagerness and desire to join the new group of missionaries where he was to become the first incorporated member.[401]

On January 15, 1985,[402] he wrote again to his bishop, reminding him of the desire he expressed seven years earlier[403] to join the new Missionary Society of St. Paul. He equally reminded his bishop that he was given permission to take the oath of temporary membership. Following his application to the internal governing council on December 11, 1984, the unanimous decision of the council approved him for permanent oath of membership while dispensing him from article 17 of the constitutions. Having stated this, he went further to apply for excardination from the diocese for the purpose of being incardinated into the Missionary Society of St. Paul. He intimated his bishop of the date for the permanent oath of membership as being January 25, 1985, the feast of St. Paul's conversion, which was very significant.

Bishop Usanga gave a positive reply six days after sending it.

DIOCESE OF CALABAR
Bishop's House P.M.B. 1044

Motto: To serve in Charity and Justice	Calabar,
Servire in Caritate et Justitia	C. R. State
Ndinam utom (Abasi) ke ima ye edinen ido	Nigeria.
	21/1/85

Your Ref....................
Our Ref......................
Rt. Rev. Msgr. Godwin P. Akpan MSP,
The National Missionary Seminary of St. Paul, Gwagwalada
P.O. Box 402, Garki Abuja
Dear Monsignor Akpan,

EXCARDINATION FROM DIOCESE TO MISSIONARY SOCIETY OF ST. PAUL

After prayerful reflection and due consultation, I hereby write to inform you that your request, reference your letter of January 18th, 1985, for permanent Excardination from the Diocese of Calabar to the Missionary Society of St. Paul is granted.

I have noted withdrawal that as by the letter dated January 18th, 1985 from His Lordship Most Rev. Dr. Anthony Sanusi, Bishop of Ijebu Ode and Ordinary of Abuja, of St. Paul, have been allowed to make your final oath of membership in the Missionary Society of St Paul.

As by this our letter of Excardination, you have our blessings, prayers, and moral support to make your final Oath and be incardinated into the Missionary Society of St. Paul.

May God, Our Blessed Mother and St. Paul guide and protect and make your missionary vocation fruitful and rewarding.

Sincerely Yours in Jesus Christ,
Brian D. Usanga
Bishop of Calabar
The Superior General and council
The Missionary Society of St. Paul, Gwagwalada

As a follow up to this letter, Most Reverend Anthony Sanusi, bishop of Ijebu Ode, wrote,

Bishop's House,
P.O. Box 322, Ijebu-Ode. 24th January, 1984.

V. Rev. Godwin P. Akpan, Rector,
National Missionary Seminary of
St. Paul Iperu—Ogun State.

Dear Msgr. Akpan,

OATH OF TEMPORARY MEMBERSHIP IN THE MISSIONARY SOCIETY OF ST. PAUL

Referring to your letter, Ref. A1/ E MOSJ/102 of January 24th, 1984, I am happy to welcome and accept your application for the oath of temporal membership in the Missionary Society of St. Paul.

I hope and pray that your admission into this Missionary Society will usher in an era of apostolic missionary activities in our country.

I assure you of the prayers and good wishes of all the bishops.

Yours Sincerely in Christ,
+Anthony S. Sanusi Bishop of Ijebu-Ode
And
Chairman, Governing Council,
National Missionary Seminary of St. Paul

The internal governing council also wrote to Monsignor Akpan about his new status and how things were progressing with him as the first priest to join the new missionary society.

THE NATIONAL MISSIONARY SEMINARY OF ST. PAUL,

P.O. BOX 11, Iperu-Remo
Ogun State, Nigeria
Established by the
Episcopal Conference of Nigeria

25th January, 1984.

Rev. Monsignor Godwin P. Akpan
National Missionary Seminary of St. Paul
P.O. Box 11
Iperu-Remo Ogun State.

Dear Monsignor,

I am writing on behalf of the four members of the Internal Council of the Missionary Society of St. Paul to whom you submitted your application, dated January twenty fourth, 1984, to be admitted to the temporary oath of membership of the society.

I am authorised to inform you in writing that your application has been unanimously approved.

We wish to say that we appreciated what a very important step you are taking before God, for yourself, for other members of the society and for the church. As the first member of the first African missionary society of secular priests, we offer you our prayerful wishes and support.

We hope that as the oldest brother in a new community, you will be a gentle, trusting and courageous witness to the missionary vocation, that through you the bonds of the society will be strengthened to unite all the members in Christ. With the guidance of the Holy Spirit, under the society's three patrons- Mary Queen of Apostles, St. Paul, St. Peter Claver and in dialogue with your brothers, may you bring the society together for the glory of God and of His kingdom.

For and on behalf of the council
Yours Sincerely in Christ Rev. James Sheerin.

The chairman of the governing council did not act independently. He acted in conjunction with the internal governing council. This accounts for separate letters, both from the chairman of the governing council, Most Reverend A. Sanusi and from the secretary of the internal governing council, Rev. Fr. James Sheerin SPS. Each letter emphasizes the same point of discussion and situation.

a. **Temporary Oath of Membership: Again, the internal governing council took the pains of communicating with Monsignor Akpan while indicating their expectation of him as an
older person in the midst of the younger people that would
be following.**

THE NATIONAL MISSIONARY SEMINARY OF ST. PAUL,
P.O. Box 11, Iperu-Remo Ogun State, Nigeria
Established by the Episcopal Conference of Nigeria.

25th January 1984

Rev. Monsignor Godwin P. Akpan
National Missionary Seminary of St. Paul P.O. Box 11
Iperu-Remo.
Ogun State.

Dear Monsignor,

I am writing on behalf of the four members of the internal council
of the Missionary Society of St. Paul to whom you submitted your application, dated January 24th, 1984, to be admitted to the temporary oath of
membership of the society.

I am authorised to inform you in writing that your application has
been unanimously approved.

We wish to say that we appreciate what a very important step your are
taking before God, for yourself, for other members of the society and for
the church. As the first member of the first African missionary society of
secular priests, we offer you our prayerful wishes and support.

We hope that as the oldest brother in a new community, you will
be a gentle, trusting and courageous witness to the missionary vocation,
that through you the bonds of the society will be strengthened to unite
all the members in Christ. With the guidance of the Holy Spirit, under
the Society's three Patrons—Mary Queen of Apostles, St. Paul, St. Peter
Claver- and in dialogue with your brothers, may you bring the Society
together for the glory of God and of His kingdom.

For and on behalf of the Council

Yours Sincerely in Christ,
Rev. James Sheerin.

In reaction to the approval letter of the governing council, he wrote again to his bishop the reception of the response to his mail. In line with all the developments, the chairman of the governing council, Most Reverend A. Sanusi gave a reply to Monsignor Akpan's letter that applied permission to be admitted into temporary oath in the Missionary Society of St. Paul.

Bishop's House,
P.O. Box 322,
Ijebu-Ode.

24th January 1984

V. Rev. Godwin P. Akpan
Rector
National Missionary Seminary of St. Paul Iperu—
Ogun State. Dear Msgr. Akpan,

OATH OF TEMPORARY MEMBERSHIP IN THE MISSIONARY SOCIETY OF ST. PAUL

Referring to your letter, Ref. A1/ E MOSJ/102 of January 24th, 1984, I am happy to welcome and accept your application for the oath of temporal membership in the Missionary Society of St. Paul.

I hope and pray that your admission into this Missionary Society will usher in an era of apostolic missionary activities in our country. I assure you of the prayers and good wishes of all the bishops.

Yours Sincerely in Christ,
+Anthony S. Sanusi
Bishop of Ijebu-Ode
And

Chairman, Governing Council,
National Missionary Seminary of St. Paul

b. The Reception of the Letter for Permanent Oath of Membership and Response

The two letters below from the chairman and the internal governing council all give positive responses to Msgr. Godwin Akpan's request and grant permission for the permanent/final oath. The internal governing council's response came before that of the bishop, the chairman of the governing council representing the episcopal conference of Nigeria.

THE NATIONAL MISSIONARY SEMINARY OF ST. PAUL,
P.O. Box 11, Iperu-Remo, Ogun State, Nigeria.

Established by the Episcopal Conference of Nigeria.
9th Jan. 1985
Very Rev. Msgr, Godwin P. Akpan, MSP
National Missionary Seminary of St. Paul
PO Box 402, Garki Abuja, FCT

Dear Monsignor Akpan,

I am authorised to write on behalf of the four members of the internal council in reply to your application of December 11th, 1984, to be dispensed from Article 17 of the constitutions and to be admitted to the permanent oath of membership in Jan 1985.

The four members considered your application in the light of your original application for membership in 1977 and of your services to the institute since then.

We wish to express again our deep appreciation of the importance of the step you propose to take, for yourself and for the missionary society of St. Paul, which will affect the salvation history of untold numbers of people. In a spirit of solidarity with you and in deep concern for the future of this young society, we ask you to take to heart this admonition to you in accordance with Article 40 of the constitutions.

We are unanimous in asking that for the future you will make a greater commitment to observing and implementing the constitutions, both in letter and in spirit. Specifically, we ask you to pay particular attention to communication and consultation with your council in keeping with Article 24 and Article 38, and to observing constitutional procedures in regard to the disbursing of the society's finances in keeping with Articles 33 and 38 No. 3.

By a majority decision, your application has been accepted, and we now recommend to the Right Rev. Ordinary of the Missionary Society of St. Paul that he should dispense you from Article 17 and admit you to the permanent oath of membership.

For and on behalf of the Council,

Yours Sincerely in Christ,
Rev. James Sheerin.

Bishop's House
P.O. Box 32, 18 January, 1985

The Rector
The National Missionary of St Paul
Abuja Campus
Gwagwalada, PO Box 402
Garki, Abuja, Nigeria

Dear Monsignor Akpan,

This is to acknowledge your request for permission to make the final oath of membership in the National Missionary Society of St. Paul.

After due consideration and consultation with the Internal Council of the Society, I am happy to inform you that you are hereby allowed to make your final oath of membership in the society according to the requirements of the constitutions.

We pray the Lord to accept and bless your holy intention and make it abundantly fruitful.

In union of prayers,
Your Sincerely in Christ,
Rt. Rev. A. Sanusi
Bishop of Ijebu-Ode/
Chairman/ Ordinary, NMS of St. Paul

After the receipt of the two letters, Monsignor Akpan was glad to do so and went on happily to take the oath on January 27, 1985. This gave six months interval before one of the first candidates received into the new group was ordained a priest.

The National Missionary Seminary of St. Paul Gwagwalada

P.O. Box 402
Abuja, Nigeria

FORMULA OF DECLARATION OF PERMANENT MEMBERSHIP

My brothers, I…Godwin…Pius…Akpan…having full knowledge of the purpose of the Missionary Society of St. Paul, do voluntarily submit myself to its constitutions. I promise, with the help of the Holy Spirit, to observe them faithfully, in my ministry as a priest, and in fellowship with my brother members. I promise and swear that I shall remain in the society permanently, and in it, under the authority of the Superiors. I will serve in any office or mission committed to me. I also promise and swear that I will proceed without delay to any place where the Superior General may send me; and that I will obey faithfully any orders given me by the Superior in accordance with the constitutions.

So help me God and these Holy Gospels.

MEMBER'S SIGNATURE.................................
DATE..............................
SUPERIOR GENERAL/DELEGATE....................................
DATE..............................
WITNESSING PRIEST..........................
DATE..............................

The processes of excardination and incardination completed, admission into the society as a temporary member sealed with temporary oath and progressing to Permanent or Final Oath of membership, Monsignor Akpan became a full member of the Missionary Society of St. Paul. This made him eligible to be appointed acting superior general of the congregation until the time that an elected superior general was to emerge.

c.   Appointment of Acting Superior General

This came directly from the Catholic Bishops' Conference of Nigeria. The letter speaks for itself. The appointment of Msgr. Godwin P. Akpan, the acting superior general of the society, could not have taken place earlier since the members to be ruled and governed were not there. The first abundant harvest took place in 1986 that witnessed eleven new young men ordained for the Missionary Society of St. Paul.

CATHOLIC BISHOP'S CONFERENCE OF NIGERIA

Force Road, Telegrams	**Telephone**	**Telex**
Lagos CATHOLISEC LAGOS	635849,636670	22592
CATSEC NIG		

Postal Address:
P.O. Box 951 Lagos, Nigeria.
November 20, 1987

Rt. Rev. Msgr. G. P. Akpan,
National Missionary Seminary of St. Paul,
Gwagwalada, P.O.
Box 402, Garki,
Abuja.

Rt. Rev. and Dear Msgr,

APPOINTMENT OF MSGR. AKPAN-RECTOR: ACTING SUPERIOR OF THE MISSIONARY SOCIETY OF ST. PAUL

I was requested by the Catholic Bishop's Conference of Nigeria, (CBCN) meeting at Awka from October 27–30 1987 to inform you that you have been appointed Acting Superior of the Missionary Society of St. Paul (Pious Association).

The appointment is for the period of one year; but can be renewed until a Superior General of the Pious Association is elected.

It is hoped that, with this appointment, the affairs of our young missionaries shall be catered for duly.

The conference is very grateful to you for your dedicated services to the seminary.

Yours ever in Christ,

_____

+ E. S. Obot
Bishop of Idah and
Secretary cc: Chairman,
Governing Council, NMS

Having been appointed acting superior general of the congregation, the governing council and the internal council moved to ratify his request to be a member of the society. The decision and petition he made earlier was slowly followed up with positive responses.

The dream of the National Missionary Seminary has gone beyond what Cardinal Ekandem had envisaged or had dreamt of and proceeded to include a community of priests that can be properly identified and called Missionaries of St. Paul even though it appears both were in his mind: the society and the seminary. The dream of the seminary gave birth to or begot Missionaries of St. Paul. At that initial stage and owing to the location of the seminary, the chairman and ordinary of the National Missionary Seminary was His Excellency Rt. Rev. Anthony Sanusi, the bishop of Ijebu Ode Diocese. His role extended even to Gwagwalada as this letter indicates until things took their proper shape and form. Monsignor Akpan was advised by the internal governing council to be gentle and act as a senior brother to the members of society.

G. What Transpired before the First Missio ad Intra and ad Extra (Internal And external Missions)

The appointment of Msgr. G. Akpan as the director of the National Missionary Seminary and the fact of his becoming the first member of the congregation contributed to its recognition with regard to its growth. It will be seen from the document below how he fought tirelessly to maintain the spirit and charism of the society by going out of his way to involve the young priests and deacons in dialogue about the future of the congregation and their existence as well as their modus operandi.

a. What Went on Before the First International Mission[404]

Sending on mission, especially outside the country, did not have a smooth and easy ride. It passed through difficulties on the national level until providence, coupled with the tenacity of the members of internal and governing council, opened the way. They needed to stand firm to see that things went through. The cohesion of thought, the single vision and purpose, aided their success in the midst of very great even vehement opposition. Providence provided an interlude within which things sorted themselves out. The first international mission began when God opened the way different from that envisaged by the organizers and planners. The governing council, the internal council, and the Episcopal Conference of Nigeria worked collaboratively to pave the way for greater growth, maturity, and autonomy necessary for a young community like that of the Missionaries of St. Paul be possible. Monsignor Akpan said,

> More importantly, it was a wonderful opportunity to share with the students my convictions about the priestly life, which to me meant focus on Christ who is the all time perfect standard for every age. What Christ expects of us, especially his friends should never be watered down. Hence the refrain to the students which was fast becoming a philosophy would ring: Only the very best is good for Christ, because if you are good, Christ wants you to be better and if you are better, he wants you to be the very best. Besides, all the Most Reverend Ordinaries of Nigeria had a standing invitation to visit the seminary at any time so as to encourage and share their experience with the students.

THE MISSIONS: After one priestly ordination in 1985, the tide has changed ever since for subsequent ordinations. In 1986, we were blessed with eleven priestly ordinations popularly known as the first eleven.

The spadework for the 1986 U.S. mission was creditably carried out with a twelve-week lecture, starting on June 8, 1985, as Rev. Peter Hogan, Josephite archivist, spoke to the seminarians about the church among Black Americans. Besides, the research for possible missions in the eighties covered dioceses of Buea, Monrovia, Freetown, and the Black Apostolate in the United States.

Before the June 1986 priestly ordination of the eleven, the idea of sending to those dioceses that applied for the MSP priests faced an uphill task in the Catholic Bishops Conference. Besides, the truly missionary dimension of the seminary/society was called into doubt. Rome through the secretary general of *Propaganda Fidei*, Archbishop Lourdisamy made a query to that effect. The then ordinary of the society, Bishop Sanusi, promptly refuted that allegation with a strong letter, part of which read, "As far as the Bishops were concerned, the Missionary dimension of the seminary/society was never in doubt."

Besides, applications for St. Paul's Missionary priests have come from the Archdiocese of Monrovia, Liberia, the Diocese of Buea in Cameroon, and Josephites in America. These applications are still under review.

On the home front, the arguments of the bishops' conference in sending to the missions outside Nigeria became so heated as to reach crisis pitch. The ordinary of the society, Bishop Sanusi, resigned in protest and a new ordinary, His Eminence Dominic Cardinal Ekandem, was appointed.

Still, the issue was not resolved. They resorted to voting. Five members of the governing council voted in favor while two abstained. At the plenary session of the conference, the new ordinary was to consult the pro-nuncio with a view to carrying out the mandate of the conference that the governing council resolved the issue. With all the wrangling, an emergency meeting of the governing council was convened. It was to be held at the rector's office in Gwagwalada on April 7, 1986. After listening to the views of those present at the meeting and in order to forestall frustration from any quarter and the possible collapse of the whole project, the governing council, in the overall interest of the Missionary Society of St. Paul, unanimously took the following decisions[405]:

That the 1986 missions suggested program be implemented.

That two of the newly ordained be assigned to work in Nigeria with:

- The vocations promotion director as his assistant.
- The spiritual year director in Iperu as an assistant.
- Contact be made with the ordinary with whom our newly ordained priests would be working through the Josephites.
- Contract agreement with the Josephites to be two years, the rest (Monrovia and Buea) three years.
- The first week of October 1986 was the accepted time of departure for the missions. Everyone would be expected to be at the mission assigned before Mission Sunday 1986.

The above decisions were sent to all the bishops on the same date with a view to any feedback for or against before the June ordinations, as the decisions would be made public after the ordination.

Although at the plenary session of the CBCN meeting held September 1986 at Ede in the then Oyo diocese, Oyo State now in Oshogbo Diocese,

Osun State, bishops still opposed the idea of 1986 missions. However, the decisions of the governing council prevailed with a mandate for one year pastoral work in Nigeria for all the subsequent newly ordained priests before going on mission.

The 1986 missions really opened the gate to the present and future missions, thus vindicating what sounded prophetic, when the then superior general of the Josephites, Rev. Fr. Filippelli, in his letter of August 5, 1982, wrote, "It is my opinion that perhaps the future spread of Christ's church will be accomplished in a great part by priests from Africa." This was highly prognosticative looking at the number of both missionary and diocesan priests from Nigeria that are in many parts of the world in the twenty-first century. Father Filippelli had given a very powerful prophecy that took just about twenty years to materialize.

The modalities of the one-year pastoral ministry within the country were delineated with supervision and monitoring. This measure aimed at ensuring a good output, useful result, and success at the end of the program, preparing the young priests for an international apostolate. The plan was well thought out and the processes thorough.

b. A Memorandum: One Year Pastoral Ministry in Nigeria before Being Sent on the Missions

The bishops' conference held in Ede, Western Nigeria, on September 11, 1986, unanimously upheld the decision of the governing council to send the newly ordained priests of the Missionary Society of St Paul to where they were assigned in Monrovia, Liberia, the Cameroon, and the United States of America, respectively. However, for future departure to the missions, the conference recommended that this be allowed after a period of one year pastoral ministry in Nigeria. Although this recommendation is motivated out of a genuine concern for the overall welfare of the newly ordained priests, a dispassionate evaluation of the situation does not see the one-year orientation as the best preparation for these reasons:

Orientation: It is now universally recognized that training for mission after ordination should be on the spot. More and more missionary congregations feel obliged by experience to send students to their future mission for part of the training. The culture, lifestyle, etc. at home invariably would be different from what to expect out there in the missions. The expected initial culture shock in a new situation is better contained in the actual situation than at the home front. In effect, it seems the areas to watch is the seminary training, which ought to be missionary-oriented.

Preserving the charism of the Missionary Society of St. Paul: The members of the missionary society of St. Paul have a duty to preserve the charism peculiar to the society. For this, the atmosphere must be consciously created and safeguarded. By their oath of membership, they are incardinated to the Missionary Society of St. Paul.

Working under another society priest member after priestly ordination on an apprenticeship basis for a year in Nigeria creates, though perhaps not intended, a de facto second-class mentality in respect of the priest member of the Missionary Society of St. Paul. How to forestall that has not yet been discussed.

Realism: After priestly ordination, every young priest assumes and expects some degree of autonomy. How, will re-adjusting to a situation at home, just for a year, knowing too well that he will have to re-adjust to another situation yet unknown outside Nigeria, prepare him for a new and unfamiliar situation outside Nigeria?

Danger of Frustration: It is highly improbable that a priest of another society, with his daily concern for his parish, will train a priest member of the Missionary Society of St. Paul for the Missionary Society of St. Paul with due respect for the charism peculiar to that society. Where there is a possible conflict in this regard, the danger of frustration within the first year of priestly ordination cannot be ruled out. To maintain the physical and the spiritual health of the young priests of the Missionary Society of St. Paul, as an interim measure, if the one-year pastoral ministry may not be shelved, certain modalities in respect of the one- year orientation are hereby suggested:

1. A mission territory within Nigeria be assigned to the Missionary Society of St. Paul for the exercise of the one-year home pastoral ministry.
2. This home ministry should be supervised either by the staff of the seminary or by the priest members of the Missionary Society of St. Paul.

3. In order to foster a healthy interaction with the members of the Missionary Society of St. Paul with a view to building up their peculiar charism, visits to the headquarters of the society should be on a regular basis.

4. Areas of the apostolate for the one-year orientation should be carefully spelt out.

5. To minimize cost and safeguard efficiency in supervising the one-year pastoral ministry, I am suggesting the ABUJA MISSION, since the headquarters of the society from where the envisaged supervision that can be effectively carried out is in Abuja.

Finally, since the Missionary Society of St. Paul, as in 1986, has eighteen permanent members—thirteen priests and five deacons—it is my considered view that their opinion on the question of doing one-year pastoral ministry in Nigeria after priestly ordination before going to the Missions should be sought before a definitive decision on the matter.

REV. MSGR. GODWIN P. AKPAN, MSP,
11/ 11/86.

In response to the letter written by Monsignor Godwin to the Father Filippelli about the posting of the young Missionaries of St. Paul's priests after their ordination, Father McManus, the vicar general who stood in for the superior general, responded indicating the absence of the superior general and the necessity of thinking about another date because of the processes it involved before getting the special Visa H-1 before the missionaries would be ready proceed to Houston for their ministerial assignment.

THE JOSEPHITES

ST JOSEPH'S SOCIETY OF THE SACRED HEART, INCO FFICE
OF THE SUPERIOR GENERAL

September 19, 1986
Rev. Msgr. Godwin P. Akpan
Rector

The Missionary Seminary of St. Paul
Gwagwalada
PO Box 402
Garki
Abuja, Nigeria

Dear Monsignor Akpan:

Father Filippelli is presently on vacation. He will return to his office on September 25. During his absence I handle his mail.

This is to acknowledge receipt of your letter of August 28, along with the enclosures certifying the ordination of the three priests who will be working here in the United States. Your letter arrived here on Saturday, September 6. On Monday September 8, I sent the materials to our attorney who handles the processing of papers at the Immigration Service. As soon as she received the letter, she phoned me to tell me that she was submitting the materials immediately to the Immigration Service along with the application forms for the H-1-Visa.

Inasmuch as you had mentioned October 5 as a possible travel date, I asked her how long it will take to process the applications. She mentioned that it would be 8 to 12 weeks because of the backlog of applications in the Immigration Office. That means that the process would not be completed until mid-November or mid-December.

She then explained the procedures to me. When the process for the H-1 Visas are approved by the Immigration Service, the Immigration Office will send a cable to the United States Embassy in Lagos informing them of the approval. In the meantime, the Immigration Office will notify our attorney of the approval. She in turn will notify us. At that time, we will communicate with you letting you know that the three priests should go to the United States Embassy in Lagos in order to sign the appropriate papers. Then the priests will be free to travel to the United States.

Since I recognise the brevity of time between our attorney's phone call to me and the projected travel date of October 5, I decided to get in touch with you as soon as possible by telephone. The only phone number I was able to obtain was the Headquarters of the Society of St. Patrick in Lagos.

I talked to a Father Moore, who said that he knew you and would get the message to you as soon as possible.

Yesterday, I received a phone call from Fr. Sheerin in Ireland. He was inquiring about the progress of the application procedure. I gave him all of the above information. He said that he was going to Nigeria and would communicate with you.

I trust that all the above information is clear. If not please get in touch with us for further clarification.

Sincerely Yours, Very Rev. Eugene P. McManus, S. S. J.

Vicar General
EPM:js

The mail of Father Filippelli to His Eminence Dominic Cardinal Ekandem was a very crucial one. It outlined all the specifics that the young priests would encounter on arrival and their reception. The aspect of the spiritual life is underscored to give prominence to the need to combine the pastoral and spiritual dimensions of their life. The missionaries would be treated in the same way with the Josephites in many things including the allowances and travels.

THE JOSEPHITES
ST JOSEPH'S SOCIETY OF THE SACRED HEART, INC.

OFFICE OF THE SUPERIOR GENERAL   JULY 28, 1986
His Eminence Dominic Cardinal Ekandem
Ordinary of the missionary Society of St. Paul
Gwagwalada
PO Box 402
Garki
Abuja, Nigeria

Your Eminence,

I was glad to hear of the Ordination of eleven young men as Missionaries of St. Paul.

Monsignor Akpan has informed me that Fr. Anthony Afangide, Fr. Felix Elosi, and Fr. Vincent Inametti have been designated to work with the Josephites in the Diocese of Galveston/Houston in the USA. Monsignor informed me that the young priests will be available after the 7th of October. We are in the process now of trying to obtain H1 Visas for them from the Department of Immigration.

After an orientation program of a few weeks, we will send them to their assignments in Houston. The priests will receive the same allowance that the Josephites receive and that is $75 a month. Naturally, their room and board will be taken care of by the parish. Their diocesan salary will be put into a special account for the Missionary Society of St. Paul. This will also include the small pension for retirement. We will take care of their medical needs and the cost of their travel arrangements.

The young priests will follow the Josephites' Rule of Life and will have regular periods of recollection. Fr. Ray Bomberger, our novice master in Houston, will be their spiritual director. They will have the use of the parish car and be close enough to one another to be able to have ordinary relationships.

The parishioners that they are being assigned to will prove to be both challenging and rewarding. The pastors are men of experience and excellent leaders, and they will be most helpful and supportive to these men in their early priesthood. We will do all that we can to make them feel very much at home and the Josephites will be brothers to them.

It is my understanding that their assignment is not two years, and hopefully, they will stay longer than that.

In my letter last year to Bishop Sanusi, I indicated to him that after a six-year period, the project could be reviewed with the hope that this will be the beginning of a long association between the Josephites and the Missionaries of St. Paul.

> Bishop Joseph Fiorenza of Galveston/Houston has been informed that the priests will be arriving in Houston at the end of October. He is delighted to have them in their diocese and is looking forward to their arrival.

Naturally, I, as superior, will be personally responsible for them, and Fr. Joseph Waters, our director for the Houston area, will be their immediate superior.

If the governing council needs any more information, please let me know as soon as possible as the mail is slow between here and Nigeria.

I wish to thank you, Your Eminence, and the bishops of Nigeria for your generosity and zeal to send these men to work in the most important apostolate in the United States. I am sure that God will bless you and the faith of the people of Nigeria.

Assuring you of my prayers, I am
Sincerely Yours in Christ
Very Rev. John L. M. Filippelli, S.S.J.
Superior General

JLMP
Msgr. Godwin Akpan

The response of the cardinal in connection with the welfare of the young missionaries streamlines the need to allow them to develop their spirituality[406] instead of living out the spirituality of the Josephites while appreciating all the offers and equality and friendship they were willing to share with the missionaries. The aspect of allowing the missionaries to live out their spirituality is one of those things that actually manifests the direction and guidance of the founder since he did not want the charism nor the spirituality of the missionaries to be confounded even at that early stage or influenced by that of the Josephites. This was clear and distinct in his mind. The Missionaries of St. Paul are distinct and special. They have to live out their particular charism.

Chapter Fourteen

ET VERBUM CARO FACTUM EST (AND THE WORD WAS MADE FLESH)

Processes of Autonomy, the First General Chapter and the Silver Jubilee

And He dwelt among us! John 1:14

In silence, we are better able to listen to and understand ourselves; ideas come to birth and acquire depth...Deeper reflection helps us to discover the links between events that at first sight seem unconnected...For this to happen, it is necessary to develop an appropriate environment, a kind of "eco-system" that maintains a just equilibrium between silence, words, images and sounds.

—Pope Emeritus Benedict XVI

TO ESTABLISH THE full autonomy of the society, necessary issues had to be looked at. One of those issues was the question of the founder. Before the resolution of the problem of the founder, the letter-head of the society bore the writing "Founded by the Episcopal Conference of Nigeria." Going through the developmental processes and the canonical aspects, the insights, the stress on the charism, the orientation, the direction given at various times and stages, the resolution of difficulties in relation to the inspirational direction gave an idea of what the final outcome could likely be. From then on, things became streamlined and followed the proper course of action.

The letters found in this section highlight the developmental stages as to how the Missionary Society/Seminary of St. Paul gained its autonomy that led to the first General Chapter. The path to the commencement of the chapter was filled with a series of obstacles. Monsignor G. Akpan, the internal governing council, CBCN, and all other groups capable of helping to resolve the issues featured very prominently. The prince, who became a cardinal and CBCN, became the central points of discussion.

Many experts featured in order to help establish the authentic founder. From the canonical point of view, those who played major roles and the input of the cardinal contributed saliently. The problem was eventually resolved. The processes followed in arriving at the solutions are handled below.

A.   Reason for Postponing the First General Assembly

A considerable amount of time was devoted to a discussion of the matter of the society's founder(s). The 1978 correspondence between the CBCN and Rome as well as society literature were seen to point to the Catholic Bishops' Conference of Nigeria as the society's multiple founders. Nevertheless, the part played by His Eminence Cardinal Archbishop Ekandem in getting the idea of a National Seminary and, later, a Missionary Seminary and Society accepted by his brother bishops, as well as in seeking material support for the enterprise, would seem to point to him as the society's founder. He had, in fact, done many of the things a founder might be expected to do.

The overriding concern of the meeting was to be faithful to what happened historically to the special part played by His Eminence as well as to the role of the Catholic Bishops' Conference as a whole. After settling on the cardinal as the founder, the meeting resolved that it should be put to the CBCN at their forthcoming meeting that His Eminence should now be acknowledged as the society's founder.

B. Preparations and Other Related Issues

a. Canonical Transformation

CBCN to transfer authority to him as the ordinary of Abuja Diocese so that he could take the necessary steps toward the canonical erection of the society. Up to this time, he had been acting in the name of the Catholic Bishops' Conference. He must now be in a position to act in his own name as the ordinary of Abuja Diocese. Once this transfer of authority had taken place, the CBCN could continue to assist and support the Missionary Society of St. Paul, but it would effectively be under the authority of the ordinary of Abuja, who would put in motion the procedure for the canonical transformation from pious association to society of apostolic life.

b. Decision on Scheduled Assembly/Chapter

The meeting addressed itself of the matter of the assembly/chapter scheduled for September 1993. Two options were considered: (1) Should the chapter go ahead as scheduled and a retroactive ratification *(sanatio)* of its decisions be sought afterward? (2) Or should it be postponed until the nihil obstat had been granted by Rome? The first of these options did not find favor with the generality of members. The general opinion was in favor of postponement. The postponement would make it possible to carry out the stipulations of the Holy Spirit for the canonical transformation of the society. When the chapter is done, it should be the real thing, not a dry run for another in two or more years after, as one participant observed. As part of the MSP pre-chapter considerations, the following decisions were arrived at:

1. There is scope for primary evangelization.
2. Its members can work together as a team.

3.   The formation process can continue under the society's non-seconded personnel.

The first General Chapter procedure established various ground rules to help the affairs of the chapter to move forward. It was established that the secretary general of the society should be the secretary of the chapter and that all the committees and subcommittees should address their presentations to the moderator whose permission was required to speak. The ground rules embraced the minutes of the assembly, the scrutineers, the steering committee, the judicial committee, the financial committee, etc.[407] The committee members made sure that everything went on very diligently and systematically.

The proposition to commence the general chapter earlier did not take place because of issues that needed to be resolved. The first major problem was that of the ordinary, then the nihil obstat situation, and an eventual *sanatio*—that is, cleansing from the root that had to be carried out by the Vatican after the whole assembly. If that were to have occurred, it means that within a space of about three years, another chapter would have taken place as a corrective measure. Consequently, the chapter was postponed until everything followed the due process.

c.   The Question of the Founder

This is a crucial point in ascertaining the authenticity of any congregation or order. The Missionaries of St. Paul getting ready for their first General Chapter did not want to gloss over this important issue, they decided to handle it properly by examining all the details that needed to be reviewed before establishing and confirming their autonomy. Their autonomy as a society of apostolic life would surely help in carrying out the General Chapter free from teething problems like reconvening of the chapter and the defect it would have incurred.

i.   The Founder of the Missionary Society of St. Paul[408]

The big question of the foundation and establishment of the society/seminary came out very strongly as far as the Catholic Bishops' Conference of Nigeria was concerned. Cardinal Ekandem accomplished many things in the line of foundation, but where did he fit in concerning "founding" and "establishing." Was it the CBCN that founded and also established the society and the seminary? That problem needed a careful resolution.

Two questions are generally raised about the founder of a religious congregation or institute of secular life or an order, be it of pontifical status or of diocesan right: the *acts of the founding and the establishment of the specific charism.*[409] It was necessary to use these two points to start the survey by looking at various passages related to the problem. The following points were raised by the special commission of inquiry into the historical origins as well as the founder of the National Missionary Seminary/Society in preparation for the chapter. They examined both sides of the coin from what the prelates said and the positions they held and finally came to a conclusion.

One of the documents tendered as a proof of foundational initiative, or rather inspiration, is the memorandum of May 15, 1976, titled "A New Ideal Of An Old Ideal, An Ideal Never Attained"[410] presented by Bishop Ekandem during the episcopal conference held in Sokoto cited in chapter 12 above. The memorandum had an addendum dated May 15 titled "Appendix" signed by the same prelate as president of the Episcopal Conference of Nigeria.[411]

The commission had some paper presentations including that of Rev. Fr. Benedict Etafo and that of Emmanuel Asuquo Akpa[412] together with members of the Missionary Society of St. Paul. The group affirmed that these two documents of the prelate authenticated his "legitimacy as the founder of the Missionary Society of St. Paul." That is, His Lordship Bishop D. I. Ekandem. The commission specified the following points of the bishop as substantiating his position as the founder:

- The training of the seminarians would take cognizance of the African situation, where the religious content of the Muslims and the animists would be studied, and
- Ecumenism in Africa would be treated in depth.
- The major achievements of Vatican Council II will not alone encourage and inspire but will see their full implementation in the seminary envisaged.

ii. The Dream Plan

The plan to found a missionary society was accepted on that day and date, Friday, May 15, 1976. It was a new idea born of an old ideal. He based his new idea on the exhortation of Pope Paul VI in Kampala in 1970 in which the Roman Pontiff called upon the church in Africa to be a missionary church.[413] The Roman pontiff said that the church in Africa must, in its turn, become a missionary church. The old ideal, which is recalled and reflected in the exhortation of the Pontiff was the Kaduna Conference Discussion of 1956 initiated by His Lordship, the same Bishop D. I. Ekandem.

Fr. Emmanuel Asuquo Akpan, one of the presenters said, "Let me touch briefly on the legal argument that a religious institute is either pontifical or diocesan. Personally, I don't know of a third possibility. On the issue of charism, an appendix of Friday, May 14, 1976, speaks for itself. I have already mentioned the document above. Cardinal Ekandem described your society in that document as an instrument of unified apostolic action in a politically divided Nigeria that we witness. May I crave your indulgence to review briefly the appendix that we have cited in this discussion."[414]

iii. Contra Voices or Objections Raised

From the opening sentence, His Lordship Bishop Ekandem, in 1976, speculated on the position, which the Holy Ghost Congregation, already sending priests to Sierra Leone, should have in the planned National Missionary Seminary. We are not told specifically as the document is so brief, but we have reasons to believe that someone objected to founding another missionary institute seeing that the Holy Ghost Congregation was already sending out missionaries to places outside Nigeria.[415]

iv. The Specificity of the Missionaries of St. Paul/Seminary

The prince-prelate went further to specify that a missionary society of his dream would have to be different from the characteristics possessed by the Holy Ghost Congregation. The new seminary of his imagination would need a sustaining organization or society to carry out a missionary program for Nigeria as a nation. The bishop wondered what form the new society would take. The first three paragraphs of his speculation are cited verbatim here. So while the Episcopal Conference established the society, Cardinal Ekandem has been the founder from the beginning. But a contrary argument runs thus: "The Nigerian Episcopal Conference is the actual founder of the society."[416]

Cardinal Ekandem wrote:

"In September 1976 the Catholic Bishops of Nigeria took a decision during their conference in Kaduna to found a society of Nigerian Missionary Priests and to establish a special seminary of missionary formation. They placed both under the patronage of the great missionary apostle St. Paul. The Bishops wished to unite the Catholics from every part of our country in the missionary work of the Church; to lead them to look beyond the confines of their own communities and to feel the solidarity of being active in the Body of Christ.[417]

"To affirm the call of the Bishops to all the Catholics in the Country to be united in facing this singular task tailored it to the young men to be open to this call thus: 'and so the leadership of the Church in Nigeria officially invites young men to accept the challenge of the Missionary Priesthood and to begin their training with the sacrifice and thoroughness which the missionary life demands.'"[418]

Furthermore, they indicated: "the Congregation for the Evangelization of Peoples has now given approval to the unanimous decision of the Nigerian Bishops to erect 'The Missionary Society of St. Paul' into a pious association."[419]

Although the first paragraph mentions the decision of the Catholic Bishops' Conference of Nigeria to establish the society/seminary, it is obvious that he placed it under the umbrella of the CBCN so that they could own it and care for it as their child, but the whole idea sprang from Bishop Ekandem. He wanted what he saw at Maynooth in Dublin to be done in Nigeria. Of course, he was not worried whether it was attributed to him or not. What he was interested in was the establishment that was taking place. History has sorted out things on its own. What he dreamed of has become existent and no longer a perceived idea in the "ideal world of Plato" but what has a *foundation in reality.*

v. The Catholic Bishops' Conference of Nigeria's Decision to Proceed with the Founding of the Society/Seminary after removing the Obstacles

Bishop Anthony S. Sanusi also wrote: "The Nigerian Episcopal Conference only arrived at a decision after all the backlog obstacles had been removed." At this point, the embattled path was positively and fairly paved as chapter 12 above indicates.

The historic decision to found a National Missionary Seminary was made by the National Episcopal Conference of Nigeria at their September meeting in Kaduna in 1976. It was a mature decision It is a fact that the three Major Seminaries in the country needed all the financial support of the Bishops; but this Seminary established by all the Bishops of Nigeria, is one with a difference The Holy Father, Pope John Paul II, further gave his encouragement by granting the Institute Canonical Status in recognising it as a Pious Association. This goes to confirm the wisdom and maturity of the decision of the National Episcopal Conference of Nigeria. "Every member of the Church in Nigeria should have a share in the missionary venture. The Bishops have given the lead, let the faithful follow."[420] The then Apostolic Pro-Nuncio to Nigeria, Most Rev. Dr. Carlo Curis, wrote: "On this occasion, I wish to congratulate the Bishops of Nigeria for this exemplary initiative."[421]

The various points raised by members of the historical committee were geared at eliminating obstacles that could impede the establishment of the fact that the prelate, Cardinal Ekandem was and is the one who founded the society/seminary, while the Episcopal Conference established the society and the seminary. It was achieved conjointly. The aspect of the founder cannot be confounded with establishment. When things were cleared, the bishops themselves did not have any objections about the founder. They saw the truth and adhered to it. When the problem of the founder and establishment was resolved, the letterhead of the society ceased to bear at the right-hand corner of the paper: "Established by the Catholic Bishops' Conference of Nigeria," as seen in the letterhead below. At that point, the calming of the storm took place.

This profile of Dominic Cardinal I. Ekandem, the prince who became a cardinal, presents everything in a flash as the founder of the Missionaries of St. Paul Society and Seminary. Some of these points have already been featured at various stages as the work progressed.

The National Missionary Seminary of St. Paul,
P.O. BOX 11, Iperu- Remo.
20th November, 1977.

THE MISSIONARY SOCIETY OF ST. PAUL

Gwagwalada,   Established by the
P.O. BOX 23,   Catholic Bishops' Conference of Nigeria
                         Abuja, Nigeria.

Your Eminence,
Your Grace,
My Lord,

FOUNDER OF THE MISSIONARY SOCIETY OF ST. PAUL

NAME: His Eminence Dominic Cardinal Ekandem
SURNAME: Ekandem
BIRTH: 1917
PLACE OF BIRTH: Ibiono—Itu L.G.A Akwa Ibom State
FATHER: Chief Paul Ino Ekandem Ubo Etok
MOTHER: Madam Nwa Ibong Umana Essien\

CURRICULUM VITAE:

Primary Education: Ibiono Village School- up to Standard 1 St. Joseph's
                     School, Anua—Standards 2-6 1928–1932
Post Primary   St. Paul's Junior Seminary attached to Christ the
1933–1937   King College Onitsha.
Probation: shall be catered for duly.

The conference is very grateful to you for your dedicated services to the seminary.

Priestly Training and Ordination

1938–1940, taught at Sacred Heart Secondary School Calabar. Post Secondary 1941–1943, studied Philosophy in Enugu Education: 1944–1947, studied Theology at St. Paul's Major

Seminary, Okpala-Owerrinta.

Priestly Ordination: Ordained Deacon in 1947

Ordained Priest on December 7, 1947 at St. Anne's Church, Ifuho by Archbishop Charles Heerey.

Episcopal Consecration

Episcopal Consecration took place: On February 7, 1954 with His Grace Archbishop Charles Heerey of Onitsha, presiding with Bishop Moynagh of Calabar as principal consecrator. Other co- consecrators were: Bishop Biechy, of Brasse-Ville in French Congo, the former Parish Priest of Anua Parish when Bishop Ekandem entered the seminary in 1933, and Bishop Peter Rogan MHF of Buea and, Archbishop Leo Taylor, OBE of Lagos.

Pastoral Ministry

1st Appointment—two months in Ifuho, from where he transferred to Afaha Obong to assist Fr. Murray SPS. Again, he assisted Fr. Pat Laffey before becoming the parish priest of Afaha Obong as well as the Manager of Schools, during which time he established a number of Schools. Named Auxiliary Bishop of Calabar in 1953 at Afaha Obong and then transferred to St Joseph's parish, Anua.

He was consecrated Bishop on February 7, 1954 in Anua. He was Father—In Charge in Anua while remaining Auxiliary to Bishop Moynagh, and also Manager of schools. While still in Anua, he formed the Catholic Teachers' Federation with its headquarters in Uyo, where the Catholic Teachers Federation hall is built. He also inaugurated the Women Catholic League (Nka Adiaha Obong), which was responsible for the establishment of Adiaha Obong Secondary School in Eniong, followed by the establishment of the Holy Trinity in Central Uruan.

Episcopal Installation

In 1963 he was transferred to Ikot Ekpene to take charge of the newly created Diocese of Ikot Ekpene. He was officially installed the Bishop of Ikot Ekpene on May 11, 1963. While in Ikot Ekpene, besides establishing some Primary Schools, he also founded such institutions as Loreto Girls' Juniorate, Eriam, Ikot Ekpene, and St. Joseph Rehabilitation Centre (Disabled Centre[422]) in Ukana Iba, and School for the Deaf and Dumb (School for the Physically impaired) in Ikot Ekpene.

Failing to get an agreement of all Nigerian Bishops for the establishment of a National seminary in Nigeria in the late 50's and early 60's, he proposed to the Holy Father, Pope Paul VI in May, 1976 his intention. The Holy Father asked him to seek the support of the Nigerian Bishops. After the proposal of the project to the Nigerian Bishops during their conference held in Kaduna in 1976, and with the result of almost unanimous vote in favour of the project; and approval was later obtained from the Holy Father in favour of the project. And so, on the 23rd of September 1977, in Ijebu Ode, the National Missionary Seminary was inaugurated.

Administrator of Port Harcourt Diocese

Between 1970 and 1973, he was appointed the Administrator[423] of the Diocese of Port Harcourt.

He was appointed Superior of Abuja Independent Mission on November 6th, 1981. He started combining the pastoral ministry of Ikot Ekpene Diocese and Abuja. That was not his first time of serving two Ecclesiastical Jurisdictions in the Church contemporaneously. Each time whenever and wherever he did that, he served diligently and convincingly to the end.

The summary of the life of Cardinal Ekandem in the curriculum vitae reconfirms him as the founder of the Missionary Society and Seminary of St. Paul. The action has, in hindsight, the undertone of growth and autonomy. Having laid the problem of the founder and establishment to rest, the structure of the institute and the institution had to be taken on board for effective governance. Such required meticulous documentation and application of the rule of law.

vi. The Internal Governing Council's Approval for Permanent Oath of Membership

The internal governing council's decision to respond positively to Monsignor Akpan's request to be a permanent member of the society/ seminary pointed to the right direction. The process of excardination/ incardination had started along with the temporary oath of membership. It was part of the consolidation process. The council through its secretary, Fr. James Sheerin, SPS, responded positively to Msgr. Godwin Akpan's letter that asked for permission to be admitted to the permanent oath of membership. When the decision was taken, the problem of the founder had not yet been resolved. That accounts for the letterhead bearing "established by the Episcopal Conference of Nigeria." Ten years after, the group overcame the difficulty, as seen above, and things moved on normally.

THE NATIONAL MISSIONARY SEMINARY OF ST. PAUL,
P.O. Box 11, Iperu-Remo
Ogun State, Nigeria
Established by the
Episcopal Conference of Nigeria
9th Jan 1985

Very Rev. Msgr. Godwin P. Akpan, M.S.P.,
National Missionary Seminary of St. Paul,
P.O. Box 402, Garki, Abuja, FCT

Dear Monsignor Akpan,

I am authorized to write on behalf of the four members of the Internal Council in reply to your application of December 11th, 1984, to be dispensed from Article 17 of the constitutions and to be admitted to the permanent oath of membership in January 1985.

The four members considered your application in the light of your original application for membership in 1977 and of your services to the institute since then.

We wish to express again our deep appreciation of the importance of the step you propose to take, for yourself and for the missionary society of St. Paul, which will affect the salvation history of untold numbers of people. In a spirit of solidarity with you and in deep concern for the future of this young society, we ask you to take to heart this admonition to you in accordance with Article 40 of the constitutions.

We are unanimous in asking that for the future you will make a greater commitment to observing and implementing the constitutions, both in letter and in spirit. Specifically, we ask you to pay particular attention to communication and consultation with your council in keeping with Article 24 and Article 38, and to observing constitutional procedures in regard to the disbursing of the society's finances in keeping with Articles 33 and 38 No. 3.

By a majority decision, your application has been accepted, and we now recommend to the Right Rev. Ordinary of the Missionary Society of St. Paul that he should dispense you from Article 17 and admit you to the permanent oath of membership.

For and on behalf of the Council,
Yours Sincerely in Christ, Rev. James Sheerin.

The letter to his bishop reveals the smooth relationship between the prelate and his clergy with a corresponding understanding among them.

THE NATIONAL MISSIONARY SEMINARY OF ST. PAUL

Gwagwalada,
P.O. Box 402,
Garki,
Abuja, Nigeria

Established by the
Episcopal Conference of Nigeria.

Jan 15, 1985.

His Lordship,
Rt. Rev. Dr. B.D. Usanga,
Bishop's House,
P.M.B. 1044,
Calabar,
Cross Rivers State.

My Lord,

About 7 years ago I manifested to you in writing my intention to join the Missionary Society of St. Paul. This was further strengthened last year when I wrote for permission for the oath of temporary membership. With your permission I took the first temporary oath of the society.

In reply to my application of the 11th of December, 1984 to the internal council to be dispensed from article 17 of the constitutions and to be admitted to the permanent oath of membership, the Internal Council "by a majority decision" has accepted my application and has recommended me to the Ordinary who has accordingly dispensed me from Article 17.

To this and, I hereby apply to you for a letter of Excardination from the diocese as the coming oath is going to incardinate me into the society.

The date for the oath of permanent membership has been fixed for the 25th of January, 1985.

While asking for your blessing,

I remain, My Lord,
Yours Sincerely in Christ,
Rt. Rev. Msgr. Godwin P. Akpan, MSP.

Msgr. Godwin P. Akpan responded in gratitude to the governing council's letter for approving and recommending him to the ordinary for action.

NATIONAL MISSIONARY SEMINARY

The Internal Council,
The Missionary Society of St. Paul,
Iperu-Remo Ogun State.
15th Jan, 1985.

Dear Confreres,

I write to thank you very sincerely for accepting my application of the 11th of December, 1984 "by a majority decision" and, in effect, recommending me to the Ordinary of the Missionary Society of St.

Paul to grant dispensation from article 17 and then admit me to the permanent oath of membership.

I treasure the solidarity thus demonstrated. I have accepted your recommendations in good spirit, asking for your prayers that the Lord will give me the wisdom and courage as a member of the Society to take such steps that will be to His greater glory and the good of the Missionary Society of St. Paul in Nigeria. With prayerful remembrance,

C. The Actual Commencement of the First General Chapter The Duties of the General Chapter

- To elect the superior general and his councilors
- To give general orientations to the government of the society
- To take decisions which foster missionary activities in accordance with the charism of the society
- To examine the state of the society, to deal with its problems, and to offer guidelines for its activities
- To evaluate the society's role in the church and in the society, the spiritual and apostolic life of its government
- To study and consider proposals, which have been put forward by members in accordance with its constitutions.[424]
- After voting for the confirmation of the Chapter Procedures, there were to be no modifications unless by absolute majority.[425]

After settling on His Eminence Dominic Ignatius Cardinal Ekandem as the founder of the congregation as and the fact of establishment by

CBCN, the founder who was providentially the ordinary of the diocese, he then acted in his full capacity to facilitate matters in order to aid the society and the seminary to progress and take root. It was not in his days that nihil obstat was obtained, it was during the time of Most Reverend John O. Onaiyekan after Cardinal Ekandem's retirement as the ordinary of Abuja. The nihil obstat was given by Rome on March 17, 1994 (Prot. 5374/94).

The approbation of the constitution took place during the time of His Grace John O. Onaiyekan, the archbishop of Abuja who became a cardinal after his appointment by Pope Benedict XIV on Thursday, January 31, 2013, and given the opportunity of serving as a member of the Congregation for the Doctrine of the Faith (CDF) and as a member of the presidential committee of the Pontifical Council for the Family.[426] His Grace Most Rev. John Onaiyekan, the ordinary of Abuja, gave the approbation of the constitution and statutes of the Missionaries of St. Paul on Easter Sunday, April 16, 1995, thus enabling the missionary institute to be erected as a society of apostolic right. With the diocesan right, the society overcame all the preexistent difficulties and began preparing seriously for the first General Chapter that took place in 1995.

D. Announcement of the New Superior General

During the first general chapter, the very reverend Fr. Felix Elosi, MSP, became the first elected superior general of the Missionaries of St. Paul. The news of the election had to reach far and wide by sending messages to all those who needed to be aware of the result of the election. With this election, Msgr. Godwin P. Akpan ceased to be the acting superior general of the society. Whenever the reality comes around the symbol must give way. This is what happened to Monsignor Akpan as the acting superior general. He handled over to the duly elected superior general who started from then on to exercise his duty of office with his newly elected members of the general council. He was succeeded by Very Rev. Hyacinth Egbebo, MSP as the second superior general and, subsequently, by Very Rev. Fr. Anselm Umoren, MSP. Each of the last two became a bishop in Bomadi in Delta State and an auxiliary bishop of Abuja in the Federal Capital Territory, respectively. Bishop Anselm Umoren, MSP was originally from Ikot Ekpene Diocese.

As an auxiliary bishop of Abuja Archdiocese, he started working with Card. John Onaiyekan, the chief shepherd of the flock.

E.   Silver Jubilee Celebration

The Silver Jubilee Preparatory Commission went to a great length to take note of the historical development of the society/seminary. They took into consideration all that happened starting from the CBCN decision to the meeting of the seminary committee, the need of Msgr. Godwin Akpan as the appointed acting rector of the seminary to go to Ijebu Ode to meet Bishop Anthony Sanusi about the site of the seminary to the first General Chapter and to the very period of preparing for the Silver Jubilee Celebration itself. They expressed in unequivocal terms the role of the St. Patrick or Kiltegan Fathers in the establishment of their society/seminary.

The involvement of the Kiltegan Fathers in the life of the young society was very crucial. In a way, in terms of the initial development of the Missionary Seminary/Society of St. Paul, the Missionaries of St. Patrick were a gift to the society. The St. Patrick Fathers who generously served in various capacities were so many extensions of that gift to which the Missionaries of St. Paul remain eternally grateful.[427]

They unanimously singled out the very reverend Fr. Thomas Greenan, SPS, for his role in terms of finding funds for the society/ seminary rehabilitation. The Bishops' Committee, the CBCN, the Catholic Bishops' Conference of Nigeria, and the Kiltegan Priests appointed to work with the society and the seminary were specifically appreciated. The same applies to the driver of Monsignor Akpan, Mr. Gregory Pius Udo, and, implicitly, the members of the Bishop's Court that received the monsignor and his driver, the parish priests of Iperu Remo and Ebute Metta, Rev. Fr. Patrick Barry, SMA, and Rev. Fr. Des Connor (Dermot Connolly), the regional superior. A lot of historical materials were reviewed apart from other committees that were put in place for the effective preparation and celebration of the Silver Jubilee. The Silver Jubilee Celebration took place a year after the second General Chapter that was held at Gwagwalada, Abuja, in 2001. The year 2002 witnessed the Silver Jubilee Celebration of the society/ seminary carried out to the greater glory of God with so many priests and many missions and seminarians including permanent members and associates of the Missionaries of St. Paul. By the year 2014, twelve years after the Silver Jubilee, the society recorded a total of 260 priests. This is a phenomenal growth with its presence in all the continents of the world. They started with three missions to the Cameroons, Liberia, and the United States of America in 1986; and by the time of the Silver Jubilee, they had graduated to twenty, adding seventeen more missions, but presently, they can be found in all the continents of the world. This was the dream of its founder, Cardinal Ekandem. It actually came to fruition. It is marvelous to see. The simplicity of sharing the Word of God with the faithful opened the way to a deeper understanding, relishing it as the Word of God; taking it to heart as the new group of missionaries started spreading that word throughout the world as the founder had envisaged. The founder started that process using his motto *In Cruce Salus* as a motivating force.

Chapter Fifteen

IN CRUCE SALUS
(IN THE CROSS IS SALVATION)

His Prophetic-Trials, Battles, Crosses and
His Religious Disposition

*Like those good helmsmen who, when battered by storm
redouble their courage and turn their vessels prow into the
most ferocious waves, which seem to be rising to swallow it.*

—St. Vincent de Paul

THE LIFE OF Dominic Cardinal Ekandem was very eventful almost from the beginning. His experiences in life, along with his convictions that were irrevocable, drew him very powerfully close to the Cross—the link to his salvation. The necessity of following the footsteps of Christ ardently so as to experience salvation coming from the Cross meant that the Cross became the focus and center of his spirituality and, indeed, of his life. His experiences even as a very young person, as a seminarian, as a young priest, as a young bishop, not forgetting his sickness, and as the administrator of Abuja Independent Mission were the background to his motto or his coat of arms that he cherished till death: *In Cruce Salus.*

St. Paul speaks of the power of the Cross joined with the Gospel thus:

> For I am not ashamed of the Gospel: it is the power of God for salvation to everyone who has faith, to the Jew first and also to the Greek. For in it the righteousness of God is revealed through faith for faith, as it is written, "He who through faith is righteous shall live. (Rom. 1: 16–17)

This text points to the idea of salvation as a fundamental outcome of the Gospel that comes with faith and the power of the Cross that Cardinal Ekandem witnessed.

Specifically, St. Paul affirms:

> For Christ did not send me to baptise, but to preach the Good news, and not to preach that in the terms of philosophy in which the crucifixion of Christ cannot be expressed. The language of the Cross may be illogical to those who are not on the way to salvation, but those of us who are see it as God's power to save. As Scripture says: *I shall destroy the wisdom of the wise and bring to nothing all the learning of the learned. Where are the philosophers now? Where are the Scribes? Where are our thinkers today?* Do you now see how God has shown up the foolishness of human wisdom? If it was God's wisdom that human wisdom should not know God, it was because God wanted to save those who have faith through the foolishness of the message that we preach. And so while the Jews demand miracles, the Greeks look for wisdom, here are we preaching a crucified Christ; to the Jews, an obstacle that they cannot get over, to the pagans madness, but to those who have been called, whether they are Jews or Greeks, a Christ who is the power and the wisdom of God. For God's foolishness is wiser than human wisdom and God's weakness is stronger than human strength. (1 Cor. 1:17–25)

St. Paul links the preaching of the Good News with faith and with divine wisdom as he contrasts it with human wisdom more so bringing out the prominence of faith in the crucified Christ that forms the basis of the resurrectional faith for those called to salvation. The language of the Cross could never have constituted an obstacle for Cardinal Ekandem, otherwise, he would not have opted for his episcopal motto of *In Cruce Salus*. He might have preferred something else! He went for it with full understanding of the underlying power propelling him unto salvation: the power of the Cross. He struck a deal but transcended it to the spiritual plane in which the Cross demonstrated the power to save. Christ, who is the power and the wisdom of God, initiates the salvific journey through the Cross, thus creating room for his followers to do the same and experience the same power of the resurrection after the passion, death, and burial so that the grain of wheat can die and germinate producing abundant fruits.

His lifelong alliance with his crucified Lord was carried out between the living God who chooses the weak things of the earth to confound the strong as seen in the above Pauline quotation in 1 Corinthians 1:17 ff. He struck the pact, or rather made a covenant, with the Lord of the Passion or entered into the Paschal Mystery of the Lord Jesus Christ through the Cross and the resurrection of Christ who conquered sin and death through the Cross and became victorious in his suffering. It is the same Lord he chose to follow who became obedient unto death even death on the Cross. It was this same obedience that disposed him to go through all the sufferings without losing sight of the Father's will and demand that motivated His Eminence to turn to the Cross where salvation was to be found instead of escaping it.

A. His Motto in Real Life

Being questioned as to what informed the choice of his motto, the cardinal recalled many things that made his heart to be captivated by the role of the Cross. He said that even Christ himself started moving on with the Cross in his life starting from the time of his public ministry. He then asked, "Who am I to reject the Cross of Christ when Christ has not rejected me and was obedient unto death, even death on the Cross?"

He was conscious of the various vicissitudes in his life being deprived of his mother at a very tender age, the role his father had to play, his experience on the way to the priesthood, and his experiences as a priest, later as bishop and cardinal made the role of the Cross very much alive in his thoughts. In order to give a central place to the Cross in his life, he used this verse to capture his vision of the priesthood, the Master that is Christ and the life after life. These lines meant so much for him that he said them with great passion, enthusiasm, and with some tears of joy intermingled in the emotion of the Cross and salvation. He rendered this so spontaneously that it was difficult to say whether it was a quotation or some inspirational rendering of one of his own intuitive perceptions in a poetic form thus:

A Priest, *Alter Christus*:
Be Thine the Master's
Cross with love to bear,
So that, Endless with Crown to Wear!

Coincidentally, the first three lines follow alphabetically: a, b, c, and the difference is in the fourth line. It could be paralleled with the manner of writing Psalm 119 where each stanza begins with a corresponding alphabet and follows one after the other.

This did not end when he became a bishop. He allowed the centrality of the Cross, its power as well as its salvific aspect to become his episcopal motto *In Cruce Salus*, In the Cross Is Salvation. The priestly and the episcopal conception of Christ and following him suggests ownership of the priest or bishop by Christ, thus becoming a *special possession* of Christ as the Hebrew wife was normally conceived as *be'ulah*. Being possessed by Christ totally conveyed many benefits, especially an eternal crown that envisages salvation not only of the body but also of the entire person in eternity.

The role of the Cross affected and colored his whole life, his thoughts and expressions, his counseling as well as his conferences and talks. He addressed a senior nursing officer (SNO) at Urua Akpan School of Nursing in Ikot Ekpene who was tormented by armed robbers sometimes twice in a week. When it became critical, it took place every other day; sometimes occurring at noonday, at early morning hours, or even at seven o'clock in the evening without allowing the nurse and her household to have supper or to pray in the house. He told the nurse that she could vacate that particular house and relocate in the compound. He exhorted her not to abandon the sick poor that she was serving even if it entailed laying down her life. She should have no fear but persist in carrying out her duty. She should do that courageously and not give in.

This recalls what St. John says in the book of Revelation: "Do not fear what you are about to suffer. Beware, the devil is about to throw some of you into prison so that you may be tested, and for ten days you will have affliction. Be faithful until death, and I will give you the crown of life" (Rev. 2:10 NRS). Every Christian is called to a life of faithful witness even on to death for the sake of Christ and his kingdom. Indirectly, the call to persevere is a general invitation to fidelity till death as the background as stamped in the Cross as a means of salvation for believers. Every follower of Christ is called to be a witness that is faithful like Christ who declares that he is a true and faithful witness (Rev. 1:5), and Philippians added obedience to death. The obedience of Jesus Christ and his faithfulness to the point of shedding blood on behalf of his brothers and sisters on the Cross sets for all believers to follow. This indicates not only a physical battle but above all a spiritual one that needs to be fought against principalities and powers. The fight has to continue on to death on the side of Christ and for the sake of his kingdom.

Being the gentle and courageous soul the cardinal was, he proceeded to say, "My dear daughter, I do not want to impose anything on you. Act according to your conscience, especially when it is properly formed according to the dictates of God." While speaking with the undertone of *In Cruce Salus,* he gave the nurse the liberty to act freely without any compulsion considering the gravity of the situation. She carefully listened to and heard him quite well but immediately shifted her base owing to the constant menace of the burglars. She moved away from the place irrespective of the fact that she was not officially transferred. She even opted to lose her monthly salary instead of losing her life and her family.

Those who discouraged her said, "You have your life and your family to take care of; do not mind him and this cross of his. That is how he colors everything with the Cross even Christ carried the Cross only once, but this one wants to carry it more than Christ did that is why he wants you to go and die in the arms of robbers. Make sure you preserve your life." A very highly placed cleric who saw the cardinal as overstretching the idea of the Cross not only in his life but in other people's lives too gave the counsel so as to discourage the woman from following the advice of the cardinal. The perception of the counselor was different from that of the cardinal. One pole was "otherworldly" while the other was "this worldly." One emphasized earthly existence with some sense of security while the other pointed out the insecurity and risks associated with hardship of discipleship coupled with the Cross transcending the spatiotemporal existence and otherworldly existence. About the Cross, Jesus says that the person who wants to follow him must take up his cross daily and follow him (Lk. 9:23). This is what informed the advice of the prelate. However, his opponents indirectly negated the Cross as the instrument of salvation.

One may ask, why did the cardinal emphasize martyrdom and holding on the fort when he knew perfectly well that death was imminent for the nurse if she did not move away from the hospital? Could he have been considered a masochist or somebody who did not value life? If he did not value life, why did he promote the existence of the hospital? Was he only interested in the cures offered by the hospital but not in the lives of the staff? If that were to be the case, why did he ensure that many of them go for training? If none of these is applicable then what was the main reason for acting like this?

First and foremost, it must be understood that Dominic Cardinal Ekandem was a man who lived out what he preached and preached what he lived. When he counseled the nurse, he meant that her suffering should be seen in the context of the sufferings of Christ who did not go back after setting his face like flint toward Jerusalem. Every person's suffering should be reflected in that of Christ who went through the Cross to save all. Consequently, none can run away from the various crosses that emerge in daily life although everyone is bound to preserve life. He rather saw the suffering of the nurse as an opportunity to triumph and use good to conquer evil. She was overpowered by the fear and the torment exacted by her heartless tormentors.

While showing love, the cardinal taught that participation in the sufferings of Christ is inevitable even if it entailed death. Everyone belongs to the Lord as St. Paul tells the Romans in chapter 14 that we belong to the Lord whether in life or in death. That sense of belonging to the Lord ignites the filial relationship that deepens the love existing between the Father and his children. The meaning of the Cross is found in love. Love forms the foundation of all the martyrs' lives. It is what the cardinal called the nurse to share in. It was a courageous call that demanded a strong faith motivated by love and the courage to answer. Perhaps she was attacked because she stood for justice and right in every situation. Her presence troubled some consciences and was a hindrance to carry out whatever they wanted to do instead of having recourse to the cardinal every time. She was paying for her loyalty to the cardinal.

To remove the Cross as a means of salvation from the cardinal's life was tantamount to removing an essential aspect of his life. He speaks of being one with the Master's Cross and bearing it with love. This is what distinguishes between a true disciple and a false one. The true disciple does everything out of love, whereas the hired laborer does whatever he carries out for the sake of money. In other words, works as a mercenary but not as the owner whose motive is to preserve, conserve, and protect cautiously but joyously.

The cross constitutes the fulcrum of thought, life, and vision of this special prelate of the church. The cardinal said that "the cross and the narrow way go together. They are an inseparable entity and cannot be severed from any Christian's life. It can neither be removed from mine. To carry the Cross with love and utter resignation demands a disciplined and mortified life. It entails dying to oneself and living in Christ. It means killing whatever is earthly and of the flesh, in other words, doing away with an inordinate type of life so as to allow the Spirit of God to take control and to flourish in the person's life. One cannot really carry the Cross in view of salvation if one is not mortified; otherwise, the temptation to give up when trials arise is always there.

The cardinal talking about his episcopal election said, "What qualifications had I? None! It was all the grace of God arising from his salvation." In his humble way he said, "My boast is in Christ." St. Paul says, "As for me, the only thing I can boast about is the Cross of our Lord Jesus Christ, through whom the world is crucified to me, and I to the world" (Gal. 6:14).

These words of Paul best express the thoughts of this humble but firm minister of God, the prelate of his own class who was never out to be praised and never even wanted himself to be praised and never pitied himself when he was criticized. He did not fall into any disproportionate concern about himself or his ministry or office as bishop. In everything, he was out to glorify God through the Cross, thus creating the inner conviction to be open to God's will at all times as dictated by the circumstances of his life. The cardinal made the words of Paul his own by saying, "The language of the Cross may be illogical to those who are not on the way to salvation but to those of us who are see it as God's power to save" (1 Cor. 1:18). He said that there was no single text that encapsulated all his thoughts; however, they all indicate the light and path for him.[428] (Cardinal Ekandem was aware of what the Cross meant; he went the whole way to embrace it.)

When he was questioned on what would be the place of Christianity if the Cross were to be removed from it he said:

> If a Cross-less Christianity were preached, there would be no need of talking about salvation, about sin, about death and resurrection about moral life or even the Sacraments for many of them especially Baptism and the Eucharist have their full expression only in the light of the Cross as blood and water flowed from his side that the Church might be the fountain of salvation. Christ himself had to go through the crooked and narrow way. He submitted to his father and prayed "Not my will but yours be done" and it was for the sake of humanity's redemption that he had to go through the agony of the Cross, died, and was buried before he rose from the dead. The whole Christ has to be accepted. Partial acceptance is a form of rejection of Christ.[429]

The cardinal expressed great dissatisfaction over some tendencies in some continents where preachers of the Gospel are afraid to talk about the Cross of Christ because of materialism and consumerism and fear of offending people or making them become afraid because suffering is mentioned. He spoke thus:

> "If Ministers have to represent Christ they have to present him well and represent him as well not in the distorted teaching. Ministers are instructed by the Holy Apostle to

preach in season and out of season." He was very emphatic while saying, "We cannot fail to be challenged by the Gospel of Christ in our daily life and in our preaching. What would it benefit me to subtract from the word of God? I hear that some priests in Nigeria base their preaching on love, money, and building-projects, have they pushed the Cross of Christ aside in order to have their way, what of justice and fair play, in this our nation that needs God's intervention and intensive prayer? He added at the end of it all "in the Cross is our Salvation."

A reaction to the choice of his motto *In Cruce Salus* is as diverse as the faces of people themselves. Some female religious when they heard about the sufferings of Cardinal Ekandem said that "it served him right to suffer because he wanted the Cross let him have it." Even among the clergy, some highly placed prelates think that the cardinal was too hard as a result of adhering rigidly to his motto. The cardinal reacting to these and many other things about his motto said, "Let people say whatever they feel. God wanted me to use this motto, and I am ready and willing to receive whatever he sends. I know what strength I draw from the Cross when I turn to Christ hanging on the Cross on my behalf. What gratitude am I to render (Ps. 16) except to cling to the Cross for salvation?"

However, one elderly woman reacting to the motto of the cardinal said:

> Being a Christian is like tying oneself with a metal or iron chain that you cannot cut; your hands are tied. You will not be able to do all the things you would like to do. You can't give in to the desires of your flesh. You can't retaliate in like manner when somebody strikes you. The life of a Christian is a difficult one, and the cardinal understood it from the beginning.[430]

Actually, the cardinal understood that to follow Christ entailed taking one's cross daily and following him. The woman in question perceived the situation in depth.

As a convert from Qua Iboe Church to Catholicism and his decision to become a seminarian—the first in Ibibio land—the various attacks and lack of understanding from friends and relations made things tough and bad to be seen with the eyes of the Cross. When the missionaries presented the message of Christianity, they presented the Cross as being central to the faith. The message was clear to the cardinal even as a boy. It inspired his values for the rest of his life.

a.   His Motto in Real Life and Consequences

The cardinal was often called upon to do many difficult things. Immediately after the Nigerian-Biafran Civil War when Bishop Godfrey Mary Paul Okoye, CSSp, the then bishop of Port Harcourt, went back to Enugu, there was a Vacant See (*Sede Vacante*). He was called upon to take charge. He said, "The authorities asked me to be the administrator of Port Harcourt along with Ikot Ekpene Diocese. I had to run the two dioceses concurrently. It was a difficult task, but I had to do it for the sake of the people's faith." When he finished his duty, there was very little recognition of his contribution. Maybe it was on the basis of the Gospel injunction that when you must have finished your duty, just say that you are an unprofitable servant who has not done more than is required of him. He was eager to balance the time spent in Ikot Ekpene and in Port Harcourt. The work entrusted to him demanded frequent movement. The roads were not wonderful in Nigeria after the war, yet all had to be done for the sake of Christ and for the good of the souls.

It was not long after that when he was made the chairman of the social department of the Catholic Secretariat of Nigeria at Lagos. He said, "In order to do the work effectively, I had to be visiting the secretariat frequently." It was the Catholic Bishops' Conference of Nigeria (CBCN) that appointed him to do that. He undertook it not minding the inconveniences and the distance. The appointment at the Catholic secretariat opened up a great link with the whole country. "In some circumstances," he added, "I had to travel to many parts of the country to clarify issues. The bishops demanded, and I accepted." He exemplified the great link between obedience, humility, and service.

In 1982, the Holy Father, Pope John Paul II, wanted somebody to go and start the mission in the Abuja Capital Territory. He wholeheartedly and willingly undertook the task. He said, "The Holy Father appointed me to be the superior of Abuja Independent Mission. I could not refuse him." Owing to his love for the church, he always spoke of the vicar of Christ as the "Holy Father." Whenever he did so, there used to be that fervent and ardent love in his tone and mannerism. He became the superior of Abuja Independent Mission, *missio sui juris*. Again he had to shuttle between Abuja and Ikot Ekpene. Abuja was not even a prefecture or a diocese; it was only an independent mission.

b. His Sickness

The cardinal had been sick for many years—for example, he started suffering from diabetes in 1962. With the sickness, he did all his work silently, without complaining. Only very close associates knew what he was suffering from. He said, "The sickness was one of the crosses the Lord sent me. I had no choice but to bear it."

At the time that the cardinal started suffering from diabetes, he had fifteen years a priest. He was only eight years old as a bishop. One of his schoolmates commenting on his sickness said, "Even as a young bishop he started injecting himself daily with insulin in order to survive. It was part of the cross he undertook."

The motto of the cardinal was very prophetic. His was a path strewn with crosses and trials form infancy even to the moment of his death. In a way he could have applied the fourth song of the suffering servant of Yahweh in Is.52:13 to 53:12 to himself. He was a man of sorrows and acquainted with grief. The extraordinary thing with him was that he was always cheerful in the midst of his sufferings. He carried his cross courageously to the end. His sickness never deterred him from doing what he was supposed to do.

It was an extraordinary charism given only to saints like St. Francis of Assisi who suffered terribly as a result of the stigmata and weeping for his sins. One of the modern saints who suffered in that way was St. Maxmilian Kolbe who suffered not only from asthma but also from tuberculosis. It was with this last sickness Kolbe established the Marian Village and promoted pilgrimage to the shrine regularly. He claimed the controversial parcel of land for our Lady from the communists with a wooden cross and fought to see that our Lady was venerated there. In the same way, the cardinal spent his life trying to do the will of God as it came to him in the midst of his sickness. Neither his sickness nor the awkward position in which he found himself deterred him from fighting his battles.

c.   His Battle with Ekpo

Ekpo masquerade and cult is part of the cultural heritage of the Ibibio land as well as Annang land and all that is called Akwa Ibom State today. It represents the ghosts of the departed ancestors. Ekpo is a purely male chauvinistic pagan cult that is secret and exclusive. The admission of members is open only to males who attain a certain age through an initiation process. At first it was practiced by specific groups of families but later opened up to all males who could shoulder the financial burden of initiation. The penalties of infringement range from fines, to destruction of property, to death. Sometimes the victim was decapitated.

In its initial stage, Ekpo emerged as a form of security for the purpose of maintaining law and order in the society. It played the role that the police force is playing now, that of maintaining law and order and prosecuting culprits and suspected criminals. In ancient societies, these functioned very well, and orderly structure of the society continued evolving from generation to generation with basic modifications as were necessary. Ekpe played a similar role in Uruan clan that has great affinity with the Efiks who equally used Ekpe as a type of police force to control the society, rid it of crime, and maintain order. Ekpo, on the other hand, produced its own surveillance unit of exposing crimes and dangers by singing with the person's name in the night.

Ekpo sometimes make a song of the offense committed and go around the village in the night performing their composition. Those who had no idea of the offense would immediately become aware of it. The person, time, and place of the offense would also be known in the process. When Ekpo Akata sings, it gives all those details. Otherwise, they would deter by punishing culprits and fining the person together with the noninitiates. The noninitiates had no privilege of going out of their houses during the season or Ekpo or when Ekpe was out. Ekpo did not only have the atrocious acts and exhibitions but also had a benign aspect of entertaining by dancing gracefully and carrying out various acrobatic displays.

Even though Ekpo was mainly for males, however, it was operated in such a way that it accommodated the oldest woman or women in the village. Such a woman or women were considered no longer as women because they were capable of keeping secret like the elderly men. This is similar to what Jesus said in the Gospels in the context of the seven brothers who married a particular woman **in** terms of passing from death to life and have no more distinctions of male and female but are like angels of God since they do not marry (Cf. Lk. 20:27–39).

Such women in the eyes of Ekpo members are effectively changed into males and can join an Ekpo group and share in the various secrets of the members. They were normally invited to join the group after consultation by the officers of an Ekpo group. They can even become the custodians of some of the artifacts of Ekpo by preserving them in their houses without betraying the confidentiality imposed on them. The artifacts were normally stored at the topmost level of their shelves before the fireplace called Utang next to the roof. That part of Utang could be regarded as attic. The Ekpo masks are normally placed very close to the wall and covered for preservation. Other items that are rarely used would be used to keep the masks and things connected with Ekpo out of the view of those who go to make use of some of those rarely used items.

Such women were revered by their fellow women and honored by the men. They were held in high esteem and could influence the decision of the men if the discussion in question was within their domain to make salient suggestions. The engrafted women acted like the men and never divulged the secrets of the group to other women and other associations. It was a high position but with a series of risks, especially beheading if found guilty.

Such cultural link continued a unified attempt at keeping and maintaining law and order in the society by a special squad of Ekpo or Ekpe where applicable. It was a successful example of what the present police force shout out but do not always mean when they say, "The police are your friends." This is said, but the people do not trust because of betrayal

442

and exposition of the informants to the culprits and making the informants become culprits. When the police say that they are friends of the people, they are claiming what was obtained in time past of cooperation between the men and the women. What the modern age cannot achieve with all the education and propaganda, the ancient society accomplished with ease. Of course, when the male organization of Ekpo began, it included young men but not children, for children had their group while looking forward to joining the adult life later. There was something to hope for.

The disciplinary aspect of Ekpo became greatly pronounced with time to the extent that it deteriorated into a "misnomer." In other words, it was created to enforce the law but became violent and generated violence. The violent nature of Ekpo, properly speaking, stemmed from the disciplinary function of Ekpo in the process of maintaining law and order. The excesses of punishment as a responsible organ of the society charged with that duty exposed the older Ekpo group, especially when it fell into the hands of undisciplined members who took laws into their hands to violence. Also, as it often happens, those charged with discipline or protecting life can even go to the extent of destroying the very life they were to protect with impunity under cover of protection. Since they are the ones in charge of such a situation, it might become very difficult to discover the truth of a matter owing to cover-up. Such can occur within any context of officialdom, that is, why an independent body or organization needs to monitor the activities of the security agents.[431]

As a secret cult Ekpo has a malicious intent of subverting the peace and order even though the initial purpose of the cult was to enforce order and promulgate injunctions and laws. Some of the subversions and hindrances of the smooth running of the society includes barring of females and all noninitiates from free movement even to places of work. On specific days of Ekpo's outing the womenfolk and men who are not initiated have to stay indoors. Nurses as well as civil servants, schoolchildren, travelers who are strangers are equally hampered. Attendance in churches whether for morning worship or devotion even on a Sunday, civil, religious as well as economic activities have to be halted. Ekpo cult is not eclectic in nature and may be good for a closed society, but not for a wider, more open society.

B.   Some Ekpo Heinous Activities

The activities of Ekpo have not changed much since the ancient times. The only difference is that the atrocious activities became greatly aggravated and the revenge attacks increased. The Akwa Ibom State Christian Association of Nigeria (CAN) calls them atrocious damages[432] and classifies them thus:

a.   Closing of Schools: Pursuing and obstructing the pupils and students from going to school renders the classrooms empty. Some pupils and students will be there, likewise some teachers,b ut surely not all will be there during Ekpo season.

b.   Attack on Churches: The same obstruction prevails. In some stations of Urua Akpan Parish in Ikot Ekpene Diocese, masquerades in 1985 and onward were reported to keep a tray for collection near the church gate. The person going to the church if allowed to approach had to pay for his entrance before going to the church. The Ekpo members said they were asking for their collection like the ministers in the church.

In 1984 in Ifa Atai in Etoi clan, a young man was attacked and beaten almost to the point of death in the apostolic church. He was eventually dragged out of the church, and the whole assembly was disrupted.

c.   Machetting: The brutal use of machete on innocent victims is a very common act. In October 28, 1986, Rev. Fr. Francis I. Umoren of happy memory was violently wounded,using the machete to cut his head, in an attempt to rescue a family from Aba in Imo State from being murdered on the Ikot Ekpene Abak Road. Realizing that Father Francis was an obstacle to their plan of extortion, maiming by violent torturing of victims, shooting with gun or bows and arrows, and wounding with a machete, they decided to use the machete on him with the intent of splitting his head in two. When he detected some movement behind him and a shadow of the human head, he instinctively jolted his head, and the blow fell on some part of his head but not with the whole weight of the arm as was originally intended. The cut was not too severe. Some of the blow fell on the bonnet of the car he drove and split part of it. The blow that fell on his head cut a part of the head and face. Blood immediately gushed out and covered his face like Christ's in Pilate's court after the "crowning with thorns." The perpetrators escaped and disappeared from the scene. The mark of sharing in the brutality and suffering of Christ during his Passion remained till his death. The scar could not be erased. It became an indelible mark almost like the invisible mark of the Sacrament of Confirmation, Ordination, or Marriage.

The same misfortune befell a youth corps member in 1989 in Uyo. In the same year, Barrister Umoh would have had his head split in two one of the nights he was returning home but, for his quick reflex, escaped the deadly blow that landed on the windscreen and bonnet of his car. The impact of that blow shattered both parts of his car.

d. Blinding with Arrows: In October 24, 1983, Master Emmanuel P. Emmanson, a minor seminarian in Queen of Apostles Seminary Afaha Obong was shot and blinded with an arrow. The thirteen- year-old boy was within the seminary fence when the incident took place. Soon afterward, the masquerade culprits escaped, but the boy had been blinded and ruined for life.

e. Attack on Women: Women who have neither right for initiation nor the opportunity of becoming members of the group owing to the exclusivity of the group are the targets of Ekpo's atrocities. Nurses as well as pregnant women, market women, those going or coming back from stream or farm, civil servants or whatever profession the person belongs to are equally targets of attack.

f. Nuns were attacked in a bus on the way to and from Urua Akpan Hospital and in many other parts of the state. Only very few escaped their attacks. Sometimes they acted as murderers and sometimes like robbers.

g. Murder: On October 29, 1984, Ms. Aniema Simon Otu—a twenty-one-year-old lady from Odoro Ikot clan was murdered in her mother's kitchen.

h. Looting and Damaging of cars, motorcycles, and bicycles are very common experiences. Many people have lost their means of transport or have had them destroyed by the same group[433].

i. Robbery: Some of the members of the cult collect money forcefully from their victims sometimes at gunpoint or threatening these unfortunate (Nigerians) citizens with a machete cut or an arrow. They make money from these people while leaving their victims in a miserably intimidated position.

There is no way the cardinal would have seen these things and been happy or even resting tranquil that nothing was happening to him. The priest whose head was wounded with a machete belonged to the cardinal, the seminarian was his own, and the hospital in Urua Akpan was in his diocese as one of the Catholic hospitals there. The nurses affected in Abak, Urua Akpan as well as Anua in Uyo Diocese made him restless as he had great concern for justice. He had pity for the populace who were tortured in this manner. He was quite aware of the enslavement of women together with the uninitiated men even as a curate in Afaha Obong or as a young bishop in Anua. The suffering touched him greatly.

He sought for a way to remedy the situation and gain freedom for the women and the uninitiated men. The struggle brought him into conflict with Chief Essien Ibanga of Anua and Chief Nyong Essien from Southern Uruan during the days of the district officers (DOs). The conflict had reached its peak when in a full assembly with the DO, Chief Nyong Essien said that Ekpo was "the display of our ancestors." Consequently, Ekpo should not be abolished. He was the authority who could have helped to stop the atrocities of Ekpo at that time, but he made it no more than a harmless tradition. He was consulted because he was a very revered chief and greatly respected by the DO.

The reaction arising from such an event did not deter the cardinal from fighting. In fact, like the battered ship in rough water, he doubled his efforts. He fought strenuously and relentlessly and with the reliance of a man who has gone through the troubled waters until he gained a partial success by letting the noninitiates in terms of men and, of course, the females to be set free. The struggle against Ekpo was not an easy one. His close friends feared very much for his safety. He was warned by his close associates just as those who were close to Abp. Oscar Romero told him that since he had refused to accept the government, those of them who had been defending him were ready to ease off and let him take care of himself. The cardinal was unperturbed and trusted in the one who had the power to set him free as Archbishop Oscar did even though the latter lasted only a little while after that rejection.

The battle against Ekpo was still raging furiously when the cardinal turned attention to many other cultural values that needed urgent attention. Many government functionaries were affected by Ekpo's atrocious exhibitions, but the government of the area was not fully involved. Many people were maimed, killed, and robbed, but the government was not moved. The experience is similar to the one found in Pharaoh's court that was smitten by the one but last plague.

Often, the press reported the various atrocities of Ekpo. A lot of priests made a series of attempts to pacify the Ekpo members by offering a cow so that Ekpo would not come out at all. Sometimes after consuming the offerings, they would turn around and become more ferocious on the ground that it was not given to the main people concerned. Paramount rulers had been approached, but not much happened. In 1989, the Corpus Christi procession—a yearly event combined with feast of Christ the King in the Catholic Church—was greatly disrupted in Urua Akpan parish because Ekpo came out "en masse" and prevented the people from coming out of their houses.

The police had earlier been alerted, and an assurance was given that there would be no problems. When somebody sneaked back to inform the police, Ekpo disappeared from the route used by the police; and when the patrol in a particular section ceased, Ekpo featured again. A few were caught and thrown into detention and large sums of money were paid for bail, yet Ekpo thrived. The next step taken by the government was to order chiefs to get license before Ekpo could feature in their villages and that the names of those involved should be noted in case there was a problem. The method helped a little, but not very much.

The recalcitrant and stubborn members never consulted the chiefs before masking. Such an action created more problems for the rulers than for the recalcitrant members of Ekpo who were always ready to escape from such vicinity after causing trouble.

What is termed Ekpo's bile of wickedness took place between 1995 and 1996 at Ifiayong Obot-Uyo in which the houses of some junior police officers and that of an inspector of police were burned down. The Ekpo members assaulted the officers. Some of the officers were wounded, and some were killed. The police reacted by burning down the whole village. Many people ran away and became refugees in other places. A lot of people were captured by the police special squad and sent into detention cells. Lives were lost; property and personal belongings were destroyed all because of the problem of Ekpo. The battle raged on till an order was issued.

Every village in which Ekpo is to be displayed has to obtain a license from the government. The license has to be obtained by the village head.

Any person intending to put on the mask in any village that has a license has to clear with the village head in case of any eventuality so as to know from where the trouble arose.

No masquerade is to feature on the main road. It is to be carried out in their squares. The police were to arrest any masquerader found on the road. Many other orders followed suit.

The wings of Ekpo were somehow broken. Some type of rest of mind returned even though some heady young men still go on furtively without respecting any of those orders about putting on the mask. All the same, the battle that began in the fifties eventually had a little success in the nineties, almost at the end of the century.

With the Ifiayong Obot in the Uruan Local Government area in which Idu is the headquarters, the pronouncement of the government over Ekpo affected all the villages from then on. The battle began by Cardinal Ekandem single- handedly was won with the government's machinery. Paul planted Appollos watered but God gave the increase (1 Cor. 3:6). It seems with time Ekpo display may be shelved in the archives of antiquity where it will only be exhumed and revisited periodically instead of being a daily occurrence. The intention of the cardinal was not to destroy Ekpo but to moderate it and turn it into a source of entertainment that will bring joy to all while retaining everything except its atrocities. The victory was not completely won because some years after this interim period of peace, when Gov. Godswill Akpabio came to the throne, he saw Ekpo as a way of promoting culture and that it should not be extinguished since the forefathers handed it down.[434]

This was the same argument adopted by Chief Nyong Essien before the DO when something should have been done about Ekpo. Such a tradition should be maintained and preserved. With the reversal of the policy, the acrimonious acts of Ekpo began again, and people started living in fear once again. He tried defending his position by saying that Ekpo as an integral part of culture can operate but should not harm any person and should be displayed to entertain and should not harm any person. In actual fact, there is no way Ekpo can be displayed without the accompanying violence except when it is displayed in a stadium during cultural display and in seminaries and schools. Any time it is displayed in the villages, they must molest, threaten, or wound or maim somebody. The season of Ekpo carries with it a fever that is not easily overcome or cured since people know what awaits them.

C. Inculturation and Foresight

The cardinal was a man of foresight, intuition, and discernment. He was ahead of his time. He was trained in the Latin tradition of the Roman Catholic Church, yet he advocated and promoted the use of vernacular in liturgical celebrations in the 1950s, long before the approbation of the Second Vatican Council in 1962. What prompted him to advocate the use of vernacular was the need for active participation in liturgical celebrations. He was not revolting against the Church. He was in the church and wanted the good of the church. He was anxious to see that the mode of conception, perception, and expression were articulated in the people's language and worship. It meant as an aid to comprehension what Latin had greatly mystified. The Efik-Iblbio language was complimentary to Latin in the context under consideration. It helped the people to understand some of the things taken for granted about the faith and culture.

Whenever the cardinal taught, even as a young priest, he taught with the simplicity and conviction of a witness. He conveyed that message with his comportment and demeanor. The python incident exemplified that aspect of his conviction and comportment. The battle against cultural values and their Christianization exposed him to many dangerous threats to his life; the python incident was that of a cultural belief.

D.   The Python Incident and the Battles Fought[435]

The Iblbio, Annangs, and Efiks believe that a human being has three types of souls. One type of soul inhabits the body *Ukpong Idem*. The second lives in an animal. The attribution of the animals to the person's soul depends on whether the person is sluggish, brisk, powerful, coward, brave, lazy, fast, quick, intelligent or dull, pugnacious, calm, avoids disturbance, or angrily aggressive. This seems to be a common belief and outlook among the Africans as such. The second type of soul called *Ukpong Ikot* seems to give a clue to the psychological study of human beings and differentiation of behaviors. Consequently, there is attribution to animals, like the lion if the person is brave, fearless, powerful, courageous and aggressive. A local animal like "Ebet" that looks like an antelope, which sleeps very much but moves very fast when awake, is likened to a very deep sleeper, the python—sluggish but very fast and powerful while moving. The crocodile and a host of other animals are described as Ukpong Ikot if people have similar characteristics. The person's soul is presumed to inhabit such an animal and lives in the deepest part of the forest or in a hole, cave or hole in a tree, river or sea so as not to be seen easily and killed. That is why people are advised not to kill such animals, especially at night when the soul is supposed to escape the body when they are asleep. Killing one of these animals is tantamount to killing the person bearing this soul. This is what the cardinal had to battle with as a very young priest.

It is believed that once the animal harboring the soul of the person is killed or harmed, the person dies at home or develops pains at the spot of the wound. The third type is *Mbukpong*, which is simply the shadow of the person. It is believed that if one's shadow is trapped or harmed, the person can also be trapped or harmed. The first type Ukpong Idem is not exposed to too much danger except the body is harmed. In case of death, the soul leaves the body and returns to God. Ukpong Idem is also the name given to a namesake to express intimacy and closeness. The second type Ukpong Ikot is similar to what St. Thomas Aquinas calls the animal soul although it is not understood in exactly the same way as that of the Ibibio.

The killing of the python took place in Afaha Obong when he became the rector of the minor seminary. As he went out to celebrate the Eucharist in a nearby village he came across a gathering of people. He did not bother himself with the group. He went and completed his assignment and met the group again on his way back. He alighted from his motorcycle and inquired what happened. They told him that Ukpong Ikot had featured, and they were trying to drive it gently back to where it came. Some people brought a wooden box trying to command the python to enter so that it could be carried to safety and never to visit home again. Others were speaking to it, urging it to go. On such a case, various names of the members of the family would be mentioned one by one with the refrain if you are so and so move away or enter the box. It takes a long time. It is always a big ceremony. Children are forbidden to appear for fear of seeing their Ukpong Ikot and dying in the process. This applies to other tribes too.

When the cardinal arrived, he told them not to bother themselves that it was just a python and not a soul connected with any human being. The three types of souls were believed to have a close connection with one another. The cardinal ordered them to kill the python. That was an abomination for mentioning such a thing. Immediately, temper rose high and people started shouting, but the cardinal, as a young priest, was serenely calm and composed. He insisted that the python should be killed and ordered somebody to carry out that order. The people became very aggravated and wanted to kill Dominic should any people die after killing the python. He was convinced of what he said and refused to budge. He ordered the python to be killed, and it was carried out. The cardinal said, "I got away with them all. They were surprised." No one died within the next three days, and the people became convinced of what the young Father Dominic said. The python incident became a means of conversion and adherence to the faith.

If the young Father Dominic had not been convinced of his faith, the mass conversion that ensued may never have taken place. His firm, persevering faith founded on Christ the rock and on the foundation of the apostles' faith expressed in a concrete situation drew many people to God. He wanted the people to experience the salvation that comes from the Cross, not the one based on human philosophy. The faith demonstrated in the context was a living faith. It went along with the legionary prayer, which says: Give us a strong and lively faith immovable as a rock...As the first priest from the area, he did everything possible to achieve the desired goal of the people's conversion and adherence to God. The young Father

Dominic was aware of the danger of putting a hand into the plough and looking back. He knew that such a person was not fit for the kingdom of God.

E.   Ukana Offot-Awa Itam: His Battles as a Young Bishop

The young bishop was a very cheerful cleric. His cheerfulness did not, however, hinder him from accomplishing difficult tasks. He was cheerful yet determined and conscious of the necessity of evangelization. It rather enhanced it, especially in a world of suffering, pain, and injustice.

When he was posted to Anua parish after his "consecration" as a young bishop, the church was already built. As a matter of fact, many of the parcels of land given to the church at the initial stage were either "evil forests" or "evil lands" where corpses of "wicked" people were buried or deposited. St. Joseph's Catholic Church land was not an exception. The whole area was given to the church but there was a little portion reserved for the clan's shrine dedicated to Ukana Offot-Awa Itam—the clan's deity. Chief Essien Ibanga was the chief of Anua at the time. He was a contemporary of Chief Nyong Essien of Southern Uruan. As a chief, Nyong Essien opposed the "deprivation of powers" of Ekpo, so did Chief Essien Ibanga oppose the destruction of the clan's shrine in front of the church.

The shrine was used for sacrifices. Other rites were also carried out there. There were constantly blood of animals, chickens feathers, heads of cocks, and skulls of various animals that were consumed or sacrificed, mashed yams, earthenware pots, carved items, some pieces of cloth stained with blood, fresh palm fronds tied around, and many other items were a constant feature at the entrance to the church. The sight was dirty and intimidating.

When Bishop Ekandem was posted there in 1954, he sought for a way of removing the shrine as quickly as possible. He pleaded with the people through the powerful Chief Essien Ibanga to transfer the shrine to another location since they voluntarily donated the land. The chief and the traditional adherents refused. The bishop did not give up, neither did he carry out his intention immediately. The bishop resorted to a dialogue, but when he realized that the dialogue met a stalemate and there was no fruitful outcome, he changed his strategy. He decided to embark on prayer for conversion, said like the "Prayer for Nigeria in Distress" after Holy Communion. Meanwhile, there was a station Catechist named Jerome from the village who used to take to his heels as soon as he approached the shrine. Jerome would never stop until he reached the church. The traditionalists never ceased sacrificing there regularly. Whether the race of Jerome the catechist was a result of fright or not wanting to set his eyes, there is another part of the story. Bishop Dominic said, "The scene was an eyesore."[436]

The prayer period was intensified, and it was carried out in the form of a retreat. It took place for two weeks. At the end of the retreat, the bishop told the congregation to come with working implements early on Saturday morning. He said, "I told the people to clear the place, uproot the trees, and level everything. The little pond was to be filled with red laterite or the red soil embedded under the black humus soil and the foundation of the Marian shrine was to commence immediately." Sisters Unah and Immaculata Offiong, both of the Handmaids Congregation, mentioned they were among the schoolgirls[437] that carried sand for the work at that time. On that same day, the foundation of the statue of Our Lady was laid and the statue installed.

F. His Internal Battles

The waves of the shock of destruction rose higher and hostilities ensued, but the Christians overcame all with prayer and silent resistance. Bishop Dominic said, "The shrine was guarded day and night until all the hostilities had a gradual death." At the end, the courage, the perseverance, and the strong and determined will of the prince-prelate prevailed. During the whole turmoil, his prayer life became greatly intensified.

a. His Battles in the Diocese and in the Presbyterium

The years between 1976 and 1978 saw Bishop Dominic Ekandem going through a very great turbulence in his life as the chief shepherd of the flock. The first major battle in the diocese began with the announcement of Bishop Ephraim Obot who was the auxiliary bishop of Ikot Ekpene Diocese as the substantive and first bishop of Idah Diocese in the then Benue State until another creation of states that caused Idah to be in Kogi State. The internal crisis and battle first started from the home front in resistance of the said transfer. Some priests grouped themselves and mobilized as many men and women as possible to put up a formidable resistance. They formed a pressure group that fronted women as a sympathetically concerned group with the supposed concern for the diocese and the bishop at heart. The *tripartite group* of the revolutionary three priests that formed the core of the events responsible for so much carnage lured the innocent women and mothers to carry placards protesting the move of the CBCN to transfer the auxiliary bishop of Ikot Ekpene, Bishop Ephraim Silas Obot, to Idah. The triad was constituted thus: the senior priest, the middle-aged, and the youngest. These three organized the demonstrations protests on the internal and external fronts. Most of the letters sent to Rome had fictitious names that could not be identified. Some bore women's names that purported to be the signatories. Day had turned to darkness and darkness into light for the center could no longer hold since all the meetings were carried out clandestinely and late into the night. Here the Hebrew greeting of Good Night, *Layillah Tob*, properly fitted the upturning and upsetting of events.

The situation simply encouraged Bishop Ekandem to become more prayerful and spend more and more time in the chapel in front of the Blessed Sacrament worshipping him while turning his eyes from time to time to the Cross from which his motto *In Cruce Salus* was derived. The following underscores the enormity of the protest and the destructive power it wielded like earthquake of great magnitude that is both frightful and mortalistic in nature. It gained the strength of an avalanche with the accompanying driving force down the slope like the melting ice in a glacial region. The reporter of the *Nigerian Chronicle*, a daily newspaper of Cross River State at the time, reported thus:

b. Women Oppose Bishop's Transfer![438]

The transfer of an indigenous Bishop has generated a rift in Ikot Ekpene diocese of the Roman Catholic Church. The entire women members of the Diocese, which is one of the largest in Nigeria, have protested against posting of their only indigenous Bishop, the Rt. Revd. Ephraim Silas Obot to the newly created Idah Diocese in Kwara state.

Bishop Obot was until his posting the auxiliary bishop of Ikot Ekpene Diocese and an assistant to Dominic Cardinal Ekandem [sic].

The women matched on a meeting to the Diocesan pastoral council last weekend where the cardinal and other dignitaries of the church sat and frowned bitterly at the transfer. They said the move was at variance with the indigenization policy of the church.

In addition, they expressed surprise at the withdrawal of the bishop who was direct assistant of Cardinal Ekanem [sic]. The women argued that already the Cardinal has great responsibilities as a member of the College of Cardinals and that he should not be bogged down with the petty diocesan administration, which was handled for him by Bishop Obot.

They pleaded that considering the load on the Cardinal's shoulder; Bishop Obot should be left to administer Ikot Ekpene Diocese, the problems of which he as a native priest is very able to tackle.

The traditional rulers in the area have received the transfer news with dismay and one of them whom our correspondent spoke with said that he suspected some political intrigue in the transfer. It is gathered that series of meetings have been going on among Christians in the area that could bring about an upheaval in the Church, which has already lost a good number to reformist denominations.

Indigenous priest from the area have kept sealed lips over the issue. Bishop Obot himself has refused to be drawn in but insiders say "the posting was news to the bishop himself" a meeting last week called at the instance [Sic] of the Diocesan council to arrange a send- off party for the bishop broke in confusion. A respected layman in the church told us "we expect Rome will do something to rescind this decision immediately in the interest of continued peace of the Catholic Church in Ikot Ekpene.

The upheaval had, at its base, ethnicity as a fundamental structure that eluded the untrained and uncouth eye. While advocating nontransfer of the bishop, it demanded the removal of Cardinal Ekandem from Ikot Ekpene Diocesan see. It was complicated and messy at the same time. The motto of the cardinal is widely pronounced in these upheavals. It was the road of thorns; he had started even from the imprisonment of the father when he got the prospectus for the minor seminary, and it trailed him through the priesthood, episcopacy, and cardinalate. The rough road he had chosen from the beginning, the road of the Cross that he had trodden ab initio had to pass through the various stages of the Passion, Calvary, reach the grave, and rise on the third day in order to witness the salvation and the crown. *In Cruce Salus* could not but hold sway both for emphasis and for realism. The idea of the transfer of Bishop Obot provoked crisis upon crisis, and everyone felt it either powerfully or slightly in the diocese of Ikot Ekpene and ostensibly throughout the entire nation. The transfer was transcultural. All the bishops and administrators of dioceses at the time were aware of. Those who read the news in the newspaper could not be aware of it too. Darkness had started descending, but Christ had promised that the gates of hell will never prevail against his church (Cf. Matt. 16:18 ff).

c. The Crisis over Bishop's Transfer[439]

Time there was when Church order was never questioned. "What is done on earth" was seen as having automatic blessing of heaven.

In the Catholic Church the infallibility of the Pope was not in doubt. But "time changes everything." And the Roman Catholic has seen quite a barrage of changes. Here the word "Roman" no more holds since the idea of indigenisation got into the church. It is now the catholic church of Nigeria. The indigenisation policy of the church first saw an end to Latin, the traditional language of saying mass.

English, the working medium in Nigeria has already given way for the celebration of the mass [sic] in the vernacular.

Time there was when Irish priest [sic] served as missionaries here. There were western world. They rode around on TRIUMPH motorcycle, and later on Volkswagen cars, ministering unto us in the "bush stations."

The only dress they could be identified with was the Sutan[440] [sic] and at times people thought they were banned from dressing like the rest of human beings. They kept their tea times and observed launch, siesta and dinner even while in the "bush" these too, have changed. In answer to the call for indigenization, sons of the soil are now priests among the flock. Unlike in the past when expatriate priests could hardly be consulted except during office hours or when "bush tour"; native priest can be met anytime, anywhere. Hardly do they have a nap at daytime (not to talk of making it a rigid schedule) because familiar as the people are with their priests sons, they feel free to wake them up from sleep when there is a problem.[441]

While it still holds true that "the prophet has no honour before his people," native priests are more committed to their people and will minister to them not only in things of the soul but in those of the body. The idea of indigenisation in the Church, needless to say is paying off."[442]

One very significant change on the Church is the attitude of church-goers. With the Catholic Church, there has been a growing urge among the laity to be brought closer to what happens in the institution. There was a time when priests, low and high, made decisions affecting the faithful and just hand them down from a pulpit during a Sunday Service. But these days there are consultations from the level of the Parish. And where this is not done even in cases where the high Clergy or Rome seemed to have the prerogative, there is the anxiety to know how and why.

This leads to an examination of the reactions that followed the transfer of Rev. Dr. Ephraim Silas Obot, Auxiliary Bishop of Ikot Ekpene, to the newly created diocese of Idah in Benue State.

Reactions came both from Ikot Ekpene, his home Diocese and from Idah. Both reactions were negative. The women of Ikot Ekpene protested over the transfer, saying it was unprecedented and politically motivated. They wanted their son to stay with them.[443] In Idah, laymen in the Diocese protested and said the imposition of the Bishop on them was arbitrary and unprecedented.

The installation of the Bishop of Idah scheduled for March 12 was put off. The dust raised was still very much in the air when Bishop Obot paid a private visit there a few weeks after the appointment was announced.

Looking first at the protest from Ikot Ekpene, one will be able to understand why the women reacted the way they did. No mother who likes her son will fail to be moved if he sets out on a distant journey. The women looked round and saw that their only indigenous Bishop was asked to leave, and they were moved. And like the mother whose only child died in a hospital's children's ward where other children struggled to live or recover, they asked why it should be theirs and not another's?

Apart from expatriate Bishops serving in some Diocese, every Indigenous Bishop is installed for his native Diocese. Perhaps because of the growing awareness in the Church the women were able to appreciate this, they were also able to know that those expatriate Bishops serving in

Nigeria came to the Country as missionary priests. The expatriate priests excelled in their jobs and were appointed and installed Bishops for the Dioceses in which they worked.

And by the word "installation," it is clear the Bishop is made for a Diocese where he will work and from where he will retire or die.

From Idah, the people saw the appointment as arbitrary. This is another way of saying that their opinion should have been sought, not just to ascertain if they would be able to work with Bishop Obot but to discuss the issue of appointment of a native priest from Idah as a Bishop.

Idah, until recently, was part of Lokoja Diocese, which is in Kwara State (Idah is in Benue State). When the new Diocese was created, the people must have seen this as a sure way to their having an indigenous Bishop.

And any more moves (as that of the appointment of Bishop Obot) to make them not realise this aspiration now was bound to evoke negative reaction.

To consider how "unprecedented" the appointment looked, there is a need to make a roll call of Bishops in Nigeria (see box). The trend of consecrating a Bishop and installing him in his home Diocese is the same the world over. The expatriate bishops were not posted from their homes after consecration, but they graduated from priests in Dioceses they are now serving.

At the level of a Bishop, it sounds unfair to want a Nigerian clergy to pack and go on postings [sic] to a place he will [have to] speak through an interpreter or learn a new language. This will alienate the flock from the Shepherd—which is part of [what] the indigenisation of the universal Church should be out to contain. In an age when the Catholic Church is losing large numbers to splinter denominations (and through acquiring new converts) everything must be done to generate a sense of belonging in the faithful.

Protests on issues like the Bishop's transfer is not likely to make the Catholic Church a democratic institution, where the laity and the clergy sit up and decide on the running of the Church. Perhaps it will eventually happen but it is very far fetched [very unlikely to happen]. Most of the problems that came up would never have occurred if the communication gap between the shepherd and the flock had been bridged.[444]

There are Laity Councils at Parish and Diocesan levels but in most cases these are forums for discussing the fixing of levies and arranging of bazaars and receptions. The clergy is learned, but the laity in their leaders and representative should be made more involved.

BISHOPS — DIOCESES[445]

RT. REV. (DR.) T. MCGUETHRICK (EXPATRIATE) — ABAKALIKI
RT. REV. P. E. EKPU — BENIN
RT. REV. B. D. USANGA — CALABAR RT. REV. M. O.
FAGUN — EKITI RT. REV. MSGR M.
ENEJA — ENUGU
RT. REV. (DR.) A. JOB — IBADAN
RT. REV. A. S. SANUSI — IJEBU-ODE
DOMINIC CARDINAL EKANDEM — IKOT EKPENE RT. REV.
(DR.) A. GBUJI — ISSELE UKWU
RT. REV. G. G. GANAKA — JOS
MOST REV. (DR.) P. JATAU — KADUNA
MOST REV. (DR.) A. O. OKOGIE — LAGOS
RT. REV. A. O. MAKOZI — LOKOJA
RT. REV. DONAL J. MURRAY — MAKURDI
RT. REV. J. E. UKPO — OGOJA
RT. REV. F. F. ALONGE — ONDO
MOST REV. (DR.) FRANCIS ARINZE — ONITSHA
RT. REV. (DR.) M. O. UNEGBU — OWERRI
RT. REV. E. S. OBOT — IDAH
RT. REV. MSGR. E. FITZGIBBON (EXPATRIATE) — PORT HARCOURT
RT. REV. M. J. DEMPSEY (EXPATRIATE) — SOKOTO
RT. REV. L. O. NWAEZEPU — WARRI
RT. REV. (DR.) P. F. SHEEHAN (EXPATRIATE) — YOLA
RT. REV. (DR.) J. T. K. COTTER (EXPATRIATE) — MAIDUGURI

The reporter gave the impression of having had an extensive survey on the issue and an impartial one, but in actual fact, he took sides when he gave the placements and territorial jurisdictions of each of the ordinaries connecting it with language and language interpretation through an interpreter or learn a new language. He saw it as being totally strange and unprecedented. He used the traditional viewpoint that he believed Rome would soon do something to forestall the upheaval that was threatening the diocese.

The priests did not refute what was published probably because those who fomented the trouble were hiding under the cloak of the women with serious anonymity but were seriously stirring the pot in the background. The women argued that the cardinal was saddled with great responsibilities, hence the necessity of having Bishop Obot, his auxiliary, to continue with the day-to- day administration of the diocese as he was wont to in the absence of the cardinal while decrying and objecting to the transfer of the auxiliary bishop.

d.   The Plot to Remove Dominic Cardinal Ekandem as Bishop of Ikot Ekpene Diocese

The dramatis personae of the plot were garbed like the Boko Haram (now in 2015) menace plaguing Nigeria with an invisible influence that causes untold hardship for the citizens of the country. Their supporters know them, and the members of the group know themselves; but they prefer to remain anonymous and faceless with a relentless effort of destabilization, anarchy, and an unfulfilled hope of overthrowing the government with wanton impunity by mass destruction of life and property without mercy and without any rational thought. Could it be that pursuing their objective, they receive support from within and coerce the nonconformists to supporting them and paying a minimum contribution of at least ten million (N10m) Naira monthly either from states or from sympathetic individuals to further their course?

What of their affiliation with Al Qaeda group, Islamic State of Iraq and Syria (ISIS), or Islamic State of Iraq and the Levant (ISIL), and some Arabic enthusiasts that give them an international link and greater sense of power? Could it be that Boko Haram flourished during the reign of President Jonathan because some senior army officers adopted the habit of releasing the Boko Haram members caught and imprisoned while paying the entire populace with disfavor to and strangling the national army? Could it be that they were aiming at preserving their numbers? Or making them unrestricted? Or making the country ungovernable? Could it be that the Muslim Brotherhood and the Organisation of Islamic Cooperation (OIC) were sympathetic to the terrorists' group by giving them regular funding or arms or training of personnel in the various arts of bombing and causing mayhem with minimum effort?

The anonymous group of clergy that supported and even acted as vanguards for these nocturnal activities, were they fronting a very plausible motive and argument to the unlearned and the simple to win sympathy? Could it be that this method was adopted to lure the Women's Organisation, the very group that was founded by the cardinal to fight against him? The women fought with the innocence of the lamb while being manipulated by wolves in sheep's clothing (Matt. 7:15). This is what Nigerians colloquially call *dog eats dog*. Jesus had said that a man's enemies are those of his own household (Matt. 10:46).

The group mobilized the Catholic Women's Organisation and their officials on their day of meeting to see that they used the women as cosignatories to the fact that they did not want Bishop Ekandem to be the bishop of Ikot Ekpene anymore. One of the women who was a great loyalist to the faction decided to present a plain sheet of paper to the women to write their names with the announcement that it was a rough sheet of attendance. The women were requested to write their names and sign. This was done, but the list was later given to the faction of priests' opposition to the bishop's peaceful service in Ikot Ekpene. The list was attached to a letter written to Rome that was to decide the case at the meeting that Bishop Ekandem was to attend.

God always writes straight on crooked lines. Nothing is impossible with him. He provided a way out of the quicksand of notoriety and criticism into which Cardinal Ekandem was to jump unconsciously in Rome, the headquarters of Christendom and Catholicism. Cardinal Ekandem could have returned to Ikot Ekpene to pack his things, bag, and baggage, perhaps flee like Prophet Ezekiel who was asked to escape through a hole in the wall while covering his face out of shame. Prophet Ezekiel, echoing the word of the Lord to him, says:

> The word of Yahweh was addressed to me as follows, "Son
> of man you are living with that set of rebels who have eyes

but never see, ears and never hear, for they are a set of rebels. You son of man, pack an exile's bundle and emigrate by daylight when they can see you, emigrate from where you are to somewhere else while they watch You will pack your baggage like an exile's bundle by daylight for them to see, and leave like an exile in the evening, making sure that they are looking. As they watch, make a hole in the wall, and go out through it. As they watch, you will shoulder your pack and go out into the dark; you will cover your face, so that you cannot see the country since I have made you a symbol for the house of Israel. (Ezk. 12:1–6)

With a plot that involved the grassroots, the situation would have been catastrophic and almost insurmountable, but God provided a way out. The Psalmist says, "When Yahweh brought Zion's captives home, at first it seemed like a dream; then our mouths filled with laughter and our lips with song" (Ps. 126:1–2). On the day of the meeting, he arrived early enough. As the cardinals interacted with one another, one of them called the attention of the bishop of Ikot Ekpene and showed him the agenda, and Ikot Ekpene's case formed part of the agenda. The cardinal in question was also very generous to indicate to Dominic Cardinal Ekandem the petition from his diocese and asked him if he could not find at least one person to refute the case; he said he could. Bishop Ekandem was permitted to photocopy the petition against him together with the names of the women and their signatures that featured in the petition.

Cardinal Ekandem took the next available flight that same night and arrived the following morning before finding his way to Ikot Ekpene, the see of the diocese. There is no gainsaying the fact that he must have prayed all through the flight, calling on our Blessed Mother to help him as he was very fund of her and devoted to her through the Holy Rosary. With the psalmist, he could have reechoed, "God, you have rejected us, broken us; You have been angry, come back to us! You have made the earth tremble, torn it apart; now mend the rifts, it is tottering still! You have allowed your people to suffer, to drink a wine that makes us reel. Hoist the standard to rally those who fear you, to put them out of range of bow and arrow, to bring rescue to those you love, save with your right hand and answer us!" (Ps. 60:3–7).

He started working to disentangle the ropes in a state of exhaustion, anxiety, and worry of returning in time for the meeting in Rome. Despite all these happenings, he worked assiduously with a concerted effort in the company of a very prominent Catholic Men's Organisation (CMO), who was one of the stalwarts of the diocese. His wife was very influential in the Catholic Women's Organisation (CWO) too. The name of that CWO member had been inserted and a forged signature appended. When she saw the list, she shuddered and shouted that she was not involved. She was not even present at the meeting, but she was made to be a cosignatory. He used that point as a basis of refuting the claim that all the women undersigned had willingly asked the cardinal to be relieved of his office, duty, and position after having toiled in the diocese for about eighteen years as a bishop. Probably, the name of the CWO officer was inserted to give credibility or to induce others to feel relaxed to write and sign as long as this other officer had written her name and signed it.

The CMO official turned round and asked the wife why she had to join those who petitioned against the bishop. The CWO officer expressed surprise and narrated how the procedure for obtaining the names and signatures took place. She wrote what she knew and gave it as an inclusion to that of the husband, and Bishop Ekandem took off that evening and arrived in Rome in preparation for his defense and to attend the meeting. The CMO official was one of those stalwarts who defended Bishop Ekandem and stood by him till he went to Abuja as Cardinal Ekandem and retired and died there.

Since he was a man of unalloyed loyalty to authority, he never relaxed in his obedience and loyalty to the succeeding prelate. The same tenacity of purpose and singularity of devotion garnished with transparency and truthfulness singled him out among equals. Cardinal Ekandem was on the verge of being thrown out with ignominy but for the timely intervention of his cardinal friend who called his attention. Thanks to Pope Paul VI who created him in consistory as a cardinal. It is equally a meraviglia Dei, the wonderful work of God, who made it possible for him to attend that meeting. Otherwise, he would only have received a letter inviting him to Rome to answer some questions or receive a delegation to come and investigate the situation as a step to relinquishing his position as the ordinary of the diocese. God, who scrutinizes everything, saw the situation ahead of time (Cf.

Ps. 139), rescued, and saved him ahead of time. The internal crisis extended even to health facilities of the diocese and left a big mark there too.

G. Dispute about Abak Hospital Land

One of the renowned members of the diocese categorically said that he was one of those who cleared the site for Mercy Hospital. The people enthusiastically voluntarily and engaged themselves in that work since they wanted the hospital to be established there. First and foremost, the proximity of the hospital to the people, the provision of services, and the attention that the patients would have gave a great sense of satisfaction to the people. That circumstance caused the people to be greatly frustrated when some people decided to sue Bishop Dominic Ekandem, the Catholic Diocese of Ikot Ekpene, and the Health Management Committee (HMC) of Mercy Hospital to court, praying the court to stop or withhold the official opening and commissioning of the hospital. Some members of the church took the summons to the bishop. He questioned in his usual manner if a prominent member of the area like Ete Idung had seen it, and they said no; he immediately ordered them to go and show it to him. The summons was taken to the diocesan council for action. He collected it and went back to Bishop Ekandem who asked what they thought of it. The bishop was told not to bother about it that the council would take care of it. The bishop said that he did not want to say anything because even though his father used to hold court in the village and his clan, he had never accompanied him nor had any person ever sued him either to village court or clan or district court. But with the summons, he would go to court; and the moment he returned from the court, no stone of the hospital would be left on another, for the buildings would be totally demolished.

Having heard Ete Idung, the bishop was assured what they were intending to accomplish and added that the bishop should hold his peace. He went to court as scheduled on the appointed day. The case against the three juridical persons was called up; the accusation was read. Ete Idung stood up and presented himself as the representative of all three. On realizing that one person represented the three juridical[446] persons addressed in the case, the magistrate said that the case was adjourned until after the official opening of the hospital before the proceedings would take place again.

After the official opening of the hospital, the case was not recalled nor the court reconvened for that purpose. In the court, the only way that Ete Idung defended the bishop and the other codefendants was to be present in court and assert that he was the representative of the three entities. Ete Idung who went to the court and stood in as a defendant in the cases on behalf of the three defendants took that bold step because of his love for the church coupled with the fact of his being a convinced Catholic and a prominent member of the diocesan pastoral council. What motivated the charge and summons was the greed of some people who wanted to claim the Abak Hospital land for their use. For that reason, they sued the Catholic bishop, the diocese of Ikot Ekpene and the Hospital Management Committee (HMC) to claim damages.

The sole defendant told the plaintiffs who came en masse that if they had any case, they should face him since he represented the three defendants. To their utter dismay and chagrin, the case was dismissed, and the accused representing the three legal entities was discharged and acquitted. It is to be noticed that the land issue in Abak Hospital has become a recurrent issue and almost a perennial problem leading to disputes, unlawful occupation of quarters not destined for some of those who go to occupy them, molestation of some of the consecrated persons who work there, shifting the boundaries, causing unnecessary disputes within the hospital, drumming up conflict between the village heads and chiefs of the area and other traditional rulers. Whether some powerful men or chiefs are behind the youth who are used to foment troubles are there or not in recent times, the emphasis has shifted to making the hospital government owned.

Some of the people who wanted to benefit excessively from the hospital want the government to take the hospital so that they could benefit without working as hard as they would have and should have done in a mission setting. Various forms of interests groups and pressure groups surge up, but the hospital is still functioning although not to its full capacity and glory. It appears that each change of leadership brings in new troubles, probably hoping that the new bishop would easily be influenced or bent to do what he should not have done if he had stayed a little longer. That called for caution and circumspection. The interesting fact is that since Dominic, later the cardinal, was soft-spoken and not easily irritated, he did not give up easily, but was very resilient in nature; much was not heard from him.

He suffered in silence like a lamb led to the slaughterhouse, he opened not his mouth (Is. 53:7).

Like Mary and Joseph when they found the child Jesus after three days in the midst of the doctors questioning and answering questions, not much was heard from him. It recalls the time he was to do probation for three years when normally it was accomplished in two years, that silent period schooled him in the providence of God, likewise total dependence on him. He shared freely when he entered the presence of the divine Lord; otherwise, he became silent and spoke less. At a certain stage, he felt like Christ on the Cross, Eli, Eli, lama sabch-thá ni? My God, My God, why have you forsaken me? (Mt. 27: 47) He was like Padre Pio who, three months (on June 4, 1918) before he received the stigmata, felt that God had totally abandoned him. He complained while appealing to Padre Benedetto, his spiritual director to come to his rescue saying, "Tears are my daily bread. I have gone astray and have lost you, but shall I find you again? Or have I lost you forever? Have you condemned me to live for all eternity far from your countenance? My Supreme Good, where are you? I no longer know you or find you. My God, my God, why have you forsaken me?"[447] Padre Pio did not know that he was undergoing a serious *dark night, transports of love, divine touches, strokes and wounds of love, transverberation and stigmatization,*[448] and powerful ascent of the mountain of God's love where he experienced a piercing through with a fiery dart that opened up on September 20, 1918, with the stigmata that attracted terrible pains as if he were pierced with a very sharp object. Cardinal Ekandem did not receive any stigmata, but he surely experienced hanging on the Cross with Jesus for the sake of the same flock of God. There are different types of sufferings. His suffering was that of betrayal by his close associates who, like Judas who betrayed Jesus with a kiss (Lk. 22:48), betrayed the cardinal with smile and soft words. That was a bitter experience. He lived through it like his Master, Christ.

It was good that Ete Idung and his group stemmed the tide of invasion and suing to court without Bishop Ekandem having to appear in court as was intended. Had he gone, it is most probable that Mercy Hospital, Abak would never have seen the light of day. Whatever was there could have been pulled down for the sake of those who were disputing the authenticity and liberty of using the land.

The uncountable number of patients treated in the eye clinic with the aid of specialists that came from Germany through the intervention of Msgr. Kenneth Enang would never have benefited from those services, not to mention the various patients that availed of the proximity of the hospital and visited for medical treatments, operations, or admissions as the needs arose. It served in that axis with the presence of the Handmaids of the Holy Child Jesus what St. Luke's Hospital, Anua served in the hands of the Medical Missionaries of Mary.

The internal battles of Cardinal Ekandem were so numerous that if all were to be penned, the prominence of *In Cruce Salus* might indirectly be obfuscated. Each of the cases, both the written ones and unwritten ones, only point to the fact that "No Cross, No Crown" as Bishop Michael Eneja of Enugu had his episcopal motto. To gain the crown, there must be total renunciation of self as well as interests while subsuming the sufferings in the sufferings of Christ in order to win the crown by experiencing salvation.

Chapter Sixteen

AD ASTRA PER ARDUA (THROUGH DIFFICULTY TO THE STARS)

Some Selected Sermons and Pastoral Letters

*Ideas become atmosphere; books beget Zeitgeist. The daily
press carries no footnotes but it has a philosophy of life,
which the gullible follow, and the wise men recognize.*

—Fulton J. Sheen

THE MATERIALS THAT will be handled here are very much in line with the title of this chapter. One of those topics is "Toward a Viable and Self-Reliant Church." The title of this booklet is focused on the church in Africa, especially in Nigeria. The Catholic Church in the vision of His Eminence should not aim at being a receiving church only, she ought to grow and become a giving church. This cannot occur without viability and reliability. There has to be some sense of self-sufficiency in order to be self-reliant. The self-reliance of the African church should not end only on the material level but should also extend to the spiritual level. Ultimately, this accounts for the conception and birth of the National Missionary Seminary and the Missionaries of St. Paul. Both were bred and born in Nigeria before extending to other countries and continents of the world.

The sermons, speeches, and pastoral letters of Cardinal Ekandem are revelations of his thoughts and personality likewise the practical expression of his mind-set concerning the theological virtues. From his conversations with those who were close to him and his insights, it can be seen that the processes of exercising them were never easy. They were strewn with thorns and thistles. Sometimes great sacrifices and self-discipline were necessary to make headway. That applies to both individuals and states or nations as the case may be. The motto of his episcopal ordination can be seen reflected in his homilies, exhortations, and pastoral letters. There can be no crown if there is no cross, and there can be no salvation if there is no cross. In other words, *In Cruce Salus*, In the Cross Is Salvation. To enjoy the beauty of the roses by cutting it, one must be ready to experience the pain of the thorns.

His speeches and sermons, homilies, colloquies, pastoral letters were geared toward production or stimulation of active faith in the living God and in his creatures, the human beings. The living faith spoken of was to manifest itself in good works and personal responsibility toward the church. As a man ahead of his time he was anxiously dedicated to promoting the interest of his brethren so that all who belong to the people of God and are consequently endowed with Christian dignity may through, their free and well-ordered efforts toward a common goal, attain to salvation (L. G. 18).

In his speeches or writings, he adopted the style of moving from the known to the unknown. In some occasions, he started with the universal and went down to the particular. Often, he used either the social or the cultural context to convey his message. Sometimes he used an event in the church to begin his preaching or speech, but he was always ready to deliver the message he had in mind. His moral courage expressed itself in his relationship with people. He spoke persuasively and convincingly to make his audience see the need for action, the bottom-line was conversion of mentality and the whole person for proper orientation.

A.   Toward a Viable and Self-Reliant Church[449]

The title as it stands is self-demonstrative. The desire to see the African Church stand on her own, strong, firm, and self-reliant instead of leaning constantly on outside help leads the African Church to maturity. It is that financial maturity as well as spiritual maturity that he envisaged. To accomplish this, he proposed various ways that the aim could be realized even at the grassroots level. Of course, when the grass root is firm and self-reliant, great heights could be reached. A great deal can be accomplished and even unimaginable things for love of the Lord. The African community, which is very religious, resembles the Jewish community, which worked for the good of the community and supported its leaders. The African community also supported its traditional priests and priests-chiefs. Both communities find fulfilment in the church. It is then the place of the members of the church as Africans to exercise their co-responsibility by supporting its leaders in the church, clergy, and religious alike in order to make the church self-reliant. The practical way in which they can support the church is through annual collection, annual harvest festival, seminary collection, supporting the aspirants to the sisterhood as well as the catechists.

The priest as a minister of God is generous in his services. The members of the church need to reciprocate this generous gesture as well by being generous themselves. The example of the widow who gave all she had is given to encourage generosity even beyond the frontiers of family, parish, and even diocese since the church is universal.[450] The priests need to know that Christ is the model; consequently, they should not live above their means or become wasteful in their expenses. They should be contented with their basic needs since the church does not try to build on the image of wealth but uses all the good things of the world to build up God's kingdom.

Generally, he conceives the church as a means of communication that works well whenever a member contributes his or her own quota.

B.   The Church in the Rise of Nigeria[451]

As one of the oldest members of the Nigerian hierarchy and as a person of great experience concerning the early beginnings of the seminary at the time, Cardinal Ekandem as the ordinary of Ikot Ekpene was asked to deliver the sermon. He willingly took up the challenge as an alumnus and did justice to it. After the introduction and greetings that followed his normal pattern, he began his sermon with the glory of the nation pointing out the glory in terms of economic boom demonstrated in the areas of educational success, medical progress, and political stability. During the 1973–1974 federal budget broadcast, he quoted the head of state and commander of the Nigerian Armed Forces, Gen. Yakubu Gowon as attributing the secret of the nation's success to God. He did not trust in his military prowess or in his ingenuity or the various decrees rolled out as normally done during any military regime but in God. This underlined the fact that God was still in control.

He pointed out that the instrument of the nation's success and development was the church. The missionaries' effort in education especially during the time of Bishop Joseph Shanahan of Southern Nigeria brought in great contribution that led to the progress of the nation. Many of those trained by the missionaries later occupied various positions in the nation and even helped foster unity and growth although ethnic division was sometimes greatly exaggerated. The clergy, the product of the missionaries' education who were both theologians and philosophers, helped the faithful have an authentic faith since the faithful do not like adulterated faith. Traditional values especially community life which is very much African is to be carefully preserved since it can lead to ecclesial and national unity. The traditional values of love and respect of elders should lead to the respect of the church's magisterium. Respect for life should lead the African theologians to defend the simple and unprotected Nigerians against birth control and abortion. This was the time that many were advocating for birth control and abortion to be passed into law in the nation and the church fought seriously against it by organizing rallies, seminars, and symposia against such moves.

He praised the laity for their unique contribution toward the foundation and building up of the church as catechists, as those who received the missionaries, by giving their children to become priests, sisters, and brothers for the service of the church. He then appealed passionately to them that since they helped in such a marvelous way they should go on financially to support the church in order to become self-reliant. He mentioned that from time to time, the government makes encouraging remarks about the church, gives civic reception and titles to the church dignitaries by the state; the church appreciates that. The state was challenged to do more since she has seen and enjoyed the contributions of the church.

He then asked, "What practical contributions is the state offering as a form of encouragement?" He went further to posit that the state has not given the desired help she is supposed to give to the church, why? Because no subsidy is given to the institutions where the clergy are neither trained nor the clerical students and their professors given any financial assistance. He calls it a poser for the government. The challenge thrown to the state is like inviting somebody for a duel, which, tactically, the state decided to adopt a tacit situation of not responding nor saying anything and allowed the situation to die naturally. What he proposed was nothing new. It used to be the living experience of the church when the church was under the missionaries who influenced many issues in the country and who were able to dialogue with men of same mind from their various European or American partners that occupied the political scenes.

The cardinal was not contented inviting the state to a duel but went further to suggest a symbiotic relationship covering mostly the financial aspect of collaboration. Furthermore, he stressed that "since the church has helped the state to grow, the state should also help the church to grow." What is advocated here is mutual understanding and friendly relationship. He was not asking for too much but for the basic right and sense of justice. He was not begging but simply conscientizing the state to wake up to her responsibility instead of adopting an ostrich posture. He defended the church against media publications that the church has failed because a member of the clergy has made a mistake that such is not correct. Jesus Christ chose twelve apostles after a whole night's prayer, but that did not make Judas not to fall off. Such blanket condemnation should not take place. Any person, in an attempt to help another, should be pitied and prayed for instead of condemnation and blaming the whole church as if the church were an individual. The church is not an individual. She is the Body of Christ. He concluded his sermon by saying that the future of Nigeria and that of the church was marked by unlimited possibilities of development and growth. He prayed that the objectives planned for be achieved. He exhorted all present that a lively presence through a fraternal

Christian life of faith in God and the goodwill of fellow Nigerian citizens would help Nigeria to grow and develop as a nation and as a church—the people whose God is the Lord.

Here he greatly demonstrated his optimistic spirit that would always overcome evil no matter the circumstances.

C. True Spiritual Leadership—A Vital Contribution to Nation Building[452]

This is the title of the sermon delivered on December 5, 1976, at the launching of Bigard Memorial Seminary, Faculty of Philosophy Ikot Ekpene, now called St. Joseph Major Seminary Ikot Ekpene, Akwa Ibom State, Nigeria.

He started in his usual way by welcoming the various categories of people that attended the celebration, remarking in a special way Most Rev. Jerome Prigione, the papal pro-nuncio's presence, as the special representative of the of the pope. He proceeded to highlight the economic prosperity of the Nigerian nation and how blessed she is with regard to mineral resources. The wealth has helped Nigeria in various developmental, educational, and medical situations. The educational program is limited to some. Seminarians are excluded, but the government needs to reconsider the situation. The unique contribution of the church is through her priests and religious since they provide above all the spiritual leadership needed for the country. The church is even in a position to do more apart from the initial contribution to supply personnel of indigenous clergy for the nation's service, hence the necessity of Nigerians training Nigerian clergy and religious.

Stephanie and Jean Bigard—mother and daughter of French origin whose contribution helped in erecting the first structures of the seminary in 1948—have given noble examples. Missio, a German catholic organization as at the time, made generous donations for the buildings, which were incomplete owing to inflation. There is no other place to turn to except the noble and generous Nigerian men and women. If these people and groups had got a name for themselves, why can Nigerians not do more to get a greater name for themselves? The gifts those who attended the launching brought would surely help to train the future spiritual leaders who will emerge from the little town of Ikot Ekpene.

i.   Beloved in Christ

An event that has brought us here today in such big numbers and involving many outstanding citizens from all the nine dioceses of the four states of Anambra, Imo, Rivers, and the Cross River must be a very significant event indeed. A church celebration in which the personal representative of His Holiness the pope, is the chief celebrant as in these solemn rites in which His Excellency the Most Reverend Jerome Prigione, titular archbishop of lauricum and personal representative of our Holy Father Pope Paul VI, is the principal celebrant, such a celebration is scheduled to commemorate an important event among us. He went on to appreciate the efforts of all who were present for the launching of the Ikot Ekpene Seminary, reflecting the difficulties many encountered to be at ceremony. He showed great appreciation.

While traveling to this place is easy for some, for others, in fact for very many, this has not been easy when we consider the physical strain of the long journey on bad roads, the expenses incurred, and many other inconveniences involved like the forgoing of other engagements. But despite these, you have not excused yourselves from coming to participate in these activities. That in itself is a contribution that has very much enriched this celebration, and I extend a very hearty welcome to you.

> Dignitaries of church and state
> My lords spiritual and temporal
> Officials of our governments,
> Chiefs and natural rulers, Men of profession,
>
> Noble citizens and friends,
> Specially invited guests,
> Staff and students of our various institutions,
> High and low
> To you all my patriotic countrymen
> I extend a hearty welcome

ii. Nigeria and Economic Prosperity

Singing our national anthem we pray that God may bless Nigeria with plenty of everything. Looking around now, we see that we are certainly being blessed with plenty of many things already. Our strong prayer now should be for wisdom to know how to use our wealth for the integral development of Nigeria, for the benefit of the small as well as the big, the poor as well the rich, and particularly for the spiritual as well as the temporal.

Massive programs of development bear testimony to the amazing wealth of Nigeria, our country, endless plans of road construction throughout the country, countrywide health scheme, and extensive programs of housing, improved air and sea communications, rural electrification and water projects, planned status of new townships, proposed new federal capital and construction of international stadium of Olympic size, all these give evidence of progress and prosperity.

iii. Seminarians as Useful Citizens Should Benefit from the National Wealth

And last month, notice was given of free education at all levels including university throughout the country. Yes, free education for Nigerians in institutions spaciously and solidly built with public funds and richly equipped campuses. We thank God for these blessings that Almighty God has poured on us through no effort of ours but through the natural resources. He has abundantly supplied to us. We pray that such continues to be the lot of our fortunate countrymen. But then what about this class of youth, our seminarians here, so intellectually active, so physically dynamic, and so morally balanced; are they Nigerians? Are they students? Will they be needed for national service, spiritual and temporal? Who provides for them? Is this a campus? Afterward, go around and have a close look and see things for yourselves; who is building up this campus? In what stage of the work are we now? These are the questions we have come to find answers for, and with that sympathy coming from our understanding of the real situation, we shall then settle down seriously, after this solemn and prayerful appeal to God for success in our endeavors, to bring help and relief to these selfless and most patriotic Nigeria youths who, through sheer miscalculation, are cut off from benefiting even in a fractional measure from our national treasury and natural resources.

As Nigerians, as students, and as institution for learning useful arts and science, these seminarians have some claim to our national budget. And those who realize the important contribution the church can make in the rise of any nation and has made to the rise of Nigeria so far come up to encourage her in the all-important work of training her priests.

iv. The Church's Unique Contribution Toward Nation-Building is through Her Priests and Religious

Here in Nigeria already, Nigerian priests are involved almost everywhere in national institutions of learning as teachers, including universities. They offer their services in national units like army chaplaincy. They are engaged in all-round social work and community development. Hence the head of state, Lieutenant General Obasanjo in his goodwill message to Nigerian bishops assembled in their national conference in Kaduna last September wrote:

> **"The church can play an important role in the social development of the nation if it produces the right caliber of priests who are disposed to offer disciplined, honest, dedicated, selfless, and patriotic leadership in their service."**

That is correct. That is what the church has already done to help Nigeria attain her present height, through her priests whose sterling qualities our head of state has so accurately summed up in his message.

Besides the initial and subsequent stages of our national development to which the church has enormously contributed, the church is even in a position to do more now by supplying a personnel of indigenous clergy for service to the nation, numerous in number, and continuous in production, since we are blessed with an abundance of vocations to the priesthood to the extent that the expansion of our existing seminary is found to be absolutely necessary.

v. Nigeria Must Now Face the Responsibility of Training her Priests and Religious

If we, your bishops, and we, your priests could go ahead with this work of expansion and future maintenance of the seminarians without bothering you in any way, we could have done it. As you yourselves can bear witness, we have offered our lives wholly and entirely in order to spread the kingdom of God, make the Gospel message effective by personal sacrifices, and render a dedicated service to the people. If we ourselves had material possessions to enable us carry on the ministry without requiring any assistance from you, we would have devoted all we have to the work and made no other demands from you except that of coming to receive the gift of faith.

This can be clearly shown from the fact that we contributed nothing in any way to the making of the expatriate priests, brothers, and sisters who are the pioneers of Christian civilization, development and progress in our country today; nor did we contribute to the building of the institutions where they received their training and were sufficiently cared for to be in a position to come out and teach us in this country.

vi. What Others Have Done for Us

And what is more, in order to start us off and put us on the road to self-sufficiency and self-reliance, the expatriate missionaries had to direct the financial resources from their own countries to ours. For instance, we are now talking of our seminary as Bigard Memorial Seminary. Why Bigard? Who is Bigard?

vii. Stephanie and Jean Bigard and the Birth of Bigard Memorial Seminary, Enugu

Our seminary is named after two French ladies: Stephanie Bigard and her daughter Jean Bigard. Realizing the importance and the usefulness of native priests in planting the faith and extending it in mission countries, these two ladies mother and daughter offered large sums of money for the education and training of native priests. It was part of that money that was used in building our seminary in Enugu in 1948. Therefore, in memory of Stephanie and Jean Bigard, the seminary is called Bigard Memorial Seminary, Enugu.

From 1951, Bigard Memorial Seminary has remained the training ground for native clergy; till now that great increase in the priestly vocations has necessitated the separation of the two houses of Bigard Memorial Seminary, leaving the theology campus in Enugu and bringing the new house of philosophy to Ikot Ekpene to form the philosophy campus.

viii. Missio and the Bigard Philosophy Campus Project

Here again we were encouraged to effect this necessary separation by Missio, a charitable Catholic German organization to which we appealed for help to solve accommodation problems. Based on the recommendation of the delegate whom Missio sent to study the situation, Missio decided to finance the extension of Enugu theology campus and the building of the new philosophy campus in Ikot Ekpene, with our cooperation. Accordingly, they voted the amount to be given to us. And if the amount had been released there, and then we might have gone far with the work before the arrival of hard times; but by the time we got through the conditions laid down by the Germans, inflation was upon us, with the result that hemmed in and obstructed with a thousand and one difficulties now, we have nowhere to go but to turn to you, our dear countrymen and women, to you our chiefs and rulers, to you our business men and women, to you our dear Nigerian people now that you are so well placed by our good and Heavenly Father who has caused Naira to fall freely like manna did for the Israelites of old.

ix.   A Poser for Nigeria

For why should the Nigerian youth of such rare and sterling qualities suffer from the want of necessary means of achieving their goals for the welfare of the whole nation in a forest or desert campus like the Bigard Philosophy Campus, as if their already voluntary self-denial and heroic sacrifices were not enough, while their counterpart with lesser dignity and less noble objectives are made to thrive in the midst of plenty, with a promise of more to come, in campuses that glitter with the splendor of earthly paradise. This is a question that our governments, federal and state, with their various departments of education and finance, will have to answer when they have time to settle down and face realities.

x. Special Appeal

Meanwhile, we your bishops, your brothers and friends, we your servants in the Lord beckon to you who have taken notice of us, to come forward and help us complete these buildings, which as you can see are all well begun. Come and help us to build up that fine body of the Catholic priesthood, which will not only continue to meet the demands of our government in bringing security and salvation to our nation but fulfill almost in every respect our Heavenly Father's will for our country. In making this call, I am confident of a great and substantial response because of the inspiration given to us and the wonderful example we have before us, of the two French ladies whose name has come to stay among us in Nigeria. If the French can secure a name for themselves in Nigeria through love, charity, and compassion for Nigerians, surely Nigerians can secure a lot more for themselves by the exercise of the self-same virtues here in their own fatherland.

In the same way on the foundation laid by the French mother and daughter of Nigerian priests and seminarians, the German Missio has erected these unfinished buildings into which our seminarians, almost three hundred of them already, have forced themselves, with almost a hundred more expected, when the institution reopens after Christmas. And who are the members of Missio—this German charitable organization that has undertaken to provide accommodation for the Nigerian students for the priesthood, for Nigerians, whose country is flowing with oil and adorned with mineral wealth. Those who have got the chance of reading the last issue of the leader where His Grace the Most Reverend Dr. Francis Arinze, our archbishop, has caused to be published some information about our German benefactors, to give us an idea of who make up this famous Missio that has decided to finance a project of this nature in our blessed country, have already learned about the condition of those who contribute to support us. From that information, you will see that the poor, the afflicted, and the bereaved, in fact the distressed, generally form the bulk of our benefactors. In which case, those of you who are not so badly affected can perhaps afford to do more with the spirit of patriotism that inspires to noble achievement at home at least, if not abroad.

However, it is very important to mention that it is with the whole-hearted support of these Catholic men and women throughout the country who are always ready to make whatever sacrifices they are called upon to make for the welfare of the Church and our nation, coupled with the cooperation of all Nigerians of good will, be they government officials, chiefs, natural rulers, or just good admirers of the Catholic Church, that we have succeeded in playing our part so far, with regard to our co-responsibility with the government, in nation building.

xi. Conclusion

And on this occasion, you do not mind assembling here in our little city of Ikot Ekpene, from far and near and from all walks of life. You have come bringing your gifts for the upkeep of our future spiritual fathers. Thus, with the eye of faith and charity, you have chosen to look at Ikot Ekpene as the Bethlehem of old, small indeed but not the least, for out of it will come forth our priests, the spiritual rulers, that will help guide the people of God, the blessed people of Nigeria.

Thank you, therefore, and may God bless you.
Dominic Cardinal Ekandem

In all his thoughts, it is obvious that the welfare of the person is paramount whether on the social, political, cultural, or religious level. For him, once something is good with the individuals who form the nation, logically, it will be good with the nation as well. Correspondingly, once something is good with the nation the same should be extended to the individuals that form the nation. The wellbeing or the nation's euphoria should be extended to all. It should not be such that some are very wealthy and others are extremely poor. There should be a balance and sharing in the bounty of the nation and of each other.

On the level of the church, there should be a sharing since the church is a community. The communal life of the African society should aid in that direction so that the church will become selfsufficient and self- reliant. This concept is very central to the thoughts of the cardinal. The church as a community should foster unity. This unity should be extended to the whole nation since the church forms part of the nation.

Since the nation has benefited greatly from the missionary activities of the church, the nation as such should help the church to be self- reliant. If the church is stronger or richer in one part, she should also be ready to help the part that is weaker.

The church as a community has the obligation of manifesting the characteristics of a community: trust, support, love, and unity. If the hierarchy in the nation is united, the unity in the church will act as an antidote against ethnicism.[453] He was very concerned about unity that is why many of his addresses as the president of the Catholic Bishops' Conference of Nigeria (CBCN) centered on unity. He said, "Unity was the thing I often spoke about in the Bishops Conference as president, for when we are united, we give an example to the nation to follow."

For Cardinal Ekandem, everything had to lead to unity and growth that would manifest in love of God and the neighbor. The growth incorporates all, the individual, the Church and the nation. The growth he had in mind was the dynamic and not static one.

D. Don't Abandon the Poor[454]

His Eminence Dominic Cardinal Ekandem

> The future leadership of Nigeria must not leave the poor to look helplessly at the gate of opportunity. Be it school, hospital, housing, fresh water, clear air or better roads, the government will have to ensure that the common man derives some benefits.

> Catholic Bishops said in a conference in Enugu that education, medical care, and these other facilities should be provided to all since majority of Nigerians are poor. "Whatever form of civilian government comes to be, there are priorities that must be got right: the nation is only strong when

united, free and committed to the rule of law and justice,"
the Bishops declared.

"There can no longer be in this nation any true God- fearing citizen
with such surplus and with an easy conscience as long as his brothers and
sisters continue to go hungry, go unhoused, unclothed, uneducated and
uncared for," the Bishops communiqué declared. They condemned the
situation where few flourish in riches and majority are left in poverty,
adding, "If there is better life ahead, then, let it be for all and not for just
a few."

The Bishops also called on Nigerians to eschew extravagant and wasteful funeral expenses characteristic of our present society and urged all to
emulate the late Pope Paul [VI] who directed in his last testament that no
monument should be constructed for him. In a communiqué issued a few
days after religious leaders had audience with the head of state Lt. General
Olusegun Obasanjo, the Bishops expressed their determination to join in
the task of ensuring peaceful, orderly and successful return to civilian Rule
in 1979. They believe that peace can be achieved if leaders practice a high
degree of accountability to their own consciences, and to those whom they
serve as well as God.

The catholic Bishops directed that all Catholics should stay from
food, drinks and other things of the flesh and bow their heads in prayer
for peace and good government for Nigeria on September 29. That day
has been proclaimed a day of fasting and abstinence. Sunday the 24th of
September is to be spent offering special prayers by the Catholics and all
Christians have been urged to do the same. In addition to all these, the
conference just ended in Enugu also directed the communiqué that catholic churches should commit the traditional October devotions to the purpose of praying for the nation.

On the international scene, the Catholic Bishops of Nigeria declared
their total commitment to the liberation of all the oppressed people of
Africa. About 30 Bishops from all over the country attended the conference, which lasted from September 11–17.

Cardinal Ekandem, in the name of the bishops, gave the high points
of the communiqué while emphasizing the necessity of caring for the
poor. The religious leaders were ready to collaborate with the government

to bring about peaceful transition from military rule to civilian government. It was truly a bold step adopted for the sake of the poor ones of the country.

E.   The Conversion of the King

In 1988, Cardinal Ekandem delivered a homily at the Federal Government College, Ikot Ekpene, Cross River State. That was almost a year before the proclamation of Akwa Ibom State as an autonomous state distinct from the mother state, Cross River State that has Calabar as the capital. His homily was in the context of the Sacrament of Confirmation. That also seemed to have been his first visit to the place within a period of about ten years in a liturgical context. It was with great enthusiasm that students and staff received him. The visit was an epoch-making history.

After the readings before the Rite of Confirmation itself, the cardinal stood up to preach. He began by thanking the Almighty God who foresees all things and knows all things before they take place who provided the opportunity for him to be there in the college to carry out his pastoral duty as the chief shepherd of his flock. He moved further to thank the school authorities for opening the doors of the school for him to accomplish the important task of coming to strengthen the young men of God in the ancient faith of the church so that the weak in faith might become strong in faith and be able to confess God with all their strength without fear or favor as the three young children in the fiery furnace did. The first reading was from the book of Daniel chapter 3 on the golden statue that King Nebuchadnezzar ordered all in his kingdom to prostrate and adore but Shadrach, Meshach, and Abednego who were the king's servants refused to prostrate before the golden statue. Their refusal was mentioned to the king and they were thrown into the burning fiery furnace. When the three young men told the king that even if their God did not rescue them, they would not adore his golden statue, the king was greatly infuriated and ordered the fiery furnace to be made seven times hotter than usual. The flame burned those who were to throw the three young men into fiery furnace to death.

The cardinal focused on the adamant faith of those three young people who refused to succumb to the threats of the king and his cohorts. He contextualized it in the school situation the children found themselves to evoke faith. Because of the faith of the three young people, they told the king that even if the God they worshipped was unable to rescue them from the fiery furnace, they would not submit to worship his gods after hearing the sound of bagpipes, horns, and so on. The king felt slighted, but at the same time, he was worried about these three children although he exercised his right to punish recalcitrance in his kingdom owing to the report made to him. He ordered the fire to be made three times hotter because of the king's anger. After carrying out his instruction, the three young men were to be thrown into the fire. The stalwarts who carried them were burned alive in the process of trying to implement the king's instruction. The three young men fell into the fiery furnace. God sent his angel to them in the fiery furnace. They were loosened and walked freely about in the fire with the angel. The king, who was very anxious and watching the whole process, sprang to his feet when he noticed that there was a fourth person in the pit. He called out to his courtiers and inquired whether there were not three people thrown into the fiery furnace, how did a fourth person looking like a son of the gods appear in the fire? He called out the three young men to come out of the fire. The calling out reflects the calling of Lazarus by Jesus at Bethany when he brought him back to life.

When his courtiers confirmed it, he ordered the three young men to be brought out. He then told everyone in his kingdom that no one should speak against the God of Shadrach, Meshach, and Abednego. The king went on to say that whoever spoke against the God of the three young men would be thrown into the fiery furnace.

Cardinal Ekandem then went on to say that it was the unflinching faith of the three young men that converted the king. He added that the faith of those who were to be confirmed could go a long way in converting others. The same applied to the others who attended that confirmation ceremony too. He exhorted all to hold on to their faith. He told the congregation that they should not fear to profess their faith or decide to follow others because they have denied their faith or fail to uphold it. They should always remember the three young men in the fiery furnace, the noble example they had given not only to the king but to the whole world including that congregation that listened to him. He reminded those to be confirmed that they had seen what it cost the young men in the fiery furnace to uphold their faith. They should remember that it was not going to be easy at all times to bear witness to faith. The three young men should be their example and encouragement. In addition, he emphasized the fact that whatever is sweet is never achieved with ease. A lot of work and effort must be involved. You cannot reach the stars without hardship or difficulties of various kinds. Do not give up because things are difficult or the context is arduous; hold on tenaciously, and at the end, the bright light will shine out in the dark.

Toward the end, he praised the Vincentian seminarians who taught Catechism in the college under the direction of the chaplain of the college, Rev. Fr. Michael I. Edem, CM who prepared everything together with the children and staff for the celebration of the sacrament. He thanked the Catholic teachers in the school and appreciated all the other teachers. He was accompanied by Rt. Rev. Msgr. Kenneth Enang, who was the parish priest of St. Vincent Catholic Church, Umuahia Road, Ikot Obong Edong, Ikot Ekpene, at the time.

The festive mood was such that the parents, the children, their friends and relations, and the Catholic staff all shared the joy of that day. The principal, Mr. Efekodo, expressed a special appreciation on behalf of the college for the honor accorded the school by the presence of His Eminence and for the fatherly disposition that made him to come over to the college to confer the sacrament. He said, "You are really the chief shepherd of the flock." Mr. Efekodo went on to implore God's continuous blessings and guidance upon him as he ministered to the people of God.

His various printed addresses can be found in one of his earliest publications titled *Shepherd among Shepherds*. It contains his addresses to the Catholic Bishops' Conference on different themes including initiating new initiatives, ministerial priesthood. As part of the third address, he emphasized the need to provide leadership in Africa, the need for unity, the future of the church in Nigeria as a major preoccupation, the need for moral authority and leadership, cautioning against the issue of ethnicity in the church, response to social issues, oneness and unity, improvement of prayer life of bishops and priests, and the necessity of having retreats. He warned against the deteriorating sense of priesthood. He emphasized the need for planning, the church's care for the neglected, the false sense of security in the priesthood and its inherent dangers, leadership by example to the new strategy of religious education after government takeover of schools, National Missionary Seminary, stock taking and to unity in the ministerial priesthood. These were issues he focused on in *Shepherd among Shepherds*.[455]

Chapter Seventeen

VOX POPULI, VOX DEI (THE VOICE OF THE PEOPLE, THE VOICE OF GOD)

His Foresights, Insights, and Awards

The hope and joy of Easter, forged in the crucible of self-denial, selfemptying, utter identification with sinners, even to the point of disgust at the bitterness of that chalice. Such were the hope and the joy which these two holy popes had received as a gift from the risen Lord and which they in turn bestowed in abundance upon the People of God, meriting our eternal gratitude.

—Pope Francis, Homily at Canonization of Sts. John XXIII and John Paul II

CARDINAL EKANDEM WAS a man of foresight and great insights even in very small things. His life was an inspiration to millions. His vision extended far and wide. It had an impact far beyond the boundaries of Eastern Nigeria.

From the onset, as a very young priest when he was made the rector of the minor seminary after Rev. Fr. Brendan Bolger, the first rector of Queen of Apostles Seminary (QUAS, or rather QAS Afaha Obong), he sought to improve the lot of the seminarians. Before his arrival, the minor seminarians were using bamboo beds. There was no iron bed (Vono bed) for them then. He was anxious on his arrival to do something.

A. Provision of the First (Iron Beds) Vono Beds at Queen of Apostles Seminary, Afaha Obong

Recapitulating the situation the Cardinal said that "the first difficulties in the seminary were how to provide solid and permanent beds for the seminarians' comfort for a meaningful stay and studies." Immediately, he began canvassing for donors. He went to various schools to talk about vocation, and in the process, he appealed to the teachers to help the seminarians be housed in moderate comfort. He persuaded them to support the seminary generously.

He suggested that a teacher should cover the cost of one bed, and where that was not possible, the person could share with some other to provide one. Whoever made a donation, their name would be written on the bed. If a convent that is those in convent schools run for girls made a donation, the name of the convent would be written there as well. The teachers responded generously. The cardinal recalled that the female teachers in convents provided the "bulk of the beds." With this method the bamboo beds that used to break easily were phased out. He was always able to perceive the situation immediately and act on it. His organizational skill was outstanding. The beds and the mattresses were provided at the same time, and the problem was solved.

When he became the rector of the seminary in 1950 or 1951, he never forgot that there were many people that worked with him, both lay and clerical. The clergy were the expatriate fathers whom he consulted frequently since he was as yet unskilled in management. He considered them not only as brothers but also as "fathers." Such respect was extended to all expatriate priests. It would have been strange for him to act otherwise since, traditionally, he was trained to respect elders. He purposely left himself open for their instruction and directives. To that effect even when he became the auxiliary bishop of Calabar in 1954 and was posted to Anua as the priest-in-charge, Bishop James Moynagh, SPS used to travel frequently from Calabar to Anua to supervise and keep an eye on him.

What Bishop Moynagh said in private to Father Michael, the principal of Holy Family College was now brought to the fore when he said that "they (the Kiltegan Priests) were sent to come and prepare those who were to take over from them since they were not going to be there forever." No wonder he made serious effort to prepare a successor in the making. Bishop Moynagh had a large heart. He was not interested in marking the failures of the new Auxiliary Bishop Ekandem and making sure that Bishop Ekandem never witnessed the light of day. He did not do that. He did not glory in victimization, hatred, unforgiveness, racial discrimination, closing of the heart to the necessity of the people of God, nor did he want to be the only cock that crows on the roof. Bishop Moynagh fulfilled God's will in this process and fulfilled the ultimate purpose of the mission. He preferred to demonstrate his fatherly love, companionship, forgiveness, and the power to exercise paternal control while giving room to his auxiliary to focus on his responsibilities. He attracted God's blessings with such disposition.

Even though the expatriate priests all joined hands "to tutor" him, he never lost his sense of autonomy. The assistance rendered by the "fathers" helped him progress smoothly. They coexisted and cooperated in working together. He was very prudent and skillful in preserving his Africanity in what was then a very European hierarchy. Very soon he revealed himself as a self-confident young priest whose confidence was based on his background, ordination, and appointment. He was a priest of God the most high, a gift he cherished very highly. He expressed this sense of gratitude and appreciation one day to Mrs. Catherine Ekpo and the late Mrs. Catherine Nyong, who visited him, when he said, "The greatest gift God has given me is the priesthood. If any other thing follows, it is an addition. That is why I cherish the priesthood and handle it delicately because it is a divine gift."[456]

The appeal that the young Reverend Father Dominic made to the teachers and lady teachers in convent schools and their generous response became the first major step in the "seminary appeal fund," which today is called "seminary collection" for the maintenance of the seminary. The teachers he turned to were in mission-controlled schools that made it easy for him to have access to them and use them in the process of evangelization.

B.   Attempt at Christianization

Among the various forms of entertainment in the seminary was Ekpo display as well as games or sports, recreation, and cultural exhibitions. As a young priest, Cardinal Ekandem never liked the "vendetta" and harmful practices of Ekpo. He loved Ekpo to be displayed though without its more negative customs. Consequently, he set out to organize Ekpo play in the seminary without some of the customs that had attracted the most criticism.

The display was made public, and people were invited to come and enjoy the rhythmic and graceful dance of Ekpo without the violence. The training involved in the dancing, the skills needed, and the harmonious movements made Ekpo display become attractive. The cardinal said, "I like Ekpo dance, but not its wilder manifestations."

In 1967, he organized a Christian rally against Ekpo's menace in OBO Market—Uruan Obo Annang—a stronghold of Ekpo. He succeeded with the rally because he had a good relationship with the traditional rulers. The two actions were greatly extolled. The rally had an effect of giving freedom to women as well as the uninitiated men to move about with an initiate instead of being locked in on such a day.

On the whole, the two actions reduced the power of Ekpo but did not deprive it of its harmful characteristic. The attempt partly failed because of the following:

Ekpo represents the spirit world, was meant to instill fear and dread on the noninitiates. To deprive it of such characteristic was to deprive it of its aura.

Turning Ekpo as a type of police force for maintaining law and order to merely a form of entertainment was not considered lightly by the initiates. The initiates saw it as trivialization of Ekpo and allowing it to lose its significance, hence they fought back. The initiates constituted a serious opposition and made the young innocent seminarians targets. The successful thing was that Ekpo members became aware of the mind of the church. They made concessions in certain aspects and gave partial freedom to noninitiates and women.

C. An Effort at Inculturation of African Values

Cardinal Ekandem attempted an inculturation process in liturgy long before the Second Vatican Council from the late fifties (1950s) he promoted the use of vernacular in liturgical worship. The bold step helped the people to understand their faith instead of using Latin, which mystified everything for them. It was almost like the anticipation of reforms in the church by Antonio Rosmini, the founder of the Institute of Charity or the Rosminians, concerning the relationship of bishops with priests, priests with priests, priests and the laity also the celebration of the liturgy and the need to widen the scope of studies of those on training for the priesthood.

On the part of Cardinal Ekandem, he encouraged traditional wedding ethos, which helped young women maintain their virginity and chastity and discouraged premarital sex that some Catholic teachers attempted to introduce as a sign of fruitfulness or fertility or testing. In order to enforce the rule of sanctity of sex and marriage, he refused those who were pregnant to put on the white veil signifying purity and virginity. To wear it was considered a contradiction since the significance would have been blurred.

The opposition caused by such a stand was immense, and he refused to budge but vehemently opposed the neo-paganistic tendency or the social pressure and manipulation inherent in such attitudes. The womenfolk were happy and backed up the attempt. They saw his movement as protecting their integrity and as a means to women's emancipation as well as autonomy. Furthermore, the female teachers in the convent schools did not want to be deprived of what they called "the white wedding." Any lady that was a culprit irrespective of her position or rank was liable to punishment. That made the women live up to their Christian calling. With a concerted effort of instruction, doubts were dispelled and the old attitudes gave way to growth because of his approach, which was always gentle but strong and firm.

In the light of the above experience, the young Bishop Dominic was seen as a Christian revolutionary. What he did and emphasized was to tap from the cultural ethos of the people elements that were already upheld as a noble sign of self-discipline, love, and respect of self as well as the customs of the people. Traditionally, unfaithfulness on the part of the unmarried and the virgins was considered as meriting death. It was considered a grievous offense. The punishment such a conduct incurred previously was burying the person together with their partner alive. This was the ancient and traditional way of dealing with unfaithfulness among the unmarried. At the time Bishop Dominic insisted on faithfulness, the stringent measure of capital punishment had given way to a more mature understanding of self-discipline, integrity, and respect of the person, but virginity and priority of marriage were nobly upheld.

D.   Reintegration of Twin Mothers

Similarly he gave the women another boost by fighting to reintegrate those who gave birth to twins. The common thing was that, if a woman gave birth to twins, she would automatically incur some prohibitions and would be ostracized. These are some of the prohibitions that took place: In times past, the twins would be killed and the mothers sent to live in the forest. Later on, the mothers were simply ostracized. In some village squares, where two roads existed, the twins' mothers were to walk on the one prescribed for them. On no account were they to walk on the usual one for fear of transferring the curse or evil trait to others.

They were not to get water from the drinking pots so as not to contaminate others. The water had to be obtained for them. They were to have their special plates and cups. The help of others was needed to help them get something, especially from the bamboo shelf above the cooking spot "utang" for them. Many other taboos were involved as well.

The Cardinal was very uncomfortable about this situation, and he fought relentlessly until there was a profound change. While Mary Slessor fought for the preservation of the lives of the twins and their mothers, Cardinal Ekandem fought for their reintegration and dignity. In Yorubaland, the twins were always seen as a blessing. One man's meat is another's poison.

E.   His Organizational Ability

Cardinal Ekandem was a man greatly gifted in many ways. As a young priest and later on as a bishop, he organized the St. Joseph Catholic League, Nka Adiaha Obong—CWO, and the Federation of Catholic Teachers Association. He harnessed the existing potentials of both the educated and uneducated. He mobilized them to become a force to reckon with. In time, they did become what they were meant to be and sometimes, even more. Referring to his organizational ability, Abp. Joseph E. Ukpo observed the following: "Cardinal Ekandem was very good in collective evangelization and organization that gave rise to the Catholic Teachers Guild, Adiaha Obong, which evolved into Catholic Women's Organisation, Catechists' Association and the like."

a. St. Joseph Catholic League

The St. Joseph Catholic League, an association of all Catholic men (educated) at the time came to existence after many years of coexistence with Ibibio Union, which was founded in the 1920s. In the late 1920s, the young Ibibio men decided to group themselves into a body, perhaps as a result of their new awareness of the need for further education.

The group formed was called Ibibio Union. The members came from many Christian denominations. They all united and worked together. Great contributions were made. The union grew and became financially viable even to the point of awarding scholarships to members who were to be trained as officers. The union succeeded to build Ibibio State College in Ikot Ekpene, now State College after being named Independence High School. The trouble and the separation came during the period of award-ing scholarships according to the zones that made up the association. The following were selected: Mr. B. U. A. Attah for Uyo, Mr. E. U. Ekpo for Abak, Mr. Ibanga U. Akpabio for Ikot Ekpene who was instrumental in establishing the State College, Mr. Nsima for Eket and Mr. Udoma E. U. for Opobo now Ikot Abasi who became the proprietor of Secondary Commercial School Opobo. Among all those chosen for the scholarship, none was a Catholic from any of the sections.

b. The Background and Formation of Catholic Teachers' League

The Catholics felt slighted and dissatisfied and decided to pull out. When they pulled out and formed the St. Joseph Catholic League, the young Bishop mobilized them into action. The association saw its exis-tence, survival, and progress as a necessity.

Rev. Fr. Uduakobong Umoren, anchoring on Rev. Fr. R. Smyth's account of the foundation of the association as the first organizing secretary narrates the events that formed the backdrop of the association. Father Smyth worked in Calabar from 1949 to 1967 at the outbreak of the Nigerian/Biafran Civil War. He was the one chosen to help Fr. Dominic Ekandem to organize the association while Father Dominic gave momentum to the spirit of the organization and vision. Father Uduakobong links the Federation of the Catholic Teachers' League with the Holy Year's Pilgrimage experience of young Fr. Dominic Ekandem when he went to Rome in 1950.2

Father Dominic passed from Rome to Dublin in Ireland and Lourdes after the pilgrimage. He witnessed the organization of the Lay Faithful in Ireland and was immediately inspired by that experience of the travels. Four years later, he translated those experiences into action.[457] On November 20, 1954, during the Marian year, while addressing over seven hundred teachers during a Holy Mass that ended a vigil of prayer arranged for teachers, the young Bishop Ekandem prevailed on the teachers to make something specific to mark the Marian year. Going further, he told them that throughout the world, people were doing something as a memorial including building of churches and erecting of statues, etc. He then challenged the gathered teachers to do something to mark the Marian year in a unique manner.

The following day, November 21, 1954, Bishop James Moynagh ordained Rev. Emmanuel Afangide, a Catholic priest at Anua. Many teachers were in attendance. Bishop Ekandem was convalescing in Anua Hospital, for medical physicians ordered a complete rest owing to the long trek from Anua to Ukana Akpa Utong, a distance of twenty-five miles that he covered while making that pilgrimage. He was physically exhausted.

It was during that period of recuperation that Mr. Gregory Nyong Edem of Nung Ukot Itam in Uyo Division remembered the passionate appeal of Bishop Ekandem at the closing ceremonies of Saturday morning for a memorial event to mark the Marian year, sent in a letter including a donation of one pound sterling[458] (£1) for the proposed Marian year project. Encouraged by this letter and donation and goodwill, he started planning for an organization of Catholic teachers that would "unite them in a spirit of charity to improve themselves and one another as architects and builders of a Christian Nation…"[459]

The Catholic Teachers' League quickly organized itself with Mr. Domingo Inyang as the very first president and Mr. Leo E. Essien as the first secretary. The league grew very fast both economically and numerically. The members had great foresight inspired by the dynamic leadership of Bishop Ekandem. They built the Holy Family College Abak. It later awarded scholarships, as did the Ibibio Union. It helped members on an individual basis, according to their needs, supported and strengthened missionary spirit in the various places that members were sent, and promoted evangelization in all its ramifications. They became very popular and strong as the year passed by.

F.   Nka Adiaha Obong—The Catholic Women's Organization

Traditionally and naturally, women in Ibibio land have been organizing themselves into groups like Ebre, Iban-Isong Nka Ikemesit and all the rest. It was not difficult for the young Bishop Ekandem to help women organize themselves in the church. Realizing how resourceful the women were, Bishop Ekandem spurred them up to undertake many things. He did not want the women to face discrimination in any way. He wanted them to be a force to be reckoned with. He spearheaded women's liberation, which is gaining much ground in today's world. He wanted the women not only to express their unity and their capacity to show concern toward one another but also to engage in projects equal to that of the men—their husbands, brothers, and relations—maybe even greater. They may not be able to accomplish everything all at once, but at least they will be able to do some things effectively.

After the Marian Year Congress in 1954, the young Bishop Ekandem got the idea of gathering the Catholic women together as he had got the men together in St. Joseph's Catholic League. He started it in Anua Parish as the cardinal himself recalled in his message to Nka Adiaha Obong during the Silver Jubilee celebration in 1979 postponed to May 1980. The association was aimed at organizing, educating, evangelizing, and positively encouraging and enhancing the growth of personal faith as a mother is the heart of the family, likewise the promotion of self-help.

The association was not limited to Anua parish alone. Since Anua parish at the **time** incorporated the following: Central Uruan, Mbak Etoi, Mbiokporo, Obio Offot, West Itam, Anua itself, Nka Adiaha Obong soon spread very quickly and extended to other parishes. Meetings were held weekly at the initial stage, especially on Sundays after the Eucharist celebration or after service where there was no priest. The executive at the time consisted of the president, the vice president, secretary, and treasurer. The work of the treasurer was lightened because most of the funds were transferred to the priest-incharge. At the time of its foundation, Madam Theresa Akpan Inyang of Ifa Atai Etoi was the first president.

Other foundation members of Nka Adiaha Obong in the then Calabar diocese were Madam Maxima Ekong from Anua, Madam Mary Ikwo Obot from Eniong, Madam Angela G. Ukpong from Obio Offot, Mrs. Rose Okon from Ibiaku Offot, Madam J. Etim from Ibiaku Issiet, Mrs. Agnes Eboh from Edem Ekpat, Mrs. Margaret Ibok from Okobo and Mrs. Theresa Akpan from Use Offot. These devoted women worked tirelessly and relentlessly to see that they laid a good foundation for growth and carried out the propaganda on initiating new members. They were apostles not only of Nka Adiaha Obong but of the good news for women and of the church as well. Later officers and members had to build on what these earlier members had started. The beginnings were tough and difficult, yet they preserved and wonderful fruits testified to their works later.

The association was for all Catholic women whether educated or not. As long as they had a few people who knew how to read and write and express themselves in English, they were able to make progress. The association is still maintaining that characteristic today. No sooner had the women organized themselves than they began to aim at building a school *Ufok Nwed Ubok Utom*, a Commercial and Domestic Science institute for their children and dependents. When they had got enough money, they started the project.

At the end of September 1963, three Daughters of Charity of St. Vincent de Paul of Mill Hill Province arrived from London to open the school known and called Adiaha Obong School of Domestic Science of Commerce at Eniong Offot. The school became as famous as Holy Family College established by the St. Joseph's Catholic League. It was a Herculean task accomplished with a Herculean good will.

Later on when the mantle of office passed from Bishop James Moynagh of Calabar to Bishop Brian D. Usanga, now Archbishop Usanga, a second Adiaha Obong technical school was established in Ekpene Ukim under the paternal guidance of the ordinary of the diocese of Bishop Usanga in 1973. This school has also grown to a great magnitude offering opportunities to both boys and girls.

One of the things that attracted numerous members and helped the association to advertise itself was the March Past. The event took place during the colonial period, or rather within the intercolonial period and the Nigerian independence in 1960. Bishop Ekandem was eager to see that one of the goals of the organization was realized. He set about organizing training and drilling the women in preparation for the March Past, which was to be part of the independence celebration. On that day October 1, 1960, the women appeared in the field.

The cardinal recalled that occasion with delight. He said, "The women marched so well as if they were a single person that the DO and all the colonial masters were very delighted and surprised to see many of the unlettered women marching side by side with the more educated ones in unison and in time to the rhythm of the drumming. It was a delightful show. Their performance won the approval of all. It was the first of its kind in the country."

The news of their excellence spread like wildfire and the name Nka Adiaha Obong became very popular. The women were very proud of themselves. Their dignity had been affirmed and enhanced. Their uniqueness had been extolled, and their excellent performance was applauded. The association needed no further advertisement. It has advertised itself very well and was only to consolidate and move on. That wonderful performance put the cardinal and Nka Adiaha Obong on a very high pedestal, and the association became a force to reckon with. No wonder then when they applied to the government to build a School for the female children and wards (even though the approval was somehow delayed because of the required logistics), the application could not be thrown away but was approved. With that approval, Nka Adiaha Obong had a school named after it. The details are contained below in the cardinal's address to the association during the Silver Jubilee Celebration. The cardinal is portrayed in all these events as an astute organizer and animator.

G.   Silver Jubilee of Nka Adiaha Obong

The Silver Jubilee Celebration of Nka Adiaha Obong occurred when most of the foundation members were still alive. Madam Rose Ekandem Nkubia was one of the officers at the time of the Silver Jubilee. She was greatly delighted to have witnessed what originated like the mustard seed growing and expanding and giving chance for all women to become part of it. This is very much in line with the slogan used by Nka Adiaha Obong that evolved to encompass CWO, the Catholic Women Organisation. The celebration of the Silver Jubilee of the association was a practical demonstration of the commitment of the women to succeed despite all odds. The achievements they accomplished resulted from their sweat. They were happy to see it, the second bishop of Calabar, Brian D. Usanga was glad, and the founder, Cardinal Ekandem, took pride in their achievements, sacrifices, and commitment.

a.   Congratulatory Message from the Founder

A MESSAGE OF APPRECIATION AND RESPECT FOR "NKA ADIAHA-OBONG" CATHOLIC DIOCESE OF CALABAR ON THE OCCASION OF THE SILVER JUBILEE OF ITS FOUNDATION MAY 1980[460]

Introduction

The news of the preparation to celebrate the Silver Jubilee of the foundation of your organisation Nka Adiaha Obong— was delivered to me by your delegates just as I was about to leave for the National Catholic Bishops' Conference which ended in Ibadan on March 1, 1980. For many reasons, I felt deeply touched by your proposal, hence my decision to send you some message of congratulations no matter how brief.

Michael I. Edem CM

Early Days

> As the founder of your Organisation, this is a very welcome news to me especially when I recall that the Catholic Teachers' Federation (founded about the same time as your organisation and which has produced Statesmen, Politicians, top-ranking Civil servants, graduate teachers, members of the Nigeria Judiciary and medical profession, and a respectable monument, the Nigeria Independence Hall, which had been erected in Uyo to welcome important visitors to the town) has not made even a hint yet, about a similar celebration.

Christian mothers of my tribe! I felt very proud of you when your society came into existence about twenty-five years ago. Today I am all the more proud of you to see that despite difficulties you have not only survived but continued to exist with a high sense of responsibility, leading to the attainment of many of your objectives.

When I remember that the beginning of your society was made with regular weekly meetings in the stations, monthly in the sections, and executive council meetings conducted also monthly in Anua the Central Mission, then we cannot help thanking God for the guidance, wisdom and strength given to the foundation members throughout Lady their heavenly Queen, in working up Nka Adiaha Obong, which under the fatherly direction of His Lordship, the Most rev. Bishop B. D. Usanga, has spread throughout the entire Diocese of Calabar.

Anua Parish, which then consisted of the following sections—Central Uruan, Mbak Etoi, Mbiokporo, Obio Offot, West ltam and Anua section itself, has therefore the distinction of being the foundation Parish of Nka Adiaha Obong.

The early days of this society were by no means easy. They members began to feel the hardships of weekly and monthly attendance at meetings with regular contributions towards their project—"Ufok Nwed Ubok Utom" which they had conceived of the welfare of their daughters. At that time they had very few well- wishers, for not even their husbands really understood what these poor women, most of them illiterate, were really up to. Their critics too far from being constructive discouraged them all the more.

It was then, to raise their morale, that I named Our Lady of Heaven as their Patron and Mary, the Maid and hardworking Housewife of Nazareth as their model. I then changed the original name of the society from Catholic Women's League to "Nka Adiaha Obong." An Association of Princesses, thus referring to the women members of the society as princesses of the Queen of Heaven. As a result of the support and protection the society received from its heavenly patron, Mary Queen of Heaven, along with the honour and dignity the women got as children of Mary, they then acquired both the courage and the strength to go ahead then with their society.

A Very Important Objective Realised

By 1961, the money contributed by the members of Nka Adiaha Obong towards their project was enough to make a start. Accordingly in 1962 an application was made to the Ministry of Education requesting permission for the opening of a Commercial and Domestic Science Institute—"Ufok Nwed Ubok Utom," which had been the dream of the society.

Fortunately by the time the permission was given in 1963, His Lordship Bishop Moynagh, the former Bishop of Calabar Diocese, had completed arrangements for the Daughters of Charity of St. Vincent de Paul to come out to Nigeria to staff the Institute. Thus in 1964 the Institute named after its founder, Nka Adiaha Obong, was opened as Adiaha Obong School of Commerce and Domestic Science, which later became known as Adiaha Obong Secondary Commercial School.

Tribute to Nka Adiaha Obong

Here let us pause and pay tribute to our Christian Mothers of Adiaha Obong Society. While the people of the Cross River State and the Nation as a whole will ever remain grateful to expatriate Missionaries of various denominations for the establishment of such famous post-Primary institutions as St. Thomas's Teachers Training College in Ogoja, Hope Waddel Training Institute and St. Patrick's College in Calabar, Mary Haney and

Boys High School in Oron, Cornelia Connelly Secondary School Uyo, Holy Child Teacher Training college Ifuho, St. Mary's T. T. C. Ediene Abak and Etinan institute, etc., we must bow our heads in gratitude and bend our knees in homage to the Christian women of our tribe, as members of Nka Adiaha Obong, who founded the famous Adiaha Obong Secondary Commercial School. The Catholic men of our community should sing high praises of their mothers, wives and sisters, who, inspired by the noble example of St. Joseph's Catholic League in establishing our famous Holy Family College in Abak, decided also on their own to establish Adiaha Obong School in Eniong for their daughters and other girls of their tribe and country.

It was therefore only right and fair that the name Adiaha Obong of which the School was thoughtlessly deprived should be resorted in honour of the founders, Nka Adiaha Obong and to commemorate the achievement of the selfsacrificing and devoted Christian women of our tribe.

Nka Adiaha Obong, be assured that all men of good will in the State, do doff their hats to you and hope that you will continue to take the lead in the initiative for self-help, selfreliance, and in offering practical guidance to your children.

Founder's Day

> I now call upon all those (Government, Communities, Societies, individuals, etc.) who have benefited in any way, from your organisation, Nka Adiaha Obong, to give you such support and recognition that will serve as an inspiration and encouragement towards greater and more spectacular achievements in the years ahead.

> A special day, for example, chosen by the Adiaha Obong Commercial School Authorities, and any other institution of their own establishment to be celebrated annually in honour of the Founders, to which the Organisation should be invited would not only serve as a mark of recognition, but would be a means of importing a practical lesson on education to the youth.

Conclusion

Nka Adiaha Obong! In your twenty-five years of existence, your work has been greatly blessed by God with many fruits, may you grow stronger ad bigger, continuing to sow, and to reap an abundance of fruits from sixty to a hundredfold, by the time you come to celebrate your Golden Jubilee. **His Eminence Dominic Cardinal Ekandem**

The Silver Jubilee Celebration of the Nka Adiaha Obong was an epoch-making event. The women were not contented to have the founder of the group, His Eminence Dominic Cardinal Ekandem, write a goodwill message. They equally wanted the bishop of Calabar Diocese, who at the time was the Most Reverend Brian D. Usanga, to do the same. The necessity of the bishop of Calabar writing the goodwill message stemmed from the fact from the foundation of the organisation taking place within Calabar Diocese when His Lordship Most Rev. James Moynagh was the ordinary of the diocese. Ikot Ekpene Diocese became an independent diocese at its creation in 1963. There was no diocese of Ikot Ekpene when its foundation took place in Anua parish in Calabar Diocese. The Silver Jubilee Celebration took place many years afterward. At that time, Cardinal Ekandem was the ordinary of Ikot Ekpene Diocese. The goodwill message of Bishop Usanga who later became the archbishop of Calabar cemented the mother-daughter relationship, affirmed, and reinserted the origin of the organization in its proper context. The officers of the Nka Adiaha Obong did not want to miss that link. They got it and got it right.

b.   Congratulatory Message by Bishop Brian D. Usanga of Calabar

SILVER JUBILEE OF ADIAHA OBONG (CWO) CALABAR DIOCESE A GOODWILL MESSAGE FROM MOST REV. DR. BRIAN D. USANGA BISHOP OF CALABAR "LOVE THE CHURCH, LOVE OUR LADY AND LOVE YOUR FELLOWMEN.[461]

My dear devoted Adiaha Obong members and followers and imitators of the Daughters of the Almighty Father—the Immaculate Virgin Mary. I join you in prayers in your celebration of the Silver Jubilee of your prestigious Association. God and our Lady have used your Organisations as effective instruments to help the Missionaries, the Church, the Bishops and Priests and Religious to evangelize, and educate our womenfolk.

We thank God that you remained loyal to and cooperated with His Eminence Cardinal Ekandem, who as Auxiliary Bishop of Calabar, founded the Organisation. You must continue to be united and work as a team to achieve your excellent aims and objectives. The Church and the State and all men of Goodwill look with pride to Adiaha Obong Secondary Commercial School, Eniong Offot, which you established from your monthly generous contributions.

I am happy to have been closely associated as the Proprietor and founder of Adiaha Obong Technical School, Ekpene Ukim, from its humble beginning. Both Schools are doing well, thank God, to your credit and to the greater Glory of God, filial devotedness to our Lady, Peace, Progress and Educational Achievement of our Nation. You are to be highly commended for upholding, defending and assisting to inculcate sound religious and Moral Education and discipline in Schools.

The Association has often singled itself out in the support and encouragements of vocations to the Priesthood and Religious Life. During Priestly ordinations and Religious Professions, you have always done well your motherly duties by advice, care and generous gifts to the newly ordained Priests and Professed Sisters. You must defend and encourage as well, the timely, worthy and faithful receptions of the Sacrament of Matrimony, defend its unity and indissolubility. You yourselves are to continue to live good exemplary Christian lives as Mothers and Housewives with deep Faith, firm Hope and boundless Charity, with unflinching loyalty and obedience to the Church, Church teaching and Church authorities.

The record of your support and encouragement's in the establishment of Junior Seminaries and Assumption Girls' Juniorate, Ndon Ebom are very commendable. Continue to pray and serve the Church in union with the Pope, the Bishops, Priests, Sisters and other Lay organisations in the Church.

Your programmes for the future are impressive. We assure you of our usual fatherly full hearted support and cooperation. Our Blessed Mother Mary, Adiaha Obong, who is directing your Association's activities and is alive in your souls and bodies when you are in the State of Grace, has been nurturing the association these twenty-five years to fulfill its aims. Through her continuous and very present participation in our redemption and her God-given power over heaven and earth and her love for us, she will continue to use her store of Graces to take care of the continuous progress and success of this society dedicated to Her. You must be united and love one another as Sisters in Christ and good daughters of Mary. Love unites, hatred divides. Strive always to serve God and the Church in Charity and Justice. Endeavour to look into the needs of all your understanding and sympathy. May God continue to pour His abundant Graces on the Association, on you the Members, your Patrons and Supporters.

> On my behalf and on behalf of all the Priests, Religious, Laity and all men of Goodwill in the Diocese, I wish our Beloved Adiaha Obong Women Association, many more years of very fruitful Apostolate. *AD MULTOS ANNOS.*
>
> **HIS LORDSHIP BISHOP JAMES MOYNAGH THE FIRST BISHOP OF CALABAR DIOCESE, BISHOP MOYNAGH HAS RETIRED AND HAS BEEN SUCCEEDED BY HIS LORDSHIP BISHOP BRIAN D. USANGA.**

H.   The Federation of St. Joseph Catholic Teachers' League

The same vivacious spirit of animation operating during the organization of the women took place with the organization of the teachers as well, it could be said that the organization of the teachers required more skill, more realism, and an abundant goodwill as well as effort to takeoff. The interesting point is that it was founded under the patronage of St. Joseph, the foster father of our Lord Jesus Christ, the patron of the universal church. Being under his care, with prayer and commitment, no mountain would have been too high to tackle.

Motive and History of Development

It is often said that traveling is a part of education. The statement very much came true in the life of His Eminence Dominic Cardinal Ekandem. It all happened during his first epoch-making journey from Obio Ibiono land to Onitsha in the Igbo hinterland. His capacity to observe did not commence when he had become a bishop. It started very early in his life.

When he got to Onitsha in 1933, he noticed something not common in his home. He had a totally different experience of meeting with teachers, headmasters, lawyers, medical doctors, engineers, clerical officers, and so on. He was greatly enthused by that experience. He was anxious to see his people make progress as well. The teachers he met in his area seemed to have been very satisfied and contented whether they were "certificated" or not, but his dissatisfaction was great. He wanted to do something. Here are his own words on the situation:

"Our people seemed to have been satisfied with only teaching. When I was doing my studies in Igboland I saw how people were helping themselves and not just being satisfied with teaching. I came home and started the 'Teachers Federation.' I wanted the teachers to help themselves to go to a higher level than they formerly were. I proposed that each should sacrifice a pound sterling (£1) each year. Many of the teachers agreed. Those who did not agree, I somehow forced them into it because I realized that education was good for them. With their contribution, the first batch of students were sent overseas, and they were successful. One of the first people to benefit from this program was Mr. Gerald Jumbo Uffot who became a lawyer and magistrate. Ladies like Patricia Edem from Calabar were among the first beneficiaries."[462]

In the above lines, the motives of establishing the association is greatly spelled out coupled with some of the first beneficiaries. He achieved this feat as a manager of schools in the district.

His Eminence Dominic Cardinal Ekandem established the association when he was an auxiliary bishop of Calabar operating from Anua during the colonial era. The establishment of the Federation of Catholic Teachers' Association came into being during the Marian year celebration in 1954.

Bishop Dominic Ekandem shortly after his "episcopal consecration" invited all Catholic teachers—male and female—to Holy Family College Oku Abak and spoke to all present very persuasively to see the need of establishing such an association and that of supporting it. After the marathon speech, the teachers pledged to form an association in all the parishes in the diocese.

The association had a humble beginning. It took off in Anua parish with Mr. Placid O. Akpan as the first president and Mr. George O. Bassey (GOB) as its first secretary. At its inception in Anua parish, it was simply christened "Catholic Teachers' Association," and then the association set out to make its "article of association" or "bylaws." A copy was sent to the bishop for approval. After the approval, the association soon spread to other parishes. The parish association then convoked and formed the Catholic Federation. It was from then christened Federation of Catholic Teachers' Association. The copies of the approved "bylaws" constitution were sent to other parishes. In this way, the pledge made to Bishop Ekandem at Holy Family College Oku Abak was redeemed. The pledge to Bishop Ekandem that each teacher would contribute one-pound sterling (£1) a year for five years toward university and teacher training education of the members of the association also became operative. The vow to make the donation for five years was renewed at the end of the term.

Aims and Objectives

a.   To enhance full participation in educational matters by the indigenous
b.   To prepare Catholics for participation in political affairs of the country

c. To provide the much-needed manpower in various fields in the society

d. To safeguard the interest of Catholic institutions in the (then) diocese of Calabar

e. To promote the interest of the association and to promote the welfare of members and foster obedience to the bishop

f. To foster effective and united directives to the moral and professional duties of teachers

g. To enhance effective evangelization[463]

Organization

The association consisted of parishes or branch chapters. The parish chapters had monthly meetings. The following committees helped in the running of the chapters: education committee, finance committee, and disciplinary committee. The branch or parish committees sent representatives who were officers to the diocesan or central council the central council held a yearly general meeting. The officers of the branches namely, the president, vice president, secretary, treasurer were members of the central council. The secretaries had to give a report of what was going on in the branches. The central council had the election committee, scholarship and project committee, and disciplinary committee. The officers of the central council were always elected at the general meeting. Non-officers were free to attend the general meetings as well. On the diocesan level, a spiritual director was always assigned.

The initial central officers elected were:

i. Etubom Maurice E. Archibong—President
ii. Mr. John I. Inoh—Secretary
iii. Rev. Fr. Reggie Smyth—Treasurer

Achievements

The Federation of Catholic Teachers' Association made it a point of duty to give university scholarship to its members every year. Two thousand pounds sterling (£ 2000) was enough to train a candidate overseas at the time. Loans were also given to members who wanted to borrow from the association at parish levels to help solve the financial problems of members.

a. Beneficiaries included medical doctors, lawyers, engineers, journalists, and teachers. These later served in both government and private establishments in the country.

b. An imposing edifice erected along Abak Road in Uyo called Catholic Teachers' Independence Hall, which served as a conference hall for both church and state until recently gained the admiration and commendation of both members and nonmembers.

c. Sportsmanship developed because of annual competition and reunion. The following items featured during the annual reunion: football matches, netball for women, and March Past. These were always thrilling moments.

d. The association opened a bookshop at No. 20A Aka Road Uyo.

e. Provision of needed manpower to Catholic schools and colleges took place.

f. Lectures and seminars were organized in parishes.

g. It achieved the defined solidarity among teachers as well as discipline and leadership to members. The association produced leaders for both church and state.

h. The association provided an effective organ of evangelization for the church and members were persuaded by the bishop and priests to join the Confraternity of Christian Doctrine (CCD) and the Legion of Mary Society.

With such wonderful achievements, the aims and objectives of the association were fulfilled. The yearly contribution of the teachers was of immense help to accomplishing all the projects enumerated as well as from their physical presence and willingness to contribute.

The cardinal recalled that difficulties crept in when the government took over the schools between 1971 and 1972, championed by the ex-administrator of East Central State (the only civilian governor at the time who later became the person in charge of education in the country). The cardinal said, "Those who understood the value of that contribution still continued paying without any constraint. During the period of contribution, he insisted that there should be adult education that would help the women to benefit from the contributions as well as men.

"When the government took over the schools and voluntary agencies and proprietors who established the schools reacted and sought for the return of the schools and compensation, what the government did after a long time was to ask the private agencies to open new schools and run them. We are still keeping our fingers crossed to see if the schools would be returned."[464]

The dream of the cardinal was almost realized when Sir Michael Otedola, the ousted civilian governor of Lagos State during the military coup[465] of Gen. Sani Abacha who became the head of state and commander in chief of the Nigerian Armed Forces toward the end of Cardinal Ekandem's life had promised to return the schools to the missions during his tenure as governor. That hope was lost immediately when the successor of Governor Otedola assumed office. The promise to give back the schools on a platter of gold to the original owners hit the rock, sank to the bottom of the sea, and never witnessed a resurgence during the lifetime of the cardinal even after a passionate plea by Bishop Joseph Ekuwem during the burial of the cardinal that schools should be returned as a tribute to him. In spite of the vicissitudes, his educational contributions are immense.

I.   Establishment of Schools

Although it could not be said that it was Cardinal Ekandem who established Queen of Apostles' Seminary in Afaha Obong, the idea of establishing it came from him. It was his brainchild. There is no doubt that "seminary cottage" was in existence, but it did not satisfy the intent of establishing it. When he realized that every person that wanted to be a priest was always sent to Onitsha to be trained, he proposed an alternative means, and that means was to establish a minor seminary in the then Calabar Diocese of which Bishop James Moynagh was the ordinary.

He noted that many of those sent to Onitsha did not go through because of distance and lack of funds to go and come back caused many to withdraw. The proposition was made even as a very young priest. He said that when he made the proposition to the bishop and the priests, it was greatly welcome news, and there was no difficulty in accepting and implementing the idea. Rev. Fr. Brendan Bolger was readily made the first rector whom the cardinal said prepared the ground for him. Even though he was not the one who implemented the idea, he was very much at the forefront of its establishment.

Loreto Girls Juniorate, Eriam Afaha Obong was established to promote vocations to the religious life. He had one single motive in establishing these institutions—the promotion of the people's good on the social economic, political, educational, moral, and religious levels. Other institutions include: Madonna Secondary School Inen, Ukanafun. The school was specifically opened for girls in the region so that they would not be lacking future leaders but would be self- sufficient with eminent leaders to pilot the affairs of women in the area and compete favorably and equitably with fellow women in the diocese, in the country and in the world. Maria Goretti Secondary School, Ikot Ekpene was established to help educate and train the young girls in the diocese to give them a sense of direction in order to be able to meet up with their counterparts in other parts of the country.

He also opened the St. Joseph School Inen Ukanafun to enable the boys to realize their potential. Holy Child Girls Secondary School, Ifuho, Ikot Ekpene after the Teachers' Training College (TTC) weaned off. St. Kizito's Comprehensive Secondary School Adiasim, Essien Udim Local Government Area, penetrated and spaced out educational facilities to every part of the diocese so as not to leave any part in a disadvantaged situation equal opportunities for all. His educational strategy worked out very well. Dominic Cardinal Ekandem loved education. He got involved in the establishment of many schools including the Holy Child Nursery and Primary School, Ikot Ekpene behind the cardinal's residence. The school became so famous that it had great influence in the state and in the country.

He established the St. Joseph Rehabilitation Center Ukana Iba, Ikot Ekpene to take care of the disabled and to rehabilitate them. Originally, the center began with the perception of Rev. Fr. P. Flanagan, SPS in conjunction with Assumption Parish, Ukana Iba. Father Flanagan began running the place as a vocational center. The center is separated from the parish church by a road leading to Ukana Akpa Utong. The disabled persons during the Nigerian-Biafran Civil War were catered for at the center after the war. The physiotherapy unit in the center, which started with the advent of the Medical Missionaries of Mary, was invited to help both medically and through physiotherapy to rehabilitate the disabled. It went on that way until the MMMs were unable to continue working in the center because of lack of enough personnel. Desiring the continuity of the good work, they suggested to Bishop Ekandem to invite the Daughters of Charity to come and take over the work.

Meanwhile, Sr. Maura Ramsbottom, MMM's regional superior consulted Sr. Peig O'Brien, DC's regional superior to take over the work. She, in turn, consulted her visitatrice, Sr. Pauline Lawlor, DC in Ireland who gave approval.[466] When the consultations were completed, the official invitation from the ordinary of the diocese, Bishop D. I. Ekandem, came. The disabled are popularly called "the physically impaired." The construction of the sisters' residence started in December 1975 and was completed in September 1978. At this time, Bishop Ekandem had been conferred the title of His Eminence Dominic Cardinal Ekandem. It was later that Mr. Peter and Mrs. Anita Kuippers Dutch CBM (Christoffel Blindenmission) volunteers personnel came through Memisa Organization and joined the staff working with the Daughters of Charity whose charism is to care for the poor and the most abandoned. Peter was a physiotherapist, while Anita was a special education teacher.[467]

The presence of Anita aided the work in the specialist institution of St. Louise's Special School for the Deaf and Dumb and the Physically Impaired. The couple, Peter and Anita, had their firstborn son whom they named Akpan, thus inculturating the name of their son according to Annang culture. Sr. Xavier Daily, DC who later went back to her original name, Sr. Alice Daly, DC and Sr. Angela Gibbons, DC took up residence on the feast of the conversion of St. Paul in 1981 as the first Daughters of Charity assigned to that work. Sr. Bridget O'Connor, DC later joined. There was a Nigerian Sr. Francesca Edet, DC who was also a member of the house. Sr. Louise O'Connell, DC was equally part of the house. The last two shuttled from Ukana Iba to Ikot Obong Edong where the St. Louise's Special School for the Deaf and Dumb, now Special School for the Physically Challenged, was cited to take care of the children that were physically impaired in the company of Anita, the special education teacher. In its diversity, it later incorporated both the "normal" children and the "impaired" ones. The spectrum of the schools quickly exemplified that.

Cardinal Ekandem said that he had to go in for the nursery and primary schools since permission was given for that, and he could open as many as possible seeing the damaged state of the educational foundation arising from the takeover of schools by the federal government from voluntary agencies. He said, "I wasted no time about it. I began it accordingly to its urgency." The International Nursery School in Ikot Ekpene is one of them.

The establishment of many institutions in Ikot Ekpene Diocese is a peculiar one in Nigeria as a result of *observation, reflection, and execution* of Cardinal Ekandem and the speed with which he brought about what he saw to be necessary. If a word were to be borrowed from Abraham Lincoln, one of the founding fathers of America, while addressing the Springfield Library Association[468] He noted that observation was a necessary base of every discovery and invention. Another aspect of the Cardinal's observation is the National Missionary Seminary in Iperu and Gwagwalada discussed in chapters 11 to 13.

J.   The Graciousness and Simplicity of the Bishop[469]

Narration by the Catholic Bishop of Aba Diocese, Most Rev. Vincent Ezeonyia, CSSp.

As a priest working in Port Harcourt Diocese at the time, Rev. Fr. Vincent Ezeonyia recalled a day that he went to see Bishop Ekandem who was the administrator of Port Harcourt Diocese after Bishop Godfrey M. P. Okoye, CSSp had been tactfully elbowed out of office because of the Nigerian-Biafran Civil War and probably for being an Igbo. One day as the bishop administrator was having a meeting with his presbyterium, Father Vincent who was at Egbema, arrived intending to see the bishop since Egbema was under Port Harcourt Diocese at that time. He waited until the crucial meeting ended and Bishop Ekandem gently took this priest by the hand as a father would to his room. That act left a very wonderful and an indelible mark in the mind of Father Vincent. On entering the house, he sat on the arm of the arm of the seat allotted to him. The bishop equally sat at the edge of the seat too. The coincidence of fact and act allowed the bishop to make a very important statement in a funny manner. After inquiring about the health of the priest and finding out how he was getting on with his apostolate, he jokingly told Father Vincent, "Both of us are almost sitting at the edge." This was construed to mean the difficulties he was facing in Port Harcourt as a diocese and the ones that the priests had in their place of pastoral engagement. Since he was new in the place and in the context of the just ended war, things were not very stable. People needed to make things change and move ahead.

The presbyteral meeting was a very crucial one. It was that meeting that caused the bishop to speak about sitting at the edge. He was not finding it very easy in that situation, yet as the chief shepherd, he had to listen to his clergy and react accordingly. He drafted a quick letter that was to become effective from that date to Bishop Unegbu of Owerri. The letter stated that from henceforth, Egbema was to cease being part of Port Harcourt Diocese and was ceded to or was to commence being part of Owerri Diocese. Automatically, Egbema became part of Owerri Diocese and severed its roots from Port Harcourt because of the civil war while being attached to Owerri. Father Vincent was obliged to do the job of delivering that momentously epoch-making message.

The bishop after hearing the priest decided to give him a letter to take to Father McCarthy who was the secretary general of the Catholic secretariat of Nigeria at the racecourse in Lagos. Father McCarthy was from the United States of America. Father Vincent had indicated that he had no car. At this point, Bishop Dominic told him that six brand new pickup vehicles had arrived at Lagos, and that he should go there with a note the bishop was about to write and take it to the secretary general, and he would be given one. Father Vincent set out for Lagos. He had never been there, but this was the opportunity to make that great journey. He arrived safely at Lagos but found it difficult to discover the location of the Catholic secretariat. After many enquiries and questions, he finally arrived at the spot.

This is what prompted Bishop Ekandem to send a written note to the secretary general, Father McCarthy did not hesitate to take Father Vincent by the hand to the wharf as Bishop Ekandem indicated. Father McCarthy showed him the six brand new pickup vans on arrival at the wharf and gave Father Vincent the liberty to pick one of his choices. He helped himself by choosing the one nearest to him. He then delivered the key of the van to him and on driving it discovered that it had only done one mile at the time. When they arrived at the secretariat, Father McCarthy gave him a pound sterling for fuel home. That was a rare commodity during the war since the Biafran currency was used in the east. It was a big surprise for Father Vincent.

K. A Man of Surprises

The unpredictable nature of Cardinal Ekandem's generosity and surprises accompanying his silent or quiet action of relating to people when he expresses goodness is something to be reckoned with. He did not give the impression that he was going to do something when the situation became tough. Always like the apostle Peter going with John through the beautiful gate of the temple and meeting a lame man from birth who requested arms from Peter and his companion John. Peter was the one who spoke. He said to the lame man, "Silver and gold, I have none but what I have I give to you, 'In the name of Jesus the Nazarene, stand up and walk!'" The man stood up and walked jumping behind them as he walked into the temple (Acts 3:6–16). Truly, the experience was a great surprise to the lame man. He already had some expectations when Peter and John drew near and when he was told, "Look at us." He was expecting something very great from them, but the reaction of Peter was totally different. That was the surprise of the man when he was made to walk instead of merely getting some money.

The experience of Martin Ekandem is similar to that of the lame man in the Gospel. One surprising experience Martin had of his uncle, left him stupefied. His expectations about Cardinal Ekandem brought a profound appreciation of his uncle's generosity.

Martin gained admission to Lincoln University in California to go and study economics and business administration in the United States of America and probably with the assurance that his uncle, Cardinal Ekandem, would take care of all expenses. To his greatest disappointment and surprise when he asked for money for his ticket, the cardinal simply told him that he did not have it. Martin thought the cardinal was making fun out of the situation without realizing he meant it. The cardinal told Martin, "Go to my brother, your father, and tell him to give you the ticket money."[470] Martin was very disappointed and downcast. He probably left the cardinal's presence without a word. Later when everything was ready, the cardinal sent for him.

At first, Martin was the one who went. Now it is the cardinal that sent for him. On his arrival at the cardinal's house, he was well received and entertained. Martin thought that since he was sent for, things would surely change and that the cardinal must have changed his mind and decided to give him money. On his arrival, the cardinal asked him to kneel down for prayer and blessing. He hesitated and said within him, "What has blessing got to do with money for a flight ticket?" He reluctantly knelt down for the prayer and blessing. After the spiritual act, Martin, who expected either a check or cash for his flight ticket, became more disappointed once again when that did not come he promised that "none of his children would ever remain poor, so as not to suffer what he went through."[471]

Martin's father, Patrick Ekandem, struggled to get the ticket money. Martin left for studies without any further reference to the uncle. He arrived safely in California. To his greatest surprise, he found an American standing with his name, Martin Ekandem, boldly written on a plate or placard. He hesitated at first and said within him, "Who is it that knows me in this foreign land?" He then mustered courage to identify himself and face whatever the outcome would be. The man introduced himself, collected his hand luggage, and went with him to wait for his suitcase. After collection, he took him home, handed over a bunch of keys to him, and showed him where he was going to stay till he was ready to leave America. Martin was stunned and immediately, he regretted why he treated his uncle that way. He used the next available opportunity he communicated with the uncle to apologize for his behavior on the final day that they met. He rather thanked the cardinal for the surprising package he prepared for him ahead of time in the United States of America without saying a word even when he was almost forced to say something. He wanted everything to be a surprise. Before blessing Martin, Dominic Cardinal Ekandem had carefully found out from him when he was intending to depart from Nigeria and what flight he wanted to take. When all these details were given, he prayed for Martin and imparted his paternal blessing. That is why he was able to arrange everything while leaving Martin in the dark to discover it in a surprising manner as he did. It is what the cardinal planned that took place even though his quietness and the whole arrangement disquieted his nephew. He did not want the left hand to know what the right hand was doing. This was part of the outstanding characteristic of Cardinal Ekandem. He wanted the Lord to know and appreciate what he was doing instead of seeking for approval of others. Martin Patrick Ekandem attended Teachers' Training College (TTC), Uyo in 1971. From there, he proceeded to Lincoln University, Oakland, California, in the United States of America. He graduated with a bachelor's degree in economics and business administration in 1975. He proceeded to Temple University, Philadelphia, and graduated in 1977. He obtained a master's degree in business administration specializing in accounting. After working in the United States of America for some time, he returned to Nigeria in 1980.

L. Provision of Benefactors/Benefactresses for his Seminarians

Whenever he found a benefactor or benefactress for any of his seminarians, he never made it known to the seminarian in question until the day of ordination. Following the example of Bishop Moynagh, Dominic, when he became a bishop and in charge of a diocese, made every effort to get benefactors and benefactresses for his seminarians. He did this very carefully but very secretly. He was not making the benefactors and benefactresses aware of the fact that the one they trained had reached the moment of ordination. Probably, this was to safeguard their good works. He was strictly observing what the Lord commanded, "Do not let your right hand know what the left is doing" (Matt. 6:3). One of the benefactors was so pleased to have trained a seminarian that after the ordination at the Cathedral of St. Anne, Ifuho, the couple who trained the newly ordained priest decided to attend the first Holy Eucharistic celebration of the new priest with his entire family. They took along with them all the furnishings a house would need to the village of the new priest. The new priest had never met them or known them, so it was a great surprise but a pleasant one. The young priest was saying, "How can a young unknown person like me be treated so highly as if I were a king by this rich family?" He was perplexed and continued to thank them and pray daily for them likewise his ordinary who made the secret arrangement.

M. Awards

The various contributions he made in various quarters merited him honors and respect in high quarters both in private and in public. The colonial masters were very concerned to give honor to whom honor was due. In this case, it was no other person than the ebullient Bishop Ekandem.

The award was given just at the close of colonialism and the start of the independence of Nigeria. It was proper during the independence in 1960 that he had his first award. Concerning the award, the cardinal said, "Seeing how beautifully our native women marched in uniform, the colonial masters could not be less impressed by the performance of these women." Realizing that Bishop Ekandem was the brain behind the women's impressive performance, the British administration decided to award him.

OBE (1960)—ORDER OF THE BRITISH EMPIRE

This was the first award he received. The OBE (1960) was given to him as a result of his contribution toward the betterment of the women's position and pride as well as his contribution to the societal growth.

CON (1965)—COMMANDER OF THE ORDER OF THE NIGER

The second award was given to him in 1965 during the reign of Dr. Nnamdi Azikiwe generally abbreviated Zik. Zik was the president and commander of the Nigerian Armed Forces at that time. The award was given to him two years after Nigeria became a republic as a result of his ingenious establishment of the Federation of Catholic Teachers' Association (FCTA). For the cardinal, any honor done to him was always seen as an honor done to the people he was working with.

CFR (1982)—COMMANDER OF THE FEDERAL REPUBLIC OF NIGERIA

This award was given to him in 1982 during the reign of Pres. Shehu Shagari, seeing his attempts to foster peaceful coexistence between the Muslims and Christians and the attempts to unify in the one entity, the Nigerian Nation. Also looking at his role in Abuja and the episcopal conference he was honored in a colorful ceremony with the award of being a commander of the Federal Republic of Nigeria.

His contributions to the nation were well recognized, and the awards were well merited. It was a great honor done to him to a great man of substance. In Cardinal Ekandem is found the combination of foresight as well as insight with his natural wisdom, which produced his vision of greater things. After all these national or political awards came the academic awards that were almost in succession.

LLD (1989)—DOCTOR OF LAW

This was an international award that went beyond the confines of Nigeria as a nation and the continent of Africa. It came across the seas. It came all the way from America. The award came seven years after being conferred with the award of commander of the Federal Republic of Nigeria.

This was in recognition of his contribution to the health sector at Mercy Hospital Abak with the establishment of a special section called the *eye unit*. This unit had made a lot of developments to solving various eye problems of many within the nation. People came from all parts of the country to the eye clinic. It was very popular and very well-known. The good results obtained encouraged many to come. What spurred it on was the team of experts that used to come from the United States of America to minister to the people just as a special team of doctors used to come from Germany to take care of those with bone problems at St. Joseph Rehabilitation Center, Ukana Iba, Ikot Ekpene and that team was later replaced by another team that comes regularly from Mka in Benue State of Nigeria to attend to those within the center and those who come from outside as outpatients.

When Cardinal Ekandem implemented these projects, he did them selflessly. He never thought of any award or recognition. It was the relief of his flock and glorification of God that was uppermost in his mind. When the team that came from Chicago in conjunction with the academic board decided to honor the cardinal because of all the good reports they have been compiling and receiving from the clinic, they decided to make his contributions to humanity public by awarding him an honorary doctorate in law. He was surprised but at the same time happy. It is all the good part of God's benevolence *misericordiam Domini in aeternum cantabo,* I will sing forever of your love Oh Lord (Ps. 89:1).

LITT. D (1990)—DOCTOR OF LETTERS

It was good that after the international award, there should be a homecoming experience of being recognized by the University of Calabar for his contribution in the field of education by establishing many prominent schools and hospitals, especially for his conscientization of the nation toward the plight of the poor, the relief of their suffering and their recognition as those made in the image and likeness of God with equal rights and privileges with human dignity irrespective of whatever must have befallen those with some disabilities. His great contribution to the ethical commission established by Pres. Shehu Shagari concerning public accountability, justice, and unity of the nation shone the beam of light on him so much so that the university dons noticed him and beckoned on him to come for the award. He appreciated it and thanked the university for its kindness.

Traditional Titles

He also received many traditional chieftaincy titles that he had forsaken when he became a member of the Catholic clergy. The same titles and honors kept on pursuing him till they met up with him. He could not, at the time, ignore them. He accepted them graciously. They conferred on him titles like *Okuku Ibiono,* the overall Ruler of Ibiono*; Obong Mfon,* Chief or King of Goodness; *Obong Emem,* Chief or King of Peace; *Adaha Unwana Ibibio,* the Fortress of Ibibio's Enlightenment; or simply *Obong Unwana,* the Chief or King of Light or Brightness; *Obong Isong,* the Chief or Ruler of the Land. It is probable that Fr. Edidiong Ekefre derived the title of his book *A Testament of Light* from this very traditional title conferred on the cardinal.

gure 1Cardinal in Chieftaincy Attire

Figure 15 Cardinal Ekandem in Chieftaincy Attire

ADDRESS BY HIS EMINENCE CARDINAL EKANDEM TO THE FEDERATION OF CATHOLIC STUDENTS ON THE OCCASION OF THEIR SILVER JUBILEE CELEBRATIONS ON 30TH AUGUST 1981 AT THE UNIVERSITY OF BENIN[472]

I thank you for this privilege and the honour done to me by this invitation. Impressed and edified by your determination, your plans and activities which I observed last August when your representatives assembled in Ibadan for the Sub-Regional Conference of the International Movement of Catholic Students, I had no hesitation in accepting this invitation knowing that the Nigerian Federation of Catholic Students is pregnant with its own possibilities. As members of the Catholic Church you have a wonderful opportunity of making substantial contribution towards nation building. The Catholic Church from the testimony of our Nigerian elders and rulers has already achieved much for this country. "The Roman

Catholic Church," remarked one of our Heads of State, "he made tremendous contributions to the Country's education and social development. We as Catholics feel rather proud to be complimented by no less a personality than our Head of State. But these remarks were made some years ago, so that the achievements recalled, refer chiefly to the work of the Missionaries in Nigeria for Nigerians. If the Church has accomplished for the Nation that amount of good works attributed to her through her expatriate missionaries who have largely contributed to their foundation—in the field of education, medical and social services—logically the church should receive not only ordinary encouragement but a meaningful support from all men of good will at least and from the government—local, state and federal. Where the contrary is the case, then there is something wrong and should be investigated. The mission of the church is to do good to all people and Nations. It has done good to our Nation and we as loyal sons and daughters of the church must make ourselves fully committed in performing this good service to our own nation—spiritual and temporal services. If the influence of the church in this country will grow stronger, then the laity has the answer.

Catholic laymen and women have the answer. You the enlightened Catholics, you the Catholic intelligentsia, have the answer. We, "Spiritual Fathers and Brothers" are like mere signposts.

From your own Catholic Families we depend for that growth and increase in vocations that will keep the Church alive, active and influential in Nigeria. So far we thank and praise God that our Seminaries, Junior and Major, are full of enough with students. The future is therefore bright. In our mission field of Nigeria, we observe the presence of lay expatriate missionaries like missionary lay teachers, teaching in educational institutions established by the Church, lay missionary doctors and nurses etc. working in mission hospitals, lay social volunteer workers, helping out in some diocese, so that in almost all aspects of the development work carried out by the Church, the clergy and the religious, were never abandoned or left alone, but volunteer lay workers and professionals were always found ready to come out and work side by side with them here in the country, a situation which is still noticeable in some dioceses at the present day.

I seize this opportunity therefore to thank a good number of Nigerian Catholic—men and women, whose faith has inspired them to being up their children well and send them on to train as priests and religious for the service of the Nation, the Church and humanity as a whole. I thank others also for adopting and sponsoring financially our young seminarians preparing for the priesthood, and those who place at the disposal of the Church for promoting the Kingdom of God in our country, their resources, their talents and their time.

But we must admit that the majority of our Nigerian Catholics have not done their best this regard not made attempts in help in solving some of the big problems facing the Church in Nigeria. With the existence of a providential organisation such as the National Federation of Catholic Students, we should confidently hope that in the very near future there will be a better understanding of the position of the Church in Nigeria with a corresponding and individually to apply effective remedy and supply relief.

Since fortunately Nigeria is now blessed with thousands of Catholic graduates and professional men and women, the church in Nigeria eagerly looks forward, not only to their cooperation and initiative in development and promotion work but to welcome them as volunteer teachers in institutions like the Seminary, and volunteer medical personnel for mission hospitals. In this way the church Nigeria which unfortunately is still largely dependent on outside help, despite all the indigenisation going on, will become viable, self-reliant and self-supporting.

N.   The Need for a National Catholic Press

> The long-standing problem of getting a good National Catholic Newspaper for Nigeria can only be effectively solved as far as I can see, but the Catholic graduates and professionals of Nigeria. The absence of such press has hit us very severely. For the past thirty or forty years, efforts have been made by the Bishops of Nigeria to set up a national press, but they have not succeeded. Their difficulties have been sabotage of funding and of personnel. Occasionally the Bishops succeeded in bringing out voluntary expatriate staff for the work, but lack of a strong financial support often forced the project to close down. The Bishops' effort, despite their determination and good intentions, as

in the case of the Leader and the Independent, our provincial papers, and the Catholic life, the bimonthly magazines, their efforts, for these difficulties, meet with feeble success and applause. This would not be the case if at any time the establishment of the Catholic national paper were to receive the support of the intellectual and material resources of our Catholic graduates and professionals all over the country.

Let, therefore, the setting up with immediate effect of a virile national press, to be maintained by you and Catholic intellectuals all over the country be one of the resolutions of your deliberations during this celebration.

O. The Menace of the Present Educational System in Nigeria

The increasing incidents and reports of violence, rioting, and destruction as the offshoot of breakdown of discipline and flouting of authority together with the abandonment of our cherished traditional and religious values on the part of our students in the various institutions of higher learning throughout the country—a situation that was formerly unheard of in the history of our education—Catholic graduates and undergraduates, I feel, can do something to help improve this situation. With this conviction and with other citizens of goodwill in the country, let them plead with our Government—Local, State, and Federal—to return to the former practice of partnership in education involving the State, the Church, and the parents. The disaster, which has befallen our Nation today, is caused by the extortion of schools from the church, the denial of the Church's right to share in the education policy of our country.

Having worked so hard for the past twenty-five years, a fruitful apostolate in our country, it is our duty as your Spiritual fathers to keep you continually in our prayers so that you may bring to perfection the good work you have so well begun.

On behalf of the Catholic hierarchy of Nigeria, I extend profound gratitude to all those who cooperate with and support you in all your endeavours, our rulers in the government, the authorities of your various institutions in which you are, our chiefs and elders as fathers of our Nation, your friends and well- wishers, particularly those who have made the big effort to be here to celebrate this occasion with you.

May God Bless and Protect Them All

The thought of the cardinal about the contributions of the Federation of Catholic Students Association (FCTA) are well spelled out. He expressed his mind on take over of schools by the government, which he accentuated as the leading factor of breakdown of discipline in schools, rioting and breakages needed to be readdressed. His speech also accentuated the need for a Catholic press as well as the state supporting the activities of the church because of the Church's contributions to the state. He equally stressed the need for educated men and women to help facilitate the indigenization process so that the church will become viable, self-reliant and self-supporting. His main concern is the growth and progress of the people—the church and the state.

P.   On Nigerians and Public Revenue

The cardinal showed his concern about public affairs, the welfare of the revered Nigerian citizens, and the necessity of justice for the sake of promoting peace by including in his Lenten pastoral letter the following:

> We have not a good reputation, rather a bad one internationally, as regards misappropriation, in so many devious ways, of public revenue. And how long it takes the State to catch up with its thieves! When did the law of God or State law ever tell us that election or appointment in public office carried with them the right to filch at will the from public office? In God's name, let us reform our lax consciences and adjust to God's Will, which many of us claim to respect.[473]

In this short exposition of his position and concern for the wellbeing of the noble citizens he hits the nail on the head regarding corruption and embezzlement of public funds with impunity without any regard to the situation of the poor or the purpose for which the funds were meant. He equally touched the aspect of lax conscience as a contributing factor to the menace of corruption and the problem of nominal Christians as Karl Rahner couched it. He did not just stop at the criticism but went further to give a piece of advice on how to proceed and make things better as the country progresses into the future.

Q. Advice for a Better Future

The foresight and insight of Cardinal Ekandem can be vividly seen in the manner he interwove common knowledge, religious, and philosophical knowledge in proffering solutions to the problem of polity and governance of the nation. His personality as one firmly grounded in the life, teachings, and history of the church manifests itself plainly in this excerpt.

> Well, I would never overstress the importance of education at all levels. But then we need to strengthen our faith the more, practising it in the public to get others attracted to it. Moreover, we should be able to produce more reliable laymen to take part in government. In the early history of the Church, we see that it was only when a Christian, Constantine became the Roman Emperor that the persecution of the Church ceased. It is not enough to criticize evil practices for all that is necessary for evil to continue is that good men do nothing to curb it. We thus insist on our laymen going into active politics using all their training on justice, integrity, compassion etc. This is the only way we can hope for a change and we must press and we must press that forward for the sake of our future.[474]

As a man of faith and a convinced Christian, he could not but bring to bear the importance of faith in the future of the nation as well as good governance. The moral principles of justice, integrity, and compassion are prominent, challenging the laymen and laywomen to take up the mantle of leadership in the emerging Nigerian politics using these moral principles as the basis of leading, guiding, and directing the citizens with compassion and equally in love, which are relevant to every human relationship and association.

Could it be that the cardinal was pointing to something he had witnessed in other parts of the world during his many travels to various continents and countries or during the regional or continental or international meetings they had been having? Could it be he hinting at the Catholics or not just the Catholics but Christians forming a political party as obtained in Europe Couched Christian Democratic Party as in the case of Germany and Italy and in flimsy manner in the United States of America in which they stand for moral principles that others may easily oppose. Can they form such a party leaving themselves open for proper Christian formation of conscience so as to act authoritatively for the good of all?

Can they persist whether they win or lose elections? Can they understand that if they win, they rule; if it happens that they fail, they know that their party has failed and begin to form a new strategy? Are the Nigerian Christians ready for such revolutionary change so as to entrench good moral principles of equality, of justice, of truth, of discipline and of fair play instead of announcing those principles verbally without implementing them? Can they form a formidable party that will embrace the whole country and see to it that justice is done in terms of voting and that the right people are elected into office without playing the politics of might is right, monetary power, or elimination by assassinating or incriminating the other in order to possess an upper hand?

From the cardinal's point of view, it is obvious that he wanted men and women who are Christians to join active or partisan politics but not to be involved in the evils of politics. Christians cannot just sit back to criticize those in power. They have to do something positive. They must be involved in politics to revolutionize it from within and not from without. The emphasis of Dominic Cardinal Ekandem is for Christians to join politics and, if possible, form their party and enjoy the freedom of the children of God by doing what is right and giving their brothers and sisters their rightful due. This is what will bring in growth into the country with the care of the poor and the weak instead of squandering the money meant for the weak and poor and leaving them in a more wretched situation.

One may ask, what of the Christians who are in politics who are already corrupted with the others in evil practices? Such an objection is right and just, but what this ecclesiastical prelate emphasizes is carrying out a revolution that will benefit the entire country and every person while respecting the rights of individuals together with the possibility of forming a Christian political party since the clergy cannot be involved in this. It is the lay faithful who have the onus or even the inalienable right of planning and executing this with the blessing of their clergy.

Was the cardinal too radical about this type of idea? Not at all! He would have reflected on what would lead Nigeria forward as Gen. Ibrahim Badamisi Babangida came up with "option A4" as open ballot system to determine the proper winner of an election. The idea may be innovative but it is not outlandish.

Cardinal Ekandem and bishops tell future government:

Don't Abandon the Poor[475]

The future leadership of Nigeria must not leave the poor to look helplessly at the gate of opportunity. Be it school, hospital, housing, fresh water, clear air, or better roads, the government will have to ensure that the common man derives some benefits.

Catholic Bishops said in a conference in Enugu that education, medical care, and these other facilities should be provided to all since majority of Nigerians are poor. "Whatever form of civilian government comes to be, there are priorities that must be got right: the nation is only strong when united, free and committed to the rule of law and justice," the bishops declared.

"There can no longer be in this nation any true God-fearing citizen with such surplus and with an easy conscience as long as his brothers and sisters continue to go hungry, go unhoused, unclothed, uneducated and uncared for," the bishops communiqué declared. They condemned the situation where few flourish in riches and majority are left in poverty, adding, "If there is better life ahead, then let it be for all and not for just a few."

The bishops also called on Nigerians to eschew extravagant and wasteful funeral expenses characteristic of our present society and urged all to emulate the late Pope Paul who directed in his last testament that no monument should be constructed for him. In a communiqué issued a few days after religious leaders had audience with the head of state Lt. Gen. Olusegun Obasanjo, the bishops expressed their determination to join in the task of ensuring peaceful, orderly, and successful return to civilian rule in 1979. They believe that peace can be achieved if leaders practice a high degree of accountability to their own consciences and to those whom they serve as well as God.

The Catholic bishops directed that all Catholics should stay from food, drinks, and other things of the flesh and bow their heads in prayer for peace and good government for Nigeria on September 29.

That day has been proclaimed a day of fasting and abstinence. Sunday the twenty-fourth of September is to be spent offering special prayers by the Catholics and all Christians have been urged to do the same. In addition to all these, the conference just ended in Enugu also directed the communiqué that Catholic Churches should commit the traditional October devotions to the purpose of praying for the nation.

On the international scene, the Catholic Bishops of Nigeria declared their total commitment to the liberation of all the oppressed people of Africa. About thirty Bishops from all over the country attended the conference that lasted from September 11 to 17.

R.   African Priests and Celibacy

The whole section on the subject of celibacy follows a variety of subjects of lesser importance. This is a great manifestation of the worth and inner strength that adorned the characteristic personality of the Cardinal Ekandem. His foresight as far as celibacy is concerned is very evident.

In the 1980s, many years after Ekandem was made a cardinal in consistory, he attended one of one those regular meetings of the cardinals in Rome. During the meeting, a discussion ensued. On the one hand it was an exciting event, but on the other hand, it created an unfortunate division that caused Cardinal Ekandem to quickly perceive the situation as awkward. He refused to join the chorus of applause and laughter that erupted concerning celibacy and the African priests. The intention was to create two different levels of observing the vow of celibacy between the Africans and the others. Recognizing what was at stake, he prepared himself for opposition that made him look for supporters who would back him up. The event did not only end there but quickly diffused itself and reached the grass root from where the smoldering fire burst into flame in a bus ride that made one enthusiastic listener keen to learn more about the situation.

The question of celibacy and the disputations surrounding it did not start with nor will it end with Cardinal Ekandem. This is a perennial problem that many regions and generations have engaged themselves from the time celibacy became part of the church's life.

There are times that opposing cardinals like Cardinal Schönborn discussed below create a theological storm about priestly celibacy. Such conflicts often lead to divisive atmosphere capable of causing much harm in the church and to her members. In all these, God who never abandons his church but cares diligently for her often preserves the church from errors and unimaginable problems and continues to set her on the right path. Some of these high-powered discussions can sometimes have their repercussions among the laity.

Many years ago when His Eminence Dominic Cardinal Ekandem was still alive, Sir Adam Bassey Nyong, KSJI, who is a colonel in his Uyo Commandery,[476] encountered some buzzing in the public bus he traveled in. The people concerned were in heated conversation about Cardinal Ekandem and African celibacy. The people talked furiously against the cardinal concerning priestly celibacy. The passengers were saying that the problem of celibacy could have been solved when at the bishops' gathering in Rome. They wanted to give African priests an option of marrying by being exempted from priestly celibacy but for the intervention of Cardinal Ekandem. They said that Cardinal Ekandem objected to it and continued to lay the burden on the clergy instead of lifting it.

The first thing about this story is that it could have been a concocted story spread through misinformation or misinterpretation or sheer ignorance. Whatever the case, there was a tendency to see celibacy as a burden rather than as a gift and a living example of Christ himself. That negative reaction prompted the listener Adam to inquire from His Eminence what the real situation was.

While in the bus, Colonel Adam decided to listen very attentively without any interruption. He was not familiar with the context of the discussion. Adam followed the normal human approach unlike Christ who adopted the nondirective approach of interaction while talking to the two disciples traveling from Jerusalem to Emmaus after his death and resurrection. On that journey, our Lord Jesus Christ took the initiative of inquiring from these travelers what they were talking about, With this approach, he drew out of them what was deeply hidden in their hearts and what caused them so much pain and disillusionment.

Eventually, he led them to the point of illumination at the table of breaking of bread.

At that point, he left them to sort out things for themselves and disappeared from their sight. His interaction caused them to decide to go back to Jerusalem after having been empowered and drawn out of their state of disillusionment and boredom. They went back to Jerusalem that same night and narrated to their companions that they had seen the Lord, that he was alive and truly risen (Cf. Lk. 24:13–35). Christ's method contrasts very strongly with that of Colonel Adam's that needed an external help and enlightenment. Adam went at the earliest opportunity to share his experience with Cardinal Ekandem about the whole affair.

He commenced his sharing by narrating his experience in the bus and went further to question the cardinal if he had any idea of what the bus passengers were saying. The first reaction of His Eminence was "Akpakap ado ommo emakop nkpo ekpekap ebup ediongo ntak mbemiso etang akpafon, emi emakop ebume kunana edidiongo!" It would have been better for them to find out what the main reason was before dabbing into what they did not know!

He then went on to share with Adam what he knew about the situation. Probably, this took place during one of the regular gatherings of the cardinals of the church in Rome. Being a member of such a prestigious body in the church and belonging to many commissions in the Vatican, he had the privilege of interacting with many delegates from varied continents and nations. Some of those discussions touched very important issues in the life of the church. One of such issues was that of celibacy.

Even though Cardinal Ekandem was held in very high esteem, perhaps, his paternal role did not embrace all. It is probable that not all shared his views on celibacy. There were some dissident voices that gave the impression that Africans were incapable of living out the celibate life effectively. Some even went to the extent of proposing that celibacy for African priests should be made optional or that they should be totally exempted because of natural weakness and inclination. Since Cardinal Ekandem was always very attentive whenever he went to any meeting, he listened, reflected, and took the discussions to heart like the Blessed Virgin after the presentation of Jesus at the temple (Lk. 2:34–35) where she was told that a sword will pierce her own heart, and after finding Jesus at the temple, Jesus said to Mary, "Did you not know that I must be in my Father's house?" Mary kept all these things in her heart (Lk. 2:49–51).

After that comment, he then went on to tell Sir Adam B. Nyong what transpired. He indicated that there was an opinion sometime in the past that African priests should be exempted from observing the priestly celibacy and that they could be allowed to marry instead. He went on to say that he was totally dissatisfied with the whole situation and sought for an occasion to voice out his protest, but he needed some support to buttress his point and give it the necessary weight it deserved. At this point, the help of another African prelate was sought. He put it in a funny manner to Sir Adam by saying, "Don't you know that some people are busybodies looking for what to do or what to say even if they have no authority to say or do it? Those who have such thoughts should have learned better and should know that celibacy is a gift of the Divine Lord. There is no need for presumption or prejudice about this noble gift given in the words of the Gospel to those who can" (Cf. Matt. 19:11).

It appears the idea of marriage by African priests is based on the age-old Gospel background whereby Peter and a few others were married and St. Paul exhorted Timothy to make sure that a bishop did not marry more than once and in the Eastern Church, priests had the liberty of marrying before diaconate and the tradition of appointing a bishop from among the unmarried clergy still exists and that the discipline of the Western Church to join celibacy and the priesthood was as a result of historical experiences. Truly, it sprang from the example of Christ, the head of the church.

Such background is not lacking at all looking at it from Peter Gill's telescope who is not the only one to construct a cloud of prejudice that Africans, or rather "black men are considered sexual predators without self-control of the mind."[477] Fr. Joseph A. Brown, SJ, a black American Jesuit gave a Loyola lecture on being black and Catholic cited what some of the American bishops echoed at home and in the Vatican about African priests reflecting their racial American background and projecting it on the Africans and their priests. The often quoted statement reflected the imputed reputation of African Americans, thereby moving from particular to generality/universal.

This prejudiced mentality found its way into the core of the church. After the speech by one of the American cardinals in the Vatican, all who were present applauded thunderously and had a very good laugh. Cardinal Ekandem was not pleased with that. During a short recess, he drew the attention of the only cardinal from East Africa that was present and questioned him why he laughed with the others after the speech and went further to ask whether he understood what was said and what abuse was directed to the African priests by making such a proposition?

Cardinal Ekandem intimated him that when they reconvened after the recess, that he was going to bring up the topic again. He wanted to counter the motion that "black men are considered sexual predators without self-control of the mind" by extension to all African priests, that no such thing as exemption should be given to Africans alone since the priesthood does not belong to the Africans but to Christ and to the universal church; Catholic priesthood is one wherever one goes. He encouraged the East African cardinal to strongly support and back up the counter-motion with powerful arguments as well. Because of his intervention, the move to apply exemption to the African priests was not only suspended but also suppressed.

His argument was "If the exemption were to have been granted to the Africans, the Europeans, the Asians, the Americans and those from Oceania might go ahead and marry, should the priestly celibacy become confused or gets into serious crisis or face a terrible defection by the others, the blame would surely point to the African priests as being the cause of downfall of the Catholic priesthood. Many other less orthodox theologians who either wittingly or unwittingly denigrated the priestly celibacy would then say, because the Africans were granted an exemption therefore, this has occurred. Noting the intricate nature of the situation, he decided not to go on with that idea." One day while sharing with his priests at table after returning from Rome, he said to those sharing the table with him that he had told the Europeans and others not to bother about Africans who practiced polygamy since this was used as a major obstacle for the Africans to live out the celibate life.

A strong point adopted in the process of trying to show the necessity of marriage for African priests was that of polygamy. The argument was that since the Africans have been marrying many wives, they would not be able to live out the vow of celibacy. They need to marry. The Europeans and others who have been marrying one wife can go ahead and live the vow of celibacy. The response of Cardinal Ekandem was that polygamy, as a background for celibacy, cannot constitute a problem at all for the Africans since celibacy entails a new life in Christ and a decision based on the grace of Christ. Those who opted for polygamy are not priests, and the priests who opt for celibacy are not undertaking their parents' lifestyle but that of Christ, the Chief Shepherd.

He went further to say that if they wanted to go and marry, they should make the choice boldly and not to try to lean on the Africans using them as scapegoats to satisfy their interest. Africans should be left out of the matter. He added an Ibibio proverb: Idoho adia asa ama adia asa, nti-nyik eketop Udo Ekperikpe, Not because the eater of asa has consumed it therefore, Udo Ekperikpe suffers hiccups. He raised his right foot and stamped it gently but continuously on the ground and added that he told them like Christ on the way to Calvary not to worry about the Africans but the deposit of faith in the whole church. Polygamy should not be used as a scapegoat to try and circumvent the glaring difficulty of celibacy of which Christ is the originator and the one who sustains those he has granted the grace. The problem of celibacy is a universal one and should not be oversimplified or used as an aspersion to the detriment of one group of persons or the other in the Church."[478] What His Eminence feared most was illusion, misleading or selective version of the Church's teaching. He preferred saying the truth in a simple and straightforward manner. He spoke the truth in love as Pope Benedict XVI titled his encyclical: *Caritas In Veritate.*[479] Truth, which is Christ, always had to prevail.

From the point of view of Divine Revelation, it is obvious that:

> This tradition, which comes from, the Apostles develops in the Church with the help of the Holy Spirit. For there is a growth in the understanding of the realities and the words, which have, been handed down. This happens through contemplation and study made by believers who treasure

these things in their hearts (Cf. Lk. 2:19, 51) through a penetrating understanding of the spiritual realities which they experience and through the preaching of those who have received through Episcopal Succession the sure gift of truth…until the words of God reach their complete fulfilment in her.[480]

The prelate remarked that there were no different standards of practicing celibacy in the church. The standard is one, and that is Christ Jesus, our Lord. It was his active and effective listening to this proposal that highlighted his foresightedness, courage, and zeal of the apostles by teaching, correcting, and leading by governing the church of God through the power of the Holy Spirit. It appears the position of Cardinal Ekandem was the same as that of St. Pope John Paul II. The pope when asked his position on married priests and in particular an Episcopalian parish and the pastor that wanted to become Catholics responded by saying:

The Holy See has specified that this exception to the rule of celibacy is granted in favour of these individual persons, and should not be understood as implying any change in the Church's conviction of the value of priestly celibacy, which will remain the rule of future candidates for the priesthood for this group.[481]

The teaching of the pope is very clear. It abhors any confusion. Here he meant that he was not ready to compromise the deposit of faith Christ handed down through the apostles. Concerning the ordination of women, he also had this to say:

In order that all doubt may be removed regarding a matter of great importance, a matter which pertains to the Church's divine constitution, in virtue of my ministry of confirming the brethren (Lk. 22:33), I declare that the Church has no authority whatsoever to confer priestly ordination on women and that this judgement is to be definitively held by all the Church's faithful.[482]

Cardinal Ekandem said that two different standards, one for the Europeans, Americans, Asians, and the other for the Africans could not coexist in the same church with the same tradition and origin. He questioned whether there were two different types of priesthoods or whether it was the same one that originated from Christ? He took up this rhetorical question by saying that if the priesthood is one, and there is one Christ, one baptism, one chalice is given to us all to drink and there is one faith in Christ, then there should be no distinction between the African priests' celibacy and that of the other continents'. All should be treated the same way. There is no high or low priesthood. It is the priesthood of Christ that entails probity of life. Catholic priesthood and celibacy derive from Christ. Those who follow him intimately undertake to walk in his footsteps and live his life.

Cardinal Ekandem's deep, loving understanding and faith conception of the universality of the Church or its Catholicity formed the bedrock of his argument concerning the Catholic priesthood and celibacy in Africa. The prelate was so passionate about the universality of the church in such a way that when one of his priests was talking about African theology, he immediately interrupted by saying that there is no African theology as such but there is only one theology that of Jesus Christ, the founder of Christianity. Every other aspect is only a contribution or an expansion of the foundation laid by Christ. No other person can lay another foundation apart from the one already laid by Christ. Christ is all in all. Once things begin from him, they will end well with him. He is never to be abandoned.

What he said about Catholic priestly celibacy became a foreboding prognostication when an Austrian cardinal presented the priestly celibacy problem to Pope Benedict XVI on behalf of his lay faithful on June 17, 2009. The presentation had this caption: "VATICAN: THE CARDINAL OF VIENNA presents a petition against celibacy for priests."

> On the eve of the opening of the Year for Priests sought by Pope Benedict XVI, the question of priestly celibacy was again forcefully raised at the Vatican. Cardinal Christoph Schönborn, one of the most influential cardinals of the Church, who is also a close collaborator of Pope Ratzinger, raised the issue. During the two days of meetings that the

Pope and the most important representatives of the Roman Curia had on June 15–16 with the Archbishop of Vienna and other representatives of the Austrian Church, discussion was not limited to the case of Gerhard Marie Wagner, the ultra-conservative priest named auxiliary bishop of Linz and later forced to step down because of a revolt by priests and laity in the diocese Cardinal Schönborn also presented a supposed "Lay Initiative" (*Laieninitiativ*), that is, a call launched at the beginning of the year by important Austrian Catholics, demanding the abolition of the celibacy requirement, the return to duty of married priests, opening the diaconate to women, and the ordination of so-called *viri probati*.[483]

If Cardinal Ekandem had left things the way the cultural and racial background had intended, the presentation of Cardinal Schönborn could have been a development of what Dominic Cardinal Ekandem approved instead of opposing it. He opposed it vehemently having perceived what was likely to emerge in the future. His vision went beyond the limits of his own time and saw the wider picture of the church's tradition.

In Italy, twenty-six women,[484] or rather mistresses of priests[485] who had been living with priests for a long time signed a letter they sent to Pope Francis asking him to make celibacy optional, that they had been living for many years with the priests in an atmosphere of love and tranquility with-out any problems and living with them in silence. In their letter, they want the pope to give them permission to come out publicly and manifest their relationship with the priests in marriage. What does this indicate, *married priests' viri probati*. Perhaps, these occurrences would have been traced to the African situation had it been granted. It would surely have muddied the water using the African priests' celibacy exemption as an excuse. The same could have applied to South America in which some of the priests look for laicisation after two three or four years of priesthood and go out to marry[486] and sometime before exiting they have already got a partner. It is notable that the growth areas in the South American church are in the more traditional areas of the church such as *Opus Dei*.

What Cardinal Ekandem did was a happy prognostication even though some people did not appreciate his foresightedness. A prophet is never appreciated in his own. His worth lies in his intuitive and infused knowledge that went beyond mere intellectual knowledge and perception. The origin was divine. It has to be recalled that when many people, including some clergy, were the advocates for women's ordination, Pope John Paul II said that the matter was of divine constitution; therefore, no one had the right to change it. All future candidates for the priesthood would have to follow that same path. It can be seen that the Church's tradition goes back to its origins and, finally, to Christ, the head of the body the church. Cardinal Ekandem foresaw the wars and the turmoils that were to come and put a refused to be sucked in. That is the spiritual vision that cannot be obtained through flesh and blood.

When Card. Peter Turkson working in the Vatican was interviewed on the issue of celibacy in Africa during the Synod of Bishops he said:

> Celibate priests already exist in our traditional religion, and also married ones, who must abstain from sexual relations for three days when they celebrate their rites. Hence, those who say that for the African mentality celibacy is inconceivable are telling an untruth.[487]

In Africa, as the history of the world knows and shows, there had been a series of intertribal wars or even village wars. Just as in the contemporary age, every war necessitates serious preparation. The same applied to the context of intertribal wars or any other wars that needed to be fought. Every warrior was supposed to have prepared himself in the traditional manner before the day of engagement with the enemy. During the whole period of preparation, they were not supposed to reach their homes nor get in touch with their wives or concubines. The forest was their home. They ate little: a roasted plantain with palm oil only throughout the whole period. They did not consume any food cooked by women except those prepared by males. They were to abstain from all forms of sexual intercourse during the period of preparation and throughout the entire period of war. No warrior dreamed of failure or defeat. That would make them become subjugated to the others. They preferred to be victorious. Hence, they observed the rule of abstention very strictly as long as they were on expedition. They believed that having sexual relationship with a woman at such period would neutralize the charms and amulets they used for war. To avoid that, they had to keep themselves pure, ready, and alert at the command to fight or advance. Celibacy is not unknown to the Africans but rather forms an integral part of the people's life. From the foregoing, it is notable that the celibate life in the traditional African context was a temporary one. That of the Catholic priesthood is not temporary but permanent since it originates from Christ who is always there—the same yesterday, today, and forever.

The same principle applies to those that were to undergo initiation rites. They had to observe their abstinence with strict religious outlook convinced that they on the way to metamorphose into a new level of existence and maturity that would initiate them into adulthood. Initiation rite was not the only one; involvement in certain masquerades also exposed those carrying it to abstain not only from sexual intercourse but also from contact with women. The idea of celibacy is not strange to the Africans in any way. They are very much at home with it. It was a predisposition for victory, for overcoming troubles of various kinds. It equally entailed disciplining oneself in order to graduate into the adulthood stage of life that Okonkwo said in Chinua Achebe's book *Things Fall Apart* that "When a small child washes his hands well, he can eat with the elders" provides an incentive to growth and maturity.

Celibacy is part of the cultural heritage of Africa. It is not foreign to it. The same is applicable to polygamy even though some people imagine that it is the biblical polygamy that encouraged them to be polygamous. That is not true since in Africa, especially in Nigeria, polygamy was practiced to enhance the labor force, as it happened in many other continents until the industrial revolution where lesser numbers of people were required to undertake a particular job since the machine took over most of it. Polygamy is no longer viewed in the same light of productivity. Those who practice it like the Muslims are attaching some religious significance to it or for personal reasons, but surely not for production of farming products.

It likewise provided the opportunity of preserving life in connection with those who carried the masquerade even though the undertaking was transient. Apart from abstaining from sexual relationship, they were meant to abstain from every type of murder or manslaughter otherwise; carrying the masquerade would lead to death. The examples given in connection with various situations in which celibacy was practiced indicate that celibacy as a value and as a gift is not foreign to the Africans but very much at home with them, notwithstanding the fact of being only for occasions and situations. Cardinal Ekandem was quite right when he foresaw what was likely to happen and nipped it at the bud. His faith, inspiration, foresight, and mystical penetration of difficult situations with divine light helped him bring to the surface what was buried in the depth. The love of the church put him on the right path where he defended the necessity of being celibate as imitators of Christ. Many African priests live and lived out their vow of celibacy in line with the teaching of Christ that those who can should undertake it (Cf. Matt. 19:11) All African priests cannot be discredited because of some who have faltered. The baby cannot be thrown away with the dirty bathwater. Cardinal Ekandem is one of those very leading clergy who practiced his celibate chaste life happily and courageously, in season and out of season, without minding the cost. This he did as long as it pleased the Lord Jesus Christ, his redeemer and master without looking at any person. He encouraged his clergy, the religious men and women to live out their lives according to the mind of Christ, irrespective of the difficulties they may encounter.

He noted in very strong terms that the risk of having Christianity without Christ, without the Cross, without suffering, death and resurrection of the Lord and his principles are very strong. One should be wary of following Christianity without a soul. Such would be shambles rather than the core of Christianity. If care is not taken, it might even be a calculated attempt to annihilate Christianity. At the same time, he admonished the laity to be faithful followers of Christ in word and in deed. He never ceased to emphasize the true nature of purity in his homilies and at ordinations or profession of the religious. He was convinced and lived out that conviction till death.

He wanted his seminarians to also live the life of celibacy. If there were any known infringements, he would not keep such a seminarian in the seminary but in his fatherly way would explain to the seminarian what the evangelical council meant and then ask him to choose a different way of life.

The celibate life of Africans was bound to the wartime and also to initiations as well as to the time the traditional priests were performing their religious duties. Celibacy was therefore tied to certain situations and was not a permanent arrangement like the celibacy in the church. What the traditional priests and those initiated into various institutions experienced was temporary while the aim of efficacy of their undertaking was success at the end of the day.

Priests in Africa command much respect from their fellow Africans because they have opted to be celibates for the sake of Christ and to follow his example of purity of heart, mind, and body. They see celibacy as a sacrifice of themselves to God by foregoing their desire for children and marriage so that they will be free to serve God and the church faithfully.

Cardinal Ekandem was absolutely right in not wanting any two classes of priests, one for the Africans and one for priests of other continents. The priesthood of Christ is one and is the same for all.

Chapter Eighteen

IN VITAM AETERNAM
(IN ETERNAL LIFE)

Death and Burial

*It might reasonably be maintained that the true object of
all human life is play. Earth is a task garden; heaven is a
playground. To be at last in such secure innocence that one can
juggle with the universe and the stars, to be so good that one
can treat everything as a joke—that may be, perhaps, the real
end and final holiday of human souls.*

—G. K. Chesterton

A.   Cardinal Ekandem's Death in the Context of World Events

MANY THINGS BOTH the good and the bad, the good and the
ugly occurred on the world scene in 1995, the year of the cardinal's
death just as they did in 1917, the year of his birth.

In November, the assassination of the Israeli prime minister Yitzhak
Rabin rocked the whole world despite the meticulous security and con-

sciousness of the Israelis. It caused many to have a rethink of life and its ephemerality. Such a perception made General Buhari, the incumbent Nigerian president, to say that only God protects in every situation. That same year the Mexican bailout took place in the collapse of their economy and financial system. The Croatian forces launched Operation Storm against Serbian forces in Bosnia and Herzegovina. As if that ethnic cleansing was not enough, they shot down an American Air Force F-16 plane on February 6 to demonstrate their readiness to exercise military prowess.[488] At its conception, it was not taken very seriously until the ethnic cleansing became so serious then the world woke from slumber but by then it was already too late.

Wheels had been set in motion. A wave of terrorism had commenced that would not easily be stopped. They destroyed the Murrah Federal Building in Oklahoma where 168 people died on April 19, 1995. They carried out the attack without compassion, mercy, or consideration of people's lives and property or resources. They were heartless and reckless. They were bent on attracting the attention of the world, which they did.

The Irish Republican Army (IRA) detonated a bomb in Manchester city centre, and two hundred people were injured, and some were maimed. As part of the unleashment of the carnage in Ireland, Veronica Guerin, an Irish journalist was shot at the traffic light on June 26 in the outskirts of Dublin to round up the first half of the year. The beginning of the second half of the year—that is, July—witnessed Dr. Ian Wilmut and his team of collaborators cloning a sheep they later named Dolly when it was born in 1996, thus marking the beginning of the cloning industry that had great moral implications for the entire world. The Belarus military shot a hydrogen balloon killing its two American pilots on September 12. In October of that year, a major breakthrough in astronomy took place. Another major star, 51 Pegasi was discovered to have a planet that is an extra solar planet revolving around it like the sun.[489] These world events included the death of Cardinal Ekandem in November of that year. Before his final exit, he underwent many bodily sufferings that caused him great pains.

B. His Last Days and Final Exit

The last days of Dominic Cardinal Ekandem did not come suddenly. He was conscious of the approaching morn. He had started leaving himself open for that moment of great departure when he celebrated his seventieth birthday anniversary. Death did not take him by surprise. Every moment of his days since after the birthday anniversary was a highly calculated and measured one. His preparation to go to the house of the Father became more pronounced from that moment of the celebration. What he used as final thoughts on his seventieth birthday anniversary souvenir is very revealing. It shows that he was waiting for death instead of death waiting for him. He adopted the wordings of the morning prayer of week two, Thursday, in the Breviary to summarize everything. He cut off some of the lines and retained some. The re- composition of the hymn suited his purpose and revealed his inner thought about his departure. It brings out his reliance on God, his willing self-disposition coupled with urgent antic-ipation that took a different turn as each day passed by. Even when he was stronger, he was quite aware that death could come at any time. He lived under the shadow of death but with eyes fixed on heaven where his Father dwells.

> Alone with none but thee, my God,
> I journey on my way
> What need I fear when thou art near,
> O king of night and day?
> More safe am I within thy hand,
> Than if a host did round me stand.
>
> My destined time is fixed by thee,
> And death doth knows its hour.
> My life I yield to thy decree
> And bow to thy control
> We leave our fate with thee and wait
> Thy bidding when to go.[490]

This redacted hymn has a lot to say about the person of the Dominic Cardinal Ekandem. It evokes total surrender, dependence, trust, the expectation of death, the yielding to God's control, the waiting and the readiness to move whenever he was to be called. All indicate that he was well prepared for what was to come. There is a saying of Fr. Charles Arminjon that "our destiny is an enigma, which reason alone cannot explain; but faith elevates our thoughts, strengthens our courage and inflames our hope."[491] When the time drew nearer, he was no longer very mobile. He perceived that the end was approaching and might come at any moment. He moved very little. He was still full of humor and sometimes laughing at himself. He compared himself to a little child learning to crawl or to walk. He descended the steps slowly but steadily.

The last days of this great man were spent between the bedroom in the ground floor and the parlor where he used to celebrate the Eucharist with those that joined him for daily morning masses in the company of Msgr. Kenneth Enang who stayed with him all the time. One could set his clock by the regularity and punctuality of his devotion and celebration. He always started the Eucharistic celebration at six o'clock in the morning. Since there was no homily, he usually finished quickly. This mode of celebration coupled with the proximity of the location to those in the residential estate, attracted many who wanted a "quick mass" before rushing off to their business or trying to escape traffic on the way to work or travel. The early celebration attracted a large crowd. Many of those people stayed at the veranda while others stood outside at whatever space was available did that with great expectation and attention. Before retiring to Abuja, he had spent some time at Anua Hospital where he was taken care of by Medical Missionaries of Mary. He was later transferred to St. Mary's Hospital, Urua Akpan, still in Akwa Ibom State. There he spent about two months between March and May 1995. At Anua and Urua Akpan, he received as many visitors as came to see him. In his usual way, he tried cheering up the visitors even though he was the one that needed to be cheered up. It was almost like Jesus Christ going to John the Baptist for baptism at the Jordan River, and John reacted by saying, "I need to be baptized by you and do you come to me?" (Matt. 3:14). Those who visited him always went back with something to reflect on. His voice had gone down, the energy waned, but the will to communicate was still very effective.

Later that year, he went to Abuja, the place he had watched germinate and grow. He returned to the same place he used to stay whenever he went from Ikot Ekpene. It was the house that was allotted to him through the instrumentality of Fr. Matthew Kukah (who became bishop of Sokoto later) and Pres. Shehu Shagari through the honorable minister of the Federal Capital Territory (FCT). A new residence had been constructed for him at Asokoro and Monsignor Inyang was working seriously to get the place ready for his transfer to it when at the last minute, he preferred to stay where he was. Presumably, this was caused by his simple nature and concern for poverty with the hope that the place can become useful in another way to the archdiocese. It was a happy prognostication because that building eventually became the center of what was known and is still known as Gaudium et Spes, where seminars, symposia, and many archdiocesan events took place including retreats for small groups.

It is worthy of note that he never lost his senses or suffered from Alzheimer's disease during the process of his transition and final journey to eternity. He remembered everything vividly including the minutest details. Where there was need to make a joke, he did not hesitate to do so in spite of his being bedfast. His body had started depreciating seriously. His face that shined formerly now started losing its brilliance. He could not walk without the help of a walking stick or even a dutiful helper, Sr. Mary Augustine, who was always available to assist and provide all the necessary support.

He was still able to lift his legs from the ground whenever he came out of the bed and stood up to walk, having walked that way from seminary days to his aging days and to the departure to the final beyond. He was as mentally alert as ever. His comportment and decorum all combined to reveal the seasoned prince and prelate that lived and survived many decades and witnessed major changes in the country, the church, and the world.

When his health deteriorated very much, the medical doctor Maureen Brennan, MMM serving at St. Mary's Hospital Urua Akpan was summoned to Abuja with great urgency. As a woman that had great respect and genuine love for the cardinal, she did not delay and had to move immediately. At her arrival, she found out that the diabetic injury had affected the small toe, and she set out to clean it as gently as she could. The cardinal's sister, Mrs. Rose Nkubia Ekandem, was there. Dr. Brennan could not leave until after his death. She noted that there was no need to administer much drug at that time since everything was slowing down and tapering to an end. Whatever food the cardinal requested for was given to him even though he could not eat much. The little he was capable of eating sustained him although not with the same gusto with which he used to enjoy his food when he was well.

All that faded with the passing days including his appetite. One who stayed with him and knew him could see that the last moments were drawing near. Dr. Brennan was very kind and gentle even though she was a tough doctor like Dr. Anne Ward, MMM who trained very many doctors and nurses in Nigeria and many parts of Africa and those from Ireland whenever they came over to Nigeria to work under her supervision. She worked with Cardinal Ekandem when he was a young auxiliary bishop at Anua. Many doctors speak of the toughness of Dr. Anne Ward, MMM who would examine all the female patients in the consulting room without writing down anything but did not confuse the drugs or the cards of any one patient with another. The nurse or doctor to work with her must always be on time. If she arrived before any of these, they would leave the consulting room or theater that day without any delays. At this time, Dr. Maureen Brennan was as calm and as docile as a lamb trying to be present to the sick cardinal. It was only in extreme conditions that she administered some minor drugs to avert too very severe pain;[492] otherwise, he was left to take life day by day and hour by hour as time passed by to avoid too much stress on him. He specifically requested[493] the assistance of Rev. Sr. Mary Augustine Okon, HHCJ, the first sister from Ndon Ebom parish who became a nurse and a very seasoned and caring sister. She ended up still as the first sister from Nung Oku Parish when that section was divided and became autonomous. It must have been this special quality of gentleness, understanding, love, and compassion that caused the cardinal to single her out and brought her close to his bedside during those parting moments. She attended to him until the very last breath. Sr. Mary Augustine enjoyed that special privilege of being sent for to come and attend to the cardinal in his last days,[494] owing to her closeness to the cardinal when she served at the children's home behind the cardinal's residence at Ikot Ekpene. He heard a great deal about her, witnessed much and experienced her caring approach to those little ones whose angels constantly see the face of God and who constitute part of what St. Vincent de Paul terms, *our lords and masters.*[495] Sr. Mary Augustine knew how to be gentle, be understanding, insist on the medication and regulations gently but very firmly while uttering the truth with love and firmness, and try to coax the cardinal to see the need of complying with doctor's regulations.[496]

The cardinal prevailed at certain times and preferred a particular food apart from the normal beans and plantain meant to aid his diabetic condition. Wheat foofoo was not very common at the time, plantain as foofoo was used but was not common either. Sometimes he asked for a little semovita or pounded yam or even though it contained carbohydrate to make a necessary change. "Amala" was all right for his condition. He sometimes requested that too.

The gentle demeanor of Sr. Mary Augustine Okon, HHCJ earned her popularity in welcoming and receiving visitors very cordially and lovingly even if they could not see the cardinal. She knew how to handle each situation. She always said, "Let me go and see, if he is awake or if he can see any person." With that type of approach, the visitors were disposed to whatever resulted from her endeavors whether seeing him for a brief moment or coming back another time. Despite the graciousness of Sister Augustine, the cardinal sometimes had the last word especially if he heard the voice of the person and recognized it. Sometimes, Sister Augustine had some difficulty especially after indicating that the cardinal was indisposed to receive visitors and that the visitor should repeat and the cardinal says, "Let him or her in." In her humble disposition, she would immediately usher in the person of the person and the cardinal himself. She was a true servant that accounts for the special trust the cardinal had for her.

Such occurrences were not very common. They took place only if the cardinal felt stronger and better that particular day. If he felt weak, Sr. Mary Augustine would make every attempt to interpret his mind and discern the situation justly and discreetly. Sister Augustine made every effort to let the person see the cardinal especially if that person came from a very long distance. Sr. Mary Augustine Okon, HHCJ lived for seventeen years after the death of her mentor and father, the cardinal, and parted the world at the age of eighty-two in 2012.

Before the hour of departure of Cardinal Ekandem came, his coadjutor and successor Abp. John Olorunfemi Onaiyekan, who became Cardinal

Onaiyekan on November 24, 2012, seventeen years after the death of the prince-prelate, Cardinal Ekandem. Abp. John Onaiyekan came and administered the last Rite of Anointing to him. He did not die immediately but took some time before he finally parted very gently without stress. He simply fell asleep on the November 24, 1995. His death was announced during the major hours of national news as part of the news program or what may be tagged in today's language: Breaking News. His remains were deposited at the *Verda Mortuary* for two weeks to prepare for the burial. Cardinal Ekandem was the originator of the two weeks preparation for burial, which started in Ikot Ekpene Diocese with the death of Very Rev. Fr. Isidore Umanah of happy memory. Although the two weeks for burial were confirmed at Father Isidore's funeral, as far as the late Father Isidore was concerned, his burial took place within seven days.

As a concluding remark after the interment, Dominic Cardinal Ekandem said, "If a priest can be buried in one week, I do not see any reason why every other person cannot be buried in two weeks. From now on, burial in the diocese commencing from a week's time will be two weeks." When this law was enacted, those mourning were not supposed to offer anything to the public in terms of food or drink since people were not supposed to spend at funerals. That was the main reason for not offering things at funerals. In Ikot Ekpene diocese at the time, the deceased compound was supposed to have been inspected, properly examined by two people—one of them being a Catechist.

It was supposed to be done immediately after the person breathed the last breath. Nothing was to be changed. This was to forestall the neglect of the beloved one that often occurred during the delay until the period for burial then the whole place would be embellished or renovated or a new building constructed while the body was kept in a mortuary, whereas the person never witnessed such luxury while alive. It was a pastoral strategy that was implemented to take care of the poor masses since the church is the church of the poor and to avoid excessive expenditure as much as possible.

C. The Funeral Ceremony

The funeral of Cardinal Ekandem took place in Abuja at Our Lady Queen of Nigeria, Garki Area 2. The funeral ceremony became a celebration of God's goodness and kindness toward his servant and chief shepherd. People from all walks of life came to the burial ground. Some of those who wanted to be there for the funeral left two days earlier. Some wanted to arrive there at all cost to the extent that when their vehicle broke down or left late, they swallowed their pride, all shame, and boarded trailers plying the North—South and South—North route of the country. Some of those arrived in Abuja about six o'clock in the morning of the burial, while some headed directly from the motor park to the funeral ground.

a. The Vigil

At the vigil celebration, all the ecclesiastical provinces had a particular period allotted for the vigil and watchfulness, always commencing with the sacrifice of the Holy Mass. Ikot Ekpene, Uyo, Port Harcourt, Ogoja, and Calabar had a special time in the early morning hours since the remains were theirs by origin. They did it happily and celebrated the Eucharist for the repose of the soul of the cardinal. The vigil took place on December 1, 1995, while the funeral celebration took place at Our Lady Queen of Nigeria (OLQN), Garki, Federal Capital Territory, on December 2, 1995.

b. Attendance

His funeral attracted people from various parts of the world and from all walks of life. Some came in person, while others sent messages or representatives. Many prelates and clergy of various ranks and file arrived from different parts of Africa and from many other countries to swell the number of the already numerous Nigerian clergy. Not all the priests who attended the funeral had a place to sit or enter the cathedral because of the numbers. The number of the clergy that remained in the sacristy and out-side the pro-cathedral of Our Lady Queen of Nigeria, Garki, Abuja, was far greater than the number that went into the place of worship.

The prelates had priority of position since this was one of their own. Consecrated women and men filled the place with various "habits" and attires. The knights and the lady auxiliaries came out with many colors and regalia. It was a national as well as an international celebration. It was apparent that, as the old saying has it in "all roads lead to Rome," on the day of the funeral of Dominic Cardinal Ekandem, all roads led to Abuja. Some generous individuals made fuel available in petrol tankers for the mourners who went to the funeral to aid in going back to their different places.

The civil authorities and military officers—in short, the different arms of the forces—featured in one way or the other. For instance, Air Vice Marshal F. J. Femi represented General Abacha, the head of state, Lt. Gen. J. T. Useni was represented by the minister of state, Dr. Mrs.

M. Ikejiani Clerk, and many others. The papal nuncio was there as was the special representative of the pope, the papal legate, His Eminence Francis Cardinal Arinze, who delivered the pope's message during the celebration. The Episcopal Conference of Nigeria demonstrated a solidarity that indicated that the elder statesman, prince, and patriarch as well as a patriarch, their senior brother in the episcopacy deserved a solemn farewell as he left for his final home.

c.   The Liturgical Celebration

The first reading was from chapter 3 of the book of Wisdom, which speaks of the destinies of the good and the bad, likewise the trials of the faithful even though their hope centered on immortality. They were tried on earth as a goldsmith purifies gold in the furnace, and their trials caused them to be accepted as a holocaust. The air of satisfaction with a life well lived and fulfilled was there. A Handmaid of the Holy Child Jesus sister with a daughter of Mary Mother of Mercy sang the responsorial psalm, which was Psalm 23, "The Lord is My Shepherd there is nothing I shall want," which is often used at funerals. The people responded enthusiastically. The Gospel was from John chapter 15 on the "vine and the branches and bearing fruits." One of the priests read the Gospel. His Grace Archbishop Brian D. Usanga, the archbishop of Calabar gave the homily.

Figure 16 Cardinal Ekandem toward the End of His Life

He began his homily with a song in Efik, Kpukpuru Nyin mi iyeda k'iso Abasi, All of us will stand before the Lord, after the formal greeting of the various people present at the funeral. Those who knew it before he continued his homily faithfully sang that hymn. He repeated some lines of the second reading from the book of Revelation that speaks of their good deeds going before them. He dwelt briefly on that point then shifted to the Gospel message that emphasized going out to bear fruits and fruits that would last.

He highlighted the fact that the entire life of the prince and patriarch was a life of service and bearing not only fruits but also enduring fruits that benefited many in all walks of life, and that his good works were surely going before him to the place of refreshment, *locum refrigerii*, after conscientiously carrying his cross and following the Lord. His Eminence followed the injunction of Christ "Go out and bear fruit." In other words, go out and evangelize and be evangelized yourself. He did that exception-ally well.

He lived and died dedicated to God. He reflected the image of the true God and served him faithfully and returned to him in the same man-ner. He obeyed God and the church to the end. He concluded with a hymn as he did at the beginning: "Savior Be My Happy Home." He then prayed that the soul of His Eminence Dominic Cardinal Ekandem should rest in perfect peace, and there was a powerful response of "Amen" from the congregation before the liturgy of the Eucharist continued.

D. Speeches by Some Dignitaries of State and Church

Some of those who spoke during the funeral ceremonies already had their messages published in the funeral brochure.

a. The first condolence message was that of the *military head of state and commander-in-chief of the Nigerian Armed Forces general Sani Abacha,* who established the Provisional Ruling Council of Nigeria after deposing Pres. Ernest Shonekan that ruled for only eighty-three days before the coup of Gen. Sani Abacha in November 1993. Air Vice Marshal Femi John Femi who condoled with Archbishop Onaiyekan and the entire Catholic Church that the death of the cardinal was a loss both to the nation and to the church and wished him a peaceful rest represented General Abacha.

b. The second message was from the *Federal Capital Territory minister of state.* It praised Cardinal Ekandem's illustriousness and selfless service to God and humanity were brought out. The minister's message equally noted his touching so many lives. Dr. Mrs. M. Ikejiani Clerk who represented him at the funeral presented the message of Lt. Gen. J. T. Useni, minister of state.

The message of condolence of the minister of state was written on behalf of the dwellers of the Federal Capital Territory Abuja expressing sympathy with the archbishop of Abuja while calling the cardinal, an illustrious son of Nigeria as well as his being an embodiment of selfless service to God and to humanity. He emphasized the fact of his touching many lives in his over forty-eight years of priestly ministry as a Catholic priest. The message was published in the funeral brochure.

c. The next message came from *Bishop Joseph Ekuwem, the bishop of Uyo Diocese.* The condolence message he sent to Abp. John Onaiyekan had already been published in the funeral program. His speech during the funeral brought out the following points: that Cardinal Dominic

Ekandem was a national figure and statesman, and a hardworking and happy man because he relied on God, worked for the unity of the country as one nation united in justice and in love. Even the unborn are grateful for having come to realize one nation; he urged the whole country to uphold it for the sake and honor of this great man. He thanked all for loving him. He appreciated the pro-nuncio, the papal legate, all the bishops, the priests, religious men and women, all the faithful, all who loved him. He said by loving him, you love us. He represented the church in Nigeria. Let her continue to experience the oneness that Abuja, the place he labored to express that unity represents. He implored the government that if they were to keep the memory of this great prince, prelate, and patriarch alive, let them return the schools and hospitals to the proprietors/ owners. At that point, there was a thunderous applause.

The next person who spoke was *Bishop Camillus Etokudo, bishop of Ikot Ekpene Diocese.* His condolence message was one of the ones published in the program. When he stood up to speak before the final commenda-tion, he thanked the pro-nuncio, the bishops, etc., who sent condolence messages to him, the successor of Cardinal Ekandem as the second bishop of Ikot Ekpene. He mentioned in his speech that he would have loved the cardinal to be buried in Ikot Ekpene since he began his life there and spent a greater part of his life ministering to the flock of God as bishop and as cardinal, and it was at Ifuho, Ikot Ekpene, and became a Catholic diocese in 1963 after its creation that he was ordained a deacon fortyseven years earlier. We shall ever remember him as a loving father and brother, a dedicated man of God and to his people, nevertheless, since providence has placed him in Abuja, and he was to be buried there. He did not object to it. The honor given to the cardinal is given to us and to the nation. He thanked all and sundry and pointed out Dr. Umanah, Dr. Ward (Anne), Dr. Brennan, the Medical Missionaries of Mary (MMM), Handmaids of the Holy Child Jesus (HHCJ), and Archbishop Onaiyekan and Msgr. Kenneth Enang for the care and attention given to the cardinal.

He spoke of the many associations he founded starting from Nka Adiaha Obong, that is the Catholic Women's Association, Catholic Men's and Catholic Youth Association. He went further to give the message left by Dominic Cardinal Ekandem that he, Cardinal Ekandem, should be buried within two weeks and that burial of the dead should be carried out in two weeks, and that will make him happy. The next point was the introduction of the cause of beatification of the cardinal whom he hoped that one day, the cardinal would be venerated at God's altar. A powerful clap resounded from the mourners as he ended his speech.

The next person who spoke was a *member of the Family of Cardinal Ekandem*. In his message, he mentioned that the cardinal was a worthy representative of their family, the church and society. He was father (patriarch) of the entire church and devoted to the church as priest, as bishop, and as cardinal. He was an exemplary man ordained in the order of Melchizedek. He was ordained and served the church for forty-eight years. He was close to the church. He used every gift he received for the common good. He was a man of the people. He prayed that his gentle soul may rest in perfect peace.

The next speaker was the chairman of the Catholic Bishops' Conference of Nigeria (CBCN), *Abp. Albert Obiefuna*, who at that time was the metropolitan archbishop of Onitsha Metropolitan See. Among the many things he said about the cardinal was his commitment to the CBCN. He underscored the fact of his living out the episcopal motto In the Cross Is (Our) Salvation. He was like one who was on the Cross, for he carried the Cross for the sake of the church and for the sake of Christ and swore never to abandon it. The Cross did not deprive him of the joy of Christian living or delay his quick reaction to situations. It rather facilitated that. Whenever he wrote or spoke, it was a reflection of the one on the Cross. His humility reflected that of Christ. His wisdom baffled many like those who were overwhelmed at the wisdom of Jesus when he was in the synagogue at Nazareth where people wondered where he got such knowledge. They asked, are his brothers and sisters not here with us? Is this not Jesus the son of the carpenter? Where did he get such knowledge? (Cf. Matt. 13:53–58) The humility of the cardinal made some people to misunderstand him, yet he remained firm in imitating Christ.

He willingly carried the Cross at all circumstances even in the context of having to travel to Abuja and back to Ikot Ekpene and taking great care of the two places without complaining. He noted that this was as a result of his burning faith for God and humanity.

Concerning wisdom, he stressed the infused knowledge of his Eminence, Dominic Cardinal Ekandem. He noted that of all the bishops in the country, he was the only one who did not go for further training after the priestly training, but there was no topic or situation that Cardinal Ekandem could not handle. This is what led the little flower, Thérèse of Lisiéux or Thérèse of the Little Child Jesus and of the Holy Face to say, "Jesus has no need of books or doctors to instruct our soul. He, the Doctor of doctors, teaches us without the sound of words. I have never heard him speak, and yet I know He is within my soul. Every moment He is guiding and inspiring me, and just at the moment I need them, 'lights' till then unseen are granted me. Most often it is not at prayer that they come but while I go about my daily duties."[497] Whenever Cardinal Ekandem spoke or reflected, he portrayed the infused knowledge, the sudden lights given just at that moment given to the mystics. In other words, Cardinal Ekandem was a mystic in disguise even though many did not know that. He was always inspired all those years he was the president of the CBCN or even the Association of the Episcopal Conferences of Anglophone West Africa (AECAWA). This insight portrays the cardinal as a great man favored by God, probably like Solomon but much more like the mystics who had special union with God. His position and stay in Nigeria as a priest, bishop, cardinal, and as cardinal archbishop has brought progress upon progress in Nigeria and upon the episcopacy.

Abp. Albert Obiefuna looked at the role of Cardinal Ekandem like that of a revered headmaster in the schools, who, on arrival, caused both the teachers and the pupils to accordingly once the headmaster was around. He compared the presence of the cardinal in the episcopal conference to that of headmaster. He prayed, "Oh Lord, please, give us another headmaster who will bring us to order and instill in us the discipline of commitment, oneness, and cooperation." His speech was interrupted by a thunderous applause. If the setting were not that of a funeral and in a church, probably, a standing ovation would have occurred. He proceeded to thank Msgr. Kenneth Enang who was very faithful to the cardinal, united with him to accomplish all that he needed to do and stood by him to the very end. He implored God's blessings upon Monsignor Enang.

The response of the chief mourner, *the Most Reverend John O. Onaiyekan* took place. He started his response by referring to the speech of the president of the Catholic Bishops' Conference of Nigeria saying, "That is our president, he has spoken as the president of our conference." He said this in his usual exuberant mood. He went on to acknowledge the messages printed in the funeral brochure. He equally acknowledged the ones sent by bishops of various dioceses including those who attended the funeral in person. He acknowledged a condolence message from Bishop Mark Unegbu who had come for the funeral and thinking that he was still around turned round to see where he sat but could not locate him. Perhaps Bishop Unegbu left after communion or after the vigil that lasted the whole night. Bishop Unegbu being a contemporary of Cardinal Ekandem at St. Paul's Seminary, Onitsha was there to pay his final respect. Among some of the dioceses that sent in messages were Warri, Umuahia, Oshogbo, and a host of others.

Archbishop Onaiyekan acknowledged and appreciated the various people and groups that made donations in cash and kind. He noted that the government had promised to send in contribution, and he told the sympathizers and mourners present there that the donations would be used in establishing Cardinal Ekandem's trust fund. The fund was to serve the purpose of Catholic education and care for the handicapped children (the physically impaired). He thanked all who came for the funeral and spoke of the cardinal as a great man.

All these took place before the final commendation. When he finished responding, he continued with the *final commendation*. This is a special prayer said in the Catholic Church for the deceased while imploring God's mercy and kindness toward the dead person. The church begs God not to judge the person as the sins committed on earth deserved but to grant a merciful judgment, deliverance from eternal death and sin of the deceased[498] through the cleansing blood of his beloved son Jesus Christ. The prayer begs Christ to carry the deceased home to the place of peace with the Father, *locum pacis*[499] *cum Patris*. The angels and saints of God are called to come to the aid of the person and to receive the soul of the defunct Christian and present it to God the most high.

God the Father is implored for the sake of his son's birth, dying, burial, and resurrection to have mercy and admit the soul of the faithful departed into his eternal abode where Lazarus will be poor no more and freedom of participation at his sacred banquet at his heavenly table with the angels and saints. The final commendation is meant to give confidence to the soul of the departed to say with certitude or with absolute certainty *Certus sum enim*, I am certain, I will see God's face instead of leaving the world in a state of uncertainty and fear. Such prayer gives confidence to the soul to appear before the Lord of Life the soul had been longing for as a result of a purified love since no tainted love can see God face to face. Abp. John Onaiyekan carried out the special ceremony, as a son would bury his father or mother. It was fitting that he did that because of the special affinity with Cardinal Ekandem as his successor in the Metropolitan See of Abuja, also as he later became one of the cardinals in the Catholic Church himself on November 24, 2012, and the third in Nigeria.

D.   The Interment

Before the casket was taken to the burial ground in the room next to the altar, one papal knight was invited to give the final salute before the priests who carried the remains began the final lap of the journey. The knight that was sought for was Sir A. T. Beka (Sir Akpan Thomas Beka, generally abbreviated, AT Beka). He served as the diocesan president till the time that His Eminence Dominic Cardinal Ekandem left Ikot Ekpene and went to Abuja, his final place of apostolate. Sir Beka went and gave the salute and moved with the bishops and those who bore the casket to the grave near the right entrance from the sanctuary. No other person was to join the bishops, the casket priest-bearers and the only knight and of course the masons who were to chuck the slabs and close the grave properly. There is no way the chamberlain, Msgr. Kenneth Enang, would not have been there. He was fully there close to the head where the body was laid. One of those who joined the group of eight that conveyed the body of Cardinal Ekandem to the grave was Very Rev. Fr. Emmanuel Idem of Calabar Archdiocese, while Father Maigari was one of the masters of ceremony for that day. He was one of the few priests who went to the grave site for the prayer at the graveside and interment.

The casket was a simple one made of plane wood that had been properly seasoned. The wood was to last for twenty-five years to take care of the length of time the construction of the cathedral church of Abuja Archdiocese was to be built. The body was to be exhumed and finally laid to rest at the cathedral of the twelve apostles after construction. The texture and durability of the wood were taken into consideration pending the completion of the cathedral. The "cardinal's hat" was placed on the casket at the side the head of the prelate, prince, and patriarch was positioned. There were lovely crucifixes on the coffin. One was on top while the other was placed at the side of the coffin where the squared part was. The crucifix was the first thing seen once the casket bearers started moving. It was after the interment that the papal legate, Francis Cardinal Arinze gave the final blessing to the congregation that was waiting almost like the group that waited for Zachariah till he came out of the Holy of Holies where he offered incense (Lk. 1:10, 11–25).

E.   Emphasis of the Different Condolence Messages

Various speeches were made. Some of the messages were read from the brochure or referred to in it. All the messages were directed to Abp. John Onaiyekan as the chief mourner and successor of the cardinal as the metropolitan archbishop of Abuja Ecclesiastical Province.

Condolence Messages

The following are among some of the condolence messages received before the time of the funeral mass and interment of Dominic Cardinal Ekandem. They were published in the funeral brochure accordingly. There were many other messages that were received on the actual day of the burial that were not printed in the funeral brochure from where the following messages were extracted.

The papal telegram emphasized the pastoral involvement of the prince-prelate and the necessity of the Christian community to be immersed in a life of service. The pope offered fervent prayers for his repose while imparting apostolic blessing.

TELEGRAM UPON DEATH OF CARDINAL EKANDEM

VATICAN CITY NOV. 25, 1995 (VIS)—Following is the text of a telegram sent by Pope John Paul to Archbishop

John Onaiyekan of Abuja, Nigeria, upon the death of Cardinal Dominic Ekandem, Archbishop- Bishop emeritus of the same archdiocese.

"Having learnt with sadness of the death of Cardinal Dominic Ekandem, I offer fervent prayers for his eternal rest and ask Almighty God to grant him the reward of his long years of service to the Gospel. Joining Your Grace and all the faithful of the Archdiocese of Abuja in mourning the loss of his devoted pastor, I pray that his devoted ministry will inspire the community to be ever more faithful in Christian life and service. As a pledge of comfort and peace in our Lord Jesus Christ, I cordially impart my Apostolic Blessing"

TGR/DEATHEKANDEM/NIGERIA:ONAIYEKAN VIS 951127(140)
Pope John Paul II

Cardinal Tomko's condolence message brought out the priestly zeal of the cardinal as one endowed with many talents, his role in the church and society, and the assurance of prayers for his repose. This message was written a few days after the announcement of death of the cardinal.

CONGREGATION
PRO GENTIUM EVANGELIZATIONE
PROF/NO.5256/95   NOVEMBER 25TH 1995.

His Grace,

The Most Reverend John O. Onaiyekan, Archbishop of Abuja, Nigeria.
(Via the Apostolic Nunciature in Lagos)

Your Grace,

Dominic Ignatius Ekandem

The Congregation for the Evangelization of Peoples is deeply saddened by the news we received earlier today of the sudden death of His Eminence Cardinal Dominic Ignatius Ekandem, Archbishop-Bishop Emeritus of Abuja.

Cardinal Ekandem who would soon have celebrated his 48th Anniversary of Priestly Ordination in a few days, served the Catholic Church in Nigeria with zeal and devotion throughout his lifetime. His contribution especially to the formation and training of the laity in Nigeria is a great testament to his pastoral solicitude. His many gifts and talents were soon recognized when, after only six years of priesthood, he was appointed the Auxiliary Bishop of Calabar in 1953, and consecrated 1st Nigeria Bishop in 1954. He then became the first Bishop of Ikot Ekpene, when the Diocese was created in 1963. in [sic] the Consistory of 24 May 1976 he was created Cardinal, by the late Pope Paul VI. His apostolic zeal and missionary spirit continued when he became the 1st Ecclesiastical Superior of the Missio "sui Juris" of Abuja in 1981, serving this new circumscription while continuing as Ordinary of his beloved Ikot Ekpene.

When, finally, the Diocese of Abuja was erected in 1989, he was promoted to the New See with the personal title of ArchbishopBishop, and continued to serve the Church both Abuja and in Nigeria until his retirement from pastoral government in 1992.

In expressing to Your Grace, and to all the priests, religious and faithful of the Archdiocese of Abuja our deep condolences at this time, we assure you of your prayer for the repose of the soul of our dear brother and friend, Cardinal Ekandem. We also extend through you to both the Diocese of Ikot Ekpene and to the entire nation of Nigeria our prayerful sympathy at this loss of a dedicated priest, Bishop, and Servant of the Lord.

Devotedly yours in Our Lord,
Joseph Cardinal Tomko Pref.

The condolence message of Bishop Ekuwem of Uyo Diocese brought out the father figure of His Eminence Dominic Cardinal Ekandem extending even to Anglophone West Africa, the sadness of his departure that will deprive many of his gentle presence while referring to the suffering he underwent and the necessity of repose at his departure. The message also stressed the cardinal's habitual attempt to follow the Master's footsteps, and that he will ever be remembered. He noted that the message of the cardinal's death was received in the diocese of Uyo on November 24 before he sent in the condolence message in a few days' time. This was part of the messages of condolences published in the burial brochure.

The message from Bishop C. A. Etokudo from Ikot Ekpene Diocese brought out the fact of his death as an irreparable loss, the debt of gratitude that Ikot Ekpene as a whole owed the cardinal in terms of promotion of vocations to the priesthood and religious life, that he was hospitable and trustworthy person, a father of peace and that of light. There was a pledge on the part of the diocese for continuous prayers, coupled with the already celebrated masses and the ones to be celebrated later. The condolence message published in the burial brochure was dated November 27 and was signed by the following on behalf of the Diocese:

Signed: Rt. Rev. C. A. Etukudoh, the Bishop of Ikot Ekpene Diocese; Barr. Cletus Udoh, Diocesan Chairman Laity Council, Fr. C. M. Udomah, the Chancellor of the Diocese and Mrs. P. I. Ekandem Director—CWO, Ikot Ekpene Diocese.

The first elected superior general of the Missionaries of St. Paul, Very Rev. Fr. Felix Elosi, MSP, also sent in a condolence message that brought out the fatherly role of Cardinal Ekandem, his status and role not only as a founder of Missionaries of St. Paul but also as the one who conceived, perceived, and fought for the implantation of the society on Nigerian soil. His condolence message addressed to the archbishop of Abuja was dated November 28, 1995, and was equally published in the burial brochure.

The next message was that of the director of the United States Liaison Office of the American Embassy, Mr. Timothy D. Andrews. He stressed, on behalf of the embassy, the developmental aspect of the cardinal's life. He added that the cardinal's death went beyond the loss to the church, Nigeria as a nation and to the whole world. He saw Cardinal Ekandem's death in a global perspective. This was one of the messages published in the burial brochure. The condolence message was dated November 28, 1995.

The death of Cardinal Ekandem went beyond the confines of the church and religious surrounding cutting through the various strata of the society embracing the Muslims where the chief imam was obliged to express his message of condolence on behalf of all the Muslims. It was marvelous to acknowledge that Abp. John Onaiyekan, the incumbent archbishop of Abuja did a fantastic work to alert all and sundry of the passing away of the first Nigerian citizen. The imam specifically noted in his condolence message titled "The Passing Away of Cardinal" that the whole Christendom and the entire world would miss that illustrious son of Nigeria, Cardinal Dominic Ekandem. The condolence message bore the address of the Abuja National Mosque written November 30, 1995, and signed by the chief imam, Ustaz Musa Muhammad. Since the message arrived early enough, it was also published in the burial brochure. It was equally addressed to Abp. John Onaiyekan, the archbishop of Abuja.

Imam Ustaz Musa Muhammad underscores the social as well as the pastoral nature of the cardinal as one *who worked for the betterment of all.* In other words, he worked without discriminating against any group, color, tribe, or religion but cut across all the boundaries. The underpinning is of great import since a non-Christian was able to pierce through the cloud of interpretation as well as the cloud of various biases and reach out to the truth. This is why Jesus Christ told the Jews that out of the mouths of babes comes the praise of God. In the case of the lepers who were cured, Jesus said, "Were not all ten made clean? Where are the other nine? Was no one found to return and give praise to God except this foreigner?" (Lk.17:11–19). That single phrase summarized the pastoral charity of this prince and patriarch who fitted into the society without any slurs likewise into the church, her mother and nurse. He has gone to enjoy *guadia sempiterna,* eternal joy, in the Kingdom of his Father whose home he returns to as the post-communion prayer for the dead implores the Almighty God to grant.[500] That place of peace, *locum pacis,* a place of perpetual light, *locum lucis sempiiternae*, is what he was struggling for all the days of his life. The prayer of all the faithful is that he be granted admittance to that sacred abode where there is no more sorrow but perpetual light and peace in the presence of the Trinity and all the saints and angels.

AD MAJOREM DEI GLORIAM,
"TO THE GREATER GLORY OF GOD."

Figure 17 Cardinal Ekandem's Grave at Our Lady
Queen of Nigeria's Chapel, Garki, Abuja, Nigeria

Epilogue

Consumatum Est

(It Is Finished)

THERE IS NOTHING that has a beginning without a corresponding end. Whatever goes up must come down. So is the life of every human person or created things in general. The death and burial of Cardinal Ekandem discussed in chapter 18 acted as a closure to the life of that great, eminent prince and patriarch. Moreover, it is not out of place to use the review of Prof. S. I. Udoidem of the University of Port Harcourt on the last book published on the cardinal a few years ago during the public presentation and launching of the book in Uyo, the capital of Akwa Ibom State, Nigeria, in 2014. Before the book review, a recapitulation of some salient points in this work will take place to refresh the memory on what went before for the purpose of maintaining the link.

His Eminence Dominic Cardinal Ekandem was born a prince in the village of Obio Ibiono in Ibiono Ibom Local Government, although at the time of his birth, Ibiono was under Itu, which is always associated with the famous Mary Slessor of Calabar. He was born a prince but he died a prelate and not only a prelate but a renounced, virtuous, towering lovely prelate and patriarch that his creativity, praxis that is what is not theoretical but practical and natural wisdom coupled with infused knowledge, partly a sign of mystical gift and closeness to God and (partly as) a relationship, which was properly humane. He was a special gift not only to Nigeria but also to the entire world as the first Nigerian cardinal putting Nigeria on a pedestal and joining the highest decision-making body in the Catholic Church. His beginnings were quiet. The twist of his life as a youth did not wind into something dangerous, rather it orientated him toward a response that was unique like that of Abraham, Isaac, and Jacob that God specially called. They passed through very difficult tests to become the patriarchs of Israel that they were and are. The life of Cardinal Ekandem passed through many huddles that even engulfed the father terribly to the point of having to forcefully send away his twentyseven wives, abandon his African traditional worship, wed with one of the women, Mary Mmatim so that Dominic could be ordained a deacon and priest of the Most High God. It was really a movement that continuously evolved itself to the flowering point in the vineyard of the Lord with all the thorns and thistles as Christ himself passed through so as to reach his glory.

Thomas Merton says, "Most human vocations tend to define their purpose not only by placing the one called in a definite relation to God but also by giving him a set place among his fellow men."[501] It is very true that the priestly vocation including the fire of love that accompanies it engulfed Dominic as a young prince in Okuku's compound. It further opened many avenues that aided him to exercise his potentials among his fellow human beings. That fire of love touched the clergy and the laity equally as exercised in his pastoral charity and outlook toward his flock both young and old. He exercised his priesthood with the freedom that this particular vocation demands aware of the fact that vocation is a mystery that is unfathomable and hidden in God and "reaches out of the obscurity of God's Providence to select, sometimes, unlikely men to be 'other Christs' and sometimes to reject those who are, in the eyes of men, best fitted for such a vocation."[502] It is possible that a perception of the fact of self-sacrifice prompted Okuku Ekandem to tell his son Dominic, "You can go. After all, I have many other children." Maybe the child he had hoped on as a would-be court clerk disappointed him when he announced he wanted to follow God as a priest. The mystery of vocation is something inscrutable.

It evolves gradually, but not in the sense of contradiction between creation and evolution as the evolutionists claim. Really evolution and creation cannot be at loggerhead as to having Darwin and God[503] at two different poles just as some people think of science and religion or reason and faith, each of this apparent contrarieties or polarities or oppositions complement each other and coexist for not just to maintain order in terms of creation and proclaim existence in terms of evolution; but whatever exists has origin thus forming a continuum of existence; and that is how Dominic Cardinal Ekandem came into the world, grew, and evolved into what God wanted him to be. He came in as a little young prince and went out a glorious prince-prelate of the Catholic Church. In him creation and evolution had a point of intersection and continued on its route until the moment of exit. There can never be two Dominic Cardinal Ignatius Ekandems. He was the only one. His uniqueness cannot be duplicated even by cloning. God is unique in his creation.

Book Review: *A Testament of Light* by Prof. S. I. Udoidem

We are here today not only to regain our past glory but also to seek for ways to sustain the glory and to harness the future that has been opened to us. The future characterized by infinite possibilities. This infinite possibility is rooted in human capacity, will, and the drive to achieve what is infinitely possible. What the future will be depends on what we do today. I am personally here today to perform my assigned responsibility as a book reviewer, because of the importance and significance of today's event. I intend to review not only the book but also the anniversary event because the two of them are ineluctable related: The memorial anniversary of, and the book on, Dominic Cardinal Ekandem.

Let me begin with a special recognition of the author of the book. He is small but mighty, young but knowledgeable, of average height but standing tall, shoulder to shoulder with the academic giants of the world. Our people say that when a child washes his hands clean, he can eat with the elders. Surely Rev. Fr. Edidiong Ekefre has washed not only his hands but also sharpened his intellect, which is why he is dining with the geniuses in the arena of intellectual intercourse. What the elders could not do, the young Father Ekefre has done, giving us an authentic story on the life and times of Dominic Cardinal Ekandem. With this book, he reminds us that there once lived a people who were blessed by God. That among the blessings was the raising of our son to the rank of a cardinal making him the first cardinal archbishop in Anglophone West Africa, the first Nigerian cardinal to participate in the conclave for the election of a pope. When Father Cosmas Nwosuh, MSP, in his book *Cardinal Dominic Ekandem and the Growth of the Catholic Church in Nigeria* attempted to tell the cardinal's story. He did well as an aggrieved political investigator, which was why when it came to the section on the Nigerian Civil War and the role of the church, he presented not only some obviously contradictory propositions but also some misleading and uncharitable insinuations coupled with politically skewed idiosyncratic innuendos about the leadership role of Cardinal Ekandem. As the Nigerian Catholic Bishops often admit, Cardinal Ekandem was an "apostle of truth." There were people who would have wished that they lied about the civil war, which was a religious war, but the cardinal spoke the truth by saying that there were Christians (Catholics) on both sides, and therefore, it was more of a civil conflict than a religious war. For that, Nwosuh grossly misrepresented him in his book. It is for this reason that I see Father Ekefre's book as a timely intervention.

In my earlier book *Hospitality as Holiness: The Genius of Cardinal Ekandem*, where I reflected on the spirituality and mission of Cardinal Ekandem and highlighted his hospitality and generous living as the hallmarks of his life, I had stated that "eternal publicity" is what we owe to our forefather, grandfather, our one and only son who blazed the trail so that we can be priests and respected Christians today. And that "the only justice that can be done to him for what he symbolized is the continuous narration of his story." His story must be told, and Father Ekefre has risen to the challenge.

His book *A Testament of Light: The Life and Times of Cardinal Ekandem* has opened a new vista in the history of Uyo Diocese. Here, I want to thank His Lordship Most Rev. John Ayah, D.D, the apostolic administrator of Uyo Diocese for the uncommon generosity and disposition of raising a private initiative of a priest in the diocese of the status of a diocesan event. This is a new dawn in Uyo Diocese. Only the memory of Cardinal Ekandem can bring this about.

This book *A Testament of Light: The Life and Times of Dominic Cardinal Ekandem*, whose presentation marks the eighteenth memorial anniversary of the passing to glory of the late Cardinal Ekandem, is a very well researched text. It has 412 pages including the 16 preliminary pages.

It consists of 20 chapters excluding the prologue, epilogue, appendix, endnotes, bibliography and index. It is published by MayFive Ltd., Ikeja, Lagos, 2013.

Chapters 1 to 3 deal with the birth, family history, and the events that led to the conversion and baptism of Tom as Dominic Ekandem. Chapter 4 deals with the story of the early missionaries and their evangelizing impact on the people of old Calabar Province, while chapter 5 singles out Dominic Ekandem as the victim and the priest. Here an insight to the tortuous journey of priesthood training from the minor through the senior seminary to ordination. It has been argued that it was the Calvary journey, which informed his motto *In Cruce Salus* (drawn from an African idiom Atudia ininge idot uwot), and in the church's grammar, "In the Cross there is salvation."

Chapters 6 to 7 presents the cardinal as a pathfinder who goes through the crucible of seminary training with humility and resignation of a man who had a conviction that evil cannot triumph good. Chapter 8 narrates his encounter with African culture and child to promote the unique identity of the African culture. Chapter 9 tells the cardinal's story as the founder of the Catholic Women's Organisation.

Chapters 10 and 11 highlight the mission of the cardinal as the good shepherd after the manner of Christ and cover his activities as a member of the Second Vatican Council. Chapters 12 and 13 tell the story of how the Nigerian Civil War affected the cardinal and how he became a hero by allowing himself to be personally bruised emotionally, psychologically, and physically, and how he recovered and became the healer by caring for those who were affected by the war, evidenced by his activities in Port Harcourt and Ikot Ekpene, the orphanages, hospital, and schools he built to take care of the underprivileged.

Chapters 14 and 15 focus on the story of how he became a cardinal and became de facto and de jure candidate for the papacy, and the story of how he participated in the election of Pope John Paul II. Chapters 16 to 20 capture his missionary engagements. His involvement in the formation of the Christian Association of Nigeria (CAN), the founding of the Missionary Society of St. Paul, and his mission of working to bring to fulfilment the injunction of Christ, "That All May Be One." He put this to practice when he was assigned to Abuja Mission where from nothing but with open hands he welcomed everyone from all parts of Nigeria, and from this he established a small community that has as a mustard seed flourished to a metropolitan see.

Chapter 20 is the last chapter. It contains the story of his last journey, his resignation to the will of God and how he died a very peaceful death. The title when the Ibibio people sent their five sons for further studies in 1938, the beneficiaries were called the beacons of light. When they came back from studies and each time that any one of them was received, a popular song was always rendered, "Show the light that we may see the way." Even in the Bible Jesus Christ described himself as the "Light and the Way." Indeed, Cardinal Ekandem in his life and times, had/has been the light for the Nigerian church and the light for the indigenous peoples of Calabar Ecclesiastical Province. Ekefre's insight in titling the book A Testament of Light is most appropriate and informative. It captures the "reason to be" of the late Dominic Cardinal Ekandem. When he first showed me the draft of the book sometime last year, he looked very discouraged by the challenges of embarking on such a project. He shared with me how an elder in the diocese had told him that he was too young to write a book on the cardinal, that Ke nsek eyen Isikwata iwuud idiok. I looked at him sternly but with facial expressions of admiration. I then asked him "Have you ever heard of the Ibibio Union Progress song that was composed in 1930?" His answer was no. I told him about the song with emphasis on the line that says, "Ibibio eyedemede ke ekem ini." I then said to him, "*K'uboro mme Ibibio eyedemede ke ekemini*, let them continue sleeping, *nsido ekpe uman afo adi-idiforo ebot*, if you have a dream and you have woken up, go ahead and work hard and bring your dream to reality." I then said to him, "*Nsek eyen isikwata iwuud idiok*, that was in the ancient times but today *nsek eyen akpe anie odudu, anie ifiok, aban afet nno adehe akeme adidok ndoro ke iwuut idiok nkwat idet idiok.*" He stood there for a while looking at me and then said, "*Mm'ekop se atang, sosongo*, Monsignor." Then he walked away quietly and did not utter another word. I am sure he got my message. With what Father Ekefre has done, you would agree with me that anyone who wakes up with a dream and works hard can bring it to reality and that *ke snsek* [sic] *eyen anyemi ono ikwat iwuut idiok.*

On my own, when I first read the manuscript, judging it with the spectacles of the canons of Western historiography, I was tempted to say that since he was not an eyewitness to the events that he is narrating, he needed to lay emphasis on the narrations as reported speeches with appropriate references. But when I went back and read the Bible from the Old Testament to the New Testament Gospels, I realized that none of the biblical narrators was an actual eyewitness to the events narrated, yet the mere forcefulness of the narrations through the influence of the Holy Spirit, under the rubrics of inspiration has authenticated their truthfulness. Also, when I reflected on the canons of African historiography, where oral history is a very important component, I was convinced that Fr. Edidiong Ekefre, in writing this book, has created a niche for himself as the Edidiong of Uyo Diocese, *adiyem edifre se Abasi akenam ono idut nnyin*, a celebrated church historian and Cardinal Ekandem's biographer. The book is very well researched. It is written in simple and lucid language, and the editing is perfect. The text when read with the eyes of faith can serve as a text for spiritual reading; it can also serve as a history of missionary activities in Calabar Ecclesiastical Province and Nigeria at large. The only area that needs a revisit in my assessment is in the area of the chronological sequence of the arrival and establishment of outposts and stations in the various locations in the province. In virtually all the books that have been written both about old Onitsha and Calabar Provinces that I have read, there are obvious conflicting reports on the chronology. Even a new book, which is already in press by Mr. Emmanuel Ushie Odey of Ogoja Diocese titled *Catholic Bishops of Calabar Ecclesiastical Province: Yesterday and Today* in which he appreciates and documents the contributions of the various ecclesiastical leaders in the history and evolution of Calabar Ecclesiastical Province, there is no agreement on the timeline. There is a need, therefore, for more research into the archives of the SMA Fathers, the Holy Ghost Fathers, and the St. Patrick Fathers to ascertain the actual sequence of events. Here I think Uyo Diocese can take the lead by commissioning Father Ekefre who has already shown signs of intellectual resourcefulness as a burgeoning church historian.

In all, Father Ekefre's book is the best so far on the subject. I therefore recommend that all those present should launch the book, and all Catholics in Uyo Diocese and indeed all Catholics and Christians in Calabar Ecclesiastical Province should have at least a copy of this book in their homes for posterity.

On the anniversary celebration, the time has come for us to have a museum full of artifacts of Dominic Cardinal Ekandem. From Obio Ibiono to Calabar, to Ikot Ekpene, to Abuja to Uyo, indeed the whole of Nigeria we can assemble memorabilia (the mass box, the chalices and ciboria he used, his cassocks and vestments, his mitre and crozier, his biretta, his shoes, etc.) in honor of Cardinal Ekandem. The time has come for us to have a library full of books and documented stories about Dominic Ekandem, his publications, sermons, talks, etc. These can serve as a source of inspiration and blessings for those who come to learn about this great spiritual leader. Thanks to Bishop John Ayah, the apostolic administrator, who has already given approval for the institution of the special prayer group devotion in honor of Dominic Cardinal Ekandem. I therefore propose that from this day henceforth, on the memorial anniversary every year we will not only dance and sing to celebrate our hero, we must tell a story about some aspect of Cardinal Ekandem's life. The diocese should make a commitment to this effect. To the people of Uyo Diocese, this is our chance. If you do not say I am, nobody will say you are. If you have a story, write it down. If you have a story but you cannot write, call Father Ekefre or Monsignor Udoidem, they will help you develop a story line. Surely, we can stand on the shoulders of our God-given giant and pierce into the higher horizons of unlimited possibilities. The Cardinal Ekandem Educational Foundation of which I am a cofounder is willing to partner with the diocese for the achievement of these noble ideas.

Begin now to support this initiative by making sure that you get a copy of Ekefre's book as a way of showing appreciation and desire to learn more about the cardinal.

Thank you, and God bless for listening.

Appendix

A.   Last Will And Testament Of Cardinal Ekandem

THIS IS THE LAST WILL AND TESTAMENT OF ME, CARDINAL DOMINIC IGNATIUS EKANDEM, Archbishop/Bishop Emeritus of Abuja in the Archdiocese of Abuja, Capital territory of Nigeria.

PREAMBLE:

It is with sentiments of personal inadequacy and of profound thanksgiving that I write this, my last will and testament. I thank our Heavenly Father for my good parents who nurtured me and handed on to me values from my tender age in the security of a happy family. I also thank God for leading me to his family on earth, the church, and for the spiritual rebirth I received, through water and the Holy Spirit, on the day of my baptism. To this amazing grace was added a vocation to the ministerial priesthood as a servant of God. In God's inscrutable ways I was, on December 7, 1947, the first indigenous priest to be ordained in the present Metropolitan Ecclesiastical Province of Calabar and, on 7th February, 1954, the first Nigerian to be ordained a bishop. There was added to this, unworthy though I was the totally unexpected appointment as a Cardinal of the Church by Pope Paul VI in 1976.

I thank God for the choice of my episcopal motto *In Cruce Salus*. I pray Him through the intercession of the Blessed Virgin Mary to help me to be faithful to this motto to the end of my life.

I thank God for the immense privilege of serving the people of God as priest, administrator, bishop, archbishop, and cardinal for several years at Calabar, Ikot Ekpene, Port Harcourt, and finally at Abuja. It has been a constant consolation for me to see the growth of the church in these jurisdictions and indeed throughout Nigeria. The small mustard seed that I knew in my youth has grown into a large and welcoming tree where all may come and find shade and sustenance for their lives.

1. I HEREBY revoke all other wills and testamentary dispositions made by me at any time heretofore.
2. I APPOINT HIS GRACE, MOST REVEREND DR. BRIAN DAVID USANGA the archbishop of Calabar Archdiocese and Metropolitan of Calabar Ecclesiastical Province, to be the sole executor of this, my will.
3. I BEQUEATH the following legacies taking cognizance of the tact that everything I own has been given to me by generous people in Nigeria and abroad to facilitate the work which God in his love and mercy has entrusted to me.
   i. My episcopal insignia the sacred vessels and vestments I use for the liturgy should be given to the ordinary of the Archdiocese of Abuja to be disposed of as he deems fit; ii. Two-thirds of my books are to be given to the National Missionary Seminary of St. Paul's, Gwagwalada; Abuja while the remaining one-third should go to Cardinal Ekandem Seminary, Uyo, Akwa Ibom State.
   ii. My vehicles are to be placed at the disposal of the Archdiocese of Abuja, except for the black Mercedes Benz car Registration No. CRS 1933 which should be given to the Archdiocese of Calabar, which gave it to me when I was made a cardinal.
   iii. One-third of my articles of secular clothing should be given to Mr. Peter Essien and the remaining two-thirds should be distributed to the poor.

4. I BEQUEATH the following pecuniary legacies:
   i. A half of all moneys due to me upon my death should go to the Archdiocese of Abuja for the poor.
   ii. Fifty percent of the remaining half should be given to Mr. Peter Essien as a gesture of my gratitude to him for all his dedicated service to me for many years
   iii. The remaining 50 percent of the balance as in paragraph 4 (ii) is to be invested in perpetuity, and the interests accruing there from should be used as mass stipends for Holy Masses for happy repose of my soul.

5. I DEVISE my real properties as follows:
   i. The plot of land allocated by my father for a house to be built for me in Obio Ibiono, which was developed by my sister chief, Mrs. Rose Ekandem Nubia, is hereby given to her together with the house she built on the plot.
   ii. To Uyo Diocese, I give the house built for me at Obio Ibiono in the diocese of Uyo on the surveyed and donated family plot of land for my retirement.

6. I DIRECT as follows:
   i. That the archdiocese of Abuja should very kindly get Mr. Peter Essien who has been serving me with great dedication, gainfully employed considering that he is an orphan. Furthermore, I request that the said archdiocese should also assist him with the education of his children when I am dead.
   ii. My funeral and burial should be as simple as possible and should take place within two weeks of the day of my demise. The funeral should take place at Abuja where I was privileged to serve the Divine Master and the people of God until my retirement and where I now reside.

7. ACKNOWLEDGMENT
   I hereby acknowledge with thanks and prayerful wishes the loyalty and dedication of barrister Mrs. Therese Nya Akan, daughter of the papal knight chief Joseph and lady knight Cecilia Nya of Calabar, in offering free legal services with regard to the preparation of this, my LAST WILL and TESTAMENT.

IN WITNESS set my hand this fifth day of June 1995.

1. The Draft Contract for Abuja

AGREEMENT BETWEEN THE ORDINARY OF DIOCESE AND THE MISSIONARY SOCIETY OF ST. PAUL

1. PURPOSE: This contract exists to regulate the relationship between the diocese of hereafter referred to as the Diocese and the Missionary of St. Paul, hereafter referred to as the Society.
2. INTERPRETATION: In the interpretation of this contract recourse shall be made to natural equity, the general law of the church, the constitutions of the Society and the custom and the pastoral situation of the diocese.
3. For the purpose of this contract the Society shall be represented by the superior of the Society or his delegate and the diocese shall be represented by the ordinary of the Diocese.
4. RELATIONSHIP OF INSTITUTE TO RECEIVING DIOCESE:
    a. The specific works of the diocese entrusted to the Society at the time of this contract coming into force are:
    b. Details of these works shall be negotiated in dialogue between the ordinary and the superior of the Society.
    c. Should the ordinary wish to relieve the Society of work entrusted to it, the authorities of the Society should be informed six months in advance.
    d. Should the Society find itself unable to continue to do the work entrusted to it, the competent superior of the Society should inform the local ordinary at least six months in advance.
5. AUTHORITY OF LOCAL ORDINARY:
    *   The Local Ordinary is the director of the apostolate and its center of unity (*Ad Gentes* No. 30) (Can. 678 §1). In all that concerns the apostolate and ministry, members of the Society working in the diocese are subject to the local ordinary in accordance with the general law of the church, the decrees of the Second Vatican Council, the guidelines issued by the Catholic Bishop's Conference of…, of the

local ordinary and subsequent decrees of the Holy See and the constitutions of the Missionary Society of St. Paul.

• The local ordinary will strive to direct the apostolic work of the diocese in such a way that he safeguards and encourages the spontaneous initiatives and activity of members in the Society, whose apostolic life is inspired the norms of their constitutions.

6. THE PRESENCE OF THE INSTITUTE WITHIN THE DIOCESE:

   A. Even while its members are actively engaged in the diocesan apostolate, the society is entitled to preserve its particular and due autonomy (Perfecta Caritatis #. 2B). (*Can. 678, s 2*)

      • The local ordinary recognizes the right of those under his jurisdiction to choose their way of life freely in accordance with the inspiration of the spirit and the right of the society to foster vocations to the society.

      • The collaboration of members of the society with diocesan priests and other religious engaged in diocesan works must be so arranged that it will not be an obstacle to the apostolic life of the Society and vice versa.

   B. Except as provided by canon law, the local ordinary shall not interfere in matters pertaining to the Society's internal observance and discipline. (Can. 587 § 1 and 2)

7. THE SUPERIORS OF THE SOCIETY:

   A. Because they belong to a (Clerical) Institute of Apostolic Life, members of the society working in the diocese have their own superiors whose appointments and duties are covered by the constitutions of the society.

   B. Without prejudice to rights not mentioned here and to those of higher authorities, it is the right of the competent society superior to:

      • Appoint those who shall exercise Society authority in the community of the Society within the diocese,

      • Call the members of the society to chapters, council meetings, assemblies and the annual retreat,

- Cal members of the society engaged in the diocesan apostolate out of the diocese to transact legitimate business of the society with due consultation with the local ordinary.

C. Without prejudice to the jurisdiction of the local ordinary the competent superior of the society shall strive to see that the members of the society faithfully fulfill the task entrusted to them by the local ordinary.

D. Should the competent society superior consider that the local ordinary is imposing duties incompatible with regular discipline, he shall consult with the local ordinary.

E. Should the local ordinary consider that one or other of the constitutions or directives of the Society is insufficiently adapted to the special conditions existing within the diocese, he shall consult with the Society's competent superior.

8. ASSIGNMENT TO AND RECALL FROM THE DIOCESE OF...OF THE SOCIETY:

A. The competent superior, respecting always the rights of higher authorities, has the right to:

- Present members of the Society for work in the diocese;
- Recall or transfer the Society's members from the diocese.
- The exercise of these rights is without prejudice to the rights of the local ordinary to put forward objections with a view to safeguarding and maintaining the pastoral activities of the diocese.

9. THE APPOINTMENT AND REMOVAL OF MEMBERS OF THE SOCIETY TO SPECIFIC DIOCESAN OFFICES:

A. In the best interest of the diocese and the society, it is desirable that there be a mutual consultation between the local ordinary and the competent Society superior concerning assignments to specific offices within the diocese. Moreover, the persons concerned ordinarily must be consulted before a final decision is made.

B. The appointment of the society members to specific offices within the diocese is subject to the following norms:

- It pertains to the competent society superior to present to the local ordinary suitable candidates for the various diocesan offices which the society is called upon to fill.
- If the local ordinary finds that the persons presented are acceptable he will give a formal written canonical appointment together with the necessary faculties.
- The local ordinary's canonical appointment will be transmitted to the individual concerned by the competent society superior who will give him his assignment.
- Should it prove difficult to come to an agreement concerning the appointment of an individual to a specific post, the competent society superior will propose two or more names for the choice of the local ordinary, if in fact there is more than one society member available for the assignment.
- Until the appointment is made public, all those concerned should observe discretion with regard to the appointment.
- In extraordinary cases, any member of the society entrusted with a diocesan office may be removed from it either by the local ordinary or by the competent Society superior. However, to provide members of the society with an opportunity to defend themselves in cases involving accusations or from any violation of prior or due process:
- There must be consultation among all parties, i.e., the local ordinary, the competent society superior and the office holder;
- All parties concerned shall be told the identity of accuser, the nature of the charges, the evidence, and other pertinent details;
- Before action is taken, sufficient time must be allowed so that an answer may be prepared.

10. TRAVEL AND LEAVE:
    A. When, for whatever reason, a member of the Society engaged in the diocesan apostolate is to be sent out of the diocese for a lengthy period of time, the following norms are to be observed:
        • If the journey is occasioned at the instance of the local ordinary, he must obtain the consent of the competent superior.
        • If the journey is occasioned at the instance of the society superior, he must inform the local ordinary in good time.
        • If the apostolate will suffer because of the absence of that member, assistance should be provided by the authority at whose instance the journey was occasioned.
        • Members of the society actively engaged in the diocesan apostolate must inform the local ordinary if, with their superior's permission, they are about to spend some considerable time outside the diocese.
    B. Members of the society assigned to work in the diocese have a right to a local leave of three weeks every year, and they shall normally proceed on a twelve weeks home leave on completion of every two years.
        • In the cases of members who go home on sick leave, the ordinary shall be responsible for their full fare while the society will be responsible for all medical expenses incurred by them while on sick leave.
11. SUPPORT AND MAINTENANCE:
    A. Over and above the provisions of the following paragraphs, the local ordinary will pay a monthly allowance for the support of each of the members of the society actively engaged in the diocesan apostolate:
        • The monthly support is to be determined by common agreement, which is to be reviewed at each annual budget period.
        • The diocese will provide housing and utilities and a vehicle.

- The Society may provide additional means of transportation if it deems it necessary and possible.
- The monthly support will be paid for the society member while he is on vacation or normal home leave.

B. The local ordinary will provide for the maintenance of parochial and other diocesan juridical persons under the administration of the Society and for their personnel in accordance with an agreed annual budget.

C. Expenses of members of the society attached to the diocese who are traveling outside it for whatever reason will be defrayed by the authority—diocesan or society—on whose behalf the journey is made.

D. The local ordinary will pay the travel expenses as follows:
- For members of the society from abroad who, while actively engaged in the diocesan apostolate, proceed on home-leave, the local ordinary shall contribute the direct (..........................—Lagos) one way or return ticket as applicable.... The society is responsible for any other expenses.
- When a member of the society actively engaged in the diocesan apostolate proceeds on annual local or diocesan leave, the local ordinary shall provide him with a means of transport or funds for securing transportation.

E. The Society will be financially responsible for all compassionate leave, i.e., in case of death or serious illness of a member of his family.

12. MONEY:

A. Donations from whatever source must be administered according to the intentions of the donor.
- Those given explicitly or implicitly for missionary or apostolic work in the diocese will fall under the diocesan temporal administration.
- All donations given to members of the society either *intuitu societatis* or *intuitu personae* accrue to the patrimony of the society, and they are to be administered

in accordance with the norms of canon law and the constitutions of the society.

- Stole fees, offerings given on the occasion of administering the Sacraments and Sacramentals are the property of the diocese, unless diocesan statutes dictate otherwise.

B. Income from the work of the diocese received under whatever title will go to the diocese if the work belongs to the diocese, or to the society if the work belongs to the society.

13. COMMENCEMENT, RENEWAL, REVISION AND TERMINATION OF CONTRACT:

A. This contract will come into effect and be binding on both parties from or thereafter from the date of its having been signed by both parties.

B. This contract will remain in force for a period of five years from the date of its commencement.

- During its term it may be modified at any time by mutual consent of the parties signatory to it. Such changes do not require submission to the superior ecclesiastical authority but are valid and effectively immediately consent is given unless another provision is made.

- Negotiations to renew or extend this contract, as well as to revise it upon its expiration, should commence at least six months prior to the date of the expiration date. In the event that neither party initiates such negotiation, the agreement is presumed to be renewed by mutual tacit consent for another period of five years.

C. Provided that, when required, notice is given by the appropriate superior ecclesiastical authorities, this contract may be terminated:

- Before its expiration by the mutual consent of the contracting parties;

- By one year's notice by either party that at its expiration it will not be renewed.

D. In case of serious disagreement concerning the application of any clause of this contract recourse shall be had to the Holy See.

In testimony of which we have affixed our signatures and our seals

DIOCESE OF.............................

ORDINARY

DATE.............................
WITNESS..........................
....
SUPERIOR OF THE MISSIONARY SOCIETY OF ST. PAUL
DATE................................
WITNESS............................

3. Final Copy of the Contract Formula

TITLE
THE CATHOLIC BISHOPS' CONFERENCE OF NIGERIA (CBCN) AND ST. PATRICK'S MISSIONARY SOCIETY, KILTEGAN

We the undersigned,

Dominic Cardinal Ekandem, archbishop of Abuja and the ordinary of the Missionary Society of St. Paul (henceforth referred to as the local ordinary) in the name of the Catholic Bishops' Conference of Nigeria and of the Missionary Society of St. Paul, on the one part, and the superior general, St. Patrick's Missionary Society, Kiltegan (henceforth referred to as St. Patrick's Society), duly represented by Very Rev, on the other hand, have agreed to sign this contract with a view to promoting fruitful collaboration between the two parties in establishing a National Missionary Institute and in fostering the missionary dimension in the Nigerian church.

ARTICLE ONE:

PURPOSE OF THE CONTRACT

This contract exists for the regulation of the mutual relationship between two juridical persons, namely the CBCN and ST. PATRICK'S SOCIETY with reference to establishing the Missionary Society of St. Paul and the formation of candidates of St. Paul's National Missionary Seminary.

ARTICLE TWO:

RELATIONSHIP OF ST. PATRICK'S SOCIETY AND THE CBCN

1. For the purpose of this contract, the CBCN shall be represented by the local ordinary and by the governing council. The competent major superior shall be the superior general of the St. Patrick's Society and shall be represented by the regional superior of St. Patrick's Fathers in Nigeria.
2. The specific work of the CBCN for which the cooperation of St. Patrick's Society is enlisted at the time of this contract are:
   - The establishment of the National Missionary Society of St. Paul.
   - The formation of the candidates of St. Paul's National Missionary Seminary.
   - The administration of St. Paul's National Missionary Seminary/Society. This administration shall be mainly concerned with the day to day running of the institute.
   - Any other suitable pastoral activity that the CBCN may deem necessary and approved by the regional superior.
3. Should the CBCN wish to relieve St. Patrick's Society of the aforementioned pastoral activity entrusted to it, the competent major superior must be informed six months in advance.
4. Should St. Patrick's Society find itself unable to continue the pastoral activity entrusted to it, the competent major superior must inform the CBCN at least six months in advance.

ARTICLE THREE:

THE AUTHORITY OF THE LOCAL ORDINARY
AND THE GOVERNING COUNCIL

1. THE "LOCAL ORDINARY" is the Superior of the Missionary Society of St. Paul,
2. The governing council is the administrative body of the Missionary Society of St. Paul and of St. Paul's National Missionary Seminary.
3. The LOCAL ORDINARY and the governing council shall strive to safeguard, encourage and direct the spontaneous initiative and activity of all those taking part in the work of the Society of St. Paul in accordance with Art. Two paragraph 2.
4. In all that concerns the work of the CBCN with regard to the Missionary Society of St. Paul's National Missionary Seminary, members of St. Patrick's Society engaged in this apostolate (initiative) are subject to the local ordinary and the governing council in accordance with the general law of the church, the decrees of the Second Vatican Council, the subsequent decrees of the Holy See, the guidelines issued by the CBCN, and subsequent decrees of the Holy See.

ARTICLE FOUR:

THE PRESENCE OF ST. PATRICK'S SOCIETY WITHIN
INSTITUTION OF THE MISSIONARY SOCIETY OF ST. PAUL
AND OF ST. PAUL'S NATIONAL MISSIONARY SEMINARY.

1. Even while its members are actively engaged in the above missionary initiative of the CBCN, St. Patrick's Society is entitled to preserve its particular character and the due autonomy (*Perfecta Caritatis* Par. 2b).
2. The local ordinary and the governing council recognize the right of those under their jurisdiction to choose their way of life freely in accordance with the inspiration of the Holy Spirit and the

right of St. Patrick's Society to foster vocations and to accept any candidates that present themselves to St. Patrick's Society. However, St. Patrick's Society shall not in any way recruit from the candidates of St. Paul's Missionary Society/ Seminary.

3. The collaboration of members of St. Patrick's Society. With other diocesan and religious priests engaged in this work must be so arranged as not to create obstacle to the apostolic life of the members of St. Patrick's Society and vice versa.

4. Except as provided by lay, the local ordinary and the governing council shall not interfere in matters pertaining to the apostolic observance and regular discipline of St. Patrick's Society.

ARTICLE FIVE:

SUPERIORS OF ST. PATRICK'S SOCIETY

1. Because they belong to a clerical society of apostolic life, members of St. Patrick's Society working in St. Paul's Missionary Society have their own religious superiors whose appointments and duties are governed by the legislation of the constitution of St. Patrick's Society (of Canon 734).

2. Without prejudice to the rights not mentioned here and to those of higher authorities, it is the right of the competent major superior to:
   - Appoint those who shall exercise apostolic authority in St. Patrick's Society within the ecclesiastical jurisdiction of Nigeria.
   - Call the members of St. Patrick's Society to chapters, council meetings, assemblies, and an annual retreat.
   - Call the members of St. Patrick's Society engaged in the St. Paul's Missionary Society out of the Missionary Society of St. Paul and of St. Paul's National Missionary Seminary to transact legitimate business of St. Patrick's Society.

3. Without prejudice to the jurisdiction of the local ordinary and the governing council, the competent major superior shall strive

to see that the members of St. Patrick's Society faithfully fulfil the task entrusted to them by the CBCN:

- Should the competent major superior consider that the local ordinary and the governing council are imposing duties incompatible with regular discipline, he shall consult with the local ordinary.
- Should the local ordinary and the governing council consider that one or another of the statutes of St. Patrick's Society is insufficiently adapted to the special conditions existing within the St. Paul's Missionary Society and St. Paul's National Missionary Seminary, they shall consult with the competent major superior of St. Patrick's Society.

ARTICLE SIX:

ASSIGNMENT TO AND RECALL FROM THE ST. PAUL'S MISSIONARY SOCIETY OF ST. PATRICK'S SOCIETY MEMBERS

1. The competent major superior, respecting always the right of higher authorities, has the right to:
   - Present members of St. Patrick's Society for work in the St. Paul's Missionary Society.
   - Recall or transfer St. Patrick's Society members there from.
2. The exercise of these rights is without prejudice to the rights of the local ordinary to put forward objections with a view to safeguarding and maintaining the activities of St. Paul's Missionary Society.

ARTICLE SEVEN:

THE APPOINTMENT AND REMOVAL OF MEMBERS OF THE ST. PATRICK'S SOCIETY TO SPECIFIC OFFICES OF THE MISSIONARY SOCIETY OF ST. PAUL.

1. In the best interest of the St. Paul's Missionary Society and St. Patrick's Society, it is desirable that there be mutual consultation

between the local ordinary and the governing council and the competent major superior concerning assignments to specific offices within the St. Paul's Missionary Society. Moreover, the persons concerned ordinarily must be consulted before a final decision is made.

2.   The appointment of St. Patrick's Society members to specific offices within the St. Paul's Missionary Society is subject to thef ollowing norms:

- It pertains to the competent major superior of St. Patrick's Society to present to the local ordinary and the governing council suitable candidates for the various offices which St. Patrick's Society is called upon to fill.

- If the local ordinary and the governing council find that the persons presented are acceptable, they will give a formal written appointment together with the necessary terms of reference and conditions of service.

- This appointment will be transmitted to the individual concerned by the competent major superior of St. Patrick's Society who will give him his assignment.

- Should it prove difficult to come to an agreement concerning the appointment of an individual to a specific post, the competent St. Patrick's Society major superior will propose two or more names for the choice of the governing council, if in fact there is more than one St. Patrick's member available for the assignment.

- Until the appointment is made public, all those concerned should observe discretion with regard to it.

3.   In extraordinary cases, any member of St. Patrick's Society appointed to a post may be removed from it either by the governing council or by the competent major superior of St. Patrick's Society. However, to provide members of St. Patrick's Society with an opportunity to defend themselves in cases involving accusations and to safeguard any violation of prior or due process: (cf 221 CC. 220.)

- There must be consultation among all parties, i.e., the governing council, the competent St. Patrick's Society Superior and the officeholder.
- All parties concerned shall be told the identity of accusers, the nature of the charges, the evidence, and other pertinent details.
- Before action is taken, sufficient time must be allowed so that an answer may be prepared.

ARTICLE EIGHT:

TRAVEL

1. When for ever reason a member of St. Patrick's Society engaged at the St. Paul's Missionary Society is to be sent out of the institution for a lengthy period of time, the following norms are to be observed:
   - If the journey is occasioned at the instance of the St. Paul's Missionary Society, he must obtain the permission of the competent St. Patrick's Society superior in good time.
   - If the journey is occasioned at the instance of St. Patrick's Society superior, he must inform the competent superior of St. Paul's Missionary Society in good time.
   - If the work will suffer because of the absence of that St. Patrick's Father, assistance should be provided by the authority at whose instance the journey was occasioned.
2. Members of St. Patrick's Society engaged in the St. Paul's Missionary Society apostolate must inform the local ordinary if, with their superior's permission, they are about to spend some considerable time outside the institution.
3. Members of St. Patrick's Society assigned to work at the St. Paul's Missionary Society have a right to three months' leave in two years, the time of such leave is to be arranged between the competent major St. Patrick's Society superior and the individual without prejudice to the particular needs in the Society of St. Paul, which might benefit from a period of six weeks'

absence each year for some members. The local ordinary must be informed in good time.

ARTICLE NINE:

SUPPORT AND MAINTENANCE

1. Over and above the provisions of the following paragraphs, the St. Paul's Missionary Society will pay monthly to the support for each of the members of St. Patrick's Society actively engaged in the St. Paul's Missionary Society apostolate:
   - The monthly allowance is to be determined by the governing council. The sum of money so determined is to be reviewed at each annual budget period.
   - The St. Paul's Missionary Society will provide housing and a vehicle.
   - A monthly allowance will be paid for a St. Patrick's Society member while he is on vacation of normal home-leave.
2. The St. Paul's Missionary Society will provide for the maintenance of the personnel (e.g., driver under the administration of St. Patrick's Society member in accordance with an agreed annual budget).
3. Expenses of members of St Patrick's Society attached to the St. Paul's Missionary who are traveling outside it for whatever reason will be defrayed by the authority on whose behalf the journey is made.
4. The St. Paul's Missionary Society will pay the travel expenses as follows:
   - For members of St. Patrick's Society who, while actively in St. Paul's Missionary Society apostolate, proceed on biannual home-leave, the St. Paul's Missionary Society shall pay 100 percent of the direct (Lagos -----X) flight, one way or return ticket as applicable. St. Patrick's Society is responsible for all other expenses when the member is on leave.
   - When member of St. Patrick's Society actively engaged in the St. Paul's Missionary Society apostolate proceeds on

sick leave and overseas medical treatment, the St. Paul's Missionary Society and St. Patrick's Society shall mutually negotiate how to defray the expenses.

5.   St. Patrick's Society will be financially responsible for all compassionate leave.

ARTICLE TEN:

FINANCE

1.   Donations from whatever source must be administered according to the intentions of the donor.
   *   Those given explicitly or implicitly for apostolic work in the St. Paul's Missionary Society will fall under the temporal administration of the St. Paul's Missionary Society.
   *   All donations given to members of St. Patrick's Society either in *intuitu societatis* or *intuitu personae* accrue to the patrimony of St. Patrick's Society, and they are to be administered in accordance with the norms of canon law and the pertinent legislation of St. Patrick's Society.
2.   Offerings given on occasion of administering the Sacraments and Sacramentals on behalf of St. Paul's Missionary Society are the property of the St. Paul's Missionary Society. All other mass stipends are personal.

ARTICLE ELEVEN:

COMMENCEMENT, RENEWAL, REVISION

1.   This contract will come into effect and be binding on both parties from the.........................19.........or thereafter, provided it has been signed by both parties.
2.   This contract will remain in force for a period of two years from the date of its commencement.
3.   During its term it may be modified at any time by mutual consent of the parties signatory to it.

4. Negotiations to renew or extend this contract as well to revise it upon its expiration should commence at least six months prior to the date of the expiration. In the event that neither party initiates such negotiation, the agreement is presumed to be renewed by mutual tacit consent for another period of two years.

5. Provided that, when required, notice is given by the appropriate ecclesiastical authorities, this contract may be terminated, before its expiration, by the mutual consent of the contracting parties, or by one year's notice by either party that at its expiration it will not be renewed.

6. In case of serious disagreement concerning the application of any clause of this contract, recourse shall be had to the sacred Congregation for the Evangelization of Peoples after all avenues of arbitration have been exhausted.

In testimony of which we have affixed our signatures and our seals.

Dominic Cardinal Ekandem.

Date: -------------------------------

Attest..............................

--Superior

General St. Patrick's Society Date: _____

Attest:_____

4. Documents About His Benefactress, Mrs. Annice Gordon and Family Members

i.   A Letter to Mrs. McDonnell

CATHOLIC DIOCESE OF IKOT EKPENE

Bishop's House
Library Avenue
P.O. Box 70
Ikot Ekpene Nigeria
June 8th 1976

Dear Mrs McDonnell,

A hundred thanks to you for your kindness and interest in finding me out and sending me that beautiful message of warm affection and prayerful good wishes.

I thank God who in his merciful love inspired you to contact me. I had been looking for a means of any contact with any of my spiritual mother's relations but found none. You have done very well indeed in presenting your good and dear self to me.

I remember you and Kilmovee. I remember the Woodlawn House where you entertained Mrs. Gordon and me. I remember the twins, Alex and all but where they are now I cannot tell. Where is my Dominican Sister? Is she the one that was in Swinford. One was Mary and the other? Please write and tell me. Let them know their Uncle is asking for them. If I can get the nun's address I would love to write to her.

For the present I wish to thank you most sincerely and to assure you of my poor prayers.

Yours in Christ
+ D. I. Ekandem

CATHOLIC DIOCESE OF IKOT EKPENE

BISHOP'S HOUSE
LIBRARY AVENUE,
P. O. BOX 70,
IKOT EKPENE,
NIGERIA.

June 8, 1976

Dear Mrs Mc Donnell,

A hundred thanks to you for your kindness and interest in finding me out and sending me that beautiful message of warm affection and prayerful good wishes.

I thank God who in His merciful love inspired you to contact me. I had been looking for a means of any contact with any of my spiritual mother's relations but found none. You have done very well indeed in presenting your good and dear self to me.

I remember you and Kilmovee. I remember the Woodlawn House where you entertained Mrs Gordon and me. I remember the Twins, Alex and all but where they are now I cannot tell. Where is my Dominican Sister? Is she the one that was in Swinford. One was Mary and the other? Please write and tell me. Let them know their Uncle is asking for them. If I can get the nun's address I would love to write to her.

For the present I wish to thank you most sincerely and to assure you of my poor prayers.

Yours in christ

+ D.I. Edem Bp

594

ii.   A Tribute to Mrs. Gordon: A Woman of Rare Courage and Generosity
5. Cardinal Ekandem's Letter to Very Reverend Father Filippelli

THE NATIONAL MISSIONARY SEMINARY OF ST. PAUL

Gwagwalada,
P.O. Box 402,
Garki,   Established By the
Abuja, Nigeria.   Episcopal Conference
2nd October 1986.   of Nigeria

Very Rev. John L.M. Filippelli S.S.J.

1130 North Calvert Street
Superior General,
The Josephites

Baltimore M.D.
21202
U.S.A.

Dear Father Filippelli,

Thank you very sincerely for your letter dated July 28, 1986, in which you outline the detailed arrangements for the three priests from the Missionary Society of St. Paul who will work in association with the Josephites in the Diocese of Galveston—Houston.

I deeply appreciate the care, which you are giving to orientation and to every aspect of their lives. This is so necessary at the beginning of a new mission.

To live close to the Josephites and follow the Josephite way of life will be an enriching experience for them. At the same time we hope they will be encouraged to discover and develop their own style of Pauline Spirituality.

Mass stipends belong to the Missionary Society of St. Paul and should normally be paid into the Society's account. Each priest has four free masses each month.

I feel sure that the commitment of the Josephite Community and the arrangements you have made will provide all the support the young priests will need at the beginning of their mission.

Wishing you every blessing
Sincerely yours in Christ.

....
Dominic Cardinal Ekandem

6. Sabbatical Leave of Msgr. Godwin Akpan, First Rector of Missionary of St. Paul, Gwagwalada

i. A letter to Fr. Robert Kearns, SSJ

The National Missionary Seminary of St. Paul

Gwagwalada
P.O. Box 402,
Abuja, Nigeria.
September 29, 1995

Very Reverend Robert Kearns, SSJ
Superior General
The Josephites
1130N Calvert Street
BALTIMORE, MD 21202

Dear Father Kearns,

Greetings from Gwagwalada.

After eighteen years of involvement in various capacities in the Missionary Society of St. Paul of Nigeria, we have a new Administration in place. Two of your men are in it, Reverend Fathers Felix Elosi and Anthony Afangide. Felix is now the Superior General and Anthony is one of his councillors. When you visit Nigeria as you mentioned in your letter, you will be meeting those who are very interested in the Black Apostolate.

While in Washington last November it was possible to see Reverend Christopher Keenan about their Sabbatical Programme at the Washington Theological Union. I have been given admission to do my sabbatical programme in the school. I raised the issue with your predecessor, Father Eugene McManus, SSJ, and last November. I am respectfully requesting for accommodation facilities in your St. Joseph's Seminary in Washington. I am expected to be in Washington for the sabbatical programme in the school in August 1996. The financial responsibility for doing the sabbatical programme will be borne by my Society.

Trusting that my request will be favourably considered.
Yours sincerely,

Rev. Msgr Godwin P. Akpan, MSP

ii.   A letter to Fr. Joseph Giordano, CICM

THE MISSIONARY SOCIETY OF ST. PAUL

P.O. BOX 3200
Barrett Station, Texas 77532-2200
Tel. (713) 328-4451
Fax (713)328-7306

August 5, 1996

Very Rev. Joseph Giordano, (cicm)
The Provincial, Missionhurst 4651, N. 25th St.
Arlington, VA 22207-3500
Tel 703-528-3800

Michael I. Edem CM

Dear Father Giordano,

I like to introduce myself as an active member of the Missionary Society of St. Paul of Nigeria. What is now a full-fledged Missionary Society of St. Paul of Nigeria started as the National Missionary Seminary of St. Paul with the sole purpose of training missionary priests for the society.

I happened to be involved from the very inception of the Missionary Institute, having been appointed by the Catholic Bishops' Conference of Nigeria, the Rector of the Seminary in 1977. While serving in that capacity from 1977 through 1987, I recall with gratitude the caring attitude in their nurturing role to our Missionary Institute of Frs. Erie, Kasanda, John Patrick and Mmani of the cicm in Nigeria.

In 1987, I was appointed by the same Bishops' Conference, the Acting Superior General of the Society as an interim arrangement in preparation for the first general chapter, which was successfully held in September 1995 with the election of the new superior general and council, thus ushering in a new Administration for the society. After 18 years of involvement in the administration of the Missionary Society of St. Paul of Nigeria, I needed a sabbatical year to which I have gained admission to do a sabbatical program with the Roman Catholic School for Ministry, the Washington Theological Union. The estimated cost in the school for an academic year is US $17,000.00. The 1-20 school form is attached. While in Nigeria I applied to Missio, Aachen for financial assistance. I got partial funding of 12,000.00 DM. Still in Nigeria I applied through the then C.I.C.M Regional Very Rev. John Patrick Ngoyi (cicm) for assistance fro the CICM community. A photocopy of the application letter is enclosed.

I am respectfully applying for financial assistance of $7,000.00 from your community to enable me to meet the essential needs of the sabbatical program. This is necessary because with the growth of my society witnessing currently 91 students in formation for the missionary priesthood, 104 priest members ministering in the Gambia, Sierra Leone, Cameroon, Botswana, Kenya, Malawi, South Africa, United States of America and Nigeria, the maintenance of these priests as well as the training of the students has not been easy financially. While awaiting your favourable consideration.

I remain
Respectfully,
Rev, Msgr. Godwin .P. Akpan, M.S.P. Enclosures.

7.   Beatification

The National Missionary Seminary of St. Paul of Nigeria

P.O. Box 23
Gwagwalada
Abuja, Nigeria.
June 21ˢᵗ 2005

The Superior General and Council
The Missionary Society of St. Paul
Gwagwalada

A MEMORANDUM

RE: INITIATING CAUSE FOR THE BEATIFICATION OF THE
FOUNDER

Encouraged by the foresight of the founder of the Missionary Society
of St. Paul of Nigeria, which foresight was progressively shared by the bishops of Nigeria in the 1970s, coupled with the doggedness of hi, which
brooked no opposition, despite the odds, such that the Missionary Society
of St. Paul of Nigeria, thought to be a dream in the 1980s, is now a reality
of major significance destined to play a significant role in the New Era
of Evangelization, as providentially guaranteed, since 1985, by the yearly
priestly ordination of talented young men with a total population of 179
priests on June 25, 2005, I strongly propose that the current Administration
of the Society of St. Paul of Nigeria, without any further delay, putting
in place, the canonical requirements for the aforementioned undertaking,
should put in motion the cause for the beautification of our founder, the
late, Cardinal Dominic Ekandem in this year of the Lord, 2005.

(Signed) Godwin P. Akpan, MSP

Bibliography

PRIMARY SOURCES

A.   His writings

EKANDEM, D. I., (Most Rev. Dr.), O.B.E, C.O.N. March, 1973, Towards a Viable and Self-Reliant Church, Aba, Cynako International Press Limited.

EKANDEM, DOMINIC I., 1974, The Church in the Rise of Nigeria, Sermon Delivered on the Occasion of the Golden Jubilee of Bigard Memorial Seminary Enugu, Nigeria, on July 29, 1974, Aba, Cynako International Press Ltd.

EKANDEM Dominic Cardinal, (His Eminence), DD, OBE, CON, December 5, 1976, True Spiritual Leadership—A Vital Contribution to Nation Building, Ikot Ekpene, De Paul Printing Press.

EKANDEM Dominic, (His Eminence), Thursday, September 1978, "Don't Abandon the Poor," in the Nigerian Chronicle, No. 1,338, (The Reporter), Calabar, Front page continued from p. 3.

EKANDEM D. I., (Most Rev. Dr.), 1979, Shepherds among Shepherds, Onitsha, Tabansi Press Ltd.

EKANDEM Dominic Cardinal I., 1979, Silver Jubilee Memoire Manuscripts (Unpublished), pp. 3, 4. He gave these to the author in 1995. The materials were typed in foolscap-sized typing sheets.

EKANDEM Dominic Cardinal I., 1995, Personal Interview Granted to the Author Regarding His Prayer Life, Urua Akpan, Essien Udim L. G. A., Akwa Ibom State, Nigeria.

EKANDEM Dominic, A New Ideal of an Old Ideal, an Ideal Never Attained, Bishop's House, Library Avenue, Ikot Ekpene, Nigeria, Friday, May 15, 1976, pp. 1–3.

EKANDEM Dominic, President, Episcopal Conference of Nigeria, Appendix, Bishop's House, Library Avenue, Ikot Ekpene, Nigeria, Friday, May 15, 1976.

EKANDEM Dominic Cardinal, April–June 1992, "Advice for the Future," Torch Magazine, Bigard Memorial Seminary Publication, No: 100, pp. 17–18 quoted in OBI Nicholas, 1998, Our Legacy; Leeway to Personal Achievements, Lagos, Jojab Ventures, p. 457.

EKANDEM Dominic Cardinal, 1987, Justice Promotes Security and Peace, Lenten Pastoral Letter, Ikot Ekpene, Akwa Ibom State, Nigeria.

EKANDEM Dominic Cardinal, Comments on the Origin of St. Joseph Catholic Teachers' League, Urua Akpan, Ikot Ekpene, Akwa Ibom State, 1995.

EKANDEM Dominic Cardinal, 1995, Comments on the Origin of Catholic Teachers' Association.

EKANDEM Dominic Cardinal, "Federation of St. Joseph Catholic Teachers' League" in Lux Catholica, Ikot Ekpene, 1981 De Paul Printing Press, 1981, pp. 12, 14.

EKANDEM Dominic Cardinal, "A Message of Appreciation and Respect for 'Nka Adiaha Obong' Catholic Diocese of Calabar on the Occasion of the Silver Jubilee of Its Foundation," in The Daughters, 1980, Adiaha Obong Catholic Women's Organisation Silver Jubilee 1955–79 (MAIDEN ISSUE), Uyo, Cross River State, May 1980, pp.2–3.

EKANDEM Dominic Cardinal, April 8, 1968, A Letter to Mother General, Gertrude Waturuocha, Bishop's House, Ikot Ekpene.

EKANDEM Dominic Cardinal, October 25, 1986, A Letter to Very Rev. Fr. John L. M. Filippelli, SSJ, Concerning the Welfare and Spirituality of the Missionaries, Gwagwalada, Abuja, Nigeria. Retrieved from Msgr. Godwin P. Akpan's Archive.

EKANDEM Dominic Cardinal, "The Necessity of the National Seminary in Nigeria" in the Ambassador Magazine, Vol.2, No. 2, Iperu Remo, Ogun State, October 1977.

B. Personal interviews granted by Cardinal Ekandem or members of the Family to the author

EKANDEM Dominic Cardinal, On Family Background Before Entry into the Minor Seminary, Oral Interview with the author, Urua Akpan, Ikot Ekpene, Akwa Ibom State, Nigeria, 1995.

EKANDEM Dominic Cardinal, 1995, On Family Financial Situation Prior to Minor Seminary, Oral interview granted to the author, Urua Akpan, Akwa Ibom State, Nigeria.

EKANDEM Cardinal Dominic, On Involvement in Pastoral Work and Cultural Understanding, Oral Interview the author, Urua Akpan, Ikot Ekpene, Akwa Ibom State, 1995.

EKANDEM Rose Nkubia, The Reaction of Family Members on Breaking the News of Going to the Seminary, Oral Interview with the author, U tuk's Avenue, Uyo, Akwa Ibom State, Nigeria, June 1995.

EKANDEM Dominic Cardinal I., On Family Background, Oral Interview with the author, Urua Akpan, Ikot Ekpene, Akwa Ibom State, April 1995.

EKANDEM Dominic Cardinal, (His Eminence), Christianity and Life in the Village, Oral Interview with the Author at Urua Akpan, Akwa Ibom State, Nigeria, 1995.

EKANDEM Dominic Cardinal I., 1995, On Prayer Life, Oral Interview with the author, Urua Akpan, Essien Udim L. G. A., Akwa Ibom State, Nigeria.

EKANDEM Vitus, On Obio Ibiono and the Origin of Okuku and Its Primacy of Position, Cardinal's Brother and Retired Civil Servant, Oral Interview with the author, Obio Ibiono, Itu LGA, Akwa Ibom State, Nigeria, April 1995.

EKANDEM Rose, (Mrs. Nkubia), Retired Teacher and Cardinal's Sister, The Story of Cardinal Ekandem's Journey to the Priesthood, Oral interview with the author. July 1995.

EKANDEM Rose Nkubia, Retired Teacher and Cardinal's Sister, On the Need to Remain Hidden, Oral Interview with the author, Utuk's Avenue, Uyo, Akwa Ibom State, Nigeria, July 1995.

EKANDEM Dominic Cardinal, On Family Background, Oral Interview with the author, Urua Akpan, Ikot Ekpene, Akwa Ibom State, April 1995.

EKANDEM Dominic Cardinal, A Private Address to the Land Officer of Ikot Ekpene Local Government Area, The Bishop's House, Cardinal Ekandem's Avenue, Ikot Ekpene, 1987.

EKANDEM Dominic Cardinal, A Response to the Speech of the Governor, Brigadier Dan Archibong, Governor of Cross River State, Ukana Iba, Ikot Ekpene, Nigeria, 1985.

EKANDEM Dominic Cardinal, On Involvement in Pastoral Work and Cultural Understanding, Oral Interview with the author, Urua Akpan, Ikot Ekpene, Akwa Ibom State, April 1995.

EKANDEM Dominic Cardinal, On Pastoral Challenges as a Young Bishop, Urua Akpan, Ikot Ekpene, Akwa Ibom State, Oral Interview with the author, April 1995.

EKANDEM Gabriel John (Dr.), Cardinal's Nephew and a member of the College of Medicine, University of Uyo, Akwa Ibom State, Nigeria, On the Choice of Mma Mary as Wedded Wife, oral conversation about Cardinal Ekandem with the author, Obio Ibiono, Ibiono Ibom LGA, Akwa Ibom State, June 2014.

SECONDARY SOURCES
Articles and Letters

AFANGIDEH. Lucy K., A Brief Account on Late Dominic Cardinal Ekandem—Archbishop of Abuja, Abuja, Handmaids Convent, An Unpublished Material made available to the author, 2014.

AKPAN Godwin (Msgr.), My Experience of Meeting Father Dominic Ekandem for the First Time, Iperu Remo, Ogun State, An Unpublished Note given to the author, 2010.

AKPAN Godwin (Msgr.), Memo on the Necessity of Active Involvement in Abuja Apostolate by the Missionaries of St. Paul, An Unpublished Document from his archive, June 21, 1989.

AKPAN Godwin P. (Msgr.), A Letter to Msgr. A. Obine, Secretary General, Catholic Secretariat of Nigeria Lagos, Uyo, Christ The King Pro-Cathedral. An Unpublished Document from his archive, August 25, 1977.

AKPAN Godwin, (Msgr.), A Memorandum: One Year Pastoral Ministry in Nigeria before Being Sent on the Missions, Gwagwalada, Abuja.

The document is from Msgr. Godwin P. Akpan's archive, November 11, 1986.

AKPAN Godwin (Msgr.), A Letter of Excardination from Calabar Diocese and Incardination into the Society Written to His Ordinary, the Bishop of Calabar, Bishop Usanga, Gwagwalada, Abuja, National Missionary Seminary of St. Paul, January 15, 1985.

AKPAN Godwin (Msgr.), A Letter of Acceptance and Appreciation to Members of the Internal Governing Council, Gwagwalada, Abuja, Nigeria, Missionary Society of St. Paul, January 15, 1985.

ANYANWU Godwin, "Enugu is the Home of Christianity-Ekandem" in Daily Star newspaper, No. 1402, Tuesday, November 30, A Publication of East Central State, Enugu, Front page, 1976.

ARINZE Francis (Archbishop), "Missionary Dimension" in the Ambassador Magazine, No. 1, Vol. 1, Iperu Remo, Ogun State, October 1977.

CATECHISM OF THE CATHOLIC CHURCH, Inspiration and Truth of Sacred Scripture, Nos. 106–108, United Kingdom, Geoffrey Chapman, 1994.

CATHOLIC BISHOPS' CONFERENCE OF NIGERIA, CBCN, Minutes of Meeting, Kaduna, September 15, 1976.

THE CATHOLIC BISHOPS' CONFERENCE OF NIGERIA, CBCN, Second Plenary Assembly of the Catholic Bishops' Conference of Nigeria, Minutes, "Congratulatory Message," Ibadan, Pastoral Institute, October 17, 1990, p. 4.

CATHOLIC BISHOPS' CONFERENCE OF NIGERIA, CBCN, Second Plenary Assembly of the Catholic Bishops' Conference of Nigeria, Minutes, October 17, 1990, p. 3.

CATHOLIC BISHOPS' CONFERENCE OF NIGERIA, CBCN, First Session, No. 2.3, "Presidential Address, cf. Working Committee 2," 1990, p. 4.

CATHOLIC BISHOPS' CONFERENCE OF NIGERIA, CBCN, Minutes, No. 4.1, March 6, 1990, p. 6.

CHRISTUS DOMINUS, Decree on the Pastoral Office of Bishops in the Church, No. 14, (FLANNERY Austin, General Editor, VATICAN II, Vol. 1), Dublin, Ireland, Dominican Publications, October 28, 1965.

CONGREGATIO PRO GENTIUM EVANGELIZATIONE, JOSEPH Cardinal Tomko, Pref. Deep Condolences at the Death of Cardinal Ekandem, Vatican City, 1995.

DEI VERBUM, The Dogmatic Constitution on Divine Revelation, No. 8. (FLANNERY Austin, General Editor, VATICAN II, Vol. 1), Dublin, Ireland, Dominican Publications, November 18, 1965.

EKERETE Julian (Sr.), Dominic Cardinal Ekandem, A Man of Rare Qualities, Immaculate Conception Secondary School/Handmaids Convent, Itak, Akwa Ibom State, An Unpublished Material given to the author, 2014.

ELOSI Felix, (MSP Superior General), Condolence, in Funeral Brochure of Cardinal Ekandem, Garki, Abuja, Nigeria, November 28, 1995. ESSIET Regina E. (Sr.), Our Dear Cardinal, Ifuho, Ikot Ekpene, Generalate Community, An Unpublished Document submitted to the author, 2014.

FILIPPELLI John L. M. (Superior General of the Josephites), A Letter to Cardinal Ekandem on Modalities of St. Paul Missionaries about to Begin Their Mission in Houston, USA, Baltimore, USA, July 28, 1986.

GILL Peter L., Editor, Priest Pulls No Punches in Loyola Lecture on Being Black and Catholic in Four County Catholic, Vol. 12, No. 1, 12–13, March 2000.

INYANG Dominic E. (Msgr.), the Vicar General of Abuja Archdiocese, On the Beginnings of Abuja Independent Mission, Garki, Area 10, Oral Interview with the author, 2010.

INYANG Dominic E. (Msgr.), the Vicar General of Abuja Archdiocese, Gambling with Feeding Money in Order to Begin a Project in the Independent Mission, Garki, Area 10, Oral Interview with the author, 2001.

IWOH Mary Anne (Mother), Ex-Superior Genral of the Handmaid Sisters, The Return Journey from Urua Inyang and Efforts to Rescue the Handmaids of the Holy Child Jesus' Refugees in 1967, An Unpublished Document given to the author, Ifuho, 2007.

IWOH Mary Anne (Mother), Ex-Mother General of the Handmaid Sisters, "Bishop Dominic Ekandem's Relationship with the Handmaids of the Holy Child Jesus," "Preface to" the Tribute to a Valiant Pioneer

Missionary, Mary Magdalen (Mother), Foundress of the Handmaids in 1973, Archival Material, 2014.

JOHN PAUL II (Pope), "Telegram upon Death of Cardinal Ekandem," Vatican City in Funeral Programme of Cardinal Ekandem, Garki, Abuja, Nigeria, December 2, 1995.

JOHN PAUL II (Pope), Apostolic Letter, Ordinario Sacerdotalis to Bishops of the Catholic Church on Reserving Priestly Ordination to Men Alone, No. 4, Vatican City, Libreria Editrice Vaticana, May 22, 1994.

McDONNELL Alex, The Continuous Death of the Gordons' Children, electronic mail sent to the author from Kilmovee, Ireland, November 11, 2015.

MCMANUS Eugene P., SSJ (Vicar General, Josephites), A Letter to Msgr. Godwin P. Akpan Concerning the Visa problem and Date of Arrival of the Missionaries at Houston, USA, September 19, 1986.

MUHAMMAD Ustaz Musa (Chief Imam, Abuja Mosque), "The Passing Away of Cardinal," in The Funeral Programme of Cardinal Ekandem, Garki, Abuja, December 2, 1995.

NYONG Adam B., The Virtues of Cardinal Ekandem, Ibiaku Obio Ndobo, Uruan LGA, Akwa Ibom State, An Unpublished Note Given to the author, 1995.

NWANRUO Theresa (Sr.) (Spiritual Daughter), My Memory of Late Dominic Cardinal Ekandem, Abuja, Handmaids Convent, An Unpublished material submitted to the author, 2014.

O'GRADY Anne, "His Eminence Cardinal Dominic Ekandem, Bishop of Ikot Ekpene, Nigeria" in Echoes of Ballaghaderreen, Ireland, 1986. OKPO Mary Joseph (Mother), Ex-General Councillor of the Handmaid Sisters, Reminiscences of the Cardinal, Unpublished materials; Iva Valley, Enugu; a 17-page handwritten notes given to the author in response to the questions asked, April 1995.

OKPO Mary Joseph (Mother), An Outline of the History of the Congregation of the Handmaids of the Holy Child Jesus 1937–1987 Golden Jubilee Celebration an unpublished manuscript cf. especially the section on "The Civil War Period—A Challenge," Ifuho, Ikot Ekpene, Cross River State, 1987.

ROCHE Paul, Distant Memories of Dominic Cardinal Ekandem, An Unpublished Material given to the author. Very Reverend Father Paul is the Director of the Daughters of Charity, England and Ireland, who worked very closely with Cardinal Ekandem up to 1978, Palace Court, United Kingdom, February 2015.

SANUSI Anthony (Bishop), A Letter of Permission to Take the Final Oath of Membership, Bishop's House, Ijebu Ode. At the time, Bishop A. Sanusi was the Chairman/Ordinary of the National Missionary Seminary of St. Paul. This letter is from Msgr. G. Akpan's archive, January 18, 1985.

SHEERIN James SPS (Internal Council Secretary), Response to Msgr. Akpan's Letter about Admission into Temporary Oath of Membership, National Missionary Seminary, Iperu Remo, Ogun State, Nigeria. The document is from Msgr. G. Akpan's archive, January 25, 1984. SHEERIN James SPS (Internal Council Secretary), A Letter Granting Permission to Msgr. Godwin Akpan to Take the Final Oath of Membership, Iperu Remo, National Missionary Seminary of St. Paul. This document is from Msgr. G. Akpan's archive, January 9, 1985.

ST. PATRICK'S MISSIONARY SOCIETY, A Short History of St. Patrick's Missionary Society in 75 Years of Missionary Service Brochure, St. Patrick's Catholic Church, Ikot Ansa, Calabar, pp. 3–5, March 17, 2007.

THE EDITOR, Silver Jubilee Brochure of Episcopal Ordination of His Eminence, Cardinal Dominic Ekandem 1954–1979, 1979.

THE EDITOR, Africa, September 1950, quoted in O'GRADY Anne, A woman of Rare Courage and Generosity in Echoes of Ballaghaderreen, Ireland. 1986.

THE EDITOR, 70TH BIRTHDAY SOUVENIR OF HIS EMINENCE, DOMINIC CARDINAL EKANDEM, DD, OBE, CON, CFR, Bishop of Ikot Ekpene and Superior of Abuja Mission, 1917–1987, 1987.

THE EDITOR, Programme for the Funeral Mass of His Eminence Dominic Cardinal Ekandem DD, DBE (Sic), CON, CFR, LLD, D. LITT, Archbishop of Abuja 1917–1995 at Our Lady Queen of Nigeria Pro-Cathedral, Garki, Abuja, Date, December 2, 1995.

THE EDITOR, THE DAUGHTERS, Adiaha Obong Catholic Women's Organisation Silver Jubilee 1955–79, Uyo, Cross River State, MAIDEN ISSUE, 1980.

THE EDITOR, The General Chapter Procedure of the Missionaries of St. Paul, Gwagwalada, Abuja, Nigeria, Unpublished Document from the archive of Msgr. Godwin Akpan.

THE EDITOR, The Ambassador magazine, Souvenir Booklet, First Issue, No. 1, Vol. 1, Iperu Remo, Ogun State, Nigeria, May 26–27, 1979. THE EDITOR, The Crisis over Bishop's Transfer in The Nigerian Chronicle, Calabar, Government Printing Corporation, Tuesday, April 4, 1978, p. 7.

THE EDITOR, Women Oppose Bishop's Transfer: Cardinal Ekandem in The Nigerian Chronicle, No. 1,154, Calabar, Government Press, Tuesday, February 7, 1978, Front page.

THE EDITOR, The Silver Jubilee of the Federation of St. Joseph Catholic Teachers' League in Lux Catholica, Ikot Ekpene, De Paul Printing Press, 1981, pp. 3–17.

THE EDITOR, Funeral Rites of Rev. Sister Mary Augustine Okon, HHCJ, 1930–2012, Seat of Wisdom Chapel, Eriam Afaha Obong, Ikot Ekpene, Akwa Ibom State, Nigeria, December 13, 2012.

THÉRÈSE of Lisiéux (St.), The Story of a Soul, London, Burns & Oates, 1964(5).

TUKU Mary (Sr.), My Daddy Dominic Cardinal Ekandem, Idah, Kogi State, Handmaids Convent, An Unpublished Material made available to the author, 2014.

UMOH Elizabeth Mary (Mother), A Letter of Resignation as Delegate of the Elected Mother General Because of Changing Situations, Handmaids Convent, Eriam, Afaha Obong, Abak, Southeastern State, An Unpublished Archival Material, July 24, 1969.

UMOH Elizabeth Mary (Mother), Delegated to Act for Mother Mary Gertrude HHCJ, Congregation of the Handmaids of the Holy Child Jesus before, during and after the Nigeria/Biafra Civil War 10th July–15th January 1970. An Unpublished Archival Material, Eriam, Abak, Cross River State, pp. 1–10. From the archive of the Handmaids, Ifuho, Akwa Ibom State, Nigeria.

USANGA Brian D. 1980, "Love the Church, Love Our Lady and Love Your Fellowmen, Silver Jubilee of Adiaha Obong (CWO) Calabar Diocese, A Goodwill Message" in The Daughters, Adiaha Obong

Catholic Women's Organisation Silver Jubilee 1955–79 (MAIDEN ISSUE), Uyo, Cross River, 1980, pp. 4–5.

USANGA Brian D., Appointment Letter as Acting Director Nigerian National Seminary, Bishop's House, Calabar. Bishop Usanga was the Bishop of Calabar Diocese and Chairman National Missionary Seminary Committee, Episcopal Conference of Nigeria, August 21, 1977.

USENI J. T. (Lt. General, Hon. Minister), Letter of Condolence, in Funeral Programme of Cardinal Ekandem, Garki, Abuja, Nigeria, November 28, 1995.

A.   Books and pamphlets

ACHEBE Chinua, 2012, There Was a Country: A Personal History of Biafra, London, England, Allen Lane, an imprint of Penguin Books.

DE PAUL Vincent (St.), 1985, Correspondence, Conferences, Documents. Vol. XIIIa, Brooklyn, NY.

DE PAUL Vincent, 2003, Correspondences, Conferences, Documents, IX, Conferences to the Daughters of Charity, Vol. 2, NY, City Press.

DE PAUL Vincent (St.) 2004, Correspondence, Conferences Documents, IX, Conferences to the Daughters of Charity, Vol. 1, Brooklyn, NY, New City Press.

DE VAUX Roland, 1961, Ancient Israel, Its Life and Institutions, trans. McHUGH John, Great Britain, Darton, Longman & Todd.

EDEM Michael I. Decision and Fulfillment of God's Promises, Port Harcourt, Nigeria, Mustard Seed Printers Ltd, 2012.

EKEFRE Edidiong, A Testament of Light: The Life and Times of Dominic Cardinal Ekandem, Lagos, MayFive Media Ltd., 2013.

ETTANG, D. A. U., Ibiono Ibom (A Synthesis of Ibionology) Calabar Newspaper Corporation, 1983.

EZEANI Emefiena, In Biafra, Africa Died: The Diplomatic Plot, London, VERITAS Lumen Publishers, 2013.

FRANCIS (Pope), Bull of Indiction of Jubilee of Mercy, Vaticana City, Libreria Editrice Vaticana, April 11, 2015.

HIGGINS Thomas, Maynooth Mission to Africa: The Story of St. Patrick's, Kiltegan, Dublin, Ireland, Gill & Macmillan, 1991.

JOHN of the Cross (St.), ZIMMERMAN Benedict, Introd by, The Living Flame of Love, London, Thomas Baker, 1919.

JORDAN P. John, Bishop Shanahan of Southern Nigeria, Dublin, Elo Press Ltd., 1971.

LONERGAN Bernard, Method in Theology, London, Darton, Longman & Todd, 1971.

MADIEBO Alexander A. (Maj. Gen.), The Nigerian Revolution and Biafran War, Enugu-Nigeria, Fourth Publishing Company, 1980. NWOSUH Cosmas K. O., Cardinal Dominic Ekandem and the Growth of the Catholic Church in Nigeria, Nigeria, Ambassador Publications, 2012.

OKWU Philomena, EDET Francesca, EKANDEM Margaret Mary, eds., Daughters of Charity of St. Vincent de Paul in Nigeria, Port Harcourt, Mustard Seed Printers Nig. Ltd., 2013.

O'MEARA Edward T., Exhortation of the New Candidates of the National Missionary Seminary, Iperu Remo, Ogun State, in The Ambassador

Magazine, Vol. 1, No. 1.Bishop O'Meara was the National Director of the Propagation of Faith, USA at the time, 1977.

PAUL VI (Pope), Evangelii Nuntiandi, an Apostolic Exhortation, to the Episcopate, to the Clergy and to All Faithful of the Entire World, Vatican City, Libreria Editrice, December 8, 1975.

PRECLIN E. & TAPIÉ V-L. The Eighteenth Century, Part I, France and the World of 1715–1789, Paris, University Press of France. The original title in French is: Le XVIIIe siècle, premiere partie—La France et le monde de 1715 à 1789, Paris, Presses Universitaires de France, 1952.

SHANAHAN Joseph, An Irish Missionary in Central Africa, Dublin, Publishing House unknown, 1923.

THE EDITOR, FUNERAL RITES OF Rt. Rev Msgr. Silas T. Umoh (October 1933–February 2, 2013) and Very Rev. Fr. Christopher C. Nkondouk (May 10, 1950–February 1, 2013, Ikot Ekpene, Iwoh Press, 2013.

THE EDITOR, Order of Christian Funerals, Approved for Use in the Dioceses of England and Wales, and Scotland, London, Geoffrey Chapman, 1990.

UDO Edet A., Who Are the Ibibio? Onitsha, FEP Publishers Ltd., 1983.
UMOREN U. E., His Eminence Dominic Cardinal Ekandem 1917–
1976, Aba-Nigeria: Cynako International Press Ltd., 1976.
WATURUOCHA Mary Gertrude (MOTHER), Memoirs of a Testimony
of an Eyewitness on the Life and Works of Mother Mary Charles
Walker RSC, Foundress of the First Indigenous Congregation
(HHCJ) In the Nigerian Church, Enugu, SNAAP Press Ltd, 2012.
WATURUOCHA Mary Gertrude (MOTHER), A Letter Stressing Blind
Obedience, Exonerating the Two Bishops, c/o Holy Child College,
Lagos, An Unpublished Congregational Circular Letter, July 16, 1968.
WEIGEL George, Witness to Hope: The Biography of Pope John Paul II,
Glasgow, Great Britain, Omnia Books Ltd. & Cliff Street Books, 2001.

INTERVIEWS AND SPEECHES

ANDREWS Timothy D., "Passing Away of His Eminence, Dominic
Cardinal Ekandem" in Funeral Brochure of Cardinal Ekandem,
Garki, Abuja, Nigeria, December 2, 1995.
BEKA A. T., An Ex-DO and Civil Servant, On the Consecration of Bishop
Dominic Ekandem, an oral interview granted to the author, Abak,
Akwa Ibom State, Nigeria, 2005.
BRENNAN Maureen (Dr.), "The Last Medical Doctor That Attended
to the Cardinal," On the Last Days of Cardinal Ekandem, Medical
Missionaries of Mary Community, Ibadan, Oyo State, Nigeria, Oral
Conversation with the author, 1996.
CAUSERO D. (Msgr.), Chargé D'Affairs, The Apostolic Pronunciature,
Message of Congratulations to His Eminence, Most Rev. Dominic I.
Ekandem in UMOREN U. E., 1976, His Eminence, Dominic Cardinal
Ekandem, First Nigerian Cardinal, Aba, Cynako International Press
Ltd., April 28, 1976.
EKUTT Patrick X. "The Priest That the Cardinal Lived with When His
House Was Under Repairs." On Liturgical Practices, Oral Interview,
Ikot Ekpene, Akwa Ibom State, Nigeria, 2010.
EKUTT Patrick X., On the Faith and Prayer Life of the Cardinal,
Conversation with the author, Ikot Ekpene Diocese, Akwa Ibom
State, Nigeria, 2010.

ENANG Kenneth. He was the rector of the Monor Seminary in Afaha Obong, Ikot Ekpene, and the project coordinator for the diocese. Cardinal Ekandem and the Finances of the Diocese, Oral Interview with the author, Okon, Ikot Ekpene Diocese, Akwa Ibom State, 2009.

EKUWEM Joseph Effiong (Bishop), On the Constitution of Cardinal Ekandem's Solid Spiritual Life, Oral Interview, Uyo, Akwa Ibom State, Nigeria, 2005.

EKUWEM Joseph Effiong (Catholic Bishop of Uyo), A Letter of Condolence, The Funeral Brochure of Cardinal Ekandem, Abuja, December 2, 1995.

ETOK Sylvanus (Msgr.). Vicar general of Ikot Ekpene Diocese and former head of Department of Religious Studies, College of Education, Uyo, Akwa Ibom State. Concerning Bishop's Residence, Oral Interview granted to the author, Immaculate Conception Catholic Church, Ikot Ekpene, Akwa Ibom State, Nigeria, September 2007.

EKPO Catherine. Former teacher and principal of many secondary schools in Akwa Ibom State, Nigeria. On the Person of the Cardinal, Ikot Ekpene, Akwa Ibom State, Oral Conversation with the author, 2010.

ETOKUDO Camillus Archibong (Most Reverend). Bishop emeritus of Ikot Ekpene Diocese Akwa Ibom State, Nigeria, before being sent to Port Harcourt Diocese in Rivers State. In Conversation about the Cardinal with the author, 2005.

ETOKUDO Camillus Archibong (Most Reverend), "Condolence Message," The Funeral Brochure of Cardinal Ekandem, Garki, Abuja, Nigeria, December 2, 1995.

EYO Sebastian O. Former student of Cardinal Ekandem as well as a retired teacher and civil servant at the time. On the Prayer Life and Probation Period of His Eminence Dominic Cardinal Ekandem, an unpublished written note submitted to the author, Uyo, Akwa Ibom State, Nigeria. July 1995.

EZEONYIA Vincent (Most Reverend). Bishop of Aba Diocese. He served in Port Harcourt Diocese under Bishop Ekandem. On the Graciousness and Simplicity of Cardinal Ekandem, Christ the King Catholic Church Compound, Bishop's House, Aba, Abia State, Nigeria, April 2008.

INYANG Paul E. Bassey, 1995, On the Person of the Cardinal, Uyo, Unpublished Write-up given to the author for this book, Akwa Ibom State, Nigeria. Mr. Inyang was a retired senior civil servant in the state at the time of the interview.

NYONG Adam Bassey. Knight of St. John and family friend of the cardinal. On Being a Good Shepherd to the Core. Oral interview granted to the author, Uyo, Akwa Ibom State, Nigeria, June 2010.

OGBUAH Lawrence (PA). Close friend of the cardinal. On the Charming Personality and Prayer Life of His Eminence Dominic Cardinal Ekandem. Oral Interview carried out by the author, Enugu, Enugu State, Nigeria, September 1997.

OBIEFUNA Albert K., Archbishop of Onitsha and president of the Catholic Bishops' Conference of Nigeria. "Cardinal Ekandem, Funeral Message" during Speeches by Some Dignitaries of State and Church, Our Lady Queen of Nigeria Pro-Cathedral, Garki Abuja, Federal Capital Territory, Nigeria, December 2, 1995.

OBOT Ephraim S. (Most Reverend). Bishop of Idah Diocese and secretary of the Catholic Bishops' Conference of Nigeria. Cardinal Ekandem and Cross-less Christianity. Oral interview with the author. Bishop's House, Idah, Kogi State, Nigeria. July 1996.

OBOT Ephraim S. (Most Reverend). The Role of the Cross in the Life of Cardinal Ekandem. Oral interview with the author. Bishop's House Idah, Kogi State, Nigeria. July 1996.

OBOT Ephraim Silas (Most Reverend). On the Spiritual Life of Cardinal Ekandem. Oral interview with the author. Bishop's House, Idah, Kogi State, Nigeria. July 1996.

OKODUA B. A., "Abuja: A Call to Development, an International Conference on the Development of Abuja Held in Abuja Directed By PMAS—Pontifical Missionary Aid Society Director, pp. 1–6. Materials come from the archive of Msgr. Godwin Akpan, MSP. April 27–30, 1992.

OKON Mary Augustine (Sr.). On Special Invitation by the Cardinal to Come to Abuja during His Dying Moment, an oral conversation with the author; Handmaids Convent, Mercy Hospital, Abak, Akwa Ibom State, Nigeria. 2010.

SHARKEY James. Kiltegan priest that served in Calabar Diocese when Ekandem was consecrated bishop. On Cardinal Ekandem's Humble Service. Oral interview with the author. St. Michael's Catholic Church, Uyo Road Parish, Akwa Ibom State, Nigeria. July 1997.

TOMBERE Regina. On Cardinal Ekandem. An unpublished written note submitted to the author. Sr. Regina Tombere is a member of the Handmaids of the Holy Child Jesus Congregation serving at Catholic Secretariat of Nigeria, Abuja, Nigeria. September 17, 2014.

UDOIDEM Sylvanus I. (Professor). Life and Service of Dominic Cardinal Ekandem: A Model to the Challenges of Priestly Life in the Modern World. Paper presented at Ifuho Cathedral, Ikot Ekpene Diocese, at the tenth anniversary of the cardinal's death. 2005.

UDOIDEM Sylvanus I., Book Review at Book Presentation of A Testament of Light: A Biography of Dominic Cardinal Ekandem, Uyo, James Moynagh Pastoral Centre, Brooks Street, Akwa Ibim State, Nigeria. 2013.

UDOMA Cosmas M. I., April 28, 1976, A Congratulatory Letter to His Eminence on Behalf of Ikot Ekpene Seminarians, Enugu, Bigard Memorial Seminary.

UDONWANKWO Emmanuel. Priest of Ikot Ekpene Diocese that worked with the cardinal. On Salient Quality of Discipline and Control of the Cardinal.

Oral interview with the author. Abiakpo Ntak Inyang, Ikot Ekpene, Akwa Ibom State. June 2010.

UDONWANKWO Emmanuel. The Special Fatherly Characteristic of Cardinal Ekandem, Abiakpo Ntak Inyang, Ikot Ekpene, Akwa Ibom State, Nigeria. June 2010.

UDONWANKWO Emmanuel. On the Cardinal's Capacity to Correct, Affirm and Identify. Oral conversation with the author. Abiakpo Ntak Inyang, Ikot Ekpene, Akwa Ibom State, Nigeria. August 2010.

UKPO Joseph Edra (Most Reverend). Bishop emeritus of Ogoja; archbishop emeritus of Calabar, Cross River State. On Cardinal Ekandem, A Man of Perception. Oral interview with the author. Archbishop's Residence, Calabar, Cross River State, Nigeria. April 2014.

UKO John Osca. Former secretary of Cardinal Ekandem. On the Prominence of Cardinal Ekandem. Recorded interview, Cassette No. 1. Inen, Ukanafun LGA, Akwa Ibom State, Nigeria. November 2007.

USANGA Brian D. (Most Reverend). Archbishop emeritus of Calabar and chairman of Seminaries' Commission, Nigeria, and the homilist at the cardinal's funeral. Homily on The Man of God, the Cardinal. Our Lady Queen of Nigeria Pro-Cathedral, Garki, Abuja, Federal Capital Territory, Nigeria. December 2, 1995.

UWEMEDIMO Rosemary. On Humility and Service of Cardinal Ekandem. Oral interview granted to the author. Oron Road, Uyo, Akwa Ibom State, Nigeria. June 1995.

GENERAL

ARMINJON Charles. The End of the Present World and the Mysteries of the Future Life, Trans., Susan Conroy & Peter McEnerny, Manchester, Sophia Institute Press. 2008.

BASSEY B. E. Ekpe Efik, a Theological Perspective, Canada, Trafford Publishers. 1998.

BENEDICT XVI (Pope), Caritas In Veritate, Encyclical Letter of The Supreme Pontiff To The Bishops, Priests, Deacons, Men And Female Religious, Lay Faithful And All People of Good Will On Integral Human Development In Charity And Truth, Rome, Libreia Editrice Vaticana. June 29, 2009.

BENGU S. M. E., Chasing Gods Not Our Own, Pietermansburg, Natal, Republic of South Africa, Shutter & Shooter, 1975.

BEREBON Paul, The Origin of Catholicism in Bodo, Ogoniland, Conversation with the Author During Pastoral Visit. 2011.

CAN, CHRISTIAN ASSOCIATION OF NIGERIA, AKWA IBOM STATE BRANCH, Ikot Ekpene AKS, DA-Lukana Press. Date? CARROLL William E., Creation and Science, United States of America, Catholic Truth Society. 2011.

DE PAUL Vincent (St.). Conferences to the Congregation of the Mission, Vol. XI, Newly Translated, Edited and Annotated from the 1921 Edition of Pierre Coste CM, NY, New City Press, 2008.

CROWLEY Roderic M. A Surprising Journey: Memoirs of Nigeria. Dublin, Ireland, Ashfield Press. 2004.

DE PAUL Vincent (St.). Correspondence, Conferences, Documents. Vol. XIIIa, Brooklyn, NY: New City Press. 1985.

EDEM Michael I., Drugs and Death: Drug Trafficking, Economic, Social and Family Implications and the Agency's Response, Port Harcourt, Nigeria, Mustard Seed Press. 2013.

EDET Sylvia. The Beginnings of the Congregation of the Handmaids of the Holy Child Jesus, 1923–1940, Calabar, Danny Press. 2013.

FRANCISCAN FRIARS OF THE IMMACULATE, KALVALAGE Francis Mary, Editor, Padre Pio: The Wonder Worker, Ignatius Press. 1999.

GAITLEY Michael E., 33 Days to Morning Glory, A Do-It-Yourself Retreat in Preparation for Marian Consecration, United States of America, Marian Press. 2012.

GILL Peter L., Editor, Priest Pulls No Punches in Loyola Lecture on Being Black and Catholic in Four County Catholic, Vol. 12, No. 1, 12–13, p. 13. March 2000.

ANDREOTTI Giulio. 1993–2012 Interview with Cardinal Peter Kodwo Appiah Turkson. "Celibacy? It's not foreign to African Culture" 30 Days: In the Church and in the world international monthly magazine no. 10. 2005.

HAGEL John. The Battle for Jerusalem. Nashville, Thomas Nelson Publishers. 1994 (5).

IZUWAH A. E. N. First vice president. The Knights of St. John, Origin and Roles: Lecture at the Initiation of Aspirants Held in Owerri, Imo State. May 15–28, 1995.

JABOTINSKY Ze'ev. The Jewish War Front. Greenwood Press, No Place of Publication indicated. 1975.

KALVELAGE Francis Mary, Editor, Padre Pio: The Wonder Worker, Franciscan Friars of the Immaculate, New Bedford, MA, USA. 2009. LINCOLN Abraham. Gettysburg Address and Other Writings. New York, Barnes and Noble Inc. 2013.

LONERGAN Bernard, Method in Theology. London, Darton, Longman & Todd. 1971.

McNAMARA Edward. "Lay Ministers Wearing a Deacon's Stole." Zenith News. The World Seen from Rome. April 21, 2015.

MERTON Thomas, No Man is an Island, Abbey of Our Lady of Gethsemani, Great Britain, Biddles Ltd, Guildford and King's Lynn, 1996.

OFFIONG Maria Immaculata, Four Faces of Mother Mary Charles Magdalene Walker, RSC: (1881–1966) A Reflection on the First Four Members, Calabar, 2012.

OLUPOHUNDA Bayo, How 2015 Elections Changed Nigeria in Punch Nigerian newspaper, March 31, 2015.

PADRE PIO, In My Own Words, Anthony F. Chiffolo., Complied By, London, Hodder &Stoughton, 2001.

PAUL VI (Pope), Evangelii Nuntiandi, an Apostolic Exhortation, to the Episcopate, to The Clergy and to All Faithful of the Entire World, Vatican City, Libreria Editrice, December 8, 1975.

SHEEN Fulton J., Those Mysterious Priests, Bangalore, ST. PAULS, 2012.

THE ACADEMY OF THE IMMACULATE, St. Thérèsè, Doctor of Little Way, Our Lady's Chapel, New Bedford, MA, USA, Franciscan Friars of the Immaculate, 1997.

THE ACTING RECTOR, Historical Development: The National Missionary Society of St. Paul, Iperu Remo, Ogun State, Undated.

THE EDITOR, Webster's Dictionary Specially Designed for Everyday Use in Home, School and Office, USA, Nichols Industries Ltd., renders moot thus: To bring up as for debate or discussion, to argue, 1998, pp. 173–174.

THE EDITOR, The Collected Works of St. Theresa of Avila, Vol. 1, trans., KAVANAUGH K. & RODRIGUEZ O., Washington, (ICS), Institute of Carmelite Studies Publications, 1987.

THE EDITOR, Breaking News: This Day, Nigerian Newspaper, March 15, 2015; PALMER Ewan, "Nigeria Elections: APC Leader, Muhammadu Buhari Defeats Goodluck Jonathan and Declared President" in International Business Times, UK Edition, Monday, May 15, Front page.

THE EDITOR, FUNERAL RITES OF Rt. Rev Msgr. Silas T. Umoh (October 1933–February 2, 2013) and Very Rev Fr. Christopher C.

Nkondouk (May 10, 1950–February 1, 2013), Ikot Ekpene, Iwoh Press, 2013.

THE EDITOR, Souvenir Programme of Events; The Ancient and Noble Order of the Knights of St. John, Holy Trinity Commandery no. 423, November 14–17, St. Anne's Cathedral, Ifuho, Diocese of Ikot, Ekpene, CRS, Friday, Aba, Cynako International Press, 1980.

THE EDITOR, Missale Romanum, Ex Decreto Sacrosancti Oecumenici Concilii Vaticani Instauratum Auctoritate Pauli PP. VI Promulgatum, Editio Typica, Typis Polyglotitis Vaticanis, MCMLXXI.

THE REPORTER, Don't Abandon the Poor, by His Eminence Dominic Cardinal Ekandem, in The Nigerian Chronicle, No. 1,338, Calabar, Front Page, 1978.

USANGA Brian D. (Archbishop of Calabar). On the Specific Marks of the cardinal. Oral interview, Sacred Heart Cathedral, Calabar, Cross River State, Nigeria. 2002.

WEIGEL George. Witness to Hope: The Biography of Pope John Paul II, Glasgow, Great Britain, Omnia Books Ltd. & Cliff Street Books, 2001.

INTERNET SOURCES

EMSPAK Jesse, Wednesday, Did Gravity Set Earth's Plate in Motion? Live Science Contributor | LiveScience.com, Yahoo News in the Internet, September 17, 2014.

https://www.history.state.gov/milestone/1945-1952/creation-Israel. https://www.history.state.gov/milestone/1945-1952/creation-Israel. Internet Source, www.google.co.uk/Lenin.and the Bolsheviks.

HAMMARSKJOLD Dag, Quotes from Dag Hammarskjold, www. Dag Hammarskjold, Quotes, Author of Markings.

HAMMARSKJOLD Dag, Markings, Stags: Forgiveness, under Quotes from Dag Hammarskjold, http://www.goodreads.com/author/quotes/946904. Dag_Hammarskj_Id. https://books.google.co.uk/books?id=Kv3d-FzEiwUC&pg=PA103&lpg=PA103&dq=cataclysm,+a+momentous+and+violent+event&source=bl&ots=6y0ZhcBgto&sig=uKn—O1p_DJlZgkywGBMHFPhlVTU&hl=en&sa=X&ved=0ahUKEwjKoIyS5O3LAhVDVBQKHWTHBWQQ6AEIJTAC#v=o-

nepage&q=cataclysm%2C%20a%20momentous%20and%20 violent%20event&f=false

GAVAGHAM Julian. On This Day—First World War begins after AustriaHungary invades Serbia, Yahoo News in Internet. July 25, 2014.

LARKIN Ernest E., Desert Spirituality in Published Articles of, p. 474, in the Internet under Carmelite Spirituality.

MOMOH Mary Angela, Erameh, Joseph Aigbodion, 1898 to 1986 Roman Catholic Nigeria. This material is found in the Internet first Nigerian Priest to be ordained, 2008.

PULLELLA Philip, Women in Love With Priests Ask Pope to Make Celibacy Optional, Reuters, Yahoo News, May 19, 2014.

SHERLOCK Ruth et. al., Found: The Bethnal Schoogirls Who Ran Away to Syria in The Telegraph, MSN News in the Internet, June 4, 2015. SLEDIORA John, St. Vincent de Paul and the Formation of Priests in FAMVIN NEWS, http://Famvin.org,/en/2013/09/ Vincent—Changed—Face-France.

SAUNDERS William P., Straight Answers, in The Anglican Catholic Herald, diocesan newspaper of Arlington (VA) diocese provided by Eternal Word Television Network, Irondale, AL 35210, www.etwn. com, September 1, 1994.

THE EDITOR, U.S. House of Representatives Votes to Sue Obama, Yahoo News; http://www.afp.com/afpcom/en/, July 30, 2014.

THE EDITOR, Demographical Data in Nigeria in the Internet.

WATSON Leon, "Dear Francis, we are each in love with a priest, please let us marry": Italian priests' mistresses in extraordinary plea to Pope to end celibacy for Catholic clergy, www.dailymail.co.uk. May 19, 2014. https://www.google.co.uk/webhp?sourceid=chrome; under the section of Historical Events For 1995, HistoryOrb.com En.wikipedia. org/wik/ Hierarchy_of_the_Catholic_Church.

234 Pulse Staff, January 11, 2015, Christianity is the Largest Religion in Nigeria, 2014 Statistics, http://www.234pulse.com/2015/01/ christianity-is-thelargest-religion-in-nigeria-2014-statistics/

Cardinal Bernadin Gantin's link and the Parish at Adelange and Guessling Hemering,https://fr.wikipedia.org/wiki/%C3%89glise_Saint-Gangoulf

OTHERS

Interrupted Lives, a film.
Video of Cardinal Ekandem's Funeral Mass

Endnotes

1. En.wikipedia.org/wik/Hierarchy of the Catholic Church.
2. More details are given in Chapter 18 on his death and burial referring to the speech of Archbishop Obiefuna.
3. THE EDITOR, 1987, *The Collected Works of St. Theresa of Avila*, Vol. 1, trans., KAVANAUGH K. & RODRIGUEZ O., Washington, (ICS), Institute of Carmelite Studies Publications, p. 60.
4. Cf. USANGA Brian D., December 2 1995, *The Man of God, The Cardinal,* Our Lady Queen of Nigeria Pro-Cathedral, Garki Abuja, Federal Capital Territory, Nigeria, chapter 18, especially the section on *Liturgical Celebration.*
5. Cf. THE EDITOR, 1979, Silver Jubilee Brochure of Episcopal Ordination of His Eminence, Cardinal Dominic Ekandem 1954–1979.
6. THE ACADEMY OF THE IMMACULATE, 1997, *St. Thérésè, Doctor of Little Way,* Our Lady's Chapel, New Bedford, MA, USA, Franciscan Friars of the Immaculate, pp. 11–12.
7. At the centre of the whole trouble of Jewish nationhood with Jerusalem as its capital, many troubles and wars brewed and fermented the ground for the spirit of nationalism that prompted the Zionist spirit to spill and galvanise the deepest longing for internationally recognized, independent nation. HAGEL John, (1994) 5, *The Battle For Jerusalem,* Nashville, Thomas Nelson Publishers examines the centrality of Jerusalem in the light of the following questions: *Why the Arab-Israeli Conflict? How does it threaten America? What does Bible Prophecy Reveal?* and finally, *Will there be Peace?* The question of Jeru-

salem cannot arise if Israel as a nation cannot stand. That provides the *raison d'* être of Zionism and Jewish involvement in the Second World War.

8. The Zionist Writer was originally called Vladimir Yevgenyevich Zhabotinsky. The name changed to proper Hebrew name Ze'ev which appears as Ze'eb but because of the rule of preceded by a vowel especially in the context of the six special letters of which 'b' is one of them it now becomes 'v'. He adopted the name when he started writing advocating fellow Jews during the WW1 to cooperate with the Allied Forces in order to have independence.

9. Cf. JABOTINSKY Ze'ev, 1940, *The Jewish War Front.*

10. https:// www. history.state.gov/milestone/1945-1952/creation-Israel.

11. https:// www. history.state.gov/milestone/1945-1952/creation-Israel.

12. The Bolshevik Revolution took place because of the corrupt nature of the Government, the poverty that engulfed the people, the distrust and lack of confidence in the of the ruling Czar, Nicholas II

13. Cf. Internet Source, www.google.co.uk/Lenin And The Bolsheviks.

14. Religious is a technical term used in the Catholic Church for both males and females that dedicate themselves to serving Christ in the Church. They belong to various groups called Congregations or Orders. These include the Active and the Contemplative Religious. The Contemplative group includes the Monks and the Nuns who live an enclosed life in Monasteries spending their time in prayer, penance and work. They live there and die in their monasteries and are buried there. Active Religious men and women who are also called, the Men Religious and the Female Religious are those who are involved in various apostolates in the Church and society having vows of poverty, chastity and obedience whereas the monks and the nuns will have stability also as part of their vows. The Active Religious are further subdivided into those who take Perpetual Solemn Vows and those who take Simple Vows. All of them are members of the Church operating within the confines of the Church and regulated by Rome through an organ called Congregation for the Religious and Secular Institutes.

15. Interrupted Lives is a film portraying the Religious Sisters of various Congregations in the Catholic Church under Communist Regime after WWII. The film shows how the Sisters developed a common

way of life, harmonious living to the surprise of their captors after being brought together from various Religious Orders and Congregations and from all parts of Russia. Their plan was to destroy the courage of the Sisters, their Congregations and Religious Life that was an indomitable challenge to their existence. They presumed that by bringing the Sisters together, they would quarrel, fight, scatter themselves and make their existence a disaster. They were stunned by the opposite reactions manifested by the Sisters. They had no alternative than to disperse the Sisters. They were sent to those that the Communists imagined the Sisters would not exercise any influence on. Unfortunately for them and fortunately for the Sisters, they influenced them by loving them.

16. GAITLEY Michael E., 2012, *33 Days To Morning Glory, A Do-It Yourself Retreat In Preparation For Marian Consecration,* United States of America, Marian Press, p. 50.

17. Cova was the actual spot that the apparition took place.

18. Moot in the context it is used indicates suggesting, or introducing or raising a question or point of discussion about a burning issue or something very important that needs urgent attention. THE EDITOR, 1998, *WEBSTER'S DICTIONARY, SPECIALLY DESIGNED FOR EVERYDAY USE IN HOME, SCHOOL AND OFFICE,* U. S. A., Nichols Industries Ltd, renders moot thus: To bring up as for debate or discussion, to argue, pp. 173–174.

19. JORDAN P. John, 1971, *Bishop Shanahan of Southern Nigeria,* Dublin, Elo Press Ltd, p. 58.

20. CSSp is an abbreviation for the Holy Ghost Fathers. The letters abbreviate the Latin *Congregationis Sancte Spiritus* or Congregation of the Holy Spirit.

21. JORDAN P. John, 1971, *Bishop Shanahan of Southern Nigeria,* pp. 62–63.

22. JORDAN P. John, 1971, *Bishop Shanahan of Southern Nigeria,* p. 60.

23. HIGGINS Thomas, 1991, *Maynooth Mission To Africa, The Story of St. Patrick's, Kiltegan,* Dublin, Ireland, Gill & Macmillan, p. 7.

24. The *Italics* are the author's and give emphasis.

25. JORDAN John P., 1971, *Bishop Shanahan of Southern Nigeria,* pp. 171–172.

26. HIGGINS Thomas, 1991, *Maynooth Mission TO Africa, The Story of St. Patrick's, Kiltegan,* p. 7.
27. JORDAN John P., 1971, *Bishop Shanahan of Southern Nigeria,* p. 172.
28. JORDAN John P., 1971, *Bishop Shanahan of Southern Nigeria,* p. 172.
29. ST. PATRICK'S MISSIONARY SOCIETY, 2007 March 17, *A Short History of St. Patrick's Missionary Society* in *75 Years of Missionary Service Brochure,* St. Patrick's Catholic Church, Ikot Ansa, Calabar, p. 3.
30. JORDAN John P., 1971, *Bishop Shanahan of Southern Nigeria,* p. 172ff
31. Episcopacy here means being raised to the rank of the Bishops or being made to join the rank of the Bishops.
32. JORDAN John P., 1971, Bishop Shanahan of Southern Nigeria, p. 173ff.
33. Cf. JORDAN John P., 1971, Bishop Shanahan of Southern Nigeria, p. 169ff.
34. JORDAN John P., 1971, Bishop Shanahan of Southern Nigeria, p. 171-173.
35. SHANAHAN Joseph, An Irish Missionary In Central Africa, Dublin, Publishing House unknown, 1923.
36. JORDAN John P., 1971, Bishop Shanahan of Southern Nigeria, p. 174ff.
37. JORDAN John P., 1971, Bishop Shanahan of Southern Nigeria, p. 175ff.
38. To assent means to agree on something in Webster's Dictionary, Specially Designed For Everyday Use in Home, School and Office, 1998, U. S.A., Nichols Industries Ltd., p. 18. Vide also, Legal-Dictionary, the freedictionary.com/ assent. The following is given in the internet: "An intentional approach of known facts that are offered by another for acceptance; agreement; consent; Express Assent is manifest confirmation of position for approval; Implied Assent is that which the law presumes to exist because the conduct of the parties demonstrate their intentions. Mutual Assent sometimes called the Meeting of the Minds of the parties, is the reciprocal agreement of each party to accept all the terms and condition in a contract.
39. ST. PATRICK'S MISSIONARY SOCIETY, *A Short History of St. Patrick's Missionary Society* in *75 Years of Missionary Service Brochure,* p. 3.

40. *St. Patrick's Missionary Society* in *75 Years of Missionary Service Brochure*, p. 3.

41. *St. Patrick's Missionary Society* in *75 Years of Missionary Service Brochure*, p. 5.

42. Culled from *St. Patrick's Missionary Society* in *75 Years of Missionary Service Brochure*, pp. 3 and 5.

43. Cf. *St. Patrick's Missionary Society* in *75 Years of Missionary Service Brochure*, p. 3.

44.

45. Postulate is an assumption of the existence of some truth that forms the basis for discussion or argument. This understanding will form the basis of its usage in this work.

46. UDO Edet Akpan, 1983, *Who Are The Ibibio?*, Onitsha, FEP Publishers Ltd., pp. 41–43.

47. UDO Edet Akpan, 1983, *Who Are The Ibibio?*, p. 9.

48. This is a system of marriage whereby the surviving brother or relative marries the wife of the deceased brother and produces children for his late brother for the continuation of the family lineage.

49. DE VAUX Roland, 1961, *Ancient Israel, Its Life and Institutions,* trans. McHUGH John, Great Britain, Darton, Longman & Todd, pp. 37–38.

50. Mourning the dead using Professional Mourners is common among the Ibibios. It entails hiring some women who incite the sympathisers, those who come to condole with bereaved family to join in mourning the deceased by recounting the litany of good things the person did while alive or the qualities and virtues of the deceased. In some places, they are not hired, they are members of the community so they join the others and make use of their talents. Even those who were not disposed to cry when they see these professionals cry bitterly and sympathetically, others will join them to cry also. This is common in Israel as indicated in the references and also in Ibibio land.

51. The taboo days are the ones in which no one is supposed to go to the form or stream like the day of rest among the Israelites as in Deut. 5:13.

52. DE VAUX Roland, 1961, *Ancient Israel, Its Life and Institutions,* p. 59; pp. 60–61.

53. Theocracy is a system of government in which priests ruled representatively on behalf of God or god.

54. Theophoric literally means God bearing Names or God carrying Names through invocation and submission to the protection of God for example: *IMA ABASI* or IMA OBONG, the love of God, *UTOM ABASI*, God's work, *IDORENYIN ABASI*—God's Hope or Hope in God, *NYAKNO ABASI*- Handed Over To God, *EDIEDIDEM* with *ABASI* as prefix means: God is King and all such names. These names can exist like Ima, Odudu, and Ukeme: Love-Charity, Strength, Power without the suffix or prefix that indicates God still renders the same meaning. These are some of the theophoric names in Ibibio land. There are myriads of them.

55. DE VAUX Roland, 1961, *Ancient Israel, Its Life and Institutions*, p. 43 especially pages 45 to 46. Circumcision is another characteristic as seen in pages 46-48.

56. ETTANG, D. A. U., 1983, *Ibiono Ibom (A Synthesis of Ibionology)* Calabar, Newspaper Corporation, p. 8.

57. UDO Edet Akpan, 1983, *Who Are The Ibibio?*, pp. 1–14.

58. ETTANG, D. A. U., 1983, *Ibiono Ibom (A Synthesis of Ibionology)*, p. 11

59. ETTANG, D. A. U., 1983, *Ibiono Ibom (A Synthesis of Ibionology)* p. 11.

60. EKANDEM Vitus, April 1995, *Oral Interview on Obio Ibiono And The Origin of Okuku and Its Primacy of Position*. At the time, he had retired from Civil Service and was resting at home as a Retired Senior Civil Servant.

61. EKANDEM Vitus, April 1995, *Oral Interview on Obio Ibiono And The Origin of Okuku and Its Primacy of Position*.

62. ETTANG, D. A. U., 1983, *Ibiono Ibom (A Synthesis of Ibionology)*, especially the section of "Coronation".

63. ETTANG, D. A. U., 1983, *Ibiono Ibom (A Synthesis of Ibionology)*, p. 11.

64. UMOREN U. E., 1976, *His Eminence Dominic Cardinal Ekandem 1917–1976*, Aba-Nigeria: Cynako International Press Ltd., p. 14

65. This is not referring to worship but to an occultic ambient where secret cult operates.

66. Cf. UDO Edet Akpan, 1983, *Who Are The Ibibio?*, pp. 120–123 for further information.
67. Cf. Section C below.
68. Libation is a traditional way of pouring wine from a cup which is generally made of calabash and calling on the Creator or the ancestors to be part of the gathering and to give their protection and guidance, security, fruitfulness and plenty in times of harvest or while fishing in the ocean. Libation often goes with some invocations. Its ritual is normally accompanied with some form of mythological outlook. If they do not want certain departed elders to participate especially those regarded to be bad people while on earth, they would immediately turn the calabash chord to their left hand and poor the wine on the floor to indicate their displeasure towards or rejection of such a spirit.
69. ETTANG, D. A. U., 1983, *Ibiono Ibom (A Synthesis of Ibionology,* p. 15.
70. Cf. The details of the bio-data of His Eminence, Dominic Cardinal Ekandem in THE EDITOR, 1987, *70TH BIRTHDAY SOUVENIR OF HIS EMINENCE, DOMINIC CARDINAL EKANDEM, DD, O. B. E., C. O. N., C. F. R., Bishop of Ikot Ekpene and Superior of Abuja Mission, 1917–1987,* Vide also Section C on Initiation into Ekong Traditional Title Taking.
71. The aspect of second burial is strongly narrated by Jordan. Cf. JORDAN P. John, 1971, *Bishop Shanahan of Southern Nigeria,* A large section of materials on second burial is found there.
72. A woman with severe curvature of the spine was normally called in the past "Hunch Back" woman but because of being politically correct and to avoid offensive word usage, likewise respect of the person, it is now rendered with the new understanding, "Woman with severe curvature of the spine.
73. DE VAUX Roland, 1961, *Ancient Israel, Its Life and Institutions,* pp. 482–483.
74. *Usen Ibet,* a taboo day that one is forbidden or prohibited to go to the fam. In the case of women, titled men and other categories of men can drink but not the women- a portrayal of male dominated society with things that favour men but detrimental to women. That was selfishness. Such days have long gone but usen ibet was meant to give

rest to the men and women from work so that they could rest. They could go to the stream but not the farm because they needed water in the home for domestic use.

75. UDO Edet Akpan, 1983, *Who Are The Ibibio?*, p. 265.

76. For more information on Ekpe, confer BASSEY B. E., 1998, *Ekpe Efik: A Theological Perspective*, Canada, Trafford Publishers. The whole book centres on that.

77. Cf. BASSEY B. E. 1998, *Ekpe Efik, A Theological Perspective*, Canada, Trafford Publishers, p. 102.

78. BASSEY B. E., 1998, *Ekpe Efik: A Theological Perspective*, p. 102.

79. *Mbre Uboikpa* is a special group of dancers for young unmarried girls who compose their songs and dance to entertain the people. If the group is very good, it can move from village to village with the leader carrying what is called *"Akpan Mbre"* which the leader must settle very well on her head so that when she is dancing, it would not fall off and disgrace the group. She is different from the person whom all other dancers must imitate when she changes her dancing steps as directed by the drummer who use the talking drum called *Obodom* to give the information.

80.

81. Culled from THE EDITOR, 1987, *70th Birthday Souvenir of His Eminence, Dominic Cardinal Ekandem, DD, O. B. E., C. O. N., C. F. R., Bishop of Ikot Ekpene and Superior of Abuja Mission, 1917-1987,* p. 5 under Biography. The same information was given personally by His Eminence, Cardinal Ekandem during the oral interview in the presence of Fr. Ekpedeme, Gaul Okon, one of the senior priests from Ibiono. The same details were narrative by the Cardinal's Sister, Madam Rose who granted interview several times to aid elucidate certain things about the family background.

82. Culled from 70th BIRTHDAY SOUVENIR OF HIS EMINENCE, DOMINIC CARDINAL EKANDEM, DD, O. B. E., C. O. N., C. F. R., Bishop of Ikot Ekpene and Superior of Abuja Mission, 1917–1987, p. 5.

83. Cf. 70Birthday Anniversary Brochure, p. 5.

84. UMOREN E. Uduakobong, 1976, *His Eminence Dominic Cardinal Ekandem 1917–1976,* p. 19.

85. Ekong is different from Ekoong mentioned above. Ekong is a group dedicated to those who had slain a slave bought with the person's money for the purpose of initiation into Ekong group of traditional warriors or simulated the slaying by using a specially sharpened knife to strike the scull of a human being bought for that purpose. They have their special dressing and signal while moving or going on a journey or travelling together for a particular ceremony in another place to perform their rituals.

86. The gradation of the sons is from Chief Vitus Ekandem.

87. GAVAGHAM Julian, July 25, 2014, *On This Day- First World War begins after Austria-Hungary invades Serbia*, Yahoo News in Internet.

88. The destruction was unprecedented owing to the fact that modern weapons and of the time were used, the killings were massive killing both the soldiers and civilians not distinguishing the soldiers from the civilians as happened in ancient wars where only the soldiers were involved. With modern weapons, the destruction of human lives and property were incalculable.

89. Personal interview with DOMINIC Cardinal EKANDEM on *His Family Background*, April 1995 in Uyo, Akwa Ibom State, Nigeria.

90. EKANDEM Cardinal Dominic (His Eminence) 1995, *Christianity And Life In the Village*, Oral Interview granted to the Author at Urua Akpan, Akwa Ibom State, Nigeria.

91. BENGU S. M. E., 1975, *Chasing Gods Not our Own*, Pietermansburg, Natal, Republic of South Africa, Shutter & Shooter. Cf. Chapter Three, Images on Religion, Section A on Opposition to he White Man's Religion, likewise Part B Western Culture As Introduced In Africa Through the Medium of the Church

92. BENGU S. M. E., 1975, *Chasing Gods Not Our Own*, Chapter 3, p. 103.

93. BEREBON Paul, 2011, *The Origin of Catholicism In Bodo, Ogoniland*, Conversation with the Author During Pastoral Visit.

94. EKANDEM Cardinal Dominic I., 1995, *On Family Background*, Personal Interview granted to the author, Urua Akpan, Ikot Ekpene, Akwa Ibom State

95. *Horarium* refers to the daily timetable or programme.

96. THE EDITOR, 2005, 10ANNIVERSARY BROCHURE OF THE DEATH OF HIS EMINENCE, DOMINIC CARDINAL EKANDEM, UYO DIOCESE, p. 37.

97. KALVELAGE Francis Mary, Editor, 2009, *Padre Pio, The Wonder Worker, Franciscan Friars of the Immaculate*, New Bedford, MA, U. S. A., p.122, A page with Padre Pio's picture and a medical report certificate bearing 1917.

98. KALVELAGE Francis Mary, Editor, 2009, *Padre Pio, The Wonder Worker, Franciscan Friars of the Immaculate*, p. 65.

99. Cf. JOHN of The Cross (St.), 1919, ZIMMERMAN Benedict, Introd by, *The Living Flame of Love*, London, Thomas Baker.

100. By October 2, 1923, Miss Mary Martin, the later Foundress of the Medical Missionaries of Mary who came on a volunteer mission as a nurse was still in the country when Sr. Mary Charles Walker RSC arrived in Nigeria.

101. EDET Sylvia, 2013, *The Beginnings of the Congregation of the Handmaids of the Holy Child Jesus, From 1923-1940,* Calabar, Danny Press, pp. x & xi.

102. WATURUOCHA Mary Gertrude (MOTHER), 2012, *Memoirs of, A Testimony of An Eye Witness on the Life and Works of Mother Mary Charles Walker RSC, Foundress of The First Indigenous Congregation (HHCJ) In the Nigerian Church,* Enugu, SNAAP Press Ltd., p. 6.

103. EDET, SYLVIA 2013, p. xi.

104. *Nna Nyin or Nna* was the official pet name the children and many others called Okuku Ekandem. Mrs. Rose Nubia or later Mrs Rose Ekandem, the sister of Cardinal Ekandem was the source of this information in July 1995 along Utuk's Avenue, Uyo.

105. Sacerdotal simply means priestly.

106. Cf. EDEM Michael I. 2012, *Decision and Fulfilment of God's Promises,* Port Harcourt, Nigeria, Mustard Seed Printers Ltd., cover page.

107. The details of meeting with the D. O. together with that of his father were narrated by the Cardinal himself while recuperating at Saint Mary's Hospital, Urua Akpan, Ikot Ekpene when the Hospital was still under the Medical Missionaries of Mary in April, 1995.

108. EKANDEM Dominic Cardinal, 1995, *On Family Background Before Entry Into The Minor Seminary*, Oral Interview granted to the author, Urua Akpan, Ikot Ekpene, Akwa Ibom State, Nigeria.

109. EKANDEM Dominic Cardinal, 1995, *On Family Financial Situation Prior To Minor Seminary*, Oral interview granted to the author, Urua Akpan, Akwa Ibom State, Nigeria.

110. NKUBIA Rose Ekandem, June 1995, *The Reaction of Family members On Breaking The News of Going to The Seminary*, oral Interview granted to the author, Utuk Avenue, Uyo, Akwa Ibom State, Nigeria.

111. PRECLIN E. & TAPIÉ V-L. 1952, *The Eighteenth Century, Part I, France And The World of 1715-1789*, Paris, University Press of France, pp. 4-10. The proper title of this work in French is: *Le XVIIIe siècle, premiere partie- La France et le monde de 1715 à 1789, Paris*, Presses Universitaires de France, pp. 4-10.

112. EDEM Michael I., 2000, Christ In The Poor, Part I, Unpublished Thesis, Rome, Salesian University, Cf. especially the part on the Clergy, pp. 101-114; Vide also, SLEDIORA John, *Saint Vincent De paul And The Formation of Priests* in *FAMVIN NEWS*, http//: Famvin.org,/en/2013/09/ Vincent- Changed—Face-France.

113. DE PAUL Vincent (St.), 1985, Correspondence, Conferences, Documents. Vol. XIIIa, Brooklyn, NY: New City, 466, 485.

114. EKANDEM Dominic I. (Cardinal), 1995, *Personal Oral Interview On Various Subjects Granted To Fr. Michael EDEM CM* at Urua Akpan, Akwa Ibom State, Nigeria. These interviews were recorded in audiocassette and transcribed later. This occurred three consecutive times before he went to St. Luke's Hospital Anua where he directed the author to go and meet some members of his family for further interviews.

115. EKANDEM Dominic I. (Cardinal), 1995, *Personal Interview Granted To Fr. Michael EDEM CM* at Urua Akpan, Akwa Ibom State, Nigeria.

116. The translation given above is a literal one. The one given by the New Revised Standard Version with Apocrypha says: 'How very good and pleasant it is when kindred live together in unity (Ps. 133:1).'

117. EKANDEM Dominic Cardinal Ignatius, 1979, *Silver Jubilee Memoir Manuscripts* (Unpublished), p. 3.

118. EKANDEM Dominic I. (Cardinal), 1995, *Personal Interview Granted To Fr. Michael EDEM CM* at Urua Akpan, Akwa Ibom State, Nigeria.

119. EKANDEM Dominic I. (Cardinal), 1995, *Personal Interview Granted To Fr. Michael EDEM CM* at Urua Akpan, Akwa Ibom State, Nigeria.

120. Mr. S. O. Eyo, April 1995, who gave his reminiscences of Dominic Ekandem as a student during an interview.

121. Cf. THE EDITOR, 2005, *Brochure of 10th Anniversary of Cardinal Ekandem's Death, Uyo Diocese*, 2005, p. 38.

122. Culled from Unpublished Notes on her *Reminiscences of the Cardinal,* April 1995—lva valley—Enugu, Nigeria.

123. EKANDEM Cardinal Dominic Ignatius, 1979, *Silver Jubilee Memoire Manuscripts* (Unpublished), pp. 3, 4.

124. Mrs. Rose Nubia/Ekandem, July 1995, A Retired Teacher and sister of Dominic Cardinal Ekandem, source of information.

125. ACHEBE Chinua, 2012, *There was a Country, A Personal History of Biafra,* Great britain, Allen Lane, An Imprint of Penguin Books, pp. 1114 especially pages 12, 13.

126. https//google.co.uk-cataclysm, a momentous and violent event marked by an overwhelming upheaval and demolition...

127. This information was collaborated by Dr. Gabriel Ekandem at the Medical School, University of Uyo, Akwa Ibom State on Pentecost Sunday, June 2014. Dr. Gabriel is one of the Grand Children of Okuku Ekandem, the trail blazer. His father John was the very first son of Okuku Ekandem and Dr. Gabriel is the son of John who was called Akpan Ekandem.

128. EKANDEM Gabriel John (Dr.), June 2014, *On The Choice of Mma Mary As Wedded Wife,* oral conversation about Cardinal Ekandem, Obio Ibiono, Ibiono Ibom LGA, Akwa Ibom State, Nigeria. Dr. Gabriel Ekandem is an Associate Professor at the College of Medicine, University of Uyo, Akwa Ibom State. He is nephew of the Cardinal Ekandem and the son of the very first son of Okuku Ekandem.

129. EKANDEM Gabriel John (Dr.), June 2014, *On The Choice of Mma Mary As Wedded Wife,* oral conversation about Cardinal Ekandem with the author, Obio Ibiono, Ibiono Ibom LGA, Akwa Ibom State.

130. NUBIA Rose Ekandem, July 1995, *The Destruction of the Roofs And Expulsion of the Wives,* oral interview granted to the author, Utuk's Avenue, Uyo, Akwa Ibom State, Nigeria.

131. Mama Rose Ekandem, 1995, the sister of Cardinal Ekandem gave this information during the interview she granted to the author in her house along Utuk's Avenue in Uyo, the capital of Akwa Ibom State, Nigeria.

132. MOMOH Mary Angela, 2008, *Erameh, Joseph Aigbodion, 1898 to 1986 Roman Catholic Nigeria* This article is found in the Internet under the title of Emerah Josph Aigbodion. The article was submitted in 2008, was researched and written by Mrs. Mary-Angela Momoh, Asst. Chief Education Officer, Delta Steel Company, Ovwian/Aladja, Delta State, Nigeria. The biography has been reviewed and approved by His Grace, Rt. Rev. Dr. Richard Burke, SPS, administrator of the Diocese of Warri and archbishop of the Catholic Diocese of Benin City (email date February 20, 2009).

133. Culled from BROCHURE OF 10ANNIVERSARY OF CARDINAL EKANDEM'S DEATH, UYO DIOCESE, 2005, p. 39.

134. SHRYANE James, July 2015, *Conversation About Irish Missionaries in Africa And Sponsorship,* Barnsley, South Yorkshire, United Kingdom.

135. Many people played a very great role in obtaining the photograph of the benefactress of Mrs. Annice Gordon who sponsored Dominic Ekandem during his days in the Seminary. People like Fr. James Shryane, Mr. Harry Freyne, Mr. Michael Gallaher, the son of Mr. Gallaher who bought the business from Mrs. Gordon, Fr. Vincent Sherlock the Parish Priest of Mr. Alex McDonnell, the cousin of Mrs. Gordon, a retired teacher who eventually provided the picture deserve very special thanks for their extra effort to obtain the photograph. May they share in the blessings of Mrs. Gordon!

136. O'GRADY Anne, 1986, *His Eminence Cardinal Dominic Ekandem, Bishop of Ikot Ekpene, Nigeria* in *Echoes of Ballaghaderreen.*

137. McDONNELL Alex, November 11 2015, *The Continuous Death of the Gordons' Children,* electronic mail sent to the author from Kilmovee, Ireland. Alex was the one who provided the photograph of Mrs. Gordon and articles on Cardinal Ekandem that featured in *Africa*

Magazine in 1950 and the one on Mrs. Gordon *A Woman of Rare Courage,* published in *Echoes of Ballaghaderreen.*

138. O'GRADY Anne, 1986, *A Woman of Rare Courage and Generosity* in *Echoes of Ballaghaderreen.*

139. EKANDEM Cardinal Dominic, 1995, *On Priestly Training And Sponsorship,* Urua Akpan, Ikot Ekpene, Akwa Ibom State.

140. THE EDITOR, September 1950, *Africa* quoted in O'GRADY Anne, 1986, *His Eminence Cardinal Dominic Ekandem, Bishop of Ikot Ekpene, Nigeria,* in *Echoes of Ballaghaderreen.*

141. Professor Martial uses the term Monsignor for Cardinal as is customary to the French and the Italians.

142. This in formation is given by Prof. Martial Jean Marie Staub o f the Department of History in Sheffield University, United Kingdom.

143. https://fr.wikipedia.org/wiki/%C3%89glise Saint-Gangoulf

144. This is something that every priest needs to emulate, the proper Christian life and relationship instead of lording it over the other or expressing racial tendencies, tribalistic, parochialisitc, corrupted, discriminatory attitudes and superiority complex. It was a life the duo lived harmoniously and joyously too. This was a meaningful co-existence of those dedicated to the priesthood of Christ Jesus the Lord who died to save all and not just a few. This communal understanding and focusing on the final destination-heaven should characterize every clergy and Consecrated person so as to avoid the wound of the heart that Antonio Rosmini spoke of in his *Five Wounds of Christ.*

145. DOMINIC CARDINAL EKANDEM, *Unpublished Materials For the Silver Jubilee Celebration in 1979,* pp. 3&4. This was collaborated by the *Personal Interview granted to Fr. Michael I. EDEM CM* in 1995 in the presence of Very Rev. Fr. Gaul Ekpedeme Okon, who became The Vicar General of Uyo Diocese in 1989 at the Creation of Uyo Diocese.

146. MSGR. GODWIN AKPAN has the same conception with Queen of Apostles Seminary Afaha Obong that gives the impression that Fr. Dominic Ekandem was the first Rector owing to the building of the Dormitory at Afaha Obong for the Minor Seminarians in 1952. Cf. Queen of Apostles Seminary, Afaha Obong, *Golden Jubilee Celebration Brochure, 1953–2003,* p. 16

147. MSGR. GODWIN AKPAN narrates his experience of meeting Father Dominic Ekandem for the first time in an unpublished note given to the author two years before his death.

148. QUEEN OF APOSTLES SEMINARY, AFAHA OBONG, 2003, *Golden Jubilee Celebration Brochure, 1953-2003*, Uyo, Inela Press, p. 16.

149. This is the name of the garment used by priests and seminarians. It is long and covers the person down to the feet.

150. UDUAKOBONG E. UMOREN, *His Eminence, Dominic Cardinal Ekandem, 1917–1976,* Aba, 27 Milverton Avenue, Cynako International Press Ltd, 1976, p. 30.

151. HOFACO is an acronym of Holy Family College.

152. This is a symbolic representation of what the mission, inclination and bent of the Bishop stands for or is aiming at. It involves a drawing with the inscriptions that look like a catch phrase in a glance focusing the attention of the viewer on what is at stake. For example, Bishop Dominic's coat of arms is *In Cruce Salus,* literally, it means: In the Cross is salvation or is our salvation to put it properly. Immediately, this focuses attention on the importance of the Cross not only in his life but also in the lives of all Christians since the Cross plays a very vital role in the History of Salvation. Every Bishop has a specific coat of arms that acts as a manifesto of what he stands for.

153. Cf. LONERGAN Bernard, 1971, *Method in Theology*, London, Darton, Longman & Todd, especially the section on Intellectual, Moral and Religious Conversion, pp. 237ff.

154. WEIGEL George, 2001, *Witness To Hope: The Biography of Pope John Paul II,* Glasgow, Great Britain, Omnia Books Ltd. & Cliff Street Books, An Imprint of HarperCollins Publishers, pp. 434–436 especially p. 435. This concerns the visit to Britain already scheduled before the Argentinian assault on Falklands, an Island that belonged to the British for 149 years. The Argentinians claimed that the British ownership of the Island infringed on their sovereignty and they aimed at retrieving it back. That was the time Pope John Paul was to visit Great Britain in late May 1982. Owing to the conflicting nature of the situation whereby Argentina a Third World country and Catholic and Britain, a First World country and Protestant involved

in war raised eyebrows from the point of view of the Argentinians how can the Pope visit a developed nation oppressing and fighting a Third World country. Many wanted the Pope to stop going whereas the British Bishops and the Catholics were ready to receive the Pope constituted a very difficult problem for the Pope. What he did was to summon the Cardinals and Bishops of both countries and initiated a discussion. Eventually, it was agreed that a political problem had to be solved through evangelical and pastoral solution. Cardinal Hume suggested that the Pope should go as an advocate of peace and messenger of reconciliation. It was equally suggested by others that after visiting Britain, he should visit Argentina too. He finished the meeting on the 22May a meeting that started on the 18of May. It took four working days to resolve what looked impossible. He finished his visit to Britain on the 2of June and on the 15, he left for Buenos Aires in Argentina. An unscheduled visit assumed the programme of a scheduled. It aimed at resolving the conflict and preach peace and reconciliation. That gathering aided the Pope to resolve the problem at stake. Similarly throwing out the idea at the Episcopal Meeting, Bishop Moynagh paved the way for his choice of the only candidate for the Bishopric as the only African.

155. WEIGEL George, 2001, *Witness To Hope: The Biography of Pope John Paul II,* pp. 566-568. The *ad limina visit* of Nigerian Bishops helped the Pope to know the Nigerian situation. That guided him in all that he did in Nigeria since he already had an idea of the situation two weeks before his arrival in Nigeria.

156. UDUAKOBONG E UMOREN, *His Eminence, Dominic Cardinal Ekandem 1917–1976, First Nigerian Cardinal,* p. 30.

157. PAUL VI (Pope), December 8, 1975, *Evangelii Nuntiandi, An Apostolic Exhortation, To the Episcopate, To The Clergy And To All Faithful of the Entire World,* Vatican City, Libreria Editrice, No. 78.

158. Marian Bishop refers to either a Bishop that is ordained during the Marian Year or within that period or is devoted to the Blessed Virgin Mary, the Mother of the Redeemer or the Mother of Jesus Christ the Lord. It is common to hear of Marian Priest or Priests as well. They have the same background and understanding.

159. Foundress is a feminine gender of Founder of a Congregation or Religious Order like St. Benedict who founded the Dominican Order, Ignatius Loyola who founded the Jesuits r the Order of Jesus or St. Clare who founded the first group of enclosed Nuns or St. Theresa of Avila who founded the Discalced Carmelite Sisters. St. Clare, St. Theresa of Avila, Mary Martin are all Foundresses together with all the other women Foundresses in the world.

160. This was a movement in the Church that attempted to unite and combine the Civil Government and the Religious Authority of the Church whereby the Government would be controlling the Church's discipline and *modus operandi*. That is why the Church as a Divine Institution founded by Christ Jesus always stresses the separation between Church and State.

161. BEKA A. T., 2005, *On the Consecration of Bishop Dominic Ekandem*, an oral interview granted to the author, Abak, Akwa Ibom State, Nigeria,

162. THE EDITOR, 2013, *FUNERAL RITES OF Rt. Rev Msgr. Silas T. Umoh (Oct. 1933-Feb 02, 2013) and Very Rev Fr. Christopher C. Nkondouk (May 10, 1950- Feb. 01, 2013,* Ikot Ekpene, Iwoh Press, p. 16.

163. Bull is a Papal Document or Letter or Charter issued by the Supreme Pontiff or Pope of the Catholic Church to commence the opening or closing of an event for example the *Bull of Indiction of Jubilee of Mercy* issued on 11April 2015 at the eve of The Divine Mercy Sunday that will take place on 12 April 2015.

164. This refers to the Church's territory whereby its legitimate authority is exercised within that area called Ikot Ekpene Diocese. In other words, it is referring to the whole area that Ikot Ekpene Diocese has the right to govern and administer in the religious context. For the Anglican Clergy that left Anglican Church to join the Catholic Church, the area in which they operate in is called *Personal Ecclesiastical Circumscription or* The *Personal Ordinariate for the Faithful From Anglican Communion.* Pope Benedict XVI was the one who established this in 2010.

165. Bishop Anthony Goko Nwedo CSSp was the first Nigerian to join the Holy Ghost Fathers and he was also the very first to be ordained a priest. He was consecrated a Bishop four years after Bishop Ekandem

whose consecration took place in 1954 thus making him to be second Bishop to be consecrated in Nigeria. Since he was installed a Residential Bishop immediately after the Consecration, he was *ipso facto* and *de iure* that is by fact and by law, the First Nigerian Residential Bishop,

166. Msgr. Sylvanus Etok, the second indigenous priest of Ikot Ekpene Diocese gave this information during my interview with him in 2007 concerning the *Bishop's Residence* while living at Immaculate Conception Catholic Church, Ikot Ekpene at the beginning of the Diocese. He is now eightyfour Years old thereby being the oldest Annang Priest in the world.

167. The number and names of the Nigerian Priests will be given under Indigenous Priests in the pages below.

168. UDOIDEM Sylvanus I., 2005, *Life And Service of Dominic Cardinal Ekandem: A Model To the Challenges of Priestly Life In The Modern World,* A Paper Presented At Ifuho Cathedral, Ikot Ekpene Diocese at the 10Anniversary of the Cardinal's Death. In this paper, he looked at the various addresses and drew conclusions pertinent for the modern age while posing important questions that challenge the modern priestly tendency to individualism that tantamount to destruction of unity both in the episcopacy and in the entire clerical life as such with a threat to the Presbyterium and if care is not taken, to the Episcopal Conference too.

169. ENANG Kenneth, 2009, *Cardinal Ekandem And The Finances of The Diocese,* Oral Interview Granted to the Author, Okon, Ikot Ekpene Diocese, Akwa Ibom State.

170. This was the method he adopted in order to evangelize the entire Diocese since the labourers were very few and the harvest very enormous. Every hand had to be on deck.

171. McNAMARA Edward, 21 April, 2015, *Lay Ministers Wearing A Deacon's Stole* in *Zenith News,* The World Seen From Rome.

172. Very Rev. Fr. Emmanuel UdoNwankwo narrated his experience of being invited to Efe in 2010 during a conversation about the fatherly role of Cardinal Ekandem because of his reaction at Priests' Meeting also called Presbyteral Meeting a few years after his Priestly Ordination in 1981. The Cardinal exhorted him to use his knowledge to defend the Church and promote her teachings for the good of the

People of God and for the promotion of God's Name and work rather than using it destructively. Invitation to Efe was not limited to young priests only; it applied to all his priests. Sometimes, he did not invite but went to the priest in person and that humbled the priests most as in the case of Msgr. S. Etok.

173. UDONWANKWO Emmanuel, 2010, *On the Cardinal's Capacity to Correct, Affirm and Identify,* oral conversation with the author, Abiakpo Ntak Inyang, Ikot Ekpene, Akwa Ibom State, Nigeria.

174. Very Rev. Fr. Emmanuel UdoNwankwo, 2010 during a conversation about Efe and its implications that revealed the salient qualities of the Cardinal.

175. UDONWANKWO Emmanuel, 2010, Conversation.

176. The source of this information is one of the Parish Priests of the particular Parish in Ikot Ekpene Diocese who prefers to remain anonymous. The story was narrated in 2008 in his village a few days after a big religious celebration in their family. He was very close to the Cardinal a s Timothy was to Paul. Paul called Timothy his son in faith (1Tm. 1:2).

177. EKUTT Patrick X, 2010, *On Liturgical Practices,* Ikot Ekpene, Akwa Ibom State, Nigeria. Ekutt was a long standing Master of Ceremonies in the Diocese together with Very Rev. Fr. John Bosco Ekandem.

178. EKUTT Patrick X., 2010, *On The Faith And Prayer Life of the Cardinal,* Ikot Ekpene Diocese, Akwa Ibom State, Nigeria.

179. EKANDEM Cardinal Dominic I., 1995, *On Prayer Life,* oral interview granted to the author, Urua Akpan, Essien Udim L. G. A., Akwa Ibom State, Nigeria.

180. EYO Sebastian O., 1995, *On the Prayer Life And Probation Period of His Eminence Dominic Cardinal Ekandem,* Uyo, Akwa Ibom State, Nigeria. Mr. Eyo was a retired Teacher and Senior Civil Servant in the State.

181. INYANG Paul E. Bassey, 1995, *On The Person of the Cardinal,* Uyo, Akwa Ibom State, Nigeria. Mr. Inyang was a retired Senior Civil Servant in the State at the time of the interview.

182. INYANG Paul E. Bassey, 1995, *On The Person of the Cardinal.*

183. OGBUAH Lawrence (PA), September 1997, *On the Charming Personality And Prayer Life of His Eminence Dominic Cardinal Ekandem,*

An Oral Interview Carried out By the Author, Enugu, Enugu State, Nigeria.

184. OGBUAH Lawrence (PA), September 1997, *On the Charming Personality And Prayer Life of His Eminence Dominic Cardinal Ekandem*

185. OGBUAH Lawrence (PA), September 1997, *On the Charming Personality And Prayer Life of His Eminence Dominic Cardinal Ekandem*

186. OBOT Ephraim Silas (Bishop), 2000, *On The Spiritual Life of Cardinal Ekandem,* oral interview granted to the author, Bishop's House, Idah, Kogi State, Nigeria.

187. ETOKUDO Camillus Archibong, 2005, *In Conversation About The Cardinal,* Ikot Ekpene, Akwa Ibom State, Nigeria.

188. EKUWEM Joseph Effiong (Bishop), 2005, *On The Constitution of Cardinal Ekandem's Solid Spiritual Life,* Oral Interview, Uyo, Akwa Ibom State, Nigeria

189. OBOT Ephraim Silas (Bishop), 2000, *On The Spiritual Life of Cardinal Ekandem,* at the Evening Session after Supper.

190. USANGA Brian D, (Archbishop), 2002, *On The Specific marks of the Cardinal,* Oral Interview, Sacred heart Cathedral, Calabar, Cross River State, Nigeria.

191. ENANG Kenneth, *On The Spirituality of the Cardinal,* Part of the Recorded Interview, Cassette No. 3, 2005, Okon, Ikot Ekpene Diocese, Akwa Ibom State, Nigeria.

192. UKO John Oscar, 2007, *On The Prominence of Cardinal Ekandem,* Recorded Interview, Cassette No. 1, Inen, Ukanafun L. G. A., Akwa Ibom State, Nigeria.

193. LARKIN Ernest E., *Desert Spirituality* in *Published Articles of,* p. 474, in the Internet under *Carmelite Spirituality.*

194. OKPO Mary John, April 1995, Unpublished Notes on her *Reminiscences of the Cardinal,* lva valley—Enugu, Nigeria.

195. NYONG Adam Bassey, April 1995, *On The Mortification of Cardinal Ekandem,* Oral Questions and Answers as one of Those who Was Very Close To Cardinal Ekandem, Uyo, Akwa Ibom State, Nigeria.

196. EKANDEM Cardinal Dominic, 1995, *On Prayer,* oral interview granted to the author, Urua Akpan, Ikot Ekpene, Akwa Ibom State, Nigeria.

197. Tonsure was a sign given to those who were on the way to the priesthood. It meant cutting off the hair at the scull of the person's head so

that wherever the person went to would be visible to all others that this was a cleric. Tonsure was a visible sign of reception or as the first stage of being received into the clerical circle and it was called **UFET EKOT** or *mfet ekot.* That was the beginning of the journey to the priesthood.

198. EKANDEM Rose Nkubia, 1995, *On the Need to Remain Hidden,* oral interview granted to the author, Utuk's Avenue, Uyo, Akwa Ibom State, Nigeria

199. EDEM Bernadette L. B., 2014, *Annual Diocesan Gathering of Catholic Women's Organisation, CWO,* oral rendering of the programme, Ibiaku Obio Ndobo, Uruan LGA, Akwa Ibom State, Nigeria. Mrs. Bernadette is a member of the Parish/Diocesan Executive Committee of the CWO. She is the one who gave information about the programme of events during such meetings. The programme is the same in all the Parishes and Dioceses in the country.

200. NYONG Adam Bassey, *On Being a Good Shepherd to the Core,* oral interview granted to the author, Uyo, Akwa Ibom State, Nigeria. Mr. Nyong had a great privilege as friend and spiritual son of the Cardinal for almost thirty years. He learnt a great deal from and shared much with the Cardinal.

201. UWEMEDIMO Rosemary, 1995, *On Humility and Service of Cardinal Ekandem,* oral interview granted to the author, Oron Road, Uyo, Akwa Ibom State, Nigeria.

202. This quotation comes from *Ignatius Catholic Study Bible New Testament,* Second Catholic Edition RSV, 2001, San Francisco, Ignatius press.

203. Cf. Chapter III, Ordination of A Priest in *The Rites,* 1991, Vol. Two, A Pueblo Book, Collegeville, Minnesota, The Liturgical Press, No. 14, p. 41.

204. SHARKEY James, July 1997, *On Cardinal Ekandem's Humble Service,* Oral Interview, St. Michael's Catholic Church, Uyo Road Parish, Akwa Ibom State, Nigeria.

205. TOMBERE Regina, 17 September 2014, *On Cardinal Ekandem,* An Unpublished written Note submitted to the author. Sr. Regina Tombere is a member of the Handmaids of the Holy Child Congregation serving at Catholic Secretariat of Nigeria, Abuja, Nigeria.

206. TOMBERE Regina, 17September 2014, *On Cardinal Ekandem,* An Unpublished written Note.

207. KIGGINS Thomas, 1991, *Maynooth Mission to Africa: The History of St. Patrick's, Kiltegan,* Dublin, Ireland, Gill and Macmillan Ltd, Goldenbridge, pp. 23-24.

208. KIGGINS Thomas, 1991, *Maynooth Mission to Africa: The History of St. Patrick's, Kiltegan,* p. 25.

209. KIGGINS Thomas, 1991, *Maynooth Mission to Africa: The History of St. Patrick's, Kiltegan,* pp. 25ff.

210. OFFIONG Maria Immaculata, 2012, *Four Faces of Mother Mary Charles Magdalene Walker, RSC: (1881-1966) A Reflection On the First Four Members,* Calabar, p. 16.

211. WATURUOCHA Mary Gertrude (MOTHER), 2012, *Memoirs of; A Testimony of An Eye Witness On The Life and Works of Mother Mary Charles Walker, RSC, Foundress of the First Indigenous Congregation (HHCJ) in the Nigerian Church;* Enugu, SNAAP PRESS LTD, p. 64.

212. WATURUOCHA Mary Gertrude (MOTHER), 2012, *Memoirs of,* p. 66.

213. WATURUOCHA Mary Gertrude (MOTHER), 2012, *Memoirs of,* p. 67.

214. EDET Sylvia (HHCJ), 2013, *The Beginnings of the Congregation of the Handmaids of the holy Child Jesus, From 1923 to 1940,* Calabar, Danny Press, p. X.

215. EDET Sylvia (HHCJ), 2013, *The Beginnings of the Congregation of the Handmaids of the holy Child Jesus,* p. X.

216. EDET Sylvia (HHCJ), 2013, *The Beginnings of the Congregation of the Handmaids of the holy Child Jesus,* p. XI.

217. OKPO MARY JOSEPH, 1987, *An Unpublished Manuscript of the History of the Congregation of the Handmaids of the Holy Child Jesus,* Ifuho, Ikot Ekpene, pp. 6, 7.

218. WATURUOCHA Mary Gertrude (Mother), 2012, *Memoirs of,* pp.155-160.

219. WATURUOCHA Mary Gertrude (Mother), 2012, *Memoirs of,* pp. 161–166.

220. Cf. MERTON Thomas, 1996, *No Man is An Island,* Abbey of Our lady of Gethsemani, Great Britain, Biddles Ltd, Guildford and King's Lynn, p. 49.

221. NWOSUH Cosmas K. O., 2012, *Cardinal Dominic Ekandem And The Growth Of The Catholic Church In Nigeria,* Nigeria, Ambassador Publications, p. 192.

222. WATURUOCHA MARY GERTRUDE (MOTHER), 2012, *Memoirs of,* p. 173.

223. NWOSUH Cosmas K. O., 2012, *Cardinal Dominic Ekandem And The Growth Of The Catholic Church In Nigeria,* Nigeria, Ambassador Publications, p. 173.

224. NWOSUH Cosmas K. O., 2012, p.173.

225. SHEEN Fulton J., 2012, *Those Mysterious Priests,* Bangalore, ST. PAULS, pp. 253-254.

226. The author was the traveller while schooling at Saint. Patrick's College, Ikot Ansa, Calabar.

227. ACHEBE Chinua, 2012, *There Was A Country, A Personal History of Biafra,* London, England, Allen Lane, an imprint of Penguin Books, p. 153.

228. Aburi Declaration was also called Aburi Accord. It took place in Accra, Ghana between 4and 5January 1967. The location was a neutral ground chosen for the resolution of the conflict.

229. ACHEBE Chinua, 2012, *There Was A Country, A Personal History of Biafra,* p. 91,

230. Cf. OKPO Mary Joseph (HHCJ), 1987, *An Unpublished Manuscript of the History of the Congregation of the Handmaids of the Holy Child Jesus,* p. 8.

231. This detail was given by Sylvanus Etok himself who confirmed the kidnapping and the location as Ngwaland. He gave this information almost forty years after the incident, which means that the experience was still very fresh in his memory.

232. SHEEN FULTON J., 2012, *Those Mysterious Priests,* Bandra, Mumbai, St. Pauls, pp. 112–113.

233. GAITLEY Michael E., 2011, *Consoling The Heart Of Jesus: A DoIt-Yourself Retreat; Inspired By The Spiritual Exercises of St. Ignatius,*

Stockbridge, Massachusetts, Marian Press, p. 343, No. 445 of *The Diary Of St. Faustina.*

234. SHEEN Fulton J., 2012, *Those Mysterious Priests,* p. 112.

235. OKPO Mary Joseph Mother, 1996, *A Scanty Sketch of—An Episodic View of Someone Who had Known him [Dominic Cardinal Ekandem] as a Seminarian from 1940-1994,* An Unpublished Manuscript on Cardinal Ekandem, Written at Iva Valley, Enugu, p. 1. This document emanated from the questions posed by the author of this book to Mother Okpo HHCJ who decided not to give oral interview but to document her thoughts and reminiscences on the man she revered so much.

236. NWOSUH Cosmas K. O., 2012, *Cardinal Ekandem And The Growth of the Catholic Church in Nigeria,* Nigeria, Ambassador Publications, pp. 207ff.

237. CROWLEY Roderic M., 2004, *A Surprising Journey: Memoirs of Nigeria,* Dublin-Ireland, Ashfield Press, pp. 26–29.

238. CROWLEY Roderic M., 2004, *A Surprising Journey: Memoirs of Nigeria,* pp. 27–30.

239. CROWLEY Roderic M., 2004, *A Surprising Journey: Memoirs of Nigeria,* pp. 26–29.

240. CROWLEY Roderic M., 2004, *A Surprising Journey: Memoirs of Nigeria,* p. 28.

241. Cf. MADIEBO Alexander A. (Maj. General), 1980, *The Nigerian Revolution And Biafran War,* Enugu-Nigeria, Fourth Publishing Company. Graphic details of how all accessory roads and airports were blocked so that no aids could come in to Biafra are given in this book.

242. Cf. WATURUOCHA Mary Gertrude (Mother), 2012, *Memoirs of: A Testimony of An Eye Witness On The Life And Works Of Mother Mary Charles Walker (RSC), Foundress of the First Indigenous Congregation (HHCJ) In The Nigerian Church,* Enugu, SNAAP Press Ltd., p. 7.

243. OKPO Mary Joseph, 1987, *An Unpublished Manuscript of the History of the Congregation of the Handmaids of the Holy Child Jesus,* Ifuho, Nigeria, pp. 19ff.

244. OKPO Mary Joseph (Mother), 1987, *An Unpublished Manuscript of the History of the Congregation of the Handmaids of the Holy Child Jesus* p. 19.

245. OKPO Mary Joseph (Mother), 1987, *An Unpublished Manuscript of the History of the Congregation of the Handmaids of the Holy Child Jesus,* pp. 19–20.

246. WATURUOCHA Mary Gertrude (Mother), 2012, *Memoirs,* p. 173.

247. OKPO Mary Joseph (Mother), 1987, *An Unpublished Manuscript of the History of the Congregation of the Handmaids of the Holy Child Jesus,* pp. 20ff.

248. Great Marian Devotees do adopt or include "Mary" in their names especially at Profession as it happened in those days when the Religious had to adopt a new name preferably a saint's name. In Latin those who adopt Mary or include Mary in their names are called 'Marius' or Mario in Italian as a feminine gender of Mary. That is why the Bishop has Mary included in his name.

249. EZEANI Emefiena, 2013, *In Biafra, Africa Died, The Diplomatic Plot,* London, VERITAS Lumen Publishers, p. 13. In the "Introduction", Ezeani has this to say: "With two super powers—Britain and Russia—on the side of the Nigerian Government with a well organised army and abundance of military hardware, why did the war against such a tiny state of Biafra drag on for about three years?" Cf. p. 60 also on the question of *Ogbunigwe* that instilled fear into the superpowers when in two months of existence already produced a bomb tagged *Ogbunigwe.*

250. WATURUOCHA Mary Gertrude, 2012, *Memoires of, A Testimony of An Eye Witness On the Life and Works of Mary Charles Walker RSC: Foundress of the First Indigenous Congregation (HHCJ) In The Nigerian Church,* pp. 176ff.

251. OKPO Mary Joseph, 1987, *An Unpublished Manuscript of the History of the Congregation of the Handmaids of the Holy Child Jesus,* pp. 17ff.

252. ACHEBE Chinua, 2012, *There Was A Country, A Personal History of Biafra,* pp. 85–89.

253. MARY Anne Iwoh, 2013, submitted this special account during the course of the research in 2013. Presently she is working in Ikot Ekpene Diocese as the Director of Education Board with her office located at the Diocesan Catholic Secretariat, Ifuho, in Akwa Ibom State.

254. Most of the material used in this section originates from Mother Mary Anne Iwoh HHCJ who wrote it down at the request of the author

while carrying out an interview with her in April 2013. The aspect about the bombing of the TTC, Ifuho compound is from Mother Mary Joseph Okpo's material on the *"An Outline of the History of the Congregation of the Handmaids of the Holy Child Jesus 1937-1987 Golden Jubilee Celebration"* an unpublished manuscript cf. especially the section on *"The Civil War Period—A Challenge"* from p. 19ff.

255. PADRE PIO, *In His Own Words.*
256. WATURUOCHA Mary Gertrude, 2012, *Memoir,* p. 174.
257. OKPO Mary Joseph (Mother), 1987, *An Unpublished Manuscript of the History of the Congregation of the Handmaids of the Holy Child Jesus,* p. 23.
258. Cf. OKPO Mary Joseph (Mother), 1987, *An Unpublished Manuscript of the History of the Congregation of the Handmaids of the Holy Child Jesus,* pp. 22ff.
259. WATURUOCHA Mary Gertrude, 2012, *Memoires of, A Testimony of An Eye Witness On the Life and Works of Mary Charles Walker RSC: Foundress of the First Indigenous Congregation (HHCJ) In The Nigerian Church,* p. 178.
260. NWOSUH Cosmas K. O., 2012, *Cardinal Ekandem And The Growth of the Catholic Church in Nigeria,* Nigeria, Ambassador Publications, p. 176.
261. Cf. Circular Letter and Conference Report of 11July 1969 whereby she signed as: m. m. Therésè HHCJ, Mother Marie Therese H.H.C.J., Vicar General of the Congregation H. H. C. J.
262. HAMMARSKJOLD Dag, *Quotes from Dag Hammarskjold,* www. Dag Hammarskjold, Quotes, Author of Markings.
263. THE EDITOR, 1979, *Silver Jubilee Brochure of Episcopal Ordination of His Eminence, Cardinal Dominic Ekandem 1954-1979,* p. 20.
264. THE EDITOR, 1979, *Silver Jubilee Brochure of Episcopal Ordination of His Eminence, Cardinal Dominic Ekandem 1954-1979,* p. 20.
265. NWOSUH Cosmas K. O., 2012, pp. 176-177.
266. I presume the PS means post script indicating an additional material to the body of the letter.
267. NWOSUH Cosmas K. O., 2012, pp. 176ff.
268. NWOSUH Cosmas K. O., 2012, pp. 176.

269. Cf. The Archival Materials of the Generalate and Itak Convent, one of the early communities that features very prominently owing to its antiquity and location.

270. WATURUOCHA Mary Gertrude, 2012, *Memoir,* p. 184.

271. OKPO Mary Joseph, (Mother), *Unpublished Manuscript,* 1987, pp. 21ff; Vide,. WATURUOCHA Mary Gertrude, 2012, *Memoir,* p. 182 last paragraph affirms that Mother travelled with many others.

272. NWOSUH Cosmas K. O., 2012, pp. 176ff.

273. THE EDITOR, July 30 2014, *US House of Representatives Votes To Sue Obama,* Yahoo News; http://www.afp.com/afpcom/en/

274. EKEFRE Edidiong, 2013, *A Testament of Light, The Life And Times of Dominic Cardinal Ekandem,* Lagos, MayFive Media Ltd, pp. 172ff. These pages corroborate what Mother Mary Joseph Okpo HHCJ said about his life being in severe danger whenever he visited the Sisters at Eriam.

275. WATURUOCHA Mary Gertrude, 2012, *Memoir,* p. 182.

276. OKPO Mary Joseph, 1995, *Reminiscences of Cardinal Dominic Ekandem,* An Unpublished Manuscript, p. 5. This manuscript was written in response to the oral interview she was to grant. She preferred to document her thoughts rather than giving an oral response to the interview at once. 277. WATURUOCHA Mary Gertrude (Mother), 2012, pp. 182.

277. DE PAUL Vincent, 2008, *Conferences To the Congregation of The Mission,* Vol. XI, Newly Translated, Edited and Annotated from the 1921 Edition of Pierre Coste CM, New York, New City Press, xxvii, Memo of Brother Bertrand Ducournuc, August 15, 1657.; also pp. 41 and 43

278. This expression appears to have an undertone of victimisation, wrestling with the facts forgetting about the right rule of conduct with a veneer of ethnicism to scatter the Congregation and turn things around at the same time, she looks at all these from the point of view of faith and the Cross, in this context she overcame the bitterness built in and surfaced in the bright sunlight of loving exhortation to the Sisters.

279. Page one of the letter ends here giving way to page two.

280. NWOSUH Cosmas K. O., 2012, *Cardinal Dominic Ekandem And The Growth of the Catholic Church In Nigeria,* p. 195.

281. NWOSUH Cosmas K. O., 2012, *Cardinal Dominic Ekandem And The Growth of the Catholic Church In Nigeria*, p. 191.
282. FULTON J. Sheen, 2012(4), *Those Mysterious priests*, Bangalore, ST. PAULS, p. 34.
283. From Jerusalem Bible Standard Edition, 1966 Edition
284. MERTON Thomas, *No Man Is An Island*, 2012, pp. 172–173.
285. It is probable that Mother Elizabeth uses the term 'tribes' as was used in the first national Anthem, "Nigeria, we hail thee, our own dear motherland, though tribe and tongue may differ in brother hood we stand…"
286. 'I heard' here is simply indicating a reported speech since she did not witness the Sister in question with another habit to indicate her continuity in the religious Life although in another Congregation.
287. 'Liberated or Liberation' was a common terminology used to refer to a place captured the Nigerian Army since other places under Biafra were considered as occupied territories. Whenever the Biafran Soldiers were defeated and driven out of a location, the term liberated or liberation was applied.
288. The Italicised word is not found in the original, it is the author's.
289. This section is found in page six of the original script.
290. That information is found in p. 7 of Mother Elizabeth Umoh's write-up.
291. Rev. Fr. John Bosco normally liked to recall this experience of having to study at Loretto Girls Juniorate and the motherly role of Mother Elizabeth and how Sister Mary Liguori taught them Biology at the time. He and all in his set always remain grateful to the Sisters and to their Ordinary, Bishop Ekandem who thought highly of them and permitted them to continue their education even when the Nigerian Soldiers occupied their school compound.
292. Page eight of the original begins here.
293. Page nine of the original starts here.
294. It is likely, this is referring to the entire Congregation.
295. Page nine ends here. What follows is in page ten.
296. Provincialisation refers to the various parts of the Congregation becoming Provinces by having their autonomy, power of governance and full operation with their councils and councillors although linked

to the General Council of the entire Congregation. The same structure that operates in the General Council operates in the Provincial Council. The Provincial Superior and the Council although independent must link up with the Congregation through the General Council since they are a constituent part of the Congregation. The Provincial Superiors have elective powers like other delegates of the General Assembly/Chapter. The Provinces carry out their election of the Provincial Superior with the Councillors before proceeding to participate in the General Assembly/

297. Chapter. Their Councillors must be elected like other members. Only the Provincial Superiors are *Ex Officio* Members likewise all the members of the General Council. The *Ex Officio* members together with the elected ones have active and passive voice. The Provincial Superiors together with other delegates have the right to elect and be elected. Each Province exists for the good of the members and for the proper functioning of the Congregation for control, ordering, governance and functionalibility. The autonomy does not indicate separation but works like the various Dioceses and Archdioceses of various countries and continents in relation to the Pope, the Vatican and the entire Church. The General Laws of the Congregation affect all. Provincial norms affect only the members of the Province.

298. Rev. Sr. Mary Elizabeth Umoh, HHCJ, 2012, Funeral Rites Brochure, May 231928–May 132012, Uyo, Inela Ventures & Publishers Ltd. 70 Dominic Utuk Avenue, p. 01. Her Funeral Rites took place at Seat of Wisdom Chapel, Eriam Afaha Obong, Abak, Akwa Ibom State where they have the Congregation's Cemetery. Where she was interred.

299. EKANDEM Dominic, 1995, *Seminary Days and Life In General,* Oral and personal Interview granted to the author at Urua Akpan.

300. NWOSUH Cosmas K. O., 2012, *Cardinal Dominic Ekandem And The Growth of the Catholic Church In Nigeria,* Iperu Remo, Ogun State Nigeria, Ambassador Publications, p. 173.

301. Cf. NWANRUO Theresa, 2014, *My Memory of Late Dominic Cardinal Ekandem,* An Unpublished Write-Up Adapted from One of Her Talks in Abuja About Her Early Involvement in Abuja Independent Mission.

302. NWANRUO Theresa, 2014, *My Memory of Late Dominic Cardinal Ekandem*, Abuja, An Unpublished Write-Up, p. 1.

303. NWANRUO Theresa, 2014, *My Memory of Late Dominic Cardinal Ekandem*, An Unpublished Write-Up, p. 2.

304. 1 Tm. 3:1–7

305. THE EDITOR, *Silver Jubilee Brochure of Episcopal Ordination of His Eminence, Cardinal Dominic Ekandem 1954-1979*, p. 7.

306. This action resembles what the early Fathers of the Church did while Christianising the pagan worship of the sun to Sun-Day, snatching it from pagan traditional worship to Christian sacred day of worshipping Christ. Bishop Ekandem uprooted the little forest in front of the Church and replaced it with the statue of the Blessed Virgin Mary.

307. EKANDEM D. I., 1973, *Dignity of the African As a Person,* An Unpublished Address Presented to the Old Boys of Holy Family College, Oku Abak in Ikot Ekpene, p. 4.

308. UMOREN E. U, 1976, *His Eminence, Dominic Cardinal Ekandem 1917–1976, First Nigerian Cardinal,* Aba, Cynako International Press Ltd, p. 55.

309. THE EDITOR, THE HANDMAIDS OF THE HOLY CHILD JESUS, 1981, *Our Mother is 100 and We are 50, Golden Jubilee*, Bodija-Ibadan, Claverianum Press, pp. 2 and 3. The Mother meant here is Mother Mary Charles Walker, the Foundress of the Congregation of the Handmaids of the Holy Child Jesus who resided at Calabar training young girls for their future life. Among these, the first set of the aspirants cropped up.

310. THE EDITOR, 1981, *The Handmaids of The Holy child Jesus, 1931–1981, Our Mother is 100 and We are 50, Golden Jubilee*, p. 3.

311. THE EDITOR, 1979, *Silver Jubilee Brochure of Episcopal Ordination of His Eminence, Cardinal Dominic Ekandem 1954-1979*, p. 17.

312. THE EDITOR, 1979, Silver Jubilee Brochure of Episcopal Ordination of His Eminence, Cardinal Dominic Ekandem 1954–1979, p. 20.

313. Part of the conversation was about legalization of abortion. There was an outright position by Nigerian Government not to legalize abortion as was done in the Western World. The Cardinal was very happy that Nigerian Government took such a bold stand and rejoiced that there was at least some sense of the sacred and respect for human life. The

conversation touched many things but they were all sacred converse that edified the soul and created room for spiritual growth.

314. SHEEN Fulton J., 2012, *Those Mysterious Priests*, p. 316.

315. SHEEN Fulton J., 2012, *Those Mysterious Priests*, p. 316.

316. NWOSUH Cosmas K. O., 2012, *Cardinal Ekandem And The Growth of The Catholic Church In Nigeria*, Nigeria, Ambassador Publications, pp. 172–175.

317. HAMMARSKJOLD Dag, *Markings, Stags: Forgiveness*, under *Quotes from Dag Hammarskjold*, http://www.goodreads.com/author/quotes/946904. Dag Hammarskj Id 1/6

318. UMOREN U. E., 1976, *His Eminence, Dominic Cardinal Ekandem, First Nigerian Cardinal,* Aba, Cynako International Press Ltd,. The text is found in pages 86-87.

319. The aspect of delivery of calls indicates what the telephone system was like in the country in the seventies. The major means of communication was being at the spot in person as was done by the *Chargé*. Things have greatly improved since then.

320. UMOREN U. E., 1976, *His Eminence, Dominic Cardinal Ekandem, First Nigerian Cardinal,* P. 87.

321. The original message does not contain 'VI' that is why it appears in square brackets.

322. Cf. ANYANWU Godwin, 1976, *Enugu Is The Home Of Christian-ityEkandem* in *Daily Star newspaper*, No. 1402, Tuesday, November 30, A Publication of East Central State, Enugu, Front page.

323. ANYANWU Godwin, 1976, *Enugu Is The Home Of Christianity Ekandem* in *Daily Star newspaper*, No. 1402, Front Page.

324. Cf. ANYANWU Godwin, 1976, *Enugu is Home of Christianity-Ekandem* in *Daily Star Newspaper*, No., 1402, Tuesday, November 30, A Publication of East Central State, Enugu.

325. ANYANWU Godwin, 1976, *Enugu is Home of Christianity-Ekandem* in *Daily Star Newspaper*, No., 1402, Front Page.

326. ANYANWU Godwin, 1976, *Enugu is Home of Christianity-Ekandem* in *Daily Star Newspaper*, No., 1402, Front Page.

327. COSMAS Udoma later became a Monsignor taking Charge of Saint Dominic's Chaplaincy in the same Building that Cardinal Ekandem dwelt for many years before the final journey to Abuja that he never

returned from. He wrote this message as the Head of Seminarians in the Theology House in Enugu. The "first in Dignity" as the Head of the Seminarians in each Diocese was normally called was also fondly nominated *Primus.*

328. Misereor is one of the agencies that gives aid to

329. EKANDEM Cardinal Dominic I., 1985, *A Response To the Speech of the Governor, Brigadier Dan Archibong, Governor of Cross River State,* Ukana Iba, Ikot Ekpene, Nigeria.

330. EKANDEM Cardinal Dominic, 1987, *A Private Address To the Land Officer of Ikot Ekpene Local Government Area,* The Bishop's House, Cardinal Ekandem's Avenue, Ikot Ekpene.

331. THE EDITOR, *Souvenir Programme of Events; The Ancient and Noble Order of the Knights of St. John, Holy Trinity Commandery NO #423,* 14Monday, Nov. 17, 1980, St. Anne's Cathedral, Ifuho, Diocese of Ikot, Ekpene, CRS, Friday, Aba, Cynako International Press, p. 5.

332. IZUWAH A. E. N., First Vice President, Thursday, 25to 28May, 1995, *The Knights of St. John, Origin And Roles: Lecture At The Initiation of Aspirants Held In Owerri, Imo State,* p. 5.

333. THE EDITOR, *Souvenir Programme of Events; The Ancient and Noble Order of the Knights of St. John, Holy Trinity Commandery NO #423,* Monday 14-Nov. 17, 1980, St. Anne's Cathedral, Ifuho, Diocese of Ikot, Ekpene, CRS, Cover Page.

334. IZUWAH A. E. N., First Vice President, Thursday, 25to 28May, 1995, *The Knights of St. John, Origin And Roles,* p. 2.

335. Cf. *Souvenir Programme of Events;* 14th Monday, Nov. 17, 1980, *The Ancient and Noble Order of the Knights of St. John, Holy Trinity Commandery NO 423,* St. Anne's Cathedral, Ifuho, Diocese of Ikot Ekpene, CRS, Friday, Aba, Cynako International Press, pp. 4&5.

336. *Souvenir Programme of Events; The Ancient and Noble Order of the Knights of St. John,* p. 18.

337. *Souvenir Programme of Events;* 14Monday, Nov. 17, 1980, *The Ancient and Noble Order of the Knights of St. John,* p. 22.

338. *Souvenir Programme of Events;* 14Monday, Nov. 17, 1980, *The Ancient and Noble Order of the Knights of St. John,* p. 19.

339. EKANDEM DOMINIC I., 1974, *The Church In the Rise of Nigeria, Sermon Delivered on the Occasion of the Golden Jubilee of Bigard*

Memorial Seminary Enugu, Nigeria, on July 29, 1974, Aba, Cynako International Press Ltd., 1974, pp. 19–20.

340. EKANDEM Dominic I., 1974, *The Church In the Rise of Nigeria, Sermon Delivered on the Occasion of the Golden Jubilee of Bigard Memorial Seminary Enugu, Nigeria, on July 29, 1974,* pp. 18–19.

341. See Maps in Figs 1&2.

342. Docility as a virtue and in the spiritual context implies openness to the Spirit, the capacity to be taught by God, to listen to hear God likewise obedience and doing his will.

343. CBCN, 1990, First Session, No. 2.3, Presidential Address, cf. Working Committee 2, p. 4.

344. CBCN, 1990, Second Session, No. 4.1, 4.30pm, March 6, p. 6.

345. CATHOLIC BISHOPS' CONFERENCE OF NIGERIA, 1990, Minutes, No. 4.1, March 6, p. 6.

346. INYANG Dominic E., 2010, *On The Beginnings of Abuja Independent Mission,* Garki, Area 10, A Verbal Interview granted to the Author. Msgr. Inyang became the first Vicar General of the Diocese. When Cardinal Ekandem died and Cardinal Onaiyekan succeeded Cardinal Dominic Ekandem, Msgr. Dominic Inyang was retained as the Vicar General. That was a special privilege on his part because he was supposed to have gone when the administration of Cardinal Ekandem terminated.

347. FLANNERY Austin, General Editor, 7 December 1965, VATICAN II, Vol. 1, *Ad Gentes Divinitus, Decree On The Church's Missionary Activity,* Dublin, Ireland, Dominican Publications, No, 39, 853.

348. UDO Aloysius, 2009, *Priestly Silver Jubilee Anniversary Celebration Brochure,* Abuja, Sub-Prints & Associates Ltd, p. 9.

349. Cf. UDO Aloysius, 2009, *Priestly Silver Jubilee Anniversary Celebration Brochure,* p. 10.

350. FLANNERY Austin, General Editor, 28 October, 1965, VATICAN II, Vol. 1, *Christus Dominus, Decree On The Pastoral Office of Bishops In The Church,* No. 14, 571.

351. Commingling is a term connected with putting a piece of the Consecrated Host into the Chalice containing the Consecrated Blood of Christ to indicated the resurrection of Christ and the union of his body and blood as obtained before his death on the Cross and pour-

ing out his blood and water while on the Cross; likewise signifying the resurrected Christ as Victor over sin and death. It also entails the sending of the piece of Consecrated Host to the Station Church as a sign of communion. It linked those Churches the Pope used to celebrate Mass in whenever he was not able to go there in person or to the Churches that were linked to the Basilica where the Pope, the Bishops, Priests and Deacons likewise the faithful worshipped together as a sign of the Church's unity and universality.

352. FLANNERY Austin, General Editor, 1965, VATICAN II, Vol. 1, *Christus Dominus,* Vol. 1, No. 6, 566-567.

353. Abuja Archdiocesan Directory, 1991, p. 5.

354. OKODUA B. A., April 27to 30, 1992, *"Abuja: A Call To Development"* This Conference took place long after the initial stages of necessity of land acquisition. The Conference was mainly on development not on acquisition which Rev. Matthew Kukah was charged with as his immediate assignment in the virgin land.

355. This means an Auxiliary Bishop that has the right of Succession to the incumbent Bishop.

356. CBCN, October 17, 1990, *Second Plenary Assembly of the Catholic Bishops' Conference of Nigeria,* Congratulatory Message, Ibadan, Pastoral Institute, p. 4.

357. CBCN, October 17, 1990, *Second Plenary Assembly of the Catholic Bishops' Conference of Nigeria,* p. 3.

358. Source, Archdiocesan Directory and Calendar, Data given in 1991.

359. DAUGHTERS OF CHARITY OF SAINT VINCENT DE PAUL, 19632013, *Golden Jubilee Celebration,* A. Mustard Seed Printer Nig. Ltd, p. 86.

360. DAUGHTERS OF CHARITY OF SAINT VINCENT DE PAUL, 1963 -2013, *Golden Jubilee Celebration,* p. 87.

361. 234 Pulse Staff, January 11 2015, *Christianity is the Largest Religion in Nigeria, 2014 Statistics,* http://www.234pulse.com/2015/01/christianity-is-the-largest-religion-in-nigeria-2014-statistics/

362. 234 Pulse Staff, January 11 2015, *Christianity is the Largest Religion in Nigeria, 2014 Statistics.*

363.

364. This is quoted from his Internationally Acclaimed Leadership Guru book of SHARMA John S., 2013, *The Monk Who Sold His Ferrari, Fable About Fulfilling Your Dreams And Reaching Your Destiny*, Mumbai, JAICO Publishing House, p. 50.

365. EMSPAK Jesse, Wed, Sep 17, 2014, *Did Gravity Set Earth's Plate In Motion?* Live Science Contributor | LiveScience.com, Yahoo News in the Internet.

366. Details of this point are given under "Historical Background" below.

367. OLUPOHUNDA Bayo, March 31 2015, *How 2015 Elections Changed Nigeria* in *Punch Nigeria Newspaper;* THE EDITOR, March 15, 2015, *Breaking News: This Day, Nigerian Newspaper,* PALMER Ewan, March 31, 2015, *Nigeria Elections: APC Leader, Muhammadu Buhari Defeats Goodluck Jonathan And Declared president* in *International Business Times,* UK Edition, Monday 15May, Front page.

368. Cf. Chapter One; *In Mente Domini, The Maynooth Fathers* above for more details on the Maynooth Fathers likewise the St. Patrick Fathers or Kiltegan Fathers or simply Kiltegans.

369. EKANDEM Cardinal Dominic, April 1995, *Missionary Seminary of St. Paul*, Personal Interview granted to the author at Urua Akpan, Akwa Ibom State, Nigeria.

370. EKANDEM Dominic, Friday, May 15, 1976, *A New Ideal of An Old Ideal, An Ideal Never Attained,* A Memo submitted to the Catholic Bishops' Conference of Nigeria in Kaduna., p. 1.

371. EKANDEM Dominic, Friday, May 15, 1976, *A New Ideal of An Old Ideal, An Ideal Never Attained,* p. 1.

372. Cf. The Document on *The Founder of the Missionary Society of St. Paul, September 16th 1995* referring to the Catholic Bishops' Conference of Nigeria Meeting in Kaduna 1976, pp. 15-16.

373. Culled from The Preparatory Document For The First General Council Of The Society, namely: The Historico-Juridical Report of The Society.

374. Cf. CATHOLIC BISHOPS' CONFERENCE OF NIGERIA, 15 September 1976, *Minutes of Meeting,* Kaduna, Kaduna State, Nigeria.

375. CATHOLIC BISHOPS' CONFERENCE OF NIGERIA, 15 September 1976, *Minutes of Meeting,* Kaduna.

376. CATHOLIC BISHOPS' CONFERENCE OF NIGERIA, 15 September 1976, *Minutes of Meeting*, Kaduna.
377. This is an Extract from the Memoirs of Monsignor Godwin P. Akpan on the Historical Development of the Seminary.
378. The material used here is part of the Historical Development of the Missionary Seminary personally given by Monsignor G. P. Akpan to the author when he visited him at Iperu after his retirement from Gwagwalada, finished his Sabbatical Leave and became part of the Iperu Community in May 2008.
379. *Historical Development*, 2008, p. 21.
380. UKPO Joseph Edra, April 2014, *Cardinal Ekandem, A man of Perception*, Calabar, Cross River State, Nigeria, Oral Interview granted to the author at Archbishop's Residence.
381. EKANDEM Dominic Cardinal, Friday, May 15, 1976, *Appendix to A New Ideal of An Old Ideal, An Ideal Never Attained.*
382. This material is extracted from page 24 of the Historical Development submitted by Monsignor Akpan during the General Assembly preparation period.
383. The above information is culled from *Historical Background/Report of* Monsignor Godwin P. Akpan as the First Acting Rector and Superior of the Seminary and Society, pp. 23 and 25.
384. Very Rev. Fr. Anthony Iffen Umoren MSP who collected this list from the present Rector or the Seminary at Gwagwalada for the purpose of this work. The contribution is well appreciated.
385. ATTENDANCE LIST WAS AS FOLLOWS:
    His Lordship, Right Rev. J.C. Onaiyekan—Chairman
    His Grace, Most Rev. A.O. Okogie—Member
    His Lordship, Most Rev. B.D. Usanga—Member
    His Lordship, Right Rev. V.V. Ezeonyia—Invited
    Very Rev. Msgr. G.P. Akpan, MSP—Member
    Very Rev. Msgr. R.C. Anasiudu—Member
    Very Rev. Fr. Dermot Connolly, SPS—Member
    Rev. Fr. Joseph Otoide, MSP—Member
    Rev. Fr. Benedict Etafo—Invited
    Rev. Fr. John Joyce, SPS—Member

ABSENT

His Grace, Most Rev. P. Y. Jatau
His Grace, Most Rev. S.N. Ezeanya
His Lordship, Right Rev. F.F. Alonge
His Lordship, Right Rev. A.O. Gbuji
Archbishop Jatau had sent a letter to say that he would be unable to attend. The meeting was informed that Archbishop Ezeanya would be unable to attend for health reasons. Bishop Gbuji had not received the letter convening the meeting. Bishop Alonge was expected but did not arrive.

AIM OF MEETING—CHAIRMAN'S OUTLINE

The chairman introduced the proceedings by stating the am of the meeting. This was to discuss formally proposals—for presentation to the CBCN—on the canonical procedure to be followed for the transformation of the Missionary Society of St Paul from its present status of Pious Association to that of the Society of Apostolic Life of diocesan right.

386. Culled from *Historical Background/Report of* Monsignor Godwin P. Akpan as the First Acting Rector and Superior of the Seminary and Society, pp. 24ff in preparation for the First General Chapter of the Society.

387. Implantation is a technical term that can refer to heart-liver transplant or the implantation of the fertilised egg or zygote implants itself into the uterus in the process of pregnancy (Vide *Implantation of Fertilised Egg* under baby Corner in the Internet). None of these implies the sense of its usage here. The implication of implantation in this case assumes the form of establishment of a new community or house or congregation or the setting up of a community in a particular locus for the first time. It can go with its own pains, nausea, and cramps as in the case of ovarian implantation that accounts for the ups and downs experienced in the process of implantation of a community or seminary as used above.

388. DE PAUL Vincent, 2003, *Correspondences, Conferences, Documents,* Vol. 9, New York, New City Press.

389. What appears under grand opening are extracts from *Ambassador Publication* covering the events of that day in October 1977 and especially from the library/ archive of Msgr. Godwin Akpan, the first rector and the first acting superior general.

390. Extract from the first publication and grand opening of the Missionaries of St. Paul in the *Ambassador Magazine.*

391. AKPAN Godwin, 1979, *Poised for the Future* in *The Ambassador Magazine,* vol. 2, nos. 2, 5.

392. This refers to missionary enterprise in a diocesan context where the priests are sent out for a particular number of years and once they complete the term of agreement they return to their country. This is what is meant by "goes and gets out."

393. The emphasis on "vocation for life" goes a long way to include immigrants from mission lands and laymen on missions, *Ecclesiae Sanctae, nos.* 23 and 24, indicating that the pastoral ministry of the Society of St. Paul Missionaries will surely include these ministerial aspects as chaplains to immigrants and lay missionaries too.

394. EKANDEM Dominic Cardinal, 1979, *The Necessity of a Missionary Seminary* in *Nigeria* in *The Ambassador Magazine,* vol. 2. no. 2, Iperu-Remo, Ogun State, 5 and also from the archives of Msgr. G. Akpan, Iperu-Remo, Ogun State.

395. JIGES John G., 1979, *Iperu-Remo as the Home of the Missionaries* in *The Ambassador Magazine,* vol. 2. no. 2, Iperu-Remo, Ogun State, 4.

396. AKPAN Godwin, 1986, *Notes on the Historical Background of the Missionaries of St. Paul,* Gwagwalada, p. 29ff. What follows is an extract from what Monsignor Akpan presented to the missionaries and to the commissions preparing for general chapter.

397. The cost indicated was adequate for 1977, but that amount cannot be all right in 2015. It costs for more than that now because of devaluation, high cost of things throughout the word, and the need of maintaining what had already been established.

398. AKPAN Godwin, 1986, *Notes on the Historical Background of the Missionaries of St. Paul,* Gwagwalada, pp. 29ff.

399. This part of the address at the opening ceremony. Realizing the great task facing the nascent institution, instead of despairing, they appealed to Nigerian Catholics to rise up and help.

400. THE EDITOR, 1979, *Benefactors* in *Ambassador magazine,* vol. 2, nos. 2, 12.

401. Cf. The letter to his Bishop written on August 8, 1977, indicating his enthusiasm and desire to join the new group of missionaries.

402. Cf. Letter of January 15, 1985, for details.

403. The seven years spoken of here is referring to the letter that Msgr. G. Akpan wrote to Bishop Usanga when he was still at Christ the King Pro Cathedral in Uyo shortly after his nomination as the acting rector of the seminary at Gwagwalada in Abuja Federal Capital Territory. The letter manifests the monsignor's intention to become a member of the new Missionary Society in the pipeline. The letter of 1977 gave weight to the seven years he alluded to in his letter while paving the way for temporary and permanent vows of membership.

404. AKPAN Godwin, 1986, *Notes on Historical Development,* Gwagwalada, pp. 27–28.

405. AKPAN Godwin, 1986, *Notes on Historical Development,* p. 28.

406. EKANDEM Dominic Cardinal, October 25, 1986, *A Letter to Very Rev. Fr. John L. M. Filippelli, SSJ, Concerning the Welfare and Spirituality of the Missionaries,* Gwagwalada, Abuja, Nigeria.

407. GENERAL CHAPTER PROCEDURE (Missionaries of St. Paul, Gwagwalada, Abuja), p. 2.

408. This Special Preparatory Commission for the General Chapter handled this aspect. The discussion took place on the 16of September 1995; one year after Abuja had been elevated to the status of an Archdiocese with His Grace Archbishop John O. Onaiyekan being the first Archbishop. As the Archbishop of Abuja, he became the proper Ordinary of the Society too. It facilitated things for the Society's progress of authentication and autonomy.

409. The Italics are the author's.

410. This title is put in a poetic manner. It gradually unfolded itself with events as time went on.

411. Chapter 12 refer.

412. Fr. Benedict Etafo and Fr. Emmanuel Asuquo-Akpan are canonists, that is, canon lawyers in the Catholic Church. They played the role of special invitees and lecturers in the seminary at the time. Father Etafo was the congregation's lawyer then. Both gave their insights concerning the point in question referring to the historical aspects of the congregational foundation to back up their points.

413. This is an indication that the Church in Africa has come of age and is ready to bear fruit and to succour those who are greatly in need.

414. Fr. Emmanuel Asuquo Akpan confirming the point during the oral interview with him about the status of the Canonical Fonder, 1995 during the period of preparation for the First General Chapter.

415. AKPAN Emmanuel Asuquo, 1995, *On the Aspect of the Canonical Fonder, A paper Presentation During Pre-Chapter Preparation,* Gwagwalada, MSP Seminary. This is part of the Historical Development of the Society/Seminary documents.

416. Cf. THE EDITOR, May 26–27, 1979, *The Ambassador magazine, Souvenir Booklet,* First Issue.

417. THE EDITOR, *The Ambassador magazine, Souvenir Booklet,* First Issue, p. 2.

418. THE EDITOR, *The Ambassador magazine, Souvenir Booklet,* First Issue, p. 2.

419. THE EDITOR, *The Ambassador magazine, Souvenir Booklet,* First Issue, p. 3.

420. THE EDITOR, *The Ambassador magazine, Souvenir Booklet,* First Issue, pp. 15–16.

421. THE EDITOR, *The Ambassador magazine, Souvenir Booklet,* First Issue, p. 5.

422. The Centre at the moment of establishment was called Handicapped Centre but with a better understanding and Conscientisation fo the people, it is now called Disabled Centre even though the major nomenclature "St. Joseph Rehabilitation Centre" still holds.

423. This is a Prelate appointed by the Supreme Pontiff to take care of a Vacant See and to serve as the Ordinary of the place.

424. All these came from GENERAL CHAPTER PROCEDURE (Missionaries of St. Paul, Gwagwalada, Abuja), p. 3. The main source of

the material was CMSP, 50, that is the Constitutions of the Missionaries of St. Paul, No. 50.

425. GENERAL CHAPTER PROCEDURE (Missionaries of St. Paul, Gwagwalada, Abuja), p. 3, No. 1.3.

426. Cf. Internet Source, WIKIPEDIA, THE FREE ENCYCLOPAEDIA, *Cardinal John Onaiyekan.*

427. THE EDITOR, 2002, *Historical Development Report,* p. 24 especially the section geared toward the Silver Jubilee Celebration.

428.

429. OBOT Ephraim S. (Bishop), 1996, *Cardinal Ekandem and Cross-less Christianity,* oral interview granted to the author, Bishop's House, Idah, Kogi State, Nigeria.

430. OBOT Ephraim S. (Bishop), 1996, *The Role of the Cross in the Life of Cardinal Ekandem,* oral interview granted to the author, Bishop's House Idah, Kogi State, Nigeria.

431. Cf. EDEM Michael I., 2013, *Drugs And Death: Drug Trafficking, Economic, Social and Family Implications and the Agency's Response,* Port Harcourt, Nigeria, Mustard Seed Press, pp. 202–207

432. Cf. CAN, CHRISTIAN ASSOCIATION OF NIGERIA—AKWA IBOM STATE BRANCH Publication Ikot Ekpene: D A Lukan Press pp. 7–13

433. CAN, CHRISTIAN ASSOCIATION OF NIGERIA, AKWA IBOM STATE BRANCH, Date? Ikot Ekpene AKS, DA-Lukana Press, pp. 8–10.

434. CAN, CHRISTIAN ASSOCIATION OF NIGERIA, AKWA IBOM STATE BRANCH, Date? Ikot Ekpene AKS, pp. 8–10.

435. EKANDEM Cardinal Dominic, 1995, *On Involvement In Pastoral Work And Cultural Understanding,* Personal Interview Granted to the author, Urua Akpan, Ikot Ekpene, Akwa Ibom State.

436. EKANDEM Cardinal Dominic, 1995, *On Pastoral Challenges As A Young Bishop*< Urua Akpan, Ikot Ekpene, Akwa Ibom State, Oral Interview Granted to The author.

437. IMMACULATA/UNAH, 2010, *The Faith Of Cardinal Ekandem In His Pastoral Work,* Personal Interview with the Sisters at Calabar And Uyo.

438. THE EDITOR, Tuesday, February 7, 1978, *Cardinal Ekandem* in *The Nigerian Chronicle,* No. 1, 154, Calabar, Government Press, Front page [Interestingly, this paper cost only 10k, a Nigerian monetary unit at the time.].

439. THE EDITOR, Tuesday, April 4th 1978, *The Nigerian Chronicle,* Calabar, Government Printing Corporation, p. 7.

440. Soutane is a white of black long dress used by the cleric as well as the Seminarians. It is also called Cassock.

441. THE EDITOR, Tuesday, April 4th 1978, *The Nigerian Chronicle,* Calabar, Government Printing Corporation, p. 7. As an addendum, it is a familiar saying that familiarity brings contempt. Part of it could be seen in this context also; although, at the same time, there is no need to be too rigid about appointments.

442. THE EDITOR, Tuesday, April 4th 1978, *The Nigerian Chronicle,* pp. 7–8.

443. The women were motivated by some of their sons that were priests. They did not begin the carrying of placards all by themselves. This is why Antonio Rosmini said that the wound of the heart of Christ is the priest's relationship with priests and eventually with the laity. In Idah, laymen in the Diocese protested and said the imposition of the Bishop on them was arbitrary and unprecedented. They started asking whether no priests in the proposed Diocese could be found worthy to be a Bishop. There were some priests who were preparing themselves for the episcopacy who became totally dissatisfied when the announcement was made and joined forces with the lay people and engineered them all the more. These situations made the arrival of Bishop Obot in Idah a very cumbersome one. He could have been chocked to death at the beginning if not for the grace of God and his willingness to do God's will.

444. THE EDITOR, Tuesday, April 4th 1978, *The Nigerian Chronicle,* Calabar, Government Printing Corporation, pp. 7–8.

445. It is very obvious that Nigeria had twenty-four Diocese by 1978 compared to fifty-two in 2015. There were three Ecclesiastical Provinces at the time, now there are nine Provinces. The growth is astronomical.

446. This is a canonical term referring to those who have rights and obligations in the Church without necessarily referring to a single person

as such but to an aggregate of persons thereby extending beyond an individual as such and does not terminate with the person.

447. FRANCISCAN FRIARS OF THE IMMACULATE, KALVALAGE Francis Mary, Editor, 1999, Padre *Pio, The Wonder Worker*, Ignatius Press, *pp.* 107, 144.

448. FRANCSCAN FRIARS OF THE IMMACULATE, KALVALAGE Francis Mary, Editor, *Padre Pio, The Wonder Worker*, p. 144. Transverberation is explained in p. 146 thus: "The Mystical writers describe the wounds of love as being deeper than what they describe as strokes of love. Moreover, the former are manifested in some external manner, either by a physical piercing of the heart (transverberation) or else by appearing in some parts of the body such as hands, feet or side (stigmatization). What St. Teresa of Avila experienced was termed "Thee Seraphs' assault" Cf. also, CANTALAMESSA Raniero, Editor, 2014 (3), *Inspiration From The Letters of Padre Pio: Words of Light*, Massachusetts, *Paraclete* Press, p. 18, The Stigmata.

449. EKANDEM D. I. (Most Rev. Dr.), O.B.E, C.O.N., *Towards A Viable And Self Reliant Church*, Aba, Cynako international Press Limited (March, 1973). At the time he was the Bishop of Ikot Ekpene and Apostolic Administrator of Port Harcourt.

450. The example of Mrs. Annice Gordon, his benefactress from Ireland could have been at the background of going beyond Parish or Diocese because, Mrs. Gordon went beyond her Diocese and country and sponsored an unknown Seminarian who eventually became her spiritual son. This is charity, this is altruism.

451. EKANDEM D. l. (Most Rev. Dr.), O. B. E, C.O.N. JULY 29, 1974, *The Church ln the Rise of Nigeria*, Aba, CYNAKO INTERNATIONAL PRESS LTD (Sermon delivered on the occasion of the Golden Jubilee of Bigard Memorial Seminary Enugu, Nigeria. The Sermon covered thirty-one pages. It was divided into three chapters with subsections 1–4 in chapters 1 and 2: Chapter 3 the longest of them all had 3 sections. Each of these was subdivided into 3 parts but the third subdivision has 4 parts. Chapter 3 was the longest of all, extending from page 18 to page 31.

452. Dominic Cardinal EKANDEM (His Eminence), D.D., O.B.E; C.O.N, *True Spiritual Leadership—A Vital Contribution to Nation Building*, Ikot Ekpene, De Paul Printing Press (Dec.5, 1976).

453. It refers to a strong emphasis on ethnic origin or prejudice based on ethnic origin.

454. EKANDEM Dominic (His Eminence), Thursday, September, 1978, *Don't Abandon The Poor*, in *The Nigerian CHRONICLE, No. 1,338,* (The Reporter), Calabar, Front page continued from p. 3. Incidentally, the paper was sold for 10 kobo then.

455. Cf. EKANDEM D. I. (Most Rev. Dr.), 1979, *Shepherds Among Shepherds,* Onitsha, Tabansi Press

456. EKPO Catherine, 2010, *On the Person of the cardinal,* Ikot Ekpene, Akwa Ibom State.

457. UDUAKOBONG E. UMOREN, *His Eminence, Dominic Cardinal Ekandem 1917–1976, First Nigerian Cardinal,* p. 69, quoted from SMYTH R. in Silver Jubilee Brochure, pp. 13-16.

458. One Pound Sterling at that time was simply known as *quid* just as the present day Nigeria speaks of a hundred K instead of a hundred thousand Naira. It was a popular slang that needed no explanation whatsoever.

459. UDUAKOBONG E. UMOREN, *His Eminence, Dominic Cardinal Ekandem 1917–1976, First Nigerian Cardinal,* p. 70.

460. Culled from THE DAUGHTERS, 1980, *Adiaha Obong Catholic Women Organisation Silver Jubilee 1955-59* (MAIDEN ISSUE) pp. 2–3.

461. Culled from THE DAUGHTERS (1980), pp. 4–5. Bishop Brian D. Usanga was the Ordinary of Calabar Diocese at the time of the celebration hence he had to send a congratulatory message.

462. EKANDEM Cardinal Dominic, 1995, *Comments on the Origin of St. Joseph Catholic Teachers' League,* Urua Akpan, Ikot Ekpene, Akwa Ibom State.

463. THE EDITOR, 1981, *The Federation of St. Joseph Catholic Teachers' League* in *Lux Catholica,* Ikot Ekpene, De Paul Printing Press, p. 13.

464. EKANDEM Cardinal Dominic, 1995, *Comments on The Origin of Catholic Teachers Association.*

465. General Sani Abacha took over from Chief Shonekon as the Head of the Interim Government in November 1993.

466. PHILOMENA OKWU, FRANCESCA EDET, MARGARET MARY EKANDEM, eds., 2013, *Daughters of Charity if St. Vincent de Paul in Nigeria,* Port Harcourt, Mustard Seed Printers Nig. Ltd., pp. 62–63.

467. PHILOMENA OKWU, FRANCESCA EDET, MARGARET MARY EKANDEM, eds., 2013, p. 63.

468. ABRAHAM LINCOLN, 2013, *Gettysburg Address and Other Writings,* New York, Barnes and Noble Inc., pp. 1 ff. The Speech took place at Springfield Illinois and it was on *Discoveries, Inventions and Improvements* delivered on 11 February 1857. The traced the origin of inventions and how mere observation on the part of Isaac Newton led to the discovery of 'Force of Gravity'. He noted that it was as a result of watching an apple fall from a tree and started questioning, investigating, coming to conclusion and beginning to implement his observation. This has led to many unimaginable discoveries. It all started from observation.

469. EZEONYIA Vincent, 2008, *On The Graciousness And Simplicity of Cardinal Ekandem,* Christ the King Catholic Church Compound, Bishop's House, Aba, Abia State, Nigeria. At th time, Vincent Ezeonyia CSSp. was the Bishop of Aba Diocese.

470. AKPAN Michael, 2014, *The Surprising Characteristic of Dominic Cardinal Ekandem, Based on The Testimony of Martin Patrick Ekandem,* A Written copy given to the author, Uyo, Akwa Ibom State.

471. AKPAN Michael, 2014, *The Surprising Characteristic of Dominic Cardinal Ekandem, Based on The Testimony of Martin Patrick Ekandem.*

472. Culled from LUX CATHOLICA, 1981, IKOT EKPENE: De Paul Printing Press, pp. 12, 14.

473. EKANDEM Dominic Cardinal, 1987, *Justice Promotes Security and Peace, Lenten Pastoral Letter,* Ikot Ekpene, Akwa Ibom State, Nigeria.

474. EKANDEM Dominic Cardinal, April–June 1992, *Advice For the Future* in *Torch Magazine,* Bigard Memorial Seminary Publication, No: 100, pp. 17–18 quoted in OBI Nicholas, 1998, *Our Legacy; Leeway to Personal Achievements,* Lagos, Jojab Ventures, p. 457.

475. THE REPORTER, 1978, *Don't Abandon The Poor, By His Eminence Dominic Cardinal Ekandem,* in *The Nigerian Chronicle,* No. 1,338, Calabar, Front Page.

476. Sir Adam B. Nyong is presently a Colonel in the Knights of Saint John International in Uyo Commandery 412. At the time of the conversation, he was a Major in the ranking of the Knighthood. He was one of the first members of the Knights of St. John in Ikot Ekpene Commandery that gave birth to Calabar and Uyo Commanderies. As an Officer, he had special privileges of seeing the Cardinal from time to time so as to discuss certain teething problems and developments with him. It was in one such visits that he voiced what he had heard in the Bus as he travelled from Uyo to Ikot Ekpene. Adam approached the Cardinal since he was accustomed to defending the faith. He had to look for some explanation to what he had heard.

477. GILL Peter L., Editor, March 2000, *Priest Pulls No Punches in Loyola Lecture on Being Black and Catholic* in *Four County* **Catholic**, Vol. 12, No. 1, 12–13; specifically page 13.

478. EKANDEM Cardinal Dominic I., 1984, *Table Conversion With His Priests,* Ikot Ekpene, Akwa Ibom State.

479. Cf. BENEDICT XVI (Pope), 29June 2009, *Caritas In Veritate,* Encyclical Letter of The Supreme Pontiff To The Bishops, Priests, Deacons, Men And Female Religious, Lay Faithful And All People of Good Will On Integral Human Development In Charity And Truth, Rome, Libreia Editrice Vaticana.

480. DEI VERBUM, 18November 1965, The Dogmatic Constitution On *Divine Revelation,* No. 8. (FLANNERY Austin, General Editor, VATICAN II, Vol. 1), Pueblo Publishers. Cf. also CATECHISM OF THE CATHOLIC CHURCH, 19974, *Inspiration And Truth of Sacred Scripture,* Nos. 106108, United Kingdom, Geoffrey Chapman.

481. SAUNDERS William P., 1 September 1994, *Straight Answers,* in *The Anglican Catholic Herald, diocesan newspaper of Arlington (VA) diocese* provided by Eternal Word Television Network, Irondale AL 35210, www. etwn.com

482. JOHN PAUL II (Pope), 22 May 1994, *Apostolic Letter, Ordinario Sacerdotalis To Bishops of The Catholic Church On Reserving Priestly Ordination To Men Alone,* No. 4, Vatican City, Libreria Editrice Vaticana.

483. RENTAPRIEST, June 17, 2009, *A conversation about the married Catholic priesthood and church reform,* http//www.laieninitiativ.at/

484. PULLELLA Philip, *May 19, 2014, Women In Love With Priests Ask Pope To Make Celibacy Optional,* Reuters, Yahoo News.

485. WATSON Leon, 19 May 2014, *'Dear Francis, we are each in love with a priest, please let us marry': Italian priests' mistresses in extraordinary plea to Pope to end celibacy for Catholic clergy, www.dailymail.co.uk*

486. This idea has strong links with what is posted in the Internet: *Future of Priestly Ministry Optional Celibacy: So All Can Be At The Table.* Podcast: Fr. Donald Cozzens on 'The *Future of Priestly Celibacy, Future Church Teleconference* November 20, 2013. It is common knowledge in some parts of South America that some of the young men become ordained to the priesthood, they labour for some years and decide to quit the priesthood and go on to marry. This is what is specified as two to three years. They =normally conclude that they have done enough by serving for those number of years.

487. ANDREOTTI Giulio 1993 to 2012 Interview with Cardinal Peter Kodwo Appiah Turkson Celibacy? It's not foreign to African Culture in *30 Days:* In the Church and in the world international monthly magazine issue no. 10–2005.

488. https://www.google.co.uk/webhp?sourceid=chrome; under the section of Historical Events For 1995, HistoryOrb.com

489. Many of the information furnished above come from the Major World Events in the Wikipedia in the Internet.

490. THE EDITOR, 1974, *Alone With None But Thee My God* in *The Divine Office- The Liturgy of the Hours According To The Roman Rite,* Vol. III, Weeks 6-34, London, Collins, 215-216. The adapted words featured in his souvenir card of the seventieth birth anniversary.

491. ARMINJON Charles, 2008, *The End of the Present World, And The Mysteries of the Future Life,* Manchester New Hampshire, Sophia Institute Press, p. 205,

492. BRENAN (Dr.) Maureen, 1996, *On The Last Days of Cardinal Ekandem,* Medical Missionaries of Mary Community, Ibadan, Oyo State, Nigeria, Oral Conversation with the author.

493. OKON Mary Augustine (Sr.), 2010 *On Special Invitation By The Cardinal To Come To Abuja During His Dying Moment,* an oral conver-

sation with the author; Handmaids Convent, Mercy Hospital, Abak, Akwa Ibom State, Nigeria.

494. THE EDITOR, 13December 2012, *Funeral Rites of Rev. Sister Mary Augustine Okon, HHCJ, 1930-2012,* Seat of Wisdom Chapel, Eriam Afaha Obong, Ikot Ekpene, Akwa Ibom State, p. 2.

495. DE PAUL Vincent (St.) 2004, *Correspondence, Conferences Documents, IX, Conferences To The Daughters of Charity,* Vol. 1, Brooklyn, NY, New City, Care of the Sick, 16March 1642.

496. The personal experience of the author while visiting the Cardinal in Abuja before his death.

497. THÉRÈSE of Lisiéux (St.), 1964(5), *The Story of A Soul,* London, Burns & Oates, p. 103. The same message is repeated verbatim in a recent book: THE ACADEMY OF THE IMMACULATE, 1997, *St. Thérèse, Doctor of Little Way,* Our Lady's Chapel, New Bedford, MA, USA, Franciscan Friars of the Immaculate, pp.11-12.

498. THE EDITOR, 1990, *Order of Christian Funerals, Approved For Use In The Dioceses of England And Wales, And Scotland,* London, Geoffrey Chapman, Option D, p. 97.

499. ARMINJON Charles, 2008, *The End of the Present World And The Mysteries of The Future Life,* Trans., Susan Conroy & Peter McEnerny, Manchester, Sophia Institute Press, P. 144.

500. THE EDITOR, MCMLXXI, *Missale Romanum, Ex Decreto Sacrosancti Oecumenici Concilii Vaticani Instauratum Auctoritate Pauli PP. VI Promulgatum,* Editio Typica, Typis Polyglotitis Vaticanis, p. 855.

501. MERTON Thomas, 1990, *No Man Is An Island,* England, Burns & Oates, p. 124.

502. MERTON Thomas, 1990, *No Man Is An Island,* p. 125.

503. Cf. CARROLL William E., 2011, *Creation And Science,* United States of America, Catholic Truth Society, pp. 39ff.

Index

671

K

J

L

M

O

P

Y

Z

www.ingramcontent.com/pod-product-compliance
Lightning Source LLC
Chambersburg PA
CBHW051127120626
46547CB00012B/706